Focus on Environmental Geology

There is one ocean, with coves having many names;
a single sea of atmosphere with no coves at all;
a thin miracle of soil, alive and giving life;
a last planet; and there is no spare.

David R. Brower

Courtesy of J. Ward

Focus on Environmental Geology

*A Collection of Case Histories
and Readings from Original Sources*

Second Edition

Selected and Edited by
Ronald Tank

New York
OXFORD UNIVERSITY PRESS
London 1976 Toronto

Foreword

For all intents and purposes, the dam on environmental geology burst on January 28, 1969. That was the day of the Santa Barbara oil blowout, a catastrophe that threatened the coast of California and the Santa Barbara Channel with between one and three million barrels of "black tide" and awakened all Americans to the environmental crisis. In fact, from the perspective of one who has toiled in the area of environmental policy since the 1950's, there is no question that this was the *one* event that triggered the increased public concern and made possible the tougher environmental laws that were written on the federal and state levels in the last few years.

Since the Santa Barbara disaster, geologists have found themselves more and more immersed in issues of acute public concern. Controversies over the Trans Alaska Pipeline, the underground nuclear test at Amchitka, and the development of a sound energy policy have made geological debates more public—and more important—than ever before. Laymen increasingly depend on geologists to help them understand the physical environment and to solve the problems we have created through the abuse of our natural resources. Thus, it is not only important for the geologist to understand the environmental aspects of his science, it is also vital that he or she communicate that understanding to the rest of us.

One of the alarming discoveries of the last several years of increased environmental concern and legislation has been how *little* we really know about what we have done to the earth—about what can be repaired and what cannot, and about what we must stop doing before it is too late. I hope that this useful anthology will encourage more students of geology to participate in the formation of public policy so that we can correct our errors before they overtake us.

Washington, D.C.   Edmund S. Muskie
November 1972

Preface to First Edition

Even though we are in the midst of an environmental crisis, there is only a small collection of books dealing with environmental geology. This is somewhat ironical, since geology is intimately concerned with the environment. Geology includes investigations of earth materials, earth processes, and the landforms that result from the interaction of natural materials and natural processes. Geological investigations also go beyond surficial phenomena to include subsurface phenomena. The geologist should therefore be well equipped to contribute much toward the solution of a variety of problems concerning the physical environment. He is experienced in evaluating the earth's capacity for providing water, mineral resources, building sites, and waste disposal sites. A knowledge of earth processes and earth structure has enhanced his appreciation of pristine environments, and the historical viewpoint inherent in much of geologic thought provides him with a unique perspective.

A higher standard of living, spectacular increases in population in recent decades, and the gradual shift of population to urban centers has led to more intensive use of the land and its resources. Under these conditions Man's relationship with his environment is brought into sharper focus, and environmental problems take on a greater significance. This has led to the development of a new branch of geology, which is commonly called environmental geology. It deals with the interrelationships of geologic processes, earth materials, and Man. It anticipates conflicts between Man and his environment, attempts to evaluate the earth's potential for providing Man with vital resources, and provides the necessary tools for planning a more harmonious relationship between Man and his environment. It relies heavily upon the traditional branches of geology but takes on a more intradisciplinary and interdisciplinary orientation. As environmental geology grows we are witnessing a broader and more obvious involvement of geology with Man's social concerns.

The readings included in this collection are intended to give the student a sense of contact with environmental geology. The readings are arranged under three major categories. The first category includes those aspects of earth processes and geologic settings that are hazardous to

Man. As Man intensifies his use of the land it is obvious that he must recognize geologic hazards and develop plans to minimize their impact. The second category of readings deals with mineral resources—prospects for the future and the impact of mineral exploitation on the environment. This is a highly controversial subject, and the readings reflect opposing points of view. The third category deals with contemporary environmental problems peculiar to urbanization.

An anthology of readings has proven to be an asset in a variety of teaching situations. "Outside reading" has been a traditional supplement to the textbook and has occasionally been used in lieu of a textbook. This has certainly been true in the area of environmental studies. A major problem has been the fact that these readings are scattered in a wide variety of professional journals, trade journals, and geological survey reports. Even the larger libraries are finding it increasingly difficult to provide the student with all of the published literature.

The selection of a limited number of readings from the vast amount of material available was difficult. A number of general papers are included to introduce each topic, while more specific and technical papers are included to illustrate applications and case histories. Some background in geology would be helpful but most of the papers should be comprehensible, informative, and stimulating to a diverse audience. Some editing has been necessary, in view of the purpose of this book, but the editing has been accomplished without detracting from the style and goals of the original source.

Each section includes introductory comments that alert the reader to the general content of the articles and their relation to each other and to environmental geology. Original references are included with each article, and a supplementary reading list is included in each section. A glossary is provided for technical terms.

The field of environmental geology is undergoing rapid development and there are bound to be differences of opinion as to what should be included in an introduction to this field. Suggestions for changes in future editions of this anthology are invited. If this book is successful, the reader will come to appreciate the vital role of geology in a broad range of environmental concerns.

I wish to express my sincere appreciation to those students at Lawrence University who offered comments on the collection of readings included in a course in Environmental Geology. These comments were most helpful in selecting the readings which appear in this anthology. I also wish to thank the authors and publishers who have permitted the inclusion of their materials.

Preface to Second Edition

The first edition of this anthology appeared only three years ago, but the pace of research and publication in environmental geology has accelerated so rapidly that an updating and revision is in order. Included among the new developments is the "dilatancy model" which has unified our thoughts about earthquake prediction and control and has enabled seismologists to enjoy unprecedented success in predicting earthquakes. A new generation of interpretive maps has become a standard tool of the geologist and has made available a more useful kind of geologic information to planning agencies. More community planning groups are now involved in flood plain zoning and management, and geology plays an increasingly important role in the preparation of required environmental impact statements. The energy crisis, which was intensified by the Arab oil embargo, is now seen to be more than a short-lived political problem. Time is running out on many communities accustomed to using unsafe waste disposal sites, and recycling of some materials has become more attractive. The necessity of protecting our water resources takes on an added urgency when it is discovered that procedures for treating polluted water may be related to the carcinogens identified in "safe" drinking water.

Several new textbooks dealing largely with topics of environmental geology are now available, new journals are being published, and established journals are including more articles on environmental concerns. We are thus faced with a greater variety of literature, new developments, and diverse approaches to presenting this information to students of geology and environmental studies. The net result is a need for an updated, expanded anthology that differs somewhat in structure from the first edition.

Part I is an introduction to the subject of environmental geology and stresses the need to communicate relevant geologic information to those who may not be trained in the earth sciences. The use of special interpretive maps as a technique for bridging the communications gap is included in this section.

Part II illustrates the wide range of geologic hazards which should act as constraints on Man's activities. Topics that represent additions to the first edition include shoreline erosion, karst topography, permafrost, surging glaciers and flood plain management.

Part III deals with mineral resources. Additions to this section include an instructive approach to dealing with estimates of resources, a comprehensive review of the energy "crisis" and an example of the considerations involved in developing an environmental impact statement.

In order to allow for more flexibility for those using the anthology in traditional introductory geology, geography, environmental studies and engineering courses, the section on urban geology has been absorbed or redistributed in new sections on water resources (Part IV), and waste disposal (Part V). Ground water reserves and geological influence on regional health are new topics appearing in Part IV and the management of radioactive waste is introduced in Part V. An epilogue illustrates the well-known conflicts between the developer and preservationist as well as the overlapping nature of the problems presented in Parts I-V.

None of the major sections stands completely as it was and some of the articles retained from the first edition have been updated with an "editor's note". The list of supplementary readings has also been updated and a list of films which would be appropriate supplements to course work has been included. Review questions appear in this edition and should help the student appreciate the broad range of concerns relating to environmental geology.

The major problem in preparing the second edition was not in deciding what to include but in deciding what might reasonably be omitted. I am indebted to those who offered comments on the articles included in the first edition of the anthology and to those who offered suggestions for the revised edition. I also wish to thank the authors and publishers who have permitted the inclusion of their materials.

RWT

Contents

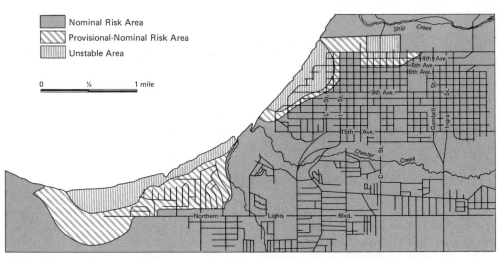

Classification of Earthquake Risk Areas, Anchorage, Alaska. From *Environmental Atlas of the Greater Anchorage Area Borough, Alaska* edited and coordinated by L. L. Selkregg. Reprinted by permission of University of Alaska, Arctic Environmental Information and Data Center. Copyright 1972.

I. Introduction

The geologist does have to bear the
added burden of carrying his work to
the user so that its potential utility
can be fully realized

Ecology is the study of the intimate relationships between organisms and their environments. It involves the lithosphere, the hydrosphere, the atmosphere, and the biosphere. Environmental geology emphasizes one aspect of this complex subject—the interrelationship of Man and his geologic environment. It involves studies of hydrogeology, topography, engineering geology, and economic geology. It is therefore a multidisciplinary field which relies heavily upon traditional branches of geology. In the first article of this anthology, John Frye presents an overview of environmental geology. The role of geologic information in solving contemporary environmental problems is made clear, but, as Frye indicates, the collection of this information must be oriented toward environmental applications. Furthermore, "the results must be presented in a form that is readily understandable to, and usable by, planners and administrators who often are unfamiliar with science and, particularly, do not have a working knowledge of the geological sciences." This is a relatively new role for the geologist and one which serves to distinguish environmental geology from some of the more traditional branches of geology.

One of the more significant applications of environmental geology is in the area of urban planning. The importance of this application has not always been realized by planning agencies, and geologists have not always been effective in demonstrating the relevance of geologic data to the planning process. The unfortunate result of the lack of communication between planners and geologists is illustrated by Ernest Dobrovolny and Henry Schmoll in Reading 2. The authors also describe the development of special purpose interpretive maps which will aid urban planners in anticipating and providing predevelopment solutions to land-use problems. Another type of special purpose map, the flood hazard map, is described in Reading 21, and references to the application of interpretive maps in other areas are included in the list of supplementary readings. These maps are products of some of the new developments in environmental geology and will be vital in the planning process. Also vital to the planning process is the support of government agencies in acquiring the needed data and in incorporating this data into policy decisions.

1 A Geologist Views the Environment

John C. Frye

When the geologist considers the environment, and particularly when he is concerned with the diversified relations of man to his total physical environment, he takes an exceptionally broad and long-term view. It is broad because all of the physical features of the earth are the subject matter of the geologist. It is long term because the geologist views the environment of the moment as a mere point on a very long time-continuum that has witnessed a succession of physical and biological changes—and that at present is dynamically undergoing natural change.

Let us first consider the time perspective of the geologist, then consider the many physical factors that are important to man's activity on the face of the earth, and, third, turn our attention to specific uses of geologic data for the maintenance or development of an environment that is compatible with human needs.

The Long View

The earth is known to be several billion years old, and the geologic record of physical events and life-forms

Frye, J. C., 1971, "A Geologist Views the Environment," *Environmental Geology Notes Number 42.* (Illinois State Geological Survey). Reprinted by permission of the author and the Illinois State Geological Survey, Urbana, Illinois. It was prepared for "Voice of America," Earth Science Series, Dr. C. F. Park, Jr., Coordinator. Mr. Frye is Executive Secretary of the Geological Society of America and Former Chief of the Illinois State Geological Survey.

on the earth is reasonably good for more than the most recent 500 million years. Throughout this span of known time the environment has been constantly changing—sometimes very slowly, but at other times quite rapidly. Perhaps a few dramatic examples will serve as illustrations. Less than 20,000 years ago the area occupied by such North American cities as Chicago, Cleveland, Detroit, and Toronto were deeply buried under glacial ice. The land on which New York City is now built was many miles inland from the seashore. And part of the area now occupied by Salt Lake City lay beneath a fresh-water lake. Twelve thousand years ago glacial ice covered the northern shores and formed the northern wall of what was then the Great Lakes, and much of the outflow from those lakes was to the Gulf of Mexico rather than to the Atlantic Ocean through the St. Lawrence River, as it is now. Although firm scientific information is not available to permit equally positive statements about atmospheric changes during the past few tens of thousands of years, deductions from the known positions of glaciers and from the fossil record make it clear that the atmospheric circulation patterns were quite different from those of the present, and studies of radiocarbon show that the isotopic content of the atmosphere changed measurably through time.

The purpose of listing these examples is to emphasize that the environment is a dynamic system that must be understood and accommodated by man's activities, rather than a static, unchanging system that can be "preserved." The living, or biological systems of the earth are generally understood to be progressively changing, but much less well understood by the public is that the nonliving, physical aspects of the earth also undergo change at an equal or greater rate.

Clearly, a dynamic system is more difficult to understand fully, and it is more difficult to adapt man's activities to a constantly changing situation than to an unchanging or static system. On the other hand, the very fact of constant change opens many avenues of modification and accommodation that would not be available in a forever constant and unchanging system.

The Problem

Although it is important that we have in mind the long-term facts concerning earth history, modern man has become such an effective agent of physical and chemical change that he has been able to produce major modifications, some of which run counter to the normal evolution of our earthly environment, and to compress millennia of normal evolutionary changes into days. These rapid modifications are, almost without exception, made by man with the intention of producing improvements and advantages for people. Problems result from the fact that by-products and side effects do occur that are neither desirable nor pleasing, and at some times and places may be hazardous or even calamitous. In some cases the undesirable side effects are unknown or are unpredictable; in other cases they are tolerated as a supposed "necessary price" to pay for the desir-able end result. It is our intent to examine the role of the earth scientist in defining some of these problems and in devising ways of minimizing or eliminating them.

The ways in which man treats his physical surroundings, produces and uses the available nonliving resources, and plans for his future needs are, of course, social determinations. However, in order that social decisions can be made in such a way that we, and our children, will not find reason to regret them, they should be made in the light of all the factual information that it is possible to obtain. If we, collectively, decide to use the available supply of a nonrenewable resource— for example, petroleum—at a particular rate, we should know how long it will last and what substitute materials are available to replace it when the supply is exhausted; if we decide to dam a river, we should know what the side effects will be in all directions, how long the facility will last, and what the replacement facility might be; if we develop huge piles of discarded trash, we should know whether or not they will cause pollution of water supplies or the atmosphere, and whether or not the terrane is sufficiently stable to retain them; if we substitute one fuel for another with the desire to abate air pollution, we should know if it will make a net over-all improvement in the pollution problem, and if it will be available in the quantity required so that man's needs can be met; and if we plan expanding metropolitan areas we should have full information on the terrane conditions at depth and on the raw material resources that will be rendered unusable by urbanization.

Role of Earth Science in Solving Problems

When we consider the role of earth science in solving problems, we see that the earth sciences can and should develop answers to all of the questions we have asked. Many of the problem areas overlap one another, but it will be easier to discuss them if we class the contributions of the earth scientist to environmental problem solving in five general categories. The first of these is collecting data for planning the proper use of the terrane, or perhaps we should say the most efficient adjustment of man's use of the earth's surface to all of the physical features and characteristics at and below the surface—particularly in expanding urban areas. Second is determination of the factors that influence the safety and permanence of disposal of waste materials and trash of all kinds—both in the rocks near the surface and at great depth in mines and wells. Third is providing information for the planning and development of safe, adequate, and continuing water supplies in locations that will serve populated areas. Fourth is the identification of rock and mineral resources to provide for future availability of needed raw materials, or of appropriate substitute materials. And, fifth is the recognition of man as a major geologic agent by monitoring the changes he has caused in his environment and by providing remedies where these changes are, or may become, harmful.

Proper Use of Land

The first of these general categories—procuring data for physical planning of the proper use of the land surface and of the rocks below the surface—covers data provided by topographic and geologic maps, by engineering geology and soil mechanics investigations, by predictions of potential landslides and other geologic hazards, and by a complete inventory of available mineral resources and future potential water supplies. Much of the geologic data needed in this category can be produced by conventional methods of research, but, to be effective, the research program must be oriented toward environmental applications. Furthermore, the results must be presented in a form that is readily understandable to, and usable by, planners and administrators who often are unfamiliar with science and, particularly, do not have a working knowledge of the geological sciences. Perhaps the best way to explain what I mean by environmental orientation is to cite a few examples.

The first example of the use of geologic research oriented for planning is a laboratory study involving clay mineralogy, petrography, and chemistry. It was prompted by numerous incidences of structural failure of earth materials. In rapidly expanding suburban residential areas there has been a great increase in the use of septic tanks and, simultaneously, a rapid increase in the household use of detergents and water softeners. A laboratory research program was initiated to study the changes induced in the clay minerals by these chemical substances when they were introduced into the near-surface deposits by discharge from septic tanks. Preliminary results showed that the materials in septic tank effluent did, indeed, produce significant and undesirable changes in the properties of some earth materials. The data made it possible to predict changes that could occur in the structural characteristics of common surficial deposits and, thus, to prevent structural failure. Therefore, the conclusions were presented to planners, health officials, architects, and other groups that might have need of the information.

In strong contrast to such a sharply focused and specific research project is a second example provided by a study of a county at the northwest fringe of the Chicago metropolitan area, into which urbanization is spreading from that metropolis. Because of impending problems, the county government organized a regional planning commission, which called upon the State Geological Survey and other agencies to collect data on the physical environment that were essential to wise, long-range planning. Where some of the fields of activity of the agencies overlapped, they cooperated informally so that they could most effectively work with the planning commission. Essential to the project were modern topographic maps of the county, and, even though much of the county had been geologically mapped previously, several man-years of geologist time were devoted to the project.

This project to characterize the physical environment involved many types of geological study. These included (1) analysis of the physical character of the major land forms within the county; (2) interpretation of the relation between geologic units near the surface and the agricultural soil units; (3) establishment of the character of the many layers of rocks and glacial deposits penetrated at depth by drilling below the surface; (4) def-inition of the occurrence and character of water-bearing strata in the near-surface glacial deposits and the deeper bedrock layers; (5) determination of the geologic feasibility of water-resource management programs; (6) determination of the geologic feasibility of waste management programs; (7) delineation of the geographic occurrence and description of the characteristics of construction material resources; (8) location of commercial mineral resources and assessment of their economic value; (9) determination of the engineering characteristics of the geologic units near the surface; and (10) geologic evaluation of surface reservoir conditions and proposed reservoir sites.

The approach to such development of data includes field work by surficial geologists, engineering geologists, ground-water geologists, stratigraphers, and economic geologists. In the laboratory, chemists, mineralogists, and stratigraphers conduct studies of the subsurface by use of cores and cuttings of the deposits at all depths; make chemical, mineralogical, and textural analyses of all deposits and rocks; determine physical properties; compile statistics; and make economic analyses of the many mineral resource situations. The results of these studies are compiled on interpretative maps, which the planning commission combines with the results of studies by specialists of other agencies and by the commission itself for preparation of maps that show the recommendations for land use. These maps, together with explanatory, nontechnical text, serve as a basis for county zoning and long-range development planning.

Development of Waste Disposal Facilities

Our second category of environmental geologic information includes those geologic data needed for proper and safe development of waste disposal facilities. Man has the propensity to produce toxic and noxious waste materials in progressively increasing quantity and in an ever-increasing variety and degree. Waste products result from manufacturing, processing, and mining—but of even greater concern is the concentrated production of waste by the inhabitants of our large cities. Traditionally, man has used fresh water to dilute liquid waste and the atmosphere to dilute the gaseous waste products of combustion. He has often indiscriminately used the land or large bodies of water for disposal of solid waste. However, even the general public is now aware of the fact that we are exhausting the capacity of fresh waters and the atmosphere to absorb our waste products. Along the sea coasts there is still the ocean—although even the ocean is being restricted as a waste disposal medium—but in the vast region of the continental interior we have no ocean in which to dump our wastes. Instead, our choices are limited to (1) selective recycling, accompanied by essentially complete purification of the residue of waste materials; (2) selective recycling accompanied by land disposal of nonrecyclable residues; or (3) the use of the rocks of the earth's crust for the total future expansion of waste disposal capacity. Geologists, who traditionally have been concerned with the discovery of valuable deposits of minerals and their extraction from the crust, now also must concern themselves with the study of the rocks of the earth's crust as a possibly safe place for the disposal and containment of potentially harmful waste products.

Petroleum geologists were introduced to one aspect of the problem of large quantity underground disposal of waste material more than a quarter century ago when it became necessary to find methods for injecting into deep wells the increasing quantities of brines produced with petroleum in oil fields. However, it was not until population densities approached their present levels that we became genuinely concerned with the most critical problems of the future—that is, the safe disposal of industrial and human waste materials in large quantity, other than by dilution. As some of these undesirable materials are destined to increase at an exponential rate in the future, it is obvious that we must devote our best geologic effort to solution of the problems of disposal. The problem of disposal of high-level and intermediate-level radioactive wastes has already attracted a major research effort, probably because these radioactive materials are obviously so highly dangerous for such a long period of time, and a body of scientific data now exists concerning their safe management.

In my own state of Illinois, solid waste disposal is generally accomplished by sanitary landfill, and frequently the State Geological Survey is asked by state and local departments of health to make geologic evaluations of proposed sites. However, precise and universally accepted criteria for this type of evaluation are only now being developed. Several disposal sites of differing geologic character are being intensively studied by coring and instrumentation of test holes, and analyses are being made of the liquids leached from the wastes and the containing deposits. In addition to laboratory study of the obvious characteristics of the containing deposits—such as texture, permeability, strength, clay mineralogy, and thickness of the units that do not transmit water (and thus protect the aquifers)—studies must be made of the less obvious effects of the seepage of liquids on the structural character of the deposit, the removal of objectionable chemicals from water solutions by the clay minerals of the containing deposits, and the microflow patterns of water in earth materials surrounding the wastes. For some of these determinations it is necessary to know the chemical composition of the liquids that pass through the wastes, as well as the chemistry and mineralogy of the deposits that contain them.

Disposal near the surface by landfill or lagooning methods requires detailed studies of the earth deposits at and immediately below the surface, with only minor data required on the deeper bedrock. On the other hand, disposal of industrial wastes in deep wells requires studies of the character and continuity of all rock layers down to the crystalline basement. Geologic data needed for deep disposal involve a combination of the types of information needed for the exploration for both oil and water, plus a knowledge of the confining beds of shale or clay. It should also enable us to predict possible changes that might be produced by the injected wastes.

A different type of pollution problem is represented by sulfur compounds and other undesirable materials released by the burning of coal, oil, and gas and discharged into the atmosphere. The earth scientist contributes to the solution of this problem by studies of the mineral matter in the coal, studies of methods of processing the coal before it is burned, studies of means of removing the harmful materials from the effluent gases produced by combustion, and research on the conversion of coal into gaseous or liquid fuels from which much of the objectionable material can be extracted.

Planning Water Supplies

The third category of concern for the earth scientist is water, its occurrence, quality, continuing availability, and pollution; its use as a resource, as a diluent for waste materials, as a facility for recreation, and as an aesthetic attribute. Many of the problems and areas of data collection for water resources fall mainly in the province of the engineer, the chemist, the biologist, or the geographer. But, it would be unrealistic to exclude water from the subjects requiring significant and major data input by the geologist, because to a greater or lesser degree geologic data is needed for the proper development and management of each of the above aspects. The occurrence, quality, availability, development, and replenishment of ground water require major attention by the geological scientist because all of these aspects are directly controlled by the character of the rocks at and to considerable distances below the surface.

Of the categories of environmental data we are discussing, water resources and water pollution are the most widely discussed in the news media and most generally recognized by the public and by municipal planners and administrators. Furthermore, an extensive cadre of earth scientists specializing in water-related problems has developed within governmental agencies and industry. There are many examples of the application of geologic data to management of water resources, ranging from dam site evaluations to the mapping of aquifers and determination of areas suitable for artificial recharge. Before we leave this category, however, I should point out that, in contrast to the rock and mineral resources of the earth's crust, water is a dynamic and renewable resource and, therefore, is subject to management. Even the long-range correction of the effects of unwise practices in the past may be possible in some cases.

Future Availability of Rock and Mineral Materials

Our fourth category is, perhaps, the most complicated aspect of environmental geology. It is the problem of assuring adequate supplies of mineral and rock raw materials for the future, and especially of assuring their availability near densely populated areas where they are most needed. We have an increasing shortage of raw material resources to meet the needs of the increasing world population, and also a mounting conflict of interest for land use in and adjacent to our urbanizing regions. Conflict exists in populated regions because buildings and pavements commonly remove the possibility of extracting the rock or mineral raw materials underneath them. While the producer of rock or mineral products is exploring for the best deposit available from both a physical and economic standpoint, the urban developer may

be planning surface installations without regard for the presence or absence of rock and mineral deposits, which he may be rendering unavailable. These unavailable resources may be urgently needed for community developments in the future, and it is important that the attitudes of the planner and mineral producer be brought into harmony, and that compatible working relations be evolved so that mineral resource development can move forward as an integral part of the urban plan. The geological sciences can supply an accurate and detailed description and maps of all of the rock and mineral resources, not only in but also surrounding urbanizing areas for a distance reasonable for transporting bulk commodities to the metropolitan centers. Grades of deposits that might have utility in the coming 25 to 50 years as well as grades currently being developed should be included in the study.

An equally important role of the earth scientists now, and more particularly in the future, lies in regions remote from the cities where exploration is needed for the raw materials and fuels required by modern society. . . . Furthermore, research by the earth scientist, directed toward the identification of substitute materials and toward meeting more exacting and different specifications for future needs, is called for if we are to keep pace with expanding human needs. Information about natural resources is just as essential a part of needed environmental data as are flood hazard maps, physical data maps for engineering projects, and aquifer maps indicating the occurrence of ground-water supplies.

Man as a Geologic Agent

Our fifth area is the recognition of man as a geologic agent, and here we have the culmination of the problems of Environmental Geology. Man's changes in his physical surroundings are made in order to obtain some real or imagined advantage for people. Some of these changes are designed to prevent natural events from happening and include levees and detention reservoirs to prevent flooding of land, revetments and terracing to prevent erosion, and irrigation to prevent the effects of droughts. But many other changes are intended to produce effects that are not in the natural sequence of things. In both cases, nature is liable to provide unplanned and undesirable side effects. It is the role of the earth scientist to determine the effects of man-made physical changes on all aspects of the physical environment before structural changes are made so that provision can be made to negate undesirable by-product effects—or, if the side effects are too severe, so that a decision against the environmental changes can be made.

A special facet of man-made changes is in the area of mineral and fuel resources. The public need and demand for energy, and for products based on mineral raw materials, is constantly increasing at the same time that increasing populations require that land resources be maintained at maximum utility. Here again, the earth scientist must add to his traditional role of finding and developing sources of energy and mineral resources the equal or more difficult role of devising methods of producing these resources in such a way that land resources have a maximum potential for other human uses. This has led to the concept of planning for multiple sequential use— that is, designing a mineral extraction operation in advance so that the land area will first have a beneficial use before the minerals need to be extracted, then be turned over to mineral extraction, and, finally, be returned to a beneficial use, perhaps quite different from the original use.

Conclusions

The earth scientist is concerned with the physical framework of the environment wherever it may be, with the supply of raw materials essential to modern civilization, and with the management of the earth's surface so that it will all have maximum utility for its living inhabitants. It is this last item that is a relatively new role for the earth scientist, and one in which he must work cooperatively with the engineer, the biologist, and the social scientist. The earth scientist must become the interpreter of the physical environment, and he must do it in the long-term context of a dynamically changing earth so that "architectural" designs will be in harmony with natural forces 50, 100, or 500 years from now, as well as with the conditions of the moment.

2 Geology as Applied to Urban Planning: an Example from the Greater Anchorage Area Borough, Alaska*

Ernest Dobrovolny and Henry R. Schmoll

Introduction

Geology commonly has been considered a study of rocks having as its main purpose the deciphering of past events, usually very remote ones. Although widely recognized as of great economic importance in the search for mineral and fossil fuel deposits, geology seemed to have little relevance to the general public and the everyday events of the present. Geologists, of course, have understood that geology deals as well with dynamic processes, and that these processes occur with as much vigor today as in the past. Except for application to engineering works of great magnitude, however, developers and the general public have often failed to recognize the relevance of these processes to many other facets of human endeavor involving use of the land.

It takes a dramatic and devastating event, like the Alaska earthquake of March 27, 1964, to forcefully draw the attention of the public to the dynamic processes of geology and the impact these processes can have on everyday life and on the economy and well being of a region. Although destruction from the earthquake was widespread throughout south-central Alaska, and some towns, notably Valdez and Seward, sustained much loss of life and property, the greatest volume of damage occurred in and around Anchorage, the largest city in the State and center of the greatest population concentration. Anchorage is located at considerable distance from the epicenter, but parts of the community were developed on areas particularly vulnerable to strong seismic shock of the duration encountered in the 1964 earthquake. Understandably, the first general public attention focused on geologic hazards associated with the seismic event, such as landslides, ground fracturing, generation of seismic sea waves, lurching, and shaking. This led in turn, however, to a wider if less immediate understanding of the role geology can and must play in the orderly development of our land and economic resources.

Existing Geologic Report

Anchorage was fortunate in having a geologic report covering the city and surrounding area (Miller and Dobrovolny 1959), which suddenly became a best-seller at least locally, and was widely cited as the chief source of background geologic information in the profusion of studies, geologic and otherwise, that rightfully accompanied

* Publication authorized by the Director, U. S. Geological Survey.

Dobrovolny, E., and Schmoll, H. R., 1968, Geology as Applied to Urban Planning: an Example from the Greater Anchorage Area Borough, Alaska, *Proceedings XXIII International Geological Congress*, vol. 12, pp. 39–56. Reprinted by permission of the authors and the Geological Survey, Prague, Czechoslovakia. The authors are on the staff of the U. S. Geological Survey.

the recovery from disaster. This new prominence for a geologic report, together with personal contacts with many geologists, served to make public officials aware of the importance of geology in fulfilling their responsibilities. The earthquake also caused a certain amout of soul searching on the part of the geologists, however, for it had become apparent that although the geologic report had correctly assessed potential dangers in the event of a strong seismic shock, little heed was paid to this warning. Obviously unless a different approach were adopted in the future there would be little need for preparing another geologic report only to have it go unused and unheeded. With this in mind it is instructive to review here the history of the old geologic report which emerged from a geologic mapping project started in 1949. A separate study of the occurrence, availability, and quality of ground water was started later the same year (Cederstrom, Trainer and Waller 1964; Waller 1964).

Anchorage was selected for an urban mapping project because the community was growing rapidly and because surficial geologic maps with engineering interpretations are of maximum usefulness in planning if available prior to a major period of development. Anchorage and vicinity was then the largest and by far the most rapidly growing community in Alaska. Much of the land surrounding the city limits was inaccessible to vehicular travel, but access roads were planned, and each year extended farther into areas suitable for homesteads and other development. And the more the surrounding land was opened up, the more Anchorage would grow as a center,

with increasingly greater development of major support facilities. Thus data on sources of natural construction material, depth to bedrock, and foundation characteristics of unconsolidated surficial deposits were needed for the design of highways, railroads, bridges, airports, hydroelectric plants, water-distribution and sewage-disposal systems, and large buildings with special foundation requirements.

A map and brief description of the geology summarizing the fieldwork of 1949 was made available in 1950. The final report was published in 1959 as U. S. Geological Survey Bulletin 1093. In addition to the regular sales and exchange distribution, about 100 copies were distributed to individuals, post offices, and institutions in Alaska.

Bulletin 1093 contains a geological map at a scale of 1 inch to the mile (1:63,360), other illustrations, tables, and a text. The map shows 29 surficial and 2 bedrock units, the division made largely on the basis of age and origin. The text describes in some detail the fairly thick sequence of surficial materials upon which Anchorage is built and refers briefly to the bedrock exposed in the adjacent mountains. Of all the map units described, only one was given a formal name, the Bootlegger Cove Clay, a light-gray silty clay of Pleistocene age that is conspicuously exposed in the bluffs along Knik Arm. The physical properties and relationship of the Bootlegger Cove Clay to other units are presented in tables and diagrams. A text section on economic geology discusses known or potential mineral resources, construction materials, and engineering problems. Among the latter are: foundation conditions, excavation, slumps and flows, drainage, and frost heave. As an example of local conditions that should be considered in development, Figure 7 (p. 95) illustrates the relationship of groundwater movement to the upper surface of the Bootlegger Cove Clay where overlain by gravel, and the associated potential health hazard resulting from contamination of the water. Bluff recession caused by active shoreline erosion is documented in Figure 6. Conditions under which landslides can be activated in the Bootlegger Cove Clay are described under slumps and flows. These problems are closely related and in one way or another have a bearing on the geologic effects produced by the 1964 earthquake.

Awareness of the 1950 and 1959 reports was limited to parts of the engineering and geologic professions. The publications served as a guide for the Alaska Road Commission in selecting parcels of land underlain by sand and gravel to be set aside as a reserve for future highway construction needs. They were used as background information by foundation engineers in preliminary site studies for some of the larger buildings, and by geologists of the Alaska Department of Highways. The bulletin was quoted in a geological field guide with respect to geologic history, and has served as a teaching aid. For several reasons the bulletin was not used as background for planning. The planning department was relatively new and its early problems concerned more pressing matters. The report is a general treatment and did not zone or classify the ground except by geologic map units. The map is not a document the planner can use directly without interpretation by a geologist.

There were no geologists on the planning staff.

After the earthquake of March 27, 1964, Bulletin 1093 was read by many and frequently cited for its warning about the susceptibility to landsliding in the Bootlegger Cove Clay. A report by the Engineering Geology Evaluation Group (1964, p. 8–10) established that all of the major landslides in the city of Anchorage were related to the physical properties of the Bootlegger Cove Clay and its distribution in relation to local topography. In a similar way Bulletin 1093 was used by the Scientific and Engineering Task Force of the Federal Reconstruction and Development Planning Commission for Alaska as a basis for preparing a preliminary map classifying "high risk" areas (Federal Reconstruction and Development Planning Commission for Alaska, 1964, maps, p. 59, 61). The principal criteria for the classification were the presence of the Bootlegger Cove Clay along steep slopes and fractures associated with landslides induced by the earthquake. The preliminary map was later modified as more definitive information derived from an emergency program of detailed geologic investigation became available.

It is evident that prior to the earthquake there was little or no communication between the authors of the geologic report and the planners and other public officials who could have used the information in it. The geologists produced their report, which was published in customary manner, and they went on to other assignments. The planners zoned the area under their jurisdiction for various and seemingly appropriate uses. The two groups went on their separate ways, essentially in ignorance of each other, largely because there was no common meeting ground for them. The geologic map was a classification of the various deposits largely in terms of origin and age; engineering characteristics that were given were largely buried in information that seemed nonrelevant to the unitiated (nongeological) reader. Furthermore, the report not only was not read by the nongeologist, but was probably not even known to him. Thus, the geologists were writing only for other geologists, as is their custom. The planners meanwhile were proceeding, as is their custom, without much consideration of the naturally occurring materials that underlie the land, without sufficient awareness of the importance of such a consideration, and without the understanding that they did need to know about the geologic map and its accompanying descriptions.

The events of the earthquake brought the two groups face to face, working in their own ways to repair the damage and look to the future. In this process the planners and other public officials recognized the need for geologic information, and the geologists saw that the conventional format of the standard geologic report was not adequate to meet this need. Consequently in any new geologic work to be undertaken, new products would have to be designed to present geologic information relevant to planning in a form that would be more readily intelligible to the nongeological professional worker. It was in this context that the Chairman of the Greater Anchorage Area Borough, a new political unit much more extensive than the city, asked the U. S. Geological Survey to begin geologic investigation that would encompass the entire Borough. Interpretive maps were especially requested, though the specific kinds of interpretations could not be defined at the time the request was made.

New Geologic Projects

The Greater Anchorage Area Borough is located in south-central Alaska (Fig. 1) and occupies most of a roughly triangular piece of land between the two estuaries at the head of Cook Inlet, Knik Arm to the northwest, and Turnagain Arm to the southwest. The western apex of this triangle and a narrow strip along Knik Arm lie within the Cook Inlet-Susitna Lowland physiographic province (Wahrhaftig 1965) and contain the city of Anchorage and its environs, including most of the land suitable for urban expansion. The remainder of the Borough lies within the Kenai-Chugach Mountains province, and is dominated by rugged, partly glacier-clad mountains with relief of as much as 6,000 feet; narrow valleys and some glacially planed shoulders provide only scattered and discontinuous areas suitable for extensive development. Thus, the greatest interest lies in a relatively small part of the Borough near the city of Anchorage, but as the Borough develops further, more and more of the marginally suitable land within the mountainous area will be brought into use, and it is vital to have basic information on this area at hand before unplanned opportunistic development is allowed to spread into unsuitable territory. The total area of the Borough is approximately 1,730 square miles (4,480 km²), of which about 240 square miles (620 km²) lies in the low-

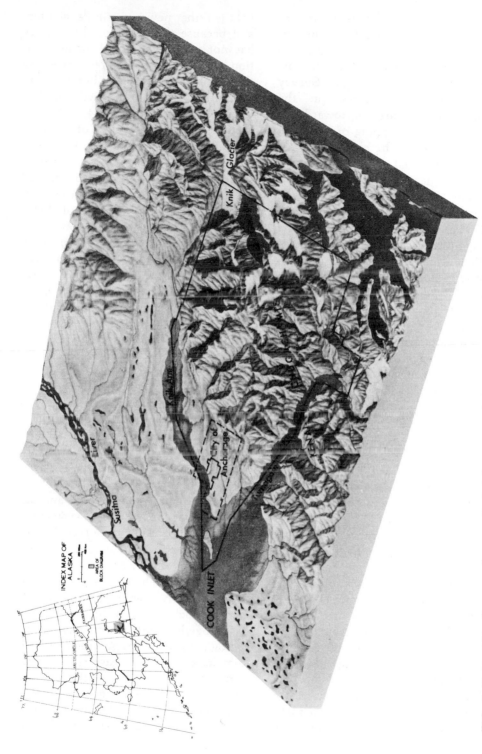

FIG. 1. Perspective diagram of upper Cook Inlet region showing physiographic setting of Anchorage. Boundaries of Greater Anchorage Area Borough and City of Anchorage shown by *solid line*; area of Figures 2, 3, 4, and 5 shown by *dashed line*.

land and the remainder in the mountains; 330 square miles (855 km²) of this part is underlain by glacier ice.

Of the two coordinated and in part interdependent U. S. Geological Survey projects now in progress in the Borough, one is directed toward the general geologic mapping of the area, with emphasis on the engineering aspects thereof, and the other toward the hydrologic aspects of the geology, especially the subsurface geology of the unconsolidated deposits in the lowland. The objective of the engineering geology project is the preparation of detailed and reconnaissance general-purpose geologic maps to provide data basic to understanding the physical features of the ground and to establish a framework within which rational land development plans can be formulated by borough officials. The hydrologic project aims to assemble and integrate the facts about the hydrologic system so that appropriate city and borough officials and their technical associates can design procedures for orderly development of the water resources.

The use of geologic maps in the search for mineral and fossil fuel deposits is well known. Geologic maps and interpretations drawn from them are also widely used in the engineering profession, generally in connection with site selection and location of construction materials for major engineering projects. Geologists are usually employed on such projects to do the geological work. The use of geologic maps in regional planning, however, has not yet become standard practice, nor, with a few notable exceptions, are geologists normally included on planning staffs. This is perhaps because the

field is rather new and still developing, and because the need for this service has not had wide enough demonstration. Geologic maps are recognized by the planning profession, but not significantly discussed in their publications (Chapin 1965, p. 254). There is further reason for neglect of geologic maps by planners. To the untrained user geologic maps are complicated; geologic information is usually plotted on a topographic base, requiring that the user see through a mass of three-dimensional data presented on a flat surface. Geologic units are shown by different colors and patterns to increase legibility, but on many such maps where contacts are intricate, the maps have the appearance of inscrutable clutter.

Nonetheless it is apparent that use of geologic maps would be of considerable benefit to the planner. Among the many considerations of regional land utilization planning are (1) development of the land for agricultural, residential, industrial, recreational, and other uses; (2) site selection for planning engineering works such as dams, bridges, highways, and other major structures; and (3) assessment and development of the hydrologic system for efficient use of water resources. Intelligent planning for land utilization therefore requires knowledge of features of the ground which may be categorized as topography, geology, and hydrology. Geologic maps on the topographic base, together with accompanying hydrologic information, provide just such knowledge, and are basic to any rational understanding of the ground conditions that the planner must have.

By itself, however, the geologic map does not convey to a planner information that is directly useful in his work. It is therefore necessary to interpret the geologic map for the planner. In parallel with the other uses of geologic maps cited above, it would be logical for the planning staff to include a geologist to interpret the geologic map at any time and for any purpose, and to participate fully in the planning process. This practice would indeed be desirable, and in the case of some large planning staffs it is followed; in the usual case of a smaller staff, however, this may not be practical. A useful alternative is the interpretive map, or a series of such maps, designed for the special needs of the planner, and based on the facts contained in the geologic map. It is this new and not at all standard approach that is being employed by the current U. S. Geological Survey projects in the Anchorage area, and interpretive maps are being produced to meet the needs of planners and other professional workers, and to some extent, the general public. Maps of this type have not had wide use in civilian application in the United States, although similar maps have been used by the military for many years (Hunt 1950).

The primary product of the engineering geology project will be the general geologic map of the entire Borough at a scale of 1 inch to the mile (1:63,360). The hydrologic project ultimately plans to produce an electric analog or mathematical model of the hydrologic system. The model can be used to examine changes in the system that would result from various stresses applied, so that reasonable forecasts can be made of the effects of various methods of operating the system for years in advance.

Each interpretive map is restricted in coverage to single or closely related topics. All maps will have a similar format, and are designed to overlay each other for easy reference. The series will be designed for publication at a scale of about 1 inch to 2 miles (1:125,000) so that the entire Borough can appear on a single sheet of manageable size. Maps of selected topics of particular importance for the lowland area may have the larger scale of 1:24,000. Some of the topics to be covered in this series are:

Slopes
Construction materials
Foundation and excavation
  conditions
Stability of natural slopes
Recreation areas
Areas of potential development of
  ground and surface water
Availability of ground-water
Depth to unconfined aquifers
Depth to confined artesian aquifers
Water-table contours
Piezometric surface
Saturated thickness
Principal recharge areas
Chemical quality of water

Each project will also produce a final report in one of the Geological Survey's standard series of papers, in which the general geology and hydrology will be discussed, and the applications thereof summarized. This report will discuss only the topographic, geologic, slope, slope stability, and construction materials maps.

Topographic Maps

The topographic map is an absolute necessity as a base on which to plot

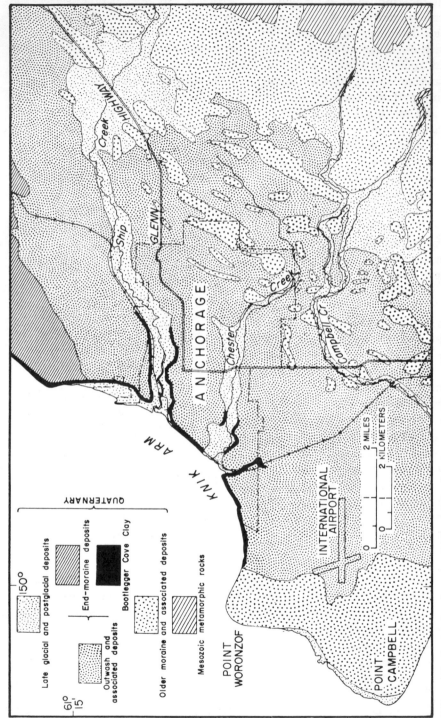

FIG. 2. Geologic sketch map of City of Anchorage and vicinity, Alaska.

data about the land. Planimetric maps used in this report were constructed from a topographic map. Figure 1 illustrates the configuration of land surface in the area. The Greater Anchorage Area Borough is covered by topographic quadrangle maps at a scale of 1:63,360 with a 100-foot contour interval in the mountains and 50-foot contour interval in most of the lowland. A special map at a scale of 1:24,000 with 20-foot contour interval covers the Anchorage metropolitan area in the lowland. Neither map shows changes caused by the 1964 earthquake. Separate topographic maps will not be included among the other maps in the series to be produced, as these maps are already widely distributed and readily available.

Geologic Map

For most of the Greater Anchorage Area Borough a conventional geologic map at a scale of 1:63,360 is adequate to show the geology. Emphasis is placed on the surficial deposits, as these are quite widespread even in the mountains in this glaciated terrane, and comprise most of the materials most critical to development. The bedrock units, on the other hand, are relatively uniform over wide areas, and for the purpose of the current project are being mapped in reconnaissance fashion. The preliminary version of the geologic map currently under revision includes six bedrock units of Mesozoic and Tertiary age, chiefly eugeosynclinal sedimentary and volcanic rocks; 23 units of Pleistocene age, chiefly of glacial origin; and 28 units of Recent age, including glacial, alluvial, and colluvial deposits. Figure 2 is a simplified version of a part of this map, at reduced scale.

Slope Map

The generalized slope map (Fig. 3) is a special kind of topographic map that summarizes the continuously variable slope information shown on the standard topographic map. Categories of slope can be chosen to meet various needs, and the map divided into units with the same slope characteristics. Such a map is necessarily generalized, because except at very large scales there usually are local slopes that do not fall within the assigned category. Inasmuch as the distribution of slopes is not random but systematic, however, it is practical to make a meaningful map. Though the slope map can be made directly from and entirely dependent upon the topographic map, its accuracy can be considerably enhanced by field observation and use of aerial photographs.

For planning purposes three primary categories of slope have been chosen: (1) slopes less than 15 percent; (2) slopes 15 to 45 percent; (3) slopes greater than 45 percent. In addition, the upper and lower categories have been subdivided, so that large areas with slopes less than 5 percent, and significant areas with many slopes greater than 100 percent are also shown. The most important division here is at 45 percent, which is the reasonable upper limit for maneuvering tracked vehicles. Figure 3 shows a part of the slope map that has been made for the entire borough.

The principal reason for making a slope map is to identify areas having the same range of slope percent, be-

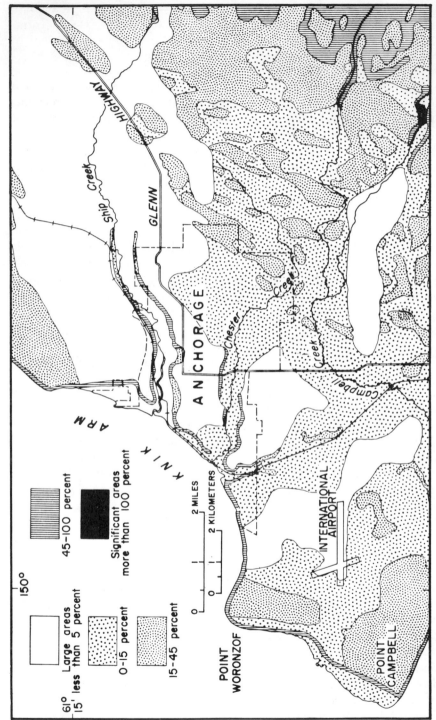

FIG. 3. Generalized slope map of City of Anchorage and vicinity, Alaska.

cause the angle of slope is a major factor in estimating slope stability. Landslides occur mainly on steep slopes and along sharp topographic discontinuities such as bluffs. They do not occur in areas of low relief that are far from breaks in topography. Identification of steep slopes is the first step in the process of isolating areas where landslides are more likely to occur. Used in conjunction with the geologic map, the slope map is a tool that leads to appraising the landslide potential of natural slopes.

Slope Stability Map

An interpretation of the stability of natural slopes in the Anchorage area is shown on Figure 4 and the map units are summarized in Table 1. The po-

tential for landslides, especially in response to seismic shock, is of principal concern here, but other types of ground movement, such as solifluction and rockfall, are also considered. The map is derived essentially from the slope map and the geologic map. The primary criterion for determining instability is the degree of slope; areas of steep and very steep slope will be the chief sites of instability. However, the degree of instability depends considerably on the geologic material underlying the slope. Thus by combining elements of the two maps the slope stability map can be prepared, showing varying degrees of stability. Generally the areas of low and moderate slopes are lumped together as having high stability. Parts of these areas adjacent to zones of low stability, how-

Table 1 Description of map units for stability map of naturally occuring slopes

Map unit	Slope stability	Landslide potential	Solifluction potential	Slopes (percent)	Geology
1	High	Very low	Very low	<45	Undifferentiated
2	Moderately high	Generally low	Generally low	45–100	Generally stable bedrock
3	Moderate	Moderately low to moderately high	Moderately low	45–100	Medium- to coarse-grained unconsolidated deposits
4	Moderately low	Moderately low to moderately high	High	45–100	Soft, frost-susceptible bedrock, chiefly argillite
5	Low (This unit is not present in the area covered by Fig. 4)	Moderately high	High (chiefly rockfalls and snow avalanches)	Commonly >100	Bedrock, fractured and in part faulted
6	Very low	High	High (chiefly slumps and earthflows)	15–>100	Unconsolidated deposits underlain by sensitive clay and silt, or incorporating ice

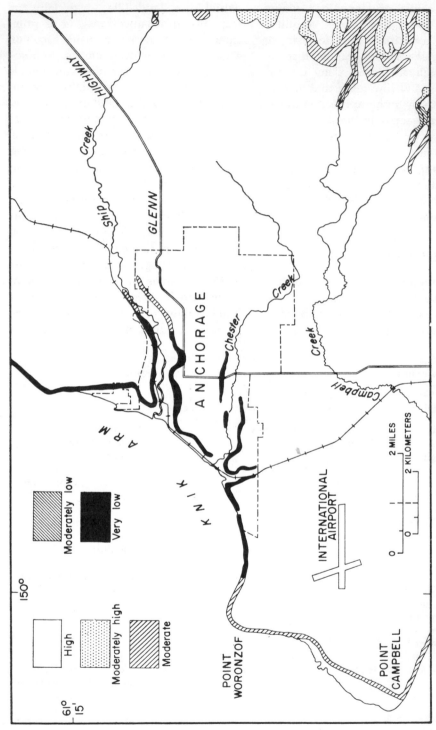

FIG. 4. Map showing stability of naturally occurring slopes, City of Anchorage and vicinity, Alaska. Map units are described in Table 1.

ever, may have potentially low stability because, for example, of the possibility that a landslide can work back from an area of steep slope and "eat" into an adjacent area of low slope; this actually happened during the 1964 earthquake. Also, the low slopes extending outward from the base of a bluff may be over-ridden by landslide debris or disturbed by pressure ridges. Such features cannot be projected on the scale of a map used here, but the potential problem area is outlined as to general location.

Figure 4 clearly shows (a) those areas which are unsuited for most development because of slope stability problems that cannot feasibly be surmounted except in unusual circumstances (units 5 and 6); (b) those areas in which slope stability presents problems that must be considered in planning and design but for which a solution can be worked out (units 3 and 4); and (c) those areas which are relatively free of slope stability problems. It must be emphasized, however, that the map is generalized, that locally within each unit the described situation may not exist, and that for particular development detailed site investigations must be made. The map is designed primarily to delineate those areas in which particular problems can be expected.

Construction Materials Map

The construction materials map is one of the most direct interpretations that can be made from the geologic map. It is essentially a lithologic map, in which geologic units of various ages and origins that have similar lithologies, and therefore similar utility as construction materials, are grouped to-gether in a single map unit. In some cases single units on the geologic map have been split into more than one lithologic unit, reflecting usually a gradational change of material within the geologic unit. Sometimes such a breakdown within a geologic unit requires additional fieldwork, and even so may have to be made arbitrarily. Thus, the transformation is not purely mechanical but requires refined geologic interpretation.

A construction materials map has been made for Anchorage based on the geologic map published in Bulletin 1093, and is confined largely to the lowland area; it has been produced at a scale of 1:24,000 and required additional field checking and laboratory analysis beyond what was done in the first survey. Six of the seven map units are for unconsolidated materials; the seventh includes all bedrock, which covers only a small part of the area and has no particular utility as a construction material. The six unconsolidated units range from gravel and commonly interbedded gravel and sand, which are of great economic importance in the area, to sand, silt, till, and swamp deposits which have relatively little utility. During the current project the entire Borough will be so mapped at smaller scale, and the large-scale map may be further refined. Figure 5 shows a part of the small-scale map.

On such a map, areas that are of interest for potential use as sources of granular construction materials can be readily seen. Though much of the land has already been preempted for other purposes, this map can still be used to select from the unoccupied areas those deposits which appear to warrant more

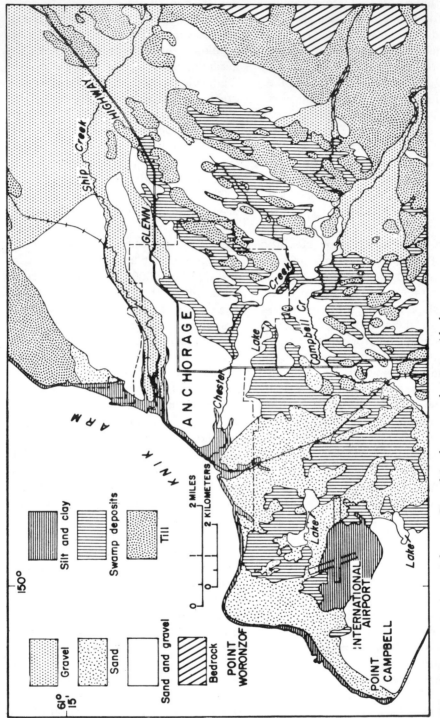

FIG. 5. Construction materials map, City of Anchorage and vicinity, Alaska.

detailed investigations. The more desirable deposits can be reserved for future use and, as part of a systematic plan, exploited prior to development of the land for other uses. It is not the intent of the map to serve as a resource map in the sense of estimating gravel reserves, or detailing the precise uses for which a particular deposit is most suited. More detailed site investigations are required for such determinations. The map does serve primarily as a guide so that the planner can know which areas are to be selected for further investigation, and which have no construction materials and can be considered for other types of development.

Recreation Areas

It has been considered appropriate to present a map showing areas particularly suited for recreational purposes, particularly those areas that are of interest for their scenic beauty or natural history, but including other areas that are less spectacular but well suited for such activities as hiking and camping, and able to accommodate large numbers of people. Chiefly esthetic considerations are involved here, and these are necessarily subjective in nature. They can less readily be derived precisely from measurements of slope or behavior of geologic materials. Nonetheless, elements of topography, geology, and hydrology play a major role in determining which areas have high esthetic appeal, and we regard that in any study of these fields such considerations should not be overlooked.

The Greater Anchorage Area Borough is fortunate in having many areas of unusual scenic interest, some of which are widely known and frequently visited; others are presently inaccessible to most people and totally undeveloped. Of special interest is Lake George, a multistage glacial lake that forms when water from a tributary valley is impounded behind Knik Glacier in the spring. In early summer the water overtops the glacier, and the river cuts a narrow gorge between steep rock and ice walls, almost emptying the lake.

The recreation potential map is intended as a guide to the planning staff, to aid in assigning priorities to development and determining degree of development that should be permitted, so that the recreation potential of the area can be realized in an orderly manner.

Conclusions

There are many elements of an economic, social, and political nature that must be considered in the planning process; these have been deciding factors in the past, and no doubt will continue to be so. Nonetheless, the physical environment deserves increased consideration, especially in areas where that environment is not as hospitable as it is in other areas where more planning experience has accumulated. This is true of large areas in the western United States that are in a general way characterized by dynamic geological processes of greater magnitude and intensity than those in the more highly developed East. It is also true, however, that in the older established cities the less problematical areas have been developed first, and those areas into which new development will extend are more likely to present physical problems. Thus there is need for wide application of the principles of planning in this era of rapid urbanization, and need for these principles to include consideration of the natural physical environment. This is true for those areas that are already well developed such as the United States, and also for the less well developed nations that will grow at ever increasing rates in the near future. And the greater the intensity of development, the greater the need for this type of planning.

In order that considerations of the physical environment gain greater prominence, geologists and others who study the physical environment should promote understanding of their work. They should meet with planners and other responsible public officials on a personal working-level basis, they should learn the jargon and needs of those individuals, and they should design their own products to be of optimum use. This statement does not imply that there should be any lessening in their own scientific pursuits, without which their work would have less and less value, but the geologist does have to bear the added burden of carrying his work to the user so that its potential utility can be fully realized. It is with this goal in mind that we believe the work of the geologic and hydrologic projects in the Greater Anchorage Area Borough can make a

contribution to the wider application of the geological sciences in the expanding area of orderly urban development.

References

Cederstrom, D. J., Trainer, F. W. and Waller, R. M. (1964): Geology and ground-water resources of the Anchorage area, Alaska. U. S. Geol. Survey Water-Supply Paper 1773, 108 p.

Chapin, F. S., Jr. (1965): Urban land use planning (2d ed.). Urbana, Univ. Illinois Press, 498 p.

Hunt, C. B. (1950): Military geology, in Paige, Sidney, chm., Application of geology to engineering practice. Geol. Soc. America, Berkey Volume, p. 295–327.

Engineering Geology Evaluation Group, 1964, Geologic report—27 March 1964 earthquake in Greater Anchorage area. Prepared for and published by Alaska State Housing Authority and the City of Anchorage, Anchorage, Alaska, 34 p., 12 figs., 17 pls.

Federal Reconstruction and Development Planning Commission for Alaska, 1964, Response to disaster, Alaskan earthquake, March 27, 1964. Washington, U.S. Govt. Printing Office, 84 p.

Miller, R. D. and Dobrovolny, E. (1959): Surficial geology of Anchorage and vicinity, Alaska. U.S. Geol. Survey Bull. 1093, 128 p.

Wahrhaftig, C. (1965): Physiographic divisions of Alaska: U.S. Geol. Survey Prof. Paper 482, 52 p. [1966].

Waller, R. M. (1964): Hydrology and the effects of increased ground-water pumping in the Anchorage area, Alaska. U.S. Geol. Survey Water-Supply Paper 1779-D, 36 pp.

Editor's note: The Arctic Environmental Information and Data Center of the University of Alaska has published an *Environmental Atlas of the Greater Anchorage Area Borough, Alaska* (edited and coordinated by Lidia L. Selkreff, 1972) which contains a variety of special purpose interpretive maps useable by the informed layman, planning personnel, and administrators who may not have a formal background in the geological sciences.

Supplementary Readings

Introduction

Cargo, D. N., and Mallory, B. F., 1974, *Man and His Geologic Environment*, Addison-Wesley Publishing Co., Inc., Mass., 548 pp.

Coates, D. R., ed., 1973, *Environmental Geomorphology and Landscape Conservation*, vol. III, Dowden, Hutchinson, & Ross, Inc., Stroudsburg, Pa., 483 pp.

Flawn, P. T., 1970, *Environmental Geology-Conservation, Land-Use Planning, and Resource Management*, Harper and Row, New York, 313 pp.

Geological Survey of Alabama, 1971, *Environmental Geology and Hydrology, Madison Co., Alabama: Meridianville Quadrangle: Geol Survey Alabama, Atlas Series 1*, 72 pp.

Lapurle, L., 1975, *Encounter With the Earth*, Canfield Press, San Francisco, Calif.

McKenzie, G. D., and Utgard, R. O., ed., 1975, *Man and His Physical Environment*, 2nd. ed., Burgess Publishing Co., Minn. 388 pp.

Menard, H. W., 1974, *Geology, Resources and Society*, W. H. Freeman and Co., San Francisco, Calif., 621 pp.

National Academy of Sciences—Committee on Geological Sciences, 1972, *The Earth and Human Affairs*, Canfield Press, San Francisco, Calif., 142 pp.

Pessl, F., Jr., Langer, W. H. and Ryder, R. B., 1972, Geologic and Hydrologic Maps for Land-Use Planning in the Connecticut Valley With Examples from the Folio of the Hartford North Quadrangle, Connecticut, *U. S. Geological Survey Circular 674*, 12 pp.

Selkregg, L. L., ed., 1972, *Environmental Atlas of the Greater Anchorage Area Borough, Alaska*, Univ. of Alaska, 105 pp.

Strahler, A. N., and Strahler, A. H., 1973, *Environmental Geoscience: Interaction Between Natural Systems and Man*, Hamilton Publishing Co., Calif., 511 pp.

Turk, L. J., ed., 1975, *Environmental Geology*, Springer-Verlag, New York Inc., New York, N. Y.

U. S. Dept. of Interior, 1973, Resource and Land Information, South Dade County Florida, *Geological Survey Investigation I-850*, 66 pp.

Wermund, E. G., ed., 1974, *Approaches to Environmental Geology, Bureau of Economic Geology Report of Investigations, No. 81*, Univ. of Texas, Austin, Texas, 286 pp.

Young, Kieth, 1975, *Geology, The Paradox of Earth and Man*, Houghton Mifflin Co., Boston, 526 pp.

Earthquake Damage, Anchorage, Alaska. Courtesy of U. S. Army.

II. Geologic Hazards and Hostile Environments

"More than ever before, local communities are seeking guidance concerning environmental hazards of all types that should be taken into account in planning for the use of land to be developed."

National Academy of Sciences

It seems appropriate to continue our analysis of the geological aspects of environmental problems by reviewing the impact of geologic processes on the environment and the activities of Man. These processes can be highly beneficial. They may, for example, produce valuable ore deposits, provide rich soil, and create spectacular scenery. The growth of economies and cultures can be directly related to many of these geologic processes. On the other hand, these same geologic processes can produce natural hazards or hostile environments that result in catastrophes. Given the highly sophisticated nature of modern technology, it would appear that Man could simply exploit the benefits and control the hazards, thereby exercising a high degree of control over his own destiny. Man's control of his own destiny is far from complete, however, because he has not understood or has frequently failed to make allowances for a variety of geologic hazards.

Part Two deals with the hazards associated with six geologic agents. There are other potential geologic hazards, but the examples cited serve to illustrate the dynamic aspects of geologic agents and their impact on Man. Most of the problems associated with these hostile forces can be avoided or minimized by utilizing adequate geologic data.

Volcanism

All mountains, islands, and level lands have been raised up out of the bosom of the earth into the position they now occupy by the action of subterranean fires.

Lazzaro Moro

Volcanism is one of the most dynamic of all earth processes and one of the most terrifying hazards. Many volcanologists consider the prediction and control of volcanic activity the ultimate goal of their discipline. As magmas begin to rise toward the surface one can anticipate earth tremors, a swelling and tilting of the local topography, increases in ground temperatures, and local changes in the earth's magnetic field and in its electrical currents. All of these phenomena can be detected by sensitive instruments.

Forewarning of an eruption might therefore come from several sources, and one must keep in mind that there are significant differences among volcanoes and their patterns of eruption. For nine days, increasing numbers of earthquakes were felt near the town of San Juan de Parangaricutiro in Mexico. On the tenth day the volcano El Parícutin was born. The people in the vicinity of Heimaey, Iceland, received almost no warning when Kirkjufell erupted at 2:00 A.M. on January 23, 1973. The events associated with the eruption of these volcanoes are vividly described in Readings 3 and 5. These volcanoes were quite different in their style of eruption, and one must be alert to these differences when engaged in forecasting activities.

In Reading 4, Dwight Crandell and Howard Waldron warn us of the hazards in the Cascade Range. Their concern is based on the past behavior of the volcanoes in this region as interpreted from postglacial strata. Their approach illustrates how one must use stratigraphic data in those instances in which the length of historical time is not sufficient to reveal the pattern of activity in dormant volcanoes. Man often complicates natural hazards through his activities, and nature, by presenting multiple hazards, frequently offers additional problems. Man's role is evident in the Cascade Range, where he has constructed numerous reservoirs and settled in valleys and lowlands well within the range of floods, mudflows, lava flows, and ash falls. It is obviously imperative to monitor the volcanoes of the Cascade Range, to recognize phenomena which might warn of an impending disaster, and to plan future developments so as to minimize the potential danger. (One cannot help wondering how many people in this area are aware of the hazardous setting and what preparations have been made to cope with a potential eruption.)

Although Man has the option to migrate to a less hazardous environment, he frequently chooses to remain in a hostile setting. Historically, there has been a tendency to view a catastrophe, such as a volcanic

Photo on page 31. Parícutin, Feb. 20, 1948 (5 years old). View from upper Casita. Only one "island" is left of prelava topography between Casita and cone. Courtesy of U. S. Geological Survey.

eruption, as the act of a vengeful god and with resignation to a fate that is beyond comprehension and control. Even with the vast amount of scientific information available today, Man's reaction to catastrophe and prediction of catastrophe frequently differs very little from that of his ancestors. Vesuvius has been intermittently active since A.D. 79, and, although thousands of people have been victims of this activity, nearby Naples continues to attract people and is today a thriving city of 1.25 million. The 1973 eruption on Heimaey caused extensive property damage. It was the fourth explosive eruption in little more than a decade, but it did not discourage resettlement.

Although it is usually difficult to change human settlement patterns, steps can be taken to reduce the possible tragic consequences. For example, one can attempt to divert lava streams from inhabited areas. Diversion techniques include the construction of walls, digging of ditches, and even bombing lava flowing in confined channels. In Reading 5, Richard Williams, Jr., and James Moore describe how sea water was used in Man's most successful attempt yet to "control" a volcano which threatened Iceland's major fishing port. The Heimaey eruption was one of the most destructive in Iceland's history, but there are plans to exploit the tephra and heat trapped within the hot lava piles. Many other communities faced with volcanic hazards are located near large bodies of water and have much to gain from the experience of "controlling" the Heimaey eruption.

3   The Mexican Volcano Parícutin*
Dr. Parker D. Trask

The new volcano in Mexico, El Parícutin (pronounced Pah-*ree*-koo-teen) is a unique geological phenomenon; for,

* Address presented before the Geologic Section of the New York Academy of Sciences in New York, October 4, 1943. Published by permission of The Director, Geological Survey, U. S. Department of the Interior.

Trask, P. D., 1943, "The Mexican Volcano Parícutin," *Science*, vol. 98, n. 2554, pp. 501–5. Reprinted with light editing by permission of the American Association for the Advancement of Science. Copyright 1943 by the A.A.A.S.

The late Dr. Trask was on the staff of the United States Geological Survey when he made his observations of El Parícutin.

before our very eyes, it has sprung into existence and has grown to a very respectable height of 1,500 feet, all within a period of 8 months. It lies within a region in which no previous volcanic activity has been known within the memory of man, though in 1759 the volcano El Jorullo, some 50 miles to the southeast, likewise suddenly was born, grew to a height of more than 1,000 feet within 5 months, and then quieted down, never more to erupt violently. Will Parícutin do likewise? That remains to be seen, for at present it is still going strong.

For the first time in their lives geologists have been able to observe in a single volcano all stages of its history. Parícutin exhibits many of the features of other volcanoes; but other volcanoes have been encountered by geologists after they have been in existence for some time, and their early history is unknown. The early history of Parícutin therefore fills important gaps in our understanding of volcanism.

To me the most outstanding aspect of this volcano is the incredible rapidity with which it grew. Within one week it was 550 feet high and within 10 weeks it was 1,100 feet in altitude. Up to this time, all the material in its cone had come from fragments that had been blown into the air from the volcano. No lava came from the cone until nearly four months after the eruption started; and then, contrary to some popular reports, it did not flow over the lip of the crater. Instead, it broke through the sides of the cone, undermining the overlying fragmental material. Lava appeared within two days of the first explosion, but it issued quietly from a fissure about 1,000 feet north of the explosive vent.

Geologists have been observing Parícutin practically from its inception. Dr. Ezéquiel Ordoñez, the grand old man of Mexican geology, despite some eight decades of age, reached the volcano, together with some associates from the Instituto Geológico de Mexico, within two days of its birth; and he has actively been watching its development ever since. Senor Téodor Flores, director of the Instituto Geológico, has devoted all available facilities of his institution to the study of Parícutin, and the passionate interest he has shown in this volcano would gladden the heart of any scientist.

Dr. William F. Foshag, of the U. S. National Museum, in charge of the war-minerals work of the U. S. Geological Survey in Mexico, has been making a systematic study of Parícutin, and I am indebted to him for practically all statements in this paper not based on my own observations. In addition, many other geologists have visited the volcano. Therefore eventually a rather complete record of its history will be available. I saw Parícutin three times: first, a week after its birth; a second time when it was nearly three months old; and once again, a month later, when I flew over it in an airplane during one of the stages when lava was pouring from the cone.

Parícutin is located in the state of Michoacan, 200 miles in airline due west of Mexico City in the Sierra Madre Occidental, which forms the west boundary of the high plateau that occupies the central part of Mexico. The volcano is situated in an area of forested hills and cultivated lowlands, and the base of the cone lies about 7,500 feet above sea level.

Parícutin is located in a region of volcanic rocks consisting of essentially the same andesitic basalt as its own lava. Several hundred volcanic cones lie within a radius of 75 miles of the volcano. These are of all ages; some are so fresh that they can hardly be more than a few hundred or a few thousand years old; others are so dissected by erosion that they must be many tens of thousands of years in age. Most of them are cinder cones— that is, cones composed of debris blown from a vent in the ground; others are composite cones consisting of both lava and fragmental material. They range in height mainly from 200 to 800 feet.

The highest rises some 4,000 feet above the surrounding country. The soil is rich and is derived from volcanic ash and interbedded lava. Most of the cones are conical and have small craters, but a few consist of rings of fragmental material, 200 feet or less in height and some hundreds of feet in diameter. One such abortive cone is situated about one mile northwest of Parícutin; another lies some miles to the east. From the air this latter cone seems to be some 3,000 feet in diameter and less than 200 feet in height. It contains within it, but somewhat off center, a similar ring-like ridge about 1,500 feet in diameter.

The first intimation that something was about to happen was an account in the newspapers about February 12, 1943, that 25 to 30 earthquakes had been felt the previous day near the town of San Juan de Parangaricútiro. Each day thereafter increasingly more tremors were reported, and on February 19 some 300 earthquakes occurred. The next day the eruptions started.

Stories of the beginning of the volcano are legion, and as time goes on they probably will become more varied. One of the most colorful is that a farmer while plowing his field turned over a stone, whereupon lava gushed forth and, like the headless horseman in the Legend of Sleepy Hollow, raced down the furrows behind him as he fled. This story of course is fantastic; in the first place, no Mexican would plow a furrow down hill, and in the second place, the Parícutin lava was too viscous to flow rapidly.

The most reliable story is that a farmer, Dionisio Pulido, while plowing noticed a column of smoke about three inches in diameter spiralling upward from a small hole in the middle of the field. Thinking that he had inadvertently started a fire he went over to the smoke and put it out by placing a stone over the hole. He continued plowing and sometime later looked around and saw smoke emerging from the ground in greater force. He went forthwith to inform the Presidente of the town of San Juan, who sent a group to see what was happening. Upon arriving at the spot three hours later these people found a hole some 30 feet in depth from which dense clouds of dark smoke were issuing. About ten that night, February 20, the first explosion occurred, and since that time the volcano has been erupting steadily.

When I first visited the volcano, on February 28, a little over one week after its inception, the explosions were coming at fairly regular intervals of 4 seconds. At times two explosions would come in quick succession; at other times the interval between outbursts was 6 or 8 seconds. In general the explosions were of about equal force, though occasional loud outbursts occurred. One was strong enough to knock me off balance while walking some 3,000 feet from the crater.

The sound from the explosions seemed to originate within the crater at about the level of the ground, though occasional explosions took place in the ash cloud 500 feet above the top of the cone. Each explosion from the crater acted like a giant gun-burst. The material was ejected from the throat of the volcano in a cylindrical column to a height of 400 to 800 feet above the top of the volcano, and at this point, like water in hydraulic jump, suddenly formed dark expanding cumulus clouds of ash that billowed upward to a height of 6,000 to 8,000 feet above the ground, where steam would begin to condense. With increasing altitude the ash cloud became progressively whiter with water vapor until some 10,000 to 12,000 feet above the ground, where it was nearly pure white. The column of vapor continued upward to about 15,000 feet and was carried eastward in a horizontal cloud bank from which columns or large puffs of vapor curled upward for another 2,000 or 3,000 feet, like ostrich plumes sewed tandem on an ermine scarf.

At this time the material ejected from the crater was thrown upward at an angle deviating from the vertical by 10°, much as if it were coming from a sharply defined conduit. As a result of this inclined direction of outburst, more material fell on the west side of the cone than on the east, thus causing the top of the cone to be lopsided. In the course of four hours the angle of ejection changed gradually back to vertical and two hours later was deviating 5 degrees to the east, thus causing the east side of the cone to build up faster than the west side.

The column of ash ascended nearly vertically but was deflected slightly eastward by the wind. Trains of cinders, one-eighth to one-half inch in diameter, rained down from the ash clouds on the lee side of the cone. They were cool, light and very porous, and they sounded like sleet as they fell on one's hat. Few cinders were falling more than two miles from the volcano. At this distance the ground was just barely covered by them. Fine particles of ash were transported greater distances than cinders, and covered the country side in delicate films for as much as 15 miles away on the leeward side. The ash and cinders were 18 inches thick 500 feet from the edge of the cone, which was the closest to the volcano my courage permitted me to approach.

At this point the ground was pockmarked with pits three to five feet in diameter where large fragments or bombs had buried themselves in the ground. The average distance between bomb-pits at this point was about 20 feet. During some 30 minutes while I was standing there, two bombs fell within 300 feet. One bomb more than four feet in diameter landed 25 feet away. For awhile as it was coming down it looked as though it might make a direct hit, and the problem was which way to run, but eventually it veered slightly and the next moment it came down with a large whoosh and whistle, and buried itself. The top was about one foot beneath the surface of the ground. A piece broken from it was hot enough to light cigarettes. Another bomb two feet in diameter, landed 50 feet to the rear, breaking an oak limb eight inches in diameter, much as if it were a cleaver cutting a bone. This bomb buried itself three feet in the ground. It came down five feet from some girls, who immediately retired to a more discreet distance.

Most of the fragmental material ejected from the volcano in this stage of its history consisted of bombs, rather than of ash or cinders. With each explosion the bombs were blown 2,000 to 3,000 feet into the air. Most of them landed on the cone; the greatest distance at which I found a bomb was 3,500 feet from the center of the volcano. The bombs went so high that it took from 10 to 15 seconds for most of them to fall, after they had reached their greatest height. They were roughly spherical and ranged in size from a walnut to a big house. Most of them were between three and five feet in diameter. The largest I saw was a block 50 feet in diameter, which was blown 300 feet above the top of the crater; that is, 850 feet above the ground. Nearly all the bombs when they landed were so thoroughly solidified as not to change in shape, though many when they struck the sides of the cone, broke into pieces. A few were still liquid when they landed and splattered out like pancakes on the ground. Bombs of this type did not penetrate the earth for more than three inches. Others rotated slowly in the air, gradually thinning in the middle, and before they fell separated into two tear-shaped bodies. Some, after coming to rest on the cone, smoked for a considerable time, certainly for as long as 15 minutes. Most of the bombs consisted of highly vesicular basalt, but a very small proportion were composed of a light medium-grained granitic rock that looked like diorite. These granitic rocks were angular, and not vesicular. They evidently were blown from the conduit through which the lava was coming.

Most of the bombs landed upon the sides of the cone, ricocheting down the side until they came to rest. The sides of the cone were remarkably even and were at an angle of 33° with the horizontal. The volcano at this time was 550 feet high and 1,700 feet in diameter at the base. The diameter of the crater at the top of the cone was 250 feet, and the orifice from which the material was ejected seemingly was about 75 feet in diameter.

The volcano at night is a magnificent, never-to-be-forgotten sight. Nearly all the bombs that are blown from the crater are red hot, and they shower up like a gigantic Fourth-of-July flowerpot. The floral effect is complicated by the fact that four or five subsequent explosions have taken place before the bombs from any one explosion have all landed. Thus some bombs are going up, some are just arching over at their highest point, and others are falling. After the bombs strike the sides of the cone they cascade down in great fiery arcs. Some come to rest on the sides; others roll to the bottom. The glow from the cone comes and goes, depending upon the number of bombs that fall and the interval between explosions. Big outbursts cover the whole volcano, and the cone progressively lightens up in an ever larger descending curtain of fiery red, as the fragments land progressively down the sides of the cone. Then, as the bombs cool, the red gradually darkens. Yet before the color finally vanishes another crop of bombs falls and the scene is repeated. Even though parts of the cone may fade into darkness before a succeeding increment of glowing bombs descends, a ring of red always remains around the edge of the cone where the rocks that roll completely down the sides come to rest.

A flow of lava first appeared in a plowed field about 1,000 feet north of the crater about two days after the birth of the volcano. In five days it had attained a length of 2,000 feet, a width of 600 feet and a thickness of 20 feet at the sides and front. It continued to grow for about 6 weeks until it was about 6,000 feet long, 3,000 feet wide and more than 100 feet high. The front and sides were steeply inclined; the top was nearly flat and consisted of blocks of congealed scraggly aa lava 3 to 15 feet in diameter.

At the time I saw the lava, five days after it first appeared, it was flowing westward down a gently sloping field at a rate of about three feet an hour in front and one foot an hour on the sides. Like a glacier the lava moved most rapidly in direction of greatest slope, and like a glacier it also developed pressure ridges as it flowed. It advanced by pushing large blocks of solidified lava, three to five feet in diameter, off the front and sides. These blocks fell down the edges of the flow, and in turn were covered by other blocks similarly spalled by the advancing lava. Gradually the molten rock inside the flow passed over the fallen blocks and incorporated them within itself, forming a volcanic flow breccia. At all times the surface of the lava was congealed, except for places from which blocks had broken off at the edges of the flow as the lava advanced. These freshly exposed places consisted of red, pasty, dense lava that solidified within a few minutes to hard rock.

Fumaroles came out of vents 6 inches to a foot in diameter and gave off dense clouds of white smoke, which, according to Foshag, is largely ammonium chloride. The ammonium chloride also condenses in a white powder around the orifices of the fumaroles, and in places a fringe of bright-orange iron chloride is also formed. Few poisonous gases seemingly are given off.

When I visited Parícutin the second time, about the middle of May, nearly three months after its birth, it was still erupting at about the same rate, but the explosions were less forceful and a much larger proportion of ash was coming out. The cone had doubled in height and the orifice from which the material was being ejected seemed to be about 150 feet in diameter. Ash was everywhere, and most of the trees within 5 miles of the volcano had been killed. The lava flow had stopped moving and was covered by 6 to 8 feet of ash. Even at Uruapan, 15 miles east of the volcano, the ash was 6 to 8 inches thick, and at San Juan, four miles to the west, it was 15 inches thick. A large part of this ash fell in one period of 36 hours early in April. Electrical discharges or lightning strokes were flashing at irregular intervals, sometimes as frequently as 30 an hour. These flashes were vertical in the cloud of ash, and generally started within a few hundred feet of the top of the cone. They ranged in length mainly from 500 to 1,500 feet, and produced sharp cracks but no loud thunder.

About four weeks after this visit, a phase of lava actively ensued. In the course of a week, 8 flows appeared, all from within the cone. Prior to this time, that is, for almost four months, no lava had come from the cone itself and there had been just the one flow. According to Foshag, each flow was preceded by a period of violent explosive activity, which terminated shortly before the lava came. While the lava was issuing from the volcano relatively few explosions took place. All these flows ruptured the sides of the cone, and those that came from the upper part of the volcano undermined the fragmental material above, leaving a large gap in the side of the cone. These gaps were rapidly filled by material blown from the crater after the lava ceased to move. One flow advanced in three days as far as the town of Parícutin, three miles to the west. When it approached Parícutin it was moving at a rate of about 100 feet an hour. Another flow on the east side of the cone spread out like a large fan at the base of the volcano. According to Foshag, this one went 1,500 feet in 15 minutes.

While one of these flows was in progress, I had the good fortune to fly over the volcano. At this time the crater was nearly full; lava extending to within 50 feet of the lip. The top of the lava in the crater was congealed, and was broken in large blocks. Ashes were issuing from a vent estimated to be 75 to 100 feet in diameter in the northwest part of the lava field within the crater, but relatively few explosions were seen. Lava was flowing from an opening on the east side of the cone. This vent was 50 to 75 feet' in width and 200 to 300 feet in height. The upper limit was 100 to 150 feet beneath the lip of the crater. The lava coming through the opening was red hot, but it soon cooled and congealed while flowing down the sides of the volcano. The cone was intact above the point of escape of lava, but according to Foshag it subsequently was undermined by the flow.

At this time, June 19th, Parícutin was 1,200 feet in altitude. By late September it had reached a height of 1,500 feet. At that time it was still exploding at about the same rate as when it started, and was showing no signs of dying. In the meantime several other flows of lava had appeared, mostly from within the cone. Parícutin truly is now a full-fledged volcano.

4   Volcanic Hazards in the Cascade Range*

Dwight R. Crandell and Howard H Waldron

Newspapers recently carried the story that the Vatican had just demoted 90 saints, including St. Januarius. You may recall that his blood is kept in

* Publication authorized by the Director, U. S. Geological Survey.

Crandell, D. R. and Waldron, H. H., 1969, "Volcanic Hazards in the Cascade Range," in *Geologic Hazards and Public Problems, Conf. Proceedings*, R. Olson and M. Wallace, eds., U. S. Govt. Printing Office, pp. 5–18. Lightly edited by permission of the senior author.
D. Crandell and H. Waldron are research geologists on the staff of the United States Geological Survey in Denver, Colorado.

vials in a cathedral in Naples and that it liquifies several times each year. One of these times is on December 16, which is the anniversary of the 1631 eruption of Mount Vesuvius. According to the newspaper article, St. Januarius has stopped the lava flows from Mount Vesuvius many times, and has repeatedly saved the Neapolitans from countless other catastrophes. Perhaps we should invoke the spirit of St. Januarius, as we discuss geologic hazards, and perhaps he should also be our patron saint.

We are pleased to report that the human casualty rate has been very low, probably nil, from volcanic erup-

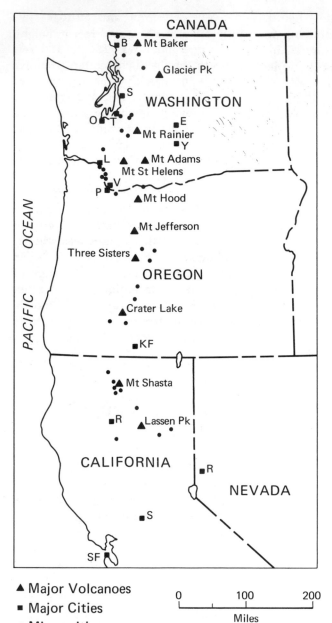

FIG. 1. Index map of Cascade Range, showing locations of major volcanoes, and major and minor cities in their vicinity.

CANADA

B ▲ Mt Baker

▲ Glacier Pk

WASHINGTON

S

O T

E

▲ Mt Rainier

Y

L ▲ ▲ Mt Adams

Mt St Helens

V

P ▲ Mt Hood

▲ Mt Jefferson

Three Sisters ▲

OREGON

▲ Crater Lake

KF

▲ Mt Shasta

R ▲ Lassen Pk

CALIFORNIA

R

NEVADA

S

SF

PACIFIC OCEAN

▲ Major Volcanoes
■ Major Cities
• Minor cities

0   100   200

Miles

tions in the Cascade Range (Fig. 1) within historic time. There is a report of an Indian who burned his leg against a lava flow from Mount St. Helens in 1844, and in 1914 a man who stood too close to the erupting crater of Lassen Peak was rather badly injured by a rock that flew out of the crater. But even he is still alive today.

So, we really cannot evaluate the dimension of volcanic hazards in the Cascade Range by the past casualty rate or by the amount of past property damage, as we can with some other geologic hazards. I think we will all agree that it's our good fortune to have volcanoes that are pretty tame. At least they are today!

This very lack of repeated eruptions in the Cascade Range is a problem in itself, for it is very difficult to predict the behavior of a volcano that has never been observed to erupt. For example, Arenal volcano in Costa Rica had been dormant for hundreds of years; in fact, it was thought to be extinct. But it erupted violently on July 29, 1968 with very little warning and killed more than 70 people in nearby villages. A year ago, if someone had asked which Costa Rican volcano might erupt next, Arenal probably would not have even been on the list; and, naturally, nothing was known about what kind of eruption could be expected.

Likewise, we don't know which of the Cascade volcanoes will be the next to erupt, but by means of a hazards evaluation study at a given volcano, we can predict some of the effects if that volcano *were* to erupt. We do this by finding the deposits of past eruptions, by dating these deposits, and by inferring what they mean in terms of kind, extent, and frequency of volcanic activity. We then assume that future eruptions most likely will follow the same pattern.

Before going any farther, however, we need to go into a little background on volcanoes so that you'll understand some of the terminology we will use later on. The best way to start is by mentioning some of the kinds of eruptions, or other processes caused by volcanism, that might be dangerous.

These are lava flows, eruptions of volcanic ash, eruptions of hot avalanches of volcanic ash and rock debris, and the formation of mudflows and floods due to an eruption. There are other volcanic processes, but we will limit our discussion to these four types.

Lava flows are the streams of molten rock that come from volcanoes. They are confined chiefly to valleys and other low areas. They may move at greatly different speeds, but most are so slow that people can easily get out of their way as they approach. The indirect effects of lava flows might be very dangerous. In fact, they may be much more dangerous than the direct effects. For example, lava flows might start forest fires or if the lava moves out onto snow and ice, it might cause very rapid melting and produce floods or mudflows.

In a *volcanic ash eruption*, great quantities of rock fragments and dust are blown high into the air by repeated explosions. And then the wind takes over. The fragments may be solid rock or pumice. Pumice is a volcanic rock full of bubbles and so light in weight that it can be transported great distances by wind for hundreds, even thousands, of miles.

Hot avalanches of ash and rock debris are a little harder to visualize. Sometimes a large volume of hot, dry fragments is blown from a crater by a volcanic explosion. The mass then avalanches down the side of the volcano, trapping air and heating it and becoming very mobile; gaining speed, it may move several miles beyond the base of the volcano. The rock fragments themselves may be giving off hot gas, which cushions and lubricates the debris so it acts just like a flow of fluid material. Such avalanches may move at speeds of 35 to more than 70 miles an hour. The temperature in the avalanche, and in the cloud of smoke and dust that rises above and accompanies it, may be hundreds of degrees centigrade, so that everything in its path is incinerated. The initial eruption of Arenal volcano in Costa Rica in July, 1968 produced one of these hot avalanches and clouds, which swept down into nearby villages. Two days later, another hot avalanche and cloud erupted just as a rescue party was moving in jeeps into the devastated area, and eight more people were killed.

The last process we'll consider is that of *floods and mudflows*. You all know what a flood is. A mudflow is simply a flood of wet mud and rock debris—it looks very much like wet concrete carrying boulders. Mudflows very commonly form on the sides of active volcanoes, chiefly because these steep slopes are frequently mantled with loose rock debris that is very unstable. When this material becomes mixed with water from rain or melting snow, or from the spillover of a crater lake, it may form a mudflow which will move many miles downstream at speeds of several tens of miles an hour.

Now, which of these volcanic events might present the greatest danger to the most people, if one of the Cascade volcanoes were to erupt? We believe that ash eruptions and mudflows are the two greatest hazards.

The degree of hazard from an ash eruption depends on the amount of material blown out, the rate and duration of the eruption, the strength and direction of the winds blowing at the time of the eruption, and also the distance people are from the volcano. On May 22, 1915, the most violent of a long series of eruptions of Lassen Peak in northern California sent a column of volcanic ash at least six miles into the air. Ash was deposited from this cloud as it drifted eastward into Nevada, and some fell as far east as Winnemucca, 100 miles downwind. But, fortunately it was a very brief eruption and only a relatively small amount of material was blown out.

Figure 2 shows an area covered by a pumice eruption at Crater Lake about 7,000 years ago. This was a catastrophic eruption. The pumice blanketed an area of several hundreds of thousands of square miles in the northwestern United States. The patterned area was covered by six inches or more of pumice, and the outer line shows the total area of the ash fall. The 6-inch fallout area has been superimposed on other volcanoes to give an idea of the area that might be most seriously affected if a similar type and scale of eruption should occur at any of them.

What are the actual hazards from volcanic ash? Breathing ash is like breathing in a duststorm; it's hard on the respiratory system as well as the eyes. Close to the volcano there may be also toxic fumes such as sulphur dioxide. Ash will destroy vegetation, including crops. It will reduce visibility for both highway and air travel, and aircraft could be damaged by flying through clouds of volcanic ash. Surface water supplies will be contaminated, both by sediment and by a temporary increase in acidity, although this acidity may go away within a few hours after the ash eruption stops. Roofs may be overloaded. A 1-inch ash fall, for example, will load a roof

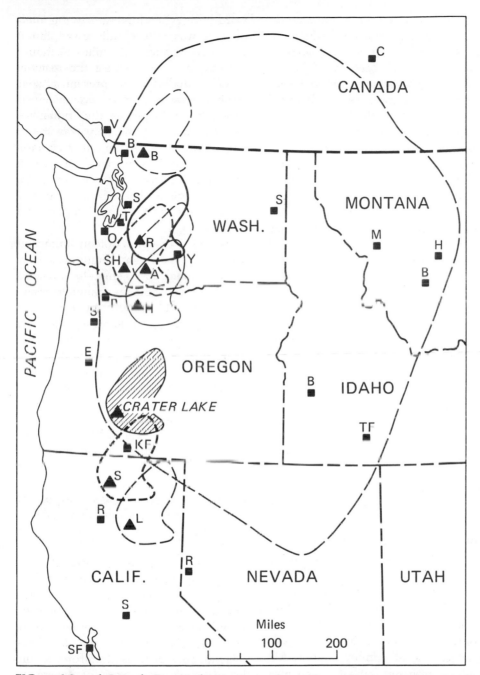

FIG. 2. Map of Cascade Range, showing area covered by pumice eruption at site of Crater Lake about 7,000 years ago. The outer line shows maximum limits of ash fall; inner line (pattern) shows area covered by 6 inches or more of pumice. The same 6-inch thickness line is shown superimposed on the other major volcanoes of the range. Data from reports by Howel Williams and H. A. Powers and R. E. Wilcox.

by about an additional ten pounds per square foot. This means perhaps a 7-ton load on a roof with a surface area of 1,500 square feet. Rainfall will increase the load, because the rain will soak into and saturate the ash. If rainfall is heavy, ash might be carried by running water into gutters, storm drains, and sewers, and it could also block streets; it may also run as mudflows if enough of the ash becomes saturated.

The U. S. Geological Survey Bulletin 1028-N, by Ray E. Wilcox, discusses the effects of volcanic ash falls; it will be a very useful reference when we have the next volcanic ash eruption here in the United States.

The other volcanic event of high potential hazard is that of mudflows and floods. The volcanoes in the Cascade Range are especially dangerous in this respect because most have a perennial snow cover, which can be melted readily by a lava flow or by a hot avalanche or by some other volcanic process. Mudflows are especially dangerous because they move at very high speeds. Generally speaking, they can move faster than water floods, and they can travel tens of miles down valley floors if they have enough volume.

Consider the unfortunate Indian who was standing at the townsite of Enumclaw in western Washington (Fig. 3) about 5,000 years ago. He was probably looking in wonder at the clouds of steam and ash rising from mighty Tahoma, the mountain he called God, and which we call Mount Rainier. Although he probably felt safe at his distance of 25 airline miles from the volcano, he didn't realize that a wall of mud hundreds of feet deep was rushing down the White River valley toward him. When he first saw the mudflow, it was still a mile away, but it was moving about 20 miles an hour.

What do you suppose the reaction would be today of the present citizens of Enumclaw in a similar circumstance? Probably the same as the Indian's— run like hell! But the only way to get out of the way of a mudflow as large as this would be by a car headed in the right direction. The right direction would be toward high ground, and this is not necessarily the direction that highways go.

We wish to point out an important difference between mudflows and floods. Floods are generally preceded by heavy rain and by gradually rising rivers. People normally can get out of the way, unless the flood is caused by a dam failure or some other sudden event. When the flood recedes, the water drains away and the danger is over, whereas, in the case of a mudflow, the mud remains forever. For example, the mudflow beneath the townsite of Enumclaw (Fig. 3) is still there, tens of feet deep. The town of Herculaneum, in Italy, five miles from the foot of Vesuvius, now lies beneath a volcanic mudflow, or rather a succession of three volcanic mudflows that total 80 feet deep, formed during the eruptions of 79 AD.

Volcanic mudflows, especially the really big ones, can occur with little or no warning. Most are likely to start during an eruption, when the volcano is hidden by clouds of smoke, steam, and ash. The upper parts of valleys heading on volcanoes, therefore, should be watched very carefully during an eruption in order to take advantage of what little warning there might be, before a mudflow comes down into a populated area.

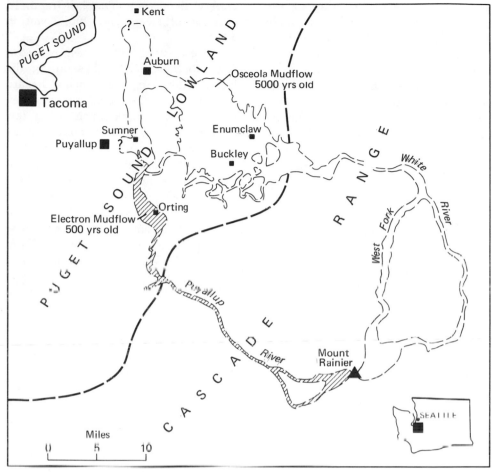

FIG. 3. Map of Mount Rainier and vicinity, showing extent of the Osceola Mudflow in the White River valley and the Electron Mudflow (pattern) in the Puyallup River Valley.

Now, we wish to appraise briefly four potentially dangerous volcanoes in the Cascade Range, which are, from north to south (Fig. 1), Mount Baker, Mount Rainier, Mount St. Helens, and Mount Shasta. These are not necessarily the only volcanoes that are potentially dangerous, or even the ones most likely to erupt next, but possibly they would threaten the largest number of people if they did erupt violently.

Very little is known about the frequency of volcanic activity at Mount Baker within the last 10,000 years, but we do know that it has erupted lava flows and volcanic ash several times. Minor eruptions of smoke or ash were reported by observers in 1843, several times between 1853 and 1859, and again in 1870. Unfortunately we know so little about Baker's behavior that we can't yet realistically assess the potential hazards there. We do suggest, however, that the chief hazard might be related to a pair of reservoirs at the southeast base of the volcano. These reservoirs are Lake Shannon and Baker Lake, which have a combined length of 18 miles. Downstream from these hydroelectric reservoirs are communities on the floor of the Skagit River valley that have more than 15,000 inhabitants. A large flood or mudflow down the east side of Mount Baker seemingly would threaten the lakes and the downstream communities as well. If a mudflow or flood raised the reservoir level very rapidly, faster than the spillways could accommodate the overflow, spillover across the dam itself could occur, with disastrous results.

Going south, we come to Mount Rainier. We know quite a lot about the past behavior of this volcano. Our studies there are described in Geological Survey Bulletin 1238, entitled Volcanic Hazards at Mount Rainier, Washington. These studies show that within the last 10,000 years there have been at least 55 large mudflows, several hot avalanches of rock debris, at least one period of lava flows, and at least 12 eruptions of volcanic ash. The last major eruption was about 2,000 years ago; it involved an eruption of lava and of pumice, and there were also several large mudflows. This extensive eruptive record doesn't necessarily mean that Rainier has been more active than Baker, but only that we have a lot more information about it. Within historic time, many eruptions on a minor scale were recorded in the 1800's, but only one produced pumice. This eruption occurred between about 1820 and 1855—we can't date it any more

closely than that. The last reported eruption of steam and smoke was in 1894.

If we assume that Rainier will continue to behave as it has during the last 10,000 years, the principal hazard will be from mudflows down valley floors. These might consist of a few million cubic yards of mud and be confined to the valley floors very close to the volcano, but there is also a possibility of a huge mudflow, like the Osceola, which covered the present site of Enumclaw. This would be a major catastrophe, comparable to or worse than the great 1902 eruption of Mount Pelée in the West Indies, which killed nearly 30,000 people. The most hazardous areas in the region around Mount Rainier, with respect to mudflows, are the low areas—the valley floors. Just how far down valley the hazard may extend depends on the size or volume of future mudflows.

To give you some idea of volume, we'll consider a few mudflows that have occurred in the past. One mudflow, which occurred about 6,000 years ago, contained about 800,000,000 cubic yards of material; it flowed down the White River valley for about 30 miles. Eight hundred million cubic yards is the equivalent of a square mile piled to a depth of 775 feet. The Osceola Mudflow (Fig. 3) occurred about 5,000 years ago. It contained a little more than 2½ billion cubic yards, that is, just a little more than half a cubic mile of material. The Osceola Mudflow covered an area of about 125 square miles in the Puget Sound Lowland in an area where at least 30,000 people now live. The Electron Mudflow (Fig. 3) occurred only about 500 years ago. It involved a little more than 200 million cubic yards and reached about 35 miles from the volcano; between 2,000 and 3,000 people live on the surface of this mud-flow today.

Two of the valleys that head on Mount Rainier are now blocked by dams. The White River valley, north-west of the volcano, is blocked by Mud Mountain Dam, built by the Corps of Engineers for flood control. It is gener-ally kept empty and has a capacity of about 170 million cubic yards. In the Nisqually River valley, 20 miles west of Mount Rainier, Alder Dam im-pounds a hydroelectric reservoir with a capacity of about 375 million cubic yards, or 332,000 acre feet. Either dam or reservoir could contain most or all of a mudflow like the Electron, if the reservoir were empty, but neither would have much effect on a mudflow as large as the Osceola.

Fifty miles southwest of Mount Rai-nier is Mount St. Helens. This is a relatively young volcano which may have been formed entirely within the last 10,000 years. About 2,000 years ago a series of big mudflows, lava flows, and hot avalanches moved south from the volcano into the Lewis River valley. Mudflows also went down the Toutle River valley, west of the vol-cano, probably at least as far as Long-view and Kelso. Mount St. Helens erupted frequently during the 1800's; many of these eruptions were actually observed in the period 1843 to 1857. Jack H. Hyde, of Tacoma Community College and the U. S. Geological Sur-vey, recently has started a hazard-evaluation study of Mount St. Helens.

Our main cause for concern with Mount St. Helens is the presence of three large lakes—hydroelectric reser-voirs—which occupy 25 linear miles of the Lewis River valley. Imagine the ef-fect if an 800 million cubic yard mud-flow were to move into the upper res-ervoir in a period of a few hours. This could set up a chain reaction that could cause half a million acre feet of water to spill over each successive dam. Downstream, below the mouth of the Lewis, more than 40,000 people live on the flood plain of the Columbia River. The city of Portland is just 20 miles upstream from the mouth of the Lewis River and essentially at tidewater. We feel that Mount St. Helens, therefore, is a possible threat to Portland and many smaller communities, especially if the volcano should erupt and send a very large mudflow, avalanche, or lava flow into these reservoirs.

Mount St. Helens seems to have been the biggest pumice producer of the Washington volcanoes. The biggest eruptions occurred about 3,500 and about 450 years ago. The one 3,500 years ago left two feet of pumice at a distance of 50 miles from the volcano, and the winds spread some of it north-ward into Canada. The eruption 450 years ago also deposited pumice to the north-northeast, but it was only about five inches thick at a distance of about 50 miles. During both of these erup-tions winds were blowing toward the north-northeast, and the sites of the present large towns were missed by the pumice falls. This is a coincidence that wouldn't be counted on in any fu-ture eruption.

The Geological Survey is now work-ing on the volcanic hazards at Lassen Peak in Lassen Volcanic National Park. The hazards there seem to be chiefly a local problem, for we see very little effect of the eruptions of Lassen be-yond the limits of the park or a zone very close to the park. So, if future eruptions follow the same pattern, we anticipate that their effects will also be limited in extent.

The Geological Survey also plans to start an appraisal of the volcanic hazards of Mount Shasta very soon. We know very little about the nature or frequency of volcanism at Shasta within the last 10,000 years, although we know there have been lava flows and ash eruptions within that period of time, and a hot avalanche may have extended down into the townsites of Weed and Mount Shasta. Much of the volcano is bordered by aprons of mudflow deposits, but we do not know how extensive they are. Although it is premature to predict future hazards from Mount Shasta, we're concerned with the possibility that a very large mudflow might extend 35 to 40 miles down the Sacramento River valley to Lake Shasta. Lake Shasta covers an area that is smaller than that now covered by the Osceola Mudflow. We can only speculate about the effects of an extremely large volcanic mudflow moving into Lake Shasta and causing the lake to spill over.

In this brief discussion of some typical volcanoes in the Cascade Range, you may have noticed a possible hazard common to each—large reservoirs within the reach of volcanic mudflows. We have read the geologists' reports on some of the damsites. The fact that there was a volcano upstream was recognized and was considered, but it was also noted that volcanic activity had been on a minor scale in historic time, and the geologists concluded that there seemed to be little or no cause for concern. Perhaps not, but we wish to suggest that the length of historic time in the case of Cascade volcanoes may not

be long enough a sample. In order to reach a meaningful conclusion, one must sample at least the last few thousand years of a volcano's history to decide whether it does or does not constitute a hazard to a reservoir.

We will conclude by mentioning a few problems and making a few suggestions. One problem when the next eruption occurs will be that of moving people out of the danger zones. People who are camping near the volcano can usually leave easily, unless roads and bridges are destroyed by mudflows and floods. We might note in passing that very few bridges near any of these volcanoes could accommodate a very large flood, and none of them could accommodate a catastrophic mudflow.

If an eruption occurred without any warning, and there were casualties, it might be dangerous to rush in with a massive rescue operation, because an even bigger eruption might follow. We suggest that the initial rescue operations be kept to an absolute minimum —just large enough for the immediate job.

Water supplies downwind are very vulnerable from an ash eruption. People should be advised to store water as soon as possible, and, if they don't leave the area, to remain indoors during falls of ash.

There is the danger of forest fires caused by volcanism. They might be much more difficult to fight during an eruption because of the reduced visibility, and roads might be impassable.

We believe that some volcanoes should be monitored, especially those that are potentially dangerous—monitored with seismographs, tiltmeters, and by periodic aerial infrared sensing to detect temperature changes on the volcanoes.

We suggest that reservoir drawdown should be considered immediately if an eruption should start at an upstream volcano. We take some satisfaction in noting that the presence of a dam is not all bad. The reservoir could accommodate a flood, if drawdown had been accomplished in time, and a dam could also impound a mudflow permanently even thought this might not have been the purpose for which the dam was constructed. But this is one way in which a mudflow could be kept out of a populated area. It is better to trap the mudflow than to chance overtopping, or perhaps destroying, the dam.

We also wish to emphasize that comprehensive studies are desirable before other dams are built in the Cascade Range—studies in which volcanic hazards are appraised in terms of the life-time expectancy for the reservoir.

Finally, when an eruption does occur, and we think it is inevitable, we hope that the news media will work with geologists and the Office of Emergency Preparedness in informing the public of what could occur and what the hazards might be, so that if people refuse to leave a potential danger zone, at least they will know enough to leave their cars parked headed in the right direction.

Editor's note: In 1972 the U S Geological Survey reported significant advances in monitoring potentially dangerous volcanoes in the Cascade Range. Seismometers were installed on Mt. Baker, Mt. Rainier, Mt. St. Helens, and Lassen Peak, and data were telemetered either to Menlo Park, California, or to the University of Washington. Seismic-event counters were also installed, and radio signals from these counters were relayed via the ERTS-1 satellite. A tiltmeter was installed on Lassen Peak, and a geodimeter network was established at Mt. St. Helens. Experiments involving continuous monitoring of fumarole activity by infrared imagery from aircraft and by recording temperatures of fumaroles was also initiated. Dwight R. Crandell reports, however, that the Geological Survey's program of monitoring the volcanoes of the Cascade Range is much reduced over what it was in 1972 (personal communication, 1974). As a precautionary measure, the National Park Service closed the Manzanita Lake visitor facilities in Lassen Volcanic National Park. Lassen Park, however, remains open to visitors.

5   Iceland Chills a Lava Flow

Richard S. Williams, Jr., and James G. Moore

Williams, R. S., Jr., and Moore, J. G., 1973, Iceland Chills a Lava Flow, *Geotimes*, v. 18, pp. 14–17. Reprinted by permission of the authors and the American Geological Institute. The authors are on the staff of the U. S. Geological Survey. Williams spent Feb. 7, 1973, on Heimaey, and Moore was there from May 3 to 5. This report is based on their observations, information from the Icelandic Ministry for Foreign Affairs, Icelandic scientists' reports through the Smithsonian Institution's Center for Short-Lived Phenomena, and published scientific reports. Icelandic scientists and officials provided logistical support and discussions of scientific and engineering aspects.

One of the most destructive volcanic eruptions in the history of Iceland seems to be waning, but only after heavily damaging the country's main fishing port, Vestmannaeyjar, on the island of Heimaey. The eruption is also notable as leading to a major attempt to control a lava flow by chilling it with sea water.

The effusive eruption is the fourth in Iceland in little more than a decade. (Earlier events: Askja, Oct. 26 to about Dec. 6, 1961; Surtsey, Nov. 14, 1963, to May 5, 1967; and Hekla, May 5 to July 5, 1970.) It is the second major eruption—the other being Surtsey— definitely known to have occurred in the Vestmann Islands archipelago since settlement of Iceland (about A.D. 874). Thorarinsson has documented at least 13 offshore eruptions (14 including

Heimaey) and about 100 onshore since settlement. 10 of the 13 previous off-shore eruptions occurred off the Rey-kjanes Peninsula, along Reykjanes Ridge, the submarine extension of the peninsula.

This ridge lies along a parallel frac-ture system about 175 km west of the northeast-trending Vestmann Islands archipelago. The Vestmann Islands group, on the southwestern continua-tion of the eastern volcanic zone, fol-low the same structural trend as the fissures, grabens, and crater rows on the mainland in the eastern neovol-canic zone, a zone of very productive and historically active volcanoes (fig. 1.)

FIG. 1. Lower left, the Vestmann Islands (after Thorarinsson and Icelandic Surveying Department). Far right, the Island of Heimaey, with the original shoreline shown as a solid line (Geodetic Institute, Copenhagen), the eruptive fissure of Jan. 23, a dashed line, and limits of the lava flows of Jan. 28 and April 30 (after Thorarinsson and others, 1973, and from maps by the Science Institute, University of Iceland).

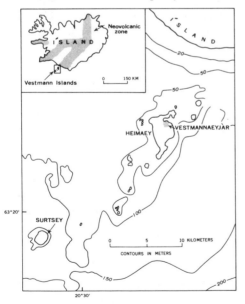

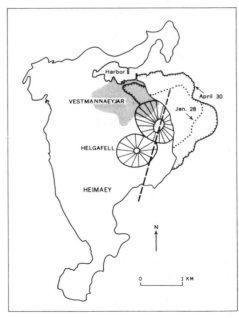

The Heimaey eruption began about 2 A.M. Jan. 23, 1973, on the eastern side of the island and about 1 km from the center of town. A fissure about 1.5 km long lengthened rapidly to nearly 2 km, traversing the island from one shore to another. A continuous curtain of fire predominated all along the fissure in the early phases, but fountaining soon retracted to a small area about 0.8 km northeast of Helgafell. Within 2 days a cinder-spatter cone grew to more than 100 m above sea level and was informally named "Kirkjufell" after a farmstead, Kirkjubaer, which it had obliterated. During the early phase, the outpouring of tephra and lava averaged about 100 cubic meters a second. A few days after the eruption began, the combination of a high rate of tephra production and strong easterly winds resulted in a major fall of tephra in Vestmannaeyjar, burying houses in the eastern part of the town. By early February the tephra fall had slackened markedly, but lava flows continued unabated, making inroads into the edge of town and threatening to fill in the harbor of Iceland's biggest fishing port.

The volcano was continuously monitored from the air and on the ground by Icelandic geologists and geophysicists; they acquired satellite thermography and imagery of the eruption from the NOAA-2 satellite and the ERTS-1 satellite under an experiment by the U. S. Geological Survey (EROS Program) and the University of Iceland (Science Institute).

By the end of February, the spatter-cinder cone reached more than 200 m above sea level. The central crater also fed a massive blocky lava flow that moved north, northeast, and east. By early May, the flow was 10–20 m high at its front, and averaged more than 40 m thick—in places 100 m. Its upper surface is littered with scoria and volcanic bombs, as well as large masses of the main cone, which broke off and were carried along with the flow. Some of these masses of welded scoria are 200 m across and stand 20 m above the general lava surface. They were rafted as much as 1 km from their original sites. Photogrammetric measurements (from aerial photographs) and geodetic measurements, made from the end of March to the end of April, indicate that it moved as a unit about 1 km long and 1 km wide at 3–8 m per day.

In addition to the advance of the flow to the north and east, large slump blocks broke loose from the cone Feb. 19 and 20 and moved west toward the southeast part of the town. In late March, a second large lava flow moved northwest on the west side of the main flow and covered many houses, a large fish-processing plant, and the power plant in the northeast part of town (Fig. 2).

By Feb. 8, the outpouring of lava had dropped from an initial estimate of 100 cubic meters per second to 60; by mid-March, to 10; and by mid-April, to about 5. By early June, activity had virtually ceased.

Thermocouple measurements of the lava indicated a temperature of $1,030°$–$1,055°C$ during the first week of the eruption, increasing later (Feb. 17) to as much as $1,080°C$.

Samples of volcanic gas of widely varying composition were collected at several places, indicating that gas fractionation operates effectively over short distances. Gas collected at sea along

FIG. 2. Panoramic view across the fishing port of Vestmannaeyjar. The outskirts (foreground) were burned and buried under some of the estimated 300 million cubic yards of volcanic debris. (Photo courtesy U. S. Geological Survey.)

the submerged part of the active eruptive fissure is dominantly CO_2; gas collected at sea, bubbling up from cooling submerged lava flows, is about 70% H_2.

Poisonous gas accumulated in low areas in eastern Vestmannaeyjar and concentrated in houses partly buried by ash and scoria. This gas is 98% CO_2 but also contains CO and methane. One person died as a result of breathing the gas in a building, and several have been overcome in houses or on the street.

Within 6 hours after the eruption began, nearly all the 5,300 residents of Heimaey had been safely evacuated to the mainland, partly as a result of the fishing fleet's being in port, but also, and more important, as a result of a foresighted evacuation plan by Almannavarnir Ríkísins, Iceland's State Civil Defense Organization.

Except for the damage to houses and

farmsteads close to the eruptive rift, the first severe property loss was caused by the heavy tephra fall a few days after the onset of the eruption. Many houses, public buildings and businesses were buried by tephra, set afire by lava bombs, or overridden by the advancing front of lava flows. Many structures collapsed from the weight of the tephra, but the shoveling of accumulated tephra from roofs saved dozens of others.

By early February, the lava had begun filling the harbor, a situation that threatened the future use of Vestmannaeyjar as Iceland's prime fishing port. The harbor on Heimaey is the best along the south coast of Iceland and is in the midst of some of the richest fishing grounds in the North Atlantic. Approximately 20% of Iceland's fish catch is landed and processed on Heimaey, which has only 2.5% of Iceland's population. As fish products represent nearly 80% of Iceland's export, the loss of the harbor would have a severe impact on the economy. Also, the flow into the harbor severed a 30,000-volt submarine power cable and broke one of the two fresh-water pipelines from the mainland.

In late March, a new surge of lava into the eastern edge of Vestmannaeyjar destroyed a large fish-freezing plant (and damaged 2 others), the local power-generating facility, and 60 more houses. By early May, some 300 buildings had been engulfed by lava flows or gutted by fire. Sixty to 70 more houses have been buried by tephra. It is estimated that half the structures on the island can be salvaged.

Short- and long-term costs will total tens of millions of dollars, a stupendous amount compared with Iceland's gross national product in 1971 of $500 million. The location of housing and other services for 5,300 persons would be equivalent in impact to finding homes for 5.3 million Americans.

Icelanders have always had to contend with volcanic eruptions, jökulhlaups ("glacier bursts"), and periods of deteriorating climate (usually caused by sea ice off the north and east coasts).

Of great interest to Icelanders and earth scientists, then, was the decision by government officials, after advice from Icelandic geologists and geophysicists, to fight the lava flows. Drawing on small experiments initiated by Thorbjörn Sigurgeirsson on Surtsey in 1967, where lava-wetting was used in an attempt to stop the flow of lava from the north slope of Surtur I toward the scientific observatory, Sigurgeirsson, with the support of other scientists, recommended that such a technique, on a much grander scale, be used on Heimaey.

As lava flows threatened to close the harbor and encroach on the heart of Vestmannaeyjar, a determined effort was begun to restrict the flow of lava to the west and north by building barriers and by pumping large amounts of sea water to cool the flows. This effort became the most ambitious program ever attempted by man to control volcanic activity and to minimize the damage caused by a volcanic eruption. Consequently the experiment is of great importance to other communities exposed to volcanic hazards.

An experiment using city water in late February indicated that spraying water on the flow did indeed slow its advance, causing the flow front to thicken and solidify. Hence, in early March, a pump ship which could deliver much more water was taken into the habor. Finally, in early April, a group of fuel pumps were purchased largely from the United States to deliver water not only to the flow front but to many sites on the surface of the flow as well.

In late April, 47 pumps mounted on barges in the harbor were delivering a total of 1 cubic meter per second of sea water to various parts of the flow at an average height of 40 m. This could lower by 200°C a volume of lava several times that of the water (Fig. 3).

The water was pumped directly on the flow front at sea level and was also pumped through 3 main 12-inch plastic pipes as much as 1 km south to the surface of the flow. Each 12-inch pipe fed several 5-inch plastic pipes, each of which could deliver as many as 200 liters per second.

FIG. 3. Rescue workers pump nearly a million gallons of water per hour over tongues of advancing molten lava in a successful effort to prevent the lava from blocking Iceland's major fishing port. (Photo courtesy U. S. Geological Survey.)

The most difficult aspect of the cooling program was to deliver large volumes of sea water to the surface of the flow some distance back from the flow front. The water effectively increases viscosity, producing internal dikes or ribs within the flow, causing the flow to thicken and ride up over itself.

First, the margin and surface of the flow is cooled with a battery of fire hoses fed from a 5-inch pipe. Then a bulldozer track is made up onto the surface of the slowly moving (up to 1 m per hour) flow. The water produces large volumes of steam, which reduces visibility and makes road building difficult. Then the larger plastic pipes are snaked up on the flow; they will not melt as long as water is flowing in them. Small holes in the wall of the pipes help cool particularly hot spots.

In each area 50–200 liters per second of water is pumped onto the lava flow, where it generally has little effect for about a day. Then the flow begins to slow in that area. Water is poured onto each point for about 2 weeks until steaming stops near the point of discharge, because by then much of the flow in a small area is cooled below 100°C. Water is delivered about 50 m back from the edge of the flow margins and front, so that a thick wall of cool rubbly lava is created at the margin, allowing the flow to thicken behind it.

The cooling of the flow margin is used in conjunction with bulldozed diversion barriers of scoria adjacent to the flow margin. The cooled flow tends to pile up against the barriers rather than rush under them as it would if the flow were more fluid.

This water-cooling program distinctly changes the surface of the main lava flow. Before watering, the surface is blocky and covered with partly welded scoria and volcanic bombs, the whole having a distinct reddish oxidized color. The general surface has a local relief of 1 m or less—the size of many of the blocks. However, large masses of welded scoria broken from the main cone stand 10–20 m above the flow surface.

After watering, the general flow surface is much more jagged, having a local relief of about 2 m. Cooling has apparently formed internal ramp structure as the more plastic interior of the flow breaks upward and rides over itself. The flow surface is black to grey and difficult to traverse. In places, closely spaced joints, perpendicular to larger joints and shears, resemble the joints in pillow basalts. In other places, salt coats fractures that were formerly deeper in the flows where cooling sea water was heated and evaporated. The change in surface texture can be readily identified on aerial photographs.

The Heimaey eruption is especially suitable to the methods that are being employed to control the lava flows. First, the initial eruptive fissure was only 1 km from the center of a large town with an important harbor; consequently, it was in the national interest to minimize damage as much as possible by supporting a control program. Second, the main lava flow was viscous and slow moving; this allowed time to plan and carry out the control program. Third, sea water was readily available. Fourth, transport by sea as well as by a local road system is good, and it was easy to move in with pumps, pipe, and heavy equipment. As a result, an ambitious program of control was attempted. This program has had an important effect on the lava flows and undoubtedly restricted their movement and reduced property loss. A final analysis of the program must await completion of many studies under way by Icelandic scientists, but other communities faced with volcanic hazards are looking to the lessons gained from the Heimaey experience.

Author's note: There was no warning of the volcanic eruption on Heimaey. Earthquakes of small magnitude in the Vestmannaeyjar archipelago were recorded on seismographs of the University of Iceland's Science Institute, but it was not until posteruption research was carried out by Sveinbjörn Björnsson that they were specifically related to Heimaey.

Reconstruction efforts were implemented within a few weeks after the eruption began and were carried out in earnest after the cessation of flow of lava into the town of Vestmannaeyjar in late March 1973. All during the eruption the Vestmannaeyjar fishing fleet was active and continued to use the port. By the summer of 1974, about 2600 residents (about one-half the total permanent population) had returned, and plans were underway to complete excavation of all homes which were salvageable and to construct, within the next two to three years, 450 homes to replace those inevocably lost under tons of lava and tephra. Heimaey has now become a vigorous fishing community, a laboratory for geologists, a major tourist attraction, but most importantly a monument and a testimony to the perseverance and courage of the Vestmann Islanders to turn, with the help of other Icelanders and foreign friends, a seemingly hopeless situation into a very bright future. (R. S. Williams, Jr., January 1975.)

Earthquake Activity and Tectonic Movements

The earth is utterly broken, it is rent asunder and is violently shaken.

Isaiah 24:19

Earthquakes appear to be more common than volcanism. Each year several large earthquakes cause catastrophic damage while numerous others are destructive locally. Although most earthquakes are associated with the well-defined Circum Pacific and Mediterranean belts, the accompanying map (Fig. 1) shows that a large number of epicenters occur outside these belts.

In Reading 6, Gordon Oakeshott describes the San Andreas fault system and its attendant earthquakes. He reviews some of the unsolved problems associated with our understanding of the fault and offers the intriguing suggestion that although the solution of these problems might enable us to predict earthquake activity, this ability might in itself create a completely new set of problems. This is because success in developing a reliable prediction system will not be without serious social, political, and economic repercussion. Social and behavioral scientists and government officials should be encouraged to develop plans which can be implemented when reliable predictions are available.

The March 1964 Alaska earthquake did much to call the attention of the American public to the hazards of earthquakes. Reading 7 describes the setting of this earthquake and its effects on Man and his physical environment. This is one of the few accounts that adequately describes the environmental impact of a large earthquake. The Alaskan earthquake occurred in a sparsely populated area,

and the loss of life and property damage were minor for a large quake.

The role of Man as a geologic agent is a popular subject among environmentalists. Although Man is a relative newcomer, his technological skills have enabled him to wield an ever-growing power over the environment. In those situations where Man has ignored geological hazards he has, on occasion, inadvertently triggered earthquakes. In 1962 a deep well at the Rocky Mountain Arsenal near Denver was used for disposing of liquid wastes. Soon afterward, earthquakes began—the first in the area since 1882. In November 1965 David M. Evans, a consulting geologist, presented data which strongly indicated that the Denver earthquakes were being triggered by the fluid-waste disposal program. His disclosure (Reading 8) reveals a strong sense of responsibility to the citizens of Denver who were becoming anxious about the sudden occurrence of earthquake activity. It hastened official action which led to a more detailed monitoring of waste disposal and tremor activity. These studies supported Evans' contention that waste disposal was a significant cause of the Denver area earthquakes. With subsequent suspension of the disposal program, the area appears to have regained its former stability. Reading 8 demonstrates the urgent need for full use of geologic knowledge before we interfere with an environment which is in equilibrium.

It is fortunate that some earthquakes have occurred at times when many people were not in the vicinity. The Alaskan earthquake occurred on Good Friday. Many stores and schools were closed, thus averting a higher death

Photo on page 57. Aerial view of the Daly City, California, area showing the trace of the San Andreas fault. Courtesy of U. S. Geological Survey.

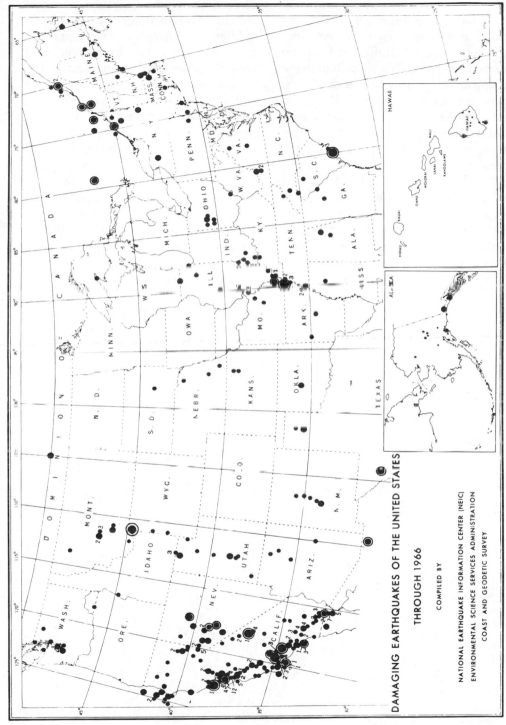

DAMAGING EARTHQUAKES OF THE UNITED STATES

THROUGH 1966

COMPILED BY

NATIONAL EARTHQUAKE INFORMATION CENTER (NEIC)
ENVIRONMENTAL SCIENCE SERVICES ADMINISTRATION
COAST AND GEODETIC SURVEY

FIG. 1. Damaging Earthquakes of the United States through 1966. (Compiled by National Earthquake Information Center (NEIC) Environmental Science Services Administration Coast and Geodetic Survey.)

toll. The San Fernando, California, earthquake of February 9, 1971, occurred at 6 A.M. when highways were relatively free of traffic and before most office and public buildings were occupied. The realization that the timing may not always be this fortuitous and that densely populated areas may be involved in the next large earthquake has stimulated research in the areas of earthquake prediction, control, and engineering. Reading 9 deals with the question of prediction and looks beyond prediction to discuss the controlled release of stored strain energy in active fault zones. The main thrust of prediction has been the search for precursors, that is, phenomena that occur prior to an earthquake. A large number of the precursors can be ex-

plained by the "dilatancy model" which serves to unify the events preceeding an earthquake and suggests a possible method for the control of at least the shallow focus earthquakes.

The International Geophysical Year and Project Vela have contributed to advances in seismology that bring the prediction and control of earthquakes within the realm of possibility. It is, however, a sobering fact that the San Fernando earthquake and several other California earthquakes occurred in areas of low seismicity and were associated with portions of a fault not previously mapped. It is obvious that, like the recent volcanic history of the Cascade Range (Reading 4), the short-term local history of the San Andreas fault system is not an adequate base for

FIG. 2. Crustal movement map showing probable vertical movements of the Earth's surface. (Prepared by National Geodetic Survey—Vertical Network Division.)

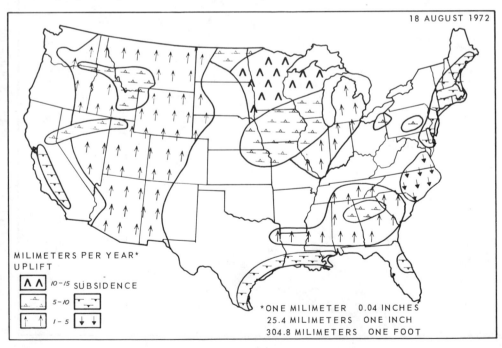

estimating risks. These readings indicate the need for additional mapping, more comprehensive information on the accumulation of strain, and reconsideration of building codes and seismic zoning.

Reid's Elastic Rebound Theory relates earthquake activity to the sudden rupturing of the earth's crust within fault zones. Movement along faults may also be slow and almost imperceptible (tectonic creep), but it can nevertheless endanger structures and present costly repair problems. Reading 10 documents the occurrences of tectonic creep in the San Andreas fault system. It is important to note that, although manmade structures are used to document and quantify the occurrence of tectonic creep, there are numerous topographic expressions of prehistoric tectonic activity. Such geomorphic features as shutterridges, offset streams, lines of springs, scarps, and sag ponds could alert the developer or planner to the hazardous setting.

Seismologists have also been able to predict episodes of tectonic creep along some portions of the San Andreas fault. It is obvious, however, that in some cases the topographic indicators have either been ignored or have not been recognized because much construction is going on in areas of active creep. It should also be noted that the occurrence of fault creep does not preclude sudden rupture and its attendant earthquakes.

Vertical tectonic movements can also present problems in the design and maintenance of engineering structures. The accompanying map (Fig. 2) shows that very few stable areas exist. The map is based on measurements made over the past 100 years and does not discriminate between movements caused by Man and those due to natural internal forces. Subsidence in some coastal areas is particularly alarming as it greatly increases drainage problems and the danger of inundation during storms.

6 San Andreas Fault: Geologic and Earthquake History*

Gordon B. Oakeshott

The San Andreas fault is California's most spectacular and widely known structural feature. Few specific geologic features on earth have received more public attention. Sound reasons for this are found in the series of historic earthquakes which have originated in movements in the San Andreas fault zone, and in continuing surface displace-

Oakeshott, G. B., 1966, "San Andreas Fault: Geologic and Earthquake History," *Mineral Information Service*, vol. 19, no. 10, pp. 159–66. Abridged by permission of the author and reprinted by permission of California Division of Mines and Geology, Sacramento, California.

Dr. Oakeshott is Deputy Director of the California Division of Mines and Geology.

* Adapted largely from Oakeshott, Gordon B., 1966, San Andreas fault in the California Coast Ranges province: California Division of Mines and Geology Bulletin 190, pp. 357–373.

ments, both accompanied and unaccompanied by earthquakes. This active fault is of tremendous engineering significance, for no engineering structure can cross it without jeopardy and all major structures within its potential area of seismicity must incorporate earthquake-resistant design features. Recently a proposal for a great nuclear power plant installation on Bodega Head, north of San Francisco, was abandoned because of public controversy over the dangers of renewed movements and earthquakes on the nearby fault. Expensive design features are being incorporated into the State's plan to transport some of northern California's excess of water to water-deficient southern California in order to ensure uninterrupted service across the fault in the event of fault movements and earthquakes in the Tehachapi area.

Geologists and seismologists the world over have directed their attention to the San Andreas fault because of: (1) the great (Richter magnitude 8.25)[1] San Francisco earthquake of 1906 and many lesser shocks which have originated in the fault zone; (2) development of the "elastic rebound" theory of earthquakes by H. F. Reid; (3) striking geologic effects of former movements and continuing surface movements in the fault zone; and (4) postulated horizontal displacements of hundreds of miles—east block moving south.

The San Andreas has been frequently and widely cited in the scientific and popular literature as a classic example of a strike-slip fault with cumulative horizontal displacement of several hundred miles; however, the geologic evidence that can be documented is highly controversial.

Location and Extent

The San Andreas fault strikes (bears) approximately N. 35° W. in a nearly straight line in the Coast Ranges province and extends southward for a total length of about 650 miles from Shelter Cove on the coast of Humboldt County to the Salton Sea. This takes it completely across geologic structures and lineation of the Coast Ranges at a low angle, then south across the Transverse Ranges and into the Salton Trough. Latest movement in the fault zone, as noted by the late Professor A. C. Lawson who named and traced it, has thus been clearly later than all major structural features of those provinces. This recent movement may, however, be an expression of renewed activity along an older fault zone that antedated differentiation of the geologic provinces now in existence. If so, we need to distinguish between such an older, or "ancestral," San Andreas fault zone and latest movements on the modern, or Quaternary, San Andreas fault proper.

The long northwesterly trend of the fault zone is interrupted in three places (see Fig. 1): (1) At Cape Mendocino, where it turns abruptly westward to enter the Mendocino fault zone, as reflected in the Mendocino Escarpment; (2) at the south end where the Coast Ranges adjoin the Transverse Ranges and the fault turns to strike east into the complex knot of major faults in the Frazier Mountain area and on emerging splits into the 50-mile-wide system of related faults, including the San Andreas fault proper, in southern California; and (3) in the San Gorgonio Pass area where the San Andreas fault proper appears to change direction again and butt into the Mission Creek-Banning fault zone which continues into the Salton Trough.

Earthquake History

Earthquake history of California is extremely short. The earliest earthquake in written records was felt by explorer Gaspar de Portola and his party in 1769 while camped on the Santa Ana River about 30 miles southeast of Los Angeles. The earliest seismographs in use in California, and also the earliest in the United States, were installed by the University of California at Lick Observatory on Mount Hamilton, and

at the University at Berkeley in 1887. The earliest seismograms of a major California earthquake are those of the San Francisco earthquake of 1906, which was recorded at seven California stations as well as elsewhere throughout the world.

One of the Bay area's largest earthquakes centered on the Hayward fault (within the San Andreas fault *zone*) in the East Bay on June 10, 1836. Surface faulting (ground ruptures) took place at the base of the Berkeley Hills from Mission San Jose to San Pablo. On October 21, 1868 another large earthquake centered on the Hayward fault with surface faulting for about 20 miles from Warm Springs to San Leandro. Maximum right-lateral (east block moving south) offset was about 3 feet.

FIG. 1. San Andreas fault zone.

In June of 1838 a strong earthquake originating on the San Andreas fault was accompanied by surface rupturing from Santa Clara almost to San Francisco. This damaged the Presidio at San Francisco and the missions at San Jose, Santa Clara, and San Francisco. Another strong earthquake centered on the San Andreas fault in the Santa Cruz Mountains on October 8, 1865. This was accompanied by ground cracks, land-slides, and dust clouds; buildings were damaged in San Francisco and at the New Almaden mercury mine, which was only a few miles east of the active part of the fault.

On April 24, 1890, a strong earthquake damaged Watsonville, Hollister, and Gilroy. Joe Anzar, who was a young boy living in the San Andreas rift valley in the nearby Chittenden Pass area at the time of that earthquake, was interviewed in 1963 by Olaf P. Jenkins and the writer. Mr. Anzar clearly remembered ground breakage, which caused Anzar Lake to drain, and landslides, which closed the railroad and highway where the fault trace crosses Chittenden Pass. He judged the motion to be stronger (at his home) than during the San Francisco earthquake of 1906.

The famous San Francisco earthquake, 5:12 a.m. local time, April 18, 1906, was probably California's greatest. Visible surface faulting occurred from San Juan Bautista to Point Arena, where the San Andreas fault enters the ocean. At the same time surface faulting also occurred 75 miles north of Point Arena at Shelter Cove in Humboldt County, probably along an extension of the San Andreas fault. The 1906 scarp viewed at Shelter Cove in 1963 clearly shows upthrow of 6 to 8 feet on the east side; there was no evidence of a horizontal component of displacement. However, offset of a line of old trees and an old fence viewed east of Point Arena in 1963 gave clear evidence of right-lateral displacement on the order of about 14 feet. The epicenter of the earthquake was near Olema, at the south end of Tomales Bay, near where a road was offset 20 feet in a right-lateral sense. Richter magnitude is generally computed at about 8.25. Damage has been estimated at from $350 million to $1 billion. An estimated 700 people were killed. A large part of the loss was due to the tremendous fires in San Francisco, which resulted from broken gas mains and lack of water owing to numerous ruptures in the lines. Most extensive ground breaking in the city was near the waterfront in areas of natural Bay mud and artificial fill.

Another of California's great earthquakes, comparable in magnitude to the San Francisco 1906 earthquake, was caused by displacement on a segment of the San Andreas fault extending through the southern part of the Coast Ranges province and on beyond across the Transverse Ranges. This Fort Tejon earthquake of January 9, 1857, probably centered in the region between Fort Tejon in the Tehachapi Mountains and the Carrizo Plain in the southern Coast Ranges. Surface faulting extended for 200 to 275 miles from Cholame Valley along the northeast side of the Carrizo Plain through Tejon Pass, Elizabeth Lake, Cajon Pass, and along the south side of the San Bernardino Mountains. Accounts of this earthquake are unsatisfactory and inconclusive, but horizontal surface displacement almost certainly amounted to several feet in a right-lateral sense.

Perhaps among California's three greatest earthquakes was that in Owens Valley on March 26, 1872. At Lone Pine, 23 out of 250 people were killed and 52 out of 59 adobe houses were destroyed. The shock was felt from Shasta to San Diego. Surface faulting at the eastern foot of the Sierra Nevada produced scarps with a maximum net vertical displacement of about 13 feet and horizontal right-lateral offset of about 16 feet. Surface faulting extended for perhaps 100 miles. This fault, of course, has no direct relation to the San Andreas.

There have been in historic times two great earthquakes (Fort Tejon and San Francisco) originating on the San Andreas fault, each accompanied by more than 200 miles of surface ruptures: one at the southern end of the Coast Ranges and one in the north. Between is left a segment, roughly 90 miles long, in the southern Coast Ranges, which has not been disrupted by surface faulting in historic time. It is interesting to note that the two ends of this segment—the Hollister area and the Parkfield area—are now the most seismically active in the southern Coast Ranges. The extreme southern segment —south of the Tehachapi Mountains— is quiet on the San Andreas fault proper, but very active on the closely related San Jacinto, Elsinore, Inglewood, and Imperial faults. In the segment marked by surface rupture in 1906, many earthquakes have originated in the central and southern part on the San Andreas fault and its auxiliary faults in the East Bay—the Hayward and Calaveras faults. However, since 1906 there have been no earthquakes on the most northerly segment from Marin to Humboldt Counties. The strongest earthquake in the Bay area since 1906 was the San Francisco earthquake of March 22, 1957, of magnitude 5.3. It originated at shallow depth near Mussel Rock, off the coast a few miles south of San Francisco; there was no surface faulting. No lives were lost, but minor damage to many homes in the Westlake-Daly City district totalled about a million dollars.

Land Forms in the Fault Zone

Extensive activity along the San Andreas fault zone in Quaternary time (last one million years of geologic time) has developed a linear depression, marked by all the features of a classic rift valley, extending the entire length of the fault and encompassing a width from a few hundred feet to over a mile and a half. Rift-valley features are particularly well expressed in the San Francisco Bay area, in the arid Carrizo Plain, and along the north side of the San Gabriel Mountains in southern California. Within the rift zone fault gouge and breccia always occur as well as a disorganized jumble of fault-brecciated rocks from both the eastern and western blocks, the result of hundreds of repeated ruptures on different fault planes in late Pleistocene and Recent time. Features of the rift valleys have resulted from: (1) Repeated, discontinuous fault ruptures on the surface, often with the development of minor graben, horsts, and pressure ridges; (2) land-sliding, triggered by earthquake waves and surface faulting; and (3) erosion of brecciated, readily weathered rock. Within the rift-valley troughs, it is common to find late Pliocene to Recent sediments.

Many of the observations made after the earthquake of 1906 are of great significance in understanding the origin and development of rift valleys and the nature of movement on the San Andreas fault: (1) open ruptures were mapped along the fault trace from San Juan Bautista to Point Arena, and at Telegraph Hill north of Shelter Cove in Humboldt County; (2) individual fault ruptures were not continuous, but extended for a few feet to a mile or a little more, with the continuations of the displacements being picked up along *en echelon* breaks; (3) the ruptures were often complex, with small grabens (downdropped blocks) and horsts (uplifted blocks) developed between breaks; (4) apparent movements were dominantly right lateral, with lesser vertical displacements; and (5) the amount of displacement varied irregularly along the fault trace, but in a gross way decreased in both directions from the maximum at the south end of Tomales Bay.

North of San Francisco, across Marin County, the fault follows a remarkably straight course approximately N. 35° W. The most prominent features are Bolinas Bay and the long, linear Tomales Bay which lie in portions of the rift valley drowned by rising sea waters following the Pleistocene glacial epoch. Between these bays, the rift zone is a steep-sided trough, in places as deep as 1,500 feet, with its lower levels characterized by a remarkable succession of minor, alternating ridges and gullies parallel to the general trend of the fault zone. Surfaces of the ridges and gullies are spotted by irregular hummocks and hollows; many of the hollows are undrained and have developed sag ponds, which are common along the San Andreas rift. Geologically Recent adjustment of the drainage in the rift zone leaves little positive evidence of the amount and direction of Recent displacement, except for that which took place in 1906. Offset lines of trees in this area still show the 13- to 14-foot horizontal right slip of 1906, and just south of Point Arena trees also serve to show the 1906 offset. In the long stretch northward from Fort Ross to a point a few miles south of Point Arena, the broad expression of the rift zone is clear, but minor features within the zone have been obscured by erosion of the Gualala and Garcia Rivers and by the dense forest cover of the area.

South of San Francisco across San Mateo County the San Andreas fault zone follows the same trend as to the north but is less straight and is complicated by several subparallel faults. Near Mussel Rock, where the fault enters the land south of San Francisco, are great landslides which obscure the trace, and for a few miles to the southeast is a succession of sag ponds, notched ridges, and rift-valley lakes within a deeply trenched valley. The long, narrow San Andreas Lake and Crystal Springs Lakes are natural lakes which were enlarged many years ago by the artificial dams built to impound San Francisco's water supply. Similar rift-valley features mark the fault southward to the Tehachapi Mountains; because of the local aridity, they are particularly clear and striking in the Temblor Range area, in the Cholame Valley, and in the Carrizo Plain. As the fault enters its eastward bend in the San Emigdio Mountains area, the rift-valley features become less striking, perhaps because the contrast between the basement rocks in the east and west blocks disappears where the fault lies wholly within granitic rocks and older schists.

South of the Tehachapi the striking rift-valley land forms continue, through sag ponds like Elizabeth Lake and Palmdale Reservoir, along the northern margin of the San Gabriel Mountains through the Cajon Pass, and along the south side of the San Bernardino Mountains. None of the offsets and other rift-valley features in this southern segment of the great fault appears to be younger than 1857.

Displacement on the Fault

In 1953, geologists Mason L. Hill and T. W. Dibblee, Jr., advanced the possibility of cumulative horizontal right-lateral displacement of possibly 350 miles since Jurassic time (135,000,000 years ago) on the San Andreas fault. This hypothesis has received very wide acceptance among earth scientists, has intrigued geologists, and has been an important factor in stimulating work on the fault. Hill and Dibblee compared rock types, fossils, and gradational changes in rock characteristics in attempting to match units across the fault. By these methods they developed suggestions for horizontal displacement (east block moving south) of 10 miles since the Pleistocene (few thousand years), 65 miles since upper Miocene (about 12 million years), 225 miles since late Eocene (about 40 million years), and 350 miles since the Jurassic. At the opposite extreme, the late Professor N. L. Taliaferro of the

University of California felt less confident about this "matching" of rock units and stated unequivocally that horizontal movement on the northern segment of the San Andreas fault has been less than 1 mile! Taliaferro believed that the principal movements on this great fault have been vertical.

Thus, geologic evidence is so varied that geologists have drawn conflicting interpretations of the geologic history and characteristics of the fault; at one extreme are those who believe that there has been several hundred miles of right slip since Late Jurassic time, and at the other are those who consider that there has been large vertical displacement on an ancient San Andreas fault and relatively small horizontal displacements in late Pliocene and Quaternary time.

Some of the latest work by geologists and engineers on the San Andreas fault in the San Francisco Bay area, and the closely related Hayward fault in the East Bay, shows that these faults are still active. In several places surface "creep," or slippage, is taking place. At the Almaden Winery a few miles south of Hollister, for example, creep occurs in spasms of movement of small fractions of an inch, separated by intervals of weeks or months. Average displacement, east block moving relatively south, is a half-inch a year. Several cases of well-substantiated right-lateral creep on the order of an eighth to a quarter of an inch per year have now been recognized along the 1868 trace of the Hayward fault from Irvington (Fremont) to the University of California stadium. Frequent earthquakes, with epicenters on these faults, also show that present-day movements are taking place.

Unsolved Problems

In spite of the interests of geologists, and the very considerable amount of time and attention given by geologists and seismologists to study of the San Andreas fault, it remains very incompletely known and understood. There is no agreement on answers to such interesting and fundamental questions as: When did the fault originate? Should the late Quaternary and "ancestral" San Andreas be regarded as different faults, developed by different stresses, and with entirely different characteristics and displacements? Have the sense and direction of displacement (presently, right slip—east block moving south) always been the same, or has great vertical movement taken place? If the latter, which is the upthrown block? (Or has this changed from one side to the other in some segments during geologic time?) If dominantly right-lateral strike slip, has the present rate of displacement or strain been about the same for the last 100 million years? Is the cumulative displacement on the fault a few thousand feet or several hundred miles? To what depth does the faulting extend—5 or 6 miles, as suggested by the depth of earthquake foci, or several times this? Is the San Andreas fault becoming more, or less, active? Are earthquakes, which center in the San Andreas fault zone, relieving stresses and thus lessening the chances of future earthquakes, or do the continuing earthquakes merely indicate a high level of seismic activity portending many future earthquakes? When may the next earthquake be expected?

Answers to these problems, so vital to our generation and generations of Californians to come, await the intensive work of geologists, seismologists, and other scientists of many disciplines. At present, fault movements and earthquakes are unpredictable; perhaps, however, our problems will become even more acute when we reach the state of knowledge which will allow prediction of earthquakes in time and place!

Notes

[1] Dr. Charles F. Richter, in 1935, devised a means of comparing the total energy of earthquakes expressed in terms of a figure now called the "Richter magnitude." The logarithm of the maximum trace amplitude in thousandths of a millimeter is taken from the measurement of earthquake waves on the seismogram of a certain standard seismometer at a standard distance from the epicenter. Constants have been worked out to make the figures comparable for other seismometers at other distances. On this scale magnitude $M = 2$ is the smallest earthquake felt. Earthquakes of $M = 4\frac{1}{2}$ to 5 cause small local damage, and $5\frac{1}{2}$–6 may cause an acceleration of one-tenth gravity and cause considerable damage. Earthquakes of 7 or more are called "major" earthquakes, and those of $7\frac{3}{4}$ and over are "great" earthquakes. Long Beach, 1933, with $M = 6.3$, was a "moderate" earthquake (but a very damaging one), Arvin-Tehachapi, 1952, at $M = 7.7$, was a major earthquake, and San Francisco, at 8.25 in 1906, was a great earthquake. Local size or strength has long been measured by an *intensity* scale based on how the earthquake is felt and its apparent damage. The commonest intensity scale in use is the Modified Mercalli.

References

Allen, C. R., St. Amand, P., Richter, C. F., and Nordquist, J. M., 1965, Relationship between seismicity and geologic structure in the southern California region: Seismological Society of American Bull., v. 55, no. 4, p. 753–797.

Bateman, Paul C., 1961, Willard D. Johnson and the strike-slip component of fault movement in the Owens Valley, California, earthquake of 1872: Seismological Society of America Bull., v. 51, p. 483–493.

Blanchard, F. B., and Laverty, C. L., 1966, Displacements in the Claremont Water Tunnel at the intersection with the Hayward fault: Seismological Society of America Bull., v. 56, no. 2, p. 291–294.

Bolt, Bruce A., and Marion, Walter C., 1966, Instrumental measurement of slippage on the Hayward fault: Seismological Society of America Bull., v. 56, no. 2, p. 305–316.

Bonilla, M. G., 1966, Deformation of railroad tracks by slippage on the Hayward fault in the Niles district of Fremont, California: Seismological Society of America Bull., v. 56, no. 2, p. 281–289.

Byerly, Perry, 1951, History of earthquakes in the San Francisco Bay area: California Division of Mines Bull. 154, p. 151–160.

California Division of Mines and Geology, 1958–1965, Geologic map of California, Olaf P. Jenkins edition, published sheets: California Division of Mines and Geology, scale 1:250,000.

California Resources Agency, 1964, Earthquake and geologic hazards conference, December 7 and 8, 1964, San Francisco, California, 154 p.

California Resources Agency, 1966, Landslide and subsidence conference, Los Angeles, California.

Cluff, Lloyd, 1965, Evidence of creep along the Hayward fault: Association of Engineering Geologists, First Ann. Joint Meeting San Francisco-Sacramento Section, paper delivered at Berkeley, Sept. 25, 1965.

Cluff, Lloyd S., and Steinbrugge, Karl V., 1966, Hayward fault slippage in the Irvington-Niles districts of Fremont, California: Seismological Society of America Bull., v. 56, no. 2, p. 257–279.

Hill, M. L., and Dibblee, T. W., Jr., 1953, San Andreas, Garlock, and Big Pine faults, California—a study of the character, history, and tectonic significance of their displacements: Geological Society of America Bull., v. 64, no. 4, p. 443–458.

Lawson, A. C., and others, 1908, The California earthquake of April 18, 1906, Report of the State Earthquake Investigation Committee: Carnegie Inst. Washington Pub. 87, v. 1, pts. 1–2, 451 p.

7   The Alaska Earthquake, March 27, 1964: Field Investigations and Reconstruction Effort

A Summary Description of the Alaska Earthquake— Its Setting and Effects

Wallace R. Hansen and Edwin B. Eckel

Introduction

One of the greatest geotectonic events of our time occurred in southern Alaska late in the afternoon of March 27, 1964. Beneath a leaden sky, the chill of evening was just settling over the Alaskan countryside. Light snow was falling on some communities. It was Good Friday, schools were closed, and

the business day was ending. Suddenly without warning half of Alaska was

Hansen, W. R. and Eckel, E. B., 1966, "A Summary Description of the Alaska Earthquake—Its Setting and Effects," *U. S. Geol. Survey Professional Paper 541*, pp. 1–37. Abridged by permission of the senior author. The authors are affiliated with the U. S. Geological Survey.

rocked and jarred by the most violent earthquake to occur in North America this century.

The descriptive summary that follows is based on the work of many investigators. A large and still-growing scientific literature has accumulated since the earthquake, and this literature has been freely drawn upon here. In particular, the writers have relied upon the findings of their colleagues in the Geological Survey. Some of these findings have been published, but some are still being prepared for publication. Moreover, some field investigations are still in progress.

Time and Magnitude

Seismologic events such as earthquakes are normally recorded in the scientific literature in Greenwich mean time. Greenwich time provides a worldwide standard of reference that obviates the difficulties of converting one local time to another. The Alaskan earthquake of 1964 thus began at about 5:36 p.m., Friday, March 27, 1964, Alaska standard time, but its onset is officially recorded in the seismological literature as 03:36:11.9 to 12.4, Saturday, March 28, 1964, Greenwich mean time.

This earthquake has become renowned for its savage destructiveness, for its long duration, and for the great breadth of its damage zone. Its magnitude has been computed by the U. S. Coast and Geodetic Survey as 8.3–8.4 on the Richter scale. Other observatories have calculated its magnitude as 8.4 (Pasadena) and 8.5–8.75 (Berkeley). These computations indicate something of the great size of the earthquake. Few earthquakes in history have been as large. In minutes, thousands of people were made homeless, 114 lives were lost, and the economy of an entire State was disrupted. Seismic sea waves swept the Pacific Ocean from the Gulf of Alaska to Antarctica; they caused extensive damage in British Columbia and California and took 12 lives in Crescent City, Calif., and 4 in Oregon. Unusually large waves, probably seiches, were recorded in the Gulf of Mexico. The entire earth vibrated like a tuning fork.

Epicenter

The epicenter of this great earthquake has been located in a forlorn wilderness of craggy peaks, glaciers, and fjords at the head of Prince William Sound, on the south flank of the rugged Chugach Mountains, about 80 miles east-southeast of Anchorage (Fig. 1). Computations by the Coast and Geodetic Survey fix the epicenter at lat. 61.1° N., long. 147.7° W.± 15 km. The hypocenter, or point of origin, was at a depth of 20–50 km. However, it is not meant to imply that the earthquake had a point source. During the quake, energy was released from a broad area south and southwest of the epicenter underlying and adjacent to Prince William Sound and the Gulf of Alaska. Epicenters of most aftershocks were dispersed throughout an area of about 100,000 square miles, mainly along the continental margin of the Aleutian Trench between Prince William Sound and the seaward side of Kodiak Island. This area coincides with a zone of tectonic uplift.

Duration and Extent

The total effect of the earthquake was intensified by the long duration of

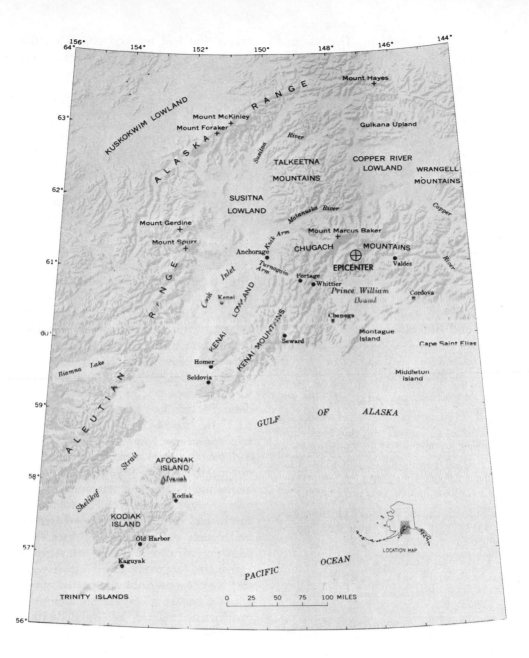

FIG. 1. Physiographic setting of south-central Alaska, including the area principally involved in the Alaska earthquake of 1964. The epicenter of the main shock is near the north end of Prince William Sound.

71   Earthquake Activity and Tectonic Movement

strong ground motion. The elapsed time can only be surmised from the estimates of eyewitnesses, inasmuch as no recording instruments capable of measuring the duration of the shock were in the affected area at the time. Several such instruments have since been installed. Some witnesses timed the quake by wrist or pocket watch, and their timings ranged from 1½ to 7 minutes or more. Most such timings ranged from 3 to 4 minutes, whether measured at Anchorage, Seward, Valdez, or elsewhere. By comparison, the great San Francisco earthquake of 1906 is said to have lasted about 1 minute.

Several factors besides the human element may influence the variation from place to place of the estimated duration of the shock. Shocks are more intense in some geologic settings than in others; the character and amplitude of seismic waves passing through one medium are unlike those passing through another of different elastic properties. Ground motion is more intense and sometimes more prolonged over thick unconsolidated fills as at Anchorage or Valdez than over firm bedrock, as in the Chugach Mountains. Under certain ground conditions the intensity of ground motion may be amplified by resonance. Motions are stronger in high buildings than in low ones, so an observer in a tall building is likely to record a longer duration than an observer in a low building. And under certain conditions, shaking may be prolonged locally after direct seismic motion has stopped: for example, if landslides or avalanches, triggered by the earthquake, are in progress in the vicinity. At any rate, even the shortest estimates indicated an earthquake of unusual duration, a du-

ration that had marked effects on the behavior of earth materials and man-made structures and on their susceptibility to damage.

The main shock was reportedly felt throughout most of Alaska, including such remote points as Cape Lisburne, Point Hope, Barrow, and Umiat on the Arctic slope of Alaska and at Unimak Island beyond the tip of the Alaska Peninsula—points 600–800 miles distant from the epicenter. The earthquake was recorded by seismographs throughout the world. It caused significant damage to ground and structures throughout a land area of about 50,000 square miles and it cracked ice on rivers and lakes throughout an area of about 100,000 square miles. Marked fluctuations of water levels in recording wells were noted at places as far distant as Georgia, Florida, and Puerto Rico.

Effects of so great an earthquake hold the utmost interest of scientists and engineers. Few earthquakes have had such marked effects on the crust of the earth and its mantle of soil. Perhaps the effects of no earthquake have been better documented. Early investigation has provided a clear picture of much that happened, but years will pass before all the effects are understood. In fact, secondary effects are still in progress. In the fjords and along the shores at tectonically disturbed tidal zones, wholesale extermination of sessile organisms has been followed by a slow restoration of the biotic balance. Marine shellfish are now seen attaching themselves to the branches of drowned spruce trees. Rivers are regrading their channels to new base levels. Long-term effects on glaciers, shorelines, and the ground-water regimen will bear further watching.

But despite its magnitude and its impressive related tectonic effects, the earthquake ranks far below many other great natural disasters in terms of property damaged and lives lost. Less violent earthquakes have killed many more people. The reasons are many: The damage zone of the Alaskan quake has a very low population density; much of it is uninhabited. In Anchorage, the one really populous area in the damage zone, many modern buildings had been designed and constructed with the danger of earthquakes in mind.

The generative area of the earthquake was also sparsely inhabited, and the long-period seismic vibrations that reached the relatively distant inhabited areas wreaked heavy damage on tall and wide-area buildings but caused mostly light damage to small one-family dwellings of the type prevalent in Alaska. Attenuation of sinusoidal seismic waves at low frequencies should vary as the square of the frequency. Thus, destructive short-period vibrations presumably were attenuated to feeble amplitudes not far from their points of origin. Most residential buildings moreover, were cross-braced wood-frame construction, and such buildings usually fare well in earthquakes.

The timing of the earthquake undoubtedly contributed to the low casualty rate. It was a holiday; many people who would otherwise have been at work or returning from work were at home. Schools were closed for the holiday. In coastal areas the tide was low; had tides been high, inundation and destruction by sea waves would have been much more severe. Nevertheless, sea waves caused more deaths than all other factors combined.

Hill (1965, p. 50) has compiled a chronological list of severe earthquakes dating back more than 1,100 years. Her list, Table 1, places the Alaskan earthquake of 1964 in a proper perspective so far as deaths are concerned.

Table 1 Severe earthquakes during last 1100 years, and resulting casualties [After Hill, 1965, p. 50]

Year	Place	Deaths
856	Corinth, Greece	45,000
1038	Shansi, China	23,000
1057	Chihli, China	25,000
1170	Sicily	15,000
1268	Silicia, Asia Minor	60,000
1290	Chihli, China	100,000
1293	Kamakura, Japan	30,000
1456	Naples, Italy	60,000
1531	Lisbon, Portugal	30,000
1556	Shenshi, China	830,000
1667	Shemaka, Caucasia	80,000
1693	Catania, Italy	60,000
1693	Naples, Italy	93,000
1731	Peking, China	100,000
1737	Calcutta, India	300,000
1755	Northern Persia	40,000

Table 1 (continued)

Year	Place	Deaths
1755	Lisbon, Portugal	30,000–60,000
1783	Calabria, Italy	50,000
1797	Quito, Ecuador	41,000
1811–12	New Madrid, Missouri, U. S. A.	
1819	Cutch, India	1,500
1822	Aleppo, Asia Minor	22,000
1828	Echigo (Honshu) Japan	30,000
1847	Zenkoji, Japan	34,000
1868	Peru and Ecuador	25,000
1875	Venezuela and Colombia	16,000
1896	Sanriku, Japan	27,000
1897	Assam, India	1,500
1898	Japan	[1] 22,000
1906	Valparaiso, Chile	1,500
1906	San Francisco, U. S. A.	500
1907	Kingston, Jamaica	1,400
1908	Messina, Italy	160,000
1915	Avezzano, Italy	30,000
1920	Kansu, China	180,000
1923	Tokyo, Japan	143,000
1930	Apennine Mountains, Italy	1,500
1932	Kansu, China	70,000
1935	Quetta, Baluchistan	60,000
1939	Chile	30,000
1939	Erzincan, Turkey	40,000
1946	Alaska-Hawaii, U. S. A.	[1] 150
1948	Fukui, Japan	5,000
1949	Ecuador	6,000
1950	Assam, India	1,500
1953	Northwestern Turkey	1,200
1954	Northern Algeria	1,600
1956	Kabul, Afghanistan	2,000
1957	Northern Iran	2,500
1957	Western Iran	1,400
1957	Outer Mongolia	1,200
1960	Southern Chile	5,700
1960	Agadir, Morocco	12,000
1962	Northwestern Iran	12,000
1963	Taiwan, Formosa	100
1963	Skopje, Yugoslavia	1,000
1964	Southern Alaska, U. S. A.	[2] 114

[1] Principally from seismic sea wave.

[2] Does not include 12 deaths in California and 4 deaths in Oregon, by drowning.

Throughout history, earthquakes have ranked high among the causes of sudden disaster and death, but many other causes have added as much or more to the misfortunes of mankind. Some of these, such as dam failures, for example, man has brought on himself. Others he has not. The great epidemics of the past are not likely to recur, but disease, famine, floods, and landslides all still take huge tolls. Single tornadoes in the American mid-continent have taken more lives than the Alaska earthquake of 1964; so have mine explosions. In East Pakistan, thousands of lives were lost in 1965 to floods and hurricanes ("cyclones"). It would be irrelevant to enlarge here on natural and manmade disasters. Hill, however, has compiled another table that sheds pertinent further light on some of the causes of human misery in the past 600 years, other than earthquakes. Wars have been omitted.

Some of the tolls listed in Hill's tables differ substantially from those reported by other authorities for the same disasters. Perhaps this difference is not surprising in view of the chaos and lack of communication that generally accompany great natural disasters and the varying casualty estimates, therefore, that appear in the subsequent literature. Nevertheless, used with caution, Hill's tables help to equate the magnitudes of past tragedies, and they provide some basis for comparing one disaster with another. Compared with the eruption of Mount Pelee in 1902, for example, or the sinking of the Titanic in 1912, the Alaska earthquake of 1964 took a small toll of lives. In view of the magnitude of the event, the relatively small size of the toll is in some ways remarkable.

Table 2   Deaths (rounded) from some of the world's worst manmade accidents and natural disasters [After Hill, 1965, p. 57]

Date	What and where	Deaths
1347–51	Bubonic plague in Europe and Asia.	75,000,000
1918	Influenza throughout the world	22,000,000
1070	Famine in China	9,500,000
1887	Flood in China	900,000
1556	Earthquake in China	830,000
1881	Typhoon in Indochina	300,000
1902	Eruption of Mount Pelee, West Indies.	40,000
1883	Eruption of Krakatoa, near Sumatra.	36,000
1941	Snow avalanche in Peru	5,000
1963	Overflow of Vaiont Dam in Italy.	2,000
1942	Mine explosion Manchuria	[1] 1,500
1912	Sinking of the Titanic	[2] 1,500
1871	Forest fire, Wisconsin	1,000
1925	Tornado in south-central United States.	700
1944	Train stalled in Italy	[3] 500
1928	Collapse of St. Francis Dam, California.	500
1960	Airliners collided over New York City.	[4] 134

[1] Actual count 1,549.
[2] Known dead 1,513.
[3] Passengers suffocated when the train was caught in a tunnel; actual count 521.
[4] Including casualties on the ground.

Aftershocks

The long series of aftershocks that followed the main Alaska earthquake gradually diminished in frequency and intensity over a period of several months. Within 24 hours the initial shock was followed by 28 aftershocks, 10 of which exceeded Richter magnitude 6. The epicenters of these shocks were disposed in a zone 50–60 miles wide reaching from Prince William Sound southwest to the Trinity Islands area south of Kodiak. Fifty-five aftershocks with magnitudes greater than 4 were recorded within 48 hours after the main earthquake, including a shock of magnitude 6.7 on March 29 at 4:18 p.m. (March 30, 02:18:05.6 Gmt). Within a week 75 shocks with magnitudes greater than 4 had been recorded by the U. S. Coast and Geodetic Survey (1964, Table 2). In the 45 days following the earthquake, 728 aftershocks were recorded. About 12,000 aftershocks with magnitudes equal to or greater than 3.5 probably occurred in the 69-day period after the main shock, and several thousand more were recorded in the next year and a half.

Previous Alaskan Earthquakes

Southern Alaska and the adjoining Aleutian Island chain together constitute one of the world's most active seismic zones. Extending from Fairbanks on the north to the Gulf of Alaska on the south, the Alaskan seismic zone is but a part of the vast, near-continuous seismically active belt that circumscribes the entire Pacific Ocean basin. Figure 2 shows the distribution of earthquake epicenters of magnitude

FIG. 2. Epicenters of major Alaskan earthquakes, 1898–1961.

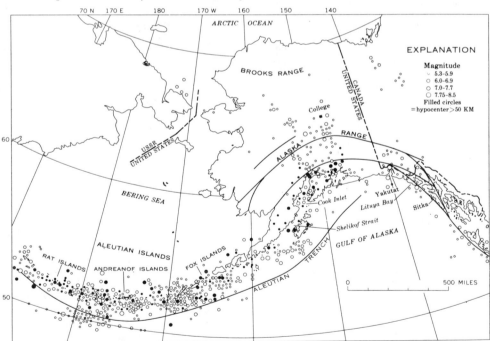

5.3 and greater recorded in Alaska since instrumental measurements began, through 1961. Between 1899 and May 1965, seven Alaska earthquakes have equaled or exceeded Richter magnitude 8, and more than 60 have equaled or exceeded magnitude 7. According to Gutenberg and Richter (1949, Table 7) about 7 percent of the seismic energy released annually on the globe originates in the Alaskan seismic zone.

This highly active zone is circumferential to the Gulf of Alaska and parallel to the Aleutian Trench. It embraces the rugged mountainous region of southern Alaska, Kodiak and the Aleutian Islands, the continental shelf, and the continental slope of the Aleutian Trench. Most of the earthquakes originate at shallow to intermediate depths—mostly less than 50 km—between the Aleutian Trench and the Aleutian Volcanic Arc.

Tectonic Effects

Tectonic effects of the Alaska earthquake of 1964 have been studied and described in detail by Plafker (1965). Crustal deformation associated with the earthquake was more extensive than any known deformation related to any known previous earthquake. From the Wrangell Mountains at the northeast to the Trinity Islands south of Kodiak, the zone of land-level changes extended southwest through the epicenter, a distance of more than 500 miles. From northwest to southeast it extended at least from the west shore of Cook Inlet to Middleton Island in the Gulf of Alaska, a distance of about 200 miles. Crustal warping may have extended inland as far as the Alaska Range and seaward out onto the continental slope of the Aleutian Trench. East along the Alaska coast, deformation died out somewhere between the Bering Glacier and Yakataga. An area of at least 70,000 square miles and possibly 110,000 square miles or more was tectonically elevated or depressed during the earthquake. Tectonic changes, both up and down, caused extensive damage to the biota in such areas as coastal forests, migratory-bird nesting grounds, salmon spawning waters, and shellfish habitats. Land-level changes at Alaskan coastal communities are shown in Table 3.

Effects on Communities

Earthquake damage to the cities, towns, and villages of southern Alaska was caused by direct seismic vibration, ground breakage, mud or sand emission from cracks, ground lurching, subaerial and submarine landslides, fires, sea waves, and land-level changes. Not all these factors caused damage in every community. Some communities were devasted by only one; the village of Chenega, for example, was destroyed by a sea wave. Overall, landslides probably caused the most damage to manmade structures and property, but sea waves took the most lives.

Effects of one factor cannot always be separated from effects of another. Thus, at Seward the waterfront was racked by vibration, slides, sea waves, fires, subsidence, and ground cracks. All these factors contributed significantly to the havoc, and all in combination wiped out the economic base of the town. Comparable damage at Valdez, plus the threat of recurrent damage in the future, forced relocation

Table 3 Summary of earthquake damages to Alaskan communities

Place	Population 1960[1]	Deaths (total, 114)	Subsidence	Uplift	Landslides		Ground cracks	Vibration	Waves	Fire
					Land	Submarine				
Afognak	190	0	×						×	
Anchorage	[2] 44,237	9			×		×	×		
Cape St. Elias	4	1			×				×	
Chenega	80	23	×						×	
Chugiak	51	0								
Cordova	1,128	0	×				×		×	
Cordova F A A airport	40	0					×	×		
Eagle River	130	0								
Ellemar	1	0			×					
Girdwood	63	0	×				×			
Homer	1,247	0	×			×		×		
Hope	44	0	×							
Kadiak Fisheries Cannery	2		×					×	×	
Kaguyak	36	3							×	
Kodiak	[3] 2,628	15	×						×	
McCord	8							×	×	
Old Harbor	193	0							×	
Ouzinkie	214	0	×						×	
Point Nowell	1	1							×	
Point Whitshed	1	1			×				×	
Portage	71	0	×				×			
Port Ashton		1							×	
Port Nellie Juan	3	3							×	
Seldovia	460	0	×							
Seward	1,891	13	×			×	×		×	×
Tatitlek				×						
Valdez	1,000	31	×			×	×		×	×
Whittier	70	13	×			×		×	×	×

[1] Alaska Depart. Health and Welfare (1964).
[2] 82,833 including military personnel.
[3] 4,788 including personnel at Kodiak Naval Station.

of the village and abandonment of the present townsite (Coulter and Migliaccio, 1966).

Most of the small coastal villages in the earthquake zone were damaged chiefly by sea waves, subsidence, or

Place	Townsite acreage (estimated)			Premises (estimated)		Type of structures damaged							
	Total	Damaged	Percent	Total	Damaged	Homes	Business and public	Military	Harbor	Water supply	Other utilities	Highways	Airports
Afognak	20	2	10	38	23	×	×		×	×	0	×	
Anchorage	4,500	700	14	15,000	750	×	×	×	×	×	×	×	×
Cape St. Elias													
Chenega	20	20	100	20	20	×							
Chugiak				0	0						×		
Cordova	200	20	10	400	40	×	×		×	×	×		
Cordova F A A airport						×	×			×	×	×	×
Eagle River	50	1	5	0	0					×			
Ellemar							×						
Girdwood						×	×						
Homer							×		×			×	
Hope	10	3	30		10	×				×			
Kadiak Fisheries Cannery				15	15	×	×		×	×	×		
Kaguyak	15			15	15	×	×						
Kodiak	285	31	11	1,100	130	×	×	×	×	×	×	×	×
McCord						×	×						
Old Harbor	30			38	35	×	×		×	×	0		
Ouzinkie	50		10	38	6	×	×		×				
Point Nowell				1	1	×							
Point Whitshed					10	×							
Portage			20			×	×				0	×	
Port Ashton					0								
Port Nellie Juan					0			×	×				
Seldovia						×	×		×				×
Seward	400	400	100	700	200	×	×	×	×	×	×	×	×
Tatitlek										×			
Valdez	300	300	100	200	40	×	×		×	×	×	×	×
Whittier	30	10	35	10	8	×	×	×	×	×	×	×	×

both. Among the larger towns, only Cordova was significantly damaged by uplift, but the native village of Tatitlek and several canneries and residences at Sawmill Bay on Evans Island were also adversely affected by uplift.

Direct vibratory damage was significant chiefly in Anchorage and Whittier, although minor vibratory damage was widespread through the area of intense shaking. At Anchorage several buildings were destroyed by vibration, and nearly all multistory buildings were damaged. At Seward, Valdez, and Whittier, ground vibrations ruptured oil storage tanks, and the spilled petroleum quickly caught fire.

Ground breakage caused extensive damage in Anchorage, Seward, Whittier, and Valdez, not only to buildings but also to buried utilities such as water, sewer, gas, electric, and telephone lines. Cracked ground resulted from the passage of sinusoidal seismic waves through the soil, from lurching, from lateral spreading of soils under gravity, especially near the heads of landslides, and from differential settlement of alluvial and artificial fills.

Mud and sand were pumped from ground cracks throughout the damage zone where water tables were shallow in saturated granular soil. At Valdez, and to a lesser extent at Seward (Forest Acres), large volumes of sediment were ejected from cracks into cellars and crawl spaces.

Submarine and subaerial landslides triggered by the earthquake caused spectacular damage in Anchorage, Seward, Valdez, Whittier, and Homer. Four large slides in built-up parts of Anchorage were caused by failures along bluff lines in soft, sensitive silty clay whose water content at critical depths exceeded its liquid limit. Failure at Anchorage was mostly subaerial, although the large Turnagain Heights slide failed partly below sea level and slipped part way down the mudflat into Knik Arm of Cook Inlet. At Valdez and Seward, violent shaking spontaneously liquified granular deltaic materials; slumping which initiated well below sea level carried away the waterfronts of both towns. The seaward slopes of the deltas, moreover, were left less stable

after the earthquake than they were before.

Estimates by the Federal Reconstruction and Development Planning Commission for Alaska, as of August 12, 1964, indicated that total property damage to Alaska by the earthquake exceeded $311 million (Fig. 3). This figure does not include loss of personal property or income. Not only was the economic base of entire communities destroyed, but the resultant loss of income severely crippled the economy of the whole State and deprived Alaska of a major share of its tax base at the time when funds were most needed to aid in restoration.

As also pointed out by the Federal Reconstruction and Development Planning Commission, the disaster struck at the heart of the State's economy, inasmuch as nearly half the people of the State reside in the stricken area. About 100,000 of the State's estimated 265,000 people live in the greater Anchorage area alone. Anchorage, because of its size, bore the brunt of property damage, but the per capita damage and the actual death toll were much greater in many smaller towns. Although the combined population of Chenega, Kodiak, Seward, Valdez, and Whittier is less than 9,000 people, each of these communities lost more lives than Anchorage.

Despite the extensive damage at Anchorage to residence and business properties, utilities, and transportation, a large segment of the economy was intact, and recovery was relatively rapid. But at many small towns and villages, where virtually entire populations were dependent on one or two industrial enterprises—fisheries, for example— the effects of the earthquake were staggering. Whole fishing fleets, harbor facilities, and canneries were destroyed.

The native villages of Chenega, Kaguyak, Old Harbor, and Afognak, all remote waterfront fishing villages, were nearly or completely destroyed by waves, especially Chenega, population 80 before the earthquake. There, 23 lives were lost, and only the schoolhouse remained of the village's buildings. Six homes were left standing at Old Harbor, where there had been about 35. There were nine homes in Kaguyak and a Russian Orthodox Church; all were carried away or destroyed. At Afognak, four homes, the community hall, and the grocery store were carried away by waves; several other homes were moved partly off their foundations (Alaska Depart. Health and Welfare, 1964b); and subsidence made the townsite uninhabitable. The sites of Chenega, Kaguyak,

FIG. 3. Earthquake damages in Alaska. From estimates by the Office of Emergency Planning (1964a).

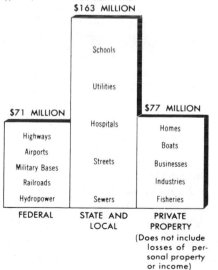

and Afognak have been abandoned in favor of new townsites.

Earthquake damages to communities of Alaska are summarized in Table 3.

Damage to Transportation Facilities

The Alaska Railroad

Damage to The Alaska Railroad, totaled about $27 million. Most of the damage was along the 150 miles of trackage between the terminal at Seward and Anchorage. Damage to the terminal and marshaling yards at Seward, was caused by submarine slumping and waves. Two railroad docks valued at $1 million were completely destroyed, together with $2 million of freight and 50 freight cars. Between Seward and Anchorage, damage was caused by direct seismic shaking, landslides, subsidence, ground cracks and lurching, and inundation by high tides. Seventeen bridges were damaged or destroyed. Ground slumping along the right-of-way was severe at Kenai Lake and at Potter. Inundation and current scour were severe near Portage. Snow avalanches covered trackage along Turnagain Arm. At Anchorage shops and rolling stock were damaged by vibration and landslides. North of Anchorage light damage was reported as far as Hurricane. Trackage just south of Matanuska was inundated by high tides.

The spur line from Portage to Whittier was also severely damaged. The port facility at Whittier was destroyed.

Highways

Highway damage resulted chiefly from destruction of bridges and cracking, collapse, or differential compaction of fills that rested on unconsolidated deposits. Estimates for repairs alone came to about $21 million. Repairs plus upgrading to higher standards may come to $55–$65 million. The Seward Highway was severely damaged between Ingram Creek and Potter, where 22 bridges were destroyed. Between Potter and Anchorage there were many pavement breaks caused by differential subsidence of fills. Lurching displaced the alignment laterally at mile 69, and just outside Valdez there were many pavement breaks where large ground cracks crossed the highway.

The partly completed Copper River Highway was severely damaged from Allen glacier to Cordova. Nearly every bridge along the route was seriously damaged or destroyed, including the famous Million Dollar Bridge. Near Kodiak, highways were severely damaged by sea waves and by tectonic subsidence.

Airports

Damage to airports was relatively minor, although loss estimates totaled about $3.3 million. Greatest damage was at Anchorage International Airport, where a life was lost when the control tower collapsed under sustained seismic vibration and where minor damage was sustained by other buildings. Also, 20,000 barrels of aviation fuel was lost from a ruptured storage tank. Runways and taxi strips were only slightly damaged.

At Elmendorf Air Force Base just north of Anchorage, the control tower was damaged by cracks from its base to a height of about 15 feet. In Cordova, Homer, Kodiak Naval Station, Seldovia, Seward, and Valdez, damage to runways and taxi strips was mostly light.

Ports and Harbors

Water transportation is one of Alaska's vital links with the outside world and is the base for one of her major industries, commercial fishing. Many Alaska communities can be reached only by water or air. The severe damage to port and harbor facilities, therefore, was a staggering blow to the State's economy and health. Moreover, destruction of The Alaska Railroad terminal and port facilities at Seward and Whittier, coupled with the destruction of the highway port at Valdez, deprived Alaska of any ice-free, all-weather ship terminals.

Ports and harbors sustained heavy damage from several different causes. Damage by direct seismic vibration generally was subordinate to other secondary causes. Submarine slides, sea waves, ground cracks, fires, subsidence, and uplift all took large tolls. Hardest hit in terms of port and harbor facilities damaged or destroyed were Seward, Valdez, Kodiak, Whittier, Cordova, and Homer.

Submarine sliding at Seward, Valdez, and Whittier generated large local waves that added to the destruction already caused by the slides and shaking. Except at Whittier, subsequent damage was then caused by seismic sea waves generated in the Gulf of Alaska or possibly by seiches. When seismic vibration sundered petroleum storage tanks in Seward, Valdez, and Whittier, the contents quickly caught fire and added to the devastation. At Seward and Valdez, burning oil that was swept into the bay by submarine sliding was carried back across the waterfront by the returning surge of water; docks, piers, and small-boat harbors were thus destroyed by water and fire. At Seward, tugs, fishing boats, and a tanker were washed ashore. At Valdez, more than 40 boats were smashed. At Whittier, the railroad port facilities were swept away.

At Kodiak, damage was caused mostly by a succession of huge seismic sea waves, intensified by tectonic subsidence of 5–6 feet. Forty percent of the business district and many homes were destroyed, as well as 30 percent of the fishing industry facilities and most of the fishing fleet. Some vessels were washed several city blocks inland where they collided with buildings and houses like great battering rams. At Kodiak Naval Station more than $11 million damage was inflicted on buildings, materials, and equipment by 30-foot sea waves and by subsidence. Piers were covered by 10 feet of water, and the buoyed-up superstructure of the cargo pier shifted off its pilings. Boat-repair shops, gear-storage buildings, and warehouses were damaged or swept out to sea.

Port and harbor facilities at Cordova were damaged chiefly by tectonic uplift of about 6 feet and subordinately by sea waves. Although the immediate effect of uplift was to minimize wave damage, it placed docks and piers beyond reach of shipping during low tides. Boats were grounded in the small boat harbor, Orea Inlet shoaled, and passages through the adjacent islands became unnavigable.

Facilities at Homer were damaged by subsidence and submarine landsliding. Wave damage was minimal. The small-boat harbor disappeared into a "funnel-shaped" pool, and a lighthouse that had been on the harbor breakwater subsided into 40–50 feet of water. Homer Spit, a gravel bar that extends 5 miles into Kachemak Bay and on which various commercial buildings and storage tanks were placed subsided 4–6 feet, partly by local compaction and lateral spreading and partly by regional tectonic lowering. During subsequent high tides, facilities on the bar were inundated.

Facilities at Seldovia sustained damage chiefly from subsidence. At Woody Island FAA facility outside Kodiak, docks and storage tanks were damaged by seismic sea waves and subsidence. A cannery at Shearwater Bay was thrown off its foundations by the earthquake and later destroyed by waves At Cape St. Elias lighthouse, about 135 miles southeast of the epicenter, a coastguardsman was injured by a rockslide and later drowned by seismic sea waves.

The Port of Anchorage was damaged by ground displacements along fractures and by direct seismic shaking. The main pier lurched laterally 5–19 inches. It sustained large longitudinal and transverse cracks, and several buildings were cracked. Gantry cranes on the pier were damaged when they jumped their tracks. Approach roads settled as much as 18 inches. Cement-storage tanks were toppled. Bulk petroleum tanks were ruptured, and large quantities of fuel were lost.

Throughout coastal areas of the damage zone many fishing vessels and other small craft were destroyed by direct wave action or by being battered against docks or the shore. Boats in harbors or tied to docks were hit hardest; vessels underway in deep water were generally undamaged; one fishing boat was sunk with all hands while underway in shallow waters near Kodiak.

Atmospheric Effects

Widespread atmospheric effects are sometimes associated with large earthquakes; some have been documented (Richter, 1958, p. 128; Benioff and Gutenberg, 1939, p. 421; Van Dorn, 1964, p. 174). An atmospheric pressure wave attributed to the Alaskan earthquake was recorded by microbarographs at Scripps Institute of Oceanography at La Jolla, Calif., more than 2,000 miles from the epicenter, and at the University of California at Berkeley. The wave traveled at acoustical velocity, reaching La Jolla 3 hours and 19 minutes after the onset of the earthquake (at 06:55 Gmt., March 28, 1964); it was, therefore, the atmospheric counterpart of the seismic sea waves generated in the Gulf of Alaska. Like the seismic sea waves, the air wave must have been caused by the tectonic uplift of the sea floor and the overlying water column. To displace the atmosphere in the form of a pressure wave, uplift must have been very rapid over a very large area, and must have coincided with the time of the most violent earth tremors.

The earthquake also generated ordinary sound waves of very low subaudible frequencies in the atmosphere. These sound waves were recorded by the National Bureau of Standards at microphone stations in Washington, D. C., Boulder, Colo., and Boston, Mass. Sound waves were radiated by the earthquake at the epicenter and by seismic waves passing through the earth remote from the epicenter, exciting the atmosphere with their passage.

Thus, the Rocky Mountains and the Mississippi delta were local sources of sound as they vibrated with the passage of the shock. In addition, Rayleigh waves (surface seismic waves) crossing the continent displaced the ground surface about 2 inches in the conterminous United States and produced strong subaudible sound waves that traveled vertically upward to the ionosphere, amplifying greatly as they ascended. The ionosphere, in turn, oscillated up and down at a rate of several hundred yards per second in motions that were detected by means of reflected radio waves broadcast from one ground station to another.

Atmospheric waves coupled to surface seismic waves were also recorded by a barograph at Berkeley. These waves started at Berkeley about 14 minutes after the onset of the quake and lasted about 4 hours.

Possible Magnetic Effects

Magnetic disturbances that began 1 hour 4 minutes before the earthquake momentarily increased the magnetic field at Kodiak by as much as 100 gammas. (Moore, 1964, p. 508). Moore has inferred a possible casual relationship between the magnetic disturbances and the earthquake, and a possible means, therefore, of predicting major earthquakes by magnetic monitoring. Why abrupt magnetic disturbances should precede an earthquake is unknown, but "one possibility is that the magnetic events which preceded the Alaska earthquake resulted from piezomagnetic effects of rocks undergoing a change in stress" (Moore, 1964, p. 509).

Biologic Effects

Probably few earthquakes have so strongly affected the fauna and flora of a region as did the Alaska earthquake of 1964. Moreover, because of the complex interrelations of one organism to another, the total biologic effects will not be known for a long time. In the littoral zones of the Prince William Sound region, of the Kenai Peninsula, Kodiak and elsewhere, large communities of organisms were adversely affected when pronounced crustal changes completely altered the ecologic setting of the shore. Broad expanses of shore and sea bottom were elevated above tide water in Prince William Sound, and innumerable marine organisms were exterminated. Effects were equally marked in the subsided upper end of Turnagain Arm near Girdwood and Portage, where coastal marshlands and forest were inundated by salt water—areas that formerly had provided winter forage for moose and nesting grounds for migratory birds. Extensive forested and grassland areas of Kodiak and Afognak Islands were drowned, also.

Hanna (1964, p. 24) has summarized the biologic effects of the earthquake in the littoral zone of Prince William Sound, and he portrays the extent of the depopulation in the following passage:

"The exposed areas spread out before the observer are many hundreds of square miles, once densely populated by a varied fauna and flora, now completely desolated. Many of the great array of marine animals that you read about when you study zoology are dead. There is now no littoral zone anywhere that the land went up 10 feet or more. Most of the soft-bodied creatures had decomposed or had become food for birds by the time of our visit, 2 months after the earthquake, so the odor was not overpowering. The great array of living marine plants, so conspicuous along most coastlines, was gone. The *Fucus* had turned black from thirst; the calcareous algae were bleached white and so were the many species of green algae. The great fields of big brown kelp were gone, but the individual stalks left their stems and holdfasts, black and bent over, a menace to the unwary footman.

"In many places there were great accumulations of dried starfish; and in one, the dried necks of clams formed a solid mass covering about a square yard. We left to speculation the manner in which these objects came to congregate. In some places a shovel could have been used to collect almost pure concentrations of small shells. Bleached remains of Bryozoa and calcareous algae were so white that the rocky beaches rivalled the snow covered adjacent mountains in brightness."

During studies that are still in progress, G. D. Hanna and George Plafker jointly examined the distribution of tectonically disturbed zones of sessile organisms. Some of these organisms, such as barnacles and various algae, grow in response to rigorous water-depth controls, and their postearthquake vertical distribution above or below mean high-tide level provides a reliable measure of land displacement where geodetic control is unavailable.

Other deleterious effects on organisms were caused by sea waves. In addition to the enormous direct destruction caused by the waves themselves, salt water invaded many coastal lakes and destroyed, at least temporarily, the fresh-water habitat. Spawning beds for salmon in some instances were destroyed by siltation in river deltas. Direct kills of eggs and fry were caused by disturbance of the gravel beds of streams.

Fish populations were also destroyed when streams and lakes temporarily lost water into ground cracks, or when streams were dammed by landslides.

On the other hand, subsidence in some areas opened miles of new spawning habitat by inundating previously impassable falls and velocity barriers in coastal streams.

The salmon fishery is one of Alaska's foremost resources, and the full impact of the quake on this fishery will not be realized until the matured 1964 hatch returns from the sea to spawn. Spawning areas for pink and chum salmon, which are intertidal spawners, received major damage in nearly all coastal sections affected by sea waves, uplift, or subsidence. On Kodiak and Afognak Island, moreover, the waves struck at a critical time when pink salmon fry were just moving from the spawning beds into the stream estuaries. Spawning areas for red and silver salmon were little affected by the earthquake.

Mortalities of dungeness crab were noted in the Copper River delta area after the earthquake, but the commercial catch appears to have been unaffected. King Crab, a deeper water species, apparently was not significantly affected by the earthquake.

Although the total crab population itself was not markedly affected by the earthquake the crab industry was severely damaged by the loss of boats, gear, harbor facilities, and canneries. The loss of fishing vessels amounted to about $7 million and of related facilities to about $13 million. To some extent the loss was offset on the market by unusually heavy catches of crab during the 1964 season, so that the crab harvest was actually larger than usual.

Much of the commercial clam habitat in Prince William Sound and in the Copper River delta was damaged or destroyed.

The effects of the earthquake on terrestrial wildlife are mixed, and some short-term effects have even been beneficial. Again, only time will disclose the long-term effects. In the mountains, some mountain goats are reported to have been killed by avalanches, and there probably was some mortality among mountain sheep, deer, and moose. Although uplift adversely affected shellfish habitats, it favorably altered nesting habitats of ducks, geese, and trumpeter swans by eliminating flood dangers. The long-term ecology may be less favorable—a new balance will be established as brush gradually invades upland areas and emergent vegetation spreads over former mudflats; nesting places will shift accordingly. In tectonically subsided areas where extensive fresh-water marshlands and meadows have been invaded by salt water, populations of moose and other grazing animals will have to readjust downward to the new restricted food supply.

Damage Outside Alaska

Secondary damage effects of the earthquake reached far beyond Alaska as seismic sea waves generated on the continental shelf in the Gulf of Alaska spread rapidly across the Pacific Ocean to Hawaii, Japan, and Antarctica. The source mechanism of the waves has been investigated by Van Dorn (1964), who concluded that the waves were caused by the sudden displacement of water in the Gulf of Alaska, accompanying the uplift of thousands of square miles of sea floor. A maximum wave height of 4 feet was reported in the Antarctic Peninsula (Palmer Peninsula), but heights in Japan were only a foot or so (Van Dorn, 1964, p. 187). Hilo, Hawaii, had a 7-foot wave, but received only minor damage. Apparently the source was directional, the waves radiating preferentially southeastward. Wave heights thus were greater along the North coast than they were in the Aleutian Islands at comparable distances from the source.

As the train of sea waves advanced southward it spread damage in British Columbia, Washington, Oregon, and California. Heavy damage was localized in Alberni and Port Alberni, B. C., in Hot Springs Cove, B. C., and in Crescent City, Calif. At Alberni and Port Alberni, damage to houses and a forest-industries complex totaled several million dollars; 260 houses were damaged, 60 heavily. Of the 17 homes at Hot Springs Cove, 5 were washed away and 10 were heavily damaged.

The coast of Washington was damaged lightly. In Grays Harbor County, the waves destroyed a bridge across the Copalis River and overturned several trailer houses.

The Oregon coast was struck by 10 to 14-foot waves. Damage was concentrated in estuaries; a family of four was drowned at De Poe Bay. At Seaside, where a trailer park was flooded as water backed up the Necanicum River, damage totaled about $250,000. At Cannon Beach, damages totaled $250,000; power and telephone services were cut off and several houses were toppled off their foundations. At Gold Coast, docks and small boats were smashed in the Rogue River.

At Coos Bay, an initial wave 10 feet above mean high water was attenuated by crossing wide tidal flats before it reached Poney Point 7 miles up the channel, but at Florence an 8-foot wave traveling up a narrow channel was negligibly dissipated.

In California, minor harbor damage was sustained as far south as San Diego where small craft were destroyed and dock installations were damaged. In San Francisco Bay, water surging through the Golden Gate set adrift a ferry boat and a house boat, and caused about $1 million damage to small boats and berthing facilities at San Rafael. At Santa Cruz, a 35-foot floating dredge was set adrift and a 38-foot power cruiser was crushed.

At Crescent City, which bore the brunt of wave damage in California, 12 lives were lost despite a 1-hour tsunami warning. Eight boats were sunk, 3 are unaccounted for, and 15 capsized. Docks, harbor facilities, and the seawall were heavily damaged. Fifty-four homes were destroyed, 13 were heavily damaged, and 24 were slightly damaged. Forty-two small business buildings were destroyed, 118 were heavily damaged, and 29 were slightly damaged. Fires were started by the rupture and explosion of 5 bulk-storage oil tanks.

The fifth seismic sea wave to arrive at Crescent City caused most of the damage and took all 12 lives. After the first wave crested at 14.5 feet above mean low low water (MLLW), a second wave slacked off at 12 feet, followed by two much smaller waves. The townspeople, thinking that the tsunami was over, had begun to return to the flooded area when the fifth wave—coming in on a high tide—crested at 20.5 feet above MLLW.

Seiches were generated in various places remote from Alaska by amplification of direct seismic vibrations. In the Gulf of Mexico off Texas—completely separated physically from any possible effects of tsunamis—waves as much as 6 feet high damaged small craft. In addition, water was agitated in many swimming pools in Texas and Louisiana. Surface-water gauges recorded fluctuations in Texas, Louisiana, Arkansas, Missouri, Kentucky, Tennessee, Alabama, Georgia, and Pennsylvania.

The ground-water regimen was affected throughout much of North America. Water-level fluctuations were noted in wells throughout the coterminous United States and at points as distant as Puerto Rico, the Virgin Islands, and Denmark. Fluctuations of as much as 6 cm were recorded in wells in Denmark. The maximum reported fluctuation was 23 feet in a well at Belle Fourche, S. D. Fluctuations apparently were greatest in a broad belt extending southeast from South Dakota and Wisconsin, through Missouri and Illinois and on through Georgia and Florida to Puerto Rico. Most level changes in wells were temporary, but some were permanent. The water in some wells was temporarily muddied.

References

Alaska Department of Health and Welfare, 1964a, Good Friday earthquake called on resources of all in State: *Alaska's Health and Welfare,* v. 21, June 1964, p. 5–7.

———, 1964b, Preliminary report of earthquake damage to environmental health facilities and services in Alaska: Juneau, Alaska Dept. Health and Welfare, Environmental Health Br., 46 p.

Benioff, Hugo, and Gutenberg, Beno, 1939, Waves and currents recorded by electromagnetic barographs: *Bull. Am. Meterorol. Soc.,* v. 20, p. 421–426.

Coulter, H. W., and Migliaccio, R. R., 1966 Effects of the March 27, 1964, earthquake at Valdez, Alaska: *U. S. Geol. Survey Prof. Paper 542–C,* 36 p.

Gutenberg, Beno, and Richter, C. F., 1949, *Seismicity of the earth and associated phenomena:* Princeton, N. J., Princeton Univ. Press, 273 p.

Hanna, G. D., 1964, Biological effects of an earthquake: *Pacific Discovery,* v. 17, no. 6, p. 24–26.

Hill, M. R., 1965, Earth hazards—an editorial: *California Div. Mines and Geology Mineral Inf. Service,* v. 18, no. 4, p. 57–59.

Moore, G. W., 1964, Magnetic disturbances preceding the Alaska earthquake: *Nature,* v. 203, no. 4944, p. 508–509.

Plafker, George, 1965, Tectonic deformation associated with the 1964 Alaska earthquake: *Science,* v. 148, no. 3678, p. 1675–1687.

Richter, C. F., 1958, *Elementary seismology:* San Francisco, W. H. Freeman and Co., 768 p.

U. S. Coast and Geodetic Survey, 1964, Prince William Sound, Alaskan earthquakes, March–April 1964: *U. S. Coast and Geod. Survey, Seismology Div., prelim. rept.,* 83 p.

Van Dorn, W. G., 1964, Source mechanism of the tsunami of March 28, 1964, in Alaska: *Coastal Eng. Conf., 9th, Lisbon, 1964, Proc.,* p. 166–190.

8   Man-made Earthquakes in Denver

David M. Evans

From April 1962 to November 1965, Denver experienced more than 700 earthquakes. They were not damaging —the greatest magnitude was 4.3 on the Richter scale—but the community became increasingly concerned. More and more people took out earthquake insurance. There was talk in the press that Denver might be removed from the list of possible sites for a $375 million accelerator to be built by the Atomic Energy Commission because it was becoming known as an earthquake area.

In November 1962, I publicly suggested that there was a direct relationship between the earthquakes and contaminated waste-water being injected into a 12,045-foot disposal well at the Rocky Mountain Arsenal, northeast of Denver.[1] Representative Roy McVicker of Colorado immediately called for a full scientific investigation of the tremors, and on March 19, 1966, the U. S. Geological Survey released the results of its studies in coöperation with the Colorado School of Mines, Regis College in Denver, and the University of Colorado.[2] The USGS concluded that "The pumping of waste fluids into a deep disposal well at the Rocky Mountain Arsenal near Denver appears to be a significant cause of a series of

minor earthquakes that have occurred just north of Denver since the spring of 1962."

Since 1942, the Rocky Mountain Arsenal has manufactured products on a large scale for chemical warfare and industrial use, under direction of the Chemical Corps of the U. S. Army. One by-product of this operation is contaminated waste-water and, until 1961, the water was disposed of by evaporation from earthen reservoirs.

When it was found that the waste-water was contaminating the ground water and endangering crops, the Chemical Corps tried evaporating the water from water-tight reservoirs. That failed, so the Corps decided to drill an injection disposal well.

It commissioned E. A. Polumbus Jr. & Associates Inc. to design the well, supervise drilling and completion, provide the necessary engineering-geology services, and manage the project. Louis J. Scopel, as an associate, was the project geologist. Another associate, George R. Downs, contributed to the initial design and acted as an adviser.

The well was drilled in NW¼ NE¼ sec. 26, T2S, R67W, Adams County, Colorado. It was completed in September 1961 at a total depth of 12,045 feet.[3]

Evans, D. M., 1966, "Man-made Earthquakes in Denver," *Geotimes*, vol. 10, no. 9, pp. 11–18. Lightly edited by permission of the author and reprinted by permission of the American Geological Institute. Copyright 1966 by A. G. I.
Mr. Evans is a consulting geologist in Denver, Colorado.

Regional Geology

The Rocky Mountain Arsenal disposal well is on the gently dipping east flank of the Denver-Julesburg Basin, just a few miles east of the basin axis. As indicated in Fig. 1, it is in a region of the subcrop of Cambro-Ordovician

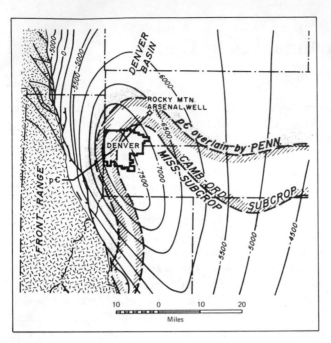

FIG. 1. Structural map of a part of the Denver-Julesburg Basin shows the location of the Rocky Mountain Arsenal Well. (After Anderman and Ackman[4])

rocks near the area where those rocks are truncated and overlain by Pennsylvanian sediments.[4] Figure 2 is a cross-section that shows the subsurface geology from the Arsenal well to the outcrop of Precambrian granite gneiss west of Denver.[5]

About 13,000 feet of structural relief exists between the top of the Precambrian in the Arsenal well and the Precambrian outcrops.

Injection in Precambrian Rocks

According to Scopel,[3] Precambrian rocks were penetrated in the Arsenal well from 11,950 feet to the total depth of 12,045. He described the rocks as bright green weathered schist from 11,950 to 11,970 and as highly fractured hornblende granite gneiss containing pegmatite intrusions from 11,970 to the bottom of the hole.

As a part of the USGS study, Sheridan, Wrucke, and Wilcox[2] analyzed the core and cuttings from the lower part of the well, and concluded that the top of the Precambrian is at 11,935. They describe the section from 11,970 to 12,045 as "migmatitic gneiss: rock containing fine-to-medium-grained hornblendic biotite-quartz-feldspar rock, containing steeply dipping open fractures, and thin calcite and ankerite-filled veinlets and microbreccias." They point out the striking similarity between the fractured Precambrian gneiss of the Arsenal well and the breccia-reef faults and fracture zones in the Precambrian outcrop of the Front Range west of Denver.

In the Arsenal well, a 5½-inch liner was cemented 5 feet into the Precambrian gneiss at 11,975 feet, and 5½-inch tubing was run to a depth of

9,011 feet, to complete the well for injection into the almost vertically fractured gneiss from 11,975 feet to 12,045.

Pumping and pressure-injection tests were made from November 1961 to February 1962 to obtain reservoir fluid samples and to determine rates and injection pressures at which the reservoir would take fluid.

A conventional oil-field pump was run in the well, and pumping tests were made. After pumping out 1,100 barrels of salt water more than the fluid lost in the hole during drilling, the well pumped down and recovery became negligible. It was concluded at the time of testing that fluid recovery was from fractures. It was believed further that as fluid was withdrawn from these fractures they were squeezed shut by compressive forces, which restricted fluid entry into the well bore.

When fluid injection tests were made, it was noticed that as fluid was injected the calculated drainage radius and formation capacity increased. That was interpreted as an indication that the reservoir consisted of fractures that expanded as additional fluid was injected.

In March 1962 the Arsenal disposal program began, and 4.2 million gallons of waste was injected. The Denver earthquakes started the next month.

The monthly volume of waste injected is shown in the lower half of Fig. 3. From March 1962 until September 1963, the maximum injection pressure is reported to have been about 550 pounds per square inch, with an injection rate of 200 gallons a minute.

At the end of September 1963 the injection well was shut down, and no fluid was injected until September 17, 1964. During the shut-down, surface evaporation from the settling basin was sufficient to handle the plant output.

From September 17, 1964, until the end of March 1965, injection was resumed by gravity discharge into the

FIG. 2. Cross-section shows subsurface geology from the Arsenal well to the outcrop of Precambrian granite gneiss west of Denver. (After M. F. and C. M. Boos and H. H. Odiorne) The line of cross-section is shown in Fig. 1.

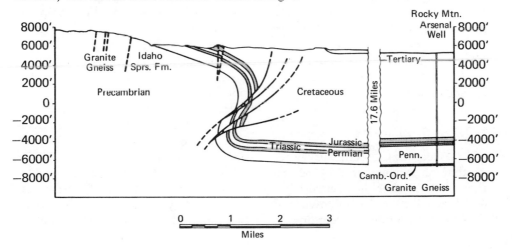

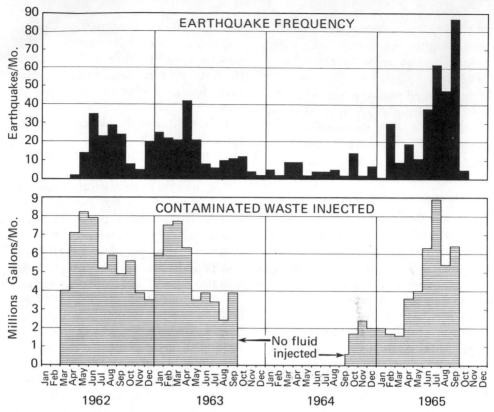

FIG. 3. Upper half: number of earthquakes per month recorded in the Denver area. Lower half: monthly volume of contaminated waste water injected into the Arsenal well.

well. No well-head pressure was needed to inject the maximum of 2.4 million gallons of waste per month into the well. Beginning in April 1965 larger quantities of fluid were injected. During April and May a maximum pressure of 1,050 pounds was required to inject 300 gallons a minute.

The Denver Earthquakes

The U. S. Coast & Geodetic Survey reports that on November 7, 1882, an earthquake was felt in Denver and nearby Louisville and Georgetown, and in southeast Wyoming. According to

Joseph V. Downey, director of the Regis College Seismological Observatory, no earthquake epicenters were recorded in the Denver area by either the C&GS or Regis between 1882 and the first earthquake in April 1962. (The Regis Observatory has been operating since 1909.)

From 1954 to 1959 a seismic station was operated at the University of Colorado in Boulder, directed by Warren Longley. As a part of the recent USGS investigation, Harold L. Krivoy and M. P. Lane analyzed the records from that station.[2] They found a few small events that might have been earthquakes in the Derby area, but they concluded that, since all those events occurred during weekday working hours, they were probably due to construction blasting or explosives disposal at the Arsenal.

From April 1962 to the end of September 1965, 710 earthquakes with epicenters in the vicinity of the Arsenal were recorded at the Cecil H. Green Observatory, Bergen Park, Colo., which is operated by Colorado School of Mines.[6]

The total number of earthquakes reported in the Denver area is plotted in the upper half of Fig. 3. The magnitude of the earthquakes reported range from 0.7 to 4.3 on the Richter scale. About 75 were intense enough to be felt. Yung-liang Wang[6] calculated the epicenters and hypocenters of the 1963–65 Denver earthquakes, and Fig. 4 shows the results of his calculations.

Most of the epicenters are within 5 miles of the well. All epicenters calculated from four or more recording stations are within 7 miles of the well. Wang[6] calculated the best-fitting plane passing through the zone of hypocenters determined from four or more recording stations. He concluded that this plane might be a fault along which movement was taking place. The plane dips east and passes beneath the Arsenal well about 6.5 miles below the surface. (See Fig. 4.)

In the USGS study,[2] J. J. Healy, W. H. Jackson and J. R. Van Schaack report that Wang's data were compiled from records of available seismographs and that most of the earthquakes plotted were with fewer than four stations and that only a few were located with four stations. Also, the four stations available to Wang in his study were not optimally placed to locate earthquakes in the vicinity of the Arsenal. Therefore the USGS set up a seismic network around the Arsenal well that would greatly improve the accuracy of earthquake location. Up to eight seismic-refraction units were in operation at the same time, and during the study from one to 20 micro-earthquakes were recorded every day.

Healy, Jackson and Van Schaack concluded that the precise USGS work showed the epicenters clustered even more closely around the Arsenal well than Wang had reported. The epicenters located by the USGS outline a roughly ellipsoidal area (which includes the well) about six miles long and three miles wide, suggesting the presence of a fault or fracture zone trending about N 60° W. The epicenters of the events studied in detail were between 4.5 and 5.5 km deep.

Pressure Injection and Earthquake Frequency

Pressure injection began in March 1962. The first two earthquakes with epicenters in the Arsenal area were recorded in April 1962.

The lower half of Fig. 3 is a graph of the monthly volume of waste injected into the Arsenal well. The total number of earthquakes recorded in the Arsenal area is plotted for each month in the upper half of the graph.

During the initial injection period, from March 1962 to the end of September 1963, the injection program was often suspended for repairs to the filter plant. In this period there does not appear to be a direct month-by-month correlation. However, the high injection months of April, May and

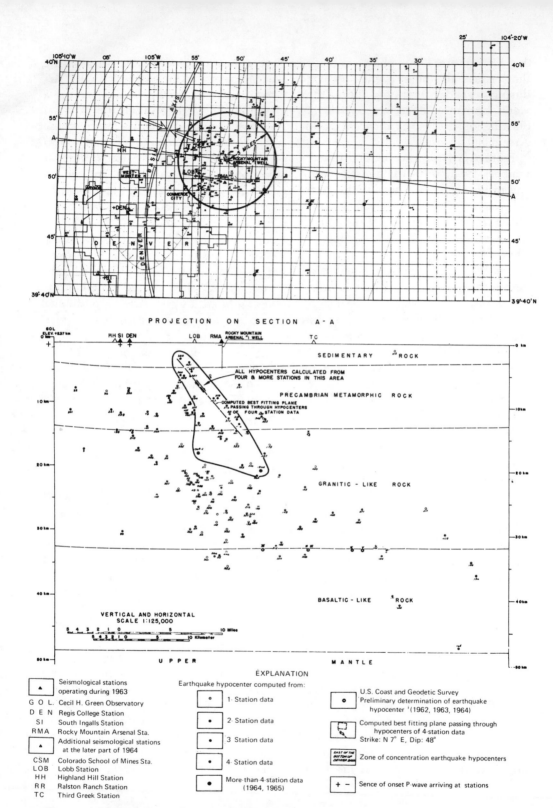

PROJECTION ON SECTION A-A

SEDIMENTARY ROCK

ALL HYPOCENTERS CALCULATED FROM
FOUR & MORE STATIONS IN THIS AREA

PRECAMBRIAN METAMORPHIC ROCK

COMPUTED BEST FITTING PLANE
PASSING THROUGH HYPOCENTERS
OF FOUR STATION DATA

GRANITIC - LIKE ROCK

BASALTIC - LIKE ROCK

VERTICAL AND HORIZONTAL
SCALE 1:125,000

UPPER   MANTLE

EXPLANATION

Earthquake hypocenter computed from:

	Seismological stations operating during 1963
G O L.	Cecil H. Green Observatory
D E N	Regis College Station
SI	South Ingalls Station
RMA	Rocky Mountain Arsenal Sta.
	Additional seismological stations at the later part of 1964
CSM	Colorado School of Mines Sta.
LOB	Lobb Station
HH	Highland Hill Station
RR	Ralston Ranch Station
TC	Third Greek Station

- 1- Station data
- 2- Station data
- 3- Station data
- 4- Station data
- More-than-4-station data (1964, 1965)

U.S. Coast and Geodetic Survey
Preliminary determination of earthquake hypocenter '(1962, 1963, 1964)

Computed best fitting plane passing through hypocenters of 4-station data
Strike: N 7° E, Dip: 48°

Zone of concentration earthquake hypocenters

+ −   Sence of onset P-wave arriving at stations

June 1962 seem to correlate with the high earthquake frequency months of June, July and August. The high injection months of February and March 1963 may correlate with the high earthquake month of April.

The period of no injection from September 1963 to September 1964 coincides with a period of minimum earthquake frequency. The period of low-volume injection by gravity flow, from September 1964 to April 1965, is characterized by two months (October and February) of greater earthquake frequency than experienced during the preceding year.

The most direct correlation of fluid injection with earthquake frequency is during the months of June through September 1965. That period was characterized by the pumping of 300 gallons a minute, 16 to 24 hours a day, at a pressure of 800 to 1,050 pounds.

There have been five characteristic periods of injection (see Fig. 5):

April 1962–April 1963; high injection at medium pressure.

May 1963–September 1963; medium injection at medium pressure.

October 1963–September 1964; no injection.

September 1964–March 1965; low injection at no pressure (gravity feed).

April 1965–September 1965; high injection at high pressure.

The average numbers of earthquakes per month are shown in Fig. 5 above the average volumes of fluid injected per month for each of those five periods. The injection for March 1962 is not used in the averages because the exact day injection was started is unknown.

Figure 5 indicates that there is a direct correlation between average monthly injection and earthquake frequency when an injection program has been carried out for several months.

The period of October, November and December 1965 provided the first check period of the correlation between earthquakes and fluid injected. From October 1 to December 20 an average of 3.8 million gallons a month were injected at an average pressure of 1,000 pounds. On December 20 the pressure was reduced to 500 pounds. From Fig. 5, it can be seen that during May–September 1963 approximately the same amount of fluid was injected at roughly half the pressure and an average of 12 earthquakes a month were recorded. With an injection pressure of 1,000 pounds, about twice as many tremors (as recorded during April–September 1965) would be expected. Allowing for the 10 days in December when the pressure was reduced, an average of about 25 earthquakes a month would be predicted. Actually, 68 shocks were recorded, for an average of slightly less than 23 a month.

During January 1966, about 2.4 million gallons were injected, and 19 shocks were recorded. On January 20, 1966, pumping was stopped; during February, 200,000 gallons were injected

FIG. 4. Earthquake hypocenters are shown here for 1963–64 as computed by seismological stations in the Denver area. All epicenters calculated from four or more recording stations are within 7 miles of the Arsenal well. All hypocenters calculated from four or more recording stations are within the area indicated on section A-A. (After Wang[6])

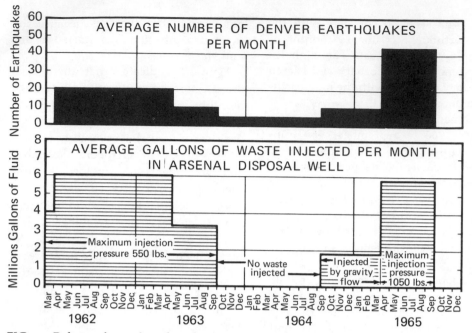

FIG. 5. Relationships of earthquake frequency and waste injection are shown here for five characteristic periods.

by gravity flow. On February 20 the well was shut in. Ten earthquakes were recorded during February at the Cecil H. Green Observatory (whose earthquake count has been used in this report).

George Bardwell[7] has made a statistical analysis of the relationship between fluid injection at the Arsenal well and earthquake frequency in the area. Even though his study did not include the effect of injection pressure, he concluded that the probability of the injection-earthquake relationship being due to random fluctuation was about 1 in 1,000.

Fluid Pressure and the Arsenal Earthquakes

Evidence gained from drilling and testing the Arsenal disposal well indicates that the Precambrian reservoir is composed of a highly fractured gneiss that is substantially impermeable. It indicates that as fluid was pumped out of the reservoir the fractures closed, and as fluid was injected the fractures opened. In other words, the pumping and injection tests indicated that rock movement occurred as fluid was withdrawn or injected at relatively low pressures.

The pressure-depth relations of the Precambrian reservoir, showing hydrostatic and lithostatic pressure variations with depth, are shown in Fig. 6. Those data were determined from a drill-stem test. As shown on the chart, the observed pressure of the Precambrian reservoir is almost 900 pounds less than the hydrostatic pressure.

Hubbert and Rubey[8] have devised a simple and adequate way to reduce by the required amount the frictional resistance to the sliding of large overthrust blocks down very gentle slopes. It arises from the circumstance that the weight of such a block is jointly supported by solid stress and the pressure of interstitial fluids. As the fluid pressure approaches the lithostatic pressure, corresponding to flotation of the overburden, the shear stress required to move the block approaches zero.

If high fluid pressures reduce frictional resistance and permit rocks to slide down very gentle slopes, it follows that as fluid pressure is decreased frictional resistance between blocks of rock is increased, permitting them to come to rest on increasingly steep slopes. The steeper the slope on which a block of rock is at rest, the lower the required increase in fluid pressure necessary to produce movement.

In the case of the Precambrian reservoir beneath the Arsenal well, the rocks were at equilibrium on high-angle fracture planes with a fluid pressure of 900 pounds less than the hydrostatic pressure before injection began.

As fluid was injected into the Precambrian reservoir, the fluid pressure adjacent to the well bore rose, and the frictional resistance along the fracture planes was thereby reduced. When, finally, enough fluid pressure was exerted over enough area, movement occurred. The elastic energy released was recorded as an earthquake.

Since the formation fluid pressure is 900 pounds subhydrostatic, merely filling the hole with contaminated waste (mostly salt water) raises the formation pressure 900 pounds, or to the equivalent of hydrostatic pressure. Any applied injection pressure above that of gravity flow increases pressure to a total higher than hydrostatic pressure. For example, an injection pressure of 1,000 pounds would raise the reservoir pressure adjacent to the well bore to 1,900 pounds, or by the amount to bring the pressure to hydrostatic (by filling the hole) plus 1,000 pounds.

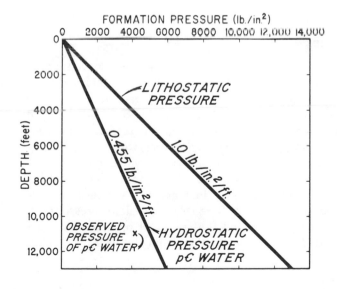

FIG. 6. Pressure-depth relations are shown here for the Precambrian reservoir at the Arsenal well.

Apparently a rise in fluid pressure within the Precambrian reservoir of 900 to 1,900 pounds is enough to allow movement to occur.

Open Fractures

The hypocenters in the Arsenal area plotted from data derived from four or more recording stations indicate that movement takes place 1.5 to 12 miles below the well. If the Precambrian fracture system extends to a depth of 12 miles, then fluid pressure could be transmitted to that depth by moderate surface injection pressure as long as the fracture system is open for transmission of that pressure.

Secor[9] concluded that open fractures can occur to great depths even with only moderately high fluid pressure-overburden weight ratios. It appears possible that high-angle open fractures may be present beneath the Arsenal well at great depths with much lower fluid pressure-overburden weight ratios than has formerly been considered possible.

Time Lag Between Fluid Injections and Earthquakes

The correlation of fluid injected with earthquake frequency (Fig. 3) suggests that the two are separated by a time lag. Bardwell[7] notes that the frequency of Denver earthquakes appears to lag waste injection by one to four months. This phenomenon is probably the same as that described by Serafim and Del Campo.[10] They describe the observed time lag between water levels in reservoirs and the pressures measured in the foundations of dams, and ascribe it to an unsteady rate of percolation through open joints in the rock mass, due to the opening and closing of the passages resulting from internal and externally applied pressures.

The time lag between waste injection in the Arsenal well and earthquake frequency is probably due to an unsteady rate of percolation through fractures in the Precambrian reservoir due to the opening and closing of these fractures resulting from the applied fluid pressure of the injected waste. The delayed application of this pressure at a distance from the well bore is believed to trigger the movement recorded as an earthquake.

Earthquakes During Shut-Down Period

In considering the earthquake frequency during the year the injection well was shut down, unfortunately neither periodic bottom-hole pressure tests nor checks of the fluid level in the hole were made. If these measurements had been made, we would know how long it took bottom-hole pressure to decline.

By the end of September 1963, about 102.3 million gallons of fluid had been injected into the well. It is believed that this injection had raised the fluid level pressure in the reservoir for some distance from the well bore. During shut-down, this elevated pressure was equalizing throughout the reservoir and at increasing distance from the well bore. As this fluid pressure reduced the frictional resistance in fractures farther from the well, movement occurred, and small earthquakes resulted.

Conclusion

The Precambrian reservoir receiving the Arsenal waste is highly fractured gneiss of very low permeability. The fractures are nearly vertical. The fracture porosity of the reservoir is filled with salt water. Reservoir pressure is 900 pounds subhydrostatic.

It appears that movement is taking place in this fractured reservoir as a result of the injection of water at pressures from 900 to 1,950 pounds greater than reservoir pressure.

Hubbert and Rubey[8] point out that rock masses in fluid-filled reservoirs are supported by solid stress and the pressure of interstitial fluids. As fluid pressure approaches lithostatic pressure, the shear stress required to move rock masses down very gently dipping slopes approaches zero.

These principles appear to explain the rock movement in the Arsenal reservoir. The highly fractured rocks of the reservoir are at rest on steep slopes under a condition of subhydrostatic fluid pressure. As the fluid pressure is raised within the reservoir, frictional resistance along fracture planes is reduced and, eventually, movement takes place. The elastic wave energy released is recorded as an earthquake.

In the present case, I believe that a stable situation in this Precambrian reservoir was made unstable by fluid pressure. It is interesting to speculate that the principle of increasing fluid pressure to release elastic wave energy could be applied to earthquake modification. That is, it might be possible to relieve the stresses along some fault zones in urban areas by increasing the fluid pressures along the zone, using a series of injection wells. The accumulated stress might thus be released at will in a series of non-damaging earthquakes instead of eventually resulting in one large event that might cause a major disaster.

Notes

[1] David M. Evans, 1966, The Denver area earthquakes and the Rocky Mountain Arsenal disposal well: *The mountain geologist*, v. 3, no. 1, p. 23–36.

[2] J. H. Healy and others, 1966, Geophysical and geological investigations relating to earthquakes in the Denver area, Colorado: U. S. Geological Survey open-file report.

[3] L. J. Scopel, 1964, Pressure injection disposal well, Rocky Mountain Arsenal, Denver, Colo.: *The mountain geologist*, v. 1, no. 1, p. 35–42.

[4] G. G. Anderman and E. J. Ackman, 1963, Structure of the Denver-Julesburg Basin and surrounding areas: in Rocky Mountain Association of Geologists' *Guidebook to the geology of the northern Denver Basin and adjacent uplifts.*

[5] C. M. Boos and M. F. Boos, 1957, Tectonics of the eastern flank and foothills of the Front Range, Colorado: American Assn. of Petroleum Geologists *Bulletin*, v. 41, p. 2,603–2,676.

[6] Yung-liang Wang, 1965, *Local hypocenter determination in linearly varying layers applied to earthquakes in the Denver area:* unpublished DSc dissertation, Colorado School of Mines.

[7] G. E. Bardwell, 1966, Some statistical features of the relationship between Rocky Mountain Arsenal waste disposal and frequency of earthquakes: *The mountain geologist*, v. 3, no. 1, p. 37–42.

[8] M. King Hubbert and W. W. Rubey, 1959, Role of fluid pressure in mechanics of overthrust faulting; part 1, Mechanics of fluid-

filled porous solids and its application to overthrust faulting: Geological Society of America *Bulletin*, v. 70, p. 115–166.

[9] D. T. Secor Jr, 1965, Role of fluid pressure in jointing, *American journal of science*, v. 263, p. 633–646.

[10] J. L. Serafim and A. del Campo, 1965, Interstitial pressures of rock foundations of dams: *Journal* of the Soil Mechanics & Foundations Division, Proceedings of the American Society of Civil Engineers v. 91, no. SM5.

9   Earthquake Prediction and Control

L. C. Pakiser, J. P. Eaton, J. H. Healy, C. B. Raleigh

The great Alaska earthquake (Richter magnitude, 8.4 to 8.6) of 27 March 1964 awakened earth scientists and public officials to the need for intensified research on earthquakes, their effects on man and his works, and possible means of reducing their hazards. Although the loss of life in Alaska (115) and property damage ($300 million) were small for such a great earthquake, the realization that an earthquake of similar magnitude could occur in densely populated coastal California, where loss of life would almost certainly be in the thousands and property damage in the billions of dollars, dramatized the urgent need for remedial action.

Following the 1964 Alaska earthquake, an Ad Hoc Panel on Earthquake Prediction was organized by Frank

Pakiser, L. C., Eaton, J. P., Healy, J. H., and Raleigh, C. B., 1969, "Earthquake Prediction and Control," *Science*, vol. 166, no. 3912, pp. 1467–74. Lightly edited by permission of the senior author and reprinted by permission of the American Association for the Advancement of Science. Copyright 1969 by the A. A. A. S.
The authors are affiliated with the U. S. Geological Survey.

Press of the Massachusetts Institute of Technology at the request of the President's Science Advisor, Donald Hornig, to study the opportunities for research on earthquake prediction. The report of the panel[1] was completed in September 1965 and released by Hornig in October. The 10-year program recommended by the panel calls for a new generation of instruments for monitoring earthquake faults in California and Alaska, extensive geological and geophysical surveys of fault zones, laboratory and theoretical studies of mechanisms of rock failure, research in prediction theory, and strongly augmented research in earthquake engineering. The panel estimated the cost of the program at $137 million.

Although the Press Panel report has not been adopted as a national program, many of its recommendations are being carried out on a modest scale by government agencies and universities. The Ad Hoc Interagency Working Group for Earthquake Research[2] reported that six federal government agencies spent $7.4 million on earthquake research in fiscal year 1967. Both the Environmental Science Services

Administration and the U. S. Geological Survey have established new earthquake-research laboratories in California. The research programs they have established are guided to a significant degree by the recommendations of the Press Panel, but they fall far short of providing the information needed for safe development of coastal California and other U. S. areas subject to earthquakes. The magnitude of the problem can be seen from the Urban Land Institute's estimate[2] that, by the year 2000, the population of California will have increased from one-tenth to one-seventh of the national total, or to about 40 million in a national population of 300 million.

In 1962, the Earthquake Prediction Research Group in Japan outlined a plan for research on the prediction of earthquakes.[3] In 1965, following the destructive Niigata earthquake of 1964, the Japanese government sponsored and provided financial support for a 5-year plan for research on earthquake prediction.[4] The program is now well advanced.[5]

Earthquakes are a cause of common concern to Japan and the United States. The National Science Foundation and the Japan Society for Promotion of Science have jointly sponsored three conferences on research related to earthquake prediction.[6] The most recent of these, held at the U. S. Geological Survey's National Center for Earthquake Research, in October and November 1968, reviewed the latest progress in Japan and the United States on studies of premonitory phenomena associated with earthquakes, and related problems.[7]

The discovery[8, 9] that injection of waste fluids in a well drilled into the Precambrian rocks beneath the Rocky Mountain Arsenal near Denver, Colorado, had triggered a series of earthquakes, and evidence that earthquakes are triggered by the impounding of water in reservoirs[10, 11] and by large underground nuclear explosions[12, 12a], have raised the possibility that earthquake hazards can be reduced by the controlled release of stored strain energy in active fault zones.

Earthquakes in California

There has been no major breakthrough in earthquake prediction since the reviews by Press[13] and Rikitake,[5] but steady progress has been made toward understanding the nature of earthquakes along the continental margins, including coastal California. An enormous amount of evidence has been marshaled in support of Hess's concept of sea-floor spreading, Wilson's transform faults, and the later ideas of Vine, Le Pichon, Isacks, Oliver, Sykes, and others, on the motions of large, rigid plates of the lithosphere that plunge downward under the island arcs and continental margins to form the major earthquake belts of the globe.[14, 15] These revolutionary new concepts provide a global tectonic framework in which we can envision, for the first time, the kinematic processes that operate to generate earthquakes at depths ranging from the shallow crust to 700 kilometers.

In this framework, the San Andreas fault system of California is seen as a transform fault associated with spreading from the East Pacific Rise and with northwestward motion of a large, rigid plate of oceanic lithosphere toward the Aleutian Islands, where it descends into the earth's mantle at a rate of about 5 centimeters per year.

Allen and others have identified areas of contrasting seismic behavior along different segments of the San Andreas fault zone in California.[16] The segments corresponding to the surface breaks of the great 1906 San Francisco and 1857 Fort Tejon earthquakes (Fig. 1) seem to be "locked" and characterized by infrequent but very severe earthquakes. At present, the seismic activity is extremely low in the locked zones, and no fault creep—the quiet, steady-to-episodic slippage along the fault—has been discovered in these segments. These segments are likely candidates for great earthquakes in the future, perhaps within the next few decades, because the crust there is capable of storing large amounts of strain energy which can be released suddenly and violently. The "active" areas between San Francisco and Parkfield, southeast of San Bernardino, and also probably northwest of Cape Mendocino seem to be characterized by fault creep, accompanied by frequent minor-to-severe (but not great) earthquakes; thus the accumulation of large amounts of stored strain energy is inhibited. In our judgment, the segment of the San Andreas fault on the San Francisco Peninsula northwest of Hollister should be considered locked, although the Hayward and Calaveras faults east of San Francisco Bay are active. The San Andreas may be locked over much of its length because of the pronounced curvature of the fault near the north

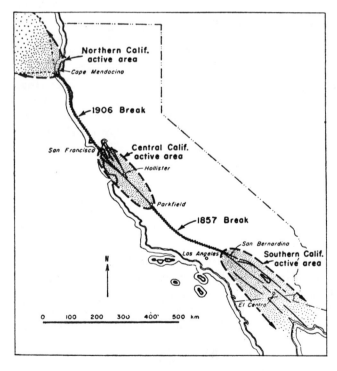

FIG. 1. Areas of contrasting seismic behavior along the San Andreas fault zone in California. [From C. R. Allen,[16] with permission]

end of the 1906 break at Cape Mendocino and near the center of the 1857 break (Fig. 1). If this pattern of contrasting seismic behavior is valid, it is clear that both Los Angeles and San Francisco are vulnerable to severe earthquake damage in the future.

The San Andreas fault zone also exhibits markedly differing patterns of seismic behavior when viewed in detail. Aftershocks of the June 1966 Parkfield-Cholame[17] earthquake lie along a narrow, near-vertical zone about 15 kilometers deep which nearly coincides at the surface with the mapped fault break. Cumulative fault creep of about 20 centimeters has been measured in this segment since 1966.

On the other hand, most of the aftershocks of a moderate earthquake that occurred southeast of Hollister at Bear Valley in 1967 were tightly clustered in a more or less spherical zone 3 kilometers in diameter and centered, just west of the San Andreas fault, at a depth of 3 kilometers. Bear Valley is near the inferred junction of the San Andreas and Calaveras faults. The center of the hypocentral zone at Bear Valley is within easy range of conventional drilling techniques and is thus available for direct observation and experimentation.

The results in the Parkfield-Cholame area and at Bear Valley were obtained from networks of portable seismographs. Seismic activity in California is also being continuously monitored by telemetered nets of short-period seismographs operated by the University of California at Berkeley, the California Institute of Technology, and the U. S. Geological Survey. In the vicinity of Hollister and Gilroy, micro-earthquakes recorded on the Geological Survey's telemetered net exhibit well-defined epicenter trends along, or near, the Sargent, San Andreas, and Calaveras faults.

In this area, as elsewhere in California, focal depths of micro-earthquakes do not exceed 15 kilometers. Crustal thickness averages about 25 kilometers. Thus, brittle behavior of the rocks in the San Andreas fault system seems to be confined to the upper crust; this implies some form of smooth slippage or flow along the faults in the lower crust and upper mantle.

Fault movements along the San Andreas system are being monitored by several federal, state, and local governmental agencies, and by universities. The most extensive fault-movement studies are the Geodimeter measurements of the State of California Department of Water Resources (now being continued by the State Division of Mines and Geology). These studies reveal a fault-movement rate that averages about 4 centimeters per year. The movement between Hollister and Cholame seems to be primarily in the form of fault creep.[18] North of Hollister, in the San Francisco Bay area, the movement is distributed primarily between the Calaveras and Hayward faults, and prominent creep has been noted at several places along the Hayward fault. No local fault movement was detected south of Cholame in the segment of the San Andreas fault that broke in 1857. These observations are compatible with the contrasting seismic behavior along different segments of the San Andreas fault zone.

Significantly, the Department of Water Resources found that earthquakes are often preceded by changes, and even reversals, in the rates of movement of the faults along which they occur.[18] Breiner and Kovach[19] have found evidence that fault-creep episodes are frequently preceded by local fluctuations in the earth's magnetic field.

Laboratory Investigations

Laboratory investigations related to the mechanism of earthquakes and the physical properties of rocks in earthquake source regions have been intensified recently in several governmental and university research institutions. Some results relevant to the problem of earthquake prediction were recently reviewed by Brace.[20] He particularly drew attention to the discovery by Raleigh and Paterson[21] that serpentine, under pressures at which it normally is ductile, becomes embrittled at high temperatures because of dehydration. Brittle fracture may, therefore, occur at depths extending into the upper mantle where hydrous phases in the mantle reach temperatures at which they dehydrate. This discovery seems to provide a mechanism for intermediate and perhaps deep-focus earthquakes as the rigid lithosphere descends into the mantle beneath island arcs and continental margins.

Byerlee and Brace[22] have shown that when two surfaces of granite or unaltered gabbro slide past one another under high confining pressure, the motion occurs through stick slip that is qualitatively similar to the shallow-focus earthquakes of the San Andreas fault system, but the confining pressures and stress drops are larger than those inferred for California. On the other hand, motion for gabbro and dunite in which olivine has been al-

tered to serpentine occurs by stable sliding similar to the behavior of the San Andreas fault system in the deep crust and upper mantle.

It is well known that seismic velocity, electrical resistivity, and magnetic susceptibility of rocks are strongly dependent on stress. Brace and Orange[23] have shown in particular that rocks under confining pressure undergo large decreases in resistivity as they become dilatant at stresses near that for fracture. Resistivity decreased following an initial increase with stress for all rocks except marble as new cracks formed in water-saturated rocks; the decrease was accompanied by a small increase in volume. This observation suggests the possibility of monitoring stress variations in fault zones by resistivity measurements obtained with surface or in-hole electrode arrays.

Man-Made Earthquakes

Man-made earthquakes have been known since Carder[10] documented the occurrence of about 600 local tremors during the 10 years following the formation of Lake Mead, in Arizona and Nevada, by Hoover Dam in 1935. Most of these tremors were microearthquakes, but one had a magnitude of about 5, and two had magnitudes of about 4. Carder concluded that the seismic activity was caused by the load of water in Lake Mead that reactivated faults in the area.

Carder's discovery remained of academic interest until Evans[8] dramatically demonstrated a correlation between the rate of injection of waste fluids and the frequency of earthquakes in the vicinity of the Rocky Mountain Arsenal well near Denver, Colorado, following the first injection of fluids in March 1962. The U. S. Geological Survey recorded the seismic activity in the vicinity of the Rocky Mountain Arsenal well, and Healy and his coworkers demonstrated[9] that the epicenters of the earthquakes occurred in a narrow, nearly linear zone about 8 kilometers long and trending northwestward, with the well near the center of the zone. Focal depths of the earthquakes ranged from 4 to 6 kilometers, just below the bottom of the 3.8-kilometer-deep Arsenal well. Following termination of fluid injection in February 1966, the frequency of the earthquakes declined, as had been expected, but in late 1966 seismic activity began again, unexpectedly, and it continued through most of 1967. The largest earthquakes, of magnitudes up to 5.5, occurred during this period and caused minor damage. The seismic activity declined again in 1968 and has continued at a low level into 1969.

Seismic radiation patterns of the first motion on seismograms recorded at the Arsenal indicate right-lateral strike-slip movement along fractures oriented parallel to the trend of the seismic zone. This led Healy and his coworkers to conclude[9] that the earthquakes were triggered by reduction of frictional resistance to faulting with increasing pore pressure, a conclusion which was supported by an analysis, according to the theory of Hubbert and Rubey,[24] of the conditions in the hypocentral zone of the earthquakes.

Stimulated by the occurrence of the earthquakes near Denver, a search for similar phenomena elsewhere led to the recognition that the Unita Basin Seismological Observatory, in Utah, had recorded a series of minor earthquakes with epicenters near the Rangely oil field in northwestern Colorado. The Rangely oil field is the site of a secondary-recovery operation involving the injection of water under pressure. To verify the location of the earthquakes, four portable seismographs were installed by the U. S. Geological Survey near the oil field in 1967 and operated for 10 days. A high level of seismic activity was recorded. At all four stations, about 20 microearthquakes were recorded strongly enough to be located.[25] These earthquakes occurred near parts of the oil field where the fluid-injection operation has produced the largest recent increases in fluid pressures (Fig. 2).

Recently Rothé[11] reviewed the association of earthquakes with the filling of reservoirs. Several examples were found, the most significant being the Koyna, India, earthquake of 10 December 1967, which had a magnitude of about 6½ and resulted in the deaths of about 200 people and in widespread destruction. The epicenter was estimated to have been within 10 kilometers of the Koyna dam, about 150 kilometers southeast of Bombay, which created a reservoir of 2 billion cubic meters in 1962 and 1963. Minor tremors had been previously recorded in the Koyna reservoir area, beginning in 1963. These events led Indian scientists to convene a special meeting in New Delhi on 19 December 1967 to consider the Koyna earthquake and its implications; the proceedings were published in a special number of the *Journal of the Indian Geophysical Union*.[26] Lee and Raleigh[27] made a fault-plane solution of the 10 December earthquake; their solution indicates that the

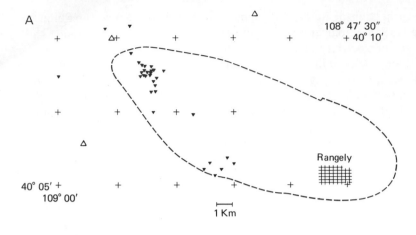

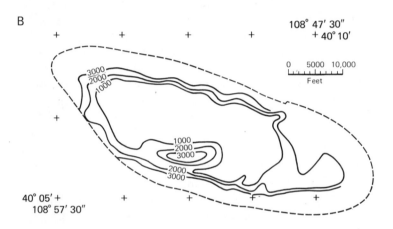

FIG. 2. Micro-earthquakes at the Rangely oil field, in Colorado. (a) Epicenters of 32 micro-earthquakes located by means of four stations. (Small inverted triangles) Epicenters; (larger triangles) stations. (b) Fluid pressures in the oil-producing horizon, the Weber sand, September 1967. Injection wells are near the perimeter of the field. Bottom hole pressure contour interval, 1000 pounds per square inch. [Pressure contours published with permission of the Chevron Oil Company]

mechanism was strike-slip faulting. From this study they concluded that tectonic strain stored in the rocks of the Koyna region was the source of the energy that released the earthquake.

Rothé[11] and Gough and Gough[28] have called attention to the earthquakes at Lake Kariba in the Kariba Gorge of the Zambezi River, Zambia. Thousands of earthquakes were recorded on a seismograph net installed after the lake was impounded by a hydroelectric dam in 1958. Gough and Gough concluded that normal faults in the area were reactivated by the reservoir load, by fault lubrication, or by both.[28] The largest of the earthquakes had a magnitude of 5.8.

Ryall and his co-workers[29] have noted numerous instances in which earthquakes were triggered by underground nuclear explosions at the Atomic Energy Commission's Nevada Test Site. In particular, they studied the Boxcar explosion of April 1968 and demonstrated that the blast triggered thousands of aftershocks in a northeast-trending zone 12 kilometers long and 4 kilometers wide.

Prior to the Benham underground nuclear explosion (yield, 1.1 megatons) of 19 December 1968, the U. S. Geological Survey installed a network of 27 seismographs in the vicinity of the Nevada Test Site.[12] Aftershocks of the explosion recorded by the network occurred as far as 13 kilometers from ground zero. Focal depths computed for the shocks ranged from the surface to a depth of about 7 kilometers. The magnitudes of the thousands of aftershocks recorded were generally small and did not exceed 5.0, as compared to the Benham magnitude of 6.3. The epicenters of the shocks migrated with time. Most were within 7 kilometers of ground zero during the first week following the explosion. After about 3 weeks the fracture zone was extended about 3 to 4 kilometers southward, and there was an accompanying increase in seismic activity. The aftershocks occurred west of ground zero, however, rather than along the zone of prominent surface fracturing to the east that developed after the Benham explosion and several earlier explosions. Analysis of the first motions of seismograms recorded from the Benham aftershocks suggest that they were triggered primarily by release of natural tectonic stress.

It is becoming increasingly evident that man can inadvertently trigger earthquakes by building dams, injecting fluids into the rocks of the earth's crust, and exploding nuclear devices underground. Earthquakes triggered by reservoirs and fluid injection have been destructive, some (as at Koyna) severely so, but, so far, seismic activity associated with explosions has occurred in the immediate vicinity of ground zero and has been less severe than the direct seismic effects of the explosions. It thus seems necessary for engineers of dams, and of fluid injection projects in particular, to give heed to the possibility that their works may trigger destructive and even death-dealing earthquakes. These discoveries also suggest the possibility of using fluid injection and perhaps explosions beneficially to control the release of stored tectonic stress and thus reduce earthquake hazards.

Outlook for Prediction and Control

Since 1964, most earth scientists have concluded that earthquake prediction is a legitimate subject for research, but they differ widely in their estimates of the prospects for success. Several developments of the 1960's lead us to conclude that the prospects for success during the next 10 years are good.

In 1965, at Matsushiro in the Nagano prefecture of Japan, swarms of earthquakes began which were so intense that as many as 600 were felt on some days. Some of the earthquakes were destructive, with magnitudes of about 5. By the time the Matsushiro seismic activity declined, in 1967, Japanese scientists had issued the first warnings of future earthquake hazards, in the form of estimates of the location and probable maximum magnitude of potentially damaging earthquakes expected over a period of a few months.[5] The warnings were based on an intensive program of leveling and Geodimeter surveys, micro-earthquake recordings, tiltmeter measurements, and geomagnetic observations. The Japanese scientists found that, without exception, swarms of very small shocks occurred in the epicentral regions of shocks that came several months later. Ground tilt was found to correlate strongly with the growth and decay of the seismic activity, and anomalous tilt was observed shortly before the occurrence of some earthquakes of magnitude about 5. Anomalous magnetic fluctuations were also observed. By continuously correlating the various changes that were occurring, the Japanese scientists were able to forecast periods of danger and to issue their warnings.

Rikitake[5] considers the Matsushiro warnings to have been a scientific success and "helpful for local governments," but notes that "those engaged in the sightseeing and hotel business were not really pleased. . . . Great care must be taken to find an adequate way of issuing a warning. . . . It is also of importance to train people . . . to properly behave in case of an earthquake warning."

In our judgment, long-range forecasting (of the order of a year) of general locations and approximate magnitudes of earthquakes, based on observed changes in the rates of vertical and horizontal motions and on seismic activity in fault zones, is attainable

in the near future. In 1955, prior to the 1964 Niigata earthquake in Japan, the rate of uplift of bench marks north of the epicenter increased to about 5 times that of the preceding years. The rate of uplift began to decrease in 1959, and later there was a tendency toward subsidence. Considerable subsidence had been observed before the earthquake occurred.[5] This suggests that an earthquake-warning system might be provided in part by leveling surveys repeated every few months or so.

The rate of movement along different segments of the San Andreas fault in seismically active areas was observed to change before the occurrence of moderate earthquakes.[18] The change was manifested as changes in the length of Geodimeter lines crossing faults: the lines lengthen or shorten depending on their orientation with respect to the fault. If a fault in a zone characterized by creep becomes locally locked, we would expect the lengthening or shortening of lines crossing the fault to slow down or stop. If the movement should be transferred to an adjacent fault, we might expect the direction of movement even to reverse. Locking or transfer of fault movement would tend to create the conditions favoring a moderate earthquake. Such locking and transfer appear to have occurred repeatedly in California,[18] and this suggests that a partial earthquake-warning system might also be provided by Geodimeter surveys repeated every few months.

Combined leveling and Geodimeter surveying, accompanied by continuous monitoring of seismic activity, appears, therefore, to offer a promising basis for a long-range earthquake-warning system.

It seems reasonable to hope that short-range prediction of earthquakes (on the order of hours or days) may be achieved through *continuous* monitoring of ground tilt, strain, seismic activity, and possibly fluctuations in the earth's magnetic field. Such monitoring should be accompanied by periodic measurement of rock stress in drill holes and by periodic or continuous observation of physical properties (for example, electrical resistivity or seismic velocity) that are stress-dependent. Short-range prediction capability cannot be achieved, however, in the absence of accelerating research on earthquake prediction along the general lines of the Press[1] and Pecora[2] reports (see [30]).

It has been demonstrated that earthquakes can be artificially triggered by fluid injection, impounding of water in reservoirs, and explosion of nuclear devices underground, and also that many earthquakes in California and Nevada occur at depths accessible to the drill. We can soberly conclude from these observations that it may be possible to develop a practical method for artificially dislodging locked sections of a major fault and to induce steady creep or periodic release of accumulating elastic strain energy along the fault to inhibit the natural accumulation of sufficient energy to produce a disastrous earthquake.[31] It is also clear that our current knowledge of the processes involved in the generation of earthquakes is insufficient to guide an engineering program for earthquake control. We suggest that an intensified program of field, laboratory, and theoretical studies aimed at im-

proving our understanding of earthquakes will not only advance the prospects for earthquake prediction but also provide an adequate basis for planning and implementing earthquake-control experiments that might ultimately provide the basis for a system of earthquake control.

Notes

[1] *Earthquake Prediction: a Proposal for a Ten-Year Program of Research* (Office of Science and Technology, Washington, D. C., 1965).

[2] *Proposal for a Ten-Year National Earthquake Hazards Program: a Partnership of Science and the Community* (Federal Council for Science and Technology, Washington, D. C., 1969). The members of the Working Group were L. Alldredge, W. E. Benson, W. Heitman, S. J. Lukasik, T. W. Mermel, L. C. Pakiser, A. J. Pressesky, W. A. Raney, H. B. Schechter, C. F. Scheffey, V. R. Willmarth, W. L. Hall (executive secretary), and W. T. Pecora (chairman). The report recommended implementation of a 10-year national earthquake hazards program along the general lines of the Press Panel report, but with less emphasis on earthquake prediction, greater emphasis on earthquake engineering, and estimated costs increased to $220 million.

[3] *Prediction of Earthquakes: Progress to Date and Plans for Further Development* (Earthquake Research Institute, University of Tokyo, Tokyo, 1962).

[4] T. Hagiwara and T. Rikitake, *Science* 157, 761 (1967).

[5] T. Rikitake, *Earth-Sci. Rev.* 4, 245 (1968).

[6] *Proceedings of the 1st (1964) and 2nd (1966) United States-Japan Conferences on Research Related to Earthquake Prediction Problems*, held, respectively, at the University of Tokyo and the Lamont Geological Observatory (available from the Earthquake Research Institute, University of Tokyo, or the Lamont Geological Observatory, Palisades, N. Y.)

[7] J. Oliver, *Science* 164, 92 (1969); see also a series of papers presented at the conference (L. Alsop and J. Oliver, Eds.), *Trans. Amer. Geophys. Union* 50, 376 (1969).

[8] D. Evans, *Mountain Geol.* 3, 23 (1966).

9 J. H. Healy, W. W. Rubey, D. T. Griggs, C. B. Raleigh, *Science* 161, 1301 (1968).

10 D. S. Carder, *Bull. Seismol. Soc. Amer.* 35, 175 (1945).

11 J. P. Rothé, *New Sci.* 39, 75 (1968).

12 *Trans. Amer. Geophys. Union* 50, 247 (1969) (abstracts of the symposium on Seismic Effects of Large Underground Nuclear Explosions, Golden Anniversary Meeting of the American Geophysical Union). See especially abstracts by J. H. Healy and R. M. Hamilton; A. Ryall, G. Boucher, W. V. Savage, and A. E. Jones; F. A. McKeown, D. D. Dickey, and G. E. Brethauer; S. W. Smith; J. Evernden; and E. R. Engdahl, W. V. Mickey, S. R. Brockman, and K. W. King.

12a R. M. Hamilton, F. A. McKeown, J. H. Healy, *Science* 166, 604 (1969).

13 F. Press and W. F. Brace, *Science* 152, 1575 (1966).

14 B. Isacks, J. Oliver, L. R. Sykes, *J. Geophys. Res.* 73, 5855 (1968).

15 H. H. Hess, in *Petrological Studies: A Volume in Honor of A. F. Buddington*, A. E. J. Engels, H. L. James, B. F. Leonard, Eds., (Geological Society of America, New York, 1962), p. 599; J. T. Wilson, *Science* 150, 482 (1965); F. J. Vine and J. T. Wilson, *ibid.*, p. 485; X. Le Pichon, *J. Geophys. Res.* 73, 3661 (1968); see also R. S. Dietz, *Nature* 190, 854 (1961).

16 C. R. Allen, in "Proceedings, Conference on the Geologic Problems of the San Andreas Fault System," *Stanford Univ. Pub. Univ. Ser. Geol. Sci. No. 11* (1968), p. 70.

17 J. P. Eaton, in "The Parkfield-Cholame, California, Earthquakes of June-August 1966: Surface Geologic Effects, Water-Resources Aspects, and Preliminary Seismic Data," *U. S. Geol. Surv. Prof. Pap. No. 579* (1967), p. 57.

18 "Geodimeter Fault Movement Investigations in California," *Calif. Dep. Water Resour. Bull. No. 116–6* (1968).

19 S. Breiner and R. L. Kovach, in "Proceedings, Conference on the Geologic Problems of the San Andreas Fault System, *Stanford Univ. Pub. Univ. Ser. Geol. Sci. No. 11* (1968), p. 70.

20 W. F. Brace, *Tectonophys.* 6, 75 (1968).

21 C. B. Raleigh and M. S. Paterson, *J. Geophys. Res.* 67, 4956 (1964).

22 J. D. Byerlee and W. F. Brace, *ibid.* 73, 6031 (1968).

23 W. F. Brace and A. S. Orange, *Science* 153, 1525 (1966).

24 M. K. Hubbert and W. W. Rubey, *Bull. Geol. Soc. Amer.* 70, 115 (1959).

25 J. H. Healy, C. B. Raleigh, J. M. Coakley, paper presented before the 64th Annual Meeting of the Cordilleran Section of the Geological Society of America, the Seismological Society of America, and the Paleontological Society of America, Tucson, Ariz., April 1968.

26 *J. Indian Geophys. Union* 5 (1968).

27 W. H. K. Lee and C. B. Raleigh, *Nature* 223, 172 (1969).

28 D. I. Gough and W. I. Gough, *Trans. Amer. Geophys. Union* 50, 236 (1969).

29 A. Ryall, G. Boncher, W. V. Savage, A. E. Jones, *ibid.*, p. 236.

30 A fairly comprehensive review of the status of research on earthquake prediction is contained in a special issue of *Tectonophysics* [6, No. 1 (1968)].

31 C. Y. King [*J. Geophys. Res.* 74, 1702 (1969)] has suggested that the fraction of stress energy released at the source of an earthquake radiated as seismic-wave energy decreases with decreasing magnitude, and is zero for fault creep. Therefore the number of small earthquakes needed to release dangerous crustal stresses should be much smaller than the number estimated on the basis of magnitude alone.

Editor's note: In recent years a number of workers in the Garm region of southern Russia, the Adirondack Mountains of New York, and the San Fernando Valley of California have suggested that there is a decrease in the relative velocities of P-waves and S-waves days or even years prior to an earthquake with a return to normal velocities just before the quake occurs. The duration and intensity of the change may even be directly proportional to the magnitude of the quake. The phenomenon may be explained by dilatancy in fluid-filled rocks which also could explain such precursory changes as electrical conductivity, ground tilts, and changes in ground elevation. The "dilatancy model" has therefore expanded application in earthquake prediction and control. References to this latest development are included in the Supplementary Readings.

In 1973 James H. Whitcomb and his colleagues discovered a significant decrease in the P-wave velocity/S-wave velocity (V_P/V_S ratio) before the San Fernando earthquake of February 9, 1971. They studied the records of nineteen earthquakes from the time period 1961 to 1970 and found they showed a large decrease of V_P/V_S in 1967 followed by a slow increase to the normal value just before the earthquake. The large precursory change was initiated three and one-half years before the earthquake, and the earthquake could have been predicted on the basis of this anomaly!

In the same year Dr. Hiroo Kanamori noted a similar anomaly while studying the seismic records of stations near Riverside, California. In this case, however, the information was used to predict a quake of magnitude four which occurred at 10:05 P.M. January 30, 1974, near Yucaipa, about sixteen miles east of Riverside, California. The event occurred at the expected site and within the expected time limit of about three months. This represents the first successful earthquake prediction for California.

Substantial progress is being reported in the application of other precursory events. Geologists of the U. S. Geological Survey were able to forecast a potentially damaging quake (Richter magnitude 5.2) that occurred Thanksgiving Day, 1974, near Hollister, California. In this case the precursors included changes in the local magnetic field accompanied by a major change in tilt direction and variations in the velocity of seismic waves. It is the first time that three different precursors have been identified for an earthquake in this country.

News dispatches from China indicate that the destructive Mukden earthquake (M-7.2) of February 4, 1975, was predicted and the population warned in time to take precautionary measures. The Chinese claim that lives were also saved by predicting ten other earthquakes during the past four years.

10 Creep on the San Andreas Fault
Fault Creep and Property Damage
Karl V. Steinbrugge and Edwin G. Zacher

Introduction

In the course of a building inspection of the W. A. Taylor Winery in April,

Steinbrugge, K. V. and Zacher, E. G., 1960, "Creep on the San Andreas Fault," Article 1: "Fault Creep and Property Damage," *Bull. Seismol. Soc. Amer.*, vol. 50, no. 3, pp. 389–96. Reprinted with light editing by permission of the senior author and the publisher. Copyright 1960, S. S. A.
Mr. Steinbrugge is professor of structural design at the University of California, Berkeley. Mr. Zacher is a consulting structural engineer in San Francisco, California.

1956, Mr. Edwin G. Zacher noticed fractures in reinforced concrete walls and displacement of concrete slabs which could not be explained by landslide or attributed to other conventional causes. The winery is on the Cienega Road about 7 miles south of Hollister, California.

An examination of geologic maps placed it in the San Andreas fault zone. On a relatively detailed geologic map Taliaferro (1949) shows the fault as a line going through the winery buildings. Since conventional explanations

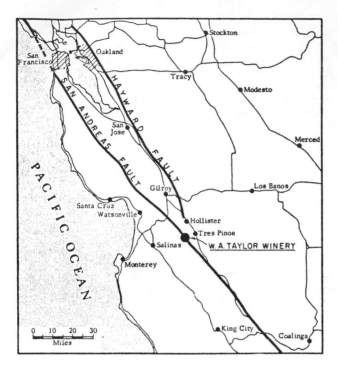

FIG. 1. Location map of W. A. Taylor Winery in California.

failed, a study was made of a possible connection between the damage and earthquakes and between the damage and possible fault movements.

Observed Damage

The observed building damage is found more or less along a straight line as may be seen in Fig. 2, and this line is oriented in the direction of the San Andreas fault. Evidence at all damage locations indicates that the westerly portion of the main building is moving northward with respect to the easterly portion; in geologic terms, this is right-lateral movement. The total movement of one portion of the building with respect to the other between 1948, when the building was constructed, and December, 1959, is almost 6 inches.

Winery employees with many years' service have known of the damage and were aware of its growth. However, its growth was slow and gave no alarm.

This shearing movement has caused reinforced concrete walls to break at three places. Figure 3 shows an offset between wall and floor slab and is one indication of the total movement. Some columns along the line of creep were so badly affected that major reconstruction was required in 1954. Concrete floor slabs have moved along construction joints or have broken, again in a right-lateral sense.

Damage outside the main building is consistent with the linearity and type of motion taking place within the building. A concrete-lined drainage ditch south of the winery, constructed about 1943, has been ruptured. In the fall of 1957 two waterlines between the winery and the drainage ditch were broken. When subsequently they were under repair, it was observed that sev-

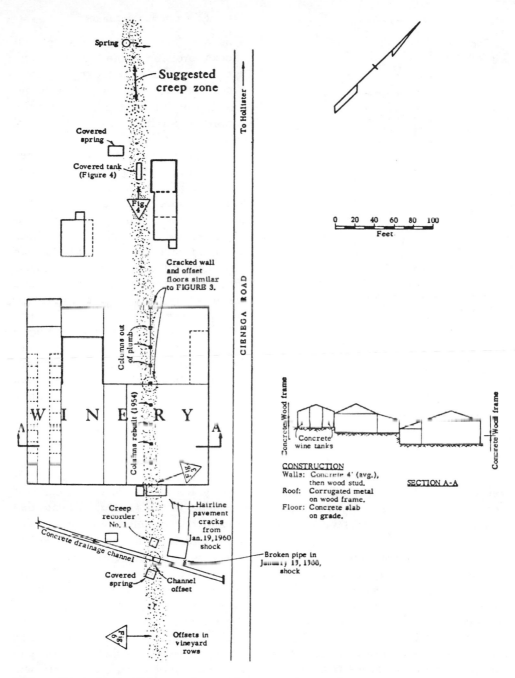

FIG. 2. W. A. Taylor Winery, showing locations of creep damage.

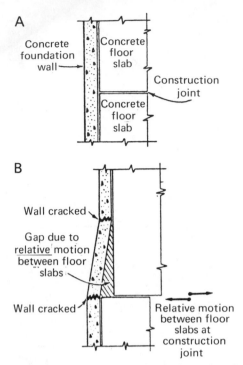

A

Concrete foundation wall →

Concrete floor slab

Construction joint

Concrete floor slab

B

Wall cracked

Gap due to relative motion between floor slabs

Wall cracked

Relative motion between floor slabs at construction joint

FIG. 3. Diagrammatic plans show the effects of creep, and may be considered as typical of all three broken walls. A: as originally built. B: effect of creep.

eral ruptures had occurred here in previous years. Another pipeline break occurred in the January 19, 1960, earthquake (Fig. 2). A covered tank in the ground and adjacent to the office building north of the winery also shows distortion due to right-lateral movement. Vineyard rows just south of the main building have offsets.

Measurements within the building have been made periodically by the authors since 1956, using as references the face of the walls, the edges of the floor slabs, and marks chiseled in the surface of the floor slabs. The data are plotted in Fig. 4, and indicate about one-half inch right-lateral movement per year.

Damage from Earthquakes

This area has had a number of felt shocks, probably more than the average for the Pacific coast region; however, the historic record makes no mention of surface faulting at this location. Four felt shocks are of special interest.

The buildings at this winery (then known as Palmtag's Winery) were damaged in the April 18, 1906, San Francisco shock (Lawson *et al.*, 1908): "At Palmtag's winery, in the hills southwest of Tres Pinos, the shock seems to have been more severe than elsewhere in the vicinity of that village. Furniture was moved, water was thrown from troughs, and an adobe building was badly cracked. One low brick winery was unharmed." A local resident who was in or near the buildings at the time, has stated to one author that "loose adobe brick" then fell from a wall. The 1906 surface faulting ended about 11 miles to the northwest.

On June 24, 1939, a local earthquake occurred which had a Modified Mercalli Intensity of VII, and its field epicenter was in the vicinity of this winery. Records of the U. S. Coast and Geodetic Survey (1939*a, b*) relate that an adobe wall pulled away from a side wall; girders pulled away from brickwork and the brickwork was badly cracked; new cracks were formed and old ones opened 1 or 2 inches in width; many fresh ground cracks appeared in the neighborhood of the building, and their general trend appeared to be northwest-southeast and at right angles thereto. The observer did not comment further on the ground cracks.

The U. S. Coast and Geodetic Survey report (1939*b*) with its accompanying photographs has been reviewed by Mr. John Ohrwall, the

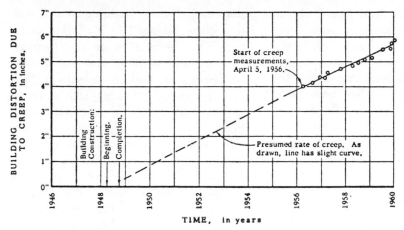

FIG. 4. San Andreas fault creep as measured by building distortions. The average creep is one-half inch per year.

present W. A. Taylor Company superintendent, who was present at the time of the 1939 shock. He says that the ground cracks were in the same location as the present movement. The parts of the winery which now lie across the creep zone have been built since 1939.

Another local earthquake, occurring on August 10, 1947, was also studied by the U. S. Coast and Geodetic Survey (1948). Their report regarding the winery states: "There was a small differential settlement at the junction of the old and new portions of one of the buildings, the older section having settled with respect to the newer. Furthermore, there was a transverse crack extending all the way across a concrete platform about 4 feet wide." Examination of the concrete-platform crack indicated local damage of no particular significance.

On January 19, 1960 (January 20, 1960, GCT), a strong local earthquake caused minor damage at the winery and also resulted in one-eighth inch of "instantaneous creep" in the building, a movement that was recorded at the

time of the shock by University of California instruments at the winery. This movement caused cracks in the floors and walls to widen, and some concrete spalling occurred. Hairline ground cracks were noted in the paving to the south of the winery (Fig. 2), and an underground pipe was broken. The ground cracks and the pipe breakage were undoubtedly associated with the one-eighth inch movement. Typical other damage: some objects were thrown from shelves, a hollow concrete block chimney cracked, catwalks over large wooden wine tanks pulled apart, and some wine barrels worked loose from their chocks.

The published historic record, plus interviews with winery employees, ruled out the creep damage as the result of an earthquake or some other obvious event, except for the January 19, 1960, earthquake.

Fault Creep

Since the winery was in the San Andreas fault zone and since the damage had been progressive, the possibility of fault creep was considered almost immediately and measurements were taken accordingly (Steinbrugge, 1957).

The winery is on a sloping site, and there are springs near and under the main building. There has been some conjecture that what is taking place may be somehow related to landslide. Springs beneath the building could facilitate the movement. However, the direction of the motion is essentially at right angles to the slope, and no noticeable downhill component of motion can be found. It would seem that landslide and other gravity effects cannot be present.

Practically all damage locations fall in a narrow straight zone as shown in Fig. 2. The bearing of this zone is essentially that of the strike of the San Andreas fault. Near-by springs, such as are often noted on a fault trace, also fall in the zone. Geologic mapping, which was done independently of the building damage, places the fault through the buildings (Taliaferro, 1949). The right-lateral movement is consistent with the right-lateral faulting known to have occurred on the San Andreas fault and is also consistent with possible creep resulting from the known regional strain pattern. The creep through the building appeared to be gradual as far as visual observation and the aforementioned crude measurements could determine, except for the earthquake of January 19, 1960.

All the foregoing is consistent with the theory of fault creep.

There is local opinion to the effect that the previous building at this site had been damaged in a similar manner. The description of the damage (skewed roof trusses), and wall offsets of about two feet in perhaps half a century, suggest that the rate of creep of one-half inch per year may have been fairly constant for many years.

Fences to the north and south of the winery show no damage or offsets which could be the result of fault creep. It is not known if the creep is markedly local, or if the fences are so situated as not to be indicative of creep.

References

Lawson, A. C., et al., 1908. The California Earthquake of April 18, 1906; Report of the State Earthquake Investigation Commission (Washington, D. C.: Carnegie Institution of Washington, 2 vols. plus atlas).

Steinbrugge, Karl V., 1957. Building Damage on the San Andreas Fault, report dated February 18, 1957, published by the Pacific Fire Rating Bureau for private circulation.

Taliaferro, N. L., 1949. "Geologic Map of the Hollister Quadrangle, California," Plate 1 of California Division of Mines Bulletin 143 (text not published).

U. S. Coast and Geodetic Survey, 1939a. Abstracts of Earthquake Reports from the Pacific Coast and the Western Mountain Region, MSA-22, April 1, 1939, to June 30, 1939. 1939b. "Central California Earthquake of June 24, 1939" (unpublished manuscript prepared by Dean S. Carder). 1948. Abstracts of Earthquake Reports from the Pacific Coast and the Western Mountain Region, MSA-55, July, August, September, 1947.

Mass
Movement

"If you wish to converse with me, define your terms"

Voltaire

Unstable sedimentary deposits represent a major hazard in many localities throughout the world. There are a number of factors which can lead to the movement of these deposits en masse. Some of the more common factors are increases in water content, changes in the slope of the topography, geologic structure, excessive loading, loss of vegetative cover, changes in the properties of the materials, shocks, and vibrations. Final movement can be rapid and with little warning. In some cases, however, movement is slow and almost imperceptible. In these cases fixed objects such as trees, fence lines, telephone poles, and gravestones may be tilted and thereby document movement. Topographic features such as scarps, hummocky surfaces, and isolated swamps or ponds without natural inlets or outlets may be the result of prehistoric landslides and should be considered indicative of possible landslide prone conditions.

Quintin Aune (Reading 11) describes an unusual clay deposit which led to earthquake-triggered landslides 75 miles from the epicenter of the Good Friday Alaskan earthquake (Reading 7). Geologists had cited the hazardous nature of these clay deposits, but the area was nevertheless developed as a fashionable suburb of Anchorage (Reading 2). Similar deposits have plagued Scandinavia and other areas where marine clays composed essentially of glacial rock flour have been elevated above sea level as a result of postglacial rebound. These clays have experienced a natural leaching of their

Photo on page 117. Aerial view of Turnagain Heights landslide, Anchorage, Alaska. Courtesy of U. S. Army.

electrolytes and are highly unstable. Mr. Aune asks if the activities of Man could also lead to the leaching of other clay deposits and set the stage for the generation of quick clays and major landslides. His suggestions should be carefully considered by those who are evaluating sites for new developments.

Most landslides are not related to the presence of quick clays. In Reading 12, William Alden describes a more common landslide setting, that is, unfavorable geologic structures and heavy precipitation. Slope failure, a process unrelated to Man's activities in this case, led to the formation of a natural dam which later failed and created the hazards associated with natural flooding. The discussion portion of Alden's paper illustrates the broad concern about this problem and the similarity between the Gros Ventre slide and slides in other localities. Reading 13 is a case study of the disastrous landslide at the Vaiont Dam in northern Italy. Adverse geologic features were the major factors contributing to this slide, but manmade conditions upset the delicate balance and more than 2000 people lost their lives in less than six minutes.

These examples of mass movement share notable similarities. The hazardous settings at Anchorage and Vaiont were well documented prior to mass movement. Development at Vaiont was a calculated risk. At Anchorage it appears that those in authority may not have been aware of the hazards involved. There were preliminary warnings of disaster at Gros Ventre and Vaiont. The warnings were, however, either unheeded or misinterpreted. Improved communications among geologists, engineers, government personnel, and the public are clearly needed to avoid similar disasters.

Reading 14 reviews the nature and distribution of permafrost. Permafrost is an unusual deposit which becomes unstable when disturbed. A variety of construction activities can cause a thawing of the permafrost, which in turn may lead to creep, landslides, slumping, and subsidence. As human activities expand in areas underlain by permafrost, it is important that we recognize the hazards and develop techniques for avoiding them.

11   Quick Clays and California's Clays: No Quick Solutions

Quintin A. Aune

The March 27 Good Friday earthquake of 1964 caused extensive damage at Anchorage, Alaska, 75 miles from the earthquake hinge belt and epicenter. Much of the damage can be related to earthquake triggered landslides. What is there about the geologic setting of Anchorage which led to localized landslide activity? U. S. Geological Survey Water-Supply Paper 1773, Geology and Ground-water Resources of the Anchorage Area, Alaska (Cederstrom et al., 1964), although written before the Good Friday earthquake, contains several clues.

The accompanying map, (Fig. 1) adapted from the ground-water study, shows distribution of earthquake-triggered landslides relative to subsurface distribution of the Bootlegger Cove

Aune, Q. A., 1966, "Quick Clays and California's Clays: No Quick Solutions," *Mineral Information Service*, vol. 19, no. 8, pp. 119–23. Lightly edited by permission of the author and reprinted by permission of California Division of Mines and Geology, Sacramento, California.
Quintin Aune is a geologist on the staff of the California Division of Mines and Geology.

Clay. These landslides contributed to a substantial part of the damage at Anchorage; they are known to have been caused by local failure of the Bootlegger Cove Clay. Major landslide failure was not uniform over the entire area underlain by the clay, but was restricted to low escarpments paralleling Knik Arm and Ship Creek in the western part of the Anchorage area.

What caused failure of the Bootlegger Cove Clay? Cederstrom et al. (1964, p. 32, and Table 4) indicate that sand in lenses in the Bootlegger Cove Clay "commonly becomes quicksand when penetrated by the (well) drill." Quicksand has the peculiar property of losing all its cohesive strength and acting as a liquid when disturbed, as by the sudden jar of a man's footsteps on the surface, or the sudden vibration of a drill—or an earthquake—beneath the surface. Some clays develop similar properties, and are called quick clays because of their analogous behavior. As we shall see below, there is reason to suspect that part of the clay fraction of the Bootlegger Cove Clay assumed the properties of a quick clay.

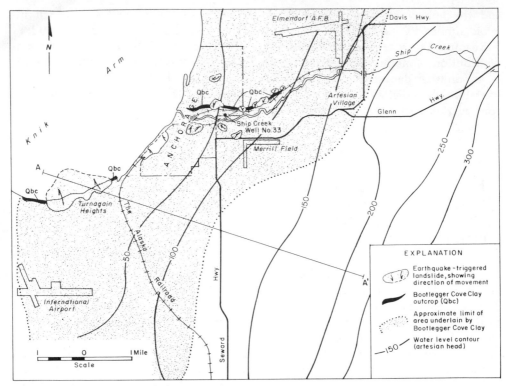

FIG. 1. Geologic map of the Anchorage area, Alaska, showing critical features of the geology pertaining to slope failures precipitated by the Good Friday Earthquake. *Adapted from text, maps, and data of the U. S. Geological Survey, Water-Supply Paper 1773, 1964.*

Quick clays are generally confined to the far north areas. They are known to have caused excessive damage in eastern Canada and Scandinavia in the past (Kerr, 1963; Liebling and Kerr, 1965). They result when a marine or brackish water clay composed essentially of glacial rock flour is elevated above sea level. Such post-Pleistocene elevation is common in the far north due to isostatic adjustment of the land surface resulting from the melting of the great overburden of glacial ice only a few thousands of years ago.

Clay derived from rock flour consists of the minutely ground up particles of many minerals, generally including several clay minerals. It is not excessively responsive to disturbance as long as the intermolecular water—the formation water—contains dissolved salt (sodium chloride). The salt acts as an electrolytic "glue" which adheres to the clay particles and provides cohesiveness and structure to the clay (Kerr, 1963, p. 134). Once the clay is elevated above sea level the salts—this natural "glue"—may be progressively flushed out by fresh groundwater. Cederstrom et al. (1964, p. 72) cite evidence to show current loss of sodium electrolyte to well water (Well #33) that penetrates the Bootlegger Cove Clay in the Anchorage area. The sodium salt may be flushed out, reducing or destroying the clay's cohesive properties, or its sodium may be replaced by calcium, greatly reducing the clay's cohesiveness. Because this process has gone on only in the past few thousand years, only portions of the clay have recently become extremely responsive to disturbance. There was, therefore, little obvious geological evidence of the clay's present instability—such as landslide scarps—until the major earthquake disturbance disrupted it at Anchorage.

As shown in the cross-section the Bootlegger Cove Clay, (Fig. 2) as defined in well-logs (Cederstrom et al., 1964), lies athwart the path of westward-flowing ground-water. It was indeed fortunate for Anchorage that the salt leaching or exchange process, sensitizing the Bootlegger Cove Clay, is a slow, incomplete one. Impermeability of the clay and position of much of the formation below sea level have significantly retarded the invasion of fresh water and "leaching" or exchange of the sodium ions.

Shown also on the cross-section and on the map is the artesian head, the level to which water from a well will rise when confined in a standing pipe. It may be seen from the cross-section

that this level is well above the ground surface in the area along the eastern margin of the Bootlegger Cove Clay but drops off rapidly as one travels west across the area underlain by the clay.

In the Anchorage area, artesian water travels in a crudely interconnected system of gravels, confined from above by impermeable till (east half of the cross-section). The westward passage of the water is impeded by the Bootlegger Cove Clay. If the clay were absent, water in the underground channels or "pipe system" would pass unobstructed to the sea and no high confining pressure could be built up, but such is not the case.

Theoretically, this relationship can be very dangerous. Confined ground water in a unified hydraulic system has much the effect of a hydraulic ram. Here, it exerts a constant pressure against the clay barrier—the Bootlegger Cove Clay—to the west. As long as that formation is coherent, and has shearing strength, it will hold together, and its molecules will not "collapse" into an unoriented liquid substance at the onset of a major shock, as an earthquake. If rendered incoherent,

FIG. 2. Geologic cross section, A-A', from Fig. 1.

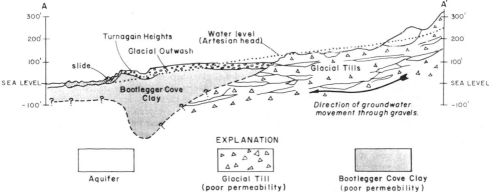

however, as it was in the disastrous quick-clay slides in eastern Canada and Scandinavia (Kerr, 1963), entire sections of the Bootlegger Cove Clay could break and glide laterally in translation movement, settling ultimately into a disheveled landslide "mush." Such a mass might flow seaward, carrying part or even all of Anchorage with it, because nearly all of Anchorage is underlain by the Bootlegger Cove Clay.

The slides at Anchorage were minor, compared to the above-inferred catastrophe, because the main earthquake shock was far distant, and because much of the Bootlegger Cove Clay is not yet a quick clay. As shown by Well #33 (Fig. 1), it is still "in the making." Perhaps the limited disaster was fortunate for Alaska. It will stimulate the residents, scientists, and engineers to recognize the problems they face, and to learn through industry and science how they can control or work around their problems at Anchorage

and elsewhere in Alaska (*Time*, 1965).

Could a similar "Good Friday" earthquake-landslide disaster happen to California? Because of the Ice-Age genesis of known quick clay deposits, California probably has no quick clays as such. It has no geological environment in which natural forces are actively flushing out the electrolytic "glue" to create structural hazards. Then does the Alaskan example apply to California? Many poorly consolidated marine and evaporite clay-bearing formations in California contain electrolytes—in the form of saline formation waters—which add to their stability. It has often been demonstrated in California that this stability may readily be disrupted during the substitution of fresh water for saline waters by a drilling mud during the drilling of oil wells (Morris et al., 1959).

California's recent geologic history is one of frequent volcanism. Volcanoes produce ash which settles into the sea or becomes concentrated in saline

FIG. 3. Cross-section of a hypothetical California landscape analogous to Anchorage. Schematic buildings represent what could be a major subdivision; irrigation losses may represent runoff from thousands of acres. Leaching of sodium ions from clay may reduce its coherence, set stage for major landslide.

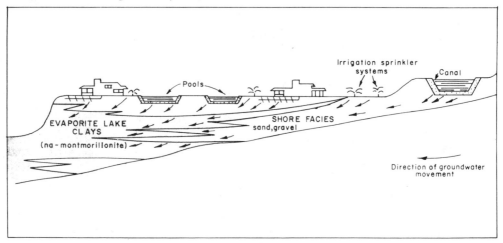

evaporite lakes, and later becomes part of the soil or of underlying marine lake bed formations or terrace deposits. Eventually the ash alters into illite and montmorillonite clay minerals. Such clays, while not reaching the extremes of quick clays, are nevertheless potentially sensitive and may even approach quick clays in this respect. As with quick clays, the sensitivity of these clays to shock or disturbance may be greatly increased by the flushing out of saline formation water with its electrolytic "glue," and substitution of fresh, "unglued" solutions in its place.

Geological processes strive toward stability. Stability of a clay deposit is a relative state. It is relative to the nature of the formation water, the type and condition of the clay, and the nature of the slope. This stability may be affected by: (1) a change in the clay through the addition of abnormal amounts of water. Certain montmorillonites will adsorb water until the "rock"—it actually becomes a gel—contains as much as 20 parts of water to one part of clay; (2) a change in salinity of the formation water, as at Anchorage; (3) a change in the slope or load conditions, by the driving of a pile or the excavation for a building foundation.

All three of these possible means of clay stability change are active to some extent in California today, in the form of man-made building excavations; canal construction and subsequent leakage of fresh canal water into salt-bearing clays; and in related activities of man. A concrete structure may give off free calcium in solution, to substitute for sodium in a clay formation electrolyte, changing the sensitivity of the clay. The number of stability changes in potentially unstable clays

may be expected to accelerate greatly in California in the immediate future, as a direct result of the transportation of vast quantities of fresh northern California water to the south to satisfy the needs of that rapidly expanding area.

This water will be delivered to areas of need, many of which are the loci of poorly consolidated clay-bearing formations, such as in the southern San Joaquin Valley, southern Coast Ranges, vast areas of the Mojave Desert, and in Los Angeles Basin region. Many of these areas contain saline clay-bearing sedimentary basins which may become vulnerable, through wastage, leakage, and plan, to fresh water invasion. This can be somewhat analogous to the Anchorage area. While disasters of the magnitude of Anchorage are unlikely, nevertheless substantial losses in life and property may result unless care is exercised.

What is our lesson from the Good Friday Alaskan earthquake? It is that change—even innocuous change, such as substitution of a fresh formation water for saline water—may breed instability in clay-bearing beds. A new residential property, and especially a "view" property which abuts against an escarpment or "free face" susceptible to landslide failure, invites disaster even without a "Good Friday" earthquake if the foundation conditions underlying the property are subjected to uncompensated stability changes. With the occurrence of a major earthquake —a potentiality in most populated areas of California—the stakes are indeed high.

Clay technology and clay mineralogy are new and dynamic branches of scientific study. Only in the past dozen years have up-to-date texts become available on these subjects. Few geologists are trained in clay problem studies and fewer laboratories are equipped to cope with them. Yet, there is a "need to know" these subjects. Great cities are growing. New ones will grow. The press is outward, to marginal development sites, to unproved development areas. Drill hole subsurface data, qualitative information on clay and pore water properties, and geologic know-how are lacking in many of these areas.

If expansion and development are to be judicious and safe, they must be accompanied by careful planning. Such planning must be based on geologic maps, which show locations of potential hazard due to past slides or presence of potentially sensitive clay formations. It must be based on complementary maps showing clay and groundwater properties of various geologic map units, so that appropriate care may be taken where potentially sensitive clays are encountered. Following such planning, competent development of an area will anticipate and prevent possible man-made "natural" disasters by utilization or preparation of foundation conditions that can resist them, and by avoiding construction of high population density developments in areas where foundation conditions are or may become too poor or unreliable to be remedied.

References

Cederstrom, D. J., Trainer, F. W., and Waller, R. M., 1964, Geology and ground-water resources of the Anchorage area, Alaska: U. S. Geological Survey Water-Supply Paper 1773.

Coulter, H. W., and Migliaccio, R. R., 1966, Effects of the earthquake of March 27, 1964, at Valdez, Alaska: U. S. Geological Survey Professional Paper 542-C, p. C1–C36.

Grim, Ralph E., 1962, Applied clay mineralogy: McGraw-Hill Book Co., Inc., New York, 422 p. Chapter 5, "Clay Mineralogy in relation to the engineering properties of clay materials," gives an excellent technical discussion of clays and foundation problems resulting from instability within clay-water systems.

Hansen, W. R., 1965, Effects of the earthquake of March 27, 1964, at Anchorage, Alaska: U. S. Geological Survey Professional Paper 542-A, p. A1–A64.

Kachadoorian, Reuben, 1965, Effects of the earthquake of March 27, at Whittier, Alaska: U. S. Geological Survey Professional Paper 542-B, p. B1–B21.

Kerr, Paul F., and Drew, Isabella M., 1965, Quick-clay movements, Anchorage, Alaska (Abstract): Geological Society of America Program, 1965 annual meetings, p. 86–87.

Kerr, Paul F., 1963, Quick clay: Scientific American, Vol. 209, no. 5 (November, 1963), p. 132–142.

Liebling, Richard S., and Kerr, Paul F., 1965, Observations on quick clay: Geological Society of America Bulletin, vol. 76, no. 8, p. 853–877.

Mielenz, Richard C., and King, Myrle E., 1955, Physical-chemical properties and engineering performance of clays: in Clays and clay technology.

Mitchell, James K., 1963, Engineering properties and problems of the San Francisco Bay mud: in California Division of Mines Special Report 82, p. 25–32.

Morris, F. C., Aune, Q. A., and Gates, G. L., 1959, Clays in petroleum reservoir rocks: U. S. Bureau of Mines Report of Investigations 5425, 65 p.

Oakeshott, Gordon B., 1964, The Alaskan earthquake: Mineral Information Service, July issue, p. 119–121, 124–125.

Schlocker, Julius, Bonilla, M. G. and Radbruch, Dorothy H., 1958, Geology of the San Francisco North quadrangle, California: U. S. Geological Survey Miscellaneous Geologic Investigations Map I-272.

Time Magazine, 1965. Anchorage's feet of clay: Time, vol. 86, no. 25, Dec. 17, 1965, p. 62.

12 Landslide and Flood at Gros Ventre, Wyoming*

William C. Alden†

A great landslide occurred on June 23, 1925, in the valley of Gros Ventre River, about 35 miles south of Yellowstone National Park (Fig. 1). The relations of the north-easterly dipping rock formations of the slide scarp and of the dam formed by the slide are

*Published by permission of the Director, U. S. Geological Survey.
† U. S. Geological Survey.

Alden, W. C., 1928, "Landslide and Flood at Gros Ventre, Wyoming," *American Institute of Mining and Metallurgical Engineers*, trans. vol. 76, pp. 347–58. Abridged and reprinted by permission of American Institute of Mining, Metallurgical and Petroleum Engineers.

shown in the diagrammatic cross-section of the valley (Fig. 2). This generalized section is based on unpublished maps and notes by Eliot Blackwelder, in the files of the U. S. Geological Survey.

Heavy rains and melting snow in the Gros Ventre Mountains had saturated clay layers in the Carboniferous strata, which dip toward the valley at angles of 18° to 21°, consequently an enormous mass of rock at the end of the north spur of Sheep Mountain became loosened and, on the afternoon of June 23, slid suddenly down into the valley. Within a few minutes this mass of debris—estimated as 50,000,000 cu.

FIG. 1. Map showing dam and lake formed by landslide blocking Gros Ventre River.

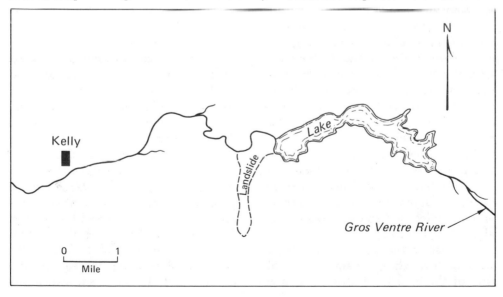

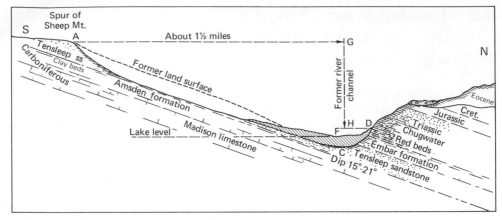

FIG. 2. Diagrammatic section (N. S.) illustrating damming of Gros Ventre River valley, Wyo., by landslide.

C-F = Height of dam (shaded) at river channel about 225 ft.

C-H = Height of dam north end of dump about 350 ft.

Geological section based on unpublished maps and notes by Eliot Blackwelder, in files of U. S. Geological Survey.

yd.—carrying on its surface a dense pine forest, rushed across the valley, piled up about 350 ft. high against the cliffs of red sandstone on the north and partly slumped back and spread so as to form a dam 225 to 250 ft. high above the lower toe of the dump. The path of the slide and the resulting dam are shown in Figs. 1 and 2. The river, which was in flood, was completely blocked and rapidly filled the basin behind the dam, so that within 18 hr. a ranch house standing 60 ft. above the river was floated off its foundation and in about three weeks the lake (shown in Fig. 1) reached a depth of about 200 ft. at the back of the dam, an average width of about ½ mile, a length of about 3 miles, and an estimated area of about 11,000 acres.

Soon after the slide, water began seeping through the dam. This took care of the inflow, which decreased as the summer came on. On Aug. 18, 1925, Depue Falck, of the U. S. Geological Survey, estimated the seepage as 500 sec.-ft. On account of this seepage the lake did not overtop the dam, and when I visited it about a month later the lake level had fallen about 9 ft. below the high-water mark.

There was considerable speculation by engineers and others as to what would occur when the snow melted in the spring of 1926. It happened that there was a light snowfall in the Gros Ventre Mountains in the winter of 1925–26, so no spring flood occurred, and conditions remained practically unchanged. In September, 1926, I crossed the dam just above the point of vigorous outflow and examined the crest of the dam from end to end. G. E. Manger, my assistant, and I climbed the mountain slope along the east margin of the scarp to its head, which my barometer indicated to be about 2100 ft. above the bed of the stream below the dam—that is, nearly four times as high as the Washington Monument.

The place where the break eventually occurred is about opposite the lowest point of the lake shore. Although there was such a mass of big blocks of rock on the outer front of the dam back of this belt of rocks, the top of this part of the dam appeared to be composed very largely of fine, loose, easily erodable material, greenish-white clay, reddish clay, and sand with fewer large stones. There was a narrow sag in the crest of the dam and the high-water mark showed that the lake had extended into this sag, but I saw no evidence at that time (September, 1926) that there had been any erosion of a channel or that water had gone over the top of the dam. I was told, however, that some water had gone over the dam, but I hardly understand how it could have done so without cutting a channel through the loose fine material.

On the steep slope adjacent to the upper half of the slide scarp we found old breaks indicating that at some time great masses of rock had started to slide, but lodged. Ranchers said, however, that no other slides are known to have occurred in this part of the valley since it was settled. There have been numerous slides farther up the valley. One of these was described by Blackwelder.[1]

Several hundred feet below the top of a scarp is a mass which started to slide, but lodged with the trees standing upon it. The declivity at the head of the scarp is 30° to 45°. Farther down it is about the same as the dip of the strata; *i.e.*, 15° to 21°. A line of

sight from the top of the scarp to the lowest point of the lake dips 17° and to the farthest high point of the dam is 13°. Limestone and sandstone are exposed in the scarp, also reddish and whitish clays such as were noted in the dam. Saturation of such clayey layers by water was doubtless the cause of the big slide.

The Flood of May, 1927

The prediction of some engineers, and the fact that there was no break in the dam for nearly two years after the slide occurred, had given rise to a feeling of security and a rather general belief that the dam would hold. In the winter of 1926–27 heavy snows fell in the Gros Ventre Mountains and a period of rapid melting, together with rain, in May, 1927, caused a rapid rise of the lake, which, on the morning of May 18, overtopped the lowest part of the dam and caused a disastrous flood. In July, 1927, in company with my assistant, Edward F. Richards, I revisited the place to see the effects of the flood and the condition of the dam and lake. From the forest ranger, C. E. Dibble, and other residents of the village of Kelly, I obtained information as to what occurred.

We found that the outflow had cut a channel nearly 100 yd. wide and about 100 ft. deep beneath the crest of the dam near its downstream face. The channel had a rather steep gradient and the head of the outlet was considerably back of the highest part of the dam, where a shallow, but a swift stream was flowing over the rocky debris. Measurement with a hand level showed the lake surface to be about 60 ft. below the high-water mark, so that there was yet probably a maximum depth of nearly 150 ft. of water in the lake.

In 1925, Herman Stabler, of the Geological Survey, estimated that, with the basin filled to the point of overflow, there would be 164,000 acre-feet impounded and that the cutting of a channel only 25 ft. deep would release about a quarter of this great amount of water, or 48,000 acre-feet. It was then predicted that sudden release of such a flood could scarcely result otherwise than disastrously. The dam did not fail as a whole, but the lake was lowered more than 50 ft. in a very short time, and disaster resulted.

The river had been slowly rising during the morning of May 18 at the village of Kelly, about 4 miles below the dam, and efforts were being made to prevent the highway bridge from being washed out. The stream had not overflowed its 10 to 15-ft. banks there up to 10 a.m. The appearance of some ranch utensils in the stream, however, warned Mr. Dibble that something was wrong at the dam. Rushing over the hills in his automobile, on the road leading up the valley, he witnessed the destruction of the buildings at Woodward's ranch about a mile below the dam and out of sight of it. He then sped back to the village and messages were sent down Gros Ventre and Snake River valleys to warn the inhabitants of the approaching flood. It is reported that about 11 a.m. there suddenly came from the mouth of the gorge above Kelly a great rush of water described as a wave 15 ft. or more in height, which caught some of the villagers as they were trying to save some of their effects. All the buildings were swept away with the rush excepting the schoolhouse and a small church and near-by cottage on a little higher level at the north edge of the village.

In 1925, Kelly had a population of 60 or 70 people, of whom a few were drowned. Besides the destruction of the buildings and their contents in this village, several ranches on Gros Ventre and Snake River were more or less damaged. Six or seven persons were drowned, some had very narrow escapes, bridges were washed out and effects of the flood were felt as far down Snake River as Idaho Falls, Idaho. It appears that there was time after the warning was given for all persons to have escaped with their lives if they had not stopped to save any of their effects. As is usually the case, however, some apparently did not appreciate the necessity for such haste. It is reported that water began to flow over the dam in three places on the afternoon before, but it does not appear that any definite watch was maintained at the dam even after flood conditions began to develop.

That which is of most interest to geologists and engineers is what actually happened at the dam. The great blocks of sandstone and limestone which it had been thought by some would retard the outflow in case of an actual break now lie on a low terrace over which the flood rushed as it swung against the north side of the gorge below the dam. Some of these blocks are 15 to 20 ft. in diameter. They are somewhat scratched and their edges are bruised. I do not know just how far down the valley such blocks were carried by the flood. The terrace on which these rocks lie corresponds to the remnant of a terrace in the cut through the dam.

The terrace along the south wall of the channel is 15 or 20 ft. above the stream. It was probably the bottom of the channel at the time the great rush of water passed through. From this the main current swung to the north side of the valley, dumping the big rocks on the inner side of the bend, and cutting into the base of the cliffs. The narrowed but still vigorous stream flow after the big rush probably cut the inner channel below the terrace. Loose and heterogeneous material formed the dam. This bluff is about 100 ft. in height and it is composed of a mixture of loose sliding sand, crushed rock, and large and small angular fragments of limestone and sandstone. Evidently such a jumble of loose porous material as composes the upper part of the dump would not form a permanent dam capable of withstanding overflow without controlling gates and adequate spillways. No trees or logs were seen buried in the rock debris. Evidently the forest trees rode down on top of the slide and were not mixed into the debris very much by rolling over. They form an almost impassable tangle of criss-crossed trees, some of them still alive, on top of the dam.

Apparently no person saw just what actually took place at the dam, but the composition of the upper part of the dam may explain why the main flood came so suddenly and with such great volume. Probably seepage increased rapidly as the lake rose and this tended to undermine at the same time as overflow at the lowest point cut the initial channel. There was an enormous quantity of water in the upper 50 ft. of the impounded body. Rapid deepening of the trench across the crest must have caused rapid slumping at the sides and

the loose material must have at once been swept out of the way, opening a broad outlet toward which the enormous body of water started moving with rapidly increasing velocity. Repeated slumpings of the sides may have caused the reported succession of wavelike crests of the flood. Driftwood was found 10 to 14 ft. above the ground in trees on the flat below Kelly, so that there was a considerable depth of water, though it is said to have spread out to a maximum width of about ¾ mile within a mile below the mouth of the gorge. From an instrumental survey made by L. C. Bishop, it has been estimated that there was in the upper 50 ft. of the lake body nearly 43,000 acre-feet of water, and apparently all of this went out. By 4 p.m. the flood had passed Kelly and the stream had receded within its banks.

So great is the width of the dam ¼ mile or more from front to back below the high-water level that after trenching the first 50 ft. the amount of material to be moved was enormously greater and the rate of deepening became very much slower. With the lowering of the lake level the sill of the outlet thus moved gradually back while the channel below the crest of the dam was further deepened another 40 ft. The lake was lowered only about 60 ft. before the rate of cutting became so slow as to end the flood.

Completed melting of the snow and cessation of rainfall also soon reduced the inflow so that on July 5, 1927, the lake had lowered only about 2 ft. farther below a fairly definite water mark. I have no information as to conditions since that date. Probably the lake slowly lowered through the summer of

1927 and through the past winter as the outlet channel deepened.

There was still an enormous amount of water impounded in July, 1927, for the lake extended 3 or 4 miles up the valley, nearly as far as before. It probably yet had a maximum depth of 100 ft. or more after the flood, for the tops of tall trees were emerging only near the borders of the lake.

What will happen in case there is another period of rapid melting of heavy snows in the mountains, together with much rainfall? Of course, one can not say definitely, but certainly the danger of such a flood as that of May, 1927, is greatly reduced. The outlet now provided may be deepened and broadened somewhat, but I see no reason to expect anything more than a normal high-water stage in the river below the dam. It may be that further deepening of the outlet may start renewed sliding on the south side of the valley. If this does not occur suddenly, it may simply retard the outflow by gradually encroaching on the stream, as has occurred in the case of an older slide about 15 miles farther up the valley. It would not, however, seem advisable to rebuild the village of Kelly on the same site on the low flat terrace directly below the mouth of the gorge.

Discussion

G. S. RICE, Washington, D. C.—Those who are interested in the question of landslides in connection with mining operations should read a very excellent paper by Professor Knox.[2] He classifies slides into "break-deformation slides" (such as those at the Panama Canal) and "gravity slides"; he also refers to mud flows. Professor Knox has gone into the question quite thoroughly. He has cited some cases of landslides in various countries, both naturally induced and those produced by artificial agencies, such as excavations and waste piles.

W. C. ALDEN (written discussion).—On Sept. 22, 1928, I again visited the Gros Ventre valley and reexamined the landslide dam. In general, conditions were about the same as at the time of my visit in July, 1927. I was informed by John A. Evans, road overseer of Teton National Forest, that there was a good deal of snow in the mountains in the spring of 1928 and the usual spring flood occurred, but resulted in little damage. Repeated freezing retarded melting of the snows and held back some of the outflow. I made a measurement which showed the lake to be approximately 60 ft. below the high-water mark, or about the same as in July, 1927. Whence it appears that the outlet has not been deepened appreciably during the intervening 14 months.

G. KNOX, Treforest, South Wales (written discussion).—I read with great interest Mr. Alden's excellent paper on the great landslide and flood at Gros Ventre, Wyoming. This is an excellent example in confirmation of the theory that water is the chief agent in the causation of landslides. In the diagrammatic section (Fig. 2) the Tensleep sandstone is shown resting on clay beds having a dip of 15° 21' towards the valley. This sandstone is no doubt semiporous and well jointed, and receives a good supply of water from the gathering ground on Sheep Mountain. With melting snow a very large percentage of the water percolates into the strata, which probably produced a slow creep of the sandstones over the clay beds. The fissures resulting from this creep enable a still greater percentage of the rainfall or melting snow to percolate down to the impervious clays. This slow movement would upset the natural drainage of the area, resulting in the lubrication of the clay and supersaturation of the sandstone, which, combined, produced conditions so unstable that the whole mass of debris suddenly rushed into the valley forming the large dam.

The Gros Ventre landslide appears to have been similar in character to the great landslide which recently took place on Mount Arbino in Switzerland, the largest known to have occurred in that country famed for landslides. The debris displaced amounted to 30,000,000 cu. m., but thanks to the vigilance of the geologists of the Swiss Topographical Service the slow creep which usually precedes these great movements was noted and warning given to the inhabitants of the villages in the valley of Arbedo.

In this case the first movement was noted as far back as 1888, and during the following 40 years the total movement was only 5 ft. 9 in. The sliding debris finally rushed down from a height of 4000 ft. over a distance of 5000 ft., forming a dam 900 ft. high in the valley below. The holding power of this dam is exercising the minds of the Swiss engineers just as that of Gros Ventre did in your country, because should this be breached a terrible disaster is likely to result.

Further movements have recently taken place higher up the valley slope and it is expected that eventually it will reach the top of the mountain 6000 ft. high. The estimated amount of debris included in the total movement is 200,000,000 cubic meters.

In South Wales there are continual movements of the mantles on the valley slopes and although not so disastrous as the landslides referred to above are a continual source of trouble and expense to the community. Most of these valleys have been formed by the erosion of the Middle coal measures, which consists of hundreds of feet of hard sandstones known as the Pennant Series. Where the valleys are confined to this series they are steep and narrow but immediately the Lower coal measures consisting of alternating beds of sandstone, shale and fireclay—with many workable coal seams—are reached, the valleys begin to widen rapidly.

In the Middle Series the eroding action of the rivers is accompanied by slides of the "rock-fall" type, but as soon as the Lower Series is reached the slides become composite in character, consisting of the mantles formed by the rock falls of the Middle Series together with the rocks resting on the clays.

The dividing line between the two series is the No. 2 Rhondda (Brithdir, Tillery or Ynysarwed) coal seam which forms a plane of saturation on the underclay below. Downhill of this saturation plane all the soil creep or "gravity" slides take place. They work backwards (uphill) towards the saturation plane forming a series of steep crags in the hard sandstones of the Middle coal measures above the saturation plane. This leads to "break deformation" slides in the hard sandstones providing fresh material for a new mantle which in turn slides into the valley.

In these cases the debris has to slide over the outcropping edges of the strata which are nearly horizontal and in this respect differ from the Gros Ventre landslide.

As the valleys provide the only suitable place for sinking the shafts from which the coal has to be worked, they have become densely populated. Apart from the necessary buildings for domestic and industrial purposes the valleys contain all the necessary public works such as railways, canals, roads, sewage, gas and water mains, etc., so that any movement in the mantle is the cause of considerable trouble.

The cause of these South Wales landslides has been somewhat obscured owing to the fact that large heaps of colliery refuse were deposited on the hillsides during the early stages of mining development. Whenever a landslide took place in which one of these masses of refuse was included the cause was attributed to the great weight of the colliery rubbish. Failing that it was attributed to mining subsidence, with the result that many colliery companies have had to pay considerable sums for damage attributed to mining operations although the real cause was landslide movement.

The natural dam formed by a landslide such as that described in Mr. Alden's paper is always a source of great danger to the district downhill of it. The debris from the "lubricating" clays while more or less mixed up in the rock boulder mess forming the dam, will usually contain a more or less definite stratum of clay near the base, as landslides move faster at the bottom than at the top of the mass. This will act as a sliding plane on which movement may ultimately be expected and the safest plan would be to gradually breach the dam during the dry season by artificial cuttings.

Notes

[1] E. Blackwelder: The Gros Ventre Slide an Active Earth Flow. *Bull.* Geol. Soc. Amer. (1912) 23, 487.
[2] G. Knox: Landslides in South Wales Valleys. *Proc.* South Wales Inst. Engrs. (1927) 43, 161.

13   The Vaiont Reservoir Disaster

George A. Kiersch

The worst dam disaster in history occurred on October 9, 1963, at the Vaiont Dam, in Italy, when some 2600 lives were lost. The greatest loss of life in any similar disaster was 2,209 in the Johnstown Flood in Pennsylvania in 1899. The Vaiont tragedy is unique in many respects because:

1. It involved the world's second highest dam, of 265.5 meters (875 ft).
2. The dam, the world's highest thin arch, sustained no damage to the main shell or abutments, even though it was subjected to a force estimated at 4 million tons from the combined slide and overtopping wave, far in excess of design pressures.
3. The catastrophe was caused by subsurface forces, set up wholly within the area of the slide, 1.8 kilometers long and 1.6 km. wide.
4. The slide volume exceeded 240 million cu. m. (312 million cu. yd.), mostly rock.
5. The reservoir was completely filled with slide material for 1.8 km. and up to heights of 150 m. (488 ft.) above reservoir level, all within a period of 30 to 60 sec. (A point in the mass moved at a speed of 25 to 30 m. per sec.)
6. The slide created strong earth tremors, recorded as far away as Vienna and Brussels.

The quick sliding of the tremendous rock mass created an updraft of air accompanied by rocks and water that climbed up the right canyon wall a distance of 240 m. (780 ft.) above reser-

Kiersch, G. A., 1965, "The Vaiont Reservoir Disaster," *Mineral Information Service*, vol. 18, no. 7, pp. 129–38. Abridged by permission of the author and reprinted by permission of California Division of Mines and Geology. The report was first published in *Civil Engineering* (vol. 34, no. 3, 1964) and the American Society of Civil Engineers has permitted its reprinting in a revised form.
Professor Kiersch is Professor of Engineering Geology at Cornell University, Ithaca, New York.

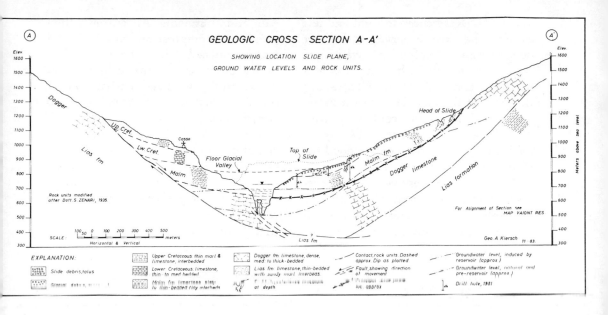

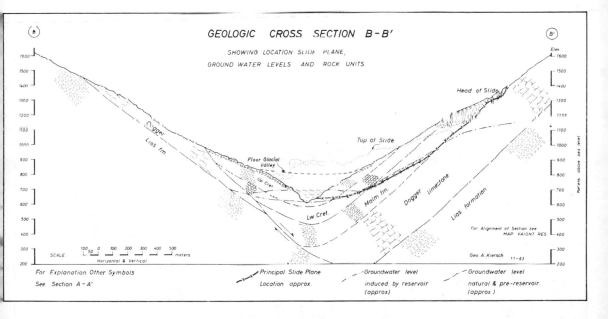

FIG. 1. On geologic cross-sections of slide and reservoir canyon, running from north to south, principal features of the slide plane, rock units and water levels are shown. For location of Sections A-A' and B-B', see Fig. 2.

voir level. (References to right and left assume that the observer is looking downstream.) Subsequent waves of water swept over both abutments to a height of some 100 m. (328 ft.) above the crest of the dam. It was over 70 m. (230 ft.) high at the confluence with the Piave Valley, one mile away. Everything in the path of the flood for miles downstream was destroyed.

A terrific, compressive air blast preceded the main volume of water. The overtopping jet of water penetrated all the galleries and interior works of the dam and abutments. Air currents then acted in decompression; this tensional phase opened the chamber-locked safety doors of all the galleries and works and completed destruction of the dam installations, from crest to canyon floor.

This catastrophe, from the slide to complete destruction downstream, occurred within the brief span of some 7 min. It was caused by a combination of: (1) adverse geologic features in the reservoir area; (2) man-made conditions imposed by impounded water

FIG. 2. Map of Vaiont Dam area and Piave River valley shows geographic features, limits of slide and of destructive flood waves.

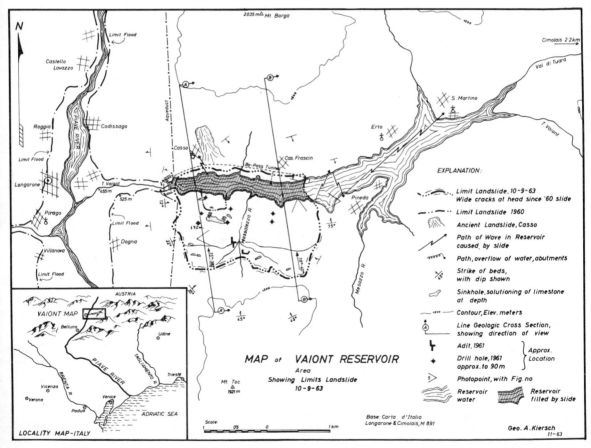

with bank storage, affecting the otherwise delicately balanced stability of a steep rock slope; and (3) the progressive weakening of the rock mass with time, accelerated by excessive groundwater recharge.

Design and Construction

Vaiont Dam is a double-curved, thin-arch, concrete structure completed in the fall of 1960. The dam is 3.4 m. (11.2 ft.) wide at the top and 22.7 m. (74.5 ft.) wide at the plug in the bottom of the canyon. It has an overflow spillway, carried a two-lane highway on a deck over the crest, and had an underground powerhouse in the left abutment. Reservoir capacity was 150 million cu. m. (196 million cu. yd., or 316,000 acre-ft.).

The way in which the dam resisted the unexpected forces created by the slide is indeed a tribute to designer Carlo Semanza and the thoroughness of construction engineer Mario Pancini.

Design and construction had to overcome some disadvantages both of the site and of the proposed structure. The foundation was wholly within limestone beds, and a number of unusual geologic conditions were noted during the abutment excavation and construction. A strong set of rebound (relief) joints parallel to the canyon walls facilitated extensive scaling within the destressed, external rock "layer." Excessive stress relief within the disturbed outer zone caused rock bursts and slabbing in excavations and tunnels of the lower canyon. Strain energy released within the external, unstable "skin" of the abutment walls was recorded by seismograph as vibrations of the medium. This active strain phe-nomenon in the abutments was stabilized with a grout curtain to 150 m. (500 ft.) outward at the base—and the effects were verified by a seismograph record. Grouting was controlled through variations of the elastic modulus.

The potential for landslides was considered a major objection to the site by some early investigators; others believed that "the slide potential can be treated with modern technical methods."

The Geologic Setting

The Vaiont area is characterized by a thick section of sedimentary rocks, dominantly limestone with frequent clayey interbeds and a series of alternating limey and marl layers. The general subsurface distribution is shown in the geologic cross sections.

Retained Stress

The young folded mountains of the Vaiont region retain a part of the active tectonic stresses that deformed the rock sequence. Faulting and local folding accompanied the regional tilting along with abundant tectonic fracturing. This deformation, further aided by bedding planes and relief joints, created blocky rock masses.

The development of rebound joints beneath the floor and walls of the outer valley is shown in an accompanying figure. This destressing effect creates a weak zone of highly fractured and "layered" rock, accentuated by the natural dip of the rock units. This weak zone is normally 100 to 150 m. (330 to 500 ft.) thick. Below this a stress balance is reached and the undisturbed rock has the natural stresses of mass.

Rapid carving of the inner valley resulted in the formation of a second set of rebound joints—in this case parallel to the walls of the present Vaiont canyon. The active, unstable "skin" of the inner canyon was fully confirmed during the construction of the dam.

The two sets of rebound joints, younger and older, intersect and coalesce within the upper part of the inner valley. This sector of the canyon walls, weakened by overlapping rebound joints, along with abundant tectonic fractures and inclined bedding planes, is a very unstable rock mass and prone to creep until it attains the proper slope.

Causes of Slide

Several adverse geologic features of the reservoir area contributed to the landslide on October 9:

Rock units that occur in a semicircular outcrop on the north slopes of Mt. Toc are steeply tilted. When deformed, some slipping and fault movement between the beds weakened frictional bond.

Steep dip of beds changes northward to Vaiont canyon, where rock units flatten along the synclinal axis; in three dimensions the area is bowl-shaped. The down-dip toe of the steep slopes is an escarpment offering no resistance to gravity sliding.

Rock units involved are inherently weak and possess low shearing resistance; they are of limestone with seams and clay partings alternating with thin beds of limestone and marl, and frequent interbeds of claystone.

Steep profile of the inner canyon

walls offer a strong gravity force to produce visco-elastic, gravitational creep and sliding.

Semicircular dip pattern confined the tendency for gravitational deformation to the bowl-shaped area.

Active dissolving of limestone by ground-water circulation has occurred at intervals since early Tertiary time. The result has been subsurface development of extensive tubes, openings, cavities and widening of joints and bedding planes. Sinkholes formed in the floor of the outer valley, particularly along the strike of the Malm formation on the upper slopes; these served as catchment basins for runoff for recharge of the ground-water reservoir. The interconnected ground-water system weakened the physical bonding of the rocks and also increased the hydrostatic uplift. The buoyant flow reduced gravitational friction, thereby facilitating sliding in the rocks.

Two sets of strong rebound joints, combined with inclined bedding planes and tectonic and natural fracture planes, created a very unstable rock mass throughout the upper part of the inner canyon.

Heavy rains in August and September produced an excessive inflow of ground-water from the drainage area on the north slopes of Mt. Toc. This recharge raised the natural ground-water level through a critical section of the slide plane (headward part) and subsequently raised the level of the induced water table in the vicinity of their junction (critical area of tensional action). The approximate position of both water levels at the time of the slide is shown in the accompanying figure (Fig. 1).

Excessive ground-water inflow in

early October increased the bulk density of the rocks occurring above the initial water table; this added weight contributed to a reduction in the gross shear strength. Swelling of some clay minerals in the seams, partings and beds created additional uplift and contributed to sliding. The upstream sector is composed largely of marl and thin beds of limestone with clay partings—a rock sequence that is inherently less stable than the downstream sector.

The bowl-shaped configuration of the beds in the slide area increased the confinement of ground water within the mass; steeply inclined clay partings aided the containment on the east, south, and west.

Two exploratory adits driven in 1961 reportedly exposed clay seams and small-scale slide planes. Drill holes bored near the head of the 1960 slide were slowly closed and sheared off. This confirmed the view that a slow gravitational creep was in progress following the 1960 slide and probably even before that—caused by a combination of geologic causes. Creep and

Fig. 3. On sketch of inner Vaiont canyon and remnants of the outer glacial valley, are shown rebound joints—old and young set—from stress relief within the walls of the valley to depths of 100 to 150 m. (330 to 500 ft.).

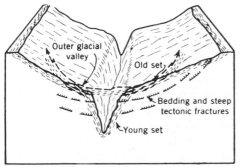

the accompanying vibrations due to stress relief were later described by Muller.

Effects of Man's Activities

Construction of Vaiont Reservoir created an induced ground-water level which increased the hydrostatic uplift pressure throughout a triangular subsurface mass aided by fractures and the interconnected system of solution openings in the limestone.

Before April 1963, the reservoir was maintained at El. 680 m. or lower, except for two months in 1962 when it was maintained at 690–700 m. In September, five months after the induced water table was raised 20 m. or higher (700–710 m.), the slide area increased its rate of creep. This action has three possible explanations: (1) a very delicate balance existed between the strength of the rock mass and the internal stresses (shear and tensile), which was destroyed by the 20-m. rise of bank storage and accompanying increase in hydrostatic pressure; (2) the same reaction resulted from the large subsurface inflow in early October due to rains; or (3) the induced groundwater level from the reservoir at El. 680 m during 1961–1962 did not attain maximum lateral infiltration until September 1963, when creep accelerated. In any case, the rate of groundwater migration into bank storage is believed to have been critical.

Evidence indicates that the immediate cause of the slide was an increase in the internal stresses and a gross reduction in the strength of the rock mass, particularly the upstream sector where this mass consists largely of marl and alternating thin beds of limestone and marl. Actual collapse was triggered by an excess of ground water, which created a change in the mass density and increased the hydrostatic uplift and swelling pressures along planes of inherent weakness, combined with the numerous geologic features that enhanced and facilitated gravitational sliding.

The final movement was sudden—no causes from "outside" the affected area are thought to have been responsible.

Sequence of Slide Events

Large-scale landslides are common on the slopes of Vaiont Valley; witness the ancient slide at Casso and the prehistoric blocking of the valley at Pineda. Movement at new localities is to be expected periodically because of the adverse geologic setting of the valley. The principal events preceding the movement on October 9 were:

In 1960, a slide of some 700,000 cu. m. (one million cu. yd.) occurred on the left bank of the reservoir near the dam. This movement was accompanied by creep over a much larger area; a pattern of cracks developed upslope from the slide and continued eastward. These fractures ultimately marked the approximate limits of the October 9 slide. The slopes of Mt. Toc were observed to be creeping and the area showed many indications of instability.

In 1960–1961, a bypass tunnel 5 m. (16.4 ft.) in diameter was driven along the right wall of the reservoir for a distance of 2 km. (6,560 ft.), to assure that water could reach the outlet works of the dam in case of future slides.

As a precaution, after the 1960 slide the reservoir elevation was generally held at a maximum of 680 m. and a grid of geodetic stations on concrete pillars was installed throughout the potential slide area extending 4 km. (2.5 miles) upstream, to measure any movement.

The potential slide area was explored in 1961 both by drill holes and by man-sized adits (see map for depth). Reportedly, no confirmation of a major slide plane could be detected in either drill holes or adit. An analysis now indicates that the drill holes were too shallow to intercept the major slide plane of October 9, and what was in all probability the deepest plane of gravitational creep started by the 1960 slide and active thereafter.

Gravitational creep of the left reservoir slope was observed during the 1960–1961 period, and Muller reports "movement of 25 to 30 cm. (10 to 12 in.) per week (on occasion) which was followed in close succession by small, local earth tremors due to stress relief within the slope centered at depths of 50 to 500 m. (164 to 1,640 ft.). The total rock mass that was creeping was about 200 million cu. m. (260 million cu. yd.)."

During the spring and summer of 1963, the eventual slide area moved very slowly; scattered observations showed a creep distance of 1 cm. (3/8 in.) per week, an average rate since the 1960 slide.

Beginning about September 18, numerous geodetic stations were observed to be moving 1 cm. a day. However it was generally believed that only individual blocks were creeping; it was not suspected that the entire area was moving as a mass.

Heavy rains began about September 28 and continued steadily until after October 9. Excessive run-off increased ground-water recharge and surface inflow; the reservoir was at El. 700m. or higher, about 100 ft. below the crest.

About October 1, animals grazing on the north slopes of Mt. Toc and the reservoir bank sensed danger and moved away. The mayor of Casso ordered townspeople to evacuate the slopes, and posted notice of an expected 20-m. (65-ft.) wave in the reservoir from the anticipated landslide. (The 20 m. was also the estimate of engineers for the height of the wave that would follow such a slide, based on experience of the slide at nearby Pontesi Dam in 1959.)

Movements of geodetic stations throughout the slide area reported for about three weeks before the collapse showed a steady increase from about 1 centimeter per day in mid-September to between 20 and 30 centimeters to as much as 80 centimeters on the day of failure.

About October 8, engineers realized that all the observation stations were moving together as a "uniform" unstable mass; and furthermore the actual slide involved some five times the area thought to be moving and expected to collapse about mid-November.

On October 8, engineers began to lower the reservoir level from El. 700 m. in anticipation of a slide. Two outlet tunnels on the left abutment were discharging a total of 5,000 cfs. but heavy inflow from runoff reduced the actual lowering of the water. The reservoir contained about 120 million cu. m. of water at the time of the disaster.

On October 9, the accelerated rate of movement was reported by the engineer in charge. A five-member board of advisers were evaluating conditions, and authorities were assessing the situation on an around-the-clock basis. Although the bypass outlet gates were open, oral reports describe a rise in the reservoir level on October 9. This is logical if lateral movement of the left bank had progressed to a point where it was reducing the reservoir capacity. These reports also mention difficulty with the intake gates in the left abutment (El. 591 m.) a few hours before the fatal slide.

Movement, Flood and Destruction

Those who witnessed the collapse included 20 technical personnel stationed in the control building on the left abutment and some 40 people in the office and hotel building on the right abutment. But no one who witnessed the collapse survived the destructive flood wave that accompanied the sudden slide at 22 hours 41 min. 40 sec. (Central European Time). However, a resident of Casso living over 260 m. (850 ft.) above the reservoir, and on the opposite side from the slide, reported the following sequence of events:

About 10:15 p m he was awakened by a very loud and continuous sound of rolling rocks. He suspected nothing unusual as talus slides are very common.

The rolling of rocks continued and steadily grew louder. It was raining hard.

About 10:40 p.m. a very strong wind struck the house, breaking the window panes. Then the house shook violently; there was a very loud rumbling noise. Soon afterward the roof of the house was lifted up so that rain and rocks came hurtling into the room (on the second floor) for what seemed like half a minute.

He had jumped out of bed to open the door and leave when the roof collapsed onto the bed. The wind suddenly died down and everything in the valley was quiet.

Observers in Longarone reported that a wall of water came down the canyon about 10:43 p.m. and at the same time a strong wind broke windows, and houses shook from strong earth tremors. The flood wave was over 70 m. (230 ft.) high at the mouth of Vaiont canyon and hit Longarone head on. Everything in its path was destroyed. The flood moved upstream in the Piave Valley beyond Castello Lavazzo, where a 5-m. (16-ft.) wave wrecked the lower part of Codissago. The main volume swept downstream from Longarone, hitting Pirago and Villanova. By 10:55 p.m. the flood waters had receded and all was quiet in the valley.

The character and effect of the air blast that accompanied the main flood wave at the dam have been described in the introduction. The destruction wrought by the blast, the jet of water, and the decompression phase are difficult to imagine. For example, the steel I-beams in the underground powerhouse were twisted like a corkscrew and sheared; the steel doors of the safety chamber were torn from their hinges, bent, and carried 12 m. (43 ft.) away.

Seismic tremors caused by the rock slide were recorded over a wide area of Europe—at Rome, Trieste, Vienna, Basel, Stuttgart, and Brussels. The kinetic energy of the falling earth mass was the sole cause of the seismic tremors recorded from Vaiont according to Toperczer. No deep-seated earthquake occurred to trigger the slide. The seismic record clearly demonstrates that surface waves ($L_1 = 3.26$ km. per sec., or about 730 mph.) were first to arrive at the regional seismic stations, followed by secondary surface waves ($L_2 = 2.55$ km. per sec. or 570 mph). There was no forewarning in the form of small shocks and no follow-up shocks—which are typical of earthquakes from subsurface sources. No P or S waves were recorded.

Pattern of Sliding

The actual release and unrestricted movement of the slide was extremely rapid. Seismological records show that the major sliding took place within less than 30 sec. (under 14 sec. for the full record of the L_1 wave) and thereafter sliding ceased. The speed of the mass movement (25 to 30 m. per sec.) and the depth of the principal slide are strikingly demonstrated by the preservation intact of the Masselezza River canyon and the grassy surface soil with distinctive "fracture" pattern.

Wave Action Due to Slide

Sketchy reports from observers at Erto described the first wave by stating that "the entire reservoir for 1.8 km. (1.1 miles) piled up as one vast curving wave" for a period of 10 sec. The strong updraft of air created by the rapid slide was confined in movement by the deep Vaiont Valley encircled by high peaks. The updraft within the confined outer valley sucked the water, accompanied by rocks, up to El. 960 m.

(885 ft. or more above the original reservoir level) and accounted for part of the force possessed by the initial wave.

At the dam, the initial wave split on hitting the right canyon wall, after demolishing the hotel building at El. 780 m. (300 ft. above the reservoir surface). Some of the water followed the canyon wall downstream and moved above and around the dam. The major volume, however, seems to have bounced off the right wall, swept back across the canyon to the left abutment and moved upslope and around the dam to at least El. 820 m. (460 ft. above the reservoir level).

The overflow waves from the right and left abutments were joined in the canyon by the main surge, which overtopped the dam, and together these constituted the flood wave that hit Longarone. Water overtopped the dam crest on the left side for some hours after the slide, strongly the next morning, and during this time also displaced water drained from pools scattered over the slide surface.

Upstream the wave generated by the slide moved first into the area opposite Pineda, where it demolished homes, bounced off the canyon wall and moved southward, hitting the Pineda peninsula. On receding from there, the wave moved northeastward across the full length of the lake and struck San Martino with full force, bypassing Erto, which went unharmed.

Conditions Since the Slide

The water level just behind the dam dropped at the rate of 50 to 80 cm. (20 to 32 in.) per day during the first two weeks after the slide. This loss is believed due in part to leakage through the intake gates for the bypass aqueduct and powerhouse conduits. Geologically, there was a substantial loss due to the new conditions of bank storage, subsurface circulation and saturation of material filling the canyon.

A pond that formed at the Massalezza River canyon, along the foot of the slide plane, dropped in level rapidly and was dry on October 24, confirming the idea of ground-water recharge to slide material and the establishment of a water table within the newly formed mass. Smaller ponds initially formed upstream from the dam along the zone of contact between the slide and the right reservoir bank. These likewise dried up by October 24 as a result of groundwater recharge and readjustment in the water table within the slide mass.

The lake level behind the slide dam rose steadily from the inflow of tributary streams. For example, two weeks after the slide, the reservoir was 13 m. (43 ft.) higher than the water level at the dam— a major problem in the future operation of Vaiont Dam.

Strong funneling craters developed during the first days after the slide in the soil and glacial debris concentrated near the toe of the slide. This cratering was of concern to some as indicating large-scale movement to come, but other conditions are the probable causes of the surface subsidence. Large blocks of rock, with some bridging action, fill the canyon and create much void space in the lower mass. Some of these spaces are filled by normal gravity shifting of fines, and ground-water circulation also distributes fines into these void spaces. Formation of craters is restricted to the section of the slide that fills the former canyon, and craters appear at intervals along its entire length. They are most extensive in the slope behind the dam.

Numerous small, step-like slide blocks occur at different levels on the main slip plane. These blocks were loosened by the movement on October 9 and have since moved slowly down the slip plane, some to the bottom of the escarpment. Talus runs are common from small V-notched canyons along the edge of the steep eastern sector of the slide.

Future of the Reservoir

The steeply dipping beds along the head of the slide will undoubtedly fail from time to time as a result of gravitational creep. Ultimately the upper most part of the slip plane will be flattened and thereby will attain a stable natural slope.

The Italian Ministry of Public Works has announced that Vaiont Dam will no longer be used as a power source. The cost of clearing the reservoir would be prohibitive because of the volume involved, the distance of 4 or 5 km. (3 miles) that waste material would have to be hauled to the Piave Valley, and the 300-m. (1,000-ft.) lift required to transport the waste over the divide west of the dam.

The bypass tunnel in the right wall of the reservoir could be ultimately used to pond water behind the dam for release through the existing outlet works. Another alternative would be to divert the reservoir water southeastward to the Cellina River drainage by a tunnel driven from the upper end of the lake. Such diversion would develop the upper catchment area of Cellina and utilize Vaiont storage, behind the slide dam, as a multi-seasonal storage astride the Piave and Cellina catchments.

Vaiont in Retrospect

Vaiont has tragically demonstrated the critical importance of geologic features within a reservoir and in its vicinity— even though the site may be otherwise satisfactory for a dam of outstanding design.

In future, preconstruction studies must give thorough consideration to the properties of a rock mass as such, in contrast to a substance, and particularly to its potential for deformation with the passage of time. An assessment that is theoretical only is inadequate. The soundest approach is a systematic appraisal that includes:

An investigation of the geologic setting and its critical features

An assessment of past events that have modified features and properties of the site rocks

A forecast of the effects of the engineering works on geologic features in the area and on the strength of the site rocks

The geologic reaction to changed conditions in the process of time.

Project plans should set forth a system for acquiring data on the interaction between geologic conditions and changes induced by project operation.

Time, in terms of the life of the project, is a key to safety and doubtless was a controlling factor at Vaiont. Since 1959, eight major dams around the world have failed in some manner. It seems imperative that the following factors be recognized:

1. Rock masses, under changed en-

vironmental conditions, can weaken within short periods of time—days, weeks, months.

2. The strength of a rock mass can decrease very rapidly once creep gets under way.

3. Evidence of active creep should be considered as a warning that warrants immediate technical assessment, since acceleration to collapse can occur quickly.

Engineering Implications

Speed of sliding movement. Rock masses are capable of translatory movement as fast as quick clays or at a liquid-like speed.

Strain energy. Its influence on a rock mass, its release and associated movement are critical. The interplay between wetting of a rock mass, buoyancy effect, and the lightening of a rock mass (1.0 or less in density) allows an accelerated release of the inherent strain energy, thereby creating more release fractures and the cycle is repeated. The net result is the increase in amount of water and a stronger buoyancy effect—both aided by the energy release phenomenon.

Potential for landslides at reservoir sites that have been in operation for many years must be studied; new projects must be evaluated for landslide potential in a more critical manner.

The tremendous amount of potential energy that is stored in a rock mass undergoing creep on an incline (as at Vaiont). With the increasing displacements, gliding friction factor drops and the velocity of mass increases. This means that a sliding mass has a potential to increase from slow creep to a fantastically high rate of movement in a brief time of seconds or minutes. The energy goes into momentum and not into deforming the interior of the sliding mass as in the typical rotational slide.

Two techniques assist the engineer today in this connection. First, he has and can use the most improved methods for observing and measuring the changes of strain within a rock mass. And second, he can use a fore-warning system in case this phenomenon acts quickly and the failure of a rock is imminent.

References

Anon. 1958. Some SADE developments: *Water Power*, vol. 10, nos. 3-6, Mar.-June 1958.

Anon. 1961. Italy builds more dams: *Engineering News-Record*, vol. 167, no. 18, pp. 30-36.

Anon. 1963. Vaiont Dam survives immense overtopping: *Engineering News-Record*, vol. 171, no. 16, pp. 22–23, Oct. 17, 1963.

Boyer, G. R. 1913. Etude géologique des environs de Longarone (Alpes venitiennes): *Soc. Géologique de France, Bulletin*, vol. 13, no. 4, pp. 451-485.

Muller, L. 1963. Differences in the characteristic features of rocks and mountain masses: 5th Conference of the International Bureau of Rock Mechanics, *Proceedings*. Leipzig, Germany, Nov. 1963.

Muller, L. 1963. Rock mechanics considerations in the design of rock slopes, in *State of Stress in the Earth's Crust*, International Conference, Rand Corp., Santa Monica, Calif., June 1963.

Pancini, M. 1961. Observations and surveys on the abutments of Vaiont Dam. *Geologie und Bauwesen*, vol. 26, no. 1, pp. 122–141.

Pancini, M. 1962. Results of first series of tests performed on a model reproducing the actual structure of the abutment rock of the Vaiont Dam. *Geologie und Bauwesen*, vol. 27, no. 1, pp. 105–119.

14   Permafrost
U. S. Geological Survey

In 1577, on his second voyage to the New World in search of the Northwest Passage, Sir Martin Frobisher reported finding ground in the far north that was frozen to depths of "four or five fathoms, even in summer," and that the frozen condition "so combineth the stones together that scarcely instruments with great force can unknit them." This permanently frozen ground, now termed *permafrost*, underlies perhaps a fifth of the earth's land surface. It occurs in Antarctica, but is most extensive in the northern hemisphere. In the lands surrounding the Arctic Ocean its maximum thickness has been reported in terms of thousands of feet—as much as 5,000 feet in Siberia and 2,000 feet in northern Alaska.

For almost 300 years after Frobisher's discovery, little attention was paid to this frost phenomenon, but in the 19th Century during construction of the Trans-Siberian Railroad across vast stretches of frozen tundra, permafrost was brought to the attention of the Russians because of the engineering problems it caused. In North America the discovery of gold in Alaska and the Yukon Territory near the turn of the century likewise focused the attention of miners and engineers on the unique nature of permafrost.

Frozen ground poses few engineering problems if it is not disturbed. But

Published by the U. S. Government Printing Office, 1973. Based on material provided by Louis L. Ray.

changes in the surface environment—such as the clearing of vegetation, the building of roads and other construction and the draining of lakes—lead to thawing of the permafrost, which in turn produces unstable ground susceptible to soil creep and landslides, slumping and subsidence, icings, and severe frost heaving. The many environmental problems stemming from the rapid expansion of human activities in areas underlain by frozen ground during and following World War II, have demonstrated that a thorough understanding of the nature of permafrost is of prime importance for wise land-use planning. Not only is it an economic requirement that the least possible disturbance be made of the frozen ground, but it is a practical necessity if the future land-use potential of the vast areas underlain by the frozen ground is to be preserved.

In the Northern Hemisphere, permafrost decreases in thickness progressively from north to south. Two major zones are distinguished: a northern zone in which permafrost forms a continuous layer at shallow depths below the ground surface and, to the south, a discontinuous zone in which there are scattered permafrost-free areas. Land underlain by continuous permafrost almost completely circumscribes the Arctic Ocean. A less clearly defined zone of so-called sporadic permafrost occurs along the southern margin of the discontinuous zone where widespread permafrost-free ground contains scattered small, isolated masses of the frozen ground.

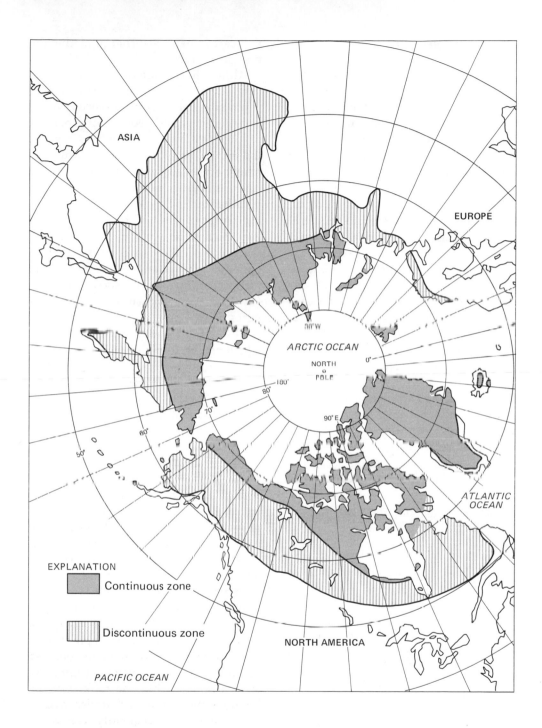

FIG. 1. Distribution of permafrost in the Northern Hemisphere.

145   **Mass Movement**

The term *permafrost*, a contraction of permanently frozen ground, was proposed in 1943 by Siemon W. Muller, of the U. S. Geological Survey, to define a thickness of soil or other superficial deposit, or even of bedrock beneath the surface of the earth in which a temperature below freezing has existed continuously for 2 or more years. When the average annual air temperature is low enough to maintain a continuous average surface temperature below 0°C, the depth of winter freezing of the ground exceeds the depth of summer thawing, and a layer of frozen ground is developed. Downward penetration of the cold will continue until it is balanced by the heat flowing upward from the earth's interior. In this manner, permafrost hundreds of feet thick can form over a period of several thousand years. Distribution and thickness of permafrost depends, however, on many factors that control surface temperatures and cold penetration. Some of these factors are: geographic position and exposure, character of seasonal and annual cloudiness, precipitation, vegetation, drainage, and the properties of

the earth materials that underlie the ground surface.

Although thawing of the surface and near surface layers may occur quickly when summer thawing exceeds winter freezing, it would require long periods of time, estimated as high as tens of thousands of years, for thawing air temperatures to penetrate and melt the thickest known permafrost. Thus, the distribution and variations of subfreezing temperatures recorded at depth in the thicker permafrost layers reflect the ancient cold temperatures of the past that are commonly assigned to the Pleistocene Epoch, the so-called Great Ice Age, which began about 3 million years ago.

The ground above the permafrost which thaws in summer and refreezes in winter is known as the *active layer*. Its thickness, like that of the underlying permafrost, depends on the many factors that influence the flow of heat into and out from the Earth's surface.

The upper surface of the permafrost layer is known as the *Permafrost Table*. When winter freezing does not penetrate to the permafrost table, an unfrozen layer remains between the base of the frozen active layer and the permafrost table. This unfrozen material, as well as the rare isolated masses of unfrozen ground present within the permafrost itself, are called *talik*, a term adopted from the Russian. The talik, like the ground ice, is a major consideration in any appraisal of the permafrost environment because unfrozen ground water, commonly concentrated within the talik, may be highly mineralized and under hydrostatic pressure. Frequently the water bursts forth to the ground surface under pressure where a point of issue

FIG. 2. Typical section of permafrost terrain.

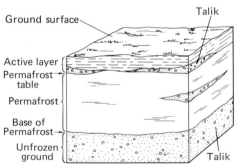

has been opened either by natural or artificial means. On reaching the surface the water may freeze, producing a thick and perhaps widespread ice sheet or an ice mound. Such *icings* may pose serious problems in areas of concentrated human activity.

In the upper part of the permafrost layer, large masses of ground ice of various shapes and origins may be present. In places in Alaska it is estimated that more than half of the volume of the upper 10 feet or so of the permafrost layer consists of ice. The ice may occur as coatings, as individual grains, veinlets and lenses, and as ice wedges that extend downward from the permafrost table.

The presence of ice-rich permafrost is readily apparent whenever the insulating effect of vegetation is modified or destroyed. Such changes trigger the thawing of the underlying permafrost and ground ice so that distinctive changes in the landscape are produced. Especially important from the standpoint of human activities is the ground subsidence that results from thawing of the ground ice and the solifluction or gravity controlled mass movement of thawed, water-saturated surficial sediments that produce a variety of land forms.

Artificial stripping of the insulating vegetation mat from the active layer or the removal or destruction of the active layer while preparing the land for agricultural use or construction projects such as roads, railroads, airfields, and buildings, disturbs the delicate thermal balance which may, unless preventive measures are taken, result in thawing of the ice masses in the underlying permafrost with consequent irregular subsidence of the land sur-

face. Even the casual crossing of tundra areas on foot or a single traverse by a wheeled vehicle may so upset the thermal balance through slight changes in the insulating properties of the vegetation mat that thawing of the underlying ground may result. Once thawing starts, its control may be difficult or even impossible.

Experience has shown that ice-rich permafrost is generally present where the active layer is relatively thin, the drainage poor, and the frozen materials are fine-grained sediments. These conditions are well developed on the Arctic Slope of Alaska where ground ice is commonly present as a honeycomb-like, polygonal network of vertical ice wedges that extends downward from the base of the active layer. Where the thermal balance has been so modified that thawing is initiated, the normal thickness of the active layer is increased, and the surface of the permafrost table is depressed below the upper part of the ground ice. Consequent melting of the tops of the ice wedges produces subsidence in the overlying ground that is reflected on the land surface by a network of shallow-to-deep interconnected furrows that form a polygonal pattern.

Where conditions are such that no polygonal ground has developed, the presence of the underlying network of polygonal ice wedges may be reflected in the character of the stream courses. The concentrated heat in the water flowing across terrain underlain by the ice-wedge polygons thaws them to produce a series of subsidence pools along the stream course at ice-wedge intersections. When viewed from the air, such stream courses with their series of pools give the impression of a string

FIG. 3. Building located south of Fairbanks is subsiding because of thawing permafrost. (Photo by T. L. Pewe, Courtesy of O. J. Ferrians, Jr., U. S. Geological Survey.)

of beads, hence the name *beaded drainage.*

When masses of ground ice thaw, subsidence may produce isolated depressions, *thermokarst pits,* or basins occupied by *thaw lakes.* Once initiated, thawing and consequent calving along the thaw shores tends to increase the lake area. If wind directions are relatively constant in the summer season, thawing may be concentrated in directions controlled by the wind and wave action along the lake shores, producing features such as the well-known "oriented lakes" of Alaska and Russia.

Curious, rounded, ice-cored hills called *pingos* are present both in areas of tundra and boreal forest. Rising above the surrounding landscape of unconsolidated, fine-grained sediments to heights as much as several hundred feet, the largest pingos may be as much as several thousand feet in diameter. Pingos are relatively ephemeral features of the landscape, believed to result from concentrations in the talik of unfrozen water under hydraulic pressure that bows up the overlying sediments and freezes. The summits of pingos may contain crater-like lakes fed by springs of fresh water that may flow throughout the year.

On the tundra of the Arctic Slope of Alaska and Canada, pingos are generally present in old lake basins that may be partly filled with swamp deposits (muskeg). In the forested areas to the south, pingos form in areas of valley-bottom alluvium adjacent to the base of steeply sloping, south-facing valley walls. Pingos in areas of boreal forests may commonly be recognized by the vegetation which grows profusely on the well-drained soils of their steeply sloping sides.

Solifluction, the slow mass movement of surficial unconsolidated water-saturated sediments downslope, is another common-place phenomenon in regions underlain by permafrost. Commonly, during the summer season of thawing, the surficial sediments become supersaturated because melt-waters are unable to percolate into the impervious permafrost below. At the interface between the frozen and unfrozen materials, these melt-waters provide a lubricant to the frozen surface over which the mobile unfrozen mass can readily slide by gravity. Sur-

FIG. 4. Ground subsidence along abandoned Copper River Railroad. (Photo by L. A. Yehle, Courtesy of O. J. Ferrians, Jr., U. S. Geological Survey.)

ficial materials may move as sheets or lobes over fronts ranging from a few to several hundreds of feet wide. Where there is a well-developed vegetation mat above the fluidlike mass of supersaturated debris, a *solifluction sheet* may move downward as a well defined sheet, or lobe, or as a series of partially overriding folds. At times the vegetation mat may rupture, and the slurry of water-saturated sediments may produce sudden destructive mud flows. Because solifluction can be triggered on slopes as low as 3°, and movement may be increased by disturbance of the normal ground conditions, it is a serious hazard at construction sites, especially those underlain by permafrost at shallow depth.

Frost heaving, commonplace in all environments where there is marked freezing and thawing of the ground, results from an upward or expanding force occasioned by swelling of the ground during freezing. The effects of this process are magnified in the colder climates where the land is underlain by permafrost, although in most areas there is generally little evidence of frost heaving under natural conditions. If surface conditions are disturbed, however, by construction or other activities permitting an increase in summer thawing with a consequent thickening of the active layer to which frost heaving is confined, it expectedly becomes a serious problem. It is necessary, therefore, to preserve the insulating value of the ground surface as much as possible so that the thickness of the active layer will be retained at a minimum, in order that the effects of frost heaving may also be kept at a minimum. This can be accomplished by not removing the vegetation mat and by increasing the surficial insulation of the ground at the construction site, generally by the addition of a coarse gravel fill.

It is readily apparent that man's uninhibited and careless use of land underlain by permafrost can produce serious problems today and in some cases, can cause lasting detrimental effects. Likewise, natural changes such as variations in climate, erosion by shifting streams, increased precipitation, unusually severe storms, earthquakes, landslides, forest fires, and many other natural phenomena can also modify the environment, producing similar adverse effects. Each modification, whether naturally or artifically induced, must be carefully evaluated, and if necessary controlled in order to minimize the detrimental effects if the vast regions underlain by permafrost are to remain continuously serviceable to man.

Suggested Reading

Ferrians, O. J., Jr. Kachadoorian, Reuben, and Greene, G. W., 1969. Permafrost and related engineering problems in Alaska: *U. S. Geol. Survey Prof. Paper 678*, 37 p.

Lachenbruch, A. H., 1968, Permafrost, *in* Fairbridge, R. W., ed., *The Encyclopedia of Geomorphology*: New York, Reinhold Publishing Corp., p. 833–839.

Muller, S. W., 1943, Permafrost or permanently frozen ground and related engineering problems: *U. S. Army, Office of Chief of Engineers, Military Intelligence Div. Strategic Eng. Study 62*, 231 p.; reprinted with corrections, 1945; also, 1947, Ann Arbor, Mich., Edwards Bros.

Ray, L. L., 1956, Perennially frozen ground, an environmental factor in Alaska: *Internatl. Geogr. Congr., 17th, and 8th Gen. Assembly, Washington, D. C., 1952 Proc.*, p. 260–264.

Erosion and Sedimentation

"Along the coastlines of the world, numerous engineering works in various states of disintegration testify to the futility and wastefulness of disregarding the tremendous destructive forces of the sea."

M. P. O'Brien

Erosion and sedimentation are less dramatic than volcanic eruptions, earthquakes, and landslides, but they affect the entire surface of the continents and have a significant impact on Man. What information is available concerning the erosion of continents? To what extent is the erosion of soils due to Man's activities? What portion is simply the result of natural phenomena? Is it possible to determine the rate of erosion? These questions are considered by Sheldon Judson in Reading 15.

From a geological point of view the zone where land and sea meet is one of the most dynamic areas and an area most vulnerable to erosion and sedimentation. In spite of its vulnerability, this zone is also one of the most desirable settings for recreation, residence, and commercial development. In Reading 16 James Rosenbaum reviews the role of manmade structures in stabilizing the shoreline environment.

A more subtle aspect of erosion is the erosion or solution which takes place in the subsurface. This can present serious construction problems and is not uncommon in humid areas underlain by limestone. The hazard is often intensified when large volumes of underground water are removed by pumping, since the water may have strengthened the rocks by floatation. Philip LaMoreaux and William Warren present a spectacular example of the sudden formation of a large solution crater (sinkhole). It is however only one of about 1000 sinkholes in an area of approximately 16 square kilometers in Alabama. This hazard is present in large areas throughout the southeastern United States.

Early soil conservation efforts were directed at the need to hold productive soils in place. The current concern reflects a change of emphasis to the effects of water-borne and deposited sediments in the aquatic environment. Sediment that adversely affects the aquatic environment originates from a number of sources, and its physical, economic, and aesthetic impact is great. A. R. Robinson presents some insights on the role of sediment as a carrier or scavenger of other pollutants in the concluding article of this section. It may be initially disturbing to note that federal and state water quality standards tend to ignore suspended sediments that may be a major pollutant of water. But is it possible to develop standards when we are uncertain about the exchange mechanism whereby a pollutant can be either taken up or released from the sediment phase? Although the forces of erosion and sedimentation are beyond the full control of Man, we should be able to better define the nature of the problem and focus our attention on programs that will reduce the adverse environmental effects.

Photo on page 151. Condominium on Sheridan Road, Chicago, April 1973. Reproduced with permission from *Chicago Daily News*. Photograph by Fred Stein.

15 Erosion of the Land,
or What's Happening to Our Continents?
Sheldon Judson

Not quite two centuries ago James Hutton, Scottish medical man, agriculturalist, and natural scientist—now enshrined as the founder of modern geology—and Jean André de Luc, Swiss emigré, scientist, and reader to England's Queen Charlotte, carried on a spirited discussion concerning the nature and extent of erosion of the natural landscape. De Luc believed that once vegetation had spread its protective cloak across the land, erosion ceased. Not so, in Hutton's opinion. He argued (Hutton, 1795):

According to the doctrine of this author (de Luc) our mountains of Tweed-dale and Tiviotdale, being all covered with vegetation, are arrived at the period in the course of times when they should be permanent. But is it really so? Do they never waste? Look at rivers in a flood—if these run clear, this philosopher has reasoned right, and I have lost my argument. [But] our clearest streams run muddy in a flood. The great causes, therefore, for the degradation of mountains never stop as long as there is water to run; although as the heights of mountains diminish, the progress of their diminution may be more and more retarded.

Judson, S., 1968, "Erosion of the Land, or What's Happening to Our Continents?" *Amer. Scientist*, vol. 56, pp. 356–74. Lightly edited by permission of the author and reprinted by permission of The Society of Sigma Xi. Copyright 1969 by The Society of Sigma Xi.
Dr. Judson is Professor of Geology at Princeton University, Princeton, New Jersey.

We know today, of course, that vegetation plays an important role in the preparation of material for erosion. We know also that although vegetation may slow the removal of material from a slope it does not stop it completely. Hutton's view is overwhelmingly accepted today. Erosion continues in spite of the plant cover, which in fact is conducive to certain aspects of erosion. The discussion now centers on the factors determining erosion, the nature of the products of this process, how these products are moved from one place to another, and at what rates the products are being produced. Hutton, in his day, had no data upon which to make a quantitative estimate of the rates at which erosion progressed. Today we, unlike Hutton, measure rates of erosion for periods of a fraction of a man's lifetime, as well as for periods of a few hundreds or thousands of years of human history. In addition, radioactive dating and refined techniques of study in field and laboratory allow us to make some quantitative statements about the rates at which our solid lands are wasted and moved particle by particle, ion by ion, to the ocean basins.

This report sets forth some of what we know about these erosional rates. We will understand that erosion is the process by which earth materials are worn away and moved from one spot to another. As such, the action of water, wind, ice, frost-action, plants and animals, and gravity all play their roles.

The destination of material eroded is eventually the great world ocean, although there are pauses in the journey and, as we will see later, the material delivered to the ocean must be in some way reincorporated into the continents.

Some Modern Records

Let us now examine some modern records of erosion of various small areas on the earth's crust, essentially determinations of rates at specific points. There is a large amount of information to be gleaned from agricultural, forestry, and conservation studies as well as from some studies by geologists.[1]

Even a casual inspection of our cemeteries demonstrates that some rock goes to pieces at a measurable rate and that rocks have differing resistance to destruction. Four marble headstones photographed in 1968 in the Princeton, N. J., cemetery indicate what can happen to marble in the 172 years involved. The marker erected in 1898 was still easily legible 70 years later, but the crisp, sharp outline of the stone carver's chisel was gone. The headstone erected 70 years earlier was still partially legible in 1968, but the stone put up in 1796 was completely illegible. In this instance the calcite ($CaCO_3$), which makes up the marble, was attacked by a carbonic acid formed by rain water and the CO_2 of the atmosphere. In general, marble headstones become illegible in the humid northeastern states after 150 to 175 years of exposure.

In contrast to the marble headstones is a marker in the Cambridge, Massachusetts Burying Ground, that was erected in 1699 and photographed in 1968. It is made of slate, often used as a headstone material in many New England cemeteries until marble became fashionable at the turn of the nineteenth century. Unlike marble it is resistant to chemical erosion. Nearly 270 years after the stone was erected the inscription stands out clearly.

Graveyards do most certainly provide examples of the impermanence of rock material as well as of the relative resistance of different rock types. The earliest study in such an environment that I have seen was by Sir Archibald Geikie, in Edinburgh, published in 1880. More recent studies have been made of the rates at which erosion proceeds on tombstones. Thus, in an area near Middletown, Connecticut, it is estimated that tombstones of a local red sandstone are weathering at the rate of about 0.006 centimeters per year (Matthias, 1967). In general, however, a graveyard does not present the best conditions for the accumulation of quantitative data.

More reliable data seem to come from agricultural stations. Here is an example. A summary of measurements has been made at 17 different stations on plots measuring 6 by 72.6 ft and under differing conditions of rainfall, soil, slope, and vegetative cover (Musgrave, 1954). Periods of record in this instance vary between 4 and 11 years. On the average, erosion from plots with continuous grass cover annually lost 75 tons per square kilometer, a lowering of about 3 meters per 1000 years. This is a dramatic demonstration of the role of plants in affecting erosion. In this instance the rate of erosion increased 100 times between grass-covered plots and well-tilled row-crop plots.

Obviously climate will also affect the

rate of erosion. For example, recent studies by Washburn (1967) in eastern Greenland show that seasonal freeze and thaw in a nearly glacial climate produce erosion rates ranging between 9 and 37 meters per thousand years. This contrasts with the rates in more temperate climates cited previously. In semiarid lands, where vegetation is discontinuous and rainfall low ($\pm$ 25 cm per year) and unpredictable, the erosion rates are high but not as high as those in the rigorous climate of northeastern Greenland. Studies of bristlecone pines in Utah and California have allowed an estimate of erosion rates on a time base of hundreds and even thousands of years (Eardley, 1967). Thus the pines, which may reach 4000 years in age, betray the amount of erosion during their lifetime by the amount of exposure of their root systems. The depth of exposed roots on living trees is a measure of the amount the land surface has been reduced since the tree began to grow. Rates of low ering in general vary with exposure (greater on north-facing slopes) and with declivity of slopes (greater on steeper slopes). On the average, the rate varies between about 2 cm per 1000 years on slopes of 5 degrees and 10 cm on slopes of 30 degrees. A total of 42 observations indicate a direct relation between the erosion rate and the sine of the slope.

A different sort of study, this one in the rain forest of New Guinea Mountains, has yielded the estimate that between 1 and 2 cm per 1000 years is lost from the area by landslides alone (Simonett, 1967). How much additional material is lost through the agency of other processes is not known.

Archaeological sites may yield in-

formation on erosional rates and have, as in the case of the bristlecone pines, a fairly long time base. Data collected in Italy show that for the sites studied the range in rates is 30 to 100 cm per 1000 years (Judson, 1968).

These are but a sample of the type of information that abounds in the literature on the rate of erosion. They are enough, however, to indicate how variable the rates can be when, as in the examples cited, the observation is for a single spot or limited area. Not only are they highly variable but they can hardly be representative of rates of erosion over large areas. It is apparent that the material eroded in one spot may be deposited nearby, at least temporarily, and thus the net loss to an area may be little or nothing. Erosion is more rapid at some spots than others for any one of many different reasons. Material removed from its position at any single spot on the landscape follows a slow, halting, devious course as natural processes transport it from the land to the ocean.

River Records

When we ask now how much material is being lost by the continents to the ocean, the spot measurements such as those reported above are of little help. We need some method of integrating these rates over larger areas. One way to do this is to measure material carried by a stream from its drainage basin at the point where the stream leaves the basin. Alternatively, the amount of sediment deposited in a reservoir or in a natural lake over a specific length of time is indicative of the rate at which the land has been worn away in the basin lying upstream. The mass of sediments accumulated in unit time can be averaged out over the area of the contributing drainage basin to produce an erosion rate. Of course the erosion rate is not uniform over the entire basin, but it is convenient for our purposes here to assume that it is.

If we examine the solid load of a stream carried in suspension past a gauging station we discover that the amount of material per unit area of the drainage basin varies considerably according to a number of factors. But, if we hold the size of the drainage basin relatively constant, we find pronounced correlation between erosion and precipitation. Figure 1 is based on data presented by Langbein and Schumm (1958) from about 100 sediment gauging stations in basins averaging 3900 sq km. It suggests that a maximum rate of erosion is reached in areas of limited rainfall ($\pm$ 25 cm per year) and decreases in more arid as well as in more humid lands.

Considering small drainage basins (averaging 78 km^2), Langbein and Schumm also show a similar variation in erosion with rainfall, but at rates which are 2 to 3 times as rapid as for the larger basins. In still smaller basins erosion rates increase even more. A small drainage basin in the Loess Hills of Iowa, having an area of 3.4 km^2 provides an extreme example. Here sediments are being removed at a rate which produces a lowering for the basin of 12.8 m per 1000 years.

We have data based on river records for larger areas. Judson and Ritter (1964) have surveyed the regional erosion rates in the United States and have shown that, on the average, erosion is proceeding at about 6 cm^2 per 1000 years. Here too, as shown in Table 1, there are variations. These appear to be related to climate as in the smaller areas already discussed. Greatest erosion occurs in the dry Colorado River basin. In examining the rates of regional erosion we note that although erosion rates increase with decrease in discharge per unit area, they do not increase quite as rapidly as

Table 1 Rates of regional erosion in the United States (After Judson and Ritter, 1964)

Drainage Region	Drainage[1] Area Km^2 $\times 10^3 \times 10^3$	Runoff m^3/sec	Load tons Km^2/yr			Erosion cm/1000 yr	% Area sampled	Avg. years of record
			Dissolved	Solid	Total			
Colorado	629	0.6	23	417	440	17	56	32
Pacific Slopes, California	303	2.3	36	209	245	9	44	4
Western Gulf	829	1.6	41	101	142	5	9	9
Mississippi	3238	17.5	39	94	133	5	99	12
S. Atlantic & Eastern Gulf	736	9.2	61	48	109	4	19	7
N. Atlantic	383	5.9	57	69	126	5	10	5
Columbia	679	9.8	57	44	101	4	39	<2
Totals	6797	46.9	43	119	162	6		

[1] Great Basin, St. Lawrence, Hudson Bay drainage not considered.

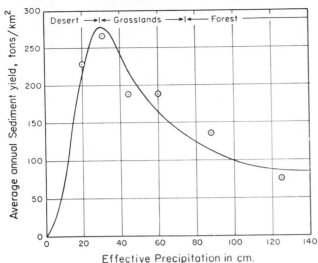

FIG. 1. Variation of the yield of sediments with precipitation. Effective precipitation is defined as precipitation necessary to produce a given amount of runoff. (After Langbein and Schumm, 1958.)

the major component, the detrital load, increases. This is so because the absolute dissolved load decreases with decreasing discharge per unit area. This inverse relation between solid and dissolved load is shown in Fig. 2.

These data suggest that on the average the United States is now being eroded at a rate which reduces the land surface by 6 cm each 1000 years. Actually the rate is somewhat less when we consider that the area of the Great Basin, with no discharge to the sea, is

not included in these figures—and that for all practical purposes the net loss from this area is presently close to zero.

Effect of Man

What effect does man's use of the land have on the rate at which it is destroyed by natural forces? Three examples are cited here:

Bonatti and Hutchinson have described cores from a small volcanic crater lake, Lago di Monterosi, 41 km

FIG. 2. Relation by regions in the United States between solid load and dissolved load in tons/km²/yr. (After Judson and Ritter, 1964.)

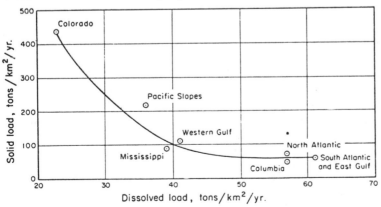

north of Rome. (See Judson, 1968, note 3.) An archaeological survey of the environs of the lake indicate that intense human activity dates from approximately the second century B.C. when the Via Cassia was constructed through the area. At this moment the cores indicate a sudden increase of sedimentation in the lake. The rate varies somewhat but continues high to the present. Extrapolation of the sedimentation rate in the lake to the surrounding watershed shows that prior to intensive occupation by man (that is, prior to the second century B.C.) the erosion rate was 2 to 3 cm per 1000 years. Thereafter it rose abruptly to an average of about 20 cm per 1000 years.

Ursic and Dendy (1965) have studied the annual sediment yields from individual watersheds in northern Mississippi. The results of their data are shown in Fig. 3. These indicate that, when the land is intensively cultivated, the rate of sediment production and hence the rate of erosion is three orders of magnitude or more above that experienced from areas with mature forest cover or from pine plantations.

Wolman (1967) has described the variation of sediment yield with land use for an area near Washington, D. C. These data are summarized in Fig. 4. They show that, under original forest conditions, erosion proceeded at the low rate of about 0.2 cm per 1000 years. With the rapid increase of farm-

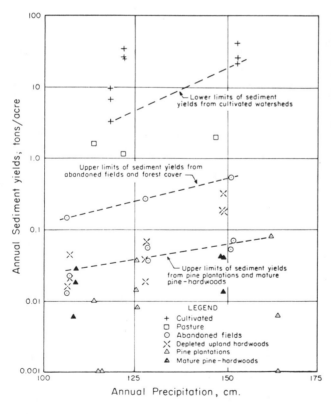

FIG. 3. Variation in sediment yields from individual watersheds in northern Mississippi under different types of land use and changing amounts of precipitation. One ton/acre equals 224 tons/km². (After Ursic and Dendy, 1965.)

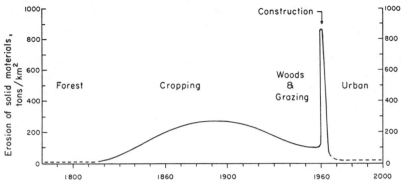

FIG. 4. A sequence of land use changes and sediment yield beginning prior to the advent of extensive farming and continuing through a period of construction and subsequent urban landscape. Based on experience in the Middle Atlantic region of the United States. (After Wolman, 1967.)

land in the early nineteenth century the rate increased to approximately 10 cm per 1000 years. With the return of some of this land to grazing and forest in the 1940's and 1950's this high rate of erosion was reduced perhaps by one-half. Areas undergoing construction during the 1960's show yields which exceed 100,000 tons per square kilometer for very small areas, which approximate a rate of lowering of 10 m per 1000 years. For completely urban areas the erosion rates are low, less than 1 cm per 1000 years.

There is no question that man's occupancy of the land increases the rate of erosion. Where that occupation is intense and is directed toward the use of land for cultivated crops the difference is one or more orders of magnitude greater than when the land is under a complete natural vegetative cover such as grass or forest. The intervention of man in the geologic processes raises questions when we begin to consider the rates of erosion for the earth as a whole and to apply modern rates to the processes of the past before man was a factor in promoting erosion.

Ian Douglas (1967) postulates that man's use of the landscape has so increased the rates of erosion that they far exceed those of the past before man became an important geologic agent. He presents persuasive data and arguments to suggest that any computation of present-day erosion rates on a world-wide basis are unrepresentative of those that pre-date man's tampering with the landscape. So, as we turn to the question of world-wide erosion, we will want to distinguish between present-day rates which are profoundly affected by man's activity and those of the immediate past before man introduced grazing, agriculture, and other activities.

Let us first attempt an estimate of erosion before man began to affect the process. It is estimated that approximately one fourth of the United States is in cropland. If this area is now undergoing a rate of erosion ten times that of its natural rate then, for the United States as a whole, the increase of rate of erosion because of man's use of the land increases the rate of the removal of solid particles from the earth's crust by a factor of a little over three times. Assuming that this is correct and that the dissolved load does not change appreciably, then, as a first approximation, the present rates of erosion listed in Table 1 for the United States would be decreased to approximately 3 cm per 1000 years, which is about 78 tons per square kilometer per year. This figure would apply then to the area of the United States before the intervention of man with intensive agricultural practices.

Rates for Entire Earth

What can we say now about the rate of erosion for the entire earth? Presented in Table 2 are data for approximately 10 per cent of the earth's surface. The table includes erosional data for the drainage basins for the Amazon, the world's largest river; the Congo; and for that part of United States covered in Table 1. Here, however, the data for the United States have been adjusted to account for the increased rates of erosion presumed to have occurred because of man's cultivation of the land. Neither the Congo nor the Amazon basins are significantly affected by man. For the 15 million square kilometers of these three areas the average rate of erosion is 3.6 cm per 1000 years, or 93 tons per square kilometer annually.

Let us accept the figures just given as representative of erosion rates prior to man's intervention in the process and use them to extrapolate to erosion rates for the whole area of the earth. The earth's land surface has approximately 151 million square kilometers, but much of this area has no streams which drain directly to the ocean. For example, a large area of western United States is without direct drainage to the sea, as is a large percentage, about 50 per cent, of Australia. Areas of little or no drainage to the sea are estimated to occupy approximately one third of the earth's surface. So for our purposes we estimate that 100 million kilometers of the earth's surface are

Table 2 Rates of erosion for the Amazon River Basin, United States and Congo River Basin

Drainage region	Drainage area Km$^2 \times$ 10^6	Load, tons $\times$ 10^6/yr			Tons Km^2/yr	Erosion cm/1000 yr
		Dissolved	Solid	Total		
Amazon River[1]						
Basin	6.3	232	548[2]	780	124	4.7
United States[3]	6.8	292	248[3]	540	78	3.0
Congo River[4]						
Basin	2.5	99	34[2]	133	53	2.0
Totals	15.6	623	830	1453	93	3.6

[1] From Gibbs, 1967.
[2] Solid load increased by considering bed load as 10% of suspended load.
[3] From Judson and Ritter, 1964. Solid load reduced to adjust for increased erosion because of man's activity.
[4] From Spronck, 1941, quoted in Gibbs 1967.

contributing sediments directly to the sea by running water. In addition to this there is a certain amount of wind erosion, and part of the materials eroded by the wind are delivered to the sea. It is even more difficult to find data on the amounts of regional erosion by wind than it is by running water. We have some preliminary estimates for the amount of eolian material which has been dumped into the oceans. These lie between 1 and 0.25 mm per 1000 years.[2] Whatever the figure, wind erosion of the land is volumetrically unimportant when compared with the amount of material carried by the streams.

We can estimate, then, the amount of sediment carried as solids and as dissolved material from the continents each year to the ocean basins as 9.3 × 10^9 tons. This figure is based on the assumption that, on the average, 3.6 cm per 1000 years are eroded from the 100 million square kilometers of land which are estimated to drain into the oceans. Further, the figure attempts to eliminate the effect on the erosion rate of man's activity. If we include an estimate for the amount of erosion by wind action then this figure increases by an amount approximating 10^8 tons. Glacier ice may add a similar amount.

We can now compare this estimate of the tonnage of eroded materials with other estimates in the following paragraphs and Table 3.

Barth (1962) presents data on some geochemical cycles indicating that weathering of the land produces on the average of 2.5 kg per cm^2 per million years. From this figure we calculate that the average tonnage per year of all material, dissolved and solid, would be 3.8 × 10^9 tons which seems low. Strakhov (1967) quotes Lopatin

Table 3. Estimates of world-wide erosion rates by various authors. All material assumed to reach the oceans

	10^9 metric tons/yr
Carried by rivers	
Dissolved load	
Livingstone (1963)	3.9
Clarke (1924)	2.7
Solid load[1]	
Fournier (1960) as calculated by Holeman (1968)	58
Kuenen (1950)	32.5
Schumm (1963) as calculated by Holeman (1968)	20.5
Holeman 1968	18.3
MacKenzie and Garrels (1967)	8.3
Combined solid and dissolved loads	
Lopatin (1950)[1]	17.5
Judson (this paper)[2]	9.3
Barth (1962)[2]	3.8
Carried by wind from land	
Calculated from various sources	0.06–0.36
Carried by glacier ice	
Estimated	0.1

[1] Does not include bed load.

[2] Solid load includes both suspended and bed load.

(1950) to the effect that annual dissolved and solid loads of the rivers total 17.5×10^9 tons of which 4.9×10^9 tons are dissolved material. Two other estimates on dissolved loads should be quoted. Clarke (1924) estimates 2.7×10^9 tons per year and Livingstone (1963) 3.9×10^9 tons per year. This last figure can be duplicated by extrapolation of the data in Table 3. Livingstone indicates that the figure might be high. Indeed new figures on the salinity and discharge of the Amazon River by Gibbs (1967) indicate that Livingstone's figure should be adjusted downward by 5 per cent.

MacKenzie and Garrels (1966) estimate that the rivers of the world carry 8.3×10^9 tons of *solid material alone* to the oceans each year. In arriving at this figure they adopted from Livingstone an average annual world-wide runoff of 3.3×10^{16} liters and an average suspended sediment concentration equal to that of the Mississippi River. If man's occupancy has indeed increased erosion rates as we have suggested, then this figure is high. Kuenen (1950) gives an estimate for solid load of 32.5×10^9 tons per year, a high estimate, the basis for which is not clear.

Even higher is the estimate of 58×10^9 tons of suspended load calculated by Holeman (1968) from data in Fournier (1960). Douglas (1967) points out that the data presented by Fournier seem to be strongly influenced by man's activity. Holeman also extrapolates data of Schumm (1963), from selected drainage basins in central United States to obtain a figure of 18.3×10^9 tons of suspended sediment per year. These data, too, are affected by man. Holeman, himself (1968), presents suspended sediment data for rivers draining 39 million square kilometers of the earth's surface, and extrapolates this to the approximately 100 million square kilometers of land surface draining to the ocean. He obtains a figure of 18.3×10^9 tons per year of suspended sediments carried annually to the oceans. The figure is strongly affected by data from the Asiatic rivers, particularly those of China, India, and the Southeast. These provide 80 per cent of the total sediment from 25 per cent of the land area in Holeman's figures. These are the same areas where the world's greatest population is concentrated and where the largest areas of intensive agriculture are located.

Let us now estimate the present rate of erosion. In this the major component is the suspended load carried by rivers. Of the data available, Holeman's appear to be the most inclusive and reliable. Allowing the bed load to be 10 per cent of suspended load and adding these two figures to the dissolved load as calculated by Livingstone, then the total material delivered annually to the sea by rivers at the present is 24×10^9 metric tons. This is about two and one half times the rate that we estimated existed before man started tampering with the landscape on a large scale (See Table 4).

Returning now to our estimate of the material produced by erosion be-

Table 4 Mass of material estimated as moved annually by rivers to the ocean before and after the intervention of man

	10^9 metric tons
Before man's intervention	9.3
After man's intervention	24

fore the serious intervention by man, we should be able to check our figure by comparing it with the amount of material deposited annually in the oceans. Thus far our only way of determining annual sedimentation rates over large areas is to average them out over the last several thousand years. Because man has only recently become a world-wide influence on erosion, this averaging serves to curtail his impact on the rate of accumulation of the sedimentary record.

What figures do we have on sedimentation in the oceans? Large areas of the ocean floor and the rates at which sedimentation takes place there are but dimly known at the present. We have data from coring of the ocean bottom but our data are scanty at best. In considering the tonnage which settles annually to the ocean floors we should distinguish between the deep oceans and the shallower oceans. As far as sedimentation goes there is probably a difference between those ocean floors lying below 3000 m and those above 3000 m. For the deep seas —those below 3000 m—current figures suggest something like 4.2×10^{-4} gm per cm^2 per year.[3] Spread over the nearly 280,000,000 km^2 of area for the deep sea, this amounts to 1.17×10^9 tons of sediments per year. Estimates for the shallower waters are probably less reliable than for the deep waters. For those waters shallower than 3000 m, about 72,000,000 km^2, I have assumed that between 10 and 20 cm of sediment accumulates every thousand years. Given a density of 0.7, there would be approximately 7 to 14×10^{-3} gm deposited for each square centimeter per year. This is equivalent to a total tonnage of between 5 and 10 $\times$

10^9 tons per year. Totaling the tonnage for the deep and shallow waters, we have a range of 6.2 to 11.2×10^9 tons. Most of this is provided by the rivers. Wind provides an estimated 10^8 tons per year. The contribution of ice is also estimated as 10^8 tons. Extra-terrestrial material is estimated by various authors as between 3.5×10^4 to 1.4×10^5 tons per year (Barker and Anders, 1968). Table 5 compares the estimate of the amount of material deposited each year in the oceans with the estimate of the amount delivered by various agents annually to the oceans. In both estimates we have tried to eliminate the effect of man.

Whether we use the rate of erosion prevailing before or after man's advent, our figures pose the problem of why our continents have survived. If we accept the rate of sediment production as 10^{10} metric tons per year (the pre-human intervention figure) then the continents are being lowered at the rate of 2.4 cm per 1000 years. At this rate the ocean basins, with a volume of 1.37×10^{18} m^3, would be filled in 340 million years. The geologic record indicates that this has never happened in the past, and there is no reason to believe it will happen in the geologically foreseeable future. Furthermore, at the present rate of erosion, the continents, which now average 875 m in elevation, would be reduced to close to sea level in about 34 million years. But the geologic record shows a continuous sedimentary history, and hence a continuous source of sediments. So we reason that the continents have always been high enough to supply sediments to the oceans.

Geologists long ago concluded that the earth was a dynamic system, being

Table 5 Estimated mass of material deposited annually in the oceans compared with estimated mass of material delivered annually to the oceans by different agents[1]

	10^9 metric tons/year
Estimated mass of material deposited in ocean	
Oceans shallower than 3000 meters	5–10
Oceans deeper than 3000 meters	1.17
Total	6.2–11.2
Estimated mass of material delivered to oceans	
From continents	
By rivers	9.3
By wind	0.06–0.36
By glacier ice	0.1
From extraterrestrial sources	0.00035–0.14
Total	~9.6

[1] Man's influence on rates of erosion is excluded from estimates.

destroyed in some places and renewed in others. Such a state would help resolve the problem of what happens to the sediments and why continents persist. Thus, although the sediments are carried from continents to oceans to form sedimentary rocks, we know that these rocks may be brought again to the continental surface. There they are in turn eroded and the products of erosion returned to the ocean. These sedimentary rocks may also be subjected to pressures and temperatures which convert them from sedimentary rocks to metamorphic rocks. If this pressure and temperature is great enough, the metamorphic rocks in turn will melt and become the parent material of igneous rock. These relationships are the well known rock cycle which has been going on as long as we can read the earth's rock record.

Inasmuch as we have been talking about the sedimentary aspects of the rock cycle, we should ask how much time it takes to complete at least the sedimentary route within the whole cycle. Poldervaart (1954) gives the total mass of sediments (including the sedimentary rocks) as 1.7×10^{18} tons. Taking the annual production of sediments as 10^{10} tons, then one turn in the sedimentary cycle approximates 1.7×10^8 years. At the present rates then we could fit in about 25 such cycles during the 4.5 billion years of earth history.

Accepting Poldervaart's figure of 2.4×10^{19} tons as the mass of the earth's crust then there has been time enough for a mass equivalent to the earth's crust to have moved two times through the sedimentary portion of the cycle.

We began this review with a brief examination of the homely process of erosion. As we continued we found that man has appeared on the scene as an important geologic agent, increasing the rates of erosion by a factor of two or three. We end the review face to face with larger problems. Regardless of the role of man, the reality of continental erosion raises anew the question of the nature and origin of the forces that drive our continents above sea level. In short, we now seek the mechanics of continental survival.

Notes

[1] Data on erosion are expressed in metric tons per square kilometer and as centimeters of lowering either per year or per thousand years. A specific gravity of 2.6 is assumed for material eroded from the land.

[2] Although data are very incomplete the interested reader will find some specific information in Bonatti and Arrhenius (1965); Delany, *et al.* (1967); Folger and Heezen (in press); Goldberg and Griffin (1964); Rex and Goldberg (1958, 1962); and Riseborough, *et al.* (1968).

[3] I use data from deep sea cores as reported by Ku, Broecker and Opdyke, 1968. In calculating weights of sediments from rates of sedimentation I have used a density of 0.7 per cm^3 (Ku, personal communication, 1968) and sedimentation rates which include original $CaCO_3$ content.

References

Barker, John L., Jr. and Edward Anders, 1968. Accretion rate of cosmic matter from iridium and osmium contents of deep-sea sediments. *Geochimica et Cosmochimica Acta*, *32*, p. 627–645.

Barth, T. F. W., 1962. *Theoretical Petrology*. 2nd edition. John Wiley & Sons, Inc.: New York and London, 416 pp.

Bonatti, E. and G. Arrhenius, 1965. Eolian sedimentation in the Pacific off northern Mexico. *Marine Geology*, *3*, p. 337–348.

Clarke, F. W., 1924. Data of geochemistry, 5th edition, *U. S. Geological Survey, Bulletin 770*, 841 p.

Delany, A. C. *et al.*, 1967. Airborne dust collected at Barbados. *Geochimica et Cosmochimica Acta*, *31*, p. 885–909.

Douglas, Ian, 1967. Man, vegetation and the sediment yields of rivers. *Nature*, *215*, Pt. 2, p. 925–928.

Eardley, A. G., 1967. Rates of denudation as measured by bristlecone pines, Cedar Breaks, Utah. *Utah Geological and Mineralogical Survey, Special Studies*, *21*, 13 p.

Folger, D. W. and B. C. Heezen. (in press), Trans Atlantic sediment transport by wind. (abstract) *Geological Society of America*. Special paper.

Fournier, F., 1960. *Climat et Erosion*, Presses Universitaires de France.

Geikie, Archibald, 1880. Rock-weathering as illustrated in Edinburgh church yards. *Proceedings, Royal Society, Edinburgh*, *10*, p. 518–532.

Gibbs, R. J., 1967. The geochemistry of the Amazon River system: Part I, *Bulletin, Geological Society of America*, *78*, p. 1203–1232.

Goldberg, E. D. and J. J. Griffin, 1964. Sedimentation rates and mineralogy in the South Atlantic. *Jour. of Geophysical Research*, *69*, p. 4293–4309.

Holeman, John N., 1968. The Sediment Yield of Major Rivers of the World. *Water Resources Research*, *4*, No. 4, p. 737–747.

Hutton, James, 1795. *Theory of the earth*. Vol. 2, Edinburgh.

Judson, Sheldon, 1968. Erosion rates near Rome, Italy. *Science*, *160*, p. 1444–1446.

Judson, Sheldon and D. F. Ritter, 1964. Rates of regional denudation in the United States. *Journal of Geophysical Research*, *69*, p. 3395–3401.

Ku, Teh-Lung, W. S. Broecker, and Neil Opdyke, 1968. Comparison of sedimentation rates measured by paleomagnetic and the ionium methods of age determinations. *Earth and Planetary Science Letters*, *4*, p. 1–16.

Kuenen, Ph. H., 1950. *Marine Geology*. John Wiley and Sons: New York and London, 551 p.

Langbein, W. B. and S. A. Schumm, 1958. Yield of sediment in relation to mean annual precipitation. *Transactions, American Geophysical Union*, *39*, p. 1076–1084.

Leet, L. Don and Sheldon Judson, 1965. *Physical Geology*. 3d edition. Prentice-Hall, Inc.: Englewood Cliffs, N. J., 406 p.

Livingstone, D. A., 1963. Chemical Composition of Rivers and Lakes. *U. S. Geological Survey Professional Paper 440-G.*, 64 p.

Lopatin, G. V., 1950. Erosion and detrital discharge. *Priroda*, No. 7. (Quoted by Strakhov, 1967.)

MacKenzie, F. T. and R. M. Garrels, 1966. Chemical mass balance between rivers and oceans. *American Journal of Science*, 264, p. 507–525.

Matthias, George F., 1967. Weathering rates of Portland arkose tombstones. *Journal of Geological Education*, 15, p. 140–144.

Musgrave, G. W., 1954. Estimating land erosion-sheet erosion. *Association Internationale d' Hydrologie Scientifique, Assemblée Générale de Rome*, 1, p. 207–215.

Poldervaart, Arie, 1954. Chemistry of the earth's crust, in *Crust of the earth*. Edited by A. Poldervaart. Geological Society of America Special Paper 62, p. 119–144.

Rex, R. W. and E. D. Goldberg, 1958. Quartz content of pelagic sediments of the Pacific Ocean. *Tellus*, 10, p. 153–159.

———, 1962. Insolubles. in M. Hill, ed. *The Sea*, Interscience: New York, vol. 1, p. 295–312.

Riseborough, R. W., R. J. Huggett, J. J. Griffin, and E. D. Goldberg, 1968. Pesticides: Transatlantic movements in the northeast trades. *Science*, 159, p. 1233–1236.

Schumm, S. A., 1963. The disparity between present rates of denudation and orogeny, *U. S. Geological Survey*, Prof. Paper 454H, p. 1–13.

Simonett, David S., 1967. Landslide distribution and earthquakes in the Bewani and Torricelli Mountains, New Guinea, in *Landscape Studies from Australia and New Guinea*, Edited by J. N. Jennings and J. A. Mabbutt, Australian National University Press: Canberra, p. 64–84.

Spronck, R. 1941. Measures hydrographique effectuées dans la region divagante du Bief Maritime du Fleuve Congo. *Brussels, Institute Royale Colonial Belge Memoire*, 156 p. (quoted by Gibbs, 1967).

Strakhov, N. M. 1967, *Principles of Lithogenesis*, vol. 1. Translated from the 1962 Russian edition by J. P. Fitzsimmons. Oliver and Boyd: Edinburgh and London, 245 p.

Ursic, S. J. and F. E. Dendy, 1965. Sediment yields from small watersheds under various land uses and forest covers. *Proceedings of the Federal Inter-Agency Sedimentation Conference, 1963, U. S. Department of Agriculture*, Miscellaneous Publications 970, p. 47–52.

Washburn, A. L., 1967. Instrumental observations of mass-wasting in the Mesters Vig district, northeast Greenland. *Meddeleser om Gronland*, 166, No. 4, p. 1–296.

Wolman, M. G., 1967. A cycle of sedimentation and erosion in urban river channels. *Geografiska Annaler*, 49-A, p. 385–395.

16   Shoreline Structures as a Cause of Shoreline Erosion: A Review

James G. Rosenbaum

Introduction

Shoreline erosion is an increasingly serious worldwide problem. In the United States alone, about one fourth of the 84,000 miles (140,000 km.) of shoreline are presently subject to ero-

Mr. Rosenbaum is a consulting geologist in Milwaukee, Wisconsin.

sion (U. S. Army, Corps of Engineers, 1971).

Along ocean coastlines, increased erosion is often attributed to a slight rise in world sea level since the turn of the century, coupled with unusually severe storms. Similarly, persons living along the Great Lakes of the United States often attribute erosion to high lake levels. In fact, it is man's activities that have disrupted fundamental shoreline processes, creating a potential for erosion which is realized whenever nature is less than benign. According to Inman and Brush (1973), two major types of man-made disruptions are:

1. Dams. Artificial impoundments behind dams act as settling basins for sediment which would otherwise nourish beaches on the coastline.

2. Shoreline structures such as harbor breakwaters, jetties, groins, and landfills. The present report will discuss how these shoreline structures cause erosion.

The Littoral Drift

Littoral drift is common to virtually all coastlines of the world and is basic to an understanding of the mechanism of erosion. Littoral drift is the term applied to sediment which moves laterally along the shore. This movement is induced by the action of waves breaking at an angle to the shore, and operates principally in the narrow zone from the breaker line to the beach (Zenkovitch, 1960; Ingle, 1966; Komar, 1971; Inman and Brush, 1973). Within this zone, sand transport is greatest where waves break in conjunction with topographic highs, as at the offshore bar and the seaward face of the beach. On a given coastline individual storms may move shore material in one direction or another, but over a longer period of time there is a well defined net movement in one direction. This net movement is the subject of the present discussion. The direction towards which material moves is termed downdrift. The direction from which material moves is termed updrift. This movement is an entirely normal process, and does not lead to a loss of shore material. Relative to a fixed observer, material moving downdrift is replaced by material which had been updrift. On a stable shoreline, sediment in the littoral zone is essentially a steady state collection of drift. Man-made structures upset this equilibrium (Fig. 2).

Consideration of the Action of a Single Structure

For many people, the presence of shoreline harbor breakwaters, jetties, groins, and landfills may be reassuring, since these engineering works signify that man has "made a stand against the sea." Ironically, such structures are actually responsible for much erosion. They alter the natural distribution of shoreline material. Areas subject to severe erosion do not occur uniformly along the shorelines, as one might expect if high water levels or storms were the principle cause of erosion (Davis et al., 1973). Instead, severely eroding shorelines are frequently downdrift of man-made structures. Field studies and reviews of case histories, (Spring, 1914; Caldwell, 1950; Johnson, 1957; Hartley, 1964; and Dyhr-Nielsen and Sorensen, 1968), laboratory tank models (Kressner, 1928; Johnson, 1948; Dyhr-Nielsen and Sorensen, 1968; Sato and Irie, 1970), and mathematical models (Bakker, 1968; Dean and Jones, 1974) have considered the effects of various man-made structures and have determined that these effects are quite predictable.

A groin is a solid, occasionally permeable, narrow structure, which projects seaward approximately perpen-

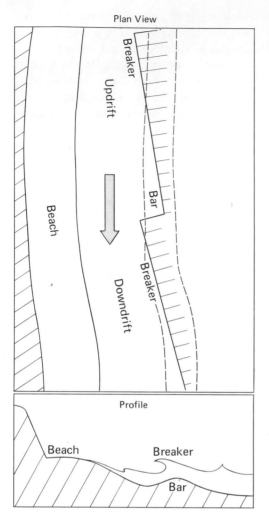

Plan View

Breaker

Updrift

Beach

Bar

Breaker

Downdrift

Profile

Beach   Breaker

Bar

FIG. 1. Normal shoreline with an off-shore bar (after Ingle, 1966). Arrow indicates the direction of the net littoral drift. Sand transport is greatest where waves break in conjunction with topographic highs; i.e., at the offshore bar and at the seaward face of the beach (Zenkovitch, 1960).

dicular to the beach. It usually rises several feet above water level. Groins are built to trap littoral drift, and by doing so cause an abnormally wide accumulation of beach material updrift, which can thus provide protection for a limited section of shoreline.

The sequence of shoreline changes following placement of a groin (or other structures attached to the shore, such as harbor breakwaters or jetties) suggests that there are two distinct

phases in the erosion history of the region downdrift.

Phase 1

During an initial phase, the groin acts as a complete barrier to littoral drift (Fig. 2a, 2b). Immediately after construction, material will accumulate updrift of the groin. As drift material continues to encounter the groin, it will also migrate seaward into water that is deep relative to the depths at which it

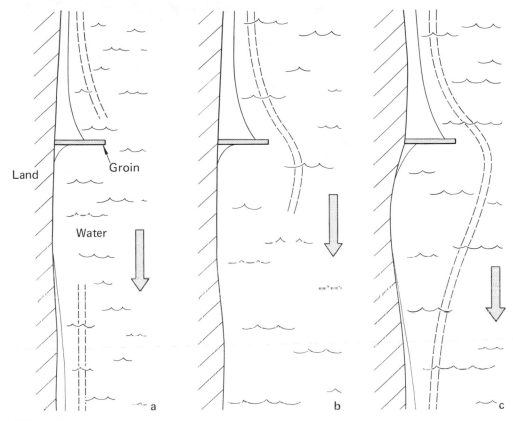

Land

Groin

Water

a   b   c

FIG. 2. Successive stages of shoreline condition after emplacement of a groin. Although not shown here, the land area downdrift of the groin may recede during the time of a and b. In Fig. 2c, a limited region downdrift of the groin remains deprived of sediment nourishment, and may continue to erode indefinitely.

would otherwise move along the shore. Flow velocities near the bottom at these greater depths are insufficient to maintain transport of most drift material, so deposition occurs. Such deposition will cause the bottom to shoal until wave action is again able to move all drift material.

The volume of material comprising the accretion updrift and offshore of the groin does not reach the shoreline farther downdrift, where it would have traveled prior to construction of the groin. Downdrift beaches will thus have a negative sand budget. The material they lose to beaches even farther downdrift will not be replaced until the impoundment capacity of the groin or jetty is exceeded.

A well known case history, in which a large structure acted as a complete littoral barrier, is the shore-attached breakwater at Santa Barbara, California (Wiegel, 1964). This breakwater was constructed in 1930. Until a dredging program was initiated to move material downdrift past the harbor, beaches were affected for up to 23 miles (38 km) downdrift (W. C. Krumbein, personal communication).

Phase 2

Beach and bar accumulation will eventually stabilize updrift and offshore of the groin. After sufficient offshore shoaling has occurred, sediment is able to continue moving past the groin (Fig. 2b) and gradually approaches the coast, as shown in Fig. 2c (U. S. Army Coastal Engineering Research Center, 1973, pp. 5–34). On barred shorelines, this transport will take place along a rebuilt outer bar (Fig. 2c), which had earlier disappeared (Fig. 2a, 2b) due to lack of sediment nourishment (Dyhr-Nielsen and Sorensen, 1970). Because this material will not reach its normal position on the shoreline for a certain distance downdrift, a section of shoreline downdrift of the groin will remain deprived of its normal sand nourishment, and will continue to erode indefinitely. In the author's experience, the length of continually eroding shoreline is frequently from 3 to 5 times the distance by which the structure projects seaward from the shore. Beaches at a greater distance downdrift, which were starved during phase 1, may return to normal (Inman and Brush, 1973). The time before onset of this recovery varies widely, depending on the size of the structure, the volume of littoral drift, and offshore topography. On Lake Michigan near Milwaukee, Wisconsin, one or two years might elapse before phase 2 is reached downdrift of a moderate size groin.

Downdrift and inshore of single-arm breakwaters, shoreline changes are commonly caused by wave refraction and diffraction (Johnson and Eagleson, 1966), as well as by the more general

nourishment problems already discussed. The altered wave regime may cause a local reversal of the littoral drift, which then removes sediment from an area downdrift and deposits it in the lee of the breakwater. Deposition will continue until the shoreline has aligned itself with the new wave front, at which time the reversed littoral drift will be eliminated. However, downdrift beaches appear to remain undernourished (Johnson and Eagleson, 1966, Fig. 9.43). A somewhat similar process takes place at detached breakwaters.

Self Propagating Nature of Shoreline Structures

Severe erosion downdrift of shoreline structures often prompts construction of additional structures in an attempt to stop that erosion. These second generation structures almost invariably cause erosion downdrift in a region which previously had been unaffected by the first generation structure. Third generation structures might then be built, causing additional erosion, and so forth (Schijf, 1959; Inman and Brush, 1973). Lawsuits brought by parties suffering erosion attributable to structures updrift may become an additional problem (Lillevang, 1965). Federal, state and local authorities may allow construction, but this will not be complete defense to such suits.

Attention has been drawn to the temporary erosion which occurs during phase 1 on shorelines far downdrift of a new groin (Fig. 2b). Installation of additional structures is a common response to this erosion. This is unfortunate, since beach nourishment on such shorelines often returns to normal

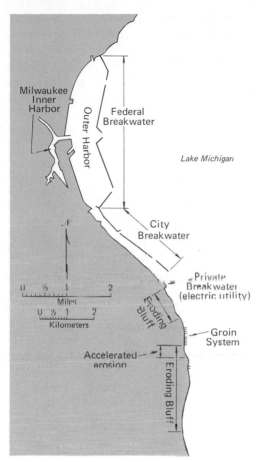

FIG. 3. Lake Michigan shoreline structures at Milwaukee, Wisconsin. The longshore drift is from north to south. The Federal breakwater was built in stages from 1881 to 1929. The city breakwater was constructed in stages from 1916 to 1930. The utility company's breakwater was built in 1920 and the groins in 1933–34.

during phase 2 (Inman and Brush, 1973). The additional structures may be needless, and may themselves cause further downdrift erosion.

The history of some major shoreline projects in Milwaukee, Wisconsin, typifies the way in which shoreline structures propagate (Fig. 3). The federal government constructed the main harbor breakwater in stages from 1881 to 1929. Construction progressed from north to south. By 1916, downdrift erosion had become severe enough to cause the city of Milwaukee to construct a rubble mound breakwater approximately 1000 feet offshore, and extending southward parallel to the shore. It terminated at a position opposite the small breakwater of a local utility. The city's rubble breakwater was built from 1916 to 1931. It was observed that the shoreline opposite the end of the structure experienced severe erosion, and that "as the breakwater was extended from year to year, the point of greatest erosion on the shore kept pace" (Milwaukee County, 1945).

The utility's landfill and small breakwater, built in 1920, probably compounded erosion to the south until 1930–1931, when its effects would have been largely masked by the overlapping city breakwater.

In 1933–1934 a system of eleven permeable groins was placed to protect the downdrift third of a 1½ mile section of eroding parkland that extended south of the termination of the new rubble breakwater. In turn, the groin system is currently responsible for accelerated erosion for at least ¼ mile to the south. To protect this and other eroding areas a citizen task force on lakefront planning has recently proposed construction of a series of offshore islands, each one being several miles long, up to a mile wide, and 3000–5000 feet offshore. If ever built, these islands, which function similar to a detached breakwater, would undoubtedly cause extremely severe erosion for many miles downdrift.

Solutions

Proposals for avoiding downdrift erosion caused by shoreline structures include building new and different structures, removing structures, bypassing sediment around structures, and zoning to forbid structures.

Artificial filling of the accretion zone updrift from a new groin is partially effective in reducing downdrift erosion (U. S. Army Coastal Engineering Research Center, 1973). It is thought that such fill allows an uninterrupted movement of drift past the structure. To be most effective, fill should not only cover the subaerial part of the new shoreline, but should also extend a considerable distance offshore. This practice is usually ignored. However, even an elaborate program of artificial filling should be followed by periodic renourishment, otherwise "starved"

beaches would be expected to occur along a region downdrift of the structure (U. S. Army, Corps of Engineers, 1973, p. 5-45). The mechanism of sediment loss would be the same as that of phase 2, outlined above (Fig. 2c).

Of course, artificial filling requires a source of fill that is hydrodynamically stable. At the present time, sources of suitable beach fill are often not readily available, partly because they have been exhausted, and partly because the process of obtaining the fill would cause physical disturbance in other sectors of the environment.

Detached offshore breakwaters parallel to the shoreline have been proposed as a solution, the concept being that they will provide shelter from wave action, but will not interfere with the littoral drift. Johnson (1957) has shown that the latter assumption is erroneous. Unless the breakwater is separated from the shore by a distance of three to six times its length, the lack of turbulence in its lee will cause sediment deposition (Inman and Frautschy, 1965). Deposits have been known to extend all the way from the shoreline out to the breakwater, forming a tombolo. Erosion downdrift will accompany this deposition. However, as discussed below, this ability of detached offshore breakwaters to trap sand may be used to great advantage.

Realization of the damaging effect of groins often prompts efforts to build seawalls, the idea in this case being that one can at least "hold the line" against the sea. However, it is recognized that because they reflect rather than dissipate wave energy, vertical impermeable walls cause a net erosion of the nearshore profile fronting the

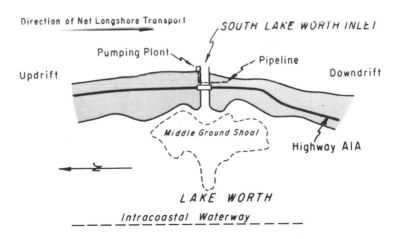

FIG. 4. Fixed bypassing plant, South Lake Worth Inlet, Florida (Figure courtesy U. S. Army Corps of Engineers).

wall (Dean and Jones, 1974). This erosion may ultimately lead to undermining and collapse of the structure. Downdrift of these structures, erosion may also accelerate (U. S. Army Coastal Engineering Research Center, 1973, pp. 5-3, 5-4). Permeable revetments, such as rubble fill, cause somewhat less erosion of the nearshore profile (A. M. Wood, 1969). On a pebble or cobble beach, a low permeable stockade projecting perhaps 1 foot (.3 m) above beach level, and aligned parallel to the shore is frequently able to trap material (Dobbie, 1946). Of course, this material is trapped at the expense of downdrift regions.

The most fruitful method of stopping erosion is to identify and treat the first cause of erosion (Schijf, 1959). Very often this will be a harbor structure, which subsequently causes other relatively minor structures to be constructed downdrift. The damaging effects of these large structures can be greatly reduced by sediment bypassing. Bypassing consists of mechanically or hydraulically moving sediment across a shoreline structure to the vulnerable region downdrift, rather than allowing the structure to shunt sediment away from shore into deep water. This approach was suggested as early as 1913 by Berridge, who commented on the disastrous accretion and erosion experienced at the shoreline harbor at Madras, India.

Most harbor breakwaters require maintenance dredging to remove littoral drift that has settled in the relatively deep, quiet water of the harbor entrance. An elementary form of bypassing could be achieved by depositing this dredged material onto the adjacent downdrift shoreline, rather than following the common practice of dumping it out at sea (Johnson and Eagleson, 1966; Watts, 1968).

The first fixed hydraulic pumping station intended for sediment bypassing was built on the updrift jetty at South Lake Worth Inlet, Florida, in 1937 (Fig. 4). Downdrift erosion was stopped from 1938 to 1942 (Caldwell, 1950; Watts, 1962). A shut down during World War II coincided with renewed erosion, which however, was stopped when pumping was resumed in 1945.

A different method of bypassing has been applied at Port Hueneme and Ventura, California. A detached offshore breakwater and small boat harbor at Ventura was completed in 1962, updrift of an older jetty system at Port Hueneme (Fig. 5). The jetty system had been deflecting sediment into the Hueneme submarine canyon, causing shoreline erosion for up to 8 miles downdrift (Watts, 1962; Tornberg, 1968). The offshore breakwater is able to trap the sediment which would otherwise be deflected into the submarine canyon. It also provides shelter for a floating hydraulic dredge which periodically pumps the trapped sand to a disposal area downdrift of the Port Hueneme jetties. This system has been notably successful in restoring the downdrift beaches. Also, because most sand is trapped before reaching the Ventura County harbor entrance, relatively little maintenance dredging of this entrance is necessary. In 1966, the U. S. Army Corps of Engineers, Coastal Engineering Research Center, reported that "This general method of bypassing is considered to provide greater assurance of effectiveness than any other thus far considered."

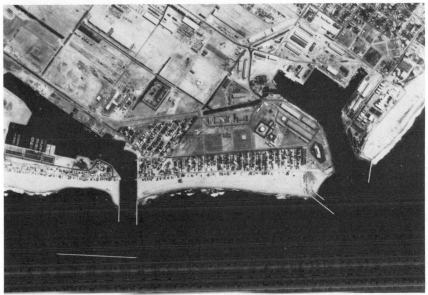

(September 1965

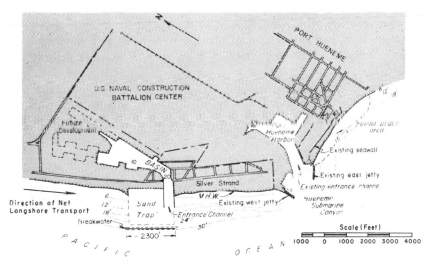

FIG. 5. Sand bypassing, Channel Islands Harbor, California. The photo was taken just after 3 million cubic yards had been dredged from the trap. (Figure courtesy U. S. Army Corps of Engineers.)

Bypassing systems are expensive to construct and maintain (Middleton, 1958), which apparently is why they are not used more widely. However, their cost should be compared to the ultimate cost of the entire proliferation of shoreline structures which would otherwise occur downdrift of the principle structure, keeping in mind that additional shoreline erosion will be caused by such a proliferation. Long sections of coastlines cluttered with engineering works also lose much of their aesthetic appeal. An important financial consideration is that bypassing systems can greatly reduce maintenance dredging of harbor entrance channels.

Once the main structure has been bypassed, consideration should be given to removal of smaller structures. Otherwise, an abundance of smaller structures might by themselves starve downdrift regions. The sequence of removal should proceed from the most updrift structure to progressively more downdrift structures.

Many cases exist in which the first cause of erosion is not an essential commercial or navigational structure, and in which the structure is not large enough to warrant a sediment bypassing system. For example, storm sewer and industrial outfalls are often built as groins. Park commissions commonly construct groins to augment the natural beach, usually at the expense of downdrift beaches. Landfills are often extended offshore and used as parking lots. These types of structures might be removed or modified. If subsequent downdrift erosion were included in the initial cost/benefit analysis of these structures, it is doubtful that they would be so attractive to public officials responsible for shoreline management.

Probably the best way of avoiding future problems in yet undeveloped areas is to require a wide buffer zone separating any future development from the shoreline (Schijf, 1959), and

to forbid the introduction of shoreline structures. This policy would greatly reduce the chance of future erosion, and would make it unnecessary to use public funds to assist those affected by erosion. Condemnation of erosion prone properties, converting them to public ownership, and forbidding construction of protective works on such properties is another possibility. In these cases, shoreline management might parallel certain aspects of flood plain management. Such programs would likely be a far wiser use of public funds than construction of additional engineering works.

Conclusions

In ignorance of the consequences, well intentioned governmental bureaus, planning agencies, and park commissions frequently recommend a new groin system, landfill, or even offshore islands as a solution to erosion problems. Although erosion may be stopped or slowed along the areas which such structures are designed to protect, erosion will merely appear at a new location downdrift.

The shore drift along Milwaukee County is lean and part of the problem becomes one of stabilizing and holding what beach now exists (Milwaukee County, 1945).

This statement is typical of the thinking that has often justified groin construction. However, it is precisely on such relatively narrow beaches that groin construction should be avoided. It is not usually appreciated that the amount of beach accumulation updrift of a groin is smaller than the amount of beach erosion and land loss which will occur downdrift as a consequence of groin construction (Schijf, 1959; Bruun and Lackey, 1962). Net erosion occurs because the scour hole downdrift of a groin continues to enlarge even after accretion updrift has stabilized.

During the past several decades, sediment bypassing systems have demonstrated their effectiveness in stopping erosion caused by major shoreline structures. Except for the possibility of more efficient and varied bypassing systems (Inman and Brush, 1973; U. S. Army Corps of Engineers, 1973), it is unlikely that any technical breakthrough will occur in the field of preventing shoreline erosion. Instead, breakthroughs must be made in public policy (Schijf, 1959; Dolan, 1972), and in an increased level of technical awareness of those responsible for shoreline management. An understanding of the continuing liability for erosion caused by shoreline structures might do much to dampen the enthusiasm of those who would advocate additional structures (Lillevang, 1965).

Agencies and individuals responsible for planning shoreline structures are slow to learn from past mistakes. M. P. O'Brien's preface to the Proceedings of the First Conference on Coastal Engineering, 1950, is as appropriate today as when first published:

Along the coastlines of the world, numerous engineering works in various states of disintegration testify to the futility and wastefulness of disregarding the tremendous destructive forces of the sea. Far worse than the destruction of insubstantial coastal works has been the damage to adjacent shorelines caused by structures planned in ignorance of, and occasionally in disregard of, the shoreline processes operative in the area.

References Cited and Selected Bibliography

Bajorunas, L., and Duane, D. B., 1967, Shifting offshore bars and harbor shoaling: *Journal of Geophysical Research*, v. 76, p. 6195–6205.

Bakker, W. T., 1968, The dynamics of a coast with a groyne system: *Proceedings of the Eleventh Conference on Coastal Engineering, American Society of Civil Engineers*, p. 492–517.

Berridge, H., 1913, Correspondence on coastal sand travel near Madras harbour, *in* Spring, F. J. E., 1914, Coastal sand travel near Madras harbour: *Min. Proc. Institution of Civil Engineers*, v. 194, p. 190.

Bruun, P., and Lackey, J. B., 1962, Engineering aspects of sediment transport including a section on biological aspects, *in Reviews in Engineering Geology*, v. 1, ed. by Thomas Fluhr and Robert F. Leggett, Geological Society of America, p. 39–103.

Bruun, P., 1962, Review of beach erosion and storm tide conditions in Florida 1961–1962: *Engineering Progress at the University of Florida, Technical Progress Report No. 13*, v. XVI, n. 11, 104 p.

Bruun, P., 1973, *Port Engineering*: Gulf Publishing Company, Houston, 436 p.

Caldwell, J. M., 1950, By-passing sand at South Lake Worth Inlet, Florida: *Proceedings of First Conference on Coastal Engineering, American Society of Civil Engineers*, p. 320–325.

Collinson, C., 1974, Sedimentological studies: a basis for shoreland management in southwestern Lake Michigan (abs.): *Geological Society of America, Abstracts with Programs*, v. 6, n. 1, p. 14.

Davis, R. A., Jr., Siebel, E., and Fox, W. T., 1973, Coastal erosion in eastern Lake Michigan—causes and effects, *Proceedings of the Sixteenth Conference Great Lakes Research, Internat. Assoc. Great Lakes Res.*, p. 404–412.

Dean, R. G., and Jones, D. F., 1974, Equilibrium beach profiles as affected by seawalls: *Transactions, American Geophysical Union*, v. 55, n. 4, p. 322.

Dobbie, C. H., 1946, Some sea defence works for reclaimed lands: *Journal of the Insti-*

tution of Civil Engineers, v. 22, n. 4, p. 257–274.

Dolan, R., 1972, Barrier dune systems along the outer banks of North Carolina: a reappraisal: Science, v. 176, p. 286–288.

Dyhr-Nielson, M., and Sorensen, T., 1970, Some sand transport phenomena on coasts with bars: Proceedings of the Twelfth Coastal Engineering Conference, American Society of Civil Engineers, p. 855–865.

Hartley, R. P., 1964, Effects of large structures on the Ohio shore of Lake Erie: Ohio Division of Geological Survey, Report of Investigation No. 53, 30 p.

Ingle, J. C., Jr., 1966, The Movement of Beach Sand: An Analysis Using Flourescent Grains: Developments in Sedimentology 5: Elsevier, 221 p.

Inman, D. L., and Brush, B. M., 1973, The coastal challenge: Science, v. 181, p. 20–32.

Inman, D. L., and Frautschy, J. D., 1965, Littoral processes and the development of shorelines: Coastal Engineering Santa Barbara Specialty Conference, American Society of Civil Engineers, p. 511–536.

Johnson, J. W., 1948, The action of groins on beach stabilization: University of California Department of Engineering, Fluid Mechanics Laboratory, Berkeley, California, Navy Department—Bureau of Ships—Contract NObs2490, Technical Report He–116–283, 21 p.

Johnson, J. W., 1957, The littoral drift problem at shoreline harbors: Journal of the Waterways and Harbors Division, American Society of Civil Engineers, v. 83, n. WW1, paper 1211, 37 p.

Komar, P. D., 1971, The mechanics of sand transport on beaches: Journal of Geophysical Research, v. 76, p. 713–721.

Kressner, B., 1928, Tests with scale models to determine the effect of currents and breakers upon a sandy beach, and the advantageous installation of groins: Bautechnik, v. 25, translated, 1930 by G. P. Specht, U. S. Army Coastal Engineering Research Center, 25 p.

Larsen, C. E., 1973, Variation in bluff recession in relation to lake level fluctuations along the high bluff Illinois shore: Illinois Institute for Environmental Quality, Chicago, 73 p.

Lee, C. E., 1953, Filling pattern of the Fort Sheridan groin system: Proceedings of the Fourth Conference on Coastal Engineering, American Society of Civil Engineers, p. 227–248.

Lillevang, O. J., 1965, Groins and effects—minimizing liabilities: Coastal Engineering Santa Barbara Specialty Conference, American Society of Civil Engineers, p. 749–754.

Middleton, S. R., 1958, Financing of sand bypassing operations: Journal of the Waterways and Harbors Division, Proceedings of the American Society of Civil Engineers, v. 84, n. WW5, paper 1875, 8 p.

Milwaukee County Committee on Lake Michigan Shore Erosion, 1945, Report: Courthouse, Milwaukee, Wisconsin, 33 p.

O'Brien, M. P., 1950, Preface: Proceedings of the First Conference on Coastal Engineering, American Society of Civil Engineers.

Sato, S., and Irie, I., 1970, Variation of topography of sea-bed caused by the construction of breakwaters: Proceedings of the Twelfth Coastal Engineering Conference, American Society of Civil Engineers, p. 1301–1319.

Schijf, J. B., 1959, Generalities on coastal processes and protection: Journal of the Waterways and Harbors Division, American Society of Civil Engineers, v. 85, n. WW1, p. 1–12.

Spring, F. J. E., 1914, Coastal sand-travel near Madras harbour: Min. Proc. Institution of Civil Engineers, v. 194, p. 153–246.

State of Illinois, 1958, Interim Report for Erosion Control: Illinois Shore of Lake Michigan: Department of Public Works and Buildings, Division of Waterways, 108 p.

Tornberg, G. F., 1968, Sand bypassing systems: Shore and Beach, v. 36, n. 2, p. 27–33.

United States Army, Corps of Engineers, Coastal Engineering Research Center, 1966, Shore Protection Planning and Design, Technical Report #4.

United States Army, Corps of Engineers, 1971, Report on the National Shoreline Study, Washington, D. C.

United States Army, Corps of Engineers,

Coastal Engineering Research Center, 1973, *Shore Protection Manual*, 3 v.

Watts, G. M., 1962, Mechanical bypassing of littoral drift at inlets: *Journal of the Waterways and Harbors Division, American Society of Civil Engineers*, v. 88, n. WW1, p. 83–99.

Watts, G. M., 1968, Field inspection of erosion problems in India, *Shore and Beach*, v. 36, n. 2, p. 34–60.

Wiegel, R. L., 1964, *Oceanographical Engineering*: Prentice-Hall Inc., 532 p.

Wood, A. M. Muir, 1969, *Coastal Hydraulics*: Gordon and Breach Science Publishers, 187 p.

Wood, S. M., 1944, Erosion of our coastal frontiers—part II: *The Illinois Engineer*, v. XX, n. 5, p. 5–34.

Zenkovitch, V. P., 1960, Flourescent substances as tracers for studying the movement of sand on the sea bed; experiments conducted in the U.S.S.R.; *Dock Harbor Authority*, v. 40, p. 280–283.

17 Sinkhole

Philip E. LaMoreaux and William M. Warren

Last Dec. 2, Hershel Byrd, a resident of rural southern Shelby County, Alabama, was startled by a rumble that shook his house, followed by the distinct sound of trees snapping and breaking. 2 days later, hunters in nearby woods found a crater about 140 m long, 115 m wide, and 50 m deep. Those events mark the time of formation and discovery of the largest recent sinkhole in Alabama and possibly one of the largest in the United States.

Aerial reconnaissance indicates that in approximately 16 square km about 1,000 sinkholes, other areas of subsidence, and internal drainage features have formed. Most of the sinks are in a limestone valley where solution activity and subsurface soil erosion are most pronounced. . . . Although the sink discovered by the hunters is on a hillside at a higher altitude, it is be-

Reprinted from *Geotimes*, v. 18, p. 15, by permission of the authors and the American Geological Institute. Copyright 1973.
Mr. LaMoreaux is the State Geologist for Alabama and Mr. Warren is on the staff of the Geological Survey of Alabama.

lieved to be hydraulically connected with the flanking valleys.

Deeply weathered Cambrian dolomites of the Knox Group underlie the low eroded ridge where the large collapse occurred, south of Birmingham. The dolomites crop out on the eastern flank of an eroded northeast-plunging anticline. The collapse occurred in white and orange residual clays; bedrock is not exposed. Steep sides are usually found in recent collapses but not in this sinkhole, probably because of its large size and unstable walls. Slumping is active on all sides (see Fig. 1), indicating that the sinkhole will continue to grow.

Two smaller sinks, one more than 15 m in diameter and 4 to 5 m deep, were discovered later about 100 m south of the large collapse. Water is standing in all 3 sinks, but the brilliant azure water in the largest is about 30 m lower than that in the smaller sinks, and its level apparently represents the altitude of the water table.

Investigations by the Alabama Geological Survey and the U. S. Geological Survey in Alabama indicate that many

FIG. 1. View of sinkhole formed December 2, 1972, in Shelby County, Alabama. The sinkhole measures 425 feet long, 350 feet wide, and 150 feet deep. (Photo by U. S. Geological Survey.)

areas underlain by carbonate rocks are prone to subsidence. Sinkhole collapses are related to natural phenomena such as heavy rainfall, seasonal fluctuations in the water table, earthquakes, or other changes in the hydrogeologic regime affecting residuum stability. Man-imposed effects such as artificial drainage, dewatering, seismic shocks, breaks in water or sewage pipes, or even over-watering of gardens may result in collapse.

Formation of sinkholes often results from collapse of cavities in residual clay that are caused by 'spalling', or downward migration of clay through openings in underlying carbonate rocks. The spalling and formation of cavities is caused by (or may be accelerated by) a lowering of the water table resulting in a loss of support to clay overlying openings in bedrock,

fluctuation of the water table against the base of residual clay, downward movement of surface water through openings in the clay, or an increase in water velocity in cones of depression to points of discharge. Collapses have occurred where spalling and resulting enlargement of cavities has progressed upward until overlying clay could not support itself, and where sufficient vibration, shock, or loading over cavities caused the clay to be jarred loose or forced down.

There are no large ground-water withdrawals from the Knox Group in the area of the December collapse. However, about 1.5 km to the east the Newala and Longview Limestones are being dewatered for limestone extraction at 1 underground and 2 recessed quarries. Small sinkholes have been a common phenomenon around the quarries for about 5 years but few collapses have been observed outside this valley. 2 km west of the collapse a municipal well has been pumped for 13 years in an adjacent valley underlain by Ketona Dolomite without development of subsidence.

Apparently the large collapse is in an area that may be affected by extensive ground-water withdrawal but the history of water levels in the area currently is unknown. Rain fell almost daily last November and concentrations of surface water were observed in December. Otherwise very little data is available and the hydrogeologic factors responsible for the collapse may only be speculated upon and can be confirmed or disproved by future investigations.

The Geological Survey of Alabama, in coöperation with the U. S. Geological Survey, has published 3 reports on investigations of similar subsidence problems on limestone terranes. We are considering plans for a long-term study on Shelby County, including use of thermal imagery and multispectral photography as well as conventional aerial photography.

18 Sediment, Our Greatest Pollutant?*

Λ. R. Robinson

Introduction

The statement is being made with great regularity that sediment is our *greatest* pollutant. The term pollution carries a connotation of something bad and undesirable. Sediment is said to be a perfect example of the definition of a

* Contribution from the USDA Sedimentation Laboratory, Soil and Water Conservation Research Division, Agricultural Research Service, United States Department of Agriculture in cooperation with the University of Mississippi and the Mississippi Agricultural Experiment Station.

Robinson, A. R., 1970, "Sediment, Our Greatest Pollutant?" Paper 70–701. Presented at the 1970 Winter Meeting, Amer. Soc. Agric. Engin. Reprinted by permission of the author and the A. S. A. E.
Mr. Robinson is the Director, U. S. D. A. Sedimentation Laboratory, Oxford, Mississippi.

pollutant, which is a resource out of place. Sediment has a two-fold effect: it depletes the land resource from which it is delivered, and it impairs the quality of the water resource in which it is entrained and deposited.[6]

President Nixon noted the seriousness of water pollution from the land in his message on the environment during February 1970. He stated: "Water pollution has three principal sources: municipal, industrial and agricultural wastes. Of these three, the most troublesome to control are those from agricultural sources: animal wastes, *eroded soil*, fertilizers and pesticides."

Secretary of Agriculture, Clifford N. Hardin, said in a recent speech before the National Farm Institute, *"Siltation is still the largest single pollutant of water."* He stated: "Our responsibility is to manage the environment for the widest range of beneficial uses, without degrading it, without risk to health or safety, and without loss of future productivity."

In a recent revision on long-range water resources research needs by the Federal Council for Science and Technology,[10] "Controlling Sediment" was one of ten important problem areas identified. The statement is made that controlling pollution caused by sediment warrants immediate increased research support.

Many people are so accustomed to to seeing muddy water in streams, ponds and reservoirs that they look upon the situation as something necessary, like taxes. Some look upon the present emphasis on pollution as a passing fad. A recent statement said that there are actually "three types of pollution: actual pollution, political pollution and hysterical pollution."[2] One can be assured that pollution in all its forms is real and must be dealt with.

The Problem

Sediment is an economic liability and the monetary loss due to sediment is high. The total annual damage from sediment in streams, not including loss of agricultural productivity of farm land lost to erosion, was estimated to be 262 million dollars in 1966.[12] This amount can be broken down as follows: deposition on flood plains, 50 million dollars; storage space destroyed in reservoirs, 50 million dollars; dredging sediment from inland navigation channels and harbors, 83 million; removal of excess turbidity from public water supplies, 14 million; removal of sediments from drainage ditches and irrigation canals, 34 million; other damages including sediment removal, cleaning, and added maintenance, 31 million.

Sediment is composed primarily of clay, silt, sand, gravel, rock fragments and mineral particles. In terms of mass alone, sediment is by far the major water pollutant. The mass of sediment loading in our streams is from 500 to 700 times that from sewage delivery. Over 4 billion tons of sediment move from the land to water courses in the average year. The average annual sediment concentration for all rivers in the United States ranges from around 200 to 50,000 parts per million.[3] Sediment concentrations for individual runoff events and for small upstream watersheds are frequently much higher than these average values. As a general rule, sediment concentrations are lowest in the more humid parts of the country and tend to increase with diminishing precipitation.

The magnitude of the sediment problems has been evaluated largely in physical terms.

> The storage capacity of man-made reservoirs is reduced about 1 million acre-feet each year by sediment.
> The Mississippi River delivers about 500 million tons of sediment to the Gulf of Mexico each year.
> Sediment yields in the Mississippi basin average about 390 tons per square mile annually.
> The 12-year average annual yield for the Pigeon Roost Creek Watershed in northern Mississippi is 2860 tons per square mile.
> Soil losses from cropland in the

Missouri basin can exceed 100 tons per acre (0.69 inches) if proper management and erosion control measures are not followed.[16]

Sediment yields from agricultural lands along the lower Mississippi range from 5 to 13 tons per acre per year. In the Southeast, sediment yields average about 7 tons per acre per year. Some sources have suggested that about 1 ton per acre per year is an acceptable sediment yield rate from croplands.[12] Despite the successes achieved in controlling agricultural erosion through scientific farming methods such as contour farming, strip cropping and terracing, soil erosion from agricultural lands continues to be extensive.

Soil losses from fraction-acre test plots in northern Mississippi indicate the possible sediment production as a result of cultural practices. Soil loss on bare fallow plots amounted to 70–90 tons per acre per year. Plots with corn planted on contoured, graded rows yielded from 1–4 tons per acre; those with corn planted up and down slopes yielded as much as 11 tons per acre of soil loss. In the same year, plots under an established grass cover yielded only 1.1 tons of sediment per acre.[9]

The 500 million tons of sediment moving to the Gulf of Mexico in the Mississippi River carry an estimated 17 million tons of plant nutrients.[16] It is estimated that 750,000 tons of phosphate are included in these nutrients, but much of this is native to the soil itself and not the result of fertilization. About 14 million tons of primary plant nutrients were applied to soils in the United States during 1967. This consisted of 6 million tons of nitrogen, 4.3 million tons of phosphate and 3.6 million tons of potash.

Approximately 50 percent of the erosional sediment is attributed to agricultural endeavors.[15] The largest single contributor of the remaining 50 percent is streambank erosion. Recent surveys in the Intermountain area of the West indicate that 66 to 90 percent of the sediment contained in many of the streams in the area comes from streambank and streambed erosion.[1] Erosion from highway and roadway construction sites is a major contributor as well as that from construction sites in urban and suburban developments. The sediment yield from highway construction areas during an average storm has been found to be 10 times greater than that from cultivated land, 200 times greater than from grassed areas and 2,000 times greater than from forested areas.

Sediments may deposit in valleys, floodplains, on alluvial fans or in stream channels. Deposition in stream channels or on floodplains may cause channels to overflow more frequently and result in additional damage. Sediments deposited on fertile alluvial soils may reduce their productivity. However, the deposition of sediment on floodplain lands may also be beneficial. Before construction of the high Aswan Dam, the annual enrichment of the Nile Valley was a classic example of an area benefited by sediment deposition. On floodplains in Nebraska, corn yields increased as much as 45% over a 3-year period after floods depositing a layer of 4 to 6 inches of sediment over the area.[4] Sediment deposition may result in incidental benefits, but there is no question that the damage caused by this misplaced soil far outweighs the benefits.

Erosion is a selective process that removes finer soil particles more rapidly than coarser particles. Both the physical and chemical properties of fine grain sediments must be considered, whereas only the physical properties of the coarse grain sediments are usually significant. The fine grain sediments, consisting of clay minerals, amorphous and organic materials, have chemically active surfaces.[5] These sediments may either sorb ions from solution or release ions to solution depending on the chemical environment. Reactions between chemicals and colloidal sediments determine the relative concentration of pollutants in solution and suspension. This will determine the pollutant transportation and deposition for a given hydraulic condition. In general, the coarse sediments serve as a buffer, modifying the erosive potential of the streamflow, and the fine sediments tend to modify the dissolved and suspended chemical load.

Sediment's Role

Recently, increased attention has been given to the role of sediment as a carrier of plant nutrients, pesticides and toxic elements such as lead, mercury, cadmium, nickel and arsenic. Plant nutrients such as nitrogen, phosphorous, potassium and certain trace elements are sorbed on sediments and may have biological significance in the eutrophication of our ponds, reservoirs and lakes. Little information is available on this aspect of sedimentation. There is also little information available on the chemical trap efficiency of reservoirs,

the contribution of chemicals adsorbed on sediment to the biological activity of the impoundment and the changes in water quality after impoundment.

Research indicates that the clays and organic fractions of sediments have active surfaces that can react with an array of chemicals. Unfortunately, this research is based on controlled laboratory studies that cannot be easily extrapolated to the field problems.

Pollutants that adhere to sediment particles are often transported at rates that are several orders of magnitude slower than dissolved pollutants. This may result in the buildup of a high concentration of pollutants in bed sediments even though the concentration dissolved in the water is well within permissible limits. If the sediment permanently assimilates the pollutant, this may be an acceptable means of waste disposal. However, in some cases, a relatively slight change in the chemical constituents of the water might cause the pollutants to be released into solution. Therefore, exchange mechanisms whereby the pollutant can be either taken up or released from the sediment phase should be considered, in addition to the transport properties of the sediment to which the pollutant is attached.

During natural sediment movement, polluted sediments may concentrate as channel deposits.[8] Subsequent transport of these polluted sediments by high-velocity flows may produce different bed sediment concentrations downstream. The pollution of bottom sediments of the lower Mississippi River by pesticides from manufacturing wastes originating near Memphis, Tennessee, is thought to be a result of this type of deposition, resuspension and transport. A recent survey of the Mississippi River sediments[1] showed no DDT at the 0.05 ppm level in the bed sediments of the lower Mississippi River. However, concentrations of up to 0.49 ppm of DDT were found in the sediments of some of the tributary streams draining from manufacturing plants. The most significant conclusion from these investigations was that the large amount of chlorinated hydrocarbons applied to crops in the Mississippi River Delta has not created widespread contamination of the streambed materials. This survey was made to determine the contribution of chlorinated hydrocarbons to massive fish kills which occurred in the river. The finding that the kill was not related to pesticides in runoff from agricultural lands has received very little attention.[16]

Federal Water Pollution Legislation has been enacted to deal with pollution problems.[7] Water quality standards, along with plans for implementing and enforcing them, are now established for all 50 states. In these standards as of 1969, not one state has set forth specific criteria on suspended solids pertaining to water quality. This is a disturbing situation since sediment has been named as the major pollutant of waters.

Besides filling stream channels, ponds and reservoirs, sediment in water increases the expense of clarification and treatment of the water used by humans. Sediment has other effects to change the environment, generally to the detriment of animal and plant life.[15] Suspended sediment impairs the dissolved oxygen balance in water and may slow the breakdown of other oxygen-demanding wastes. Reduced oxygen supply hurts fish life. If the dissolved oxygen content goes much below 4 parts per million, most fish will die from asphyxiation. Fish population is also reduced by sediment blanketing fish spawning grounds and fish food supplies.

Bottom sediments in ponds, lakes and streams have been reported to be a source of water-soluble nutrients available to algae and other microorganisms. In shallow water, the bottom sediments support aquatic plants that live, die and decay, contributing nutrients and organic matter to eutrophying lakes and ponds. Sediment-water equilibria should be evaluated to determine changes in nutrient solubility and availability from transported or deposited sediments.

The magnitude of the sediment pollution problem tends to obscure the benefits of proper sediment concentrations. Generally overlooked is the fact that a flowing stream is a dynamic body which has energy to transport sediment. Unless flowing in a channel that is nonerodible, such as concrete, the stream will attempt to transport sediment up to its energy ability, and may erode or degrade the bed or surface to obtain this material. If the load exceeds the available energy, then deposition occurs. Therefore, the flowing stream must be considered to be almost a living body and treated as such.[11] All the sediment moving in a natural stream cannot be eliminated.

Sediment pollution of nutrient-rich waters may help prevent eutrophication and the accompanying water quality deterioration. Sediment may receive chemicals from the solution phase and may serve as a trap or sink to remove the materials from the flowing stream.

Other Factors

Each ton of sediment carries about 1 pound of phosphorus fixed to its surface.[16] By contrast, the amount of phosphorus delivered in metropolitan sewage amounts to about 2 pounds per person per year. This phosphorus largely accrues from use of detergents. Thus, sewage effluent from a city of one million people will carry at least 1000 tons of phosphorus per year.

Phosphorus is attached to soil surfaces so tenaciously that only minute quantities are ever released to solution in the water. For each pound of phosphorus per ton of suspended sediment, not more than 10 percent of the phosphorus is available for plant nutrition.[15] Algae grows vigorously if the water contains only 0.1 ppm of phosphorus and growth is stimulated by only 0.05 ppm. To prevent algae growth, phosphorus content must be below 0.01 ppm.

Phosphorus from farmlands may be transported into streams and lakes in solution in the runoff and adsorbed on the sediment contained in the runoff. The total amount of phosphorus released from sediment is largely a function of the sediment concentration. Sediments can be expected to adsorb-desorb phosphorus from solution during transport. However, sediments deficient in phosphorus can adsorb significant amounts of phosphorus from solution. Research has shown that a Memphis soil, at sediment concentrations of 10,000 ppm, is capable of reducing the phosphorus concentration in solution from sewage effluent from 6.6 ppm to 4.3 ppm.[14]

Research has shown that the surface chemistry of sediments may vary appreciably during runoff events. The ratio of cations sorbed on suspended sediments to those in solution reaches a maximum of 0.8 in eastern streams and may be 3 or more in western streams. The maximum ratio for a stream in Mississippi was found to be 1.9 with a minimum near 1.0. Maximum ratios for the stream usually occur at the peak of suspended sediment concentration.[5] Concentration of agrichemicals in solution are frequently higher in the initial runoff from farmlands. The major portion of the dissolved chemical load is transported at or near the peak water discharge. Significant quantities of K, Ca and Mg were found to be transported in association with sediment.

Research has also shown that lake bottom sediments can effectively remove dissolved phosphates from solution.[13] Studies in Minnesota have indicated that sedimentation can effectively remove dissolved phosphate from lake waters. Apparently, sediments transported into the lake waters in this area are not a major source of soluble phosphates.

Summary

Sediment becomes a pollutant when it occupies water storage reservoirs, fills lakes and ponds, clogs stream channels, settles on productive lands, destroys aquatic habitat, creates turbidity that detracts from recreational use of water, as well as when it degrades water for consumptive or other uses, increases water treatment costs, or damages water distribution systems. Sediment is also the carrier of other pollutants such as plant nutrients, insecticides, herbicides and heavy metals. There is evidence that bacteria and virus are carried by sediments and this possibility should be investigated.

Because of erodible boundaries and the energy available in flowing streams, sediment will continue to be produced and carried by moving water and will carry with it available pollutants. It is primarily the larger sediment particles that are most readily controlled by available technology. However it is the fine particles that are the principal carriers, the more active chemically, and transported further before deposition. There are not yet adequate means for controlling the amount of clay and colloidal fractions which make up the bulk of the sediment problem. This is true both at the source and in the final deposition.

It is true that sediment is our greatest pollutant of waters in terms of volume. However, sediment may be a carrier of other pollutants and in some instances actually remove and deposit these pollutants from the solution. In this case, sediment acts as a scavenger.

If there is to be control of sediment pollution, there must also be control of other pollutants associated with the sediments. Sediment control practices, such as soil conservation measures, must be applied more thoroughly and effectively throughout the country.

Notes

[1] Barthel, W. F., J. C. Hawthorne, J. H. Ford, G. C. Bolton, L. L. McDowell, E. H. Grissinger and D. A. Parsons. 1969. Pesticide residue in sediments of the lower Mississippi river and its tributaries. Pesticide Monitoring Jour. 3(1): 8–66.

[2] Bellinger, E. H. 1969. Severity of Lake Erie's pollution debated. Chemical and Engineering News 47 (21): 43 p.

[3] Glymph, L. M. and C. W. Carlson. 1966. Cleaning up our rivers and lakes. ASAE Paper No. 66–711. 14 p.

[4] Glymph, L. M. and H. C. Storey. 1967. Sediment—its consequences and control. AAAS Pub. 85. p. 205–220.

[5] Grissinger, E. H. and L. L. McDowell. 1970. Sediment in relation to water quality. Water Resources Bull. 6(1): 7–14.

[6] Joint Task Force of the U. S. Dept. of Agriculture and the State Universities and Land Grant Colleges. 1968. A National program of research for environmental quality-pollution in relation to agriculture and forestry. 111 p.

[7] Klein, C. L. 1969. Sediment pollution and water quality standards. Proceedings of the National Conf. on Sediment Control, Washington, D. C. p. 26–30.

[8] McDowell, L. L. and E. H. Grissinger. 1966. Pollutant sources and routing in watershed programs. Proceedings of the 21st Annual Meeting, SCSA. p. 147–161.

[9] McGregor, K. C., J. D. Greer, G. E. Gurley and G. C. Bolton. 1969. Runoff and sediment production from north Mississippi loessial soils. Mississippi State University, Experiment Station Bull. 777. 30 p.

[10] Office of Science and Technology, Executive Office of the President. 1969. Federal Water Resources Research Program for FY 1970. Federal Council for Science and Technology. 47 p.

[11] Robinson, A. R. 1969. Technology for sediment control in urban areas. Proceedings of the National Conf. on Sediment Control. p. 41–47.

[12] Stall, J. B. 1966. Man's role in affecting the sedimentation of streams and reservoirs. Amer. Water Resources Assn. Proceedings of the 2nd Annual Amer. Water Resources Conf. (University of Chicago) p. 79–95.

[13] USDA North Central Soil Conservation Research Center, Morris, Minnesota, Annual Report. 1968.

[14] USDA Sedimentation Laboratory, Oxford, Mississippi, Annual Report. 1969.

[15] Wadleigh, C. H. 1968. Wastes in relation to agriculture and forestry. USDA Pub. 1065. 112 p.

[16] Walker, K. C. and C. H. Wadleigh. 1968. Water pollution from land runoff. Plant Food Review, No. 1. 4 p.

Floods

"Humans are attracted to settlement in flood hazard areas by the very characteristics—water supply and floodplain terrain—which contribute to the damage potential"

Jacquelyn L. Beyer

Like erosion and sedimentation, floods are natural and recurrent events. They become a problem when Man attempts to compete with a river for the use of the floodplain or when he encroaches upon the coastal margins. There is no complete record of flood damages, but it is a sobering fact that despite numerous programs designed to alleviate floodplain problems, property damage on the floodplain continues to increase. From a global perspective, floods are the most universally experienced natural hazard and involve greater loss of life than do other hazards. In Reading 19 Jacquelyn Beyer presents an overview of this problem.

An unusual hazard is presented by glacier dammed lakes. The major hazard presented by these lakes is catastrophic flooding which occurs when the ice dams fail. This is becoming an increasingly critical problem in Alaska because most development has taken place and continues to take place along rivers which flow from glaciers. The glacier-clad volcanoes of Alaska and the Cascades Range (Reading 4) are also susceptible to outburst floods even when dammed lakes are not present. In Reading 20, Austin Post and Lawrence Mayo document the nature of these hazards and offer recommendations for mitigating the dangers.

As urban pressures force increased development on flood-plains, it becomes necessary to develop new techniques to reduce the hazards associated with development. The concept and application of flood-hazard mapping are reviewed in Reading 21.

Floods exact a costly toll both in loss of lives and property damage while measures to control floods often result in heavy ecological losses. Ecologically acceptable solutions must be found. James Goddard in Reading 22 presents several case histories where flood-plain management incorporated solutions which are both ecologically and economically sound.

19   Global Summary of Human Response to National Hazards: Floods

Jacquelyn L. Beyer

Definition

All streams are subject to flooding in the hydrological sense of inundation of riparian areas by stream flow which exceeds bank full capacity. In arid regions the channel itself, not usually filled with water, is "flooded" at times of high runoff. The point at which the channel discharges an overbank surplus is the flood stage. This may not, however, coincide with the amount of

Reprinted from *Natural Hazards, Local, National, Global*, ed. by G. F. White with the permission of the author and publisher. Copyright 1974 by Oxford University Press, Inc.

Photo on page 188. Flood of March 12, 1963, on North Fork Kentucky River at Hazard, Kentucky. A graphic example of man and nature competing for a river floodplain. Photograph by Billy Davis, "Courier-Journal and Louisville Times."

water outside the normal channel which will cause damage to human works. It is also possible to calculate the stage of high water which is the threshold for damage to property or dislocation of human activities. Frequently the use of the term "flood stage" is based on such a perception of the event, and is therefore a definition subject to change as conditions of floodplain occupance change. This paper is not concerned with coastal flooding.

Spatial Extent

Floods are the most universally experienced natural hazard, tend to be larger in spatial impact, and involve greater loss of life than do other hazards. Floods can occur on both perennial and ephemeral stream beds or in an area where no defined channel exists, such as in an arid region subject to cloudburst type storms. The problem is compounded for human adjustment by the fact that few other hazards present the ambivalent Januslike aspect of good and evil. Humans are attracted to settlement in flood hazard areas by the very characteristics—water supply and floodplain terrain—which contribute to the damage potential.

For this reason it is not surprising to find that historic attempts have been made to resolve the conflict between the need for riparian occupance and the inevitable damage, as Wittfogel describes it: "Thus in virtually all major hydraulic civilizations, preparatory (feeding) works for the purpose of irrigation are supplemented by and interlocked with protective works for the purpose of flood control" (Wittfogel, 1957, p. 24). Less elaborately

organized preindustrial societies have also worked out ecological adjustments to flooding. Familiar examples of peasant adaptation to periodic flooding include the traditional agricultural organization along the lower Nile, now altered by the construction of the high Aswan dam, and the village rice culture of the lower Mekong, which will eventually be affected by flood-control components of the Mekong basin development. Another such example is the people of Barotseland in northwest Zambia where migration to higher ground is the organized response to the annual seasonal inundation of the reaches of the upper Zambezi which mark the coreland of Barotse occupance. Changes in socioeconomic patterns as such societies industrialize will undoubtedly accelerate the damage from floods. Familiar adjustments such as migration will fall outside the range of choice. Alternative workable adjustments may be inhibited by lack of knowledge, technology, and/or capital.

For industrial societies the twentieth-century concept of multiple-purpose river basin planning, now widely diffused (United Nations, 1969a), involves the consideration of flood damage reduction along with planning for beneficial use of water.

In summary, the potential for flooding is global in nature and can occur, with the proper combination of factors, whenever there is precipitation. This precipitation may range from uniform and general to sporadic and highly localized. Adjustments to hazards must be made in the context of both universality and randomness. In addition there needs to be sensitivity to beneficial uses for floodplains and water courses.

Damage Potential

Types of floods are so varied in origin, duration, strength, timing, volume, depth, and seasonality that it is difficult to identify damage potential except in the most general terms. The amount of damage and the damage potential in any flood-hazard area is very closely related to the nature of occupance and to the stage of economic development as well as to the physical parameters. There also seems to be an inverse relationship between property damage as measured in monetary terms and loss of life. Societies which have much to lose in terms of structures, utilities, transportation facilities, etc., also have the technological sophistication to ensure better monitoring, warnings, evacuations, and rehabilitation—all of which contribute to lowering the human costs. Conversely, preindustrial societies, especially with dense rural populations, do not suffer large property losses but are less well equipped to provide preventative or rescue measures for people.

Clearly the main damage agent is the water itself, overflowing normal channels and inundating land, utilities, buildings, communications, transportation facilities, equipment, crops, and goods which were never meant to operate in or withstand the effects of water. In addition, high velocity of running water operates as a damage agent either directly or indirectly. In the latter case, debris carried by the water or dislodged materials batter structures, people, and goods. Debris and silt carried by the water and left behind as the water recedes operate as further damage agents.

Damage is considered to be either direct or indirect (primary or second-ary). Such a classification is useful in any assessment which attempts to clarify the benefits of a damage reduction program. Loss of human life is the most dramatic and certainly the easiest to identify as a direct result of flood events. Loss of livestock may be especially costly in rural zones.

In agricultural areas, damage involves inundation of land accompanied by erosion and/or loss of crops. It is in such cases that the season of flooding is especially significant. Water damages farm equipment, stored materials (seed, fertilizer, feed), disrupts irrigation systems and other water supply, and disrupts communication.

Urban facilities are all subject to water and force damage—buildings of all kinds, public facilities, utilities, transportation, waterway facilities, and open space. Machinery, manufacturers, goods in retail establishments, household furniture can all be damaged by water, debris, and silt.

Indirect damages are generally associated with health and general welfare although such amenities as scenic values, recreational services, and wilderness preservation may also be taken into account. Normal public-health services are subject to greater pressures in the face of disruption of transportation and utilities, especially water supply. Contamination and pollution are more probable, epizootics emerge, stagnant water is left as a flood legacy, and general morbidity increases. Flooding affects the normal sources of food and shelter and hence adversely affects health conditions. Opposed to these considerations is the possibility that emergency relief operations might provide better health care and food than is normally available to some communities counter-acting, to some extent, the effects of both direct and indirect damages (White, 1945).

Benefits

Rivers in flood clearly are hazardous for many kinds of human use, but a complication in planning for amelioration of the hazard is presented by the benefits of naturally flowing rivers, including overbank flooding. "Control" of flooding by protective works, especially, may negate benefits from soil nutrient renewal and fisheries. Restrictions on use of floodways will provide for damage reduction and also enhance community values through preservation of open space. In some parts of the world, exemplified by India and Bangladesh, the rhythms of agricultural production are dependent upon water brought by major storms and renewal of fertility through siltation. In such cases serious weather modification efforts should proceed only after careful assessment of the total benefit-cost pattern.

Damage Assessment

Assessment includes the costs of repair, including temporary repairs; replacement and cleanup; and loss of improvements and inventories. Emergency costs are also involved. Loss of business and employment during flood disruption is also a direct cost associated with the physical damage. Similarly the transfer of public economic development funds to flood emergency and control programs represents a deferred opportunity which may be especially significant as a social cost in developing nations.

There are no comprehensive calculations of global damage from floods. In many cases, local flooding in areas remote from communications may not even be recorded. There are immense difficulties for any inventory of flood consequences including those of cost, technical expertise, comparability of data collected, allocation of losses to proper causes, and time. A pilot survey of global natural disasters by Sheehan and Hewitt (1969) provides some information for the 20 years 1947–67 for most of the world—the USSR is the major country excluded. During this period Asia (excluding the USSR) led in loss of life, with 154,000 deaths. Europe (excluding the USSR) followed with 10,540 deaths. Africa, South America, and the Caribbean area each recorded 2,000–3,000 deaths. During the same period 680 lives were lost to floods in North America, and 60 in Australia, totaling for all these regions 173,170 deaths.

This total can be compared with the 269,635 deaths attributed to all . . . other hazards . . . and if it is considered that many of the other categories—e.g., tornadoes, typhoons, hurricanes, and tidal waves—also involve flooding, the death loss is the most impressive comparison. Table 1 will give some idea of the magnitude of the hazard in terms of area affected, people involved, and property damage.

Damage Factors

The factors which should be taken into account in assessing the damage potential for flooding in any basin include the following.

Frequency

Flood flows can occur on the average as often as once every 2 years in temperate climates and as infrequently as once in 1,000 years elsewhere. The recurrence of a particular flood flow can be predicted with reasonable accuracy over a long time span if sufficient stream-flow data are available over a long period. This emphasizes the certainty of the event, not its timing, which is not predictable since flood flows are assumed to be random events.

Frequency is a physical parameter clearly related both to perception and adjustments. The greater the frequency the more accurate is the perception of the hazard by floodplain occupants and the greater is their willingness to consider a wider range of adjustments, including alternative sites for their activities. This is demonstrated by variations in community decision making which can be correlated with frequency of flooding (Kates, 1962).

Magnitude (depth)

Magnitude of a flood may be expressed in physical, or probabilistic terms. The physical measures are rate of flow measured in cusecs, m³/sec (cubic meters per second), or river stage in meters (or feet) above some datum (reference) point. Both of these require carefully established measuring installations to obtain reliable data. Flow can be graphically plotted versus stage to give a stage-discharge relationship which can then be useful in predicting damages. This relationship can be quite complex, and considerable care should be exercised in its use.

The probabilistic measure is a statistical method of ordering various magnitudes of flow and stating the probability that a given flow will be exceeded. Under this procedure, a 5-year flood is a flow or stage which will be equaled or exceeded 20 times, on the average, in a 100-year time span. The statistical method has validity only in areas where good flow records over a long period of time (at least 30 years) are available, although some simulation can be done. The ability to determine probability of flood magnitudes is not the same as the ability to state when such floods will occur. Some of the parameters upon which magnitude depends and which are useful in classifying the flood characteristics of a given area include the type, intensity, duration, areal extent, and distribution of precipitation; basin size and shape; floodplain topography; surface conditions of soil; and land use. There is an effort in Japan, for example, to elaborate a system of flood-hazard classification through the use of landform analysis. It is suggested that such analysis will provide for predictability of flood current, ranges of submersion, depth of stagnant water, and length of period of stagnation (Oya, 1969).

Depth can be important in terms of both the kinds of damage and possible adjustments, e.g., floodproofing of structures.

Rate of Rise

This is the time from flood stage (or zero damage stage) to flood peak and is a measure of the intensity of the flood. As Sheaffer (1961) notes, this time between flood stage and flood peak represents an adjustment time during which persons affected by flooding can engage in activities to lessen the damage. Generally, people will not respond to the danger of flooding until at least flood stage, so this time period is critical. It is clear that there is a relationship between the

Table 1 Significant historical flood events

Date	Place	Deaths	Property damage
June 1972[a]	Eastern U. S.	100+	$2 billion
June 1972[a]	Rapid City, S. D.	215 (est.)	$100 million
May 11–23, 1970[b]	Oradea, Rumania	200	225 towns destroyed
January 25–29, 1969	Southern California	95	
July 4, 1969	Southern Michigan and Northern Ohio	33	
August 23, 1969	Virginia	100	
May 29–31, 1968	Northern New Jersey	8	$140 million
August 8–14, 1968	Gujarat, India	1,000	
January–March 1967	Rio de Janeiro and São Paulo states	600+	
November 26, 1967	Lisbon	457	
January 11–13, 1966	Rio de Janeiro	300	
November 3–4, 1966	Arno Valley, Italy	113	Art treasures in Florence and elsewhere destroyed
June 18–19, 1965	Southwest U. S.	27	
June 8–9, 1964	Northern Montana	36	
December 1964	Western U. S.	45	
October 9, 1963	Belluno, Italy	2,000+	Vaiont Dam overtopped
November 14–15, 1963	Haiti	500	
September 27, 1962	Barcelona	470+	$80 million
December 31, 1962	Northern Europe	309+	
May 1961	Midwest U. S.	25	
December 2, 1959	Frejus, France	412	Malpasset Dam collapsed
October 4, 1955	Pakistan and India	1,700	5.6 million crop acres at loss of $63 million
August 1, 1954	Kazvin District, Iran	2,000+	
January 31–February 1, 1953	Northern Europe	2,000+	Coastal areas devastated
July 2–19, 1951	Kansas and Missouri	41	200,000 homeless, $1 billion
August 28, 1951	Manchuria	5,000+	
August 14, 1950	Anhwei Province, China	500	10 million homeless; 5 million acres inundated
July–August 1939	Tientsin, China	1,000	Millions homeless
March 13, 1928	Santa Paula, Calif.	450	St. Francis Dam collapsed
March 25–27, 1913	Ohio and Indiana	700	
1911	Yangtze River, China	100,000	
1903	Heppner, Ore.	250+	Town destroyed
May 31, 1889	Johnstown, Pa.	2,000+	
1887	Honan, China	900,000+	Yellow River overflowed; communities destroyed
1642	China	300,000	

[a] Press reports.

[b] Adapted from Table of Disasters/Catastrophes, *New York Times Encyclopedic Almanac* *(1970), p. 1228;* (1972), pp. 322–33.

nature of the drainage system and the rate of rise—upstream areas will have a more rapid rise and shorter duration of flooding than will downstream areas.

Seasonality

This is one of the more significant factors for agricultural damage and probably the main basis for the adjustments made by preindustrial riverine societies. Clearly the hazard increases where the growing season is limited and coincides with the season of flooding. Winter floods might also account for increased loss and disruption in urban areas where heating and sanitary facilities are needed to guard against increase in disease and discomfort.

Duration

The time of inundation for flood flows can vary from a few minutes to more than a month. The duration is highly correlated to the rate of rise and fall of flood crests except where drainage of land area is impeded by obstructions. Flood duration is dependent upon such parameters as source of runoff; runoff characteristics including slope and surface conditions; nature of obstructions impeding recession of waters; and man-created controls such as reservoirs, levees, and channelization.

Nature of floodplain occupance

This includes the density of settlement; types of facilities; extent of fixed facilities, buildings, and equipment; and value of facilities. Obviously every increase in such occupance will increase the potential damage and call for some kind of adjustment, whether protec-

tive works, warning systems, and public relief capabilities, or a willingness to accept the losses.

Efficacy of Forecasting and Warning Systems

The ability to forecast the occurrence of overbank flooding is limited to a time span in which the hydrologic conditions necessary for flooding to occur have begun to develop. The formulation of a forecast for flood conditions requires information on current hydrologic conditions such as precipitation, river stage, water equivalent of snowpack, temperature, and soil conditions over the entire drainage basin as well as weather reports and forecasts.

In small headwater regions a forecast of crest height and time of occurrence is all the information required to initiate effective adjustments since the relatively rapid rate of rise and fall makes the period of time above flood stage relatively short. In lower reaches of large river systems where rates of rise and fall are slower it is important to forecast the time when various critical stages of flow will be reached over the rise and fall. Reliability of forecasts for large downstream river systems is generally higher than for headwater systems.

Warning time for peak or overbank conditions can range from a few minutes in cloudburst conditions to a few hours in small headwater drainages to several days in the lower reaches of large river systems. As with forecasting, the time and reliability of the warning increase with distance downstream where adequate knowledge of upstream conditions exists.

Clearly the amount of information required, the data collection network necessary for collecting the information, the technical expertise required for interpretation, and the communication system needed to present the information in time to potential victims are such as to preclude many poor and developing nations from having an adequate service. The World Meteorological Organization of the United Nations, through its World Weather Watch and Global Data Processing System, hopes to coordinate efforts to improve forecasting. A recent report (Miljukov, 1969) notes that quantitative precipitation forecasts for 24–49 hours in advance are provided in parts of Australia, Byelorussian SSR, Cambodia, Canada, Czechoslovakia, France, Federal Republic of Germany, Hong Kong, India, Iraq, Japan, Mauretania, Norway, Pakistan, Philippines, Rhodesia, Romania, Sweden, Ukrainian SSR, the USSR, and the U. S. Precipitation forecasts for hydrological purposes are provided in Australia, Canada, Czechoslovakia, France, Federal Republic of Germany, India, Iraq, Japan, the USSR, and the U. S. The report also notes: "Precipitation forecasts are not accurate and reliable enough, in the present state of meteorological science, for use in the preparation of quantitative forecasts of river discharges" (Miljukov, 1969, p. 10). Most developing nations will have to rely on much less data than are ideally needed for forecasting and warning, which in turn will lessen the effectiveness of this factor with respect to flood losses.

Efficacy of Emergency Services
The helplessness of many small and poor societies is exemplified by the situation in Bangladesh during the tropical cyclone of 1970. Where resources are not available for planning, for the physical effort of relief and evacuation, and for coordination with other activities, little will be done outside of contributions of international aid agencies. Even in more developed areas, local conditions of transportation and public attitudes will lessen the usefulness of emergency aid, e.g., the disaster at Buffalo Creek, West Virginia, in 1972. The more elaborate and dependable such services are, however, the more there is a tendency to rely on such aid as a major adjustment and to reject consideration of less costly and more effective adjustments. There clearly must be provisions for first-level emergency aid where settlement already exists and where alternative moderations of the hazard are difficult to implement or costly, but these should normally not supplant other measures to reduce losses.

The Range of Adjustments and Their Adoption

The accompanying table (Table 2) suggests that the cumulative experience of centuries provides for any society or group wishing to alleviate the social and economic costs of flood losses a choice of methods, to be used singly or in strategic combinations. Much of the wisdom with respect to the need for such strategies, adapted to local conditions of basin hydrography, settlement characteristics, and economic capabilities, has been gained in industrial nations after painful and costly trial and error. It has been suggested (Goddard, 1969) that developing nations need not repeat the errors of the past, that they have models for actions

Table 2 Adjustments to the flood hazard

Modify the flood	Modify the damage susceptibility	Modify the loss burden	Do nothing
Flood protection	Land-use regulation and changes	Flood insurance	Bear the
(channel phase)	Statutes	Tax write-offs	loss
Dikes	Zoning ordinances	Disaster relief	
Floodwalls	Building codes	volunteer	
Channel	Urban renewal	private	
improvement	Subdivision regulations	activities	
Reservoirs	Government purchase of	government aid	
River diversions	lands and property	Emergency measures	
Watershed treatment	Subsidized relocation	Removal of persons	
(land phase)	Floodproofing	and property	
Modification of	Permanent closure of low-level	Flood fighting	
cropping practices	windows and other openings	Rescheduling of	
Terracing	Waterproofing interiors	operations	
Gully control	Mounting store counters on wheels		
Bank stabilization	Installation of removable covers		
Forest-fire control	Closing of sewer valves		
Revegetation	Covering machinery with plastic		
Weather	Structural change		
modification	Use of impervious material for		
	basements and walls		
	Seepage control		
	Sewer adjustment		
	Anchoring machinery		
	Underpinning buildings		
	Land elevation and fill		

Source: Adapted from Sewell (1964), pp. 40–48; and Sheaffer, Davis, and Richmond (1970).

and policies which would provide a much more coherent and suitable response to the flood hazard. It is clear, even with such models, that adaptation to local circumstances in any society will not be a simple matter. It is increasingly evident that various combinations of individual psychology, institutional inertia, costs, governmental policies and philosophies, and historical precedents help to condition the choice of adjustments.

Modify the Flood

This category includes engineering works affecting the channel which represent the most widely accepted feasible adjustment with the possible exception of bearing the loss. Such protective works are justified where benefits exceed the costs of implementation and especially where high damage potential exists for relatively intensive settlement in urban and industrial situations. In such cases the high value of fixed facilities will justify levees, dams, and channelization even when 100 percent protection cannot be guaranteed. While benefits accrue to both private and public sectors, the costs are necessarily largely public. Partly for this reason this adjustment strongly tends to encourage persistent settlement and even attracts, through a false sense of security, further floodplain encroachment. On the other hand, such engineering works are important components of multiple purpose projects which are directed toward comprehensive land and water planning and they can be complemented, for floodplain management, with other measures. A major problem is to encourage engineers and officials to think in terms of nonstructural alternatives or supplements to protective works.

Watershed treatment practices have more subtle implications with respect to flood control and are frequently more significant for their contribution to improved *in situ* land management. All such measures have their limitations with respect to major flood events. There may be some contribution to lowering the depth in small floods and to lengthening the flood-to-peak interval, but essentially the appeal of such practices is lower costs. About 90 percent of the costs for such practices are public while benefits accrue largely—about 85 percent—to private land users. Land treatment measures often complement and make more effective protective measures but will also tend to encourage continued settlement for flood-prone areas.

Weather modification is a fairly recent technique with respect to flood control and too little is known about its effectiveness. One major problem, even given scientific certainty about effectiveness, will be the necessity to allay public fears that tampering with weather processes will increase rather than lessen floods. Recent news stories of the use of weather modification techniques in the Indochina war will not make this task easier (Shapley, 1972). The immediate postflood news reports from the 1972 Rapid City,

South Dakota, flood suggest that this has already become an issue. Costs for weather modification are entirely public while benefits are about equally divided between private users and the public.

Modify the Damage Susceptibility

Given that there may be a need to encroach on floodplains or to accept present settlement patterns, certain measures are possible which are either less costly than protective works or bearing the loss, or which will lessen the actual damages even more. There is also a greater shift of cost bearing to private interests, especially in the case of floodproofing, with resultant increased awareness of the need for flood adjustments.

Land-use regulation, including changes in occupance, is especially suitable where there is competition for floodplain land for uses other than agricultural or recreational. The legislative and police powers of the state can be used to control and guide development of floodplains. According to Goddard, in the United States "about 35 states have adopted regulations and 500 additional places in 41 states have them in adoption process" (Goddard, 1971). Encouraging this is the 1969 Federal Flood Insurance Act which provides for governmental flood insurance subsidy to individuals in communities which agree to adopt floodplain regulation guidelines. These measures tend to encourage more efficient and less costly use of floodplains and there is a greater shared responsibility between floodplain users and authorities. Strong leadership and a commitment to long-range planning and rational allocation of land uses are also prerequisites to widespread adoption of such measures.

Floodproofing and structural changes (including land elevation) provide for even larger shifts of costs as individual users may bear all the costs and share benefits with the public on an equal basis. Such adjustments are most appropriate where flooding is not intense either in velocity or depth and where some warning time is possible. Floodproofing especially requires a network of forecasting and warning facilities along with a flood-hazard information program which will encourage preflood adjustments. Structural modifications are possible for existing structures as well as for new structures although this will increase costs. In many cases it would be too expensive to modify old buildings. Some types of buildings are better suited to modification than others but clearly damage reduction is related to size of structures and costs of modification. These adjustments tend to encourage persistent occupance and lose effectiveness where flood frequency is low. At the same time they place more responsibility on the user and thus heighten sensitivity to and knowledge about the flood hazard.

Modify the Loss Burden

There is much more emphasis in this category on humanitarian responses rather than calculated economic rationale, based on the inevitability of flooding and the unlikely possibility of preventing all damage by eliminating floodplain occupance. Losses will thus occur even in the face of widespread use of appropriate adjustments. When people suffer trauma and loss there can be little question of a social obliga-

tion to provide assistance. The dilemma for rational flood damage reduction, however, is that relief measures and emergency assistance unless properly designed tend to encourage persistent occupance and reluctance to accept more rational adjustments.

Insurance and tax write-offs will not decrease flood losses but there will be a spreading of loss over time and a shift of some costs to the general public. As the flood insurance program has been worked out in the United States, the insurance subsidy by the government to private carriers must be coupled with community planning for land use regulation and other adjustments to lessen potential damage. In Hungary, where levees and flood fighting are the principal adjustments, agricultural insurance was extended in 1968 to cover flood damages (Bogardi, 1972). Whether this works as an incentive for private adjustments is not clear. There is obviously a sensitive line between encouraging further encroachment or private irresponsibility and alleviating the damages to those who must occupy floodplains. Purchases of insurance, according to recent reports after the June 1972 floods in the eastern U. S., have not been commensurate with the danger nor with the benefits to eligible individuals. Problems resulting from a hazard insurance program which was not thoroughly planned have been noted.

Disaster relief is a necessary adjustment in order to lessen the immediate impact of a flood event and to ease the implementation of rehabilitation efforts. Whether government or private, the major disadvantage is that such measures, necessary though they may seem when disaster strikes, strongly encourage the belief that nothing else need be done.

The effectiveness of emergency measures depends largely upon the nature of the flood hazard (ideal combination of high flood frequency, low velocity and depth, long flood-to-peak interval, and short duration) and the quality of forecasting. The immediate governmental obligation is generally seen to be the removal of persons and property from flood threatened areas.

Do Nothing

Bearing the loss is still the major adjustment for large numbers of floodplain occupants in developing countries (Ramachandran and Thakur, chap. 5), and is frequently modified in developed nations only by the widespread expectation of relief and emergency measures. In all cases, however, it is clear that an increasing effort to clarify public interest in floodplain situations will restrict the choice of doing nothing and management strategies will become more common (Sheaffer, Davis, and Richmond, 1970).

Reduction of Loss

One element in the acceptance by any group of decision makers of a particular mix of components in a flood damage reduction program is the assessment of the comparative return from each possible choice of adjustment or combination of adjustments. If damage assessment after the fact of flooding is extremely difficult, it is even more difficult to predict what the damage will be under a set of assumptions about responses of various kinds. White and Burton have suggested methods whereby maximum damage

reduction and minimum cost can be calculated for particular situations (White, 1964; Burton, 1969). Such methods may hopefully provide an additional planning tool in those situations where encroachment onto the floodplain is neither as intensive as in some industrial countries nor necessary. Some such tool is essential also to ensure the most efficient allocation of scarce resources, whether of materials, man-power, or money.

The relative contributions of each possible adjustment to reduction of potential damage can only be crudely measured at present. Such measurement is further complicated by the fact that only infrequently is a single adjustment adopted. Clearly any protective works which provide for 100 percent security under any feasible flood condition will provide 100 percent loss reduction although costs of providing such protection are likely to be unacceptable. Such security is highly improbable, both because of costs and imperfect knowledge of potential floods. The damage reduction to structures may range from 40 to 100 percent, dependent upon the size of the flood experienced and the nature of structures (White, 1964).

Watershed treatment data are inconclusive with respect to damage reduction and there are no data available for weather modification. Land-use regulation and change can provide for up to 90 percent damage reduction dependent upon the effectiveness of the regulations and the speed of application.

Data from one United States town (White, 1964) suggest that even minimal floodproofing of present structures under conditions of frequent but shallow flooding can be very effective, reducing damages by 60–85 percent. Great depths and/or high velocities would call for consideration of flood-proofing as part of building design.

Emergency action increases in effectiveness where there is a long flood-to-peak interval, high flood frequency, low depths, short duration, and low velocity. Where such conditions prevail, and assuming adequate warning facilities plus personnel and equipment, emergency action can reduce damages by 15 to 25 percent. A lower range of 5 to 10 percent is more probable.

"Adequate" warning would seem to be a minimal requirement for communities subject to flood hazard, but it is not simple nor inexpensive to provide a good system. Meteorological services and communications are part of the costs. Even given an excellent network of knowledge about the physical event, it may be difficult to convey that information to persons who will have to make adjustment decisions. Factors involved in a less than optimal warning system include:

1. Reluctance of officials to give false alarms.
2. Lack of complete coverage of median used to transmit warnings (radios, telephones, etc.)—communities and individuals may not be able to afford facilities.
3. Reluctance of people to see themselves affected by distant events (storms, runoff).
4. Individual interpretation of warning messages, especially where several messages may be contradictory or the messages may be incomplete.

5. Failure to provide exact information about what recipients of warnings are to do.
6. Impossibility of warning in time for much else than rapid evacuation.
7. Dramatic warning signals triggering an influx of the curious which negates warning advantages.

Flood insurance and tax subsidies spread the burden through time and shift much of the loss to the general public but do not reduce damage.

Another indication of the relative efficacy of various adjustments in reducing damage is the importance placed on them in national and regional plans. A recent report on Hungary (Bogardi, 1972), for example, suggests that reduction of damages is to be achieved largely through levee construction and maintenance, flood fighting, and, to some extent, insurance. Recommendations for Malaysia (Flood Control, 1968) are for a flood-control program involving better data collection and improved organization for relief and evacuation, combined with structural controls, land-use regulations, and flood-resistant crops. It is estimated that these measures would reduce anticipated damage from presently known levels of flooding by 50 percent. This report does not consider dams in catchment areas justifiable for flood control alone. Engineering works are still considered primary tools for India although some attention is being given to catchment area management and weather modification. The Japanese have extended their management approach to include regulatory measures (Oya, 1969). A comprehensive summary of national efforts to cope with floods as one of many natural hazards would probably justify a comment in a report from the United Nations (1969b): "Although there is still a considerable gap in many countries between the needs for governmental action and the actual institutional framework, new administrative patterns have evolved in others which responded to the need for a more coordinated and system oriented approach to resource administration."

Perception of Hazard and Adjustments

The global nature of the flood hazard is suggested not only by maps of large floods and by tables of deaths, but also by reference to international interest in the problem. The special agencies of the United Nations are involved in a wide spectrum of activities, including hydrological and meteorological data collection, flood forecasting methods, world catalogue of large floods, problems of health due to floods, and relief and aid to victims. Agencies involved include the Economic Commission for Africa, Economic Commission for Asia and the Far East, World Meteorological Organization, World Health Organization, and UNESCO. In many cases small nations will have to rely on technical help and assistance through United Nations channels. There is a discernible diffusion of efforts to plan and implement comprehensive programs including Canada, Japan, United Kingdom, and the United States. Because river basin management is so popular as an economic development tool, this opens the door for widespread consideration of comprehensive flood control as a component of such programs.

From the global and national institutional viewpoints there is probably adequate sensitivity to the nature of the problem, if not to the possible range of adjustments. At the individual level, it is more difficult to judge whether the knowledge gained in recent years about perception of the hazard in the United States (Kates, 1962; Burton and Kates, 1964; James, Laurent, and Hill, 1971) is applicable to individual perception in developing or industrializing nations—or even industrial nations with different social and political conditions. A summary of some of the findings of these hazard perception studies, especially of floodplain occupants in Georgia, may be listed in the form of planning guidelines (adapted from James, Laurent, and Hill, 1971):

1. It cannot be assumed that accurate knowledge of the flood hazard will inhibit all persons from moving onto the floodplain.
2. The flood hazard itself will process people over time in terms of perception of the hazard and willingness to make adjustments. Management programs can short-circuit the unhappy experiences of those who remain unaware of the hazard and reluctant to adopt adjustments by preventing their settlement (e.g., through insurance programs).
3. Prospective floodplain occupants who are initially unaware cannot be swayed by large amounts of technical information; they also tend to be people who avoid contact with public

officials and are not observant with respect to natural features.

4. In contrast, people who are knowledgeable about the flood hazard and settle anyway on floodplains will be responsive to more sophisticated information than is usually presented.

5. Delineation of flood-hazard areas on a map is ineffective as a form of communication.

6. Officials who disapprove of settlement on floodplains or who think in technical terms about risk will not be effective with those who are unaware of the risk.

7. Those who know about the flood hazard will be sensitive to depths, if not to frequency, and will therefore be open to flood proofing and possibly insurance as adjustments.

8. Time reduces awareness of the hazard, especially for those moving into a hazard area where indications of past flood events are not evident.

9. The wave of concern for environmental issues has brought with it evidence that those who are unaware of the flood hazard, but who have a concern for environmental damage, may respond more to appeals that land-use regulations are ecologically sound than to information about potential property damage.

10. Flood damage sufferers who contact, or who are contacted by, officials are a biased sample in terms of response to flood hazard. Frequently this bias is associated with speculation as a motive for owning floodplain property.

11. Upstream development frequently becomes the scapegoat for downstream floodplain users threatened by floods.

12. Floodplain users who are alienated from government or authority because of other contacts are poor candidates for participation in floodplain management programs.

13. Extended delays in programs to reduce flood losses will increase alienation and make user participation more unlikely.

14. Encouragement of particular users should be part of policy, e.g., it should be made easy for those who are unaware of the hazard and/or reject adjustments to leave and be replaced by those who know something about the hazard and will be willing to adopt reasonable adjustments, including insurance and flood proofing or structural change. Where even these adjustments are too costly in the light of potential damage the policy should be to consider purchase and reversion to open space and recreational use.

It is hard to believe that persons would vary much with respect to a number of factors involved in determining the degree of knowledge about flood events, anticipation of future events, and willingness to consider various possible adjustments. Confirmation of this belief awaits further investigations of human response in diverse societies.

References

Baroyan, O. V. (1969) "Problems of health due to floods." Tbilisi, USSR: United Nations Inter-regional Seminar on Flood Damage Prevention Measures and Management.

Bogardi, I. (1972) "Floodplain control under conditions particular to Hungary." International Commission on Irrigation and Drainage, 8th Congress.

Burton, Ian. (1969) "Methods of measuring urban and rural flood losses." Tbilisi, USSR: United Nations Inter-regional Seminar on Flood Damage Prevention Measures and Management.

———, and Kates, Robert W. (1964) "The perception of natural hazards in resource management." *Natural Resources Journal* 3 (2):412–41.

Flood Control, Report of the Technical Subcommittee for (1968) Government of Malaysia: Director of Drainage and Irrigation.

Goddard, James E. (1969) "Comprehensive flood damage prevention management." Tbilisi, USSR: United Nations Interregional Seminar on Flood Damage Prevention Measures and Management.

———. (1971) "Flood-plain management must be ecologically and economically sound." *Civil Engineering—ASCE* 000:81–85.

James, L. Douglas, Laurent, Eugene A., and Hill, Duane W. (1971) *The Flood Plain as a Residential Choice: Resident Attitudes and Perceptions and Their Implications to Flood Plain Management.* Atlanta: Georgia Institute of Technology, Environmental Resources Center.

Kates, Robert W. (1962) *Hazard and Choice Perception in Flood Plain Management.* Chicago: University of Chicago, Department of Geography, Research Paper No. 78.

Miljukov, P. I. (1969) "Review of research and development of flood forecasting methods." Tbilisi, USSR: United Nations Inter-regional Seminar on Flood Damage Prevention Measures and Management.

Oya, Masahiko (1969) "Flood plain adjustments, restricted agricultural uses, zoning, and building codes as damage prevention measures." Tbilisi, USSR: United Nations Inter-regional Seminar on Flood Damage Prevention Measures and Management.

Sewell, W. D. F. (1964) *Water Management and Floods in the Fraser River Basin.* Chicago: University of Chicago, Department of Geography, Research Paper No. 100.

Shapley, Deborah. (1972) "News and comment." *Science* 176: 1216–20.

Sheaffer, John. R. (1961) "Flood-to-peak interval." In Gilbert F. White, ed., *Papers on Flood Problems.* Chicago: University of Chicago, Department of Geography, Research Paper No. 70.

———, Davis, George W., and Richmond, Alan P. (1970) *Community Goals—Management Opportunities: An Approach to Flood Plain Management.* Chicago: University of Chicago, Center for Urban Studies. Report by Institute for Water Resources, Department of the Army, Corps of Engineers.

Sheehan, Lesley, and Hewitt, Kenneth. (1969) "A pilot survey of global natural disasters of the past twenty years." Toronto: University of Toronto, Natural Hazards Research Working Paper No. 11.

United Nations. (1969a) *Integrated River Basin Development.* New York: rev. reprinting.

———. (1969b) "Some institutional aspects of adjustments to floods." Tbilisi, USSR: Resources and Transport Division, Department of Economic and Social Affairs, United Nations Inter-regional Seminar on Flood Damage Prevention Measures and Management.

White, Gilbert F. (1945) *Human Adjustment to Floods: A Geographical Approach to the Flood Problem in the United States.* Chicago: University of Chicago, Department of Geography, Research Paper No. 29.

———. (1964) *Choice of Adjustment to Floods.* Chicago: University of Chicago, Department of Geography, Research Paper No. 93.

Wittfogel, Karl A. (1957) *Oriented Despotism: A Comparative Study of Total Power.* New Haven, Conn.: Yale University Press.

20 Glacier Dammed Lakes and Outburst Floods in Alaska

Austin Post and Lawrence R. Mayo

Introduction

Glaciers in Alaska cover an area of about 73,361 square kilometers (28,317 square miles). They are most highly concentrated along the Pacific Coast and in the south-central part of the State. Many of these glaciers, as elsewhere in the world, flow across the mouths of adjoining valleys and cause lakes to form behind the ice streams. These glacier ice dams are subject to repeated failure. Because most Alaskan communities and transportation routes are situated along rivers which flow from glaciers the hazards presented by glacier dammed lakes are serious. The damage by floods from these lakes will increase if people encroach into areas where flooding occurs.

Glacier dammed lakes in south-central and southeastern Alaska and in adjacent Canada which drain into rivers entering Alaska are included in this study. Such lakes are numerous in this area; 750 glacier dammed lakes have been plotted. . . . The number and size of individual lakes vary enormously during the seasons and from year to year; the total number of lakes plotted provides an indication of their abundance.

Not included in this report are the few, very small lakes dammed by glaciers that are widely scattered in the

Abridged from *U. S. G. S. Hydrologic Investigations Atlas HA–455*, 1971, 10 pp.
The authors are on the staff of the U. S. Geological Survey.

Brooks Range, Alaska Peninsula, Kodiak Island, and Aleutian Islands.

The major hazard presented by glacier dammed lakes is catastrophic flooding which occurs when the ice dams fail. In many places flooding occurs annually; there are many exceptions and the situations change rapidly from one year to the next.

It should be noted that large quantities of water can also be stored in or under glaciers and may create serious floods even though no surface lake is visible. Such catastrophic floods have occurred in Iceland so frequently (Thorarinsson, 1953) that the Icelandic term "jökulhlaup" is now used internationally to describe them. In the State of Washington floods of this nature have been observed from at least four glaciers (Richardson, 1968). Thus, glaciers with no visible lakes may present unusual flood hazards. However, one cannot identify from aerial photographs or maps those glaciers which are likely to produce large jökulhlaups except to note a common association of glacier outburst floods with glacier-clad volcanoes. Any glacier may produce an outburst flood, but only visible glacier dammed lakes and glaciers on volcanoes are included in this report. The largest glacier outburst floods in Alaska are from the release of glacier dammed lakes.

The purpose of this report is to present an up-to-date assessment of the hazardous glacier outburst floods in Alaska by mapping the present extent of glaciers, the location of glacier

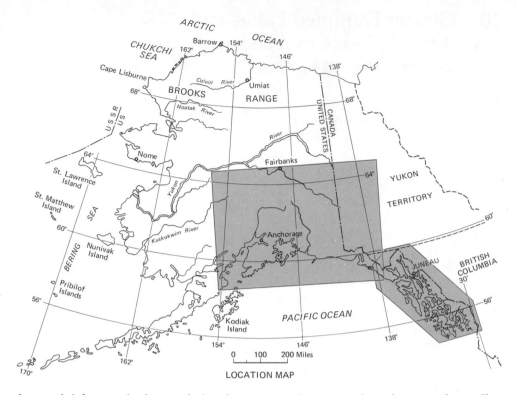

ARCTIC OCEAN
CHUKCHI SEA
Barrow 154°
162°
Cape Lisburne
68°
BROOKS RANGE
Colvill River
Umiat
146°
138°
68°
Noatak River
U.S.S.R
U.S.
River
Nome
64°
Fairbanks
64°
YUKON TERRITORY
St. Lawrence Island
Yukon
St. Matthew Island
60°
BERING SEA
Kuskokwim River
Anchorage
60°
Nunivak Island
JUNEAU
BRITISH COLUMBIA
30°
Pribilof Islands
56°
PACIFIC OCEAN
56°
Kodiak Island
154°
146°
138°
170°
162°
0   100   200 Miles

LOCATION MAP

dammed lakes and glacier-clad volcanoes, presenting the recent history of
several prominent glacier dammed
lakes, and delineating areas where outburst flooding may be expected. Avoiding particularly hazardous situations is
advised and recommendations are
made for monitoring a few lakes which
cause very large or potentially damaging floods.

. . .

The Formation of Glacier Dammed Lakes

Glacier dammed lakes form in a number of different situations. The largest
lakes, which present the greatest hazards, occur in ice free tributary valleys
blocked off by active valley glaciers.
Most common are small lakes situated

in alcoves and niches in the valley
walls along the margins of glaciers and
in depressions formed where tributary
valley glaciers join. A few lakes are
located slightly above the regional firn
line; the large majority occur along
the lower reaches of glaciers.

No attempt is made here to classify
glacier dammed lakes as to manner of
formation such as by active or stagnant ice, or by advancing or retreating
glaciers. Glacier dammed lakes can be
formed, change size, or be destroyed
in so many ways in various geomorphic
settings that a complete classification
would be both cumbersome and of
very little practical value.

Once a depression is closed off by a
glacier it begins to fill with meltwater
and rain runoff from the surrounding
basin. The resulting lake continues to

fill until the water overflows a bedrock saddle or initiates a self dumping process at the ice dam. Filling continues at a reduced rate during the winter by water draining from the porous old snow in the higher areas of nearby glaciers. Winter snowfall also adds to the lake height.

Most large ice-dammed lakes fill until they reach depths where the ice dam becomes unstable. Summit Lake, British Columbia released in 1961 and 1965 when the water depth equaled 0.82 of the ice thickness (computed from data reported by Mathews, 1965). The maximum possible depth is that necessary to float the dam, which is approximately 0.9 of the ice thickness. The lake in the Snow River basin in September 1970 rose to a depth of 0.9 of the ice dam level before drainage began.

How Glacier Dammed Lakes Release

The release of glacier dammed lakes may be initiated by the formation of a channel under, through, or over the ice in one or more of the following ways:

1. Slow plastic yielding of the ice due to hydrostatic pressure differences between the lake and the adjacent, less dense ice (Glen, 1954).
2. Raising of the ice dam by floating (Thorarinsson, 1939).
3. Crack progression under combined shear stress due to glacier flow and high hydrostatic pressure (Nichols and Miller, 1952).
4. Drainage through small, preexisting channels at the ice-rock inter-

face or between crystals in the ice.
5. Water overflowing the ice dam, generally along the margin (Liestøl, 1956).
6. Subglacial melting by volcanic heat (Tryggvason, 1960).
7. Weakening of the dam by earthquakes (Tryggvason, 1960).

Once a leak is established the initial opening can be expanded rapidly by melting (Liestøl, 1956). The lake water is usually slightly above the melting temperature (Gilbert, 1969); in addition heat is supplied by conversion of potential energy of the water into heat energy during its passage through the ice. The rate of increase of tunnel cross-section area due to melting must be related to the water discharge and the heat available. The size of the passage at any time is therefore related to the volume of water which has already passed through it. In addition to melting, mechanical scouring strips partially melted ice crystals from the tunnel walls increasing the tunnel diameter. In the early stages of outbreak the water discharge increases slowly at first and then faster and faster—in at least one case, Lake George in Alaska, the increase followed an exponential law (Meier, 1960). This accelerating rate of increase occurs until the discharge reaches extremely high values. As the lake drains the lowering of the lake then reduces the water and energy available, and the discharge decreases abruptly. Because plastic flow of the ice is usually too slow to close the opening as rapidly as the water pressure is reduced, the channel remains open long enough for most reservoirs to drain completely. The time required for a lake to release varies from a few hours to several days. So many factors combine to influence the intensity and duration of flooding that quantitative generalizations are not possible with present data.

Occasionally, at least, a lake may drain with no flood resulting (Lindsay, 1966). Data from lakes where streamflow records exist indicate that the lakes usually drain rapidly enough to present flood hazards at least a few kilometers downstream from the glacier terminus. For example, small lakes on Martin River Glacier were observed by Tuthill and Laird (1966, p. 21–22) to fill and release in the summer of 1964, causing local flooding on the outwash plain at the head of Lake Charlotte near the Bering River. Even where there is no evidence of past flooding, one should assume that any glacier dammed lake may drain abruptly and rapidly with little or no advance warning.

Characteristics of Floods from Glacier Dammed Lake Outbursts

A large majority of the smaller lakes fill and empty one or more times each year. A tiny glacier dammed lake at Gulkana Glacier in the Alaska Range filled and drained at three-day intervals during the 1970 summer (gaging station 15-4780.4). Two small lakes adjacent to Lemon Creek Glacier near Juneau drained several times during the summer of 1967 (C. Zenone, oral commun., 1968). Aerial photographs taken each year show that most of the small lakes and many of the larger ones have drained by late August. Seasonal cycles in subglacial water

pressure may be present (Mathews, 1964) and may affect the dumping cycle.

Although most small glacier lakes appear to have drained by late summer, the time of glacier lake release is not related to weather patterns in any simple way. Regardless of the time of year, glacier dammed lakes release whenever they fill to critical levels. Several of the large lakes drain annually. . . and others drain only once each 2 to 4 years. The longer time period occurs where the lake basins are so large that they require several years for filling.

Although most glacier dammed lakes are not large, the rapid draining which can take place may result in extremely large floods. For example, Summit Lake, British Columbia dammed by Salmon Glacier has a maximum size of only 4.2 square kilometers (1.6 square miles). On November 30, 1965, it released and produced a flood peak of 3,100 cubic meters per second (110,000 cubic feet per second). Nonoutburst floods are compared to outburst floods by relating their unit discharge, the peak flow divided by the source area. This technique can be used to illustrate that relatively small lakes are capable of producing a very large flood. For an outburst flood from Summit Lake this unit discharge was 750 cubic meters per second per square kilometer of lake surface (70,000 cubic feet per second per square mile). By comparison, the unit discharge for nonoutburst floods in the same basin is on the order of 1 cubic meter per second per square kilometer (100 cubic feet per second per square mile). It is because of the extremely abrupt release of water that even very small glacier dammed lakes can present serious local hazards.

Areas flooded by glacier dammed lake releases are subject to serious damage. Wide flood plains are inundated to unusual depths and the high discharge rates can produce rapid erosion, deposition, and stream channel changes. The measured scour and fill of the Snow River streambed during outburst flooding during September 19–23, 1970 was 1.2 meters (4 feet) of scour and 0.7 meter (2 feet) of fill at point locations in the stream (Leveen, written commun., 1970). At Knik River, 2.4 meters (8 feet) of scour and 1.2 meters (4 feet) of fill occurred locally in the channel from July 9–11, 1965 (Leveen, written commun., 1966). Photographs show 7.5 meters (25 feet) of fill at Sheep Creek near Valdez.

Serious damage may occur in spring, summer, or fall, especially when the outburst flood is superimposed on already high discharge due to melting snow or severe storms. In some places particularly hazardous situations are presented when lakes dump during the winter. Small or moderate floods at that time of year can create great damage. For instance, in January 1969 an unnamed lake . . . dammed by Skilak Glacier was released. The peak flow would have been minor if it had occurred during the summer for it caused a rise of Skilak Lake of only 0.3 meter (0.8 foot) (Harry Hulsing, oral commun., 1969). Despite this, the resulting increase in flow from the lake was sufficient to fracture the ice on Kenai River, forming great ice jams that plugged the channel at Soldotna. During a bitter cold night the backwater from these ice jams inundated roads, homes, and businesses with freezing water.

Another example is a winter flood (Fig. 2), undoubtedly from the breakout of Van Cleve Lake, which took place while the famous Million Dollar Bridge across the Copper River was

1909 OUTBURST FLOOD ON COPPER RIVER

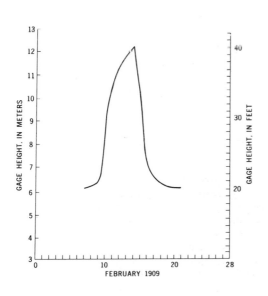

FEBRUARY 1909

FIG. 2. Flood on Copper River at Miles Glacier measured by A. O. Johnson in 1909 (Ellsworth and Davenport, 1915, p. 49), judged to be from Van Cleve Lake. This remarkable wintertime flood caused damage to the Copper River and Northwestern Railroad during its construction. Data are river stage measurements referenced to an arbitrary datum.

under construction. O'Neel and Hawkins (1910, p. 1) reported "On February 10th, 1909, some unknown disturbance took place in Miles Glacier, and although the weather was cold, the river rose 20 feet, taking the ice out completely, and doing some damage to the temporary track across the delta below."

Difficulties in Flood Prediction from Glacier Dammed Lakes; Flood Histories of Five Rivers

Magnitudes and frequencies of future floods from storms or snow melt can be predicted from long-term stream-flow records. For example, it may be possible to estimate the largest flood to be expected, on the average, once in 10 years or once in 100 years. Future floods from most glacier dammed

lakes, however, cannot be estimated reliably using these standard statistical procedures, because the hydrologic characteristics of the drainage basin may change suddenly and discontinuously. Glacier dammed lakes which have no previous record of flooding may abruptly begin dumping, the flood sequence may change drastically, or the reservoir may cease filling due to changes in the damming glacier. For even short-term predictions of individual floods from glacier dammed lakes, up-to-date information on both the glaciers and the lakes is required in addition to the historical record.

Some of the reasons for difficulty in prediction are illustrated in the following flood histories of five rivers. Graphs showing the flood histories of four of these rivers are included in Figures 3–6.

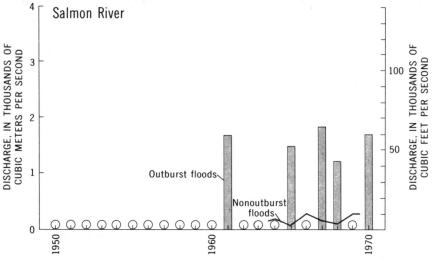

FIG. 3. The greatest average daily discharges (bars) from the release of Summit Lake, British Columbia are many times higher than the greatest average daily discharge each calendar year due to ice melt and rainfall (black line) (gage No. 15–80). Years with no outburst flood are indicated by an open circle. Momentary peak discharges during the day can be 50 percent higher than the daily average discharge at this flashy stream. The 1961 discharge was not measured and is estimated here only to indicate that an outburst did occur (Mathews, 1965, p. 49, and U. S. Geological Survey, 1954–70).

Salmon River

This river had no outburst floods from before 1890 to 1960, during which time Summit Lake, British Columbia impounded behind Salmon Glacier, drained over a bedrock saddle to the basin occupied by former Tide Lake (Field, 1958a; Hanson, 1932, p. 335–336; Haumann, 1960, p. 104–105; Mathews, 1965). A highway, bridge, and the town of Hyder meanwhile were built in the Salmon River valley. In 1961, Summit Lake unexpectedly and abruptly drained under Salmon Glacier and flooded the valley causing severe damage. Since 1961 the river has experienced four more glacier out-

burst floods from the lake. Here, an unexpected period of lake dumping followed a long history of lake stability.

Knik River

The Knik River near Palmer is famous for destructive outburst flooding from Lake George, which in recent years has been the largest glacier dammed lake in Alaska. Since 1918, at least, the lake emptied annually (Stone, 1963b), a pattern which continued until 1963 when no ice dam formed. Lake George again annually refilled and dumped between 1964 and 1966. The annual flooding of Knik River was so regular between 1918 and 1963 that

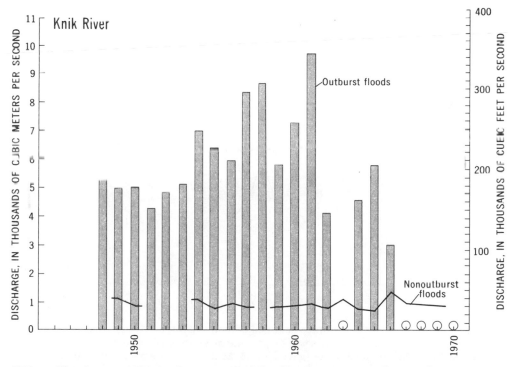

FIG. 4. The draining of Lake George caused flooding far in excess of nonoutburst floods on the Knik River (gage No. 15–2810). The greatest daily average discharges during the breakouts (bars) are compared with the greatest nonoutburst daily discharges (black line) for the same calendar years. The lake failed to refill (open circle) in 1963 and 1967 to the present.

flood experts, bridge maintenance crews, and tourists reserved a week in July or August for the event. Because of this spectacle the area has been designated as a Natural Landmark by the National Park Service. Between 1966 and 1971, Knik Glacier failed to form an ice dam and the lake was not filled. In this case, a period of regular lake dumping lapsed briefly and later ceased abruptly.

The peak discharges from 1949 to 1966 changed systematically rather than randomly as is usual for nonoutburst floods. From 1949 through 1961, there was a significant rise in the peak discharges; then during the later phase of the lake, 1962–66, the peak discharges were lower than during the preceding decade. The cause of these latter changes was undoubtedly due to a thinning of the ice at the glacier terminus. Lake George will reform in the future if Knik Glacier thickens

and advances a small amount. Although this change is fairly likely, it cannot be predicted with assurance from the data presently available.

Snow and Kenai Rivers

Outburst floods on the Kenai River above Skilak Lake originate from a glacier dammed lake at the headwaters of the Snow River. The first recorded outburst on this river was in December 1911 (Ellsworth and Davenport, 1915, p. 114). Outburst flooding continued, usually during November, December, or January, causing ice jams and overflow icings that damaged railroad and highway bridges (E. Estes, oral commun., 1970). The Kenai River has been gaged near Cooper Landing since 1947. Until 1961 the peaks of glacier outburst floods at this location were generally lower than the annual peaks due to snow and ice melt and rainstorms. Since 1961, all of the out-

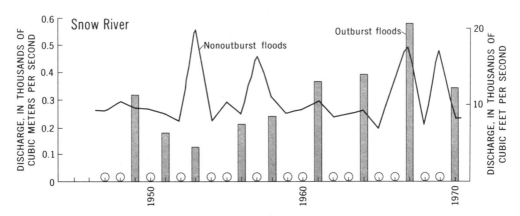

FIG. 5. Release of water from an ice dammed lake in the Snow River valley has produced high flows of about the same magnitude as storms, where measured downstream at the outlet of Kenai Lake (gage No. 15–2580). Data are average daily discharge for the highest flow each calendar year. Bars indicate maximum daily outburst discharge, black line indicates maximum daily discharge from nonoutburst sources. The lake release period was usually 2 years prior to 1958 but since has changed to each 3 years. It may be possible to predict future breakouts of this lake because the lake releases at regular intervals and the peak discharges change systematically.

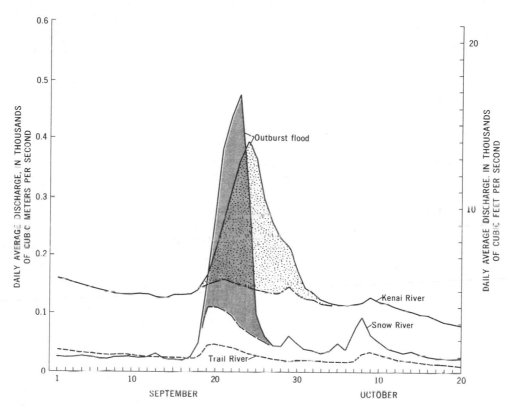

FIG. 6. Glacier outburst flood in September 1964 caused by the dumping of the glacier dammed lake at the head of Snow River. The flood passed the Snow River gage (No. 15 2435) before entering Kenai Lake; the Kenai River gage (No. 15–2580) is located at the outlet of Kenai Lake. The daily average discharge recorded by the two gages shows downstream lowering and attenuating effects of lake and streambank storage on the floodwaters. Momentary peak discharge was 8 percent higher than peak daily flow shown for Snow River. The amount of water due to the lake release (Snow River, in grey; Kenai River, dotted) is superimposed on the normal runoff. The discharge of nearby Trail River is shown for comparison. (U. S. Geological Survey, 1965, 1966; Kenai River data, unpublished revisions.)

burst peaks have exceeded the annual storm peaks.

The change of outburst peak discharge has been quite regular: from 1949 to 1953, the peaks decreased; from 1953 to 1967, increased; and in 1970 again decreased. These changes are judged to be related to gradual gains and losses in the glacier size and therefore are not random. Glacier ice occupies part of the basin; as this ice melts the volume of water impounded increases in proportion and the resultant outburst flood is greater. The lake volume inferred from flood hydrographs ranged from a minimum of 94 million cubic meters (3.3 billion cubic feet) in 1953 to a maximum of 175 million cubic meters (6.2 billion cubic feet) in 1967. The time interval between lake releases also may be related to small gains or losses in glacier size. Lake releases occurred at 2-year intervals (with one 3-year exception) from 1949 to 1958, during the period with low peak discharges. Since 1958 the interval has been 3 years and the peak discharges have been higher. In this case the magnitude and frequency of outburst floods has changed markedly but systematically in a few decades.

Tazlina River

This river basin contains four major dumping lakes—two formed by Tazlina Glacier and two others by Nelchina Glacier. Photographs (Ragle, Sater, and Field, 1965a, p. 24–27) indicate that draining of the Nelchina Glacier lakes occurred sometime between April 14 and September 11, 1964, but no definite outburst floods appear on Tazlina River hydrograph for that year. Evidently the lake discharge was not rapid enough to create floods. During some other years two outbursts occur indicating the rapid release of at least two lakes on different dates. The large 1962 flood was produced by the combined release of the two largest lakes adjacent to Tazlina Glacier (Balvin, 1963), while a 1970 flood originated at Nelchina Glacier (D. K. Stewart, oral commun., 1970). The flood which destroyed the Copper River railway bridge at Chitina during a period of clear weather in August 1932 . . . could have been caused by the release of one or more lakes in the Tazlina River basin. The flood history at Tazlina River is much **more** complex than for the other examples

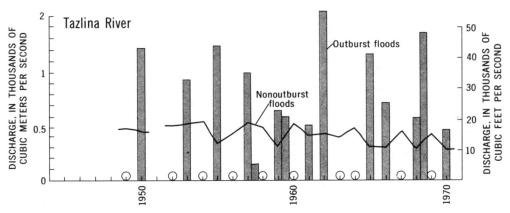

FIG. 7. Four major glacier dammed lakes release in the Tazlina River basin causing highest average daily discharges (bars) at gage No. 15–2020 which are often higher but sometimes lower than the nonoutburst highest daily discharges (black line) each calendar year. Some years have no glacier outburst (open circles), while other years have two outbursts. Outbursts were identified by comparing the hydrographs for Klutina and Tonsina Rivers with nearby Tazlina River. Momentary peak discharges are 5 to 10 percent higher than the daily averages shown here. Until the lake dumping sequence in the basin is determined and each lake is monitored, accurate predictions of future breakouts cannot be made for this complex sequence.

because more than one major lake is involved. The magnitude and frequency of outburst floods on the Tazlina River cannot be predicted using the historical flood record because the changes have not been systematic.

Bering River

Berg Lake . . . impounded by Bering Glacier has a complex history and presents one of the greatest potential floods of any glacier dammed lake in Alaska. When observed by Martin (1908, p. 46–48, pl. 2; also in Ellsworth and Davenport, 1915, p. 36, pl. 2) five smaller lakes occupied bays of the present large lake and the water level stood at an altitude of about 247 meters (810 feet). Strandlines as much as 60 meters (200 feet) higher indicated former levels of the lake. Martin writes "The level of the lake is oscillating. The absence of vegetation on the lower terraces shows that it has fallen in recent years. In June, 1905, it was rising several inches per day. The outlet of the lake, which is beneath the ice at the end of the long point south of First Lake, becomes choked with debris at irregular intervals. The water then rises until the pressure clears the outlet, or till the water can flow on the surface around the end of the point, when the lake is emptied, causing severe floods in the valley of Bering River."

At some unknown date since Martin's observation, but judged to have been prior to 1940 from the vegetation present in 1948, thinning of Bering Glacier lowered the ice dam and the lake level became fixed, discharging over a bedrock spillway at an altitude of about 207 meters (680 feet). Despite the lowering of the lake surface, the area of the lake has increased from 12.2 kilometers (4.7 square miles) in 1905 to 28 square kilometers (11 square miles) in 1970 because of the melting of a large ice tongue that formerly filled most of the basin. For a period of 30 or more years there have been no outburst floods from Berg Lake.

Catastrophic draining will occur in the near future if the ice dam continues to thin, for the situation is again becoming unstable. The ice dam now holding Berg Lake could be rapidly eroded, releasing the entire lake in a few hours. This could create a devastating flood sweeping the Bering River valley with a peak flow far exceeding 30,000 cubic meters per second (1,000,000 cubic feet per second).

Some Special Outburst Flood Settings

Former Lakes Dammed by Glaciers

In addition to the glacier dammed lakes already mentioned, a number of lakes that have not formed for several decades are of unusual interest. Several of these lakes will have no chance to reform in the foreseeable future because the damming glaciers have now completely melted away. An example is former Endicott Lake near Glacier Bay (shown on an 1892 map by Reid, 1896, pl. 86, and on International Boundary Commission map, Sheet No. 10, 1907, and later, greatly enlarged due to glacier melt, in a U. S. Navy 1929 aerial photograph).

In recent years the Alaska Highway Department has considered the feasibility of constructing a highway by way of the Taku River valley to the capitol city of Juneau. Glacier related problems were studied by Miller (1963, p. 195–200). A large lake was impounded in this valley by an advance of Taku Glacier more than 200 years ago (Lawrence, 1950, p. 208–211, fig. 6). This glacier then retreated but has readvanced 5 kilometers (3.5 miles) in the past 80 years. If this rate of advance continues, the lake could reform in about 50 years. Slowing and possible culmination of the advance before closing off the Taku River seems likely due to the great increase in glacier width as the ice spreads out in the broad Taku River valley.

Large lakes in the Alsek River valley were impounded behind Lowell and Tweedsmuir Glaciers in Canada and probably the Alsek Glacier in Alaska in recent centuries. Recent (Holocene) Lake Alsek (Kindle, 1953, p. 21–22, map 1019A), impounded by Lowell Glacier, was the largest glacier dammed lake formed in Western North America since the disappearance of the Cordilleran Ice Sheet during the late Pleistocene. At its highest level 200 or more years ago, the lake extended up the Alsek and Dezadeash Rivers with a total length of 83 kilometers (52 miles) and covered an area of 250 square kilometers (97 square miles) including the present site of the Alaska Highway at Haines Junction. A slightly smaller lake formed in the same basin about 120 years ago. A major flood on the Alsek delta occurred in 1909 (Tarr and Martin, 1914, p. 158) which presumably was caused by the draining of a lake dammed by Lowell Glacier. Scoured valley walls, giant ripple marks on outwash deposits and sparse, youthful vegetation in the lowland areas provide spectacular evidence of the passage of gigantic floods from Lowell Glacier down the Alsek valley to the sea.

Temporary Lakes Caused by Periodically Surging Glaciers

Both Lowell and Tweedsmuir Glaciers, which dammed former lakes as mentioned above, have surface features, such as folded medial moraines, which result from periodic surges (unusually rapid flow with accompanying advance of the terminus) that occur at intervals of about 20 years. Strong surges of either of these glaciers could again repeatedly form lakes which, when released, could flood the lower Alsek Valley. Lowell Glacier is of particular interest because its surface features suggest that it is subject not only to small surges, such as observed in 1950 and 1968, but also to very large surges occurring at intervals of perhaps 80 to 150 years. Should one of these large surges occur, the ice dam in the Alsek Valley would recreate Recent (Holocene) Lake Alsek which might inundate parts of the Alaska Highway and cause devastating floods downstream when the lake water was released.

Another hazardous situation could be produced by a strong surge of Black Rapids Glacier in the Alaska Range. This glacier evidently dammed the Delta River about 1830 ± 40 years judging from description of the scene by Mendenhall (1899, p. 328) and moraines dated by Reger and Péwé (1969). A surge of similar magnitude could inundate part of the Richardson Highway and create severe floods in the Delta and Tanana River valleys. More than 200 surging glaciers have been identified in Alaska and adjacent Canadian provinces (Post, 1969). Practically all surging glaciers block lateral valleys during their rapid advances, causing glacier dammed lakes to form and resulting in floods when the lakes release (see Figs. 8 and 9).

Other Potential Future Lakes

Advancing glaciers can block side valleys forming new lakes. A striking example of this may occur around 1990 if the vast Hubbard Glacier, 120 kilometers (74 miles) in length and covering an area of 3,800 square kilometers (1,470 square miles), continues to advance at its current rate. The ice will close off Russell Fiord, a 45-kilometer (28-mile) long arm of the sea, which will then become a fresh water lake. ... A glacier dammed lake was charted in this valley "by the Russian Booligin in 1807 and Lieut. Khromtchenko in 1823" (Tarr and Martin, p. 108). This lake, at an altitude of 50 meters (160 feet), overflowed to the south as indicated by underfit streams in the area today.

New lakes can also form adjacent to receding glaciers as the ice melts from lateral embayments; this is now occurring at two points in Desolation Valley. ... Other sites for potential lakes ... are in large depressions presently occupied by nearly stagnant glacier ice.

Outburst Floods Caused by River Icings

In interior Alaska during winter months, river icings (aufeiss) occur in many places and in some situations build up at the outlets of lakes. Outburst flooding may occur when these ice dams fail. In March 1971, H. Livingston, K. Kahler, and A. Tatro of the Alaska Department of Highways observed a flood which covered a portion of the Richardson Highway near Rainbow Mountain with freezing slush.

Outburst Floods from Glaciers on Volcanoes

Although few ice dammed lakes are known to exist on Alaska's glacier sheathed volcanoes ... these peaks present unusual flood hazards.

The Icelandic and Washington jökulhlaups all occurred in volcanic areas or on volcanic peaks. A direct relationship between vulcanism and these floods has not been determined for most cases. Alaskan ice-sheathed volcanoes doubtless present similar flood hazards and catastrophic outburst floods may occur without warning. These volcanoes, many of which are intermittently active, present even greater hazards when eruptions occur.

Very rapid melting of glacier ice can result from release of volcanic heat. During the eruption of Redoubt Volcano, beginning on January 24, 1966, a large amount of water and mud descending from the summit crater destroyed the upper reaches of an unnamed glacier and covered the lower part with debris. ... The flood waters then proceeded down Drift River (Wilson and Forbes, 1969, p. 4511). The 1953 eruption of Mount Spurr (Juhle and Coulter, 1955; Nielsen, 1963, p. 136–138) melted the glacier ice located in the crater of Crater Peak, eroded a deep gorge in the side of the mountain and swept away part of the margin of an unnamed glacier. The resulting mudflow dammed Chakachatna River forming a lake more than 8 kilometers (5 miles) in length. These two relatively small eruptions serve to emphasize the

FIG. 8. Tikke Glacier, Canada. This view of a surging glacier was taken in August 1965 when a surge was moving rapidly down the glacier. Lateral valleys to the right of the glacier do not contain lakes. Farther up the glacier on the left side the fast-moving ice recently has dammed the lateral streams. (Photo courtesy U. S. Geological Survey.)

FIG. 9. Tikke Glacier in August 1966 after culmination of the surge shown in progress in Fig. 8. The advancing ice has now formed dams blocking both side valleys on the right side of the glacier. This is only one of nearly 200 surging glaciers in Alaska and Canada which can be expected to form hazardous lakes periodically. (Photo courtesy U. S. Geological Survey.)

flood hazards that could be presented by large eruptions.

Summary

Floods resulting from Alaska glacier dammed lakes present a serious and increasing hazard to the growing population of the State. The number of lakes varies widely during the seasons and from year to year; the 750 lakes identified in this report indicate their abundance. Large lakes are most frequently found where valley glaciers block off ice-free side valleys; most commonly the lakes are small and located along the glacier margins below the firn line.

Although most smaller lakes fill in early summer and have drained by late August, the time of dumping of glacier dammed lakes occurs when the basins fill to critical levels and has little relationship to weather patterns. Thus flooding may occur at any time of year. Floods superimposed on high discharge due to meltwater runoff or storms create unusual hazards in summer; in winter even small floods can raise the ice on rivers causing ice jams and serious flooding.

Usual methods of storm flood frequency analysis should not be applied to floods from glacier dammed lakes. Due to changes in the glaciers, new lakes may form, old ones may be destroyed, or the frequency and/or volume of discharge may be altered. Each lake has a unique past and future, and up-to-date data on the lakes and glaciers are required for even short-term flood predictions. Flood histories of Salmon, Knik, Kenai, Tazlina, and Bering Rivers illustrate how variable the lake discharge regimes can be.

New lakes may form where glaciers advance; Hubbard Glacier may block Russell Fiord around 1990 creating a lake 45 kilometers (28 miles) in length. Lakes may also form subglacially or in depressions on or adjacent to receding glaciers. In the past 200 years several very large former lakes have disappeared due to melting or retreat of glaciers; a large former lake dammed by Taku Glacier probably will not reform in 50 years even though the glacier has been advancing strongly since 1890. Recent Lake Alsek, largest glacier dammed lake in Western North America in recent centuries which rose to high levels about 120 and 200 years ago, could reform if Lowell Glacier were to surge strongly. Many other surging glaciers form lakes when advancing; a strong surge of Black Rapids Glacier could block the Delta River creating major floods.

Large floods can also be released from glaciers with no visible lakes. Lakes dammed by river icings in interior Alaska can create outburst floods. Glacier sheathed volcanoes present serious outburst flood hazards particularly when eruptions occur; recent eruptions of Redoubt Volcano and Mount Spurr produced floods resulting from glacier melt.

Conclusion: A Need for Recognizing Hazardous Areas and for Monitoring of Glacier Dammed Lakes

Floods from the outburst of glacier dammed lakes have caused considerable loss of property, damage to transportation links, and some danger to human life in Alaska. As man and his works move into new areas in or below glacier-clad mountains, the hazards created by glacier dammed lakes will become increasingly serious. The dangers can be mitigated by two actions: recognition of hazardous areas and surveillance of dangerous lakes in order to provide flood warnings.

U.S.G.S. Atlas HA 455 delimits specific areas of known or presumed hazard from glacier dammed lake outbursts. Detailed studies can define the dangers more precisely. Flood inundation mapping should be done for each future outburst flood in especially hazardous areas. Areas where flood data should be collected are identified in the table.

All flood hazards from glacier dammed lakes should be carefully evaluated by studying hydrological, glaciological, historical, and other pertinent data before planning highways, pipelines, and other economic improvements in downstream areas. Wherever practical, present and potential outburst flood areas should be avoided. All structures in hazardous zones should be engineered to withstand stream erosion and deposition, severe flooding, and winter ice jams.

For some situations monitoring of lake levels and ice jam characteristics is suggested. This monitoring can take many forms. Periodic aerial photography, as a first step, yields information on long-term changes in the lake and its bounding glacier. Sensors such as water-stage indicators might eventually be placed on certain lakes; preferably these would be tied to real time data acquisition systems so that warning of approaching danger could be recognized immediately. Because of the systematic nature of changes in outburst flood frequency and magnitude in certain cases (for example, Lake George and the lake above Snow River) prediction of outbursts can be made utilizing, in addition to hydrological information, glaciological data such as mass balance or changes in glacier thickness. Existing glacier research programs at nearby locations might provide relevant data.

Most major hazards in nature, such as earthquakes and major storms, are virtually impossible to predict. Glacier dammed lakes, especially the large ones, are clearly visible so that there is little need for ignorance about the location or extent of the hazard. Furthermore, simple monitoring or study of individual lakes makes possible approximate predictions of outburst frequency, magnitude, and perhaps even timing.

References

Alaska Department of Highways, 1970, Photographs of Nizina River bridge before, during, and after flood of June 1934; Emergency work follows lake dumping near Hyder: Alaska Dept. Highways Newsletter, v. 3, no. 8, 10 p.

Balvin, A. W., 1963, Tazlina River reconnaissance: Alaska Dept. Highways report, 25 p.

Bateman, A. M., 1922, Kennecott Glacier, Alaska: Geol. Soc. America Bull., v. 32, p. 527–539.

Bolton, D. F., 1959, Report on the failure of the Sheep Creek bridge at Mile 19, Richardson Highway: Dept. Commerce, U. S. Bur. Public Roads, Juneau, 6 p.

Capps, S. R., 1916, The Chisana-White River District, Alaska: U. S. Geol. Survey Bull. 630, 130 p.

Dawson, G. M., 1889, Report on an exploration in the Yukon District, N.W.T., and adjacent northern portion of British Columbia, 1887: Geol. and Nat. His. Survey of Canada, Ann. Rep., new ser., V. 3, pt. I, for 1887–88, The Stikine River, p. 46B–64B.

Doell, R. R., 1963, Seismic depth study of the Salmon Glacier, British Columbia: Jour. Glaciology, v. 4, no. 34, p. 425–437.

Eisenhuth, H. P., 1968, Index of surface-water records to September 30, 1967, Alaska: U. S. Geol. Survey Circ. 585, 18 p.

Ellsworth, C. E., and Davenport, R. W., 1915, A water power reconnaissance in south-central Alaska: U. S. Geol. Survey Water Supply Paper 372, 173 p.

Field, W. O., 1958a, Geographic studies of mountain glaciation in the Northern Hemisphere, Pt. 2a, Chap. 1, Glaciers of the Coast Mountains: Am. Geog. Soc., 95 p.

———— 1958b, Geographic study of mountain glaciation in the Northern Hemisphere, Pt. 2a, Chap. 3, Glaciers of the Chugach Mountains, Alaska: Am. Geog. Soc., 45 p.

Fisher, David, 1969, Subglacial leakage of Summit Lake, British Columbia, by dye determinations: Ottawa; Canada, Dept. Energy, Mines and Resources, Inland Waters Branch, 11 p. mimeographed report.

Gilbert, Robert, 1969, Some aspects of the hydrology of ice-dammed lakes: Observations on Summit Lake, British Columbia: Univ. British Columbia, Dept. Geology, MA Thesis, 93 p.

Glen, J. W., 1954, The stability of ice-dammed lakes and other waterfilled holes in glaciers: Jour. Glaciology, v. 2, no. 15, p. 316–318.

Hanson, George, 1932, Varved clays of Tide Lake, British Columbia: Royal Soc. Canada Trans., Sec. IV, p. 335–339.

Haumann, Dieter, 1960, Photogrammetric and glaciological studies of Salmon Glacier: Arctic, v. 13, no. 2, p. 74–110.

Hayes, C. W., 1892, An expedition through the Yukon District: Natl. Geog. Mag., v. 4, p. 117–159.

Hoffman, J. E., 1970, Master plan for the proposed Keystone Canyon State Park: Univ. Alaska Inst. Social, Economic, and Government Research, No. 25, 90 p.

Indermuhle, V. C., 1961, Preliminary report on the waterpower resources of Snow River, Nellie Juan Lake and Lost Lake, Kenai Peninsula, Alaska: U. S. Geol. Survey open-file report, 55 p.

International Boundary Commission, 1952, Establishment of the Boundary between Canada and the United States, Tongass Passage to Mount St. Elias: U. S. Dept. State, Washington, D. C., 365 p.

Jackson, B. L., 1961, Potential waterpower of Chakachamna Lake, Alaska: U. S. Geol. Survey open-file report, 20 p.

Juhle, Werner, and Coulter, Henry, 1955, The Mt. Spurr eruption, July 9, 1953: Am. Geophys. Union Trans., v. 36, no. 2, p. 199–202.

Kerr, F. A., 1928, Second preliminary report on Stikine River area, British Columbia: Canada Geol. Survey Summ. Report, Pt. A, p. 11A–26A.

———— 1934, The ice dam and floods of the Talsekwe, British Columbia: Geog. Rev., v. 24, p. 643–645.

———— 1936, Extraordinary natural floods of Talsekwe River, Taku District, northern British Columbia and southeastern Alaska: Royal Soc. Canada Trans., Ser. 3, v. 30, sec. 4, p. 133–135.

Kindle, E. D., 1953, Dezadeash map-area, Yukon Territory: Canada Geol. Survey Mem. 268, 68 p.

Knudsen, D. C., 1951, Alaska's automatic lake drains itself: Natl. Geog. Mag., v. 99, no. 6, p. 835–844.

Kuentzel, M. A., 1970, Flood hydrology of Alaskan glacier-dammed lakes: Trans Alaska Pipeline System report, 9 p.

Lawrence, D. B., 1950, Glacier fluctuations for six centuries in southeastern Alaska and its relation to solar activity: Geog. Rev., v. 40, no. 2, p. 191–223.

Liestøl, Olav, 1956, Glacier dammed lakes in Norway: Norsk Geog. Tidsskr., v. 15, p. 122–149.

Lindsay, J. F., 1966, Observations on the level of a self-draining lake on the Casement Glacier, Alaska: Jour. Glaciology, v. 6, no. 45, p. 443–445.

Mandy, J. T., 1936, North-Western Mineral Survey District (No. 1): Ann. Report Minister of Mines of Prov. British Columbia 1936, pt. B, 63 p.

Marcus, M. G., 1960, Periodic drainage of glacier-dammed Tulsequah Lake, British Columbia: Geog. Rev., v. 50, no. 1, p 89–106.

Martin, G. C., 1905, The petroleum fields of the Pacific Coast of Alaska, with an account of the Bering River coal deposits: U. S. Geol. Survey Bull. 250, 64 p.

———— 1908, Geology and mineral resources of the Controller Bay region, Alaska: U. S. Geol. Survey Bull. 335, 141 p.

Mathews, W. H., 1964, Water pressure under a glacier: Jour. Glaciology, v. 5, no. 38, p. 235–240.

———— 1965, Two self-dumping ice-dammed lakes in British Columbia: Geog. Rev., v. 55, no. 1, p. 46–52.

———— 1971, The record of two jökulhlaups: Internat. Assoc. Sci. Hydrology, Cambridge Symposium 1969, Pub. 95 (in press).

McConnell, R. G., 1904, The Kluane Mining District: Canada Geol. Survey 1904 Ann. Report.

Meier, M. F., 1960, The outbreak of a glacier-dammed lake [abs.]: Jour Geophys. Research, v. 65, no. 4, p. 1315.

Mendenhall, W. C., 1899, A reconnaissance from Resurrection Bay to the Tanana River, Alaska, in 1898: U. S. Geol. Survey 20th Ann. Report, Pt. 7, p. 265–340.

Miller, M. M., 1952, Preliminary notes concerning certain glacier structures and glacial lakes on the Juneau Ice Field: Am. Geog. Soc., Juneau Icefield Research Project rept. no. 6, p. 49–86.

———— 1963, Taku Glacier evaluation study: Alaska Dept. Highways, 200 p.

———— 1970, The 1970 Glaciological and Arctic Sciences Institute Juneau Icefield and Taku-Atlin Region, Alaska-B.C.-Yukon: Mich. State Univ. Glaciological and Arctic Sciences Inst., Ann. Report no. 11, 36 p.

Moffitt, F. H., 1938, Geology of the Chitina Valley and adjacent area, Alaska: U. S. Geol. Survey Bull. 894, 137 p.

Moffitt, F. H., and Capps, S. R., 1911, Geology and mineral resources of the Nizina District, Alaska: U. S. Geol. Survey Bull. 448, 111 p.

Muir, John, 1915, Travels in Alaska: Boston, Houghton Miffin Co., 325 p.

Nichols, R. L., and Miller, M. M., 1952, The Moreno Glacier, Lago Argentino, Patagonia: Jour. Glaciology, v. 2, p. 41–50.

Nielsen, L. E., 1963, A glaciological reconnaissance of the Columbia Glacier, Alaska: Arctic, v. 16, no. 2, p. 134–141.

O'Neel, A. C., and Hawkins, E. C., 1910, Copper River bridge near Miles Glacier: Copper River and Northwestern Railway engineers report, 9 p.

Post, Austin, 1967, Effects of the March 1964 Alaska earthquake on glaciers: U. S. Geol. Survey Prof. Paper 544–D, 42 p.

———— 1969, Distribution of surging glaciers in western North America: Jour. Glaciology, v. 8, no. 53, p. 229–240.

Ragle, R. H., Sater, J. E., and Field, W. O., 1965a, Effects of the 1964 Alaskan earthquake on glaciers and related features: Arctic Inst. North America Research Paper 32, 44 p.

———— 1965b, Effects of the Alaska earthquake on glaciers and related features: Arctic, v. 18, no. 2, p. 135–137.

Reger, R. D., and Péwé, T. L., 1969, Lichenometric dating in the central Alaska Range; in Péwé, T. L., ed., The Periglacial environments: McGill-Queens Univ. Press, p. 223–247.

Reid, H. F., 1896, Glacier Bay and its glaciers: U. S. Geol. Survey 16th Ann. Report, 1894–1895, Pt. I, p. 415–61.

Richardson, Donald, 1968, Glacier outburst floods in the Pacific Northwest: U. S. Geol. Survey Prof. Paper 600–D, p. D79–D86.

Russell, I. C., 1898, The glaciers of North America: Geog. Jour., v. 12, p. 558.

Scidmore, E. R., 1899, The Stikine River in 1898: Natl. Geog. Mag., v. 10, no. 1, p. 1–15.

Stone, K. H., 1955, Alaskan ice-dammed lakes: Arctic Inst. North America, Proj. ONR-67, 86 p.

———— 1963a, Alaskan ice-dammed lakes: Assoc. Am. Geographers Annals, v. 53, p. 332–349.

———— 1963b, The annual emptying of Lake George, Alaska: Arctic, v. 16, no. 1, p. 26–40.

Tarr, R. S., and Martin, Lawrence, 1914, Alaskan glacier studies: Natl. Geog. Soc., 498 p.

Thorarinsson, Sigurdur, 1939, The ice dammed lakes of Iceland with particular reference to their values as indicators of glacier oscillations: Geog. Annaler, Arg. 21, Ht. 3–4, p. 216–242.

223   Floods

——— 1953, Some new aspects of the Grimsvötn problem: Jour. Glaciology, v. 2, no. 14, p. 267–275.

Tryggvason, E., 1960, Earthquakes, jökulhlaups and subglacial eruptions: Jökull, Årg. 10, p. 18–22.

Tuthill, S. J., and Laird, W. M., 1966, Geomorphic effects of the earthquake of March 27, 1964 in the Martin-Bering Rivers area, Alaska: U. S. Geol. Survey Prof. Paper 543-B, 29 p.

U. S. Geological Survey, 1957, Compilation of records of quantity and quality of surface water of Alaska through September 1950: U. S. Geol. Survey, Water-Supply Paper 1372, 255 p.

——— 1964, Compilation of records of surface water of Alaska, October 1950 to September 1960: U. S. Geol. Survey Water Supply Paper 1740, 83 p.

——— 1961–70, 1960–69, Surface water records of Alaska: Anchorage, Alaska, Water Resources Division, published annually.

Wilson, C. R., and Forbes, R. B., 1969, Infrasonic waves from Alaskan volcanic eruptions: Jour. Geophys. Research v. 74, no. 18, p. 4511–4522.

21   Flood-Hazard Mapping in Metropolitan Chicago

John R. Sheaffer, Davis W. Ellis, and Andrew M. Spieker

Introduction

The effective management of flood plains consists of more than building detention reservoirs and levees. As urban pressures are forcing more and more developments on flood plains, such devices as flood-plain regulations and flood proofing are coming into wider use. These devices, however, require information as to what areas are likely to be flooded. The need for flood-plain information is further intensified by Federal legislation such as the National Flood Insurance Act of 1968 (Title XIII, Public Law 90–448) and recent Federal policies on use of flood plains (U. S. Congress, 1966; Executive Order 11296).

The present report describes how these needs are being met in the Chicago SMSA (Standard Metropolitan Statistical Area) by a cooperative program involving the six counties of the metropolitan area—Cook, Du Page, Kane, Lake, McHenry, and Will—the Northeastern Illinois Planning Commission, the State of Illinois, and the U. S. Geological Survey. This unique flood-mapping program, in progress since 1961, has resulted in coverage of nearly the entire six-county metropolitan area by maps showing the flood hazard. Figure 1 is a map of the area showing the extent of coverage in June 1969. Quadrangles showing an HA (U. S. Geological Survey Hydrologic Investigations Atlas) number are published and available for sale at the Northeastern Illinois Planning Commission, or the U. S. Geological Sur-

Sheaffer, J. R., Ellis, D. W., and Spieker, A. M., 1969, "Flood-Hazard Mapping in Metropolitan Chicago" U. S. Geol. Survey Circ. 601-C, 14 pp.

Mr. Sheaffer is affiliated with the Center for Urban Studies, The University of Chicago. Davis Ellis and Andrew Spieker are on the staff of the U. S. Geological Survey.

vey, Washington, D. C. Quadrangles without an HA designation are in progress or are scheduled for future mapping. At present this coverage is about 85 percent complete. Metropolitan Chicago is the only large metropolitan area in the United States for which this information is so widely available.

The purpose of this report is to describe how the program originated and is being carried out, the outlook for improving this program to meet the changing needs of the rapidly urbanizing metropolitan area, and the various ways flood maps can be used by individuals and public and private institutions.

Flooding in Metropolitan Chicago

Floodflows in the rivers and waterways of Metropolitan Chicago have periodically spilled from their channels and inundated the adjacent lowlands or flood plains. The earliest recorded flood in the Chicago area occurred on March 29, 1674, when the explorer priest Marquette and his companions were driven from their camp near Damen Avenue by high water coming through Mud Lake, from the Des Plaines River. However, such overflows did not become hazards, except possibly to navigation, until development of the flood plains gave the floods something to damage.

In retrospect, it is conceivable that if adequate land-use planning, based on sound hydrologic data in conjunction with regulatory and flood-proofing measures, had guided the development of our flood plains, there would be little, if any, improper use today and no major flood problems would exist.

Flood damages have been steadily increasing as urban sprawl has engulfed many flood plains and subdivisions have been located on sites subject to flooding. The absence of accurate information on these areas subject to flooding has been a limitation on efforts to formulate a comprehensive flood damage reduction program. The need for this information is particularly acute in Metropolitan Chicago and other topographically, similar regions of flat terrain and poorly developed drainage, where the flood plains are not readily perceptible to the human eye.

The Concept of Flood-Hazard Mapping

Flood-hazard mapping is a means of providing flood-plain information for planning and management programs. Such information should be designed to assist officials and private interests in making decisions and alternative plans concerning the development of specific lands subject to flooding. Proper use of flood-hazard mapping will help to:

1. Prevent improper land development in flood-plain areas.

2. Restrict uses that would be hazardous to health and welfare and which would lead to undue claims upon public agencies for remedy.

3. Encourage adequate stream channel cross-section maintenance.

4. Protect prospective home buyers from locating in flood-prone areas.

5. Preserve potential for natural ground-water recharge during flood events.

6. Guide the purchase of public open space.

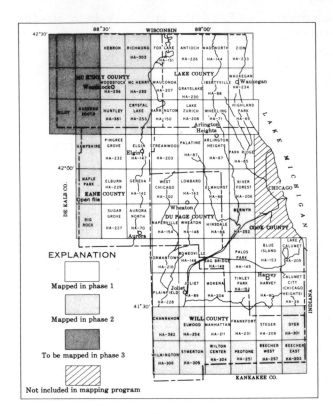

FIG. 1. The Chicago metropolitan area showing location of quadrangles included in flood-hazard mapping program.

7. Avoid water pollution resulting from the flooding of sewage treatment plants and solid waste disposal sites that were located on flood plains.

What is a Flood-Hazard Map?

A flood-hazard map uses as its base a standard U. S. Geological Survey topographic quadrangle which includes contours that define the ground elevation at stated intervals. Each of the quadrangles covers an area 7½ minutes of longitude wide by 7½ minutes of latitude deep, or approximately 57 square miles. The scale of the flood maps is 1:24,000, or 1 inch equals 2,000 feet. The area inundated by a particular "flood of record" is superimposed in light blue on the map to designate the "flood-hazard area." Also marked on the flood-hazard map are distances (at ½-mile intervals) along and above the mouth of each stream and the locations of gaging stations, crest-stage gages, and drainage divides. Figure 2 shows part of the Elmhurst quadrangle, a typical flood map.

Profiles and Probabilities

Accompanying the flood-hazard map are explanatory texts, tables, and graphs, which facilitate their use. One set of graphs shows the linear flood profiles (see Fig. 3) of the major streams in the quadrangle; from them, the user can tell how high the water rose at any given point during one or more floods.

Another valuable tool (Fig. 4) is a set

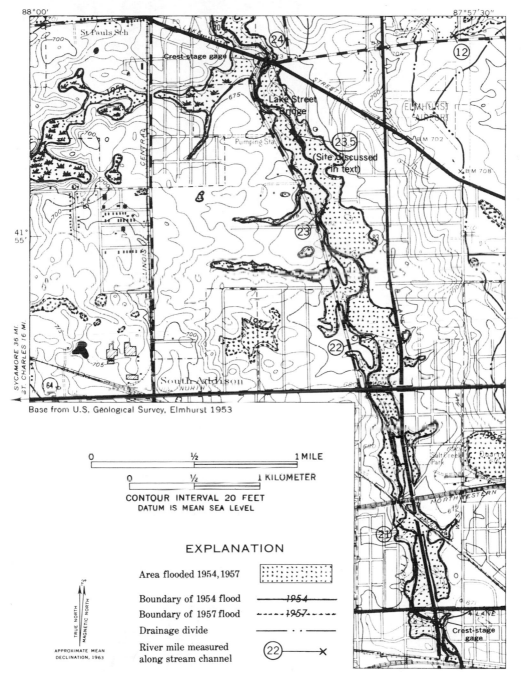

FIG. 2. Flood-hazard map of part of the Elmhurst quadrangle. Adapted from Ellis, Allen, and Noehre (1963).

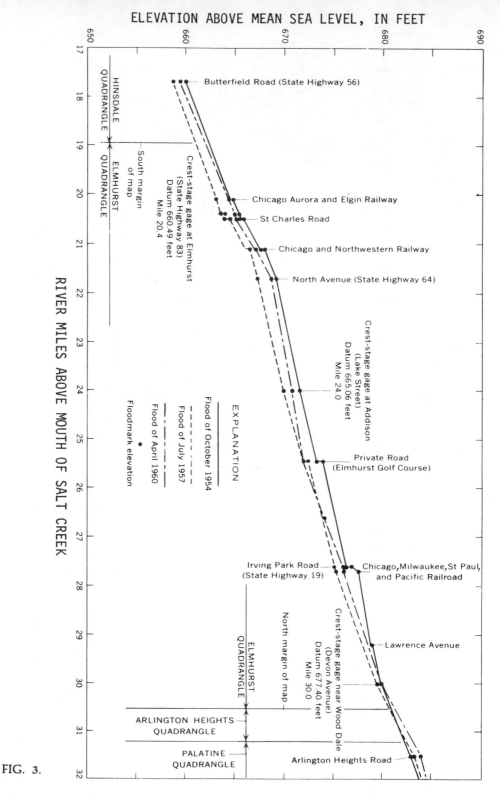

FIG. 3.

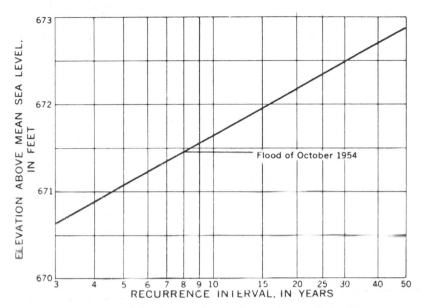

FIG. 4. Frequency of floods on Salt Creek at Addison (Lake Street).

of graphs showing probable frequency of flooding at selected gaging stations. These charts indicate the average interval (in years) between floods that are expected to exceed a given elevation. Frequencies can also be expressed as probabilities which make it possible to express the flood risk or "flood hazard" for a particular property; for example, a given area may have a 5-percent chance of being inundated by flood waters in each year.

How to Use a Flood-Hazard Map

To illustrate the use of a flood-hazard map, assume that you own property along Salt Creek, near Elmhurst and about half a mile south of Lake Street. Perhaps you plan to build there, and you want to know the risk of being flooded. You examine the Elmhurst quadrangle flood-hazard map (Fig. 2) and note that your property is located

at a point 23.5 miles above the mouth of Salt Creek. (The river miles are shown on the map.)

One of the graphs accompanying the map is a flood-frequency curve for Salt Creek (Fig. 4). This curve, however, is for a particular point on Salt Creek—the Lake Street Bridge. To apply the flood-frequency relationship to your own property will require an adjustment for the water-surface slope between the two points. So you consult another graph, the one which shows profiles or high-water elevations, of floods along Salt Creek (Fig. 3). There, you find that at the Lake Street Bridge (river mile 24) the 1954 flood crested at 671.5 feet, while at the point you are interested in (river mile 23.5) the crest was at 671 feet.

Returning now to the flood-frequency curve, you find that the 1954 flood has an 8-year "recurrence interval," meaning that, over a long period of time, floods can be expected to reach or exceed that level on an average of once every 8 years. That level, you have already found, is 671.5 feet at Lake Street and 671 feet at your property. Another way of thinking of it is this: if you were to erect a building on your property at 671-foot elevation, the chances of a flood reaching the structure in any given year would be approximately one in eight. These are only odds—probabilities—and the actuality may be better or worse. But the odds are poorer than most property owners are willing to accept, so you will probably want to seek better odds at higher ground.

Suppose you were willing to accept a flood risk of one every 25 years: What is the ground elevation at which a building should be situated to enjoy that much security?

The flood-frequency curve indicates that, at the Lake Street Bridge, an elevation of 672.3 feet corresponds to the 25-year recurrence interval. You now plot this elevation at river mile 24 on the flood-profile chart and draw a straight line through the point you have plotted and parallel to the 1954 flood profile. You now have the profile for a flood with a 25-year recurrence interval, and it shows that the elevation reached by such a flood at your property would be 671.8 feet. Using the line you have drawn, you can determine corresponding elevations (for the same recurrence interval) at other points along Salt Creek. And, of course, you can use the method outlined to approximate the elevation at your property for other recurrence intervals—up to 50 years.

The Metropolitan Chicago Flood-Mapping Program

It was determined that flood-hazard mapping could meet some of the needs that had become evident in Metropolitan Chicago. However, it was also recognized that flood-hazard mapping of such a large area could not be accomplished overnight. It would require financing, time, careful planning, and data. The flood-mapping program is a cooperative effort, financed jointly by the six counties of Metropolitan Chicago, the Northeastern Illinois Planning Commission, the State of Illinois, and the U. S. Geological Survey. Funds offered by the six counties through the Planning Commission which serves in an administrative and coordinating role, are matched on a one-to-one basis with Federal funds. The actual mapping is done by personnel of the U. S. Geological Survey. In 1968 the State of Illinois entered into a separate, though similar, cooperative agreement with the U. S. Geological Survey to assist with part of the financing. The flood-mapping program was carried out in phases. The first phase extended from July 1, 1961 to June 30, 1966. Phase 2 extended from July 1, 1966 to June 30, 1969. The formulation of a phase 3 is currently (1969) being discussed among the principal agencies involved.

Phase 1

In phase 1 of the program, flood maps were prepared for 43 7½-minute quadrangles in the six-county area. One flood atlas, U. S. Geological Survey Hydrologic Investigations Atlas HA–39, "Floods in the Little Calumet River basin near Chicago Heights, Ill.," had been prepared previously by the Geological Survey as a prototype for the program. Each quadrangle is given the name of a principal city or prominent geographic feature located on the map. The location of these quadrangles is shown in Fig. 1.

The scope of phase 1 is shown in Table 1 and Fig. 1. The average cost of preparing a flood map initially was estimated as $6,250, or a cost to the local agencies of $3,125, and the initial agreements between local agencies and the Planning Commission were prepared on this basis. Early in the program, however, it was found that, for several quadrangles, particularly in Lake County, there was need for supplemental contours on the flood-plain areas. These were provided under a supplemental agreement among the appropriate agencies. Partly because of this change, and partly because of steadily rising costs throughout the 5-year period of the program, the total expenditure for phase 1, including the supplemental contours, the preparation of inundation maps for 43 quadrangles, and the installation and operation to June 30, 1966, of the initial 229 crest-

Table 1 Scope of phase 1 of flood-mapping program, July 1961 to June 1966

Counties	Quadrangles mapped
Cook	[1]13
Du Page	6
Kane	6
Lake	10
McHenry	1
Will	8
Total	44

[1] Includes Calumet City quadrangle. Chicago Heights, which was prepared as a pilot project, was not included as part of program.

stage gages, was $299,860, or about $6,975 per quadrangle.

Another item of possible interest to those who may plan similar programs is the expenditure of manpower. All operations were conducted from the Survey subdistrict office at Oak Park, near the geographic center of the area. A total of 37,372 direct man-hours were required to complete phase 1; this indicates an average of 869 direct man-hours per quadrangle. There was, however, considerable variation for the individual quadrangles, ranging from a maximum of 1,455 man-hours to a minimum of 520 man-hours. Man-hours required for providing the supplemental contours are not included in these figures, as this part of the work was performed under a contractual arrangement with the Topographic Division of the Geological Survey.

Because of insufficient hydrologic data in much of the area, it was necessary to establish 229 crest-stage gages to record instantaneous flood peaks so that flood profiles and flood-plain limits could be better defined along the approximately 1,000 miles of streams located in the 43 quadrangles.

Preparation for phase 2 of the flood-mapping program involved the installation of an additional 165 crest-stage gages in McHenry, Kane, and Will Counties in 1963. The installation of these gages was necessary because the hydrologic events on many of the streams in southern Will County and western Kane and McHenry Counties had never been recorded. These gages are located in 19 quadrangles which were scheduled for mapping during phase 2. The costs were covered by supplementary cooperative agreements with the affected counties.

A flood-hazard mapping program can lead to other related hydrologic studies. A study of the role of flood-plain information and related water resource management concepts in comprehensive land-use planning (Spieker, 1969) was made by the Geological Survey, at the request of the Planning Commission, in 1965–67. This study used the Salt Creek basin in Cook and Du Page Counties as a demonstration area to illustrate principles which govern the effects of alternative land-use practices, particularly uses of the flood plains, on the overall water resources of the area. Emphasis was placed on the interrelationship of the various components of the hydrologic system, particularly the interrelationship between surface water and ground water.

Phase 2

Phase 2 involved the preparation of 19 additional flood maps. (See Fig. 1.) In addition, the 394 crest-stage gages, including those located in areas already mapped, were kept in operation as part of phase 2 to extend the hydrologic records. The completion of phase 2 will make flood maps available for the en-

tire metropolitan area with the exception of the western part of Mc-Henry County and the completely urbanized area of Chicago and the close-in suburbs in Cook County. This area, which comprises four quadrangles, was not mapped because urbanization has obliterated nearly all the natural flood plains and overbank flooding is generally not a problem.

The scope of phase 2 is presented in Table 2. A proportionally larger share of the local cost was allocated to Mc-Henry and Will Counties because a major part of the work was done in those two counties. In 1967, the State of Illinois, through the Division of Waterways of the Department of Public Works and Buildings entered into a separate cooperative agreement with the Geological Survey to assume part of Will County's share of phase 2 mapping. The cost of mapping in phase 2 was $174,600, of which $86,200 was provided by local agencies and $88,400, by the Geological Survey. (The difference of $2,200 was due to supplemental allotments of Survey funds, unmatched by local funds, to partially cover interim increases in Federal salary rates.) At the comple-

Table 2 Scope of phase 2 of flood-mapping program, July 1966 to June 1969

Counties	Quad-rangles mapped	Total number of gages	Gages having peak dis-charge data
Cook	2	70	8
Du Page		36	12
Kane	3	58	11
Lake		40	11
McHenry	6	52	8
Will	8	138	19
Total	19	394	69

tion of phase 2, the total cost of flood mapping in the metropolitan area was $474,460. (This cost includes operation of the entire network of 394 crest-stage gages to June 30, 1969.)

The Formulation of Phase 3

Providing adequate flood information in an urban area is a continuing activity. Floods will continue to occur and will provide new and additional information. Spreading urbanization can alter both the frequency and the patterns of flooding. Paving and covering of the land tends to accelerate storm runoff and increase flood peaks. Manmade changes in the channel cross section can alter flooding patterns. Examples of such changes are bridges, culverts, fill on the flood plain, and building on the flood plain. These changes take place at a rapid pace in a fast growing area such as Metropolitan Chicago.

To keep up with these changes will require periodic revision of the flood-hazard maps. Many of the maps are based on information which is 8 years old. Additional flooding and a great deal of urbanization has taken place during these 8 years. The crest-stage gage network has provided a wealth of data to document these flood events and to help in analyzing the changes resulting from urbanization.

Phase 2 of the flood-mapping program terminated in 1969. In continuing the program into its third phase, the following four activities should be considered.

1. Continued operation of the existing network of crest-stage gages. The crest-stage gage network is believed to be the densest such network in the country. About 8 years of record will be available at the completion of phase 2 of the program. As urban development continues, the continued availability of flood-stage information will be increasingly important. Such data would be valuable in determining rates if a flood-insurance program became operational.

2. Evaluation of the crest-stage gage network for adequacy and relevance. Although the existing network is one of the most comprehensive in the country, there exists a need for its review to eliminate redundant gages and to add new ones where needed. The 8 years of record would be useful in this evaluation.

3. Extension of the program to unmapped areas. At the completion of phase 2 all of the six-county metropolitan areas except the completely urbanized central city and the western 40 percent of McHenry County will be mapped. The remainder of McHenry County is already planned for inclusion in phase 3. Before the metropolitan area expands into Kankakee and Kendall Counties, the flood-mapping program should be extended there to provide a part of the basis for orderly growth.

4. Periodic and systematic revision of the flood maps prepared in phases 1 and 2. All existing maps should be evaluated as to their adequacy and a systematic program should be planned for updating the maps where urbanization and additional flood data warrant it. This should be a continuing process. Examples of maps greatly in need of revision are the Calumet City (HA–39) and Arlington Heights (HA–67) quadrangles. In addition to mapping floods of record, consideration should be given to defining floods of given frequencies:

for example, at 25-, 50-, and 100-year recurrence intervals. Even though the cost of such a mapping program would be considerably greater than that of mapping historical floods, the maps would provide a more sound and consistent basis for considering the element of risk in planning and decision making. Profiles at the selected frequencies also should be included in future mapping. This kind of flood information would be especially useful in determining premium rates under the National Flood Insurance Act of 1968. It has been agreed,[1] for example, that the area inundated by the 100-year flood should define the regulatory area under the Flood Insurance Act.

Continuation of the cooperative flood-hazard mapping program along these lines will assure that local governmental bodies, industries, utilities, developers, and citizens of Metropolitan Chicago will have more and better flood information which can be used in furthering the region's orderly development.

The Crest-Stage Gage Network

The Northeastern Illinois Planning Commission and the U. S. Geological Survey's cooperative flood-mapping program required the establishment of a network of crest-stage gaging stations.

A crest-stage gage is a rather simple device that records the maximum elevation of floods. These gages are mounted on wingwalls or piers of highway bridges and culverts or anchored in concrete along stream banks. After the gages are mounted, levels are run from nearby benchmarks to establish datum (zero) of the gages referred to mean sea level, datum of 1929. The

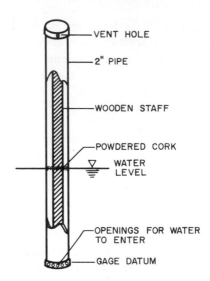

FIG. 5. Typical crest-stage gage.

base of these gages is set above normal water levels so that they record only flood elevations. The sketch in Fig. 5 illustrates how the gage functions. Water enters the gage through specially designed holes at the bottom of the pipe. Finely ground cork at the bottom of the gage floats on the water surface and comes in contact with the wooden staff located inside of the pipe. As the water recedes, the cork adheres to the staff and provides a record of the maximum stage of the flood.

After a flood, the crest-stage gage is serviced by opening the gage, withdrawing the staff, and measuring the distance from the base of the staff to the top of the cork line. After the measurements are made, the cork is removed from the staff, any debris that has collected is removed from the holes at the base of the gage, new cork is added, and the gage is reassembled. It is then ready to record the elevation of the next flood. By adding the depth of water recorded on the staff (gage height) to the gage datum, the elevation of the flood in feet above mean sea level is determined.

Usefulness of Flood-Hazard Maps in Urban Development

The main purpose of flood-hazard mapping, as stated previously, is to make available information which can be used to bring about the orderly and beneficial use of areas subject to flooding. A wide range of institutions and devices exists through which this information can be put to use. The following outline presents the general categories of flood-plain information use:

1. Regulation of private development:
   a. By public institutions:
      (1) Building, subdivision, and zoning regulations.
      (2) Sewer connection permits.
      (3) Public financial institutions (that is, Federal Housing Administration, Veterans Administration).
      (4) Land management and use criteria of the flood insurance program.
   b. By private institutions:
      (1) Financial institutions.
      (2) Private utilities (that is, gas, electric).
2. Purchase of property for public use:
   a. Forest preserve districts (county).
   b. Parks and recreation facilities.
   c. Municipal parking lots.
3. Development of public facilities:
   a. Highways and streets.
   b. Sewer extensions, treatment plant locations.
4. Guidelines (planning) for future development.

Following is a résumé of how the flood-hazard maps have actually been used to give direction to urban development in the Chicago metropolitan area.

Regulation of Private Development

One of the most frequently employed devices of flood-plain management is flood-plain zoning. The zoning authority is usually delegated to local governments, villages, and cities. County governments may exercise zoning powers in the unincorporated areas.

The Northeastern Illinois Planning Commission (1964) has prepared a model flood-plain zoning ordinance for the assistance of county and local governments. This model is the basis for many of the flood-plain zoning ordinances that have been adopted by Metropolitan Chicago communities.

Progress in the adoption of flood-plain zoning ordinances by county and municipal governments has been varied. As of late 1968 three of the six metropolitan counties—Cook, Du Page, and Lake—had adopted such ordinances. Kane County does not have a flood-plain zoning ordinance as such, although its zoning ordinance and subdivision regulations set forth conditions for subdivision development in flood-hazard areas. As of October 1968, 94 of the 117 Cook County municipalities located in the Metropolitan Sanitary District had adopted flood-plain zoning ordinances. There are 20 Cook County municipalities within the Sanitary District which do not have recognized flood hazards. An additional three are revising ordinances which have been rejected as unsatisfactory. Outside of Cook County, only a few municipalities have adopted flood-plain zoning ordinances.

One of the reasons for the large number of Cook County municipalities taking action is the policy adopted in 1967 by the Metropolitan Sanitary District regarding the issuance of sewer permits. The policy states that: "No permits shall be issued by the Metropolitan Sanitary District for sewers to be constructed within a flood-hazard area, as delineated on the maps prepared by the United States Geological Survey in cooperation with the Northeastern Illinois Planning Commission, until the local municipality has adopted a flood-plain zoning ordinance which meets the approval of the Sanitary District."

"Permits in undeveloped areas will not be approved until Cook County adopts flood-plain zoning regulations."

"The ordinance shall include but not be limited to the following:

1. Restrictions on residential development.

2. Provisions for establishing permanent flood way channels through acquisition of rights-of-way, including easements for maintenance and improvements.

3. Requirements for flood proofing buildings within the flood-hazard areas. The ordinance shall be adopted before September 1, 1967."

This policy has proved highly effective in encouraging municipalities to adopt flood-plain zoning ordinances. In addition, Cook County has adopted a flood-plain ordinance which applies to all its unincorporated areas.

Financial institutions, public and private, can exert a powerful influence over the location of private urban development. Where flood-plain informa-tion is available, these institutions are generally reluctant to finance housing development in flood-hazard areas. The financing of housing in flood-prone areas is a risk that financial institutions would rather not assume, provided that there exists a knowledge of this risk. In the Chicago metropolitan area the Veterans Administration and the Federal Housing Administration routinely check the location on the U. S. Geological Survey's flood-hazard maps of new housing developments which they are considering financing. These agencies as a matter of policy will not finance developments in areas known to be subject to flooding. A large number of private financial institutions (banks, savings and loan companies) make similar use of the flood-hazard maps.

Private utility companies can influence urban development by where they choose to extend—or not to extend—gas and electric lines. By recognizing that development on flood plains is not wise, utility companies are in an excellent position to prevent their development by refusing to service them. Flood-hazard maps thus can be useful to utility companies by helping them to identify those areas where they might wish to discourage development.

Purchase of Property for Public Use

The public development of flood-hazard areas for recreation or aesthetic purposes has long been recognized as a technique of flood-plain management. Green belts, or undeveloped areas along streams, can provide breaks in the monotony of urban sprawl. The construction of municipal parking lots is another example of public use of flood plains. Identification on flood-hazard maps of those areas subject to flooding can assist public officials in acquiring these lands at a reasonable price.

The Du Page County Forest Preserve District is now engaged in a long-range program of land acquisition whose purpose is to develop a major green belt along the West Branch of the Du Page River. The U. S. Geological Survey's flood-hazard maps have been extremely useful in providing guidelines for land purchase. Also, they have been helpful in negotiations for public open space acquisition in Cook and Lake Counties.

Development of Public Facilities

Public facilities frequently lead urban development into flood-hazard areas. The State Division of Highways has made frequent use of the flood-plain maps in their highway planning process. Proper planning of access can tend to discourage improper flood-plain development.

The location of sewage treatment plants and sanitary landfills is also influenced by flood-plain information. An example of such use is found in "Rules and Regulations for Refuse Disposal Sites and Facilities" (Illinois Department of Public Health, 1966, p. 1). This document states that: "sites subject to flooding should be avoided . . . or protected by impervious dikes and pumping facilities provided." Thus, flood-plain information becomes involved in all decisions regarding the establishment of disposal sites and facilities and is cited by the State Geological Survey in their site-evaluation reports.

Guidelines (Planning) for Future Development

Planning, or the formulation of guidelines for future development, provides the overall framework in which the previously discussed uses of flood-hazard maps are implemented. It is in the planning process that the broad, long-range goals and objectives are set out. These objectives can be attained by alternate tactics.

The importance of wise management of the flood plains has been recognized by the Regional Planning Agency for Metropolitan Chicago, Northeastern Illinois Planning Commission, almost from its inception. Examples of how the flood-hazard maps are influencing long-range planning can be found in the two following policy statements taken from the Northeastern Illinois Planning Commission's comprehensive general plan for Metropolitan Chicago (Northeastern Illinois Planning Commission, 1968, p. 7): "Lands unsuited for intensive development due to flooding, unstable soil conditions, or where the provision of essential public services and facilities is difficult, should be maintained in suitable open space use." And on page 11: "Intensive urban development should be directed so as to avoid flood plains, protect ground water deposits, and preserve lands particularly suited for multi-purpose resources management programs."

Notes

[1] Consensus of Seminar on Flood Plain Management held at the Center for Urban Studies, University of Chicago, December 16-18, 1968, at the request of the U. S. Department of Housing and Urban Development.

References

Bue, C. D., 1967, Flood information for flood-plain planning: U. S. Geological Survey Circular 539, 10 p.

Ellis, D. W., Allen, H. E., and Noehre, A. W., 1963, Floods in Elmhurst quadrangle, Illinois: U. S. Geol. Survey Hydrol. Inv. Atlas HA-68.

Illinois Department of Public Health, 1966, Rules and Regulations for Refuse Disposal Sites and Facilities: Illinois Dept. Public Health, Springfield, Ill., 7 p.

Mitchell, W. D., 1964, Some problems in flood mapping in Illinois: Natl. Acad. Sci.—Natl. Research Council Highway Research Board, Highway Research Rec. 58, p. 42–43.

Northeastern Illinois Planning Commission, 1964, Suggested flood damage prevention ordinance with commentary: Northeastern Illinois Planning Comm., Chicago, Ill., 28 p.

———— 1968, A regional armature for the future: The comprehensive general plan for the development of the northeastern Illinois counties: Northeastern Illinois Planning Comm., Chicago, Ill., 12 p.

Sheaffer, J. R., 1964, The use of flood maps in northeastern Illinois: Natl. Acad. Sci. —Natl. Research Council Highway Research Board, Highway Research Rec. 58, p. 44–46.

Sheaffer, J. R., Zeizel, A. J., and others, 1966, The water resources in northeastern Illinois—Planning its use: Northeastern Illinois Planning Comm. Tech. Rept. 4, 182 p.

Spieker, A. M., 1969, Water in metropolitan area planning: U. S. Geological Survey Water-Supply Paper 2002. (In press.)

U. S. Congress, 1965, A unified national program for managing flood losses: U. S. 89th Cong., 2d sess., House Doc. 465, 47 p.

22 Flood-Plain Management Must Be Ecologically and Economically Sound

James E. Goddard

Over the past 35 years in the U. S., some $8 billion has been spent for dams, levees and channelization to limit flood losses. Yet over that same 35 years, losses due to floods have risen, as shown in the reports "Changes in Urban Occupance of Flood Plains," by Gilbert F. White & Associates, Univ. of Chicago, 1958; "Types of Agricultural Occupance of

Reprinted from *Civil Engineering*, v. 41, pp. 81–85, by permission of the author and the American Society of Civil Engineers. Copyright 1971 ASCE.
Mr. Goddard was on the staff of the Tennessee Valley Authority and the Corps of Engineers. He is currently a consulting engineer in Tucson, Arizona.

Flood Plains," by Ian Burton, Univ. of Chicago, 1962; and House Document 465, "A Unified National Program for Managing Flood Losses," 1966. The average annual potential flood losses are now well over $1 billion.

Such data as these led to the conclusion that flood-control works are not the entire answer. Better agricultural practices and land control over development in flood plains, to hold the rainwater and snowmelt on the land longer and to wisely limit occupation and investment in flood plains must be part of the answer, though difficult to achieve.

In and near the cities, especially, a

judicious blend of flood-control measures—and regulatory measures—is required. A few cities are finding that their work in tackling flood problems has had broader results, with the effort leading to redevelopment of the entire town.

Following are case histories of flood-damage prevention illustrating positive ecological and environmental effects.

Channelization

In "Crisis on our Rivers," in *Reader's Digest*, December 1970, James Nathan Miller charged that federal agencies are blindly channelizing rivers and streams in order to foster development and stop flooding, but that for ecological and other reasons it would be better to forbid channelization and stop flood-plain development. There may be cases where Mr. Miller's advice should be followed; however, in many instances development either cannot be stopped or need not and there will be little ecological price to pay. Following are examples to support this statement.

Bear Creek—Alabama and Mississippi
Bear Creek winds through fertile bottomlands, from northwest Alabama into northeast Mississippi before it empties into Pickwick Lake on the Tennessee River. Trees crowd its banks and, in places, almost choke off its normal flow. Most of the time, stream and neighbors remain at peace. But several times each year, heavy rains swell the flow and a smoldering controversy is resumed.

It happens that farmers and owners of flood-prone bottomland propose channelization, for it would mean re-lief from flooding of their lands. But to the sportsmen and fish and wildlife biologists, channelization would mean uprooting the creek's complex system of plant and animal life which nature has established over many years. They cite studies which indicate reductions of up to 90 percent in both the weight and number of game fish per acre following stream channelization.

A solution has been found which largely satisfies both interests. Floodways are being built by the Tennessee Valley Authority in areas where channelization is required to provide flood protection to some 17,600 acres of potentially productive land. These wide and shallow floodways cut diagonally across the meandering river channel, at a higher level than the existing streambed. Low flows will continue to be handled by the old streambed, with its ecology largely undisturbed. But during floods, the surplus flow will be handled by the shallower but larger-capacity floodways. (See Fig. 1.) When not in use these grassed flood-ways will be dry and hardly noticeable as their broad, flat bottoms and gently sloping sides provide pasture and walkways for livestock.

A similar application is the separate, auxiliary floodway built by the Corps of Engineers to bypass floods on the Arkansas River around Wichita, Kansas, and thus preserve the waterfront through the city.

Coastal Marsh near Houston
On the low coastal lands east of Houston, about 75 percent of the 36,000-acre East Bay Bayou watershed was in a rice-then-pasture rotation. Rice production requires intricate irrigation and water-disposal systems. July and August are not only the high-

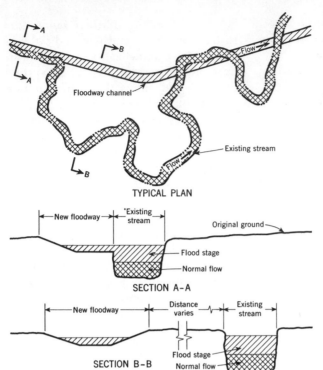

TYPICAL PLAN

Floodway channel

Existing stream

Flow

SECTION A-A

New floodway — Existing stream — Original ground

Flood stage
Normal flow

SECTION B-B

New floodway — Distance varies — Existing stream

Flood stage
Normal flow

FIG. 1. In Bear Creek, both ecology and development have been served. Most of the time, all flow is through the deeper but constricted natural channel, thus preserving the river ecology. During floods, the overflow passes through the new channel, thereby avoiding flooding of adjacent lands and making them developable.

rainfall months, but also rice-harvest time when floods can ruin a crop. Drainage is into the narrow, shallow East Bayou (see Fig. 2) that twisted through the marsh to the coast. During heavy rains the stream overflowed, dumping excessive fresh water into the marsh.

However, the brackish water, with salinity one-fourth to one-half that of sea water due to occasional high tidewaters lapping over a high rim near the coast, is excellent habitat for muskrats, ducks and geese. It also supports some of the best livestock grazing to be found. But during years of heavy rainfall, the excessive fresh water often diluted the brackish water. This damaged wildlife habitat, dumped sediment into the marsh, and reduced livestock forage from plants thriving under brackish conditions.

Watershed planners and biologists agreed on a plan to channelize East Bay Bayou and add spoil banks along both sides. To permit regulating the amount of fresh or saline water going into or out of the marsh, and thus controlling brackishness and flood heights, 10 semi-automatic two-way gates and 16 other flap gates were installed in the spoil banks (see Fig. 2).

As a result of this regulation, duck and geese hunting flourishes with 134,000 man-days annually in the region; muskrat trapping provides more than 3,500 pelts; commercial fishing in the bayou exceeds 20,000 lb annually; range grasses in the marsh have been improved and flood damages to the rice crop have been sharply reduced, nearly doubling the income. This was a cooperative effort of the U. S. Agriculture Department's Soil Conserva-

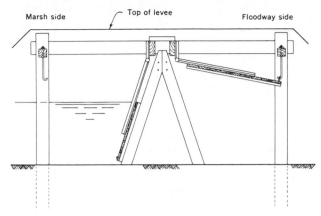

FIG. 2. East Bay Bayou floodway, near Houston; ten of these semi-automatic, two-way gates in spoil banks on either side of floodway maintain proper levels and mixtures of brackish-fresh water to benefit both agriculture and wildlife. When the right-hand gate is lowered, water will flow to the right, but not to the left.

tion Service, with the U. S. Bureau of Sport Fisheries and Wildlife, and the Texas Parks and Wildlife Department.

Danger if Flood Problem is not Tackled

It is unfortunate that many cities and counties are permitting bad flood-plain practices to continue.

This seems to be happening in the Upper Mill Creek Watershed that lies 10 miles north of Cincinnati in Ohio, and within the influence of that major city. Of the 50-sq-mi watershed, about three sq mi are subject to one to three floods per year.

Despite the flood hazard, farming continues and industrial development is accelerating. Private levees built to protect private lands restrict flows because of their haphazard location. When one looks at the situation as a watershed-wide problem, they are a bad partial solution. Cost of industrial flood damages will triple from $200,000 to $678,000 annually in a few years if nothing is done.

A plan to alleviate the situation, as prepared by the Soil Conservation Service, included four flood-retarding and one multipurpose structure and some channel improvement—but there have

been delays in implementation. The proposed project would cost $4.6 million, with average annual benefits of $0.9 million, and average annual costs of $0.2 million, for a benefit-cost ratio of about 4 to 1.

Landowners and governments are aware of the danger of inaction. Local sponsors know that delays will bring increased costs, and thus threaten the economic feasibility of the program, because of increasing encroachments of new construction in the flood plain, of housing and utility lines and industrial plants. This construction should not be permitted because of the negative effect on the economy and ecology. Three of five sites proposed for flood-control structures have already been seriously affected by the developments.

Unfortunately, this watershed is just one of hundreds of such cases in which unwise practices are continuing. Engineers must increase their efforts in arousing greater public understanding that will spark appropriate action.

Sometimes, Relocation is the Answer

Prairie du Chien, a town of about 6,000, is on the Mississippi River in

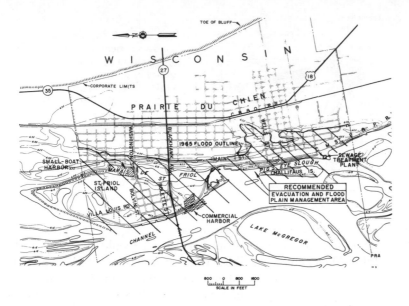

FIG. 3. Map of Prairie du Chien, Wi., showing flood plain. It is
proposed that the area shown be evacuated and that 205 buildings be
removed from the flood plain. Most would be relocated to higher
ground.

Wisconsin. The river valley at this point is some 8,000 ft wide between high cliffs, and the Mississippi normally is confined to two channels, each 1,000 ft wide. The town is in the valley, and is occasionally flooded, usually by the combination of spring snow melt and spring rains. (See Fig. 3, showing flood plain.)

Thorough investigation determined that levees, walls and upstream reservoirs were neither technically sound nor economically justified. The most feasible solution was found to be evacuation and flood-plain regulations. Such a plan has been recommended by the Board of Engineers for Rivers and Harbors, and by the Chief of Engineers (Corps of Engineers).

The proposed solution provides for local ownership of project lands and for federal flowage easements. Implementation of flood-plain regulations and other land management is to be by nonfederal governments. About 48 buildings would be purchased and torn down, 157 relocated, 33 raised above 100-year flood level, and seven flood-proofed. Relocation sites would be graded and landscaped and utilities installed. Sites of razed buildings would be cleared of debris, filled, and graded as necessary to make them safe and attractive. Historical sites (this is an early fur-trading post) and business-complementing open-space use can remain, if they are floodproofed. City and state interests plan to develop the evacuated flood plain for recreation and tourism uses, during periods of other than flood flow, as demand for those uses warrants.[1]

Flood Proofing of Buildings in the Flood Plain

Sometimes it is not feasible or not desirable to move buildings out of the flood plain. And there are often major advantages or needs for new buildings in flood plains. An alternative is to make them water-tight to above flood level.

A good example is found in St. Bernard Parish (county), east of New Orleans, La. Most of the land is low marshland, typically about 1.5 ft. above sea level. The lowlands extend inland for varying distances of about 20 to 50 miles. These Louisiana coastal areas have experienced many severe hurri-canes and lesser storms. Perhaps even more damaging than the winds are the hurricane-induced flood waters, which push inland from the Gulf. Thus flood protection is required.

There are flood levees in portions of St. Bernard Parish, but extending them around additional areas is not economically justified. A recent Corps of Engineers study indicated that the most practical approach would be to flood-proof structures, including constructing buildings with their lowest floor at least 12 ft above mean sea level (see Fig. 4). An alternative, if a building is not so constructed, would be early evacuation to protected areas.

FIG. 4. New Sabastian Roy School replaced one destroyed by Hurricane Betsy south of New Orleans, La. It was flood proofed by elevating the lowest floor 10 ft to level of 100-year flood. The open ground level, paved, will be used for recreation. (Photo courtesy U. S. Corps of Engineers.)

Land Filling

Land can be filled and buildings constructed thereon.

An example is found in Waterloo, Iowa (pop. 74,000) on the Cedar River. Some 4,200 acres are in the flood plain; this land holds most of the city's commercial development, 46 industrial plants, more than 5,000 homes, water and sewage plants, municipal buildings, and many schools, churches, etc.

Fill available from river-channelization dredging will be placed behind a new levee-road, and this filled land will be available for flood-safe construction. Behind about two miles of the berm, some 1,500 acres of filled land will be available.

Flood-Proofing

Individual buildings, both new and existing, can be flood proofed. Details are contained in the report, "Introduction to Flood Proofing," by John R. Schaeffer, Center for Urban Studies, University of Chicago, 1967.

Other Management (non-structural) Solutions

By habit, training, and historic precedent, civil engineers and officials tend to think first of structural solutions to a problem. In the case of flood problems, there are important non-structural alternatives that must also be considered. Generally, the optimum solution will be a combination of several approaches, both structural and non-structural. Three of the many non-structural techniques or management tools are flood-plain regulations, flood insurance, and flood forecasting.

Flood-Plain Regulations

One of the outstanding programs, which by its very nature provides and insures opportunities for ecological and environmental-quality enhancement and preservation is that of flood-plain regulations. In this type of program, a community or state uses its police powers to guide and control use and development of flood-plain lands.

Generally zoning ordinances, subdivision regulations, building codes, and similar ordinances are enacted which will: (1) provide for open areas or floodways which will permit floods to pass without so constricting the flow as to unduly raise the flood level and thus worsen the problem, and (2) require floors of buildings in the remainder of the flood plain (outside the open floodway) to be higher than selected flood elevations, or that buildings be flood-proofed to this elevation.

The benefits of such regulations are seen in the case of Lewisburg, Tn. Because it had not adopted flood-plain regulations, the construction of some 20 houses was halted (the city wanted to wait to see the regulations before issuing a building permit). Had these homes been built, they would have been under 6 to 10 ft of water in the flood that occurred four months later.

Several states have active, effective statewide programs of this type, requiring regulation, including Nebraska, Connecticut, Iowa, Minnesota, and Wisconsin. Wisconsin also has a shorelands program to preserve nature and to guide development along the shores of its many lakes and streams. (See "Wisconsin's Shoreland Management Program," December 1970 issue, p. 80.) California, Washington, Oregon and New Jersey also have programs designed to lead to wise use. Tennessee, North Carolina, and others have still different approaches. But many of these programs need to be strengthened and the remaining two-thirds of the states need to act. One acre in 16 in the U. S. is in a flood plain, and most states have not done enough.

Over the past 15 years, about 360 communities throughout 35 states have adopted regulations and 500 additional places in 41 states have them in adoption process. This is heartening but this is a discouragingly small fraction of the 5,200 significant-size towns and cities wholly or partially in flood plains.[2]

Help is available to the cities and states. Reports containing hydrologic and hydraulic data outlining the local flood situation are prepared by the Corps of Engineers, TVA, and others. These are the basis for designing the needed regulations.

Flood Insurance

A Federal Flood Insurance Program, authorized by Congress in 1968, for the first time makes flood damage insurance available at premiums which large numbers of owners are willing to pay. Already nearly 100,000 policies have been written.

As intended, the federal law is proving to be a spur to responsible development (or non-development, if indicated) of the flood plain. For example, availability of the insurance has led scores of cities and counties, such as Alexandria, Va. and Santa Cruz County, Az., to adopt their first flood-plain regulations. More than 500 others, from Fairbanks, Al. to Maricopa County, Az. to Palm Beach, Fl., are in the process of adopting regulations. If the cities and counties do not pass such regulations, their landowners cannot continue to get the insurance.

Flood Forecasting

The forecasting of flood stages, and then temporary evacuation, permit continued occupation of innumerable areas where other measures that may upset ecology have not been taken.

In recent years the U. S. Weather Service has improved its techniques, more of the data required for reliable forecasting are available, organization for implementing disaster and relief plans are improved, and public awareness is greater.

A good example of benefits to be derived from flood forecasting was Operation Foresight of the Corps of Engineers, Associated General Contractors, and others. This was in the spring of 1970 for the upper Mississippi River Valley when record flood stages hit cities on the Mississippi, Red, and Souris rivers causing more than $100 million in damage. Relying on accurate stage forecasts, levees were raised by earthmoving equipment provided at cost by regional contractors, other remedial structural action was taken, many structures floodproofed, and some areas evacuated in an effort estimated to have saved $190 million in flood damages (CE, June 1969, p. 99).

Conclusion

Today "ecology" is a popular watchword in the mass media and the federal government. "Development" is currently out of favor in much of the land. Clearly, in the past too little attention has been paid to conservation and ecology. Some construction projects were undertaken which should not have been, or which should have been modified. But today, to some engineers the danger seems to be that some construction projects are being held up or cancelled, despite their being ecologically acceptable on balance; they are held up because there is political capital to be gained in so doing, or because politically there is no choice but to kill the projects.

Stopping all river channelization, or all flood-plain and water-resource development, is not the answer. In some individual cases, yes; in others, no. Needed today is a team effort by development interests and conservation interests.

Human beings also are part of the environment. America has never needed the decent middle, honest center ground of discussion and compromise as it does now. Hopefully, knowing that man cannot live by ecology alone, public-spirited members of environmental groups will curb harmful pursuits of some of their leaders in the interest of more constructive approaches. And, hopefully, the engineering profession will take the steps necessary to be the effective catalyst.

Today all federal agencies have the same worthy objectives. The differences and misunderstandings rise from the methods of reaching these goals. Through close cooperation of all parties and better public understanding of both sides of the issues, channelization, flood-plain regulations, and other flood-plain management measures can be used, but wisely.

The federal government is moving in the right direction: the federal Water Resources Council was established in 1965 to coordinate the actions of federal agencies; a Presidential Task Force report of 1966 on managing flood losses is gradually being implemented; and in 1970 Congress instructed the Secretary of the Army (Corps of Engineers) to prepare and promulgate by 1972 appropriate guidelines for an ecological impact assessment and statement with each federal project.[3]

But the goals are not yet reached. Today developers are asked to fully consider alternative ways to reach goals; this costs more money, manpower, and time than have been available in the past. Government must meet this need without further delay.

Public understanding is needed. In public discussions by the media and government officials and representatives, reason should replace emotion, and both sides of a question should be aired, not just the conservation or the construction side. Engineers and ecologists and environmentalists must work more closely together as partners, and must develop evaluation measures in addition to economic (the dollar is not the only measure of well being).

Notes

[1] The flood-plain management plan for Prairie du Chien has been authorized by Congress in the Water Resources Development Act of 1974. Funds have been provided to initiate the first phase of planning. It is anticipated that Phase I studies should be completed by July 1976 [Ed.]

[2] As of July 1, 1973, the Corps of Engineers had completed about 870 Flood Plain Information Reports involving 2500 places. As a result 750 communities had adopted flood-plain regulations or strengthened existing

regulations. An additional 780 communities had regulations in process of adoption. Many communities have also acted on information developed by themselves or agencies other than the Corps. [Ed.]

[3] Environmental Impact Statements are required by Section 102 (2)(c) of the National Environmental Policy Act of 1969 (Public Law 91-190) and prepared according to Council on Environmental Quality Guidelines for Statements on Proposed Federal Actions Affecting the Environment, dated August 1, 1973. The requirement applies to all planning, design, construction, management, and regulation of civil works activities of the Corps of Engineers. [Ed.]

Supplementary Readings

General

Leet, L. D., 1948, *Causes of Catastrophe,* McGraw-Hill Book Co., Inc.

Leet, L. D., and Judson, S., 1971, *Physical Geology,* 4th ed., Prentice-Hall, New Jersey, 687 pp.

Olson, R. A., and Wallace, M. M., 1969, *Geologic Hazards and Public Problems,* Conference Proceedings (May 27–28, 1969), U. S. Office of Emergency Preparedness, 335 pp.

Putman, W. C., 1971, *Geology,* 2nd ed. revised by A. B. Bassett, Oxford Univ. Press, New York, 586 pp.

White, G. F., 1974, *Natural Hazards; Local, National, Global,* Oxford Univ. Press, New York, 288 pp.

Volcanism

Bullard, F. M., 1962, *Volcanoes: in History, in Theory, in Eruption,* University of Texas Press, Austin, Texas.

Crandell, Dwight R., 1971, Postglacial Lahars from Mount Rainier Volcano, Washington, *U. S. Geological Survey Prof. Paper No. 677.*

Crandell, Dwight R., and Mullineaux, Donal R., 1967, Volcanic Hazards at Mount Rainier, *U. S. Geol. Survey Bull. 1238,* 26 pp.

Eaton, J. P., Richter, D. H., and Ault, W. V., 1961, The Tsunami of May 23, 1960, on the Island of Hawaii, *Seismological Soc. of Amer. Bull.* v. 51, pp. 135–57.

Jaggar, T. A., 1945, Protection of Harbors from Lava Flow, *Amer. Jour. Sci.,* v. 243-A, pp. 333–35.

Keller, G. V., Jackson, D. B., and Rapolla, A., 1972, Magnetic Noise Preceding the August 1971 Summit Eruption of Kilauea Volcano, *Science,* v. 175, pp. 1457–58.

Lear, J., 1966, The Volcano that Shaped the Western World, *Saturday Rev.,* v. 49 (Nov. 5, 1966), pp. 57–66.

Mason, A. C., and Foster, H. L., 1953, Diversion of Lava Flows at Oshima, Japan, *Amer. Jour. Sci.,* v. 251, pp. 249–58.

MacDonald, G. A., 1972, *Volcanoes,* Prentice-Hall, New Jersey.

Maiuri, A., Bianchi, P. V., and Battaglia, L. E., 1961, Last Moments of the Pompeians, *Natl. Geog.,* v. 120, pp. 651–69.

Richter, D. H. et al., 1970, Chronological Narrative of the 1959–60 Eruption of Kilauea Volcano, Hawaii, *U. S. Geological Survey Prof. Paper 537-E.*

Tyrrell, George W., 1931, *Volcanoes,* Oxford Univ. Press.

Wexler, Harry, 1952, Volcanoes and World Climates, *Sci. Amer.,* v. 186, n. 4, pp. 74–80.

Wilcox, Ray E., 1959, Some Effects of Recent Volcanic Ash Falls with Especial Reference to Alaska, *U. S. Geol. Survey Bull. 1028-N,* pp. 409–76.

Williams, Howell, 1951, Volcanoes, *Sci. Amer.,* v. 185, n. 5, pp. 45–53.

Earthquake Activity and Tectonic Movements

Anderson, D. L., 1971, The San Andreas Fault, *Sci. Amer.,* v. 225, n. 5, pp. 52–67.

Bernstein, J., 1954, Tsunamis, *Sci. Amer.* v. 191, n. 2, pp. 60–63.

Dickinson, W. R., and Grantz, A., eds., 1968, Proceedings of Conference on Geologic Problems of San Andreas Fault System, *Stanford Univ. Pubs. Geol. Sci.,* v. 11, pp. 70–82.

Eckel, E., 1970, The Alaska Earthquake March 27, 1964: Lessons and Conclusions, *U. S. Geol. Survey Prof. Paper 546,* 57 pp.

Fairbridge, R., 1958, Dating the Latest Movements of the Quaternary Sea Level, *Trans. N. Y. Acad. Sci.,* Ser. II. v. 20, n. 6, pp. 471–82.

Fairbridge, R., 1960, The Changing Level of the Sea, *Sci. Amer.* v. 202, n. 5, pp. 70–79.

Flint, R. F., 1971, *Glacial and Quaternary Geology* (chap. 12, Fluctuation of Sea Level, and chap. 13, Glacial-Isostatic Deformation), John Wiley & Sons, Inc., New York, 892 pp.

Fuller, M. L., 1914, The New Madrid Earthquake, *U. S. Geol. Survey Bull. 494.*

Gutenburg, B., 1941, Changes in Sea Level, Postglacial Uplift and Mobility of the Earth's Interior, *Bull. Geol. Soc. Amer.,* v. 52, n. 5, pp. 721–22.

Hagiwara, T. and Rikitake, T., 1967, Japanese Program on Earthquake Prediction and Control, *Science,* v. 166, no. 3912, pp. 1467–74.

Hammond, A. L., 1973, Earthquake Prediction (II): Prototype Instrumental Networks, *Science,* v. 180, pp. 940–41.

Hess, H. H., 1946, Drowned Ancient Islands of the Pacific Basin. *Amer. Jour. Sci.,* v. 244, pp. 772–91.

Hodgson, J. H., 1964, *Earthquakes and Earth Structure,* Prentice-Hall, New Jersey, 166 pp.

Kisslinger, C., 1974, Earthquake Prediction, *Physics Today,* v. 27, pp. 36–42.

Lomnitz, C., 1970, Casualties and Behavior of Populations During Earthquakes, *Bull. Seismological Soc. Amer.* v. 60, pp. 1309–13.

Lomnitz, Cinna, 1973, Global Tectonics and Earthquake Risk, *Developments in Geotectonics,* v. 5, Elsevier, Amsterdam, 334 p.

National Academy Sciences, 1971, *The San Fernando Earthquake of February 9, 1971: lessons learned from a moderate earthquake on the fringe of a densely populated region,* Wash. D. C.

Palmer, D., and Henyey, T., 1971, San Fernando Earthquake of 9 February 1971: Pattern of Faulting, *Science,* v. 172, pp. 712–15.

Parkin, E. J., 1948, Vertical Movement in the Los Angeles Region, 1906–1946, *Trans. Amer. Geophys. Union,* v. 29, n. 1, pp. 17–26.

Press, F. and Brace, W. F., 1966, Earthquake Prediction, *Science,* v. 152, n. 3729, pp. 1575–84.

Radbruch, D. et al., 1966, Tectonic Creep in the Hayward Fault Zone California, *U. S. Geological Survey Circular 525.*

Reid, H. F., 1914, The Lisbon Earthquake of November 1, 1755, *Seismol. Soc. of Amer. Bull.,* v. 4, pp. 53–80.

Rogers, T. H., 1969, A Trip to An Active Fault in the City of Hollister, *Mineral Information Service,* v. 22, n. 10, pp. 159–64.

Russell, R. J., 1957, Instability of Sea Level, *Amer. Scientist,* v. 45, p. 414–30.

Ryall, A., Slemmons, D. B., and Gedney, L. D., 1966, Seismicity, Tectonism, and Surface Faulting in the Western United States During Historic Time, *Seismol. Soc. Amer. Bull.,* v. 61, n. 12, pt. 2, pp. 1529–30.

Scholz, C. H., Sykes, L. R., and Aggarwal, Y. P., 1973, Earthquake Prediction: A Physical Basis, *Science,* v. 181, pp. 803–10.

Steinbrugge, K. V., 1968, *Earthquake Hazard in the San Francisco Bay Area: a continuing problem in public policy,* Univ. California Press, Berkeley, Calif.

Wallace, R. E., 1974, Goals, Strategy, and Tasks of the Earthquake Hazard Reduction Program, *U. S. Geological Survey Circular 701,* 26 pp.

Whitcomb, J. H., Garmany, J. D., and Anderson, D. L., 1973, Earthquake Prediction: Variation of Seismic Velocities before the San Francisco Earthquake, *Science,* v. 180, pp. 632–35.

Mass Movements

Arora, H. S., and Scott, J. B., 1974, Chemical Stabilization of Landslides by Ion Exchange, *California Geology,* v. 27, pp. 99–107.

Black, R. F., 1954, Permafrost—a Review, *Geol. Soc. Amer. Bull.,* v. 65, pp. 839–56.

Kerr, Paul F., 1963, Quick Clay, *Sci. Amer.*, v. 209, n. 5, pp. 132–42.

Leighton, F. B., 1972, Origin and Control of Landslides in the Urban Environment of California, *Proceedings 24th Session, International Geological Congress, section 13*, pp. 89–96.

McDowell, B., and Fletcher, J., 1962, Avalanche! 3,500 Peruvians Perish in Seven Minutes, *Natl. Geog.*, v. 121, pp. 855–80.

Sharpe, C. F. S., 1938, *Landslides and Related Phenomena*, Columbia Univ. Press, New York.

Shreve, R. L., 1968, The Blackhawk Landslide; *Geol. Soc. Amer., Spec. Paper No. 108.*

Terzaghi, K., 1950, Mechanism of Landslides, *Geol. Soc. Amer., Berkey Volume*, pp. 83–123.

Varnes, D. J., 1958, Landslide Types and Processes, chap. 3 in *Landslides and Engineering Practice, Highway Research Board, Spec. Rept. 29.*

Zaruba, A., and Mencl, V. 1968, *Landslides and Their Control*, Elsevier Pub. Co. Amsterdam, 205 pp.

Erosion and Sedimentation

Dendy, F. E., 1968, Sedimentation in the Nation's Reservoirs, *Jour. Soil and Water Conservation*, v. 23, n. 4, pp. 135–37.

Dolan, R., 1973, Man's Impact on the Barrier Islands of North Carolina, *Amer. Scientist*, v. 61, pp. 152–62.

El-Ashry, M. T., 1971, Causes of Recent Increased Erosion along United States Shorelines, *Geol. Soc. Amer. Bull.*, v. 82, pp. 2033–38.

Gorsline, D. S., 1966, Dynamic Characteristics of West Florida Gulf Beaches, *Marine Geology*, v. 4, pp. 187–206.

Guy, H. P., 1970, Sediment Problems in Urban Areas, *U. S. Geol. Survey Circular 601-E*, 8 pp.

Guy, H. P., and Ferguson, G. E., 1970, Stream Sediment: an Environmental Problem, *Jour. Soil and Water Conservation*, v. 25, pp. 217–20.

Hester, N., and Fraser, G., 1973, Sedimentology of a Beach Ridge Complex and its Significance in Land-Use Planning, *Env. Geol. Notes No. 63*, Ill. State Geol. Survey, 24 pp.

Ippen, A. T., ed., 1966, *Estuary and Coastline Hydrodynamics*, McGraw-Hill, New York.

Johnson, J. W., 1956, Dynamics of Nearshore Sediment Movement, *Amer. Assoc. Petroleum Geologist Bull.*, v. 40, p. 2211–32.

Krumbein, W. C., 1950, Geological Aspects of Beach Engineering in Paige, S. (Ed.) *Application of Geology to Engineering Practice*, Geol. Soc. Amer.

Legrand, H. E. and Stringfield, V. T., 1973, Karst Hydrology—A Review, *Jour. of Hydrology*, v. 20, pp. 97–120.

Martinez, J. D., 1972, Environmental Geology at the Coastal Margin, *Proceedings, XXIV Int. Geol. Congress, Symposium 1*, pp. 45–58, Montreal, Canada.

Newton, J. G., and Hyde, L. W., 1971, Sinkhole Problem in and near Roberst Industrial Subdivision, Birmingham, Alabama, recon. Geol. Survey Alabama Bull. 68, 42 pp.

Schwartz, M. L., 1967, The Bruun Theory of Sea Level Rise as a Cause of Shore Erosion, *Jour. Geol.*, v. 75, n. 1, pp. 76–92.

Shepard, F., 1973, *Submarine Geology*, (3rd ed.), Harper and Row, New York.

Shepard, F. P., and Wanless, H. R., 1970, *Our Changing Coastlines*, McGraw-Hill, New York, 539 pp.

Stall, J. B., 1966, Man's Role in Affecting Sedimentation of Streams and Reservoirs, pp. 79–95, in Bowder, K. L., ed., *Proceedings, 2nd Ann. Amer. Water Resources Cong.*, 465 pp.

Trask, P. D., ed., 1950, *Applied Sedimentation*, J. Wiley, N. Y., 707 pp.

Warren, W. M. and Wielchowsky, C. C., 1973, Aerial Remote Sensing of Carbonate Terranes in Shelby County, Alabama, *Ground Water*, v. 11, pp. 14–26.

Floods

Brahtz, J. F., 1972, *Coastal Zone Management: multiple use with conservation*. Wiley Interscience, N. Y., 352 pp.

Bue, C. D., 1967, Flood Information for Flood-Plain Planning, *U. S. Geol. Survey Circ. 539*, 10 pp.

Dougal, M. D., ed., 1969, *Flood Plain Management, Iowa's Experience*, Iowa State University Press, Ames, Iowa, 270 pp.

Emerson, J. W., 1971, Channelization: A Case Study, *Science*, v. 173, pp. 325–26.

Fisk, N. H., 1952, Geological Investigations of the Atchafalaya Basin and the Problem of Mississippi River Diversion, *Corps of Engineers, U. S. Army Waterways Exp. Station, Vicksburg, Miss.*

Hinson, H. G., 1965, Floods on Small Streams in North Carolina, Probable Magnitude and Frequency, *U. S. Geol. Survey Circ. 517,* 7 pp.

Hoyt, W. G., and Langbein, W. B., 1955, *Floods,* Princeton Univ. Press, Princeton, N. J.

Judge, J., 1967, Florence Rises from the Flood, *Natl. Geog.,* v. 132, pp. 1–43.

Leopold, L. B., 1962, Rivers, *Amer. Scientist,* v. 50, pp. 511–37.

Leopold, L. B., 1968, Hydrology for Urban Land Planning, *U. S. Geol. Survey Circular 554.*

Rantz, S. E., 1970, Urban Sprawl and Flooding in Southern California, *U. S. Geol. Survey Circular 601-B.*

Schneider, W. J., and Goddard, J. E., 1974, Extent and Development of Urban Flood Plains, *U. S. Geol. Survey Circular 601-J.*

U. S. Geological Survey Water-Supply Papers (series includes descriptions of severe floods which occur each year), U. S. Gov. Printing Office, Washington, D. C.

Films

Volcanism

Case History of a Volcano (National Educational Television, 1966: 30 min.)

Eruption of Kilauea, 1959–60 (U. S. Geological Survey, 1960: 25 min.)

The Heimaey Eruption: Iceland 1973 (University of Waterloo, 1974: 28 min.)

Volcanoes: Exploring the Restless Earth (Encyclopedia Britannica, 1973: 18 min.)

Earthquake Activity and Tectonic Movements

The Alaska Earthquake, 1964 (U. S. Geological Survey, 1966: 22 min.)

An Approach to the Prediction of Earthquakes (American Educational Films, 1967: 27 min.)

The San Andreas Fault (Encyclopaedia Britannica, 1973: 21 min.)

San Francisco—the City that Waits to Die (Time-Life, 1971: 58 min.)

The Trembling Earth (National Educational Television, 1968: 30 min.)

Tsunami (National Ocean Data Center, 1965: 28 min.)

Mass Movement

Mud (National Association of Conservation Districts, 1968: 20 min.)

Erosion and Sedimentation

Barrier Beach (ACI Films, 1971: 20 min.)

The Beach—a River of Sand (Encyclopaedia Britannica, 20 min.)

Erosion—Leveling the Land (Encyclopaedia Britannica, 1964: 14 min.)

The New Jersey Shoreline (Environmental Films, Inc., 1971: 18 min.)

Waterbound—The Carolina Barrier Islands, (North Carolina State Univ., 1974: 20 min.)

Floods

Storm—Tropical Storm Agnes (U. S. Defense Civil Preparedness Agency, 1974: 29 min.)

III. Mineral Resources and the Environment

Bingham Canyon Mine, Utah. Photo courtesy of U.S. Bureau of Mines and R. H. Dott, Jr.

The readings in Part Two dealt with the geologic hazards that limit Man's use of the physical environment. They illustrate that there are environmental limits that function, or should function, as constraints on the activities of Man. Part Three deals with natural resources. Readings 23 to 26 focus on the limits of these resources. Readings 27 to 31 consider the environmental impact of Man's intensive exploitation of these resources.

Outlook for the Future

"Better methods for estimating the magnitude of potential mineral resources are needed to provide the knowledge that should guide the design of many key public policies"

V. E. McKelvey

Pliny the Elder described the earth as "gentle and indulgent, ever subservient to the wants of man." Today, however, we often express concern about the ability of the earth to provide sufficient materials, energy, and food. Questions concerning the magnitude of resources arise in conjunction with a variety of problems at the local, national, and international levels. Decisions concerning price structure, import-export policies, research and development programs, exploration activities, population controls, rationing, conservation, land-use, and so on, are influenced, in part, by our estimates of the magnitude of our resources. We must know not only what exists now and can be produced under present economic and technologic conditions, but we must also know the potential represented by undiscovered deposits and known deposits that can not be profitably produced at the present time. In Reading 23 V. E. McKelvey, Director of the U. S. Geological Survey, presents a comprehensive system of resource classification and terminology that brings out the classes of resources that need to be taken into account when inventorying our mineral base. He also points out that a resource inventory is dynamic and may change rapidly with economic, technologic, exploration, and production activities.

Many scientists, engineers, and economists have expressed grave doubts about the adequacy of our resources while others are more optimistic. In Reading 24 Alvin Weinberg presents an optimistic view of the future but one that implies a drastically altered, energy-intensive world. Cheap nuclear power as an almost limitless energy source is the basis for his optimism. The cheap and almost limitless energy is applied to the desalination of sea water, the electrolytic reduction of metaliferous ores, and the development of a highly rationalized agro-industrial complex. While Weinberg recognizes the need for population control—a difficult social problem—he attempts to demonstrate how technology can be used to expand our resources.

Preston Cloud (Reading 25) suggests that, "the technological fix is not a panacea but an anesthetic," and he challenges other fundamental premises underlying the concept of "unlimited mineral resources." While acknowledging the role of economics and technology in evaluating current and potential resources, he is careful to demonstrate that these are not the sole factors governing the availability of mineral resources. They may, however, buy time in which to find better solutions.

It is clear that there are fundamental differences in assessing the magnitude of our resources, but the short-term problems of energy supply are real and with us today. A comprehensive overview of the energy "crisis" is presented in Reading 26.

Solar energy facility near Odeillo, France. Photo courtesy of Combustion Engineering Incorporated.

23 Mineral Resource Estimates and Public Policy

V. E. McKelvey

Not many people, I have found, realize the extent of our dependence on minerals. It was both a surprise and a pleasure, therefore, to come across the observations of George Orwell in his book *The Road to Wigan Pier*. When describing the working conditions of English miners in the 1930s he evidently was led to reflect on the significance of coal:

Our civilization . . . is founded on coal, more completely than one realizes until one stops to think about it. The machines that keep us alive, and the machines that make the machines are all directly or indirectly dependent upon coal. . . . Practically everything we do, from eating an ice to crossing the Atlantic, and from baking a loaf to writing a novel, involves the use of coal, directly or indirectly. For all the arts of peace coal is needed; if war breaks out it is needed all the more. In time of revolution the miner must go on working or the revolution must stop, for revolution as much as reaction needs coal. . . . In order that Hitler may march the goosestep, that the Pope may denounce Bolshevism, that the cricket crowds may assemble at Lords, that the Nancy poets may scratch one another's backs, coal has got to be forthcoming.

To make Orwell's statement entirely accurate—and ruin its force with complications—we should speak of min-

eral *fuels*, instead of coal, and of other minerals also, for it is true that minerals and mineral fuels are the resources that make the industrial society possible. The essential role of minerals and mineral fuels in human life may be illustrated by a simple equation,

$$L = \frac{R \times E \times I}{P}$$

in which the society's average level of living (L), measured in its useful consumption of goods and services, is seen to be a function of its useful consumption of all kinds of raw materials (R), including metals, nonmetals, water, soil minerals, biologic produce, and so on; times its useful consumption of all forms of energy (E); times its useful consumption of all forms of ingenuity (I), including political and socio-economic as well as technologic ingenuity; divided by the number of people (P) who share in the total product.

This is a restatement of the classical economists' equation in which national output is considered to be a function of its use of capital and labor, but it shows what capital and labor really are. Far from being mere money, which is what it is popularly thought to mean, capital represents accumulated usable raw materials and things made from them, usable energy, and especially accumulated knowledge. And the muscle power expended in mere physical toil, which is what labor is often

Reprinted with light editing from *American Scientist*, v. 60, pp. 32–40, with the permission of the author and the publisher. Copyright 1972 by Society of Sigma Xi. Dr. McKelvey is the Director of the U. S. Geological Survey.

thought to mean, is a trivial contribution to national output compared to that supplied by people in the form of skills and ingenuity.

This is only a conceptual equation, of course, for numerical values cannot be assigned to some of its components, and no doubt some of them—ingenuity in particular—should receive far more weight than others. Moreover, its components are highly interrelated and interdependent. It is the development and use of a high degree of ingenuity that makes possible the high consumption of minerals and fuels, and the use of minerals and fuels are each essential to the availability and use of the other. Nevertheless, the expression serves to emphasize that level of living is a function of our intelligent use of natural resources, and it brings out the importance of the use of energy and minerals in the industrial society. As shown in Fig. 1, per capita

Gross National Product among the countries of the world is, in fact, closely related to their per capita consumption of energy. Steel consumption also shows a close relation to per capita GNP, as does the consumption of many other minerals.

Because of the key role that minerals and fuels play in economic growth and in economic and military security, the extent of their resources is a matter of great importance to government, and questions concerning the magnitude of resources arise in conjunction with many public problems. To cite some recent examples, the magnitude of low cost coal and uranium reserves has been at the heart of the question as to when to press the development of the breeder reactor—which requires an R & D program involving such an enormous outlay of public capital that it would be unwise to make the investment until absolutely necessary. Simi-

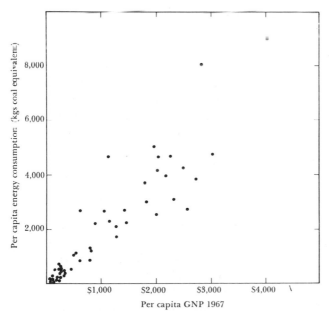

FIG. 1. Per capita energy consumption compared to per capita Gross National Product in countries for which statistics are available in the United Nations *Statistical Yearbook* for 1967.

larly, estimates of potential oil and gas resources are needed for policy decisions related to the development of oil shale and coal as commercial sources of hydrocarbons, and estimates are needed also as the basis for decisions concerning prices and import controls.

Faced with a developing shortage of natural gas, the Federal Power Commission is presently much interested in knowing whether or not reserves reported by industry are an accurate indication of the amount of natural gas actually on hand; it also wants to know the extent of potential resources and the effect of price on their exploration and development. At the regional or local level, decisions with respect to the designation of wilderness areas and parks, the construction of dams, and other matters related to land use involve appraisal of the distribution and amount of the resources in the area. The questions of the need for an international regime governing the development of seabed resources, the character such arrangement should have, and the definition of the area to which it should apply also involve, among other considerations, analysis of the probable character, distribution, and magnitude of subsea mineral resources.

And coming to the forefront is the most serious question of all—namely, whether or not resources are adequate to support the continued existence of the world's population and indeed our own. The possibility to consider here goes much beyond Malthus' gloomy observations concerning the propensity of a population to grow to the limit of its food supply, for both population and level of living have grown as the result of the consumption of nonre-

newable resources, and both are already far too high to maintain without industrialized, high-energy, and high mineral-consuming agriculture, transportation, and manufacturing. I will say more about this question later, but to indicate something of the magnitude of the problem let me point out that, in attaining our high level of living in the United States, we have used more minerals and mineral fuels during the last 30 years than all the people of the world used previously. This enormous consumption will have to be doubled just to meet the needs of the people now living in the United States through the remainder of their lifetimes, to say nothing about the needs of succeeding generations, or the increased consumption that will have to take place in the lesser developed countries if they are to attain a similar level of living.

Concepts of Reserves and Resources

The focus of most of industry's concern over the extent of mineral resources is on the magnitude of the supplies that exist now or that can be developed in the near term, and this is of public interest also. Many other policy decisions, however, relate to the much more difficult question of potential supplies, a question that to be answered properly must take account both of the extent of undiscovered deposits as well as deposits that cannot be produced profitably now but may become workable in the future. Unfortunately, the need to take account of such deposits is often overlooked, and there is a widespread tendency to think of potential resources as consisting merely of materials in known deposits producible under present economic and technologic conditions.

In connection with my own involvement in resource appraisal, I have been developing over the last several years a system of resource classification and terminology that brings out the classes of resources that need to be taken into account in appraising future supplies, which I believe helps to put the supply problem into a useful perspective. Before describing it, however, I want to emphasize that the problem of estimating potential resources has several built-in uncertainties that make an accurate and complete resource inventory impossible, no matter how comprehensive its scope.

One such uncertainty results from the nature of the occurrence of mineral deposits, for most of them lie hidden beneath the earth's surface and are difficult to locate and to examine in a way that yields accurate knowledge of their extent and quality. Another source of uncertainty is that the specifications of recoverable materials are constantly changing as the advance of technology permits us to mine or process minerals that were once too low in grade, too inaccessible, or too refractory to recover profitably. Still another results from advances that make it possible to utilize materials not previously visualized as usable at all.

For these reasons the quantity of usable resources is not fixed but changes with progress in science, technology, and exploration and with shifts in economic conditions. We must expect to revise our estimates periodically to take account of new developments. Even incomplete and provisional estimates are better than none at all, and if they differentiate known, undiscovered, and presently uneconomic resources they will help to define the supply problem and provide a basis for policy decisions relating to it.

The need to differentiate the known and the recoverable from the undiscovered and the uneconomic requires that a resource classification system convey two prime elements of information: the degree of certainty about the existence of the materials and the economic feasibility of recovering them. These two elements have been recognized in existing terminology, but only incompletely. Thus as used by both the mining and the petroleum industries, the term *reserves* generally refers to economically recoverable material in identified deposits, and the term *resources* includes in addition deposits not yet discovered as well as identified deposits that cannot be recovered now (e.g. Blondel and Lasky 1956).

The degree of certainty about the existence of the materials is described by terms such as *proved*, *probable*, and *possible*, the terms traditionally used by industry, and *measured*, *indicated*, and *inferred*, the terms devised during World War II by the Geological Survey and the Bureau of Mines to serve better the broader purpose of national resource appraisal. Usage of these degree-of-certainty terms is by no means standard, but all of their definitions show that they refer only to deposits or structures known to exist.

Thus one of the generally accepted definitions of *possible* ore states that it is to apply to deposits whose existence is known from at least one exposure, and another definition refers to an ore body sampled only on one side. The definition of *inferred* reserves agreed to by the Survey and the Bureau of Mines permits inclusion of completely concealed deposits for which there is specific geologic evidence and for which the specific location can be described, but it makes no allowance for ore in unknown structures of undiscovered districts. The previous definitions of both sets of terms also link them to deposits minable at a profit; the classification system these terms comprise has thus neglected deposits that might become minable as the result of technologic or economic developments.

To remedy these defects, I have suggested that existing terminology be expanded into the broader framework shown in Fig. 2, in which degree of certainty decreases from left to right and feasibility of recovery decreases from top to bottom. Either of the series of terms already used to describe degree of certainty may be used with reference to identified deposits and ap-

plied not only to presently minable deposits but to others that have been identified with the same degree of certainty. Feasibility-of-recovery categories are designated by the terms *recoverable, paramarginal,* and *submarginal.*

Paramarginal resources are defined here as those that are recoverable at prices as much as 1.5 times those prevailing now. (I am indebted to Stanley P. Schweinfurth for suggesting the prefix *para* to indicate that the materials described are not only those just on the margin of economic recoverability, the common economic meaning of the term *marginal.*) At first thought this price factor may seem to be unrealistic. The fact is, however, that prices of many mineral commodities vary within such a range from place to place at any given time, and a price elasticity of this order of magnitude is not uncommon for many commodities over a space of a few years or even months, as shown by recent variations

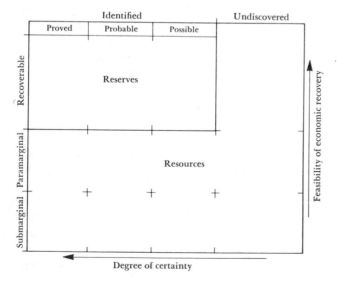

FIG. 2. Classification of mineral reserves and resources. Degree of certainty decreases from left to right, and feasibility of recovery decreases from top to bottom.

in prices of copper, mercury, silver, sulphur, and coal. Deposits in this category thus become commercially available at price increases that can be borne without serious economic effects, and chances are that improvements in existing technology will make them available at prices little or no higher than those prevailing now.

Over the longer period, we can expect that technologic advances will make it profitable to mine resources that would be much too costly to produce now, and, of course, that is the reason for trying to take account of submarginal resources. Again, it might seem ridiculous to consider resources that cost two or three times more than those produced now as having any future value at all. But keep in mind, as one of many examples, that the cutoff grade for copper has been reduced progressively not just by a factor of two or three but by a factor of ten since the turn of the century and by a factor of about 250 over the history of mining. Many of the fuels and minerals being produced today would once have been classed as submarginal under this definition, and it is reasonable to believe that continued technologic progress will create recoverable reserves from this category.

Examples of Estimates of Potential Resources

For most minerals, the chief value of this classification at present is to call attention to the information needed for a comprehensive appraisal of their potential, for we haven't developed the knowledge and the methods necessary to make meaningful estimates of the magnitude of undiscovered depos-

its, and we don't know enough about the cost of producing most presently noncommercial deposits to separate paramarginal from submarginal resources. Enough information is available for the mineral fuels, however, to see their potential in such a framework.

The fuel for which the most complete information is available is the newest one—uranium. As a result of extensive research sponsored by the Atomic Energy Commission, uranium reserves and resources are reported in several cost-of-recovery categories, from less than $8 to more than $100 per pound of U_3O_8. For the lower-cost ores, the AEC makes periodic estimates in two degree-of-certainty categories, one that it calls *reasonably assured reserves* and the other it calls *additional resources*, defined as uranium surmised to occur in unexplored extensions of known deposits or in undiscovered deposits in known uranium districts. Both the AEC and the Geological Survey have made estimates from time to time of resources in other degree-of-certainty and cost-of-recovery categories.

Ore in the less-than-$8-per-pound class is minable now, and the AEC estimates reasonably assured reserves to be 143,000 tons and additional resources to be 167,000 tons of U_3O_8—just about enough to supply the lifetime needs of reactors in use or ordered in 1968 and only half that required for reactors expected to be in use by 1980. The Geological Survey, however, estimates that undiscovered resources of presently minable quality may amount to 750,000 tons, or about two and a half times that in identified deposits and districts. Resources in the

$8-$30-a-pound category in identified and undiscovered deposits add only about 600,000 tons of U_3O_8 and thus do not significantly increase potential reserves.

But tens of millions of tons come into prospect in the price range of $30–$100 per pound. Uranium at such prices would be usable in the breeder reactor. The breeder, of course, would utilize not only U^{235} but also U^{238}, which is 140 times more abundant than U^{235}. Plainly the significance of uranium as a commercial fuel lies in its use in the breeder reactor, and one may question, as a number of critics have (e.g. Inglis 1971), the advisability of enlarging nuclear generating capacity until the breeder is ready for commercial use.

Until recently the only information available about petroleum resources consisted of estimates of proved reserves prepared annually by the American Petroleum Institute and the American Gas Association, plus a few estimates of what has been called ultimate production, i.e. the total likely to be eventually recovered. A few years ago, however, the API began to report estimates of total oil in place in proved acreage, and the Potential Gas Committee began to estimate possible and probable reserves of natural gas, defining them as consisting of gas expected to be found in extensions of identified fields and in new discoveries in presently productive strata in producing provinces. It also introduced another category, *speculative resources* —equivalent to what I have called "undiscovered"—to represent gas to be found in nonproducing provinces and in presently unproductive strata in producing provinces.

In 1970 the National Petroleum Council released a summary of a report on *Future Petroleum Provinces of the United States*, prepared at the request of the Department of the Interior, in which it reported estimates of crude oil in the combined probable–possible class and in the speculative category. In addition, NPC estimated the amounts that would be available under two assumptions as to the percent of the oil originally in place that might be recovered in the future (Table 1). NPC did not assess the cost of such recovery, but the average recovery is now about 30 percent of the oil in place, and NPC expects it to increase gradually to about 42 percent in the year 2000 and to 60 percent eventually. The NPC estimates do not cover all potentially favorable areas either on land or offshore but, even so, in the sum of these various categories NPC sees about twelve times as much oil remaining to be discovered and produced as exists in proved reserves alone.

The Potential Gas Committee's estimates of potential gas resources similarly do not cover all favorable areas, but they indicate that resources in the probable, possible, and speculative categories are about twice that of proved reserves and past production. Because about 80 percent of the gas originally in place is now recovered, paramarginal and submarginal resources in ordinary gas reservoirs are not as large as for crude oil. Paramarginal and submarginal gas resources may be significant, however, in kinds of rocks from which gas is not now recovered, namely impermeable strata and coal. In the Rocky Mountain province, for instance,

Table 1 Some estimates of U. S. crude oil reserves and resources (in billions of barrels)

	In identified fields or structures		In undiscovered fields and structures ("speculative")
	Proved	Probable–Possible	
Recoverable at present rate[1]	31 (API)	74 (NPC)	67 (NPC)
Additional at 42% recovery	47 (NPC)	22 (NPC)	21 (NPC)
Additional at 60% recovery	69 (NPC)	40 (NPC)	37 (NPC)
Oil originally in place	388 (API)[2]	227 (NPC)	209 (NPC)
Total oil originally in place	2200 (Hendricks-Schweinfurth)		
Ultimate production[2]	190 (Hubbert); 353 (Moore); 433 (Weeks); 450 (Elliott and Linden); 432–495 (NPC); 550 (Hendricks-Schweinfurth)		

[1] Average recovery is 30 percent of oil in place.

[2] Includes past production of 86 billion barrels.

Haun, Barlow, and Hallinger (1970) recently estimated potential gas resources in ordinary reservoirs to be in the range of 100–200 trillion cubic feet, but pointed out that gas in impermeable strata which might be released by nuclear stimulation would be several times that amount. Gas occluded in coal—now only a menace in this country as a cause of explosions—is already recovered in some European mines and is also a potentially large resource.

The uncertainties concerning potential coal resources center not on their total magnitude, as they do for oil and gas, but on the amounts available at present prices. Because coal beds have great lateral continuity, geologic mapping and stratigraphic studies make it possible to project them long distances from their outcrops and to categorize them in terms of thickness of beds, thickness of overburden, rank of coal, and other features that affect cost.

The Geological Survey has prepared such estimates, but the cost of recovering coal in the various categories has yet to be determined. Coal in beds more than 14 inches thick totals at least 3.3 trillion tons in the United States, but estimates of the amounts minable at present prices have ranged from 20 to 220 billion tons (see U. S. Office of Science and Technology, *Energy R & D and National Progress*). Because 20 billion tons represents nearly a 40-year supply at present rates of consumption, it is easy to see why the studies needed to determine how much would be available at various costs have not been undertaken. The question is by no means only of academic interest, for the nuclear power development program was justified in part in its early years on the assumption that reserves of low-cost coal were extremely limited, and part of the continued growth of the nuclear power industry is said to be the result of the difficulty power companies are having in acquiring low-cost reserves.

Quantifying the Undiscovered

Considering potential resources in the degree-of-certainty, cost-of-recovery framework brings out the joint role that geologists, engineers, mineral technologists, and economists must play in estimating their magnitude. Having emphasized the importance of the economic and technologic side of the problem, I want now to turn to the geological side and consider the problem of how to appraise the extent of undiscovered reserves and resources.

It is difficult enough to estimate the extent of unexplored resources of the inferred or possible class. In fact, it is even difficult to estimate measured or proved reserves with a high degree of accuracy until they have been largely mined out. Thus estimates of proved reserves prepared in advance of appreciable production commonly have an error of about 25 percent, and the error in estimates of incompletely explored deposits is usually much larger. Generally the combination of the geologist's inherent conservatism and the lack of information on the geology of concealed areas leads to estimates that err in being too low rather than too high.

One eminent mining geologist reported that, having recognized these effects, he once arbitrarily tripled his calculations to arrive at an estimate of the ore remaining in a producing district; twice the amount of his inflated estimate, however, was found and mined over the next 20 years, and more was in prospect. To match many

such stories are at least a few prematurely deserted mills and mine installations built on the expectation of finding ore that did not materialize. Both kinds of experiences emphasize the difficulty of appraising the extent of mineral deposits even in partly explored areas. In the light of such experiences one is justified in asking—as many well-informed people have—whether estimates of the magnitude of undiscovered deposits can have enough reliability to make them worthwhile.

The fact that new districts are still being discovered for nearly every commodity and that large areas favorable for the occurrence of minerals of all kinds are covered by alluvium, volcanics, glacial drift, seawater, or other materials that conceal possible mineral-bearing rocks or structures assures us that undiscovered deposits are still to be found. Qualitatively, at least, we know something about the distribution of minerals with respect to other geologic phenomena and, if this is so, we have a chance of developing quantitative relations that will give us at least a start.

Two principal approaches to the problem have been taken thus far. One is to extrapolate observations related to rate of industrial activity, such as annual production of the commodity; the other is to extrapolate observations that relate to the abundance of the mineral in the geologic environment in which it is found.

. . .

The rate methods, however, have an inherent weakness in that the phenomena they analyze reflect human activities that are strongly influenced by economic, political, and other factors that bear no relation to the amount of oil or other material that lies in the ground. Moreover, they make no allowance for major break-throughs that might transform extensive paramarginal or submarginal resources into recoverable reserves, nor do they provide a means of estimating the potential resources of unexplored regions. Such projections have some value in indicating what will happen over the short term if recent trends continue, but they can have only limited success in appraising potential resources.

Even the goal of such projections, namely the prediction of ultimate production, is not a useful one. Not only is it impossible to predict the quantitative effects of man's future activities but the concept implies that the activities of the past are a part of an inexorable process with only one possible outcome. Far more useful, in my opinion, are estimates of the amounts of various kinds of materials that are in the ground in various environments; such estimates establish targets for both the explorer and the technologist, and they give us a basis for choosing among alternative ways of meeting our needs for mineral supplies.

The second principal approach taken thus far to the estimation of undiscovered resources involves the extrapolation of data on the abundance of mineral deposits from explored to unexplored ground on the basis of either the area or the volume of broadly favorable rocks. In the field of metalliferous deposits, T. B. Nolan pioneered in extrapolation on the basis of area in his study of the spatial and size distribution of mineral deposits in the Boulder Dam region and in his conclusion that a similar distribution should prevail in adjacent concealed and unexplored areas. Lewis Weeks and Wallace Pratt played similar roles with respect to the estimation of petroleum resources—Weeks extrapolating on the basis of oil per unit volume of sediment and Pratt on the basis of oil per unit area. Many of the estimates of crude oil that went into the NPC study were made by the volumetric method, utilizing locally appropriate factors on the amount of oil expected per cubic mile of sediment. Olson and Overstreet have since used the area method to estimate the magnitude of world thorium resources as a function of the size of areas of igneous and metamorphic rocks as compared to India and the United States, and A. P. Butler used the magnitude of sandstone uranium ore reserves exposed in outcrop as a basis for estimating the area in back of the outcrop that is similarly mineralized.

. . .

I have suggested another variant of the areal method for estimating reserves of non-fuel minerals which is based on the fact that the tonnage of minable reserves of the well-explored elements in the United States is roughly equal to their crustal abundance in percent times a billion or 10 billion (Fig. 3). Obviously this relation is influenced by the extent of exploration, for it is only reserves of the long-sought and well-explored minerals that display the relation to abundance. But it is this feature that gives the method its greatest usefulness, for it makes it possible to estimate potential resources of elements, such as uranium and thorium, that have been prospected for only a short period. Sekine tested this method for Japan

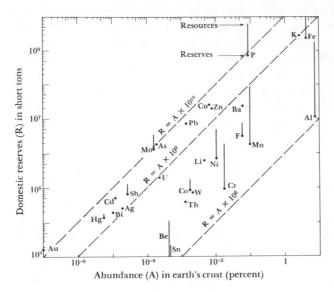

FIG. 3. Domestic reserves of elements compared to their abundance in the earth's crust. Tonnage of ore minable now is shown by a dot; tonnage of lower-grade ores whose exploitation depends upon future technological advances or higher prices is shown by a bar.

and found it applicable there, which surprised me a little, for I would not have thought Japan to be a large enough sample of the continental crust to bring out this relationship.

The relation between reserves and abundance, of course, can at best be only an approximate one, useful mainly in order-of-magnitude estimates, for obviously crustal abundance of an element is only one of its properties that lead to its concentration. That it is an important factor, however, may be seen not only in its influence on the magnitude of reserves but also in other expressions of its influence on the concentrations of the elements. For example, of the 18 or so elements with crustal abundances greater than about 200 parts per million, all but fluorine and strontium are rock-forming in the sense that some extensive rocks are composed chiefly of minerals of which each of these elements is a major constituent. Of the less abundant elements, only chromium, nitrogen, and boron have this distinction.

Only a few other elements, such as copper, lead, and zinc, even form ore bodies composed mainly of minerals of which the valuable element is a major constituent, and in a general way the grade of minable ores decreases with decreasing crustal abundance. A similar gross correlation exists between abundance of the elements and the number of minerals in which they are a significant constituent.

. . .

Need for Review of Resource Adequacy

Let me return now to the question of whether or not resources are adequate to maintain our present level of living. This is not a new question by any means. In 1908 it was raised as a national policy issue at the famous Governors' Conference on Resources, and it has been the subject of rather extensive inquiry by several national and international bodies since then. In spite of some of the dire predictions about the future made by various people in the course of these inquiries, they did not lead to any major change in our full-speed-ahead policy of economic development. Some of these inquiries, in fact, led to immediate investigations that revealed a greater resource potential for certain minerals than had been thought to exist, and the net effect was to alleviate rather than heighten concern.

Now, however, concern about resource adequacy is mounting again. The overall tone of the recent National Academy of Sciences' report on *Resources and Man* was cautionary if not pessimistic about continued expansion in the production and use of mineral resources, and many scientists, including some eminent geologists, have expressed grave doubts about our ability to continue on our present course. The question is also being raised internationally, particularly in developing countries where concern is being expressed that our disproportionate use of minerals to support our high level of living may be depriving them of their own future.

Personally, I am confident that for millennia to come we can continue to develop the mineral supplies needed to maintain a high level of living for those who now enjoy it and to raise it for the impoverished people of our own country and the world. My reasons for thinking so are that there is a visible undeveloped potential of substantial proportions in each of the processes by which we create resources and that our experience justifies the belief that these processes have dimensions beyond our knowledge and even beyond our imagination at any given time.

Setting aside the unimaginable, I will mention some examples of the believable. I am sure all geologists would agree that minable undiscovered deposits remain in explored as well as unexplored areas and that progress in our knowledge of regional geology and in exploration will lead to the discovery of many of them. With respect to unexplored areas, the mineral potential of the continental margins and ocean basins deserves particular emphasis, for the technology that will give us access to it is clearly now in sight. For many critical minerals, we already know of substantial paramarginal and submarginal resources that experience tells us should be brought within economic reach by technologic advance. The process of substituting an abundant for a scarce material has also been pursued successfully, thus far not out of need but out of economic opportunity, and plainly has much potential as a means of enlarging usable resources.

Extending our supplies by increasing the efficiency of recovery and use of raw materials has also been significant. For example, a unit weight of today's steel provides 43 percent more structural support than it did only ten years ago, reducing proportionately the amount required for a given purpose. Similarly, we make as much electric power from one ton of coal now as we were able to make from seven tons around the turn of the century. Our rising awareness of pollution and its effects surely will force us to pay even more attention to increasing the efficiency of mineral recovery and use as a means of reducing the release of contaminants to the environment. For similar reasons, we are likely to pursue more diligently processes of recovery, re-use, and recycling of mineral materials than we have in the past.

Most important to secure our future is an abundant and cheap supply of energy, for if that is available we can obtain materials from low-quality sources, perhaps even country rocks, as Harrison Brown has suggested. Again, I am personally optimistic on this matter, with respect both to the fossil fuels and particularly to the nuclear fuels. Not only does the breeder reactor appear to be near enough to practical reality to justify the belief that it will permit the use of extremely low-grade sources of uranium and thorium that will carry us far into the future, but during the last couple of years there have been exciting new developments in the prospects for commercial energy from fusion. Geothermal energy has a large unexploited potential, and new concepts are also being developed to permit the commercial use of solar energy.

But many others do not share these views, and it seems likely that soon there will be a demand for a confrontation with the full-speed-ahead philosophy that will have to be answered by a deep review of resource adequacy. I myself think that such a review is necessary, simply because the stakes have become so high. Our own population, to say nothing of the world's, is already too large to exist without industrialized, high energy- and mineral-consuming agriculture, transportation, and manufacturing. If our supply of critical materials is enough to meet our needs for only a few decades, a mere tapering off in the rate of increase of their use, or even a modest cutback, would stretch out these supplies for only a trivial period. If resource adequacy cannot be assured into the far-distant future, a major reorientation of our philosophy, goals, and way of life will be necessary. And if we do need to revert to a low resource-consuming economy, we will have to begin the process as quickly as possible in order to avoid chaos and catastrophe.

Comprehensive resource estimates will be essential for this critical examination of resource adequacy, and they will have to be made by techniques of accepted reliability. The techniques I have described for making such estimates have thus far been applied to only a few minerals, and none of them have been developed to the point of general acceptance. Better methods need to be devised and applied more widely, and I hope that others can be enlisted in the effort necessary to do both.

References

Allais, M. 1957. Methods of appraising economic prospects of mining exploration over large territories. *Management Sci.* 2:285–347.

Armstrong, F. C. 1970. Geologic factors controlling uranium resources in the Gas Hills District, Wyoming. 22nd Annual Field Conf. *Wyoming Geological Assn. Guidebook*, pp. 31–44.

Blondel, F., and S. F. Lasky. 1965. Mineral reserves and mineral resources. *Econ. Geology* 60:686–97.

Bush, A. L., and H. K. Stager. 1956. Accuracy of ore-reserve estimates for uranium-vanadium deposits on the Colorado Plateau. *U. S. Geol. Survey Bull.* 1030–D: 137.

Buyalov, N. I., N. S. Erofeev, N. A. Kalinin, A. I. Kleschev, N. M. Kudryashova, M.

S. L'vov, S. N. Simakov, and V. G. Vasil'ev. 1964. *Quantitative evaluation of predicted reserves of oil and gas.* Authorized trans. Consultants Bureau.

DeGeoffroy, J., and S. M. Wu. 1970. A statistical study of ore occurrences in the greenstone belts of the Canadian Shield. *Econ. Geology* 65:496–504.

Elliott, M. A., and H. R. Linden. 1968. A new analysis of U. S. natural gas supplies. *J. Petroleum Technology* 20:135–41.

Griffiths, J. C. 1962. Frequency distributions of some natural resource materials. 23rd Tech. Conf. on Pet. Prod., Sept. 26–28. *Min. Ind. Expt. Sta. Circ.* 63:174–98.

Griffiths, J. C. 1966. Exploration for natural resources. *Operations Research* 14:189–209.

Halbouty, M. T., A. A. Meyerhoff, R. E. King, R. H. Dott, Sr., H. D. Klemmer, and T. Shabad. 1970. World's giant oil and gas fields: World's giant oil and gas fields, geologic factors affecting their formation, and basin classification, Part 1. *Geology of Giant Petroleum Fields.* Memoir no. 14. Am. Assn. of Petroleum Geologists, pp. 502–28.

Halbouty, M. T., R. E. King, H. C. Klemme, R. H. Dott, Sr., and A. A. Meyerhoff. 1970. Factors affecting formation of giant oil and gas fields, and basin classification: World's giant oil and gas fields, geologic factors affecting their formation, and basin classification, Part 2. *Geology of Giant Petroleum Fields.* Memoir no. 14. Am. Assn. of Petroleum Geologists, pp. 528–55.

Harris, D. P., and D. Euresty. 1969. A preliminary model for the economic appraisal of regional resources and exploration based upon geostatistical analyses and computer simulation. *Colo. School of Mines Q.* 64:71–98.

Haun, J. D., J. A. Barlow, Jr., and D. E. Hallinger. 1970. Natural gas resources, Rocky Mountain region. *Am. Assn. Petroleum Geologists Bull.* 54:1706–18.

Hendricks, T. A. 1965. Resources of oil, gas, and natural gas liquids in the U. S. and the world. *U. S. Geol. Survey Circ.* 522.

Hendricks, T. A., and S. P. Schweinfurth. 1966. Unpublished memorandum quoted in *United States Petroleum through 1980* (1968). Washington, D. C.: U. S. Dept. Interior.

Hubbert, M. K. 1969. Energy resources. In *Resources and Man.* National Academy of Sciences–National Research Council, San Francisco, Calif.: W. H. Freeman & Co., pp. 157–239.

Inglis, D. R. 1971. Nuclear energy and the Malthusian dilemma. *Bull. Atomic Scientists* 27(2):14–18.

Kaufman, G. M. 1963. *Statistical Decision and Related Techniques in Oil and Gas Exploration.* Englewood, N. J.: Prentice-Hall.

Lasky, S. G. 1950. Mineral-resource appraisal by U. S. Geological Survey. *Colo. School Mines Q.* 45:1–27. See also his (1950) How tonnage and grade relations help predict ore reserves. *Eng. Mining J.* 151 (4):81–85.

Lowell, J. D. 1970. Copper resources in 1970. *Mining Eng.* 22(April): 67–73.

McKelvey, V. E. 1960. Relation of reserves of the elements to their crustal abundance. *Amer. J. Sci.* (Bradley Vol.) 258-A:234–41.

Moore, C. L. 1966. *Projections of U. S. Petroleum Supply to 1980.* Washington, D. C.: U. S. Dept. Interior, Office of Oil and Gas.

National Academy of Sciences–National Research Council. 1969. *Resources and Man.* San Francisco, Calif.: W. H. Freeman & Co.

National Petroleum Council. 1970. *Future Petroleum Provinces of the United States —A Summary.* Washington, D. C.: National Petroleum Council.

Nolan, T. B. 1950. The search for new mining districts. *Econ. Geology.* 45:601–08.

Oil and Gas J. 1969. Vast Delaware-Val Verde reserve seen. 67(16):44. (re: Zimmerman and Long)

Olson, J. C., and W. C. Overstreet. 1964. Geologic distribution and resources of thorium. *U. S. Geol. Survey Bull.* 1204.

Orwell, G. 1937. *The Road to Wigan Pier.* (Am. edition, N. Y.: Harcourt, Brace & World, 1958.)

Potential Gas Committee. 1969. Guidelines for the estimation of potential supply of natural gas in the United States. In *Potential Supply of Natural Gas in the United States (as of December 31, 1968).*

Golden, Colo.: Colo. School Mines Fdn., Inc., pp. 21–30.

Pratt, W. E. 1950. The earth's petroleum resources. In L. M. Fanning, ed., *Our Oil Resources*, 2nd ed. New York: McGraw-Hill, pp. 137–53.

Rodionov, D. A. 1965. *Distribution Functions of the Element and Mineral Contents of Igneous Rocks: A Special Research Report*. Authorized trans. Consultants Bureau, pp. 28–29.

Sekine, Y. 1963. On the concept of concentration of ore-forming elements and the relationship of their frequency in the earth's crust. *Internat. Geol. Rev.* 5:505–15.

Slichter, L. B. 1960. The need of a new philosophy of prospecting. *Mining Eng.* 12:570–76.

Slichter, L. B., et al. 1962. Statistics as a guide to prospecting. *Math and Computer Applications in Mining and Exploration Symp. Proc.* Tucson: Arizona Univ. Coll. Mines, pp. F-1–27.

U. S. Office of Science and Technology. 1965. *Energy R & D and National Progress*. Washington, D. C.: U. S. Govt. Print. Off.

Weeks, L. G. 1958. Fuel reserves of the future. *Am. Assn. Petroleum Geologists Bull.* 42:431–38.

Weeks, L. G. 1950. Concerning estimates of potential oil reserves. *Am. Assn. Petroleum Geologists Bull.* 34:1947–53.

Weeks, L. G. 1965. World offshore petroleum resources. *Am. Assn. Petroleum Geologists Bull.* 49:1680–93.

Zapp, A. D. 1962. Future petroleum producing capacity of the United States. *U. S. Geol. Survey Bull.* 1142-H.

24 Raw Materials Unlimited

Alvin M. Weinberg

A technologist like me is confused by the difference in attitude toward the world's resources displayed on the one hand by economists, and on the other hand by many demographers and geologists. One would expect the economists to be pessimists since their distinguished predecessor David Ricardo was such a pessimist. It was he who predicted that we would always have to extract raw materials from ever-poorer natural resources; even if we controlled our population, we would have to pay more and more for our basic raw materials and therefore our

Weinberg, A. M., 1968, "Raw Materials Unlimited," *Texas Quarterly*, vol. 11, no. 2. Reprinted with light editing by permission of the author and the publisher.

Mr. Weinberg is the former director of the Oak Ridge National Laboratory, Oak Ridge, Tennessee.

economic situation would inevitably decline. Yet economists, when asked about the future, tend to be very jaunty: technology will more than keep pace with the depletion of natural resources. This view is best summarized by Harold Barnett, professor of economics from Washington University, in an article "The Myth of Our Vanishing Resources" (*Trans-Action 4*, 6–10. June 1967). Barnett starts by quoting Keynes, "The ideas of economists and political philosophers, both when they are right and when they are wrong, are more powerful than is commonly understood." He then goes on to say that the idea that our natural resources are vanishing is just a myth. For example, although the demand for minerals between 1870 and 1957 increased about fortyfold, the cost of a unit of minerals decreased to a level only one-fifth as large as it was in 1870. The yearly decline in the unit cost of minerals up to World War I was about 1 per cent per year and in the period from 1919 to 1957 about 3 per cent per year.

The key to Professor Barnett's optimism is energy. This is asserted by the geologist Dean F. Frasché in a National Academy report on natural resources where he speaks of the connection between energy and minerals: "The extraction of mineral raw materials from low-grade rock is a problem in the application of energy—at a price." (*Mineral Resources*, A Report to the Committee on Natural Resources, National Academy of Sciences, Publication 1000-C, p. 18. December 1962.) "Total exhaustion of any mineral resource will never occur: Minerals and rocks that are unexploited will always remain in the earth's crust. The basic problem is how to avoid reaching a point where the cost of exploiting those mineral deposits which remain will be so costly, because of depth, size, or grade, that we cannot produce what we need without completely disrupting our social and economic structures." This is indeed the problem: we can always get iron at a cost; we can always get aluminum at a cost. What we really are concerned with is that the costs of these basic raw materials do not rise so precipitously that a segment of the economy which now represents say 2 per cent of our total expenditure jumps to 20 or 30 per cent. If jumps of that order occur, the living standard of the society will deteriorate seriously. And, according to Frasché, the key to maintaining our mineral and other resources at a reasonable price is cheap, inexhaustible energy. As long as we can get energy at a very low price, we can get other natural resources economically: in short, cheap energy ultimately would provide the technological basis for Professor Barnett's lack of concern about the future.

In sharp contrast to this view is the alarmingly pessimistic view held, by and large, by demographers. Their argument is simple: if you don't finally limit the population, then Malthus will finally be proved right. With this view, again, one cannot quarrel. Of course, the population eventually will have to level off if we are not to sink to an animal-like existence.

How many people can the earth ultimately support at a level of comfort that would be considered acceptable? Is the present population already too large as some insist; or is seven billion, the figure suggested by others, too large; or the extraordinary estimate of Professor Richard Meier, University of California, Berkeley, of between thirty-five and fifty billion by the twenty-second century? With fifty billion people the entire world will be one vast city. Could we survive in a totally urbanized world? Obviously life would be very different from what it is today, and, to our mind, very much less worth living.

I shall present a rather optimistic point of view about these huge questions. Yet I want to make clear that nothing I say implies opposition to attempts to keep the population of the earth at some manageable level. The burden of my remarks is that technology may prove the optimists—that is the economists and the technologists —right in the short run; but of course, the demographers and the geologists— in short, the pessimists—are right in the long run unless we act most urgently to control population.

Why does an old-time nuclear scientist like me find ground for optimism in the face of the unmitigated pessimism expressed by the Paddocks in their book *Famine—1975!* (William and Paul Paddock, *Famine—1975!*, Little, Brown and Co., Boston 1967)? It is because of four major technological advances: cheap nuclear energy, cheap desalination, high-yielding grains, and cheap electrolytic hydrogen which, when taken together, provide the means for forestalling the Malthusian catastrophe at least for a while. I shall describe where we stand in each of these technologies, and shall show how they can be used, in principle, to expand our resources of minerals and of foods. Whether in fact they will be used is a difficult social question that I am unable to deal with.

Nuclear Energy

First, I mention the major breakthrough in the cost of nuclear power. The dimensions of this breakthrough are so massive as to have caught the nuclear power people themselves by surprise. For the past twenty years people said that nuclear power was going to be competitive ten years from today (and it really didn't make any difference when today was, it was always ten years hence). Then, in 1962, the General Electric Company executed a firm price bid with the Jersey Central Power & Light Company for a 515 megawatt boiling water reactor, the famous Oyster Creek reactor, at a capital cost of around $130 per kilowatt—lower than the capital cost for conventional plants of the same size.

This was the signal for the rush to nuclear power, and in the past year rather better than half of all of the new central generating plants that have been ordered by the utilities, are nuclear. There are now fifty million kilowatts of electrical capacity in operation, on order, or under construction in the United States, and with an additional ten million kilowatts planned it seems that there is little sign of this activity abating. The costs are a little hard to judge at the moment; the most detailed analysis of the cost of nuclear power was given by TVA, in connection with its Browns Ferry Plant. The estimated energy generating costs for the Browns Ferry reactors is about 2.37 mills per kilowatt hour. This is lower than would be the corresponding costs for a privately owned utility, since the fixed charges in the TVA system are around 6 per cent as compared to the 12 per cent charges for a private utility. If the TVA fixed charges were at 12 per cent, their costs would go up to perhaps 3.3 mills per kilowatt hour.

Since Browns Ferry the price of nuclear reactors has gone up. But it seems very likely that very large boiling or pressurized water reactors will be available for about $125.00 to $135.00 per kilowatt; though this is somewhat higher than the price of coal-fired plants, the over-all cost of energy from the current generation of water reactors should still be competitive with energy from fossil fuel costing around 22¢ per million British thermal units. This would mean that nuclear reactors will probably be used for at least 60 per cent of all new steam capacity in the United States during the next decade.

The reactors now being sold in the

United States burn the rare isotope of uranium, U^{235}. The cost of the fuel cycle includes the cost of the U^{235} which is burned, the cost of refabricating unspent fuel, the fixed charges on the fuel held in inventory, and the insurance on fuel. These fuel cycle costs now total about 1.5 mills per kilowatt hour, with an expectation that for the first twelve years of operation of reactors like Browns Ferry the fuel cycle might average only 1.2 mills per kilowatt hour. This corresponds to fossil fuel at about 15¢ per million British thermal units. Of course the higher capital cost of the nuclear plant diminishes the advantage nuclear fuel enjoys over fossil fuel.

There are many of us who believe that the cost of nuclear energy ought to fall significantly below the figure that I have quoted. First, with respect to capital costs, one might ask why was it that despite all the very gloomy predictions which became quite fashionable about nuclear energy in the late forties and early fifties the General Electric Company offered a reactor at a capital cost that was quite competitive with the capital cost for a fossil fuel plant? The main reason really was that the early thinkers about the nuclear energy business were thinking about much smaller reactors than the ones that are now being built. For example, in 1947 the economists Walter Isard and Vincent Whitney ("Atomic Power and the Location of Industry," *Harvard Business Review 28*, 45–54 [March 1950]; see also Isard and Whitney, "Atomic Power and Economic Development," *Bulletin of the Atomic Scientists 5*, 73–78 [March 1949]) made the flat statement that nuclear energy would never become competitive with fossil fuel, and particularly the capital costs of nuclear plants would always exceed those of fossil fueled plants. Their error was in thinking too small. To these economists, 75 megawatts was a very big plant, and 200 megawatts was about as large as their imagination could visualize. Yet now we are constructing many reactors with capacities of more than a million kilowatts. There is no basic reason, at least for some types of reactors, why individual reactors should not produce 2,000 megawatts or even 3,000 megawatts of electricity. Now devices of this sort scale rather favorably; the larger the reactor, the smaller the price per kilowatt. Moreover, as the energy demands of society increase, the unit size of each energy producing device can also be expected to increase.

There are several other reasons why some experts believe that the costs of very large nuclear power plants ought eventually to be less than a hundred dollars per kilowatt. For example, I mention the possibility of generating electricity at 400 cycles rather than at 60 cycles. A 400 cycle generator is only about a sixth as large as a 60 cycle generator, and therefore the higher frequency generator should be much cheaper. Of course, higher frequency is unusable if the reactor is tied in with a 60 cycle system; however, if the energy is used on the spot, say for chemical processing, or is transmitted by direct current, the frequency of generation is unimportant.

But we cannot achieve really cheap energy, unless we can significantly lower the fuel cycle cost, which in the present generation of reactors is rather higher than 1 mill per kilowatt hour. The reason it is this high is because the U^{235} burned in the reactors is a rather expensive fuel. One gram of separated U^{235} costs about $10.00 and, when converted to electricity at 45 per cent thermal efficiency, contributes about 1 mill per kilowatt to the cost of the fuel cycle. But, in breeder reactors the fuel is the much cheaper and abundant U^{238} or Th^{232}. At $8.00 per pound, a gram of U^{238} or Th^{232} costs about 2¢. Thus the intrinsic cost of the fuel in a breeder reactor is only one five-hundredth the cost of the fuel in the current "burner" reactors.

Even if the cost of uranium or thorium increased tenfold, as would happen when we deplete our rich reserves, the intrinsic cost of the fuel is negligible—about .03 mill per kilowatt hour. And it is on this account that some of us believe we see the possibility of getting energy at extremely low cost, possibly as low as 1.5 mills or even 1 mill per kilowatt hour for the entire cost. Moreover, once we achieve reactors that burn sizeable parts of the uranium and thorium instead of just the rare U^{235}, we have an essentially inexhaustible energy source. I don't have to tell geologists that there is only a certain amount of uranium at $8.00 per pound; but if one goes to $80.00 or even $200.00 per pound then the amount of uranium that one can extract from the earth increases vastly. But the intrinsic cost of the fuel even at $100.00 per pound is still so small that we must consider rocks containing uranium and thorium at such low concentrations perfectly useable as fuel. At $80.00 per pound, there must be vast amounts of thorium and uranium in the earth's crust. For example, John Adams from Rice University, a

few years ago showed that the Conway granites contain about thirty million tons of thorium available at around $40.00 per pound.

Even if we make rather extravagant estimates of how much energy we shall need in the future, the thorium in the Conway granite alone, the thirty million tons, is almost surely enough to keep society in adequate energy resources for something like a thousand years. If one goes to $120.00-per-pound granites, it is a little foolish to ask how long this energy resource would last. It will undoubtedly supply our energy for millions and millions of years, provided we develop a breeder reactor that burns the abundant isotope U^{238} and thorium.

Where do we stand in the development of breeder reactors? Several experimental "fast" breeder reactors based on the U^{238} plutonium cycle are now operating. There have been three such reactors in the United States; there is one in England; there is one in France; and there is one in the Soviet Union. These reactors represent a rather difficult technology because the reactors are very compact and they have to be cooled with sodium. The sort of difficulty that has been encountered is illustrated by the Fermi reactor near Detroit. An inadvertent blockage of one of the channels caused a fuel element to melt. As a result, the reactor has been sitting idle for the last year while technicians tried to fish out the damaged fuel element. Still, the Russians and the British are taking a very aggressive and optimistic attitude toward fast breeders: the British have started to build a 250 megawatt fast breeder reactor, and the Russians are planning two fast breeder reactors, one at 250 megawatts electric, another at 600 megawatts electric.

Although the fast breeder reactor represents the main line of breeder development, there is another, to my mind more attractive, possibility based on thorium. This reactor type uses molten fluoride salts as its fuel. In the molten salt breeder a mixture of molten uranium fluoride, thorium fluoride, lithium fluoride, and beryllium fluoride circulates through a graphite matrix. The salt enters the graphite at about 1150° F. and emerges at about 1300° F. It gives its heat up to raise steam that operates a turbine. The great advantage of the molten salt system is that the uranium and thorium are always in liquid form, and thus the newly bred uranium can be extracted from the reactor relatively simply. We have been running a small molten salt reactor very successfully at the Oak Ridge National Laboratory for more than two years. At the moment we are trying to get money to build a larger version of the reactor.

To summarize, then, with respect to nuclear power itself, I am highly optimistic, especially about the molten salt breeders. One must take seriously the probability that inexhaustible, and ubiquitous energy at between 1 and 2 mills per kilowatt hour will be available within, say, fifteen years.

Desalination

The situation with respect to desalting the sea, using nuclear or other energy sources, can be summarized about like this. The thermodynamic minimum amount of energy required to desalt a thousand gallons of sea water is about three kilowatt hours. At two mills per kilowatt hour the energy cost would be 6¢ per thousand gallons, and this, of course, is the theoretical minimum cost to get fresh water from the sea. Since all real desalting plants operate irreversibly, the actual cost of desalted water is greater than the theoretical minimum. To approach the thermodynamic minimum, the distillation plants require an infinite number of stages. An infinite number of stages would cost an infinite amount, so one in practice must use more energy to save on the number of stages. If nuclear energy costs as little as I have suggested, and in particular, if we combine the desalting plant with an electrical plant so that the steam to energize the still is merely waste from the exhaust of the turbine, then our economic optimum will be a very cheap still utilizing very few stages. Moreover, there are new advances in heat transfer technology which ought further to lower capital costs of large sea water stills. We now have designs on the drawing board which suggest that even with present day reactors, desalted water might cost as little as 15¢ per thousand gallons, as compared with the 22–25¢ per thousand gallons expected at the new Metropolitan Water District Plant in Los Angeles. Many of us believe that when advanced breeders become available this cost will go down to perhaps less than 10¢ per thousand gallons.

The New Grains

The third major development may possibly be the most important technological development of the century, but it is one that has received very little attention. I refer to the extraordinary development, largely under the aegis of the Rockefeller Foundation, of the new high-yielding grain crops. These new varieties of corn and wheat have converted Mexico from an importer of grain to an exporter of grain. The new wheats, developed jointly by Rockefeller and the Mexican government, are particularly important because they do so well in the environment of West Pakistan and in the Ganges basin of India. In West Pakistan just six or eight years ago the population was going up, and the food per capita was going down; now the two are coming very much closer together. And the Rockefeller people are optimistic about what can be done in introducing these varieties into India. Last year a half million acres in India were planted in Mexican wheat; this year about six million acres are expected to be so planted. Since the yields of these varieties are three times that of the older types, the over-all increase in output should be very significant.

Can desalted sea water be used to raise these new grains at acceptable costs? Ordinarily about two thousand gallons of water are needed to supply the 2,400 calories for a man's daily food. Now if the water costs 15¢ per thousand gallons, then 2,000 gallons would cost 30¢ per day—obviously too much for an underdeveloped country. But, if one assumes that the average yield demonstrated with the Mexican-Rockefeller Foundation wheat can be achieved and if one assumes that fertilizer and water are available when needed and that agriculture is conducted scientifically, then it appears that only 200 gallons of water would

be needed per person per day. This estimate was first put forward by Dr. R. Philip Hammond, originally from the Los Alamos Scientific Laboratory and now at Oak Ridge, and it has been verified by agricultural experts at the Rockefeller Foundation.

If one can achieve anything close to 200 gallons per day, then at 15¢ per 1000 gallons this comes to about 3¢ per day for the water needed to feed a person with a modest but adequate diet. This is in a range that is interesting for underdeveloped countries. The Rockefeller Foundation is sufficiently interested in this line of thinking that it is examining the possibility of trying out this new kind of highly rational desert agriculture based on distilled water. I hope that a pilot farm might be started within the next year or so in a coastal desert.

Cheap Electrolytic Hydrogen; Electrolytic Metals

The fourth development, a spin-off from space technology and from submarine technology, is to some extent still a gleam in peoples' eyes. I refer to the development of very high current electrodes for the electrolytic production of hydrogen. Ordinarily in electrolytic production of hydrogen, one assumes that the current density is 150 amperes per square foot. As a result of developments in fuel cell technology it is possible now to anticipate electrode densities of 1,500 amperes per square foot. If this technology is now scaled up to the large-scale production of hydrogen and if one then assumes that electrical energy is available at around 2 mills per kilowatt hour, one comes out with costs of hydrogen which are surprisingly interesting—about 21¢ per thousand standard cubic feet, assuming one sells the oxygen at $4.00 per ton. Now 21¢ per thousand standard cubic feet is not the cheapest hydrogen that one can get but neither is it the most expensive; some of our consultants tell us this is comparable to hydrogen from natural gas costing about 37¢ per million British thermal units. Moreover, since sea water is ubiquitous, we have in principle here a way of producing hydrogen, indefinitely, at a price that is quite acceptable even today.

Hydrogen is the universal reducing agent; insofar as much of extractive metallurgy requires reducing agents, the availability of cheap hydrogen extends our mineral resources. Thus hydrogen can be used instead of coke to produce iron. The Bethlehem Steel Company has a pilot plant near Los Angeles which produces about 40,000 tons per year of hydrogen iron. Professor Arthur Squires, a well-known chemical engineer, estimates if energy costs 2 mills per kilowatt hour, hydrogen iron competes with steel by the usual blast furnace process. Or to mention another possibility that involves electrolysis, magnesium can be used as a structural metal instead of aluminum. Can magnesium from sea water compete with aluminum? My impression is that it can: if, for example, we extract *anhydrous* magnesium chloride from sea water concentrates and then electrolyze the salt, the magnesium will be cheaper than aluminum; some estimates put the market for magnesium at perhaps 25 to 30 per cent of that for aluminum if anhydrous magnesium chloride can be won readily from sea water.

In my examples of electrolytic production of hydrogen, iron, and magnesium, I have given instances of how cheap electricity can be converted into basic materials. The elasticity of demand for electricity for energy-intensive processes ought to be very high: that is, with power available at, say, 2 mills per kilowatt hour, many more industrial processes will be performed electrically than when power costs 3 mills per kilowatt hour. If we were to plot the cumulative number of industrial processes performed electrically versus cost of electric power, we would get a curve such as Fig. 1 in which the number of industrial processes based on electricity increases sharply as the cost of energy decreases. If electricity delivered to the plant were really costless, we probably would reduce iron electrolytically, hydrogenate coal to make liquid fuel, gasify coal with electric heat, etc. etc. In other words, the incentive toward extremely low-cost power is not simply that we would thereby save on processes that already use electricity. It is rather that we would choose to perform many industrial processes in an energy-intensive manner: we would substitute energy for raw materials such as coke, or natural gas, or high quality ores whose geographic distribution is uneven and capricious.

It is for this reason that I consider the achievement of very low-cost energy through the molten salt breeder reactor to be a matter of the highest urgency. It is not merely that with the molten salt breeder reactor we shall have a practically infinite source of energy, nor that we believe it will be cheaper than the non-breeder. It is rather that, because of the aforemen-

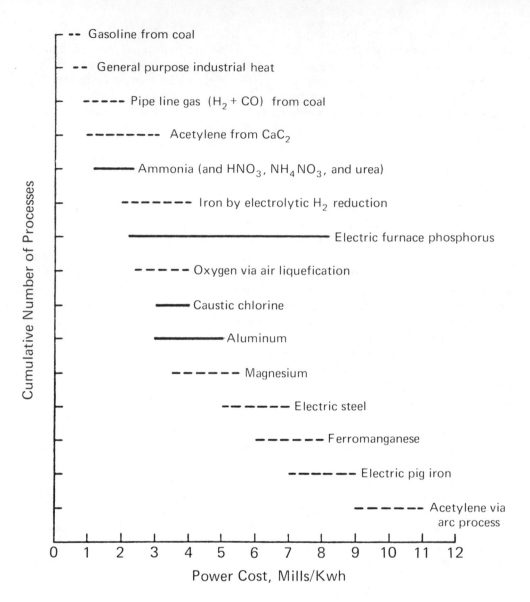

FIG. 1. Elasticity of the demand for power.

tioned elasticity of demand for electrical energy, the very cheap nuclear energy source could become the basis for a new kind of industrial development in which energy-intensive processes replace raw material-intensive processes.

The Agro-Industrial Complex

Can we combine cheap energy, relatively cheap desalting, highly rationalized agriculture, and production of hydrogen and other energy-intensive industrial materials into economically viable agricultural and industrial complexes in which the basic raw material is electrical energy rather than coal or petro-chemicals? At Oak Ridge we have studied such nuclear powered agro-industrial complexes. An example is summarized in Table 1.

The complex centers around two reactors producing 2,000 megawatts of electricity and a distillation plant producing 500 million gallons of water per day. Included in this complex is land under intensive cultivation based on distilled water. The agriculture is so highly rationalized that we prefer to use the words "food factory" rather than farm. Fertilizer is applied exactly at the right time, the water requirements of the plants are continuously monitored, and so on. This particular complex produces ammonia, electrorefines phosphorus, produces caustic chlorine, and salt. We have looked at a variety of cases; the one summarized

in the table costs perhaps $900,000,000 to build, and its annual income is about 15 percent of the investment. The food factory would occupy 180,000 acres and would produce enough food to feed perhaps two and one half to three million people.

The idea of a nuclear powered agro-industrial complex has received a good deal of attention. Recently a team of a half dozen people from Oak Ridge visited India to talk with their counterparts there and determine the extent to which massive technological packages of this sort might make some dent on the bitter problems facing India. I would like to close therefore by describing a variant of this scheme which I hope we shall hear a great deal more about in the next few years. The President's Science Advisory Commitee last year, in its report on world food problems (*The World Food Problem*, A Report of the President's Science Advisory Committee, U. S. Government

Table 1 Agro-industrial complex, light water reactors

Electric capacity	2,000 Mwe
Water capacity	500,000,000 gals/day
Investment	
Reactor	$160,000,000
Turbogenerator	135,000,000
Water plant	240,000,000
Industrial complex	230,000,000
Food factory	110,000,000
Town	20,000,000
Electric grid	5,000,000
	$900,000,000
Number of Workers	8,200
Annual Value of Products	
Industrial Products	$230,000,000
Agriculture	100,000,000
	$330,000,000
Annual operating expense	$194,000,000
Income less expense	$136,000,000
Annual return on investment	15%

Printing Office, Washington, D. C., May 1967), suggested that probably there are large amounts of ground water in the Gangetic Plains of India and that in the Indian climate this ground water can possibly be used to irrigate crops in the dry season. About the same time, a distinguished agricultural scientist, Professor Perry R. Stout of the University of California, Davis, while visiting Uttar Pradesh in India, was struck by the similarity between the topography, geology, and soil in this area and that in the San Joaquin Valley in California. The flourishing agriculture of the San Joaquin Valley is based on pumping ground water for irrigation. At present the agriculture in Uttar Pradesh is confined to the monsoon season, which lasts about four months during the year. If, however, a hundred thousand tube wells, each about twenty feet deep and each powered by about a five horsepower motor, could be dug, then one would be able to irrigate something like five million acres, and the water would be available for two crops and, if one is lucky, three crops could be produced here, because the climate is so equable. Moreover, if the new varieties of wheat I mentioned earlier were now introduced and if there were available sufficient ammonia fertilizer, Stout estimates that within ten years of the onset of such a project the yield of wheat in this area could be increased not by 10 per cent, not by 30 per cent, but by factors between four and ten. Now what are the problems? Well, I will skip the social problems because I'm sure that these will come out in discussion, but the first problem is the hydrology of the area. The hydrology has not really been studied, and one does not really know that all that ground water is there. But most geologists think that there is probably plenty of ground water. At least there are right now in this area about nine thousand tube wells, generally run by oxen or by diesels. At any rate, the monsoon rainwater has to go somewhere, and it is Perry Stout's belief that the ground water is being replenished each year. The second problem is electrical energy to power the tube wells and to produce the ammonia. Stout, therefore, proposes that a million kilowatts of electricity be installed. It doesn't have to be nuclear; there is coal about six hundred miles away in this area. If the Uttar Pradesh project is successful here, Stout proposes extending the project to a million tube wells. The total cost of this entire one million tube well project with the required energy sources and distribution system would be ten billion dollars. But the return would be extraordinary. Stout estimates that the extended project could convert India from an importer of $800,000,000 worth of food each year to an exporter of food!

Let me close in the following vein: I don't want anybody to misunderstand; I am not saying that these technological gimmicks based on energy should substitute for aggressive direct attacks on the population problem. But, on the other hand, I reject the attitude expressed in the book *Famine—1975!* —an attitude that pre-empts the future by saying that nothing can be done about the future of India. Ten billion dollars for the Stout Plan spent over five years in India is not all that big a sum of money. Though one million tube wells seem excessive, in West Pakistan alone in the last two years, forty thousand tube wells have been drilled. These wells have been drilled not by people just saying we have to drill forty thousand tube wells, but rather, by the farmers themselves. The Paddocks and other soothsayers of doom to the contrary notwithstanding, these farmers are not dumb, they're smart; and when they see that they are going to get the fertilizer and that the irrigation is going to work, they will drill the tube wells. I leave you with this possibility. I stand accused of being an optimist, but if we were not to some extent optimistic, we would to this extent not be human.

25 Realities of Mineral Distribution

Preston E. Cloud, Jr.

Introduction

. . . Optimism and imagination are happy human traits. They often make bad situations appear tolerable or even good. Man's ability to imagine solutions, however, commonly outruns his ability to find them. What does he do when it becomes clear that he is plundering, overpopulating, and despoiling his planet at such a horrendous rate that it is going to take some kind of a big leap, and soon, to avert irreversible degradation?

Dr. Weinberg, with his marvelous conception of a world set free by nuclear energy [Reading 24] sees man at this juncture in history as comparable to the frog who was trying, unsuccessfully, to jump out of a deep rut. A second frog came along, and, seeing his friend in distress, told him to rest awhile while he fetched some sticks to build a platform from which it would be but a short leap to the top of the rut. When frog number two returned, however, his friend was nowhere to be seen. A glance around soon revealed him sitting at the top of the rut. "How did you get up there?" the second frog exclaimed. "Well," said the first frog, "I had to—a hell of a big truck came down the road." In this story we are the first frog, the truck is overpopulation, pollution, and dwindling mineral resources, and the extra oomph that gets us out of the rut is nuclear power—specifically the breeder reactor, and eventually contained fusion.

The inventive genius of man has got him out of trouble in the past. Why not now? Why be a spoil-sport when brilliant, articulate, and well-intentioned men assure us that all we need is more technology? Why? Because the present crisis is exacerbated by four conditions that reinforce each other in a very undesirable manner: (1) the achievements of medical technology which have brought on the run-away imbalance between birth and death rates; (2) the hypnotic but unsustainable national dream of an ever-increasing real Gross National Product based

Reprinted from, *Texas Quarterly*, v. 11, pp. 103–26 by permission of the author and the publisher.
Mr. Cloud is Professor of Biogeology at the University of California, Santa Barbara.

on obsolescence and waste; (3) the finite nature of the earth and particularly its accessible mineralized crust; and (4) the increased risk of irreversible spoilation of the environment which accompanies overpopulation, overproduction, waste, and the movement of ever-larger quantities of source rock for ever-smaller proportions of useful minerals.

Granted the advantages of big technological leaps, therefore, provided they are in the right direction, I see real hope for permanent long-range solutions to our problems as beginning with the taking of long-range views of them. Put in another way, we should not tackle vast problems with half-vast concepts. We must build a platform of scientific and social comprehension, while concurrently endeavoring to fill the rut of ignorance, selfishness, and complacency with knowledge, restraint, and demanding awareness on the part of an enlightened electorate. And we must not be satisfied merely with getting the United States or North America through the immediate future, critical though that will be. We must consider what effects current and proposed trends and actions will have on the world as a whole for several generations hence, and how we can best influence those trends favorably the world over. Above all, we must consider how to preserve for the yet unborn the maximum flexibility of choices consistent with meeting current and future crises.

Rhetoric, however, either cornucopian or Malthusian, is no substitute for informed foresight and rational action or purposeful inaction.

What are the problems and misconceptions that impede the desired progress? And what must we invest in research and action—scientific, technological, *and* social—to assure a flexibility of resource options for the long range as well as for the immediate future? Not only until 1985, not only until the year 2000, not only even until the year 2050, but for a future as long as or longer than our past. In the nearly five billion years of earth history is man's brief stay of now barely a million years to be only a meteoric flash, and his industrial society less than that? Or will he last with reasonable amenities for as long as the dinosaurs?

Nature and Geography of Resources

Man's concept of resources, to be sure, depends on his needs and wants, and thus to a great degree on his locale and place in history, on what others have, and on what he knows about what they have and what might be possible for him to obtain. Food and fiber from the land, and food and drink from the waters of the earth have always been indispensable resources. So have the human beings who have utilized these resources and created demands for others—from birch bark to beryllium, from buffalo hides to steel and plastic. It is these other resources, the ones from which our industrial society has been created, about which I speak today. I refer, in particular, to the nonrenewable or wasting resources—mineral fuels which are converted into energy plus carbon, nuclear fuels, and the metals, chemicals, and industrial materials of geological origin which to some extent can be and even are recycled but which tend to become dispersed and wasted.

All such resources, except those that are common rocks whose availability and value depend almost entirely on economic factors plus fabrication, share certain peculiarities that transcend economics and limit technology and even diplomacy. They occur in local concentrations that may exceed their crustal abundances by thousands of times, and particular resources tend to be clustered within geochemical or metallogenic provinces from which others are excluded. Some parts of the earth are rich in mineral raw materials and others are poor.

No part of the earth, not even on a continent-wide basis, is self sufficient in all critical metals. North America is relatively rich in molybdenum and poor in tin, tungsten, and manganese, for instance, whereas Asia is comparatively rich in tin, tungsten, and manganese and, apparently, less well supplied with molybdenum. The great bulk of the world's gold appears to be in South Africa, which has relatively little silver but a good supply of platinum. Cuba and New Caledonia have well over half the world's total known reserves of nickel. The main known reserves of cobalt are in the Congo Republic, Cuba, New Caledonia, and parts of Asia. Most of the world's mercury is in Spain, Italy, and parts of the Sino-Soviet bloc. Industrial diamonds are still supplied mainly by the Congo.

Consider tin. Over half the world's currently recoverable reserves are in Indonesia, Malaya, and Thailand, and much of the rest is in Bolivia and the Congo. Known North American reserves are negligible. For the United States loss of access to extra-continental sources of tin is not likely to be offset by economic factors or technological changes that would permit an increase in potential North American production, even if present production could be increased by an order of magnitude. It is equally obvious that other peculiarities in the geographical distribution of the world's geological resources will continue to encourage interest both in trading with some ideologically remote nations and in seeking alternative sources of supply.

Economic geology, which in its best sense brings all other fields of geology to bear on resource problems, is concerned particularly with questions of how certain elements locally attain geochemical concentrations that greatly exceed their crustal abundance and with how this knowledge can be applied to the discovery of new deposits and the delineation of reserves. Economics and technology play equally important parts with geology itself in determining what deposits and grades it is practicable to exploit. Neither economics, nor technology, nor geology can *make* an ore deposit where the desired substance is absent or exists in insufficient quantity.

Estimated Recoverable Reserves of Selected Mineral Resources

Consider now some aspects of the apparent lifetimes of estimated recoverable reserves of a selection of critical mineral resources and the position of the United States with regard to some of these. The selected resources are those for which suitable data are available.

Figure 1 shows such lifetimes for different groups of metals and mineral

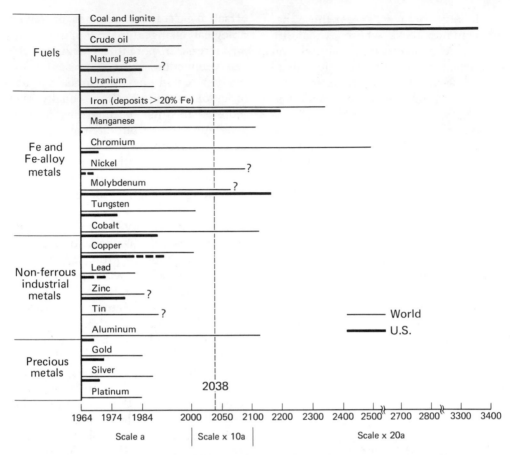

FIG. 1. Lifetimes of estimated recoverable reserves of mineral resources at current mineable grades and rates of consumption (no allowance made for increasing populations and rates of consumption, or for submerged or otherwise concealed deposits, use of now submarginal grades, or imports). (Data from Flawn, 1966).

fuels at *current* minable grades and rates of consumption. No allowance is made for increase of populations, or for increased rates of consumption which, in the United States, tend to increase at twice the rate of population growth. Nor is allowance made for additions to reserves that will result from discovery of submarine deposits, use of submarginal grades, or imports —which may reduce but will not eliminate the impact of growth factors. Data

are from the U. S. Bureau of Mines compendia *Mineral Facts and Problems* and its *Minerals Yearbooks*, as summarized by Flawn (*Mineral Resources*, Rand McNally, 1966). The thin lines represent lifetimes of world reserves for a stable population of roughly 3.3×10^9 at current rates of use. The heavy lines represent similar data for a United States population of about 200 million. Actual availability of some such commodities to the United

States will, of course, be extended by imports from abroad, just as that of others will be reduced by population growth, increased per capita demands, and perhaps by political changes. The dashed vertical line represents the year 2038. I have chosen this as a reference line because it marks that point in the future which is just as distant from the present as the invention of the airplane and the discovery of radioactivity are in the past.

The prospect is hardly conducive to unrestrained optimism. Of the nineteen commodities considered, only fourteen for the world and four or five for the United States have assured lifetimes beyond 1984; only ten for the world and three for the United States persist beyond the turn of the century;

FIG. 2. Estimated recoverable reserves of minerals (above sea level) for which U. S. reserve estimates exceed, equal, or fall only slightly below those of the U.S.S.R. plus Mainland China. (Data from Flawn, 1966).

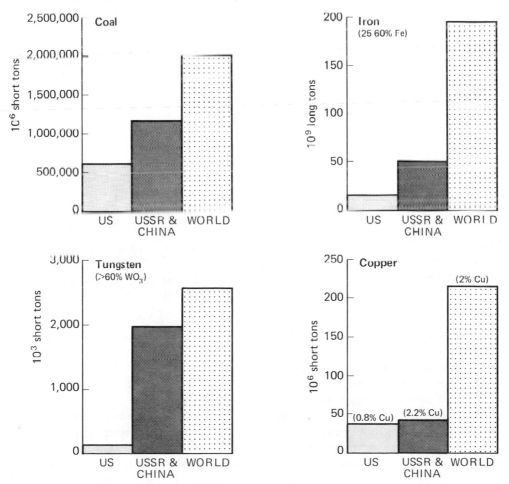

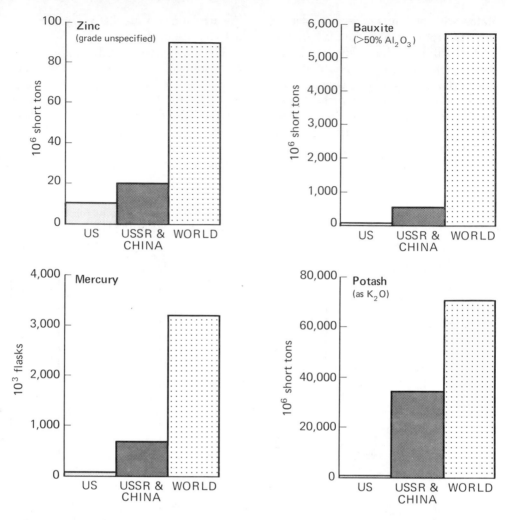

FIG. 3. Estimated recoverable reserves of minerals (above sea level) for which U. S. reserve estimates are less than those of the U.S.S.R. plus Mainland China. (Data from Flawn, 1966).

and only eight for the world and three for the United States extend beyond 2038. I do not suggest that we equate these lines with revealed truth. Time will prove some too short and others perhaps too long. New reserves will be found, lower-grade reserves will become minable for economic or technological reasons, substitutes will be discovered or synthesized, and some critical materials can be conserved by waste control and recycling. The crucial questions are: (1) how do we reduce these generalities to specifics; (2) can we do so fast enough to sustain current rates of consumption; (3) can we increase and sustain production of industrial materials at a rate sufficient to meet the rising expectations of a world population of nearly three and

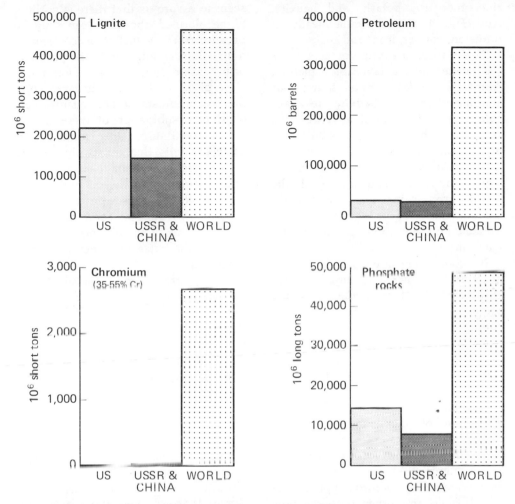

FIG. 4. Estimated recoverable reserves of minerals (above sea level) for which U. S. reserve estimates are less than those of the U.S.S.R. plus Mainland China. (Data from Flawn, 1966).

one-half billion, now growing with a doubling time of about thirty to thirty-five years, and for how long; and (4) if the answer to the last question is no, what then?

A more local way of viewing the situation is to compare the position of the United States or North America with other parts of the world. Figs. 2 to 4 show such a comparison for sixteen commodities with our favorite measuring stick, the Sino-Soviet bloc. Figure 2 shows the more cheerful side of the coin. The United States is a bit ahead in petroleum, lignite, and phosphate, and neither we nor Asia have much chromium—known reserves are practically all in South Africa and Rhodesia. Figure 3, however, shows the Sino-Soviet bloc to have a big lead in zinc, mercury, potash, and bauxite. And Fig. 4 shows similar leads in tungsten, copper, iron, and coal.

Again there are brighter aspects to the generally unfavorable picture. Ample local low grade sources of alumina other than bauxite are available with metallurgical advances and at a price. The United States coal supply is not in danger of immediate shortage. Potassium can be extracted from sea water. And much of the world's iron is in friendly hands, including those of our good neighbor Canada and our more distant friend Australia.

No completely safe source is visible, however, for mercury, tungsten, and chromium. Lead, tin, zinc, and the precious metals appear to be in short supply throughout the world. And petroleum and natural gas will be exhausted or nearly so within the lifetimes of many of those here today unless we decide to conserve them for petrochemicals and plastics. Even the extraction of liquid fuels from oil shales and "tar sands," or by hydrogenation of coal, will not meet energy requirements over the long term. If they were called upon to supply all the liquid fuels and other products now produced by the fractionation of petroleum, for instance, the suggested lifetime for coal the reserves of which are probably the most accurately known of all mineral products, would be drastically reduced below that indicated in Fig. 1—and such a shift will be needed to a yet unknown degree before the end of the century.

The Cornucopian Premises

In view of these alarming prospects, why do intelligent men of good faith seem to assure us that there is nothing to be alarmed about? It can only be because they visualize a completely nongeological solution to the problem, or because they take a very short-range view of it, or because they are compulsive optimists or are misinformed, or some combination of these things.

Let me first consider some of the basic concepts that might give rise to a cornucopian view of the earth's mineral resources and the difficulties that impede their unreserved acceptance. Then I will suggest some steps that might be taken to minimize the risks or slow the rates of mineral-resource depletion.

The central dilemma of all cornucopian premises is, of course, how to sustain an exponential increase of anything—people, mineral products, industrialization, or solid currency—on a finite resource base. This is, as everyone must realize, obviously impossible in the long run and will become increasingly difficult in the short run. For great though the mass of the earth is, well under 0.1 per cent of that mass is accessible to us by any imaginable means (the entire crust is only about 0.4 per cent of the total mass of the earth) and this relatively minute accessible fraction, as we have seen and shall see, is very unequally mineralized.

But the cornucopians are not naive or mischievous people. On what grounds do they deny the restraints and belittle the difficulties?

The five main premises from which their conclusions follow are:

Premise I—the promise of essentially inexhaustible cheap useful energy from nuclear sources.

Premise II—the thesis that economics is the sole factor governing availability of useful minerals and metals.

Premise III—the fallacy of essentially uninterrupted variation from ore of a metal to its average crustal abundance, which is inherent in Premise II; and from which emanates the strange and misleading notion that quantity of a resource available is essentially an inverse exponential function of its concentration.

Premise IV—the crucial assumption of population control, without which there can be no future worth living for most of the world (or, worse, the belief that quantity of people is of itself the ultimate good, which, astounding as it may seem, is still held by a few people who ought to know better—see, for instance, Colin Clark, *Population Growth and Land Use*, Macmillan, 1967).

Premise V—the concept of the "technological fix."

Now these are appealing premises, several of which contain large elements of both truth and hope. Why do I protest their unreserved acceptance? I protest because, in addition to elements of truth, they also contain assumptions that either are gross oversimplifications, outright errors, or are not demonstrated. I warn because their uncritical acceptance contributes to a dangerous complacency toward problems that will not be solved by a few brilliant technological "breakthroughs," a wider acceptance of deficit economy, or fall-out of genius from unlimited expansion of population. They will be solved only by intensive wide-ranging, and persistent scientific and engineering investigation, supported by new social patterns and wise legislation.

I will discuss these premises in the order cited.

Premise I

The concept of essentially inexhaustible cheap useful energy from nuclear sources offers by all odds the most promising prospect of sweeping changes in the mineral resource picture, as Dr. Weinberg so brilliantly argued. We may be on the verge of developing a workable breeder reactor just in time to sustain an energy-hungry world facing the imminent exhaustion of traditional energy sources. Such a development, it has been persuasively stated, will also banish many problems of environmental pollution and open up unlimited reserves of metals in common crustal rocks. There are, unhappily, some flaws in this delightful picture, of which it is important to be aware.

As Dr. Weinberg has told you, uranium 235 is the only naturally occurring spontaneously fissionable source of nuclear power. When a critical mass of uranium is brought together, the interchange of neutrons back and forth generates heat and continues to do so as long as the U^{235} lasts. In the breeder reactor some of the free neutrons kick common U^{238} over to plutonium 239, which is fissionable and produces more neutrons, yielding heat and accelerating the breeder reaction. Even in existing reactors some breeding takes place, and, if a complete breeding system could be produced, the amount of energy available from uranium alone would be increased about 140 fold. If thorium also can be made to breed, energy generated could be increased about 400 fold over that now attainable. This would extend the lifetime of visible energy resources at demands anticipated by 1980 by perhaps 1000 to 3000 years and gain time to work on contained nuclear fusion.

The problem is that it will require about 275,000 short tons of $6.00 to $10.00 per pound U_3O_8 (not ore, not uranium) to fuel reactors now on order to 1980, plus another 400,000 tons to sustain them until the turn of the century, burning only U^{235} with currently available enrichments from slow breeding (Charles T. Baroch, U. S. Bureau of Mines, oral comment). Only about 195,000 of the 675,000 tons of uranium needed is known to be available at this price, although known geologic conditions indicate the possibility of another 325,000 tons. Thus we now appear to be about 155,000 tons short of the U_3O_8 needed to produce the hoped-for 150,000 megawatts of nuclear energy on a sustained basis from 1985 until the end of the century without a functioning breeder reactor. Unless we find a lot more uranium, or pay a lot more money for it, or get a functioning complete breeder reactor or contained nuclear fusion within ten or fifteen years, the energy picture will be far from bright. There is good reason to hope that the breeder will come, and after it contained fusion, *if* the U^{235} and helium hold out—but there is no room for complacency.

If and when the breeder reactor or contained fusion does become available as a practicable energy source, however, how will this help with mineral resources? It is clear immediately that it will take pressure off the fossil "fuels" so that it will become feasible, and should become the law, to reserve them for petrochemicals, polymers, essential liquid propellants, and other special purposes not served by nuclear fuels. It is also clear that cheap massive transportation, or direct transmittal of large quantities of cheap electric power to, or its generation at, distant sources will bring the mineral resources of remote sites to the market place—either as bulk ore for processing or as the refined or partially refined product.

What is not clear is how this very cheap energy will bring about the extraction of thinly dispersed metals in large quantity from common rock. The task is very different from the recovery of liquid fuels or natural gas by nuclear fracturing. The procedure usually suggested is the break-up of rock in place at depth with a nuclear blast, followed by hydrometallurgical or chemical mining. The problems, however, are great. Complexing solutions, in large quantity also from natural resources, must be brought into contact with the particles desired. This means that the enclosing rock must be fractured to that particle size. Then other substances, unsought, may use up and dissipate valuable reagents. Or the solvent reagents may escape to ground waters and become contaminants. Underground electrolysis is no more promising in dealing with very low concentrations. And the bacteria that catalyze reactions of metallurgical interest are all aerobic, so that, in addition to having access to the particles of interest, they must also be provided with a source of oxygen underground if they are to work there.

Indeed the energy used in breaking rock for the removal of metals is not now a large fraction of mining cost in comparison with that of labor . and capital. The big expense is in equipping and utilizing manpower, and, although cheap energy will certainly reduce manpower requirements, it will probably never adequately substitute for the intelligent man with the pick at the mining face in dealing with vein and many replacement deposits, where the sought-after materials are irregularly concentrated in limited spaces. There are also limits to the feasible depths of open pit mining, which would be by all odds the best way to mine common rock. Few open pit mines now reach much below about 1,500 feet. It is unlikely that such depths can be increased by as much as an order of magnitude. The quantity of rock removable decreases exponentially with depth because pit circumference must decrease downward to maintain stable walls.

It may also not be widely realized by non-geologists that many types of ore bodies have definite floors or pinch-out downward, so that extending exploitative operations to depth gains no increase in ore produced. Even where mineralization does extend to depth, of course, exploitability is ultimately limited by temperature and rock failure.

Then there is the problem of reducing radioactivity so that ores can be handled and the refined product utilized without harm—not to mention heat dispersal (which in some but not all situations could itself be a resource) and the disposal of waste rock and spent reagents.

Altogether the problems are sufficiently formidable that it would be foolhardy to accept them as resolved in advance of a working efficient breeder reactor plus a demonstration that either cheap electricity or nuclear ex-

plosions will significantly facilitate the removal of metals from any common rock.

A pithy comment from Peter Flawn's recent book on *Mineral Resources* (Rand McNally, 1966, p. 14) is appropriate here. It is to the effect that "average rock will never be mined," It is the uncommon features of a rock that make it a candidate for mining! Even with a complete nuclear technology, sensible people will seek, by geological criteria, to choose and work first those rocks or ores that show the highest relative recoverable enrichments in the desired minerals.

The reality is that even the achievement of a breeder reactor offers no guarantee of unlimited mineral resources in the face of geologic limitations and expanding populations with increased per capita demands, even over the middle term. To assume such for the long term would be sheer folly.

Premise II

The thesis that economics is the sole, or at least the dominant, factor governing availability of useful minerals and metals is one of those vexing part-truths which has led to much seemingly fruitless discussion between economists and geologists. This proposition bears examination.

It seems to have its roots in that interesting economic index known as the Gross National Product, or GNP. No one seems to have worked out exactly what proportion of the GNP is in some way attributable to the mineral resource base. It does, however, appear that the dollar value of the raw materials themselves is small compared to the total GNP, and that it has decreased proportionately over time to something like 2 per cent of the present GNP, as I recall. From this it is logically deduced that the GNP could, if necessary, absorb a several-fold increase in cost of raw materials. The gap in logic comes when this is confused with the notion that all that is necessary to obtain inexhaustible quantities of any substance is either to raise the price or to increase the volume of rock mined. In support of such a notion, of course, one *can* point to diamond, which in the richest deposit ever known occurred in a concentration of only one to twenty-five million, but which, nevertheless, has continued to be available. The flaw is not only that we cannot afford to pay the price of diamond for many substances, but also that no matter how much rock we mine we can't get diamonds out of it if there were none there in the first place.

Daniel Bell (1967, Notes on the Post-industrialist Society II: *in* the *Public Interest*, no. 7, p. 102–118) comments on the distorted sense of relations that emerges from the cumulative nature of GNP accounting. Thus, when a mine is developed, the costs of the new facilities and payroll become additions to the GNP, whether the ore is sold at a profit or not. Should the mine wastes at the same time pollute a stream, the costs of cleaning up the stream or diverting the wastes also become additions to the GNP. Similarly if you hire someone to wash the dishes this adds to GNP, but if your wife does them it doesn't count.

From this it results that mineral raw materials and housework are not very impressive fractions of the GNP. What seems to get lost sight of is

what a mess we would be in without either!

Assuming an indefinite extension of their curves and continuance of access to foreign markets, economists appear to be on reasonably sound grounds in postulating the relatively long-term availability of certain sedimentary, residual, and disseminated ores, such as those of iron, aluminum, and perhaps copper. What many of them do not appreciate is ... that the type of curve that can with some reason be applied to such deposits and metals is by no means universally applicable. This difficulty is aggravated by the fact that conventional economic indexes minimize the vitamin-like quality for the economy as a whole of the raw materials whose enhancement in value through beneficiation, fabrication, and exchange accounts for such a large part of the material assets of society.

In a world that wants to hear only good news some economists are perhaps working too hard to emancipate their calling from the epithet of "dismal science," but not all of them. One voice from the wilderness of hyperoptimism and overconsumption is that of Kenneth Boulding, who observes that, *"The essential measure of the success of the economy is not production and consumption at all, but the nature, extent, quality, and complexity of the total capital stock, including in this the state of the human bodies and minds included in the system"* (p. 9 *in* K. E. Boulding, 1966, "The economics of the coming spaceship Earth," p. 3–14 *in* Environmental Quality in a Growing Economy, Resources of the Future, Inc.,·The Johns Hopkins Press). Until this concept penetrates widely into the councils of government and the conscience of society, there will continue to be a wide gap between the economic aspects of national and industrial policy and the common good, and the intrinsic significance of raw materials will remain inadequately appreciated.

The reality is that economics per se, powerful though it can be when it has material resources to work with, is not all powerful. Indeed, without material resources to start with, no matter how small a fraction of the GNP they may represent, economics is of no consequence at all. The current orthodoxy of economic well-being through obsolescence, over-consumption, and waste will prove, in the long term, to be a cruel and preposterous illusion.

Premise III

Premise III, the postulate of essentially uninterrupted variation from ore to average crustal abundance is seldom if ever stated in that way, but it is inherent in Premise II. It could almost as well have been treated under Premise II; but it is such an important and interesting idea, whether true or false, that separate consideration is warranted.

If the postulated continuous variation were true for mineral resources in general, volume of "ore" (not metal) produced would be an exponential inverse function of grade mined, the handling of lower grades would be compensated for by the availability of larger quantities of elements sought, and reserve estimates would depend only on the accuracy with which average crustal abundances were known. Problems in extractive metallurgy, of course, are not considered in such an outlook.

This delightfully simple picture would supplant all other theories of ore deposits, invalidate the foundations of geochemistry, divest geology of much of its social relevance, and place the fate of the mineral industry squarely in the hands of economists and nuclear engineers.

Unfortunately this postulate is simply untrue in a practical sense for many critical minerals and is only crudely true, leaving out metallurgical problems, for particular metals, like iron and aluminum, whose patterns approach the predicted form. Sharp discontinuities exist in the abundances of mercury, tin, nickel, molybdenum, tungsten, manganese, cobalt, diamond, the precious metals, and even such staples as lead and zinc, for example. But how many prophets of the future are concerned about where all the lead or cadmium will come from for all those electric automobiles that are supposed to solve the smog problem?

Helium is a good example of a critical substance in short supply. Although a gas which has surely at some places diffused in a continuous spectrum of concentrations, particular concentrations of interest as a source of supply appear from published information to vary in a stepwise manner. Here I draw on data summarized by H. W. Lipper in the 1965 edition of the U. S. Bureau of Mines publication *Mineral Facts and Problems*. Although an uncommon substance, helium serves a variety of seemingly indispensable uses. A bit less than half of the helium now consumed in the U. S. is used in pressurizing liquid fueled missiles and space ships. Shielded-arc welding is the next largest use, followed closely by its use in producing controlled atmospheres for growing crystals for transistors, processing fuels for nuclear energy, and cooling vacuum pumps. Only about 5.5 per cent of the helium consumed in the United States is now used as a lifting gas. It plays an increasingly important role, however, as a coolant for nuclear reactors and a seemingly indispensable one in cryogenics and superconductivity. In the latter role, it could control the feasibility of massive long-distance transport of nuclear-generated electricity. High-helium low-oxygen breathing mixtures may well be critical to man's long-range success in attempting to operate at great depths in the exploration and exploitation of the sea. Other uses are in research, purging, leak detection, chromatography, etc.

Helium thus appears to be a very critical element, as the Department of the Interior has recognized in establishing its helium-conservation program. What are the prospects that there will be enough helium in 2038?

The only presently utilized source of helium is in natural gas, where it occurs at a range of concentrations from as high as 8.2 per cent by volume to zero. The range, however, in particular gas fields of significant volume, is apparently not continuous. Dropping below the one field (Pinta Dome) that shows an 8.2 per cent concentration, we find a few small isolated fields (Mesa and Hogback, New Mexico) that contain about 5.5 per cent helium, and then several large fields (e.g., Hugoton and Texas Panhandle) with a range of 0.3 to 1.0 per cent helium. Other large natural gas fields contain either no helium or show it only in quantities of less than 5 parts per 10,000. From the latter there is a long jump down to the atmosphere

with a concentration of only 1 part per 200,000.

Present annual demand for helium is about 700 million cubic feet, with a projected increase in demand to about 2 billion cubic feet annually by about 1985. It will be possible to meet such an accelerated demand for a limited time only as a result of Interior's current purchase and storage program, which will augment recovery from natural gas then being produced. As now foreseen, if increases in use do not outrun estimates, conservation and continued recovery of helium from natural gas reserves will meet needs to slightly beyond the turn of the century. When known and expected discoveries of reserves of natural gas are exhausted shortly thereafter, the only potential sources of new supply will be from the atmosphere, as small quantities of He^3 from nuclear reactor technology, or by synthesis from hydrogen—a process whose practical feasibility and adequacy remain to be established.

Spending even a lot more money to produce more helium from such sources under existing technology just may not be the best or even a very feasible way to deal with the problem. Interior's conservation program must be enlarged and extended, under compulsory legislation if necessary. New sources must be sought. Research into possible substitutions, recovery and re-use, synthesis, and extraction from the atmosphere must be accelerated—*now* while there is still time. And we must be prepared to curtail, if necessary, activities which waste the limited helium reserves. Natural resources are the priceless heritage of all the people; their waste cannot be tolerated.[1]

Problems of the adequacy of reserves obtain for many other substances, especially under the escalating demands of rising populations and expectations, and it is becoming obvious to many geologists that time is running out. Dispersal of metals which could be recycled should be controlled. Unless industry and the public undertake to do this voluntarily, legislation should be generated to define permissible mixes of material and disposal of "junk" metal. Above all the wastefulness of war and preparation for it must be terminated if reasonable options for posterity are to be preserved.

The reality is that a healthy mineral resource industry, and therefore a healthy industrial economy, can be maintained only on a firm base of geologic knowledge, and geochemical and metallurgical understanding of the distribution and limits of metals, mineral fuels, and chemicals in the earth's crust and hydrosphere.

Premise IV

The assumption that world populations will soon attain and remain in a state of balance is central to all other premises. Without this the rising expectations of the poor are doomed to failure, and the affluent can remain affluent only by maintaining existing shameful discrepancies. Taking present age structures and life expectancies of world populations into account, it seems certain that, barring other forms of catastrophe, world population will reach six or seven billion by about the turn of the century, regardless of how rapidly family planning is accepted and practiced.

On the most optimistic assumptions, this is probably close to the maximum number of people the world can support on a reasonably sustained basis,

even under strictly regularized conditions, at a general level of living roughly comparable to that now enjoyed in Western Europe. It would, of course, be far better to stabilize at a much smaller world population. In any case, much greater progress than is as yet visible must take place over much larger parts of the world before optimism on the prospects of voluntary global population control at any level can be justified. And even if world population did level off and remain balanced at about seven billion, it would probably take close to one hundred years of intensive, enlightened, peaceful effort to lift all mankind to anywhere near the current level of Western Europe or even much above the level of chronic malnutrition and deprivation.

This is not to say that we must therefore be discouraged and withdraw to ineffectual diversions. Rather it is a challenge to focus with energy and realism on seeking a truly better life for all men living and yet unborn and on keeping the latter to the minimum. On the other hand, an uncritical optimism, just for the sake of that good feeling it creates, is a luxury the world cannot, at this juncture, afford.

A variation of outlook on the population problem which, surprisingly enough, exists among a few nonbiological scholars is that quantity of people is of itself a good thing. The misconception here seems to be that frequency of effective genius will increase, even exponentially, with increasing numbers of people and that there is some risk of breeding out to a merely high level of mediocrity in a stabilized population. The extremes of genius and idiocy, however, appear in about the same frequency at birth from truly heterogeneous gene pools regardless of size (the data from Montgomery County, Maryland, are really no exception to this). What is unfortunate, among other things, about overly dense concentrations of people is that this leads not only to reduced likelihood of the identification of mature genius, but to drastic reductions in the development of potential genius, owing to malnutrition in the weaning years and early youth, accompanied by retardation of both physical and mental growth. If we are determined to turn our problems over to an elite corps of mental prodigies a more surefire method is at hand. Nuclear transplant from various adult tissue cells into fertilized ova whose own nuclei have been removed has already produced identical copies of amphibian nucleus-donors and can probably do the same in man (Joshua Lederberg, 1966, *Bull. Atomic Scientists*, v. 22, no. 8, p. 9). Thus we appear to be on the verge of being able to make as many "xerox" copies as we want or need of any particular genius as long as we can get a piece of his or her nucleated tissue and find eggs and incubators for the genome aliquots to develop in. Female geniuses would be the best because (with a little help) they could copy themselves!

The reality is that without real population control and limitation of demand all else is drastically curtailed, not to say lost. And there is as yet not the faintest glimmer of hope that such limitation may take place voluntarily. Even were all unwanted births to be eliminated, populations would still be increasing at runaway rates in the absence of legal limitation of family size, as Dr. Erlich has so pas-sionately argued. The most fundamental freedom should be the right not to be born into a world of want and smothering restriction. I am convinced that we must give up (or have taken away from us) the right to have as many children as we want or see all other freedoms lost for them. Nature, to be sure, will restore a dynamic balance between our species and the world ecosystem if we fail to do so ourselves—by famine, pestilence, plague, or war. It seems, but is not, unthinkable that this should happen. If it does, of course, mineral resources may then be or appear to be relatively unlimited in relation to demand for them.

Premise V

The notion of the "technological fix" expresses a view that is at once full of hope and full of risk. It is a gripping thought to contemplate a world set free by nuclear energy. Imagine soaring cities, of aluminum, plastic, and thermopane where all live in peace and plenty at unvarying temperature and without effort, drink distilled water, feed on produce grown from more distilled water in coastal deserts, and flit from heliport to heliport in capsules of uncontaminated air. Imagine having as many children as you want, who, of course, will grow up seven stories above the ground and under such germ-free conditions that they will need to wear breathing masks if they ever do set foot in a park or a forest. Imagine a world in which there is no balance of payments problem, no banks, or money, and such mundane affairs as acquiring a shirt or a wife are handled for us by central computer systems. Imagine, if you like, a world in which the only problem is boredom, all others being solved by the state-maintained system of genius-technologists produced by transfer of nuclei from the skin cells of certified gene donors to the previously fertilized ova of final contestants in the annual ideal-pelvis contest. Imagine the problem of getting out of this disease-free world gracefully at the age of 110 when you just can't stand it any longer!

Of course this extreme view may not appeal to people not conditioned to think in those terms, and my guess is that it doesn't appeal to Dr. Weinberg either. But the risk of slipping bit by bit into such a smothering condition as one of the better possible outcomes is inherent in any proposition that encourages or permits people or industries to believe that they can leave their problems to the invention of technological fixes by someone else.

Although the world ecosystem has been in a constant state of flux throughout geologic time, in the short and middle term it is essentially homeostatic. That is to say, it tends to obey Le Chatelier's general principle— when a stress is applied to a system such as to perturb a state of near equilibrium, the system tends to react in such a way as to restore the equilibrium. But large parts of the world ecosystem have probably already undergone or are in danger of undergoing irreversible changes. We cannot continue to plunder and pollute it without serious or even deadly consequences.

Consider what would be needed in terms of conventional mineral raw materials merely to raise the level of all 3.3 billion people now living in the world to the average of the 200 mil-

lion now living in the United States. In terms of present staple commodities, it can be estimated (revised from Harrison Brown, James Bonner, and John Weir, 1947, *The Next Hundred Years*, Viking Press, p. 33) that this would require a "standing crop" of about 30 billion tons of iron, 500 million tons of lead, 330 million tons of zinc, and 50 million tons of tin. This is about 100 to 200 times the present annual production of these commodities. Annual power demands would be the equivalent of about 3 billion tons of coal and lignite, or about ten times present production. To support the doubled populations expected by the year 2000 at the same level would require, of course, a doubling of all the above numbers or substitute measures. The iron needed could probably be produced over a long period of time, perhaps even by the year 2000, given a sufficiently large effort. But, once in circulation, merely to replace losses due to oxidation, friction, and dispersal, not counting production of new iron for larger populations, would take around 200,000 tons of new iron every year (somewhat more than the current annual production of the United States), or a drastic curtailment of losses below the present rate of 1 per cent every two or three years. And the molybdenum needed to convert the iron to steel could become a serious limiting factor. The quantities of lead, zinc, and tin also called for far exceed all measured, indicated, and inferred world reserves of these metals.

This exercise gives a crude measure of the pressures that mineral resources will be under. It seems likely, to be sure, that substitutions, metallurgical research, and other technological advances will come to our aid, and that not all peoples of the world will find a superfluity of obsolescing gadgets necessary for the good life. But this is balanced by the equal likelihood that world population will not really level off at 6.6 or 7 billion and that there will be growing unrest to share the material resources that might lead at least to an improved standard of living. The situation is also aggravated by the attendant problems of disposal of mine wastes and chemically and thermally polluted waters on a vast scale.

The "technological fix," as Dr. Weinberg well understands, is not a panacea but an anesthetic. It may keep the patient quiet long enough to decide what the best long-range course of treatment may be, or even solve *some* of his problems permanently, but it would be tragic to forget that a broader program of treatment and recuperation is necessary. The flow of science and technology has always been fitful, and population control is a central limiting factor in what can be achieved. It will require much creative insight, hard work, public enlightenment, and good fortune to bring about the advances in discovery and analysis, recovery and fabrication, wise use and conservation of materials, management and recovery of wastes, and substitution and synthesis that will be needed to keep the affluent comfortable and bring the deprived to tolerable levels. It will probably also take some revision of criteria for self-esteem, achievement, and pleasure if the gap between affluent and deprived is to be narrowed and demand for raw materials kept within bounds that will

permit man to enjoy a future as long as his past, and under conditions that would be widely accepted as agreeable.

The reality is that the promise of the "technological fix" is a meretricious premise, full of glittering appeal but devoid of heart and comprehension of the environmental and social problems. Technology and "hard" science we must have, in sustained and increasing quality, and in quantities relevant to the needs of man—material, intellectual, and spiritual. But in dealing with the problems of resources in relation to man, let us not lose sight of the fact that this is the province of the environmental and social sciences. A vigorous and perceptive technology will be an essential handmaiden in the process, but it is a risky business to put the potential despoilers of the environment in charge of it.

The Nub of the Matter

The realities of mineral distribution, in a nutshell, are that it is neither inconsiderable nor limitless, and that we just don't know yet in the detail required for considered weighing of comprehensive and national long-range alternatives where or how the critical lithophilic elements are concentrated. Stratigraphically controlled substances such as the fossil fuels, and, to a degree, iron and alumina, we can comprehend and estimate within reasonable limits. Reserves, grades, locations, and recoverability of many critical metals, on the other hand, are affected by a much larger number of variables. We in North America began to develop our rich natural endowment of mineral resources at an accelerated pace before the rest of the world. Thus it stands to reason that, to the extent we are unable to meet needs by imports, we will feel the pinch sooner than countries like the U. S. S. R. with a larger component of virgin mineral lands.

In some instances nuclear energy or other technological fixes may buy time to seek better solutions or will even solve a problem permanently. But sooner or later man must come to terms with his environment and its limitations. The sooner the better. The year 2038, by which time even current rates of consumption will have exhausted presently known recoverable reserves of perhaps half the world's now useful metals (more will be found but consumption will increase also), is only as far from the present as the invention of the airplane and the discovery of radioactivity. In the absence of real population control or catastrophe there could be fifteen billion people on earth by then! Much that is difficult to anticipate can happen in the meanwhile, to be sure, and to place faith in a profit-motivated technology and refuse to look beyond a brief "foreseeable future" is a choice widely made. Against this we must weigh the consequences of error or thoughtless inaction and the prospects of identifying constructive alternatives for deliberate courses of long-term action, or inaction, that will affect favorably the long-range future. It is well to remember that to do nothing is equally to make a choice.

Geologists and other environmental scientists now living, therefore, face a great and growing challenge to intensify the research needed to ascertain and evaluate the facts governing availability of raw material resources, to integrate their results, to formulate better predictive models, and to inform the public. For only a cognizant public can generate the actions and exercise the restraints that will assure a tolerable life and a flexibility of options for posterity. The situation calls neither for gloomy foreboding nor facile optimism, but for positive and imaginative realism. That involves informed foresight, comprehensive and long-range outlooks, unremitting effort, inspired research, and a political and social climate conducive to such things.

Conclusions and Proposed Actions

Every promising avenue must be explored. The most imperative objective, after peace and population control, is certainly a workable breeder reactor— with all it promises in reduced energy costs, outlook for desalting saline waters and recovering mineral products from the effluent wastes, availability of now uselessly remote mineral deposits, decrease of cutoff grades, conservation of the so called "fossil" "fuels" for more important uses, and the reduction of contaminants resulting from the burning of fossil fuels in urban regions.

But, against the chance that this may not come through on schedule, we should be vigorously seeking additional geological sources of U^{235} and continuing research on controlled nuclear fusion.

A really comprehensive geochemical census of the earth's crustal materials should be accelerated and carried on concurrently, and as far into the future as may be necessary to delineate within reasonable limits the metallogenic provinces of our planet's surface, including those yet poorly-known portions beneath the sea. Such a census will be necessary not only in seeking to discover the causes and locations of new metalliferous deposits, but also in allowing resource data to be considered at the design stage, and in deciding which "common rocks" to mine first, should we ever be reduced to that extreme. Of course, this can be done meaningfully only in context with a good comprehension of sequence and environment based on careful geologic mapping, valid geochronology, perceptive biogeology, and other facets of interpretive earth science.

Programs of geophysical, geochemical, and geological prospecting should meanwhile be expanded to seek more intensively for subglacial, subsoil, submarine, and other concealed mineral resources in already defined favorable target areas—coupled with engineering, metallurgical, and economic innovation and evaluations of deposits found.

Only as we come to know better what we have, where it is, and what the problems of bringing it to the market place are likely to be will it be feasible to formulate the best and most comprehensive long range plans for resource use and conservation. Meanwhile, however, a permanent, high-level, and adequately funded monitoring system should be established under federal auspices to identify stress points in the mineral economy, or likely future demands, well in advance of rupture. Thus the essential lead time could be allowed in initiating search for new sources or substitutes, or in defining necessary conservation programs.

Practices in mixing materials during fabrication and in disposal of scrap metal should be examined with a view to formulating workable legislation that will extend resource lifetimes through more effective re-use.

Management of the nation's resources and of wastes from their extraction, beneficiation, and use should be regarded in the true democratic tradition as national problems and not left entirely to the conscience and discretion of the individual or private firm. Where practices followed are not conducive to the national, regional, or local welfare, informed legal inducement should make them so.

Research into all phases of resource problems and related subjects should be maintained at some effective level not dependent on political whimsey. It would be a far-sighted and eminently fair and logical procedure to set apart some specific fraction of taxes derived from various natural resources to be ploughed back into research designed to assure the integrity of the environment and the sufficiency of resources over the long term.

Much of the work suggested would naturally be centered in the U. S. Department of the Interior and in various state agencies, whose traditionally effective cooperative arrangements with the nation's universities should be enlarged.

[Universities] . . . are also central to the problem of sustaining a healthy industrial society. For they are the source of that most indispensable of all resources—the trained minds that will discern the facts and evolve the principles via which such a society comes to understand its resources and to use them wisely. The essential supplements are adequate support and a vision of the problem that sweeps and probes all aspects of the environmental sciences the world over. The times cry for the establishment of schools and institutes of environmental science in which geologists, ecologists, meteorologists, oceanographers, geophysicists, geographers, and others will interact and work closely together.

I can think of no more fitting way to close these reflections than to quote the recent words of Sir Macfarlane Burnet (p. 29, *in* "Biology and the appreciation of life," The Boyer Lectures, 1966, ABC, 45p.)—"*There are three imperatives: to reduce war to a mini-mum; to stabilize human populations; and to prevent the progressive destruction of the earth's irreplaceable resources.*" If the primary sciences and technology are to be our salvation it will necessarily be in an economic framework that evaluates success by some measure other than rate of turnover, and in the closest possible working liaison with the environmental and social sciences.

Notes

[1] In January 1974 the federal government terminated its helium storage and conservation program. [Ed.]

26 The Energy "Crisis"
What Impact? What Solutions?

Foreign Policy Association

"My candle burns at both ends;
It will not last the night;
But oh, my foes, and oh, my friends—
It gives a lovely light."
　　　　　—Edna St. Vincent Millay

There was an eerie beauty to the sight of Manhattan lighted only by a full moon and the flicker of candles. But the great Northeast power failure of November 9, 1965, which plunged 25 million people into darkness and confusion for up to 12 hours, was also an eerie reminder of how crippled our civilization would be without electricity. And it turned out to be a first,

Reprinted from, *Great Decisions, 1974* by permission of Foreign Policy Association, Incorporated. Copyright 1974.

dramatic omen of energy cutoffs to come. Over the past few years we have become accustomed to recurrent, brief but exasperating breakdowns in fuel and electric service. A hot summer brings brownouts from airconditioner overloads on the power supply. A cold winter brings "chillouts" from shortages of heating fuel. At any time of year the car owner may find the gasoline pump empty and the householder may find a Save-a-Watt notice with his electric bill urging him to use his various appliances sparingly.

Is America in the throes of an energy "crisis"? Are we actually running out of the power to keep our mechanized, motorized, electrified society going? Before the outbreak of the Middle East war, assessments differed. "For the next three decades," warned John A. Carver Jr. of the Federal Power Commission, "we will be in a race for our lives to meet our energy demands." Secretary of the Interior Rogers C. B. Morton held that there was no crisis now, only a potential one. Others argued that there was no shortage of resources—only a lack of intelligent policies for their acquisition and use.

But on one point there was less dispute. The energy demands of the U. S. and the other industrialized nations of the world are fast outpacing the world's supply of fuels that are at the same time *abundant, safe, clean* and *cheap*. Something will have to give.

Hard Choices Ahead

The world's appetite for energy doubles every 15 years. This means that in 1985 it will devour twice the amount of fuel—primarily the fossil fuels—it consumed in 1970. Of the world's major nations, only two are expected to remain wholly self-sufficient in these fuels: the Soviet Union and China. The U. S. is already a net importer and could well find itself competing with the other leading deficit areas, Western Europe and Japan, for available supplies.

Americans constitute one-twentieth of the world's population but consume one-third of its energy output. Three items account for the most dynamic growth in American consumption since the 1950's: the automobile, the jet plane and the airconditioner. Together they have pushed the demand for transportation fuel and electric power up to half of our total energy consumption (see Table 1). And at bargain rates. Our gasoline, heat and electricity costs are far lower than, say, Europe's. "The simple fact," says one oil executive bluntly, "is that we are spoiled rotten."

But the energy "joyride," as others call it, is now over. Ahead of us are hard choices and compromises. The trouble is, How can we agree on the compromises when we disagree so strongly on the priorities? Is it more important that our fuels be plentiful— or nonpolluting—or inexpensive, since we cannot have it all ways? Here a

Table 1 United States gross consumption of energy resources—1970
(in trillions of BTU's)

Consuming sector	Petroleum	Natural gas	Coal	Hydro-power	Nuclear	Total by sector	
Industry	5,069	10,500	5,560	—	—	21,129	(31%)
Electricity Generation, Utilities	2,263	4,025	7,824	2,647	208	16,967	(25%)
Transportation	15,756	671	9	—	—	16,436	(24%)
Household and Commercial	6,349	7,350	399	—	—	14,098	(20%)
Nonenergy uses[1]	180	—	—	—	—	180	(0.2%)
Total by resource:	29,617	22,546	13,792	2,647	208	68,810	
	(43%)	(33%)	(20%)	(4%)	(0.3%)		(100%)

[1] Primary chemicals manufactured from petroleum feedstocks.
Source: U. S. Dept. of the Interior.

conflict of interest divides the businessman, the scientist, the environmentalist, the economist, the government official and, not least, the taxpayer-consumer.

Take the environmental interest. Except for the windmill, no conventional power source is 100-percent clean. Our tough new antipollution and conservation standards put added constraints on our energy supplies, both at the production end (strip-mining, damming rivers, drilling offshore for oil and gas, building new electric-power plants) and at the consumption end (the burning of high-sulfur coal, fuel oil and high-octane gasoline). Moreover, many of the processes for improving environmental quality themselves call for extra quantities of energy—to run machinery for removing air pollutants, treating sewage and recycling wastes. Where is it to come from? S. David Freeman, a former White House energy adviser now with the Ford Foundation, sums up the view of many professionals in the field: "Energy demands and environmental goals are on a collision course."

Or take the consumer interest in low prices. This conflicts with the industrialist's need for investment capital to explore and exploit new sources of conventional fuel, with the scientist's need for research funds to develop the energy technology of the future, and with the consumer's own desire for cleaner technology today. Nearly all observers are convinced that energy will have to become more expensive to bring supply into line with demand; in the words of former Secretary of Commerce Peter G. Peterson, "Popeye is running out of cheap spinach." But how can we see to it that

higher costs are fairly allocated? Will the small individual consumer be saddled with exorbitant rates for home heat and electricity while the big industrial customer benefits from bulk discounts? And how much, if at all, will rising prices reduce demand?

Can Consumption be Curbed?

Demand is of course the heart of the energy problem. Must we use as much as we do?

Some analysts see only one radical solution: switch our entire industrial machine into lower gear. By their reasoning, economic growth itself is the root cause of the energy crunch.

Most observers, however, contend that savings in energy are possible *without* major changes in our lifestyle. Technology itself can provide some of the means, e.g. by improving the efficiency of electricity. Only about a third of the fuel now burned in power generators is actually converted into electricity; the bulk of its heat is wasted. Some of the waste could be eliminated by better generating techniques. The remainder could be piped from the power plant to provide central heating to nearby communities a common practice in Scandinavia. And further losses which occur in the conduction and consumption of electricity could be reduced by better transmission technology and appliance design.

We would also waste less fuel if we insulated our houses better. We could use more solid materials than glass, which lets heat escape in winter and penetrate in summer, for the walls of high-rise commercial buildings. (The twin skyscrapers of the new World

Trade Center in New York City use more electricity each day for heating, cooling and lighting than is consumed by the entire city of Schenectady, with some 80,000 inhabitants.) And enormous savings could be made in the transportation sector. If we drove cars with less horsepower we could get more mileage per gallon. If we moved less traffic by automobile and truck and more by urban mass transit and intercity railroad, the same passengers and freight would cover the same distances on much less fuel.

Our fuel resources could be allocated more efficiently. Natural gas is particularly suited to home heating because it is the cleanest of the fossil fuels. But more than two-thirds of our scarce domestic supply is consumed by factories and utilities that could easily burn (and remove pollutants from) more abundant fuels such as coal and residual fuel oil.

In his energy policy message of April 18, 1973, President Nixon recommended "a national energy conservation ethic" founded on voluntary savings by consumers (turning out lights, tuning up automobiles) and by industry (labeling major appliances for their "energy efficiency"). On June 29 he went further and called for a spe-cific 5 percent cut in nationwide energy consumption over the coming year, announcing that offices of the Federal government would set the example with a 7 percent reduction in their own consumption. The President also appointed Governor John A. Love of Colorado to head a new Energy Policy Office in the White House. On November 7 the President announced the goal of national energy self-sufficiency by 1980 while proposing new measures to cope with shortages resulting from the Middle East war. These included further cuts in the use of energy by the government; reductions in fuel allocated for aircraft and in oil to heat homes and factories. The President also asked Congress to enact legislation providing for even more drastic conservation measures—if necessary, gasoline rationing.

Some observers believe that rationing will have to become a standard feature of our national energy policy in any event, at least in the short run. We will explore the short-run supply problems, with their international as well as domestic implications, later in the discussion. First, to put them into perspective, it is worth reviewing some of the *long-run* options for solving them.

Long-run Solutions: the Sun's the Limit

The world of the 21st century will consume most of its energy in the cleanest form known: electricity. It will produce more and more energy from sources and techniques that are only beginning to be known today, although many of the conventional fuels we rely on now should still be in use.

But there are limits to the latter.

The world's known petroleum reserves could theoretically be exhausted soon after the turn of the century, and natural gas is in even shorter supply. Hydropower is at best a supplementary source; the world has only so many waterfalls and river sites suitable for dams. The U. S. now derives 4 percent of its power from hydro-electric generators and the proportion is not expected to change. But there is one conventional resource that the U. S. possesses in enough abundance to fill our *entire* energy needs for at least the next 300 years: the dirtiest of the fossil fuels, coal.

Comeback For King Coal?

To Americans over 30, the chug of the steam locomotive and the clatter of coal pouring down the cellar chute are half-forgotten sounds from a not-too-distant past. King Coal's long reign as America's No. 1 fuel came to an end after World War II. It lost virtually all of its railroad and residential market and much of its factory business to oil, and was spared from oblivion mainly by the demands of the steel and utility industries. Today it supplies 20 percent of our energy needs, compared to 70 percent a generation ago, even though our reserves of bituminous coal and lignite are estimated at 1.6 trillion tons—between one-fifth and one half of total world deposits.

"We're draining America dry of its oil and gas while all that coal just sits there," comments S. David Freeman. Recent oil and gas shortages have, however, sparked a modest comeback for coal: 1972 production approached 600 million tons for the first time since 1948. Yet it remains an underemployed giant. As Freeman puts it, "There are two things wrong with coal today. We can't mine it and we can't burn it."

The trouble with deep underground mining is its danger and expense. The physical risks of explosions, cave-ins, "black lung" disease and other deep-mine hazards have now been lessened by the provisions of the Federal Coal Mine Health and Safety Act of 1969. But the law's new precautions have had little effect on the low morale of miners (aggravated by union political battles), have further lowered worker productivity and may add as much as $1 per ton to the already high cost of extraction. Although deep mining still accounts for about half of U. S. coal output, most observers foresee its continuing decline; not a single new underground mine has been opened since the early 1960's.

The trouble with open-pit or strip-mining of coal near the surface—the safest, simplest and cheapest method of extraction—is the pockmarked wasteland it leaves in its wake. With time, some strip-mined terrain is restored by nature, but much remains "dead" unless man invests the money and effort to replace and replant the topsoil. The U. S. possesses plenty of coal beds shallow enough to be stripped, including the huge low-sulfur deposits in the Fort Union and Powder river regions of Montana, Wyoming and the Dakotas. But do we want to see the range lands of the northern Plains states, one of our last great unspoiled frontiers, gouged into a barren "lunar landscape"—another Appalachia? If not, we seem to have only two choices: leave the coal alone, or set strict legal standards for mining practices and land reclamation. The Department of the Interior is planning to pursue the latter policy because, up to now at least, the coal industry's record of voluntary restoration has not been impressive. Even so, as *Fortune* magazine points out, the cost of good land reclamation nowhere near cancels out the cost advantage of open-pit production—$1.50 per ton cheaper than deep-mined coal.

The trouble with burning coal is its pollution of the air. The sulfurous smoke, fly ash and other noxious by-products of its combustion kill crops, corrode metal and afflict people with a variety of respiratory, eye and heart ailments. More and more urban communities have effectively banned coal through "London laws" (so called after the first major city to adopt them, in 1956) which forbid the burning of fuels with more than 1 percent sulfur content.

Techniques for removing sulfur from coal before burning or from its stack gases after combustion are still in the experimental stage. But the most promising answer to the air-pollution problem, with the most exciting potential for our long-term fuel needs, seems to be the conversion of coal into synthetic oil or methane gas—the chief constituent of natural gas. We already have several coal-gasification pilot plants aided by Federal research funds, and a West German process that has been used successfully in Europe is also being introduced here. How soon the technology evolves into commercial reality depends on how much we invest. Some experts maintain that if we were willing to spend $5 billion between now and 1985, we could then have over two dozen plants converting 500 million tons of dirty coal into 6 trillion cubic feet of clean gas every year. In the long run, in a new guise, coal might once again be king.

Nuclear Energy: Three Stages

Of all the fuels of the future, nuclear energy has turned in the most disappointing performance so far. After more than two decades of scientific and commercial development, subsidized by nearly 85 percent of all Federal funds spent on energy research, it still accounts for a smaller proportion of U. S. energy consumption than old-fashioned wood-burning. The former head of the Atomic Energy Commission (AEC), James R. Schlesinger, sees the "romance of the atom" ending amid vehement opposition from environmentalists, spiraling plant costs and impending uranium shortages.

We are still in the first stage of atomic energy: the fission or "burner" reactor. This produces power by the fission (splitting) of the extremely rare uranium-235 atom, comprising less than 1 percent of natural uranium. Burners require tremendous quantities of water for cooling and discharge 50 percent more waste heat than fossil-fuel generators. The result is thermal pollution and damage to marine life in the river, lake and coastal waters along which the plants are situated. The danger to human life is hotly debated. So far there have been more than a dozen emergency shutdowns of nuclear plants but no accidents, and the long-term effects of possible radioactive "leaks" remain to be seen. One leading scientist, Dr. Edward Teller, calculates that a man could lean against a nuclear plant for the rest of his life and absorb no more radiation than he would from sleeping next to his wife, from the potassium in her blood. Moreover, the plants emit no air pollutants and, once the initial high construction costs have been met, can be run as cheaply as fossil-fuel plants. Today the U. S. has about 30 operating nuclear plants producing close to 4 percent of our electricity; the AEC estimates that by 1980 the figures will have risen to 160 plants and 23 percent.

By then the U. S. may have reached the second stage of nuclear energy: the "fast breeder" reactor. Here we lag behind other countries in commercial development, although experimental work has been under way since 1951. Last July the world's first breeder plant went into commercial production at Shevchenko, U. S. S. R., on the shore of the Caspian Sea. The second will soon be ready in Scotland and another is under construction in France. The fast breeder's great advantage over the fission reactor is fuel economy. As its name implies, it generates more atoms than it consumes (and uses the abundant U-238 isotope of uranium), making it a self-perpetuating energy producer. But it also has a great disadvantage. One of its waste products is highly radioactive plutonium, which remains lethal for at least a quarter of a million years. How can it be safely transported and disposed of? Unless we find some way to bury it deep in the earth's core or rocket it into outer space, we will be burdening future generations with the "perpetual care" of toxic wastes.

Most scientists see the breeder reactor as only an interim technology, to conserve the supply of uranium fuel until we attain the third and "ideal" stage of atomic energy: controlled thermonuclear fusion. The big challenge is in the word "control," for the process of fusing hydrogen atoms under intense heat and pressure has been understood ever since the development of the hydrogen bomb. There is no fuel problem: an unlimited supply of hydrogen exists in seawater. There is next to no waste problem: the only

radioactive product is tritium, which is less dangerous than wastes from fission reactors and could probably be recycled through the system. And eventually the thermal-pollution problem might be solved by converting a fusion reaction directly to electricity, bypassing the steam-generating phase which produces the excess heat.

There have been some encouraging developments in recent fusion research, including the use of powerful light beams from lasers to trigger a controllable reaction. But even the most optimistic scientists doubt that fusion power will be economically feasible in this country much before 1990 (though many predict that the Russians will achieve an earlier breakthrough; we are already borrowing some of their experimental techniques). Sometime beyond the turn of the century, however, it is hoped that this clean, safe, inexhaustible source of electricity will be supplying at least half of our energy needs—restoring the romance of the atom.

Wind, Water, Earth and Sun

Nature offers a wide range of other nonpolluting, infinitely renewable energy resources. The problem is how to harness them. How, for example, can the principle of the lowly windmill be elevated to a point where the enormous power of atmospheric winds and storms can be captured, stored and applied where needed? How can the greatest source of hydropower, the ocean tides, be exploited? There are two tidal-power plants in operation today, one in the Soviet Union and one near St. Malo in France. At least 50 more estuary sites exist—including, in

North America, the Bay of Fundy and Alaska's Cook Inlet—where giant tides might be dammed to generate electricity, but most are remote from the major energy markets. Can fuel be derived from organic wastes? Yes, but not very much.

There are three other possibilities, however, that hold more promise.

One is hydrogen. It can be collected in the form of a gas by passing an electric current through seawater. It can then be burned in either gas or liquid form for heating and transportation fuel and to generate electric power. The drawbacks are that hydrogen is not a primary fuel (energy must be expended to obtain it) and has a dangerously low ignition point. (The most notorious accident was the explosion of the hydrogen-gas zeppelin *Hindenburg* at Lakehurst, N. J. in 1937.) The merits are its abundance and cleanliness: the only waste product is harmless water vapor which eventually returns to the oceans—a complete natural cycle. There is growing excitement about hydrogen's potential as a staple fuel in our economic future. If the potential is fufilled, so will a prediction made a hundred years ago by the novelist Jules Verne, many of whose other scientific prophecies have since come true. "I believe," says a character in Verne's *The Mysterious Island*, "that water will one day be employed as fuel, that hydrogen and oxygen which constitute it, used singly or together, will furnish an inexhaustible source of heat and light. . ."

Another inexhaustible source is geothermal energy: steam heat from the earth's core, used to drive the turbines of electric generators. Geothermal power plants are already operating in Italy (where underground steam was first harnessed in 1904), the Soviet Union, Japan, New Zealand, Iceland, Mexico and the U. S. (in California's Sonoma Valley). Others are planned or under construction, and scientists believe that at least 80 nations have suitable geological conditions for them. The simplest way to exploit the earth's heat is to tap steam produced naturally by underground water coming into contact with molten rock at relatively shallow depths. This occurs particularly in the zones of volcanic and earthquake activity where hot springs, geysers, etc. are common. But it is also possible to create the steam by drilling into hot dry rock and injecting a current of water from above. Geothermal wells have some unpleasant environmental side effects that need to be dealt with, such as noise, odor and corrosive mineral salts, and much of the steam is not dry enough for efficient generation of electricity. But operating costs are low and reserves are practically unlimited. The U. S. alone is believed to have the energy equivalent of 900 trillion barrels of petroleum in accessible subterranean heat, and last year Washington began a geothermal leasing program on 59 million acres of Federal land in 14 Western states. "In 50 years," says Dr. Joseph Barnea, director of the UN's resources and transport division, "geothermal energy will be recognized as an energy resource of even greater significance than petroleum."

Ultimately, the world's most significant energy resource may turn out to be the most basic of all: the sun. Up to now its mammoth potential has been exploited only minimally, for heating water and buildings and for supplying electricity to spacecraft. Because solar power is so diffuse and uneven, the problem—as with wind power—is to concentrate and store it. How can its heat be "collected" in sunbaked tropics and exported to colder and cloudier regions? One experiment now under study is for a solar "farm" in the Arizona desert to produce electricity. Another involves placing a giant satellite in permanent orbit 22,000 miles in space, which would capture rays from the sun, convert them to microwaves and beam the current to a receiving station on earth. Experts agree that, given the research funds, we need not wait until the next century for solar radiation to become an efficient and economic energy source.

But in the fiscal year 1974 the Federal government spent only about $870 million for research and development (R&D) on *all* the new energy sources— liquid and gaseous fuels from coal, nuclear fusion, geothermal and solar power, etc.—combined. President Nixon has called for a Federal R&D effort totaling $10 billion over a five-year period, beginning in the 1975 fiscal year. It is far from certain that this amount of public money can be raised. But if it can be, we will hasten the day when the new technology is a commercial reality and we are freed from our critical dependence on natural gas and petroleum.

Short-run Crisis:
Are We Running Out of Gas?

"Gas Heats Best!" the ads used to proclaim. And too many customers agreed. By 1970, when 55 percent of all American homes were heated by gas, the utility companies had had to stop promoting it; there was no longer enough to go around.

Back in the 1930's natural gas—as distinct from old-fashioned "city gas" produced from coal—was regarded as a nuisance by-product of oil, with which it is often found, and was burned off the tops of oil wells in Texas and Oklahoma. Then the construction of large-diameter pipelines during World War II introduced it to urban markets as a boiler fuel that was at once clean, convenient and cheap. In the postwar period the market jumped an average 6 percent a year—to a point where gas now supplies a third of our entire energy consumption. But at the *present* consumption rate of 23 trillion cubic feet a

year, our proved domestic reserves could theoretically run out by 1985.

Will it happen in practice? Probably not. What will avert it? Some combination of four alternatives: new discoveries of domestic gas, bigger imports of foreign gas; rationing of gas; much higher prices for it—in effect, rationing by market forces.

Price Deregulation: Pros and Cons

Up to now natural gas has been the only fuel subject to government price regulation. The Federal Power Commission maintains a ceiling, averaging 20 cents per thousand cubic feet, on the wellhead price of gas sold to interstate pipelines, meaning on all gas delivered to markets beyond the handful of gas-producing states. In April, 1973 President Nixon proposed lifting the ceiling. He asked Congress for legislation to "deregulate" gas.

The main argument of the Administration, the gas industry and others who favor deregulation is that holding gas prices at "artificially" low levels, below those of competing fuels, discourages production by making it unprofitable. The industry has little incentive to exploit deep-lying reserves of discovered gas and to explore possible new sources unless the capital costs are met by a fair market price. Higher market prices will, at the same time, encourage conservation and more efficient use of supplies. Big utilities and manufacturing plants will switch their business to residual fuel oil and coal, releasing more gas to the residential and commercial market. Americans have a clear-cut choice, say the advocates of deregulation: cheap gas in ever-shorter supply, or more costly gas in adequate quantities—a classic application of the law of supply and demand.

On the other side of the fence are various consumer groups, economists, congressmen, utility executives and state and local officials who argue that the gas companies can easily afford to produce more *without* a price hike. "What they are really saying," maintains Charles F. Wheatley Jr. of the American Public Gas Association, "is they want a far greater profit than the substantial profit (15 percent) they are currently earning on their production of natural gas." Joseph C. Swidler, a former chairman of the Federal Power Commission, warns that deregulation will result in "astronomical windfalls" for gas producers. Some critics of the oil and gas industry complain that we have no way of verifying whether the gas shortage is genuine or artificial, contrived by a self-serving "oligopoly." "The only information avail-

able," says Senator Philip A. Hart (D–Mich.), ". . . comes from the industry—which would benefit enormously by price increases." The Federal Trade Commission has, in fact, been investigating the industry's published figures on domestic gas reserves.

Proved and Potential Reserves

According to the *Oil & Gas Journal*, America's *proved*, recoverable reserves of gas at the beginning of 1973 totaled 271.5 trillion cubic feet (see Table 2). This is less than a 12-year supply at current consumption rates. Estimates of our *potential* reserves range from a 65-year to a 300-year supply. A good part of the potential, however, may turn out not to exist. Some may be confirmed but not readily recoverable—e.g. deep underwater deposits at the outer edges of the continental shelf. Some may be recoverable only at extreme environmental risk—e.g. nuclear explosions to release an estimated 317 trillion cubic feet of gas "trapped" in tight underground rock formations in the western U. S.

Our natural gas supplies will be supplemented by synthetic gas manufactured from other fuels: coal, as described earlier, as well as naphtha (a petroleum feedstock) and perhaps organic wastes. And we have begun turning more to foreign sources.

Looking Abroad

In 1970 imports accounted for about 4 percent of our total gas consumption. Nearly all came from Canada (the rest from Mexico, a marginal source). Our northern neighbor is regarded as the most desirable foreign supplier, not least because the cheapest and most

Table 2 Worldwide oil and natural gas—proved reserves as of January 1, 1973. Area totals and selected major producing nations

	Oil (billion barrels)	Natural Gas (trillion cubic feet)
World total	666.9	1,882.9
Asia-Pacific	34.4	122.2
China	19.5	21.0
Indonesia	10.0	5.5
Australia	2.1	36.2
U.S.S.R.	75.0	635.4
Middle East	355.9	344.2
Saudi Arabia	138.0	50.0
Iran	65.0	200.0
Kuwait	64.9	33.0
Iraq	29.0	25.0
Africa	106.4	189.0
Algeria	47.0	105.0
Libya	30.4	27.5
Nigeria	15.0	40.0
Europe	12.1	178.4
Western Hemisphere	79.6	405.7
U. S. (incl. Alaska)	36.8	271.5
Canada	10.2	55.0
Venezuela	13.7	34.6
Misc. unaccounted for Area totals	3.5	8.0

Source: *Oil & Gas Journal*

efficient way to transport gas is by overland pipeline. But Canada's National Energy Board has ruled against increasing gas exports to the U. S. much above present levels (about two-fifths of Canadian production) on the grounds that the country's recoverable reserves are not sufficient. Geologists are convinced that enormous deposits of gas and petroleum lie buried under the ice fields of the Canadian Arctic. But these are only beginning to be tapped and will be enormously costly to extract and deliver to market.

So we have begun to look overseas for imports of liquefied natural gas (LNG). Algeria, with 105 trillion cubic feet of gas reserves, is one promising source. Small quantities of Algerian gas are already arriving on our East Coast and the El Paso Natural Gas Company has signed a contract with Algiers for the purchase of a billion cubic feet a day over a 20-year period, beginning sometime after 1975. Other companies are investigating possible LNG imports from Australia, Nigeria and Latin America. But the biggest source of all—"our ace in the hole," according to one commentator—is Siberia.

With 635 trillion cubic feet of proved gas reserves, the Soviet Union possesses more than a third of the world total and nearly two and a half times as much as the U. S.—and is eager to sell its gas for hard currency. Two major Soviet-American deals are now in the planning stage. One project, labeled North Star, would jointly develop the Urengoiskeye gas field in western Siberia, believed to be the world's largest, and ship the LNG from the Arctic port of Murmansk to the U. S. East Coast. The other, a tripartite venture with Japan, would pipe gas from the big Yakutsk deposits in eastern Siberia to the Pacific port of Nakhodka for shipment to Japan and the U. S. West Coast. Each project entails a mutibillion-dollar investment: exploration and drilling equipment, installation of pipelines, construction of liquefaction plants and a fleet of LNG tankers. The necessary financing and government clearances for both projects are still pending. Even if they were assured in time to start work today, we would not be getting sizable deliveries of Soviet gas much before the end of the decade. But by 1980, the North Star venture alone could be supplying more than 10 percent of the projected gas consumption of 13 Eastern states.

Various objections have been voiced to a large-scale LNG import program. On political grounds, Is it wise to let the U. S. become dependent on the U. S. S. R. for a strategically vital resource? On environmental grounds, Do we want LNG tanker ports and gas revaporization plants along our heavily populated coasts? And on purely economic grounds, Is it worth it? The East Coast wholesale price of Algerian gas will be roughly twice as high, and Soviet gas at least three times as high, as what utilities now pay interstate pipelines for domestic gas. Wouldn't the retail customer be better off if the money were invested right here in the U. S. in coal-gasification plants and exploration for new gas reserves?

Other analysts point out, however, that by the time foreign LNG begins arriving here in volume, its price will be more competitive with domestic gas; the latter will by then be more expensive. To many energy experts, the issue of imports is not a Yes-or-No proposition. We are going to have to buy *all* the gas we can obtain, they say, from every available source, at whatever prices the market dictates, for as long as we rely on it as one of our basic fuels. But that reliance should gradually diminish. "On the basis of what is known now," concedes physicist Robert H. Williams of the University of Michigan, "the long-term future for natural gas is not bright."

Where the Oil Is

The long-term outlook for oil, which now supplies roughly half of the world's total energy needs, may not be much brighter than that for natural gas. At the current consumption rate the world has only a 35-year supply of proved, recoverable petroleum re-

serves. And consumption is rising by 8 percent a year—faster than the rate of new oil discoveries. The biggest consumer, the U. S., now burns 30 percent of the total: close to 6 billion barrels in 1972. By 1980, it is estimated that our demand will climb to 8.8 billion barrels; by 1985, to 9.5 billion. Where will it come from?

Certainly not all from domestic sources. Everyone agrees that the U. S. can never again be self-sufficient in oil. We are already importing about a third of our needs. The big issues for the years ahead are: How much of our oil will have to come from abroad? Which countries will supply it, and on what terms? How will we pay for it? And what effects will our dependence on foreign sources of oil—often called the most political of commodities— have on U. S. foreign policy in general?

Suppose we wanted to minimize our dependence on imports as far as possible. How much oil could we hope to derive from American sources?

Domestic Sources

With one conspicuous exception, our proved reserves of 37 billion barrels are already being exploited to the maximum. On land and offshore, wells are pumping at capacity around the clock, producing about 4 billion barrels a year. The exception is Alaska, where 10 billion barrels in Prudhoe Bay and other North Slope fields await the construction of a pipeline across the Arctic wilderness—delayed by environmental protests.

Elsewhere, our unexplored reserves can only be guessed at. Estimates of oil buried along the outer continental shelf of the Atlantic Coast range from less than 10 billion to nearly 170 billion barrels. Rocky Mountain shale deposits in Colorado, Utah and Wyoming might be able to yield 80 billion barrels of oil. One leading petroleum geologist, M. King Hubbert, whose earlier predictions have proved more accurate than many, now believes that fields already identified in the "lower 48" states, including the continental shelves, represent between 68 and 85 percent of the total U. S. reserves that will ever be discovered.

The oil industry, however, takes a more optimistic view. It promises significant increases in domestic production if the following strategy is adopted: Accelerate exploration on the Gulf of Mexico continental shelf and inaugurate it on the Atlantic Coast. Help defray the high development costs with government financial incentives to the industry. Expedite the delivery of Alaskan oil to market. Simultaneously, relieve some of the demand for oil by aggressive exploitation of coal reserves, deregulation of natural gas prices, development of the Rocky Mountain shale deposits, etc.

The Administration endorses a good part of this strategy. In his April 18, 1973 energy message, President Nixon asked Congress to grant the oil industry a new tax credit on its investments in exploration (12 percent if the new wells yield oil, 7 percent for dry holes), over and above the special tax deduction for the depletion of existing oil wells that the industry has long been allowed. He also asked for speedy licensing of a trans-Alaska pipeline. And he promised that the Department of the Interior would step up the sale of Federal leases for drilling in offshore waters.

But there is strong opposition to this "game plan" in Congress, the big Northeast states and elsewhere. The oil industry, say its critics, hardly needs extra financial incentives to maximize domestic output. And the environmental objections are legion. Every governor from Maine to Maryland, for example, is opposed to oil drills, with the accompanying risk of oil spills, in the waters off the Atlantic Coast.

Yet even if the entire game plan were given the green light, no one expects the results to satisfy our soaring oil needs into the next decade. "No matter how much domestic oil we develop," concedes Secretary of the Interior Morton, "you still come up short about 50 percent, and that 50 percent will have to be made up from imports from other countries."

Foreign Suppliers

Which countries will make up our oil deficit?

Some of the world's producing areas can be discounted as major suppliers to the U. S. because their oil is urgently needed in other, nearer consumer markets. Indonesia, Australia and other Asian-Pacific producers will ship the bulk of their output to Japan. Algeria, Libya, Nigeria and other African producers will ship most of theirs to Europe. Oil from the recently discovered North Sea fields, estimated to contain some 12 billion barrels, is also earmarked for Europe, particularly Britain and West Germany. Western Europe's appetite for oil is growing so fast (by 7 percent a year) that by 1980 its consumption should equal or surpass that of the U. S., and North Sea production will at best fill only 15 percent of its needs.

As for the U. S. S. R., with twice the oil reserves of the U. S., its domestic needs are soaring as Soviet industry switches from coal to cleaner fuels and Soviet society enters the automobile age. So are the needs of Moscow's chief export customers: its Eastern European allies. To the extent that Moscow continues selling oil to hard-currency customers, Western Europe will probably continue to have first call on it, with Japan another candidate.

Western Hemisphere countries now supply 70 percent of our oil imports, but the proportion will shrink as the total volume swells. Canada today has little surplus oil for sale. It consumes almost as much as it produces and imports almost as much as it exports. This may change, however, as two promising (but expensive) new sources are developed: the rich tar sands along the Athabasca river in northern Alberta, which probably contain over 300 billion barrels of recoverable oil, and the oil fields under Ellesmere, Baffin and other Canadian Arctic islands, which are just beginning to be tapped.

On the other hand, Venezuela—our biggest foreign supplier up to now— is fast running dry. At the 1972 production rate of 1.2 billion barrels (down 9 percent from the previous year), the recoverable reserves of the Lake Maracaibo region would be exhausted by 1984. The Orinoco basin is believed to contain close to a trillion barrels of "heavy" oil, of which at least one-tenth (100 billion barrels) is recoverable with present technology. But the foreign oil companies—whose present Venezuelan concessions are due to expire in 1983–84—are so far unprepared to invest the enormous amounts of capital needed to exploit the Orinoco deposits.

Elsewhere in Latin America there are promising new finds in the Amazon basin on the eastern flank of the

Andes. Ecuador has already begun to export the Amazon oil, and Peru and Colombia should soon follow suit. But based on currently proved reserves, the output of all the South American countries combined, plus small amounts from Trinidad-Tobago and other Caribbean producers, will be able to supply only a fraction of the future oil needs of the U. S.

Inevitably, then, we turn to the Middle East—more specifically, the Persian Gulf region. With 53 percent of total world reserves it is by far the earth's richest reservoir of oil. Saudi Arabia alone possesses more than one-fifth of the world supply. Much Persian Gulf oil is "easy" oil, flowing freely from just beneath the surface. Its distance from major markets is of little significance in an era of super-tankers. And despite rapidly rising prices it remains the world's least expensive oil to produce.

Scrapping the Import Quotas

In 1972 only 178 million barrels of Mideast oil—a tenth of our total imports—passed through the U. S. quota barrier. The barrier had been erected by the Eisenhower Administration in 1959. In recent years it was lowered sporadically, mostly in favor of Canadian and Venezuelan oil, as domestic fuel ran short. Then, effective May 1, 1973, President Nixon scrapped the quotas across the board. In their place he instituted a system of graduated "license fees" (equivalent to tariffs).

Besides facilitating the entry of for-eign oil, the new arrangement is intended to stimulate the search for domestic oil; the price of the latter will become more competitive with imports because of the license fees. The fees are also designed to spur the construction of new refineries in the U. S.: as a consequence, crude oil will come into the country at a much cheaper rate than gasoline and other finished products.

But here again, the proliferation of refineries—especially along the East Coast—is running headlong into environmental opposition. Another problem is the unloading of tankers bringing oil from overseas. The U. S. has no port facilities, present or planned, to accommodate supertankers weighing upward of 150,000 tons—of which nearly 500 will be in service by the end of 1975. One alternative is to continue "exporting pollution" by having foreign crude refined at Caribbean ports before being shipped here in product form. Another is President Nixon's proposal for construction of offshore terminals for supertankers: "We can expect considerably less pollution if we use fewer but larger tankers and deepwater facilities."

But these environmental dilemmas can, in principle at least, be resolved by compromise decisions here at home. Far more troublesome, since the decisions are not ours alone to make, are the foreign policy implications—strategic, political and monetary—of America's ever-deepening dependence on the oil kingdoms of the Middle East.

Environmental Impact

"The American Colossus was fiercely intent on appropriating and exploiting the riches of the richest of all continents—grasping with both hands, reaping where he had not sown, wasting what he thought would last forever."

Gifford Pinchot
Breaking New Ground

In Reading 27 Hubert Risser states, "The problem that confronts the mineral industry today is that of finding ways to comply with the requirements for environmental quality protection and still provide the nation with the minerals it requires at an acceptable cost." He explores the alternatives involved in reducing environmental effects and reviews current and proposed regulations which apply to mineral production, transportation, and utilization. It behooves industry to take the present concern for the environment seriously; and the consumer must be prepared to pay a fair share of the cost of environmental protection.

Man's exploitation of natural resources has led to a variety of environmental problems. The magnitude of surface mining and the problems which result from this form of exploitation are reviewed in Reading 28. Less than 1 per cent of the total land area of the United States has been disturbed by surface mining, but the effects go well beyond the mine site. Mining activity not only influences the quality of the land, it also has far-ranging impacts on air, water, and plant and animal life. Furthermore, surface mining affects some portion of every state and frequently conflicts with other demands for land use. Surface mining will increase greatly in future years. Technological advances will enable us to mine ore at greatly accelerated rates and also, if Alvin Weinberg is correct, to consider lower grade ores. In view of the fact that the rehabilitation of mine sites has been

Photo on page 316. Courtesy of U.S. Bureau of Mines, R. L. Williams.

discouragingly slow, it is imperative that technological advances be applied to rehabilitation as well as exploitation.

Subsurface mining activities can also have adverse effects on the environment. Underground mining of solid resources and the withdrawal of underground fluids—water, oil, and gas—can cause the subsidence or sinking of the land. Specific examples and case histories of subsidence are presented in Reading 29. This Reading documents the magnitude of the problem in western United States and the economic and political impact of this phenomenon. Subsidence at Long Beach, California, for example, by 1962 had reached 29 feet and caused more than 100 million dollars in damages. The draining of peat bogs, the irrigation of certain soils, and the application of surface loads can also cause subsidence. In some instances subsidence can lead to catastrophic failures of dams or levees, and public agencies and private developers should be aware of the problem and of the methods for stopping or reducing subsidence.

Many investigators have pointed out that the subsea mineral resources of the world are vast. In 1947 the petroleum industry turned to offshore prospecting and exploitation as a natural extension of the development of numerous onshore prospects. Since then, offshore petroleum production has increased to the point where it now accounts for 18 per cent of the world's total production. It is estimated that offshore production will account for one-third of the world's total by 1980, and will rise to one-half of the world's total during the 1980's. During normal development of a prospective oil pool about 6½ miles southeast of Santa

Barbara, California, a blowout occurred on January 28, 1969, during completion of the fifth well being drilled from Platform A on Federal Tract OCS P-0241. The well flowed uncontrolled until February 7 and spilled oil over a large part of the channel and adjacent beaches. The problem was compounded by moderate and steady seepage long after the well was brought under control.

The Santa Barbara incident cannot be looked upon as typical of offshore development activity. Of 9000 wells drilled on the Outer Continental Shelf only twenty-five have experienced blowouts. But the incident served to raise many questions about the adequacy of offshore drilling technology and regulations and about our ability to cope with an oil spill. It also raised the question of the advisability of drilling in a hazardous geologic setting. The Santa Barbara Channel, located in an area of high seismicity, is subject to earthquakes, tsunamis, and seiches. Furthermore, oil reservoirs in the channel are often inadequately sealed, and it can be anticipated that weak traps will leak oil if their equilibrium is disturbed during drilling activity.

Harvey Molotch vividly describes the activities, emotions, frustrations, and confusion surrounding the blowout at Santa Barbara (Reading 30). It is obvious that the degree of sophistication which characterizes petroleum exploration and drilling did not characterize the industry's efforts to control the oil spill. The environmental, economic, social, legal, and political implications of this inadequacy are sweeping. The problem of oil spillage goes beyond drilling and includes the transportation, refining, and marketing of oil. It appears that progress is being made in a broad range of areas through the cooperation of industry, government, and the public, but there remains a need for more extensive organization, coordinated laws, and more research.

It would of course be advantageous to anticipate the social, economic, political, and environmental impact of resource development if we are to achieve a better balance between the losses and gains that are associated with development activities. Environmental impact analysis is the process by which we can predict the far-reaching effects of our attempts to exploit natural resources. Perhaps the most ambitious efforts to develop an environmental impact statement are those directed at the proposed Trans-Alaska pipeline project. In Reading 31 David Brew reviews these efforts and demonstrates how environmental considerations enter into the decision-making process. It is obvious that there are many interacting components and that special analytical techniques must be developed for each project.

27 Environmental Quality Control and Minerals*

Hubert E. Risser

During the past several years an increasing concern for the quality of our national environment has arisen. Within the last two years the volume of articles and speeches—of criticism, accusations, and demands—has crescendoed and shows no signs of subsiding.

Some persons, whether sincerely concerned or merely seeking attention, have gained national prominence by declaring that the nation will be doomed within the next year, 5 years, or 10 years. Other voices are more moderate, but nonetheless insistent that many of the patterns of activity and material consumption within the United States must be altered, if not totally abandoned.

Most of the environmental effects that concern our nation today are not the result of deliberate intent or disregard. They are the by-product of activities aimed at very worthwhile goals. The farmer who applies nitrate or other fertilizer that can run off his field to add to pollution in streams and rivers is only trying to make his land more productive and obtain a larger

crop yield. The housewife who uses phosphate detergent hopes to make her clothes cleaner. Those who mine by surface methods are attempting to produce materials at the lowest practicable cost.

As is true of many activities, efforts to correct or avoid the detrimental effects of mineral production will bring into play factors that are not anticipated or desired. Ultimately, the goal must be that of achieving the best balance possible.

Although various activities have come under criticism, it appears, at least to those of us who are connected in any way with minerals, that minerals have been a special target—not only the production of minerals but their transportation, processing, and utilization as well.

There are perhaps three principal reasons why so much attention has been focused on minerals.

1. By virtue of their manner of occurrence and their physical and chemical makeup, minerals are actually an integral part of the environment. Therefore, their production, movement, or utilization without modification of the environment would be entirely unrealistic.

2. The quantities involved are so huge and mineral production and consumption activities so widespread geographically that their effects are observable to everyone. As sources of energy, as metallic and nonmetallic materials, and as plant foods, minerals are directly related to or involved in almost every form

* Presented at the Annual Meeting of the American Association of Petroleum Geologists, Houston, Texas, March 31, 1971.

Risser, H. E., 1971, "Environmental Quality Control and Minerals," *Environmental Geology Notes Number 49*, Illinois State Geological Survey. Reprinted with light editing by permission of the author and the Illinois State Geological Survey, Urbana, Illinois.

The late Dr. Risser was a Mineral Economist with the Illinois Geological Survey and a special advisor and assistant to the Director, U. S. Geological Survey.

of industrial, economic, and recreational activity. Between 3 and 4 billion tons of solid fuels and minerals, 5 billion barrels of liquid fuels, and 22 trillion cubic feet of natural gas are consumed each year. Furthermore, the rate of use of some minerals has been doubling every 9 to 15 years.

3. Many mineral materials are so durable they remain as scrap long after the product has served its useful purpose. Reclamation may not be economic, but the production of new materials is criticized because old materials are so obviously available.

Minerals and the Environment

The problem that confronts the minerals industry today is that of finding ways to comply with the requirements for environmental quality protection and still provide the nation with the minerals it requires at an acceptable cost. The environmental components we most frequently think of are the atmosphere, the water, and the land, but recently increased public attention has been turned to plant and animal wildlife as well.

FIG. 1.

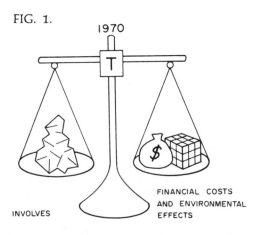

1970

INVOLVES

FINANCIAL COSTS
AND ENVIRONMENTAL
EFFECTS

Let's examine for a moment the relation between the environment and mineral production and use. Any production of minerals will, without exception, involve financial costs and will result in some effects on the environment. The balance of these three factors is illustrated in Fig. 1, where mineral production on the one hand is accompanied by costs and environmental effects on the other. In some instances these effects may consist only of the void left by removal of the minerals. In other instances the effects may be detrimental, completely benign, or even beneficial. The nature and extent of the effects will vary in degree and character, depending on the type of mineral, the manner of its occurrence, the method of production used, and other factors. But its very removal will cause some modification of the environment.

If we accept the premise that any mineral production or use will inevitably carry with it some environmental effects and financial costs, a logical corollary appears to be that our steadily expanding demand for and use of minerals will, other things being equal, also result in an increase in the magnitude of these effects. Thus an increase in the mineral output on the left side of the scale in Fig. 1 brings a parallel increase on the right side.

Although greater mineral output is accompanied by increases in both total costs and over-all environmental effects, from the public standpoint a significant difference exists between these factors that cannot be ignored by the mineral industry. Production expenditures quickly become identified as unit costs, and the cost of each unit to the consumer may not change significantly as total quantity produced increases.

On the other hand, seldom, if ever, are the incremental environmental effects (unless expenditures are made to correct them) identified with, or allocated to, the additional units of material produced or energy consumed. Instead, within a given mining area the total cumulative environmental effects are observed in their entirety rather than as a series of discrete units.

To provide for the industrial growth of our nation and supply the demands of a growing population for material goods and energy, a steady increase in the use of minerals of all types has occurred. Expansions in the output of fuels and metals have tended to parallel each other, increasing on the average of about 3 percent per year.

The growth in use of nonmetallics, which consist primarily of construction and plant-food materials, has been considerably more rapid than that of metals. An especially significant aspect of this growth is the extremely large total quantity of minerals material involved. The combined output of the major construction minerals—crushed stone, sand, and gravel—currently amounts to about 1.8 billion tons per year and it is projected to reach 5.6 to 8.0 billion tons per year by 2000 (U. S. Bur. Mines, 1971, p. 22). Because most

construction activity normally occurs in or near large centers of population and industrial activity, most production of construction materials is highly visible to a large segment of the public and is therefore subjected to increasing objections and regulations.

Reducing Environmental Effects

Once we recognize that environmental effects are inherent in the production and use of any mineral, we might ask what, if anything, can be done to reduce the undesirable or adverse effects. One obvious way would be to decrease the amount of mineral materials produced and consumed (Fig. 2). Through such a reduction, both the total environmental effects and the total (but not necessarily the unit) production expenditure would be reduced. But there has been as yet no indication that this alternative is acceptable to the American public. The consumption figures of a few mineral commodities (Fig. 3) gives evidence to the contrary. Not only has the production of minerals expanded to provide for population growth, but it also has provided a dramatic increase in the average per capita consumption.

Consumption of electric power, most

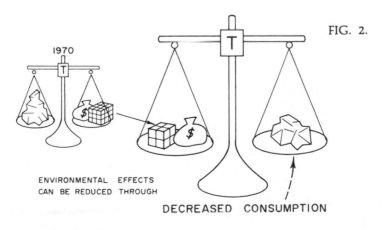

FIG. 2.

ENVIRONMENTAL EFFECTS CAN BE REDUCED THROUGH

DECREASED CONSUMPTION

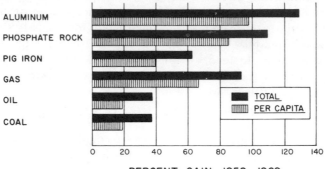

PERCENT GAIN, 1958–1969

of which is generated by mineral fuels, has been doubling every 10 years, and in the 1970s it is expected to equal the total amount consumed during the past 70 years.

Another way to reduce environmental effects is through increased expenditures (Fig. 4). Increased costs may result from changes made in production procedures to protect the environment, from expenditures to restore the environment after production has occurred, or from expenses related to other types of action, such as installation of pollution-control devices.

In the past, the minerals industry's primary assignment has been to provide minerals to meet the nation's needs at the lowest possible cost. In at least some cases, environmental protection now is taking precedence over lowest cost as the prime objective. An added demand now is that these mineral materials be produced with a minimum of undesirable environmental disruption.

While some members of the public no doubt partially realize that increased costs will be involved in this shift of emphasis, it is doubtful that the general public fully recognizes the extent of these costs or the fact that these increased production costs must ultimately be borne by the consumer through increased prices if production is to continue.

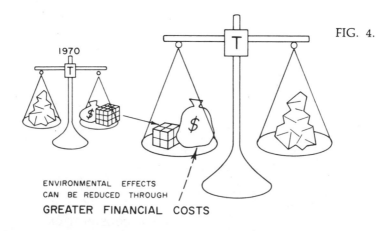

FIG. 4.

ENVIRONMENTAL EFFECTS CAN BE REDUCED THROUGH **GREATER FINANCIAL COSTS**

As the effort toward environmental improvement progresses and the relative magnitudes of both the costs and benefits become more apparent, a greater public tendency to balance one against the other may develop. It may be decided that, beyond a certain point, the incremental benefits do not justify the added costs. Nonetheless, there is a public mood today that reflects a strong conviction that the quality of the environment must be protected from further deterioration, and the official government attitude reflects that public mood. An effort to point out the magnitude of the costs involved in complying with new regulations is unlikely to receive much sympathetic attention today. Nor will the fact that a proposed regulation or procedure appears completely impractical or infeasible necessarily mean that legislation requiring such procedure will not be enacted.

Still another way in which some environmental effects may be reduced is through improved technology in the production and use of minerals (Fig. 5) Such technological improvements may or may not result in increased costs. They may, in fact, bring the desired results at a reduced cost. But new tech-

nology does not just happen. Its development requires time, concerted effort, and increased investment.

Effects of Environmental Regulation

Some of the impact of environmental regulations is already apparent, and the effect of many others will be felt during the next few years. New regulations will be applied to production, transportation, and utilization of mineral materials. A brief review will serve to point out some of these.

Mineral Production

Increasingly stringent regulations controlling production techniques and reclamation procedures have recently been enacted. Some proposals have been made that would completely halt certain types of mineral production because of their effects on the environment. Already pits and quarries have been banned in some urban areas and strip mining has been prohibited in certain regions. Proposals have been introduced in Congress to halt all offshore drilling and both in Congress and in certain state legislatures to prohibit strip coal mining completely.

The banning of pits and quarries by

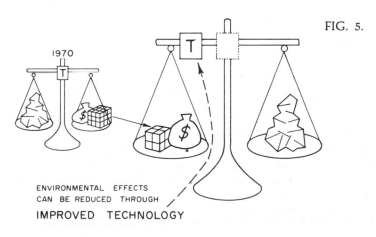

FIG. 5.

ENVIRONMENTAL EFFECTS
CAN BE REDUCED THROUGH
IMPROVED TECHNOLOGY

zoning ordinances makes near-by short-haul resources unavailable and increases the transportation cost and, in turn, the delivered price of construction materials to builders within the metropolitan area.

The proposed banning of further offshore drilling would make inaccessible more than 9 percent of the nation's known oil reserves and almost 13 percent of the known gas reserves. In addition, it would remove from exploration large areas that offer some of the greatest potential for the future discoveries that will be required to meet our fuel needs. If the proposed ban on offshore drilling were extended to current production, a significant portion of the current oil and gas output would be halted.

The total prohibition of strip mining of coal would eliminate about one third of the current output in the United States. At present there would be no means of replacing, through underground mining, the approximately 200 million tons per year of strip coal that would be lost, and there would be other effects also. In 1969, underground mining costs were, on the average, about 40 percent higher than strip mining costs. In the same year, about 22,000 men produced almost 200 million tons of coal from strip mines. To produce the same amount of coal from underground mines would have required about 27,000 additional miners because underground miners have a lower average of productivity. The total coal mining labor force would thus need to be increased by 21.5 percent at a time when there is a shortage of mining manpower. Too, since underground mining recovers only about 50 percent of the coal in the ground, nearly twice as much coal resource would be exhausted in providing the same amount of output. Finally, the loss of lives in underground coal mining has historically been about 3½ times that for the same production by strip coal mining.

Complete banning of strip mining of all solid minerals other than coal would have even more impact, because 94 percent of the nation's production of nonfuel minerals comes from surface mining operations.

Transportation

The transportation of solid minerals has not, in general, resulted in major environmental problems, although the noise and traffic of trucks has been partly responsible for objections to pits and quarries in and near metropolitan areas.

Recently, much more attention has been directed to the effects of oil spillage, occasionally from ruptured pipelines but most frequently from waterborne shipments. Oil spillage is not a new problem. A publication issued in 1925 dealt with pollution of bathing beaches by oil spilled from ships along the east coast from Connecticut to Florida, parts of the Gulf Coast, and the Pacific Coast (U. S. Public Health Service, 1925).

As the water transportation of oil increases, problems of tanker spillage also are likely to increase. Our own increasing dependence on foreign sources will bring more of these shipments to our shores. The increased size of tankers should reduce the number of tankers required and perhaps the incidence of tanker accidents. On the other hand, as tanker size increases, any accidents that do occur are likely to have far greater effects. A tanker of 372,400 DWT (dead weight tons) capacity is reported currently under construction, and one of 477,000 DWT capacity is reportedly being planned (Industry Week, 1971). The cargoes of two ships of this size will exceed the reported 794,000 tons of combined capacity of 95 ships sunk by U-boats in World War II (Bachman, 1971). Some of these ships, with their cargoes still intact, are reported to remain on the ocean bottom off the east coast of the United States.

The oil transportation project currently receiving the greatest attention is the proposed Alyeska Pipeline from Prudhoe Bay to Valdez, Alaska (Fig. 6). Construction is being delayed pending further study of potential environmental effects of the construction and operation of the pipeline and the designing of methods to control these effects. The greatest uncertainty relates to the impact of the passage of oil through the pipes at high temperatures in an Arctic environment. Anyone who has worked at construction in Arctic areas is aware of the problems that permafrost can bring, even for normal, small-scale excavations.

Nearly 500 oil pipeline leaks were reported to have occurred in the United States in 1968. Most of these resulted in only minor spillage, and only about one fifth involved spills of as high as 1,000 to 12,000 barrels (Carter, 1969). Because of the operating conditions that will prevail in Alaska and the large spillage likely to occur if the 48-inch pipeline should be ruptured, it is considered especially critical that pipeline breaks should be prevented.

Attention has also been called to the possibility of oil spills along the Canadian Pacific Coast from tankers moving between Valdez and the coastal ports of the western United States. To avoid this danger it has been proposed that, instead of crossing Alaska, the pipeline be constructed along an alternative route through Canada to the United States border (Wall Street Journal, 1971). Although the Canadian route would avoid some of the mountainous terrain of northern Alaska and the zone of high seismic activity in Alaska, a much longer pipeline would be needed.

Whatever the final outcome, the cost

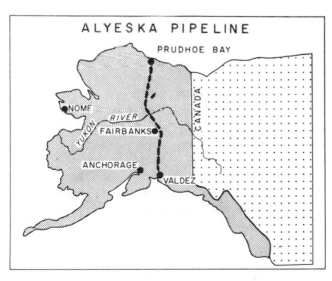

ALYESKA PIPELINE   FIG. 6.

of the delays and of compliance with environmental regulations will add significantly to the cost of the oil when it is finally delivered in the United States.[1]

Mineral Utilization

A third type of environmental quality regulation affecting minerals is directed at the consumer rather than the mineral-producing industry. These consumer-directed regulations may well have greater impact than those applying to mineral production activities, for already they are radically changing the patterns of mineral use.

One of the proposals would prohibit the use of tetraethyl lead in gasoline. Besides altering the refinery product, the prohibition of lead as a gasoline additive, if fully implemented, would immediately reduce the market for lead by about 20 percent and create a drastic impact on the producers of lead and associated minerals.

Recent discoveries of the transformation, through bacterial action, of metallic mercury to highly toxic methyl mercury have led to laws for control of spillage of mercury into lakes and other natural waters. The modification of processes has led to a reduction in the loss of mercury, which, in turn, has resulted in a significant decline in demand for that metal.

Perhaps the most dramatic and far-reaching impact has been that resulting from recently proposed and already established sulfur dioxide emission standards for fuels. The standards are such that much of the coal currently being produced and most of the reserves throughout the country cannot meet them without the use of emission control devices on combustion units. Un-fortunately, such control devices have not yet proved effective on a commercial basis. In an effort to comply with the new air quality standards, fuel consumers attempted to procure natural gas as a substitute for coal. As present supplies of gas cannot even meet the growth in the traditional markets, the sudden additional demand for gas as a substitute fuel could not be met.

Unable to get either low-sulfur coal or natural gas, utilities and large industrial firms attempted to obtain low-sulfur residual fuel oil. Residual traditionally had been so low in value that only a minimum amount was produced by most refiners. Because there was so little low-sulfur residual to meet the sudden demand, it quickly became a premium product with a premium price.

Hopefully, within the next few years, satisfactory devices and techniques for the control of sulfur oxide emission will be available so that high-sulfur coal can be burned without violating air quality standards. In the future, coal will also be processed into sulfur-free synthetic pipeline gas to supplement the declining reserves of natural gas and into liquid fuel to supplement natural petroleum products. In the meantime, it will be necessary to use those fuels that are available, for in many instances there are no alternatives to either doing that or shutting down.

Conclusions

The widespread concern for the environment and the intensity of the demand for corrective action appear to be rather recent phenomena, but they do have a history extending back several decades. Expression of environmental concern has taken many forms, and some of the demands and regulations resulting from it are beyond the present technology and capability of the nation. It is to be hoped that demands that are patently unreasonable or impossible to comply with will give way to a more rational approach. But for the minerals industry to think that all of the present concern for the environment is merely a passing public fancy would be a serious mistake.

The mineral producers of this nation and the world, and the mineral consumers as well, are faced with a future in which mineral costs will increase as prices rise to cover the additional costs of environmental protection activities.

It is too early to measure accurately just what price increases will be required and what impact on demand these increases will ultimately have. The nation's industrial growth for two centuries has been assisted by the availability of low cost energy and mineral materials.

Secretary of the Interior Rogers C. B. Morton was recently quoted as stating:

Now, because we have finally achieved the measure of concern for the environment that we should have summoned 30 years ago, these social costs are at last going to be charged to the proper accounts. Those who benefit from the production and consumption of energy will be asked to pay the full tab, and for the first time the user will have some feel for the true cost of the energy he consumes.[2]

Although the statement referred specifically to energy, it applies equally to all other mineral products.

The Secretary is correct in that the consumer ultimately will pay the full tab. But for the minerals industry to take this too literally and become complacent about allocation of environmental costs could be extremely hazardous. The public still has the option of paying the cost or doing without. There is at present no way of pinpointing the level at which the consumer will balk at paying increased prices.

It behooves the industry to pass along the necessary costs involved in protecting the environment and to identify these costs as such for the public. But it is also extremely important that the minerals industry continue to produce and provide its products at the lowest possible cost.

Notes

[1] In November 1973 Congress authorized the construction of the Trans-Alaska pipeline from Prudhoe Bay to Valdez. Construction began in the spring of 1974, and the first pipe was laid in 1975. The pipeline will cost approximately 6 billion dollars and will have the capacity to deliver two million barrels of crude oil per day when it opens in 1977. [Ed.]

[2] (AGI Report, 1971.)

References

AGI Report, 1971, National Petroleum Council (March 4): The AGI Report, Geo-Times Newsletter, v. 4, no. 10, p. 1.

Bachman, W. A. [Sr. ed.], 1971, U-boat as a polluter: Oil and Gas Jour., v. 69, no. 2, p. 13.

Carter, L. J., 1969, North slope: Oil rush: Science, v. 166, no. 3901, p. 85–92.

Industry Week, 1971, Oil supertankers becoming more super: Industry Week, v. 168, no. 3, p. 26.

U. S. Bureau of Mines, 1971, Minerals yearbook 1969, Metals, minerals and fuels: U. S. Bur. Mines, Dept. Interior, Washington, D. C., v. 1, 2, 1194 p.

U. S. Public Health Service, 1925, Oil pollution at bathing beaches: Reprint no. 980 from the Public Health Reports, v. 39, no. 51, p. 3195–3208.

Wall Street Journal, 1971, Ruckelshaus says delay trans-Alaska pipeline, study Canadian route: March 15, 1971, p. 14.

28 Surface Mining, Its Nature, Extent, and Significance

U. S. Department of the Interior

Stated in the simplest terms, surface mining consists of nothing more than removing the topsoil, rock, and other strata that lie above mineral or fuel deposits to recover them. In practice, however, the process is considerably more complex.

When compared with underground methods, surface mining offers distinct advantages. It makes possible the recovery of deposits which, for physical reasons, cannot be mined underground; provides safer working conditions; usually results in a more complete recovery of the deposit; and, most significantly it is generally cheaper in terms of cost-per-unit of production. Surface mining is not applicable to all situations, however, because the ratio between the thickness of the overburden that must be moved in order to recover a given amount of product places a definite economic limitation upon the operator. While this ratio may vary widely among operations and commodities owing to differences in the characteristics of the overburden, types and capacities of the equipment used, and in value of the material being mined, it is nonetheless the factor that primarily determines whether a particular mining venture can survive in a competitive market.

"Surface Mining, Its Nature, Extent, and Significance," in *Surface Mining and Our Environment*, Strip and Surface Mine Study Policy Committee, U. S. Department of the Interior, 1967, 124 pp. Reprinted with light editing.

The procedure for surface mining usually consists of two steps: Prospecting, or "exploration,"—to discover, delineate, and "prove" the ore body—and the actual mining or recovery phase. Topography and the configuration of the deposit itself strongly influence both. Exploration techniques generally employed consist of either drilling to intersect deeper-lying ore bodies, or excavating shallow trenches or pits to expose the ore. Although drill sites or excavations associated with exploration are usually small, their large number constitutes a serious source of surface disturbance in some of the Western States. Surface methods employed to recover minerals and fuels are generally classified as (1) open pit mining (quarry, open cast); (2) strip mining (area, contour); (3) auger mining; (4) dredging; and (5) hydraulic mining.

Open pit mining is exemplified by quarries producing limestone, sandstone, marble, and granite; sand and gravel pits; and, large excavations opened to produce iron and copper. Usually, in open pit mining, the amount of overburden removed is proportionately small compared with the quantity of ore recovered. Another distinctive feature of open pit mining is the length of time that mining is conducted. In stone quarrying, and in open pit mining of iron ore and other metallics, large quantities of ore are obtained within a relatively small surface area because of the thickness of the deposits. Some open pits may be mined for many years—50 or more; in fact, a few have been in continuous operation for more than a century. However, since coal beds are comparatively thin—the United States average being about 5.1 feet for bituminous coal and lignite strip mined in 1960—the average surface coal mine has a relatively short life.

Area strip mining usually is practiced on relatively flat terrain. A trench, or "box cut," is made through the overburden to expose a portion of the deposit, which is then removed. The first cut may be extended to the limits of the property or the deposit. As each succeeding parallel cut is made, the spoil (overburden) is deposited in the cut just previously excavated. The final cut leaves an open trench as deep as the thickness of the overburden plus the ore recovered, bounded on one side by the last spoil bank and on the other by the undisturbed highwall. Frequently this final cut may be a mile or more from the starting point of the operation. Thus, area stripping, unless graded or leveled, usually resembles the ridges of a gigantic washboard. Coal and Florida phosphate account for the major part of the acreage disturbed by this method, although brown iron ore, some clays, and other commodities are mined in a similar manner.

Contour strip mining is most commonly practiced where deposits occur in rolling or mountainous country. Basically, this method consists of removing the overburden above the bed by starting at the outcrop and proceeding along the hillside. After the deposit is exposed and removed by this first cut, additional cuts are made until the ratio of overburden to product brings the

operation to a halt. This type of mining creates a shelf, or "bench," on the hillside. On the inside it is bordered by the highwall, which may range from a few to perhaps more than 100 feet in height, and on the opposite, or outer, side by a rim below which there is frequently a precipitous downslope that has been covered by spoil material cast down the hillside. Unless controlled or stabilized, this spoil material can cause severe erosion and landslides. Contour mining is practiced widely in the coal fields of Appalachia and western phosphate mining regions because of the generally rugged topography. "Rim-cutting" and "benching" are terms that are sometimes used locally to identify workbenches, or ledges, prepared for contour or auger mining operations.

Anthracite strip mining in Pennsylvania is conducted on hillsides where the coal beds outcrop parallel with the mountain crests. Although most of the operations are conducted on natural slopes of less than 10 degrees, the beds themselves vary in pitch up to 90 degrees. Beds that are stripped are thicker than in the bituminous fields, most varying from 6 to 20 feet, and can be mined economically to much greater depths. Because of the angles at which the beds lie, the methods employed may not be correctly identified either as contour or area mining, but rather as a combination of both. In a few instances, the operations may resemble open pits and quarries, while others are long, deep narrow canyons.

Auger mining is usually associated with contour strip mining. In coal fields, it is most commonly practiced to recover additional tonnages after the coal-overburden ratio has become such as to render further contour mining uneconomical. Augers are also used to extract coal near the outcrop that could not be recovered safely by earlier underground mining efforts. As the name implies, augering is a method of producing coal by boring horizontally into the seam, much like the carpenter bores a hole in wood. The coal is extracted in the same manner that shavings are produced by the carpenter's bit. Cutting heads of some coal augers are as large as seven feet in diameter. By adding sections behind the cutting head, holes may be drilled in excess of 200 feet. As augering generally is conducted after the strip-mining phase has been completed, little land disturbance can be directly attributed to it. However, it may, to some extent, induce surface subsidence and disrupt water channels when underground workings are intersected.

Dredging operations utilize a suction apparatus or various mechanical devices, such as ladder or chain buckets, clamshells, and draglines mounted on floating barges. Dredges have been utilized extensively in placer gold mining. Tailing piles from gold dredging operations usually have a configuration that is similar to spoil piles left by area strip mining for coal. Dredging is also used in the recovery of sand and gravel from stream beds and low-lying lands. In the sand and gravel industry most of the material (volume) produced is marketed, but in dredging for the higher-priced minerals virtually all of the mined material consists of waste that is left at the mine site. Some valuable minerals also are recovered by dredging techniques from beach sands and sedimentary deposits on the continental shelf.

In *hydraulic mining* a powerful jet of water is employed to wash down or erode a bank of earth or gravel that either is the overburden or contains the desired ore. The ore-bearing material is fed into sluices or other concentrating devices where the desired product is separated from the tailings, or waste—by differences in specific gravity. Hydraulic mining was extensively used in the past to produce gold and other precious metals, but is practiced only on a limited scale today. As both hydraulic mining and dredging create sedimentation problems in streams, some States exercise strict controls over these techniques, either through mining or water-control regulations.

Regardless of the equipment used, the surface mining cycle usually consists of four steps: (1) Site preparation, clearing vegetation and other obstructions from the area to be mined, and constructing access roads and ancillary installations—including areas to be used for the disposal of spoil or waste; (2) removal and disposal of overburden; (3) excavation and loading of ore; and (4) transportation of the ore to a concentrator, processing plant, storage area, or directly to market.

Reclamation may not be considered by a majority as an integral component of the mining cycle. Experience here and abroad has demonstrated, however, that when reclamation of the land is integrated into both the pre-planning and operational stages, it can be done more effectively and at a lower cost than as a separate operation. This is particularly true because much of the machinery used in the mining operation can be easily used in reducing peaks of spoil piles, segregating toxic materials, and establishing controlled drainage from the site.

The rapid expansion of surface mining since World War II may be attributed primarily to the development of larger and more complex earth-moving equipment. Equipment used today includes bulldozers, loaders, scrapers, trucks up to 100-ton capacity, and a miscellany of other devices. A shovel is now working that can handle 185-cubic yards in one "bite," with a monster having a 200-cubic yard bucket on the engineers' drawing boards. Draglines of up to 85-cubic yard capacity are in operation and larger ones are being planned. Clamshells and wheel excavators are used where conditions permit. There are floating dredges, tower excavators, drag scrapers, and augers; and to move the overburden and ores beyond the reach of the basic excavating machines, tram or rail cars, conveyor belts, overhead cable buckets, and pipelines.

Extent

An estimated 3.2 million acres of land, 5,000 square miles, had been disturbed by surface mining in the United States prior to January 1, 1965. This total includes only the excavation, or pit, and areas required to dispose of waste or spoil from the mining operation alone. An additional 320,000 acres have been affected by mine access roads and exploration activities. About 95 percent of the acreage disturbed by surface mining is attributable to but seven commodities: Coal for approximately 41 percent of the total; sand and gravel, about 26 percent; stone, gold, clay, phosphate, and iron, together, about 28 percent; and, all others combined, 5 percent.

Table 1 Land disturbed by strip and surface mining in the United States, as of January 1, 1965, by mineral and type of mining[1] [Thousand acres]

Mineral	Strip Mining			Quarry-open pit			Dredge, hydraulic, and other methods	Grand total[2]
	Contour	Area	Total	Into hillside	Below ground level	Total		
Coal[3]	665	637	1,302					1,302
Sand and gravel	38	258	296	82	371	453	74	823
Stone	6	8	14	100	127	227		241
Gold		8	8	1	3	4	191	203
Clay	10	26	36	22	44	66	7	109
Phosphate	28	49	77	13	93	106		183
Iron	7	31	38	30	96	126		164
All Other	11	12	23	59	81	140		163
Total	765	1,029	1,794	307	815	1,122	272	3,188

[1] Data by method of mining estimated on basis of information obtained by random sampling survey.
[2] Data compiled from reports submitted by the States on U. S. Department of the Interior form 6-1385X, from Soil Conservation Service, U. S. Department of Agriculture, and estimates prepared by the study group.
[3] Includes anthracite, bituminous, and lignite.

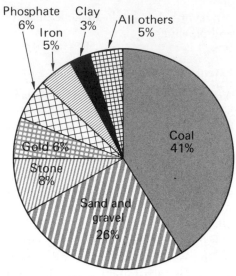

Phosphate 6%
Clay 3%
Iron 5%
All others 5%
Gold 6%
Stone 8%
Coal 41%
Sand and gravel 26%

Total = 3.2 million acres

FIG. 1. Percentage of land disturbed by surface mining of various commodities as of January 1, 1965.

Harmful off-site effects are also an important component of the surface mining picture. These effects include stream and water-impoundment pollution from erosion and acid mine water; isolation of areas by steep highwalls; and, the impairment of natural beauty by the creation of unsightly spoil banks, rubbish dumps, and abandoned equipment. All of these add appreciably to the total that must be considered as being adversely "affected" by surface mining.

Unreclaimed Acreage

The total acreage needing reclamation can only be approximated because definitions of two key words, "reclamation" and "adequacy," are a matter of individual judgment. Professionals in many scientific disciplines can agree on certain essential elements, but the many variables involved preclude a general agreement on a definition of "adequate reclamation" that would be applicable at any given time and for every geographic location. From a survey conducted by the Soil Conservation Service and data submitted by certain States it is concluded that probably only one-third of the total acreage disturbed by surface mining has been adequately reclaimed—either by natural forces or by man's own effort. Thus, approximately two-thirds of the acreage (about 2.0 million) still require some remedial attention.

Annual Increase in Disturbed Acreage

The annual increment to the total disturbed acreage is not known exactly, but can be calculated roughly. Based on data reported by producers to the U. S. Department of the Interior it is estimated that 153,000 acres of land were disturbed in 1964 by strip and surface mining. Sand and gravel accounted for 60,000 acres; coal, 46,000; stone, 21,000; clay and phosphate rock, each 9,000; and the remaining minerals accounted for 8,000 acres. This annual rate of disturbance is expected to increase in future years with an increased demand for minerals and solid fuels and a further diminution in the grade of mineral deposits available for exploitation. Indicative of this trend is the fact that surface mining production of all metals and non-metals increased from 2.5 billion net tons of crude ore (including waste) in 1960 to 3.0 billion in 1965. Strip-mine production of coal (anthracite, bituminous, and lignite) increased from 138 million net tons to 185 million over the same period.

Significance

The economic potential of any nation is founded primarily upon its soil, its waters, and its mineral deposits. Where these are deficient, the economic well-being of the nation will depend upon the ability of its people to import raw materials required to manufacture and compete successfully in world trade.

The United States is blessed with a wealth of natural resources, needing only to import a small portion of its total mineral requirements. Tens of thousands of firms are engaged in the production of semi- and finished goods. These industries are supported, in turn, by a wide variety of extractive and processing activities and services. The extractive industries are the primary source of metallic ores and non-metallic minerals and fuels—with agriculture and forestry contributing a wide range of products. Our population, with its varied skills, completes the design and confirms an old truth: Man creates nothing—it is only through his ability to produce crops, convert, process, and synthesize that his civilization flourishes.

The importance of surface mining to the extractive industries is easily measured. In 1965, for example, surface mining accounted for about four-fifths of the total ore and solid fuels produced. Economists recognize that the extractive mineral industries are primarily suppliers of basic materials, rather than producers of end products. Some appreciation of the extent to which other industries depend upon the mineral industries can be obtained through an examination of the Input-Output table prepared by the Office of Business Economics, U. S. Department of Commerce, which divides the national economy into 82 industrial sectors and shows the interchange of goods among them. Although the data are not current, the patterns have not changed appreciably. For example, the table indicates that 76 percent of all coal mined is used directly (almost entirely as an energy source) by 56 industries to produce other products. The remaining 24 percent represents exports, consumption by individual and public establishments, and intra-company transfers.

Although the relationship of coal to other industrial activities is quite clear, the influence of some other minerals is not always so direct and easily recognized. Examples of indirect, but equally important influences, can be found in iron and ferroalloy ore mining. Over 81 percent of all the iron and ferroalloy ore mined is consumed by the primary iron and steel industry. Yet, output of this industry is used as direct input for 55 of the 82 industrial categories. It is evident that the real value to our economy of the minerals and fuels obtained by surface mining can be measured only by adding to their prices as crude materials the "value added by manufacturing," a concept that entails an evaluation of their contribution to a finished product. But, the story does not end there. As a consumer, the minerals industry is also a substantial contributor to the economy. The products of 49 or more industries are needed to equip and maintain the coal, iron, ferroalloy mining industries, and petroleum and natural gas producers.

FIG. 2. Total acreage disturbed by surface mining as of January 1, 1965.

EXPLANATION

⊥ = 50,000 Acres

Table 2. Land disturbed by strip and surface mining in the United States as of January 1, 1965, by commodity and State [Acres]

State	Clay	Coal (bituminous, lignite and anthracite)	Stone	Sand and gravel	Gold	Phosphate rock	Iron ore	All other	Total
Alabama [1]	4,000	50,600	3,900	21,200	100		52,600	1,500	133,900
Alaska [2]		500		2,000	8,600				11,100
Arizona [1]	2,700		1,000	7,200	1,200			20,300	32,400
Arkansas [2]	600	10,100	900	2,600			100	8,100	22,400
California [2]	2,700	20	8,000	19,900	134,000		900	8,500	174,020
Colorado [1]	2,000	2,800	6,200	15,500	17,100		25	11,400	55,025
Connecticut [1]			100	16,100				100	16,300
Delaware [2]	200		200	5,200			100	10	5,710
Florida [1]	13,200		25,300	3,900		143,600		2,800	188,800
Georgia [1]	e 1,300	e 300	e 6,800	e 1,200			e 100	e 12,000	1 21,700
Hawaii [2]								10	10
Idaho [2]	500		700	11,200	21,200	3,100	35	4,200	40,935
Illinois [2]	1,400	127,000	5,700	9,000					143,100
Indiana [2]	1,500	95,200	10,200	18,000				400	125,300
Iowa [1]	1,300	11,000	12,200	17,600			6	2,300	44,406
Kansas	1 1,100	2 45,600	1 7,500	1 5,100				1 200	59,500
Kentucky [1,2]	1 2 2,400	1 2 119,200	1 3,900	1 1,700				1 500	127,700
Louisiana [1]	900		100	29,700			50		30,750
Maine [1]	1 1,200		1 4,400	28,200	12		100	1,700	34,812
Maryland	1 2 1,200	2 2,200	1 2,200	1 18,800			1 20	1 800	25,220
Massachusetts [1]	700		1,200	36,400			1,100	900	40,300
Michigan [2]	600		7,700	25,200			2,200	1,200	36,900
Minnesota [1]	600		3,900	41,600	3		67,700	1,600	115,403
Mississippi [2]	2,700		400	26,500			30		29,630

State									Total
Missouri [2]	6,600	31,800	8,400	3,800			200	8,300	59,100
Montana [2]	900	1,500	10	[e]13,500	5,600		10	6,200	26,920
Nebraska [2]	100		4,300	23,700			600	200	28,900
Nevada [1]			1,600	5,500	5,600		700	19,500	32,900
New Hampshire [2]			100	8,000				200	8,300
New Jersey [2]	1,400		2,000	27,600			1,000	1,800	33,800
New Mexico [2]	13	1,200	100	400	40		100	4,600	6,453
New York [1]	1,700		12,500	42,200	5		700	600	57,705
North Carolina [1]	5,800	10	6,000	18,400	2,200	300	100	4,000	36,810
North Dakota	[1]800	[2]7,700	[2]2,300	[1]26,100					36,900
Ohio	[1]10,200	[2]212,800	[1]21,000	[1]28,100		[1]4,000		[1]600	276,700
Oklahoma [2]		23,500		[e]2,500			1,400		27,400
Oregon [2]	100		300	1,300	6,300		10	[1]1,400	9,410
Pennsylvania	[1]10,400	[2]302,400	[1]24,400	[1]23,800	[1,2]2		[1]8,800	[1]400	370,202
Rhode Island [1]			20	3,600					3,620
South Carolina [1]	10,900		1,400	10,400	200	8,100	100	1,600	32,700
South Dakota	[2]2,000		[2]900	[e]28,000			[2]3,300		34,200
Tennessee [2]	2,700	29,300	4,400	18,400		27,000	5,300	13,800	100,900
Texas [1]	6,800	2,900	21,900	122,300			9,600	2,800	166,300
Utah [2]	600		200	2,200		10	500	2,000	5,510
Vermont			[2]2,300	[1]4,000				[2]400	6,700
Virginia	[1,2]1,100	[2]29,800	[1]4,300	[1]13,100	[1]600	[1]100	[1,2]7,700	[1,2]4,100	60,800
Washington [2]	500	100	1,300	5,700	400		20	800	8,820
West Virginia [2]	300	192,000	2,800	300			100		195,500
Wisconsin [2]	100		9,000	26,400	5		49		35,554
Wyoming	[1,2]3,500	[1,2]1,000	[1,2]300	[1,2]200		[2]800	[1,2]300	[2]4,300	10,400
Total	108,513	1,301,430	241,430	823,300	203,167	183,110	164,255	162,620	3,187,825

[e] Estimate.

[1] Data obtained from Soil Conservation Service, U. S. Department of Agriculture.

[2] Data compiled from reports submitted by the States on U. S. Department of the Interior form 6-1385X.

Impact on Environment

Environment is defined as "the surrounding conditions, influences, or forces which influence or modify." Within this context there are physical, biological, social, physiosocial, biosocial, and psychosocial factors. Thus, the all-inclusive term, "environment." encompasses almost every aspect of life and living. The environment is ever-changing. Throughout geologic time the earth has been subjected to a continuing cycle of orogeny, erosion, transportation, and deposition. Natural land disturbances are neither new nor intrinsically bad; but, to these natural phenomena a new dimension has been added—man.

Surface mining frequently shocks the sensibilities, not so much by what is done as by the sheer magnitude of man's accomplishments. He literally has moved mountains, and some of his surface excavations are so vast as to resemble craters on the moon. Surface mining destroys the protective vegetative cover, and the soil and rock overlying the mineral deposit is frequently left in massive piles cast onto adjoining land. The result is a drastic reshaping of the surface, an alteration of normal surface and sub-surface drainage patterns. Square miles of land may be turned over to a depth of 100 feet or more and valleys rimmed by mile after mile of contour benches. Massive landslides have blocked streams and highways, waters have been polluted by acid and sediment, land areas isolated, and economic and esthetic values seriously impaired.

Our derelict acreage is made up of tens of thousands of separate patches. In some regions they are often close together. Where one acre in ten is laid waste, the whole landscape is disfigured. The face of the earth is riddled with abandoned mineral workings, packed with subsidence, gashed with quarries, littered with disused plant structures and piled high with stark and sterile banks of dross and debris,

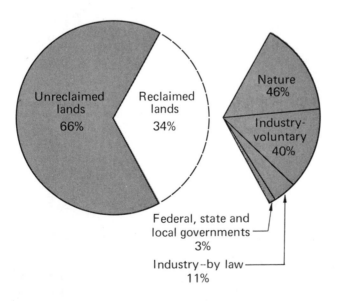

FIG. 3. Status of land disturbed by surface mining as of January 1, 1965.

Table 3 Status of land disturbed by strip and surface mining in the United States as of January 1, 1965, by State (Thousand acres)

State	Land requiring reclamation[1]	Land not requiring reclamation[1]	Total land disturbed[2]	State	Land requiring reclamation[1]	Land not requiring reclamation[1]	Total land disturbed[2]
Alabama	83.0	50.9	133.9	Nebraska	16.8	12.1	28.9
Alaska	6.9	4.2	11.1	Nevada	20.4	12.5	32.9
Arizona	4.7	27.7	32.4	New Hampshire	5.1	3.2	8.3
Arkansas	16.6	5.8	22.4	New Jersey	21.0	12.8	33.8
California	107.9	66.1	174.0	New Mexico	2.0	4.5	6.5
Colorado	40.2	14.8	55.0	New York	50.2	7.5	57.7
Connecticut	10.1	6.2	16.3	North Carolina	22.8	14.0	36.8
Delaware	3.5	2.2	5.7	North Dakota	22.9	14.0	36.9
Florida	143.5	45.3	188.8	Ohio	171.6	105.1	276.7
Georgia	13.5	8.2	21.7	Oklahoma	22.2	5.2	27.4
Hawaii	(3)	(3)	(3)	Oregon	5.8	3.6	9.4
Idaho	30.7	10.3	41.0	Pennsylvania	229.5	140.7	370.2
Illinois	88.7	54.4	143.1	Rhode Island	2.2	1.4	3.6
Indiana	27.6	97.7	125.3	South Carolina	19.3	13.4	32.7
Iowa	35.5	8.9	44.4	South Dakota	25.3	8.9	34.2
Kansas	50.0	9.5	59.5	Tennessee	62.5	38.4	100.9
Kentucky	79.2	48.5	127.7	Texas	136.4	29.9	166.3
Louisiana	17.2	13.6	30.8	Utah	3.4	2.1	5.5
Maine	21.6	13.2	34.8	Vermont	4.2	2.5	6.7
Maryland	18.1	7.1	25.2	Virginia	37.7	23.1	60.8
Massachusetts	25.0	15.3	40.3	Washington	5.5	3.3	8.8
Michigan	26.6	10.3	36.9	West Virginia	111.4	84.1	195.5
Minnesota	71.5	43.9	115.4	Wisconsin	27.4	8.2	35.6
Mississippi	23.7	5.9	29.6	Wyoming	6.4	4.0	10.4
Missouri	43.7	15.4	59.1	Total	2040.6	1147.2	3187.8
Montana	19.6	7.3	26.9				

[1] Compiled from data supplied by Soil Conservation Service, U. S. Department of Agriculture.
[2] Data compiled from reports submitted by the States on U. S. Department of the Interior form 6-1385X, from Soil Conservation Service, U. S. Department of Agriculture, and estimates.
[3] Less than 100 acres.

Table 4 Land disturbed and production at strip and surface mines in the United States in 1964 for selected commodities, by ownership and geographic areas [1]

Geographic area	Clay — Acres disturbed				Clay — Production		Coal — Acres disturbed				Coal — Production	
	Private	Per cent	Public	Per cent	Thousand short tons	Per cent [2]	Private	Per cent	Public	Per cent	Thousand short tons	Per cent [2]
New England	37	100.0			290	64.0						
Middle Atlantic	386	99.5	2	0.5	2,136	41.1	5,246	94.0	334	6.0	15,365	45.3
South Atlantic	672	99.6	3	.4	8,413	56.8	3,888	95.7	173	4.3	7,992	38.9
East North Central	304	98.4	5	1.6	5,704	51.6	14,674	95.9	629	4.1	58,782	86.2
East South Central	238	99.2	2	.8	1,384	37.8	4,004	96.9	126	3.1	25,603	72.6
West North Central	458	99.8	1	.2	2,152	49.8	1,896	99.9	2	.1	4,913	92.9
West South Central	1,749	98.8	21	1.2	4,753	71.3	469	71.3	189	28.7	3,202	92.9
Mountain	487	64.2	272	35.8	1,873	84.1	534	91.0	53	9.0	6,352	93.9
Pacific	460	98.3	8	1.7	1,557	34.9	10	25.0	30	75.0	528	68.6
Total	4,791	93.8	314	6.2	28,262	53.4	30,721	95.2	1,536	4.8	122,737	70.3

Geographic area	Stone — Acres disturbed				Stone — Production		Sand and gravel — Acres disturbed				Sand and gravel — Production	
	Private	Per cent	Public	Per cent	Thousand short tons	Per cent [2]	Private	Per cent	Public	Per cent	Thousand short tons	Per cent [2]
New England	51	100.0			7,148	43.3	462	94.3	28	5.7	13,102	22.9
Middle Atlantic	556	99.3	4	0.7	46,721	49.5	692	98.4	11	1.6	23,910	32.7
South Atlantic	1,271	93.3	91	6.7	27,644	18.7	1,756	95.7	78	4.3	19,465	29.7
East North Central	954	98.1	18	1.9	69,380	45.8	3,035	94.7	170	5.3	104,792	57.2
East South Central	344	84.3	64	15.7	6,763	13.3	342	87.2	50	12.8	6,554	29.3
West North Central	1,588	98.3	27	1.7	51,915	65.7	4,218	93.3	305	6.7	36,290	32.1
West South Central	1,420	100.0			33,143	40.0	4,593	93.3	329	6.7	25,865	42.2
Mountain	319	67.4	154	32.6	9,060	37.4	2,519	72.3	967	27.7	42,813	41.5
Pacific	414	77.2	122	22.8	8,243	10.4	1,182	36.7	2,036	63.3	57,313	30.2
Total	6,917	93.5	480	6.5	260,017	35.8	18,799	82.5	3,974	17.5	330,104	38.0

[1] As reported voluntarily by producers on U. S. Department of the Interior forms 6-1386X and 6-1387X.

[2] Per cent of production reported and published in the U. S. Bureau of Mines Minerals Yearbook, 1964.

Note: Phosphate rock; land reported disturbed in 1964 totaled 2,450 acres, only 20 acres of which was publicly owned. Production reported, 20,740,000 net tons, or 28 per cent of the United States total. Of total land disturbed, 81 per cent was in the South Atlantic States; 15 per cent in the East South Central States; and, 4 per cent in the Mountain States.

and spoil and slag. Their very existence fosters slovenliness and vandalism, invites the squatter's shack and engenders a "derelict land mentality" that can never be eradicated until the mess itself has been cleared up. Dereliction, indeed, breeds a brutish insensibility, bordering on positive antagonism, to the life and loveliness of the natural landcape it has supplanted. It debases as well as disgraces our civilization. . .

Although the preceding paraphrased excerpts from "Derelict Land" were written to describe conditions in Great Britain, they are equally relevant to certain mining districts in the United States. To many individuals, natural beauty may exist only in a particular national monument, mountain, forest, park, lake, or well-remembered scenic view. However, this narrow concept is giving way to an awareness that natural beauty is everywhere and in everything.

There is no question that many surface-mining operations blight the landscape. Nearly 60 percent of the more than 690 surface mine sites examined could be observed from public-use. areas. Where the sites contrasted with greener suroundings, they could be considered unsightly, or even repellent. In arid, or desert, areas public concern is less evident because of the sparse population and the mine sites are somewhat similar in appearance to the surrounding areas.

It was found in the majority of cases (78 percent), that no abandoned structures or equipment had been left on the site of the operation; however, about one-third of the areas visited were being used illegally by the public to discard garbage, rubble, junked vehicles, and construction materials. Such misuse endangers public health and safety and destroys the appearance of an area. In addition mine fires, which cost the Nation millions of dollars annually, are often started by burning trash and other materials in abandoned coal strip pits.

As yet, only a small percentage (about 0.14 percent) of the total land area of the United States has been disturbed by surface mining. But the effects are evident in every State, varying from small prospecting trenches in the West to the widespread disturbances of Appalachia. Effects of such mining upon the environment also vary widely, depending upon the steepness of the terrain, amount of precipitation, temperature, chemical characteristics of the mineral, and method of mining.

Basic Disturbances

Surface mining affects the environment in three ways. To some degree, it influences the quality of our air, land, and water; and, through these, animal and plant life.

Air

Although air pollution is one of our more serious environmental problems, surface mining, per se, cannot be considered a major contributor. However, the dust and vibrations resulting from blasting and movement of equipment during mining operations can be annoying and, in densely populated areas, a public nuisance. Some abandoned surface mines and waste piles also may be a source of air-borne dust.

Land

Two factors that are essential to the establishment of vegetation on surface-mined areas are the physical and chemical characteristics of the spoil. The spoil material was considered suitable for agricultural use at only 25 percent of the sites observed during the random-sampling survey. Where excessive stoniness exists (at about 20 percent of the sites inspected) the possibility of getting a quick vigorous cover is hampered by the rapid run-off and lack of soil. Most of the remaining 55 percent might be receptive to tree or herbaceous type plantings if climatological conditions are favorable.

There were no serious erosion problems at about 60 percent of the areas examined primarily because some vegetation had been established and the slope of the land was relatively gentle before and after mining. Most of the remaining sites showed evidence of erosion in the form of gullies less than one-foot deep; but, at 10 percent of the sites gullies were found that exceeded this depth. Sediment deposits were found in 56 percent of the ponds and 52 percent of the streams on or adjacent to the sample sites.

Spoil bank materials which have a pH of 4.0 or less are lethal to most plants. A pH of 7.0 is neutral; values higher than 7.0 indicate alkalinity. Free acid may be leached enough in 3 to 5 years to permit planting, but the leaching process will not improve soil conditions if erosion is allowed to expose more sulfuritic minerals in the spoil. Although some plants achieve successful growth in spoil with a pH range under 5.0, most plants require a less acid environment for successful growth. Of the measurements taken on spoil banks, 1 percent showed a pH of less than 3.0 and 47 percent, a range between pH 3.0 and 5.0.

About 15 percent of the spoil banks are covered with vegetation sufficient to provide adequate site protection. Another 15 percent have fair to good cover which, with more time and some spot planting, should suffice to protect the areas and speed renewal of the soil. Twenty percent will require direct seeding, seedlings, and fertilization. About 30 percent of the sites inspected had little, or no, cover and will, therefore, require extensive treatment. On the remaining 20 percent of the sites examined, vegetation will be extremely difficult to grow because of excessive stoniness or toxic conditions. It was also observed that wide variations occur in the rate at which natural revegetation takes place because of differences in physical and chemical characteristics of the spoil, and proximity to seed sources.

It was assumed for the random-sampling survey that, generally, mined land had been used prior to mining for purposes similar to those on adjoining tracts, and that, if left untreated by man, the mining site would eventually regain the same types of cover. Field observations made during the survey showed this to be largely untrue, however, because only about one-half of the areas assumed to have been forested had returned to forest and land classified as idle had increased almost fourfold. Land which had been devoted to crops and human occupancy, of course, had not voluntarily returned to these uses. Curiously, most land assumed to have been grassland had returned to grass. Clearly then, in most cases, natural forces will need a strong assist from man if mined sites are to be brought back to their former uses.

When natural vegetation is removed

by exploration and mining activities, the area becomes virtually useless for wildlife because it becomes barren of food, nesting, and escape cover. Even in the most arid areas of the country, erosion eventually follows removal of vegetation, and the resulting silt and sediment may affect fish and wildlife habitat. Thus, except in a few limited areas of the Midwest, poorer soils and vegetative cover resulting from surface mining create less favorable wildlife habitat. However, the rough broken ground found at many sites does afford protection from hunters for some species.

Water

Although basic to human existence, water is perhaps America's most abused resource. The surface mining industries are not the major contributor to the degradation of our water supplies on a national basis, yet in many areas such as Appalachia, they are a significant source of pollution.

Chemical pollution of water by surface mines takes many forms. The polluted water may be too acid, too alkaline, or contain excessive concentrations of dissolved substances such as iron, manganese, and copper. High concentrations of dissolved minerals may make the water unsuitable for certain purposes, but not for others; for example, water unsuitable for domestic use because of chemical content may often be used by industry, and some forms of aquatic life may flourish in it.

Sulfur-bearing minerals are commonly associated with coal, and are a major cause of water pollution. When exposed to air and water, they oxidize to form sulfuric acid. This acid may enter streams in two ways: (1) Soluble acid salts formed on the exposed spoil surfaces enter into solution during periods of surface run-off, and (2) ground water, while moving to nearby streams, may be altered chemically as it percolates through spoil, or waste dumps.

Acid drainage is but one of several adverse chemical effects caused by surface mining. Even in minute concentrations, salts of metals such as zinc, lead, arsenic, copper, and aluminum are toxic to fish, wildlife, plants, and aquatic insects. Indirectly associated with acid drainage are the undesirable slimy red or yellow iron precipitates ("yellow boy") in streams that drain sulfide-bearing coal or metal deposits. Of the streams receiving direct run-off from surface mine sites, 31 percent of those examined contained noticeable quantities of precipitates. Water discoloration was recorded at 37 percent of the streams adjacent to the sites observed, suggesting chemical or physical pollution. The discoloration occured most frequently in connection with the mining of coal, clay, sand and gravel, peat, iron, stone, and phosphate rock.

Streams are also polluted by acid water from underground mines, preparation plants, and natural seepage from unworked coal and other pyritic material. Because of the intermingling of effluents from these sources, it is difficult, if not impossible, to determine the quantity of acid that comes from surface mining alone. Many authorities believe, however, that not more than 25 percent of the acid load created by coal mining can be attributed directly to surface operations. Many streams in the Appalachian region are affected to various degrees by acid drainage from both surface and underground mines.

Although acid conditions are associated with coal mining conducted elsewhere, the problems are not usually so severe because the topography is not as rugged, rainfall is less profuse, pyritic materials oxidize more slowly, and, in some cases, limestone formations act as a neutralizing agent. Where acidity is neutralized by alkaline water, or limestone, the concentration of certain dissolved substances still may remain high and the water may not be usable without treatment.

Acid mine drainage affects fish and wildlife in several ways. Acid changes the water quality of streams into which it is discharged and, although the concentration may not be lethal to fish or wildlife, it may bring about changes in their physical condition and rate of growth. However, acid may be present in such concentration as to be directly lethal to fish or tend to suppress or prevent reproduction of the most desirable species.

The Bureau of Sport Fisheries and Wildlife reported that in the United States some 5,800 miles of streams (about 57,000 acres) and 29,000 surface acres of impoundments and reservoirs, are seriously affected by surface coal mining operations. The Bureau reported that, in 1964, 97 percent of the acid mine pollution in streams and 93 percent in impoundments, resulted from coal mining operations. Similar data were obtained by a United States Geological Survey reconnaissance conducted in 1965, which disclosed that water quality at 194 of 318 sampling sites in Appalachia was measurably influenced by acid mine drainage. None of these data, however, reflect the percentage of damage that can be attributed to surface mining alone.

Access roads built of pyritic waste material may also be sources of acid water. In past years, some highway departments have hauled waste from the mines for road building purposes. This practice is not generally followed today, and is forbidden in some States; however, roads built of this material continue to acidify rainwater passing over them—despite long periods of leaching. In addition, some privately constructed mine-access roads are being built of pyritic material.

Roads opened on National Wildlife Refuges by prospectors frequently result in broken levees; interfere with controlled burning; increase human activity, which interferes with the nesting and breeding of birds and animals; and, restrict animal movements. The distance that each species, or even individual animals, will place between themselves and the disturbance varies greatly, but some species will leave an area entirely when their natural habitat is invaded by people and equipment.

Physical pollution is most serious in areas typified by high-intensity storms and steep slopes, particularly during and shortly after mining. In areas undisturbed by strip mining within the Appalachian region, the average annual sediment yield ranges from about 20 to 3,000 tons per square mile of watershed, depending upon land use. Research conducted in Kentucky indicated that yields from coal strip-mined lands can be as much as 1,000 times that of undisturbed forest. During a four-year period, the annual average from Kentucky spoil banks was 27,000 tons per square mile while it was estimated at only 25 tons per square mile from forested areas.

Erosion and sedimentation problems

from surface mining are less severe in arid regions; however, even in such areas, storms do occur during which large quantities of sediment are discharged from mine workings, spoil heaps, and access roads. At some idle surface mines in arid country, the effects of wind and water erosion are still evident on steep spoil banks that were abandoned many years ago.

One of the major causes of sedimentation problems is the failure to control surface run-off following rainstorms. In areas outside Appalachia, 86 percent of the surface-mined areas investigated were found to have adequate run-off control. Areas lacking sufficient control were confined almost exclusively to the surface mining of coal, phosphate, manganese, clay, and gold.

Some 7,000 miles of stream channels have had their normal storm-carrying capacity reduced according to the Bureau of Sport Fisheries and Wildlife. It was observed that the normal water-carrying capacity of about 4,500 miles of these streams had been moderately to severely affected. The remaining 2,500 miles had been affected only slightly (debris reducing channel by less than one-third of capacity). Sediment generally was not a significant problem on small streams located more than two miles from the sample site.

Substandard access and haulage roads, and others built in connection with prospecting activities, are a major source of sediment. Based on the sample data, 95 percent of these roads were less than 3 miles long, but the proximity of many to natural stream channels had considerably increased their potential for sedimentation damage. The roads were fairly passable in the majority of cases; however, approximately 15 percent were eroded to a point that would make them difficult to traverse by ordinary vehicles.

Beneficial Effects of Surface Mining

When massive rocks are fragmented during surface mining, the resulting piles of material contain considerably more void space than existed in the fractures, partings, and pore spaces of the undisturbed rock. As a result, certain desirable hydrologic effects may occur. The danger of floods is diminished because a significant portion of the rainfall is trapped in depressions and behind the spoil banks where it sinks into the earth to augment groundwater supplies, rather than running off rapidly to nearby streams. Because water stored in the banks moves slowly, drainage will continue for a long time before the water level declines to that of adjacent streams. Thus, streams near surface-mined areas often maintain a longer sustained flow during dry weather than those draining undisturbed ground. This phenomenon was verified through field studies conducted in the Midwest by the Indiana University Water Research Center, but it occurs less frequently in most of Appalachia because of the rapid run-off.

In the Western United States, some surface mines have exposed groundwater sources and made water available where none existed before. This water has proved invaluable to livestock and wildlife. At some surface mining operations along mountainsides, the pits impound surface run-off from torrential rains, minimize the sediment load of streams draining the area, and effect considerable ground water recharge as well.

In California, piles of dredge tailings are quite permeable. However, because of their irregular conformation, they undoubtedly inhibit surface run-off to a greater degree than the original slopes, thus making some contribution to flood control and ground-water recharge. In Alaska, dredge mining for gold has destroyed the permafrost and the resulting tailings and mined area are considered premium property for residential and industrial development.

Many mine-access roads, when properly repaired and maintained, can be of considerable value since they may be used to promote the multiple-land-use potential of extensive areas. Accessibility for fire protection, recreation, and management activities, can' mean the difference between use and isolation. For example, by improving fire protection, investments can be made more safely in growing timber, and hazards to human and wildlife considerably reduced. Where massive equipment was used in the mining process, the access roads were usually well constructed, and the cost of repairing and maintaining them would be low. By converting some of these roads to public use, tourism might also be encouraged because many of the sites examined (33 percent) were located in areas that afforded spectacular views of mountains, valleys, and lakes.

Surface mining has created many opportunities to develop recreational areas where none existed before. Water in the form of small ponds or lakes, and the spoil piles themselves, frequently provide a pleasant topographic change in areas of virtually flat land. Examples may be found in flat coastal areas and in such States as Kansas, Illinois, Indiana, Ohio, and California.

Related Problems

Although on-site and some off-site conditions associated with strip and surface mining are discussed, this report does not cover waste materials resulting from processing mineral ores and preparing solid fuels for market. Neither does it explore problems associated with waste brought to the surface from underground operations, mine fires, surface subsidence, acid drainage from underground mines, possible accumulations of spent oil shale, seepages of oil and brine, mining on the continental shelf, and conflicting land uses. However, some of these problems are discussed briefly in the following sections to alert the reader to their significance, and to outline some of the efforts being taken to resolve them.

Bureau of Mines Solid Waste Disposal Program

Under Public Law 89-272, the Solid Waste Disposal Act, the Secretary of the Interior has delegated responsibility to the Bureau of Mines for a study of problems associated with the disposal, or use, of solid wastes resulting from the extraction, processing, or utilization of mineral or fossil fuels. To discharge this responsibility, the Bureau has initiated two types of projects:

a. Economic and resource-evaluation investigations aimed at identifying the causes of waste disposal problems in the mineral and fossil fuel industries; and

b. scientific and engineering research to develop methods of utilizing, or

FIG. 4. Active operation adjacent to reclaimed areas—Sand and gravel.
Photo by T. Hazlett, courtesy of National Sand and Gravel Association.

*otherwise disposing of, a variety of in-
organic waste materials.*

The economic and resource-evaluation studies are directed toward determining the magnitude, nature, and
location of solid waste piles; identifying problems in terms of priority; appraising the effectiveness of current
disposal practices, including costs and
possible profits that might accrue from
further beneficiation or treatment; and,
estimating the quantity of waste that
may accumulate from future operations. A series of case studies will be
included that will attempt to evaluate
specific waste piles from the standpoint
of public health and safety (such as

burning culm banks) and the extent to
which they retard industrial or urban
development. In addition to wastes
that may still contain some mineral
values, slag dumps and tailings will be
investigated to determine whether they
are potential sources of road materials
and lightweight aggregates.

The current research program includes projects at Bureau research installations, grants-in-aid to universities
and colleges, and one contract to private industry. Research by the Bureau
includes projects designed to produce
a clean steel scrap from automobile
bodies; to develop technically- and
economically-feasible methods of re-

covering and utilizing the metal content of red-mud residues of the alumina industry; to use auto scrap and non-magnetic taconite ores for the production of marketable magnetic iron oxide concentrates; to develop new or improved methods of salvaging metal from municipal wastes; and, to devise processes for the production of marketable products therefrom.

Grants-in-aid include studies on grass and other plants that might flourish on waste piles; use of mine and mill wastes in manufacturing bricks, lightweight block, structural clay products, or as aggregates for concrete; potential uses for spent oil shale; recovery of valuable products from mine dumps; and, removing contaminating metals from automobile scrap. The private contract is for the purpose of developing techniques to remove and recover copper from auto scrap melted in a cupola. Iron ingots suitable for use in iron or steel foundries will be produced and copper recovered from the slag, thus providing from auto scrap two metals which have well-established markets.

Mine Fires and Subsidence

A coal formation is a vast bed of combustible fuel. Mining makes oxygen available and all that is required to initiate combustion is a source of heat. One of the most common causes of coal mine or waste bank fires is the practice of burning trash or rubbish in strip pits or near the banks. Mine fires not only have a demoralizing effect upon a community, they pose a menace to public health and safety by emitting noxious gases and fumes, endanger surface lands and property, and destroy valuable resources. Of the more

than 200 mine fires located in the United States in 1964, many had been burning for years, a few for several decades. These fires, with nearly 500 waste bank fires, thus exert a considerable adverse effect upon the environment in certain areas. An insidious aspect of these types of fire is that, because of their proximity to each other, a mine fire may ignite a culm bank and vice versa.

Underground mining removes that part of the surface support supplied by the mineral extracted. Regardless of the type of mining and roof support used, subsidence usually occurs when the ore body, or coal seam, is relatively near the surface. Surface subsidence resulting from underground mining has caused loss of life and millions of dollars of damage to buildings, streets, water mains, and sewage lines in built-up areas. In addition, subsidences disrupt drainage patterns and permit surface water to infiltrate underground mine workings, thus frequently creating enormous underground impoundments in abandoned mines. Where the water is acid, its return to the surface, either by pumping or gravity flow, presents a serious pollution problem in the receiving streams.

Disposal of Spent Oil Shale

About one-half barrel of oil may be recovered from a ton of oil shale by a number of retorting processes. It is estimated that, for a 50,000 barrel-per-day operation, the disposal problem would involve 100,000 tons of spent shale per day. "High-grading" and unwise plant practices could waste large amounts of oil shale, resulting in enormous spoil piles of low-grade shale, and create stream and air pollution problems. Underground mining could induce surface subsidence that might adversely affect the recovery of minerals that lie above the oil shale deposits in some places.

Oil Seepage and Brines

Leaks in well casings and the disposal of brines and other wastes seriously contaminate fresh water supplies in many of the older oil fields. Leaks that allow brines to percolate downward to the ground water reservoir and the presence of permeable sands beneath some disposal pits are two of the major sources of contamination. Another major problem lies in locating oil wells which may be contaminating ground water. After they are found, the procedure is to clean and cement them from the bottom to seal off permeable formations. However, the problems mentioned require continued study.

Ocean Floor Mining

Ocean floor mining is emerging as a source of future mineral supply. Though in its infancy, commercial operations are being conducted for (1) shells off the coast of Iceland, in San Francisco Bay, and in the Gulf of Mexico; (2) tin off the coasts of Indonesia and Thailand; (3) diamonds off South-West Africa; (4) aragonite in Florida; and (5) iron sand in Ariaka Bay, Kyushu, Japan. Oil and sulfur have long been recovered from off-shore deposits, and gold dredging in off-shore areas of Alaska is being actively investigated. Effective disposal of the tailings (waste) without seriously impairing the utilization of other marine resources and creating objectionable on-shore waste piles appears to be the most important problem so far encountered.

Conflicting Mineral Land Use Problems

Surface mining often disturbs other resources. In many instances, timber is removed, wildlife habitat disrupted, natural streams diverted or contaminated, roads are built in undisturbed areas, and holes drilled. There is also the question of whether the initial mining operation will reduce our mineral-resource base by interfering with or precluding entirely the ultimate recovery of other underlying minerals. The demand for land to support both urban growth and mineral development (particularly sand and gravel) also creates serious social and political questions in densely-populated areas. In addition, when reclamation is contemplated, disagreements often occur as to the type of land use that will contribute most to society.

A nationwide study by the Bureau of Mines that is scheduled for completion in fiscal year 1967 is aimed at determining the effect of mineral extraction on land values. Although primary efforts will be directed toward urban centers and scenic and recreational areas, other locales will be included. The study will attempt to delineate problems of land rehabilitation and end-use following various types of mining such as strip, open pit, quarrying, and underground. Conditions under which mined-out land may enhance in value as well as some of the factors that lead to deterioration of value will also be determined. A special feature will deal with methods of handling future, or potential, land conflicts in order to maximize the utilization of the Nation's mineral resources and yet minimize the objectionable economic and sociologic after-effects of mining.

References

Hundreds of reports have been published on many aspects of surface mining and mined-land reclamation. The subject matter varies widely, ranging from technical details of a single problem in a small water-shed to in-depth studies of problems in areas the size of Appalachia. Because of the sheer volume and diversity of the subject matter covered by the literature, no attempt has been made to compile a comprehensive list of references. Rather, to assist those who might wish to delve further into pertinent writings, the following bibliographies are presented:

Berryhill, Louise R. Bibliography of the U. S. Geological Survey Publications Relating to Coal, 1882-1949. U. S. Geol. Survey Circ. 86, Jan. 1951, 52 pp.

Bituminous Coal Research, Inc., for the Coal Research Board, Commonwealth of Pennsylvania, Mine Drainage Abstracts. A Bibliography, 1910-63. 1964.

Bowden, Kenneth L. A Bibliography of Strip Mine Reclamation, 1953-60. Dept. of Conserv., The Univ. of Mich., 1961, 13 pp.

Funk, David T. A Revised Bibliography of Strip Mine Reclamation. U. S. Forest Service. Central States Forest Expt. Sta. Misc., Release 35, 20 pp.

Lorenz, Walter C. Progress in Controlling Acid Mine Water: A Literature Review. U. S. BuMines Inf. Circ. 8080, 1962, 40 pp.

Pacific Southwest Inter-Agency Committee. Annotated Bibliography on Water Quality in Pacific Southwest Inter-Agency Committee Area, 1950-63. Dec. 1965, 94 pp.

U. S. Department of Agriculture, Forest Service. Annotated List of Publications, Central States Forest Expt. Sta., Jan. 1965-Mar. 1966, 18 pp.

The following publications include comprehensive lists of references that are directly related to the subject matter indicated in the titles.

Averitt, Paul. Coal Reserves of the United States—A Progress Report, January 1, 1960. U. S. Geol. Survey Bull. 1136, 1961, 116 pp.

Bauer, Anthony M. Simultaneous Excavation and Rehabilitation of Sand and Gravel Sites. Nat. Sand and Grav. Assoc., Silver Spring, Md., 1965, 60 pp.

Biesecker, J. E., and J. R. George. Stream Quality in Appalachia as Related to Coal-Mine Drainage, 1965. U. S. Geol. Survey Circ. 526, 1966, 27 pp.

Brooks, David B. Strip Mine Reclamation and Economic Analysis. Natural Resources J. v. 6, No. 1, Jan. 1966, pp. 13–44.

Derelict Land, A study of industrial dereliction and how it may be redeemed. Civic Trust, 79 Buckingham Palace Road, London S. W. 1, 1964, 70 pp.

Federal Water Pollution Control Administration, Region VIII. Disposition and Control of Uranium Mill Tailings Piles in the Colorado River Basin. U. S. Dept. of H. E. W., Mar. 1966, 36 pp. and 28 p. Appendix.

Forest Service, Eastern Region and the Soil Conservation Society of America. Strip Mine Reclamation (a digest). U. S. Dept. Agr., Rev., 1964, 69 pp.

Johnson, Craig. Practical Operating Procedures for Progressive Rehabilitation of Sand and Gravel Sites. Nat. Sand and Grav. Assoc., Silver Spring, Md., 1966, 75 pp.

Kinney, Edward C. Extent of Acid Mine Pollution in the United States Affecting Fish and Wildlife. U. S. BuSport Fish. and Wildlife Circ. 191, 1964, 27 pp.

Ministry of Housing and Local Government, Her Majesty's Stationery Office. New Life for Dead Lands, Derelict Acres Reclaimed. Brown, Knight and Truscott, Ltd., London and Tonbridge. 1963, 30 pp.

Research Committee on the Coal Mine Spoil Revegetation in Pennsylvania. A guide for Revegetating Bituminous Strip-Mine Spoils in Pennsylvania. 1965, 46 pp.

The Council of State Governments. Proceedings of a Conference on Surface Mining, Roanoke, Virginia, April 1964. Surface Mining—Extent and Economic Importance, Impact on Natural Resources, and Proposals for Reclamation of Mined-Lands. 1964, 64 pp.

Udall, Stewart L. Study of Strip and Surface Mining in Appalachia. An Interim Report to the Appalachian Regional Commission. U. S. Dept. of the Int. June 1966, 78 pp.

29 Land Subsidence in Western United States*

Joseph F. Poland

Introduction

Volcanic eruptions, earthquakes, tsunamis, and landslides are instantaneous events that often have disastrous consequences. On the other hand, land subsidence due to man's activities, which I will be discussing in this paper, ordinarily is a relatively slow process that may continue for several decades. Subsidence may produce conditions or stresses that trigger some instantaneous event such as the failure of a dam or a levee, and public agencies should be aware of such potential hazards; but in many areas that have experienced appreciable subsidence, the problems created, although of considerable economic significance, are not hazards to human life.

Subsidence may occur from one or more of several causes, including withdrawal of fluids (oil, gas, or water), application of water to moisture-deficient deposits above the water table, drainage of peat lands, extraction of solids in mining operations, removal of solids by solution, application of sur-

face loads, and tectonic movements (including earthquakes).

In western United States, the subsidences of appreciable magnitude and area have been caused chiefly by the withdrawal of fluids, but also by application of water to moisture-deficient deposits and drainage of peat lands. This paper, therefore, will be limited to a brief description of these three types of subsidence, the problems created, and remedial measures, actual or potential.

Subsidence of Organic Deposits Due to Drainage

The peat lands which underlie roughly 450 square miles of the Sacramento-San Joaquin Delta constitute one of the largest areas of organic deposits in western United States. These peat deposits are as much as 40 feet thick. Drainage of the Delta islands for agricultural use began shortly after 1850. The land surface of many of the islands, initially about at sea level, is now 10 to 15 feet below sea level. Protective levees have been raised as the island surfaces have subsided. Leveling by Weir shows that the surface of Mildred Island subsided 9.3 feet from 1922 to 1955 at an average rate of 0.28 foot per year. Weir (1950) concluded that the causes of the subsidence were (1) oxidation of the deposits dewatered by lowering the water table to permit cultivation (by aerobic bacteria primarily, and probably the major cause), (2) compaction by tillage machinery,

* Publication authorized by the Director, U. S. Geological Survey.

Poland, J. F., 1969, "Land Subsidence in Western United States," in *Geologic Hazards and Public Problems*, May 27-28, 1969, Conference Proceedings, Olson, R. A. and Wallace, M. W., eds. U. S. Govt. Printing Office, pp. 77–96. Lightly edited by permission of the author. The paper was originally read before the conference and illustrated with slides.
Mr. Poland is a research hydrologist with the Ground Water Branch of the U. S. Geological Survey, Sacramento, California.

(3) shrinkage by drying, (4) burning, and (5) wind erosion.

The lower the island surfaces sink below the water surface in the Delta channels, the greater the stress on the protecting levees. This past winter, a levee reach on Sherman Island failed and the island was flooded. Although the water is being pumped out of Sherman Island, the levee-maintenance problem will increase in the Delta as continued drainage for cultivation lowers the island surfaces farther.

Subsidence Due to Application of Water (Hydrocompaction)

Locally, along the west and south borders of the San Joaquin Valley, moisture-deficient alluvial-fan deposits above the water table have subsided 5 to 15 feet after the application of water (Lofgren, 1960). These deposits are composed chiefly of mudflows and water-laid deposits and have higher clay content than the non-subsiding deposits, according to Bull (1964), who concluded that the compaction by the overburden load occurred as the clay bond supporting the voids was weakened by wetting.

This near-surface subsidence, or hydrocompaction, has been a serious problem, resulting in sunken irrigation ditches and undulating fields and has damaged canals, roads, pipelines, and transmission towers. It is particularly serious in construction and maintenance of large canals. As a preventive measure, deposits of this type along about 20 miles of the San Luis section of the California Aqueduct and along about 50 miles of the Aqueduct in Kern County were precompacted by prolonged wetting, prior to canal con-

struction. The estimated cost of this operation was $25 million.

According to Lofgren (1969), moisture deficient alluvial deposits that compact on wetting also have been reported in Wyoming, Montana, Washington, and Arizona, where subsidence of as much as 6 feet after wetting has created problems in engineering structures. Also, moisture-deficient loessial deposits as much as 100 feet thick covering extensive areas in the Missouri River basin have caused problems in the construction of dams, canals, and irrigation structures. Precompaction by wetting has been the usual solution, once this property of the sediments is recognized.

Subsidence Due to Withdrawal of Fluids

Subsidence due to withdrawal of fluids is by far the most common type of man-made regional subsidence. It may occur over oil and gas fields or over intensively exploited ground-water reservoirs. In either case, the cause is the same. The withdrawal of water reduces the fluid pressure in the aquifers and increases the effective stress (grain-to-grain load) borne by the aquifer skeleton. In ground-water reservoirs, the increase in effective stress in the permeable aquifers is immediate and is equal to the decrease in fluid pressure. The aquifers respond chiefly as elastic bodies. The compaction is immediate, but usually is small and mostly recoverable if fluid pressures are restored.

On the other hand, in the confining clays or the clayey interbeds, which have low hydraulic conductivity and high compressibility, the vertical escape of water and adjustment of pore pressure is slow and time-dependent. In these fine-grained beds, the stress applied by the head decline becomes effective only as rapidly as pore pressures decay toward equilibrium with pressures in adjacent aquifers. It is the time-dependent nature of the pore-pressure decay in these fine-grained beds that complicates the problem of predicting compaction or subsidence.

Intensive ground-water withdrawal and decline of head in heterogeneous confined aquifer systems in unconsolidated to semiconsolidated deposits of late Cenozoic age have produced the major areas of subsidence in western United States. Therefore, I will first review the dimensions and problems of subsidence due to ground water withdrawal, and then comment briefly on subsidence of oil fields.

Subsidence Due to Ground-Water Withdrawal

In the Houston-Galveston area of the Texas Gulf Coast, 1 to 6 feet of subsidence has occurred over an area of about 1,500 square miles. This is due almost wholly to lowering of artesian head in the ground-water reservoir, although there are subsidiary depressions due to oil-field subsidence.

In south-central Arizona, subsidence of 1 to 3 feet has been defined by leveling in several areas where water levels have been lowered 150 to 250 feet. The maximum known subsidence in southern Arizona is in the Eloy-Casa Grande area where subsidence of 7.5 feet occurred between 1949 and 1967. The extent of the area is not defined.

At Las Vegas, Nevada, subsidence of 3 feet was indicated by leveling in 1963.

Figure 1 shows the principal areas of subsidence in California. In the Sacramento-San Joaquin Delta, we have the organic deposits that I described earlier. The areas of subsidence due to ground-water withdrawal include the Santa Clara Valley, which is at the south end of San Francisco Bay, and where about 250 square miles have been affected and maximum subsidence by 1967 was 13 feet in San Jose. Then we have the large area in the San Joaquin Valley extending from about Los Banos on the west side south to Wasco on the east side, and the area at the south end which is referred to here as the Arvin-Maricopa area. The maximum subsidence in the San Joaquin Valley is on the west side and was about 26 feet in 1966. To the south, in southern California, the location of the Wilmington oil field is shown, and about 20 miles to the northwest of the Wilmington oil field is the Inglewood oil field in the Baldwin Hills (not shown).

There is one other area of subsidence that I might mention. That is Antelope Valley (Lancaster area in Fig. 1). It is just north of the San Gabriel Mountains and at least 160 square miles have been affected; subsidence in Lancaster is at least 3 feet.

Figure 2 shows the magnitude and extent of subsidence in the San Joaquin Valley but not for the same period of time in all areas, because the year span is determined by the available leveling control. The maximum subsidence is on the west side of the valley southeast of Los Banos.

As of 1963, subsidence exceeded 20 feet west of Fresno, and extensive areas had subsided 12 to 20 feet. On the east side, in the area between Tulare and Wasco, maximum subsidence was 12

FIG. 1. Areas of land subsidence in California. Major subsidence due to fluid withdrawal shown in black; subsidence in Delta caused by oxidation of peat.

feet by 1962; and that is the latest leveling control in that area. South of Bakersfield the maximum subsidence was 8 feet in 1965, which is the latest complete leveling in that area. The total area that is affected by more than one foot of subsidence exceeds 3,500 square miles or almost a third of the San Joaquin Valley. Each of the subsiding areas is underlain by a confined aquifer system in which the water level has been drawn down 200 feet or more —on the west side as much as 450 feet—by the intensive withdrawal. The dotted line is the position of the California Aqueduct which passes through the western and southern areas of subsidence.

The land subsidence in the Santa Clara Valley from 1960 to 1967 is shown in Fig. 3; it was nearly 4 feet in San Jose in the 7 years, and this happened to be the period of most rapid land subsidence in the Santa Clara Valley. The total subsidence has been about 13 feet in downtown San Jose. You will note that from 1960 to 1967 there was about 2 feet of subsidence at the south end of San Francisco Bay.

Figure 4 illustrates the change in altitude (subsidence) of a bench mark in downtown San Jose, where the elevation changed from 98 feet above sea level to about 85 feet above sea level from 1912 to 1967, representing a sub-

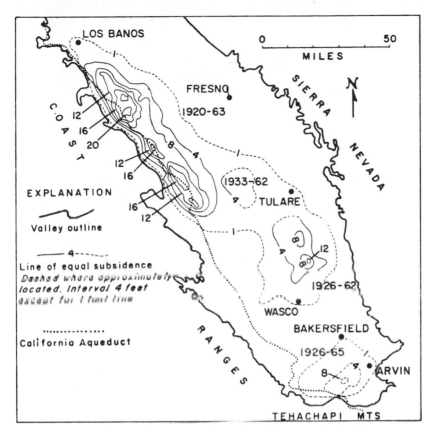

FIG. 2. Map showing the magnitude and areal extent of subsidence in southern San Joaquin Valley.

sidence of 13 feet. The hydrograph shows the fluctuation of water level in a nearby well. I call your attention to the fact that during a period of artesian-head recovery from 1936 to 1943, the subsidence stopped; it presumably began again about 1947 and reached its steepest rate of about 0.7 foot a year in the early 60's, due to the rapid decline in head from 1959 to 1963. The rate of subsidence in San Jose has decreased substantially in the past 2 years because there has been a winter water-level recovery of about 30 feet above levels of the middle 1960's.

Figure 5 shows the relation of the subsidence of 25 feet occurring in western Fresno County in the San Joaquin Valley between 1943 and 1966 and a decline of approximately 400 feet in the water level in nearby wells. This bench mark is at the locus of maximum subsidence in the San Joaquin Valley.

Subsidence can be measured by two methods: by repeated leveling of bench marks at the land surface, which is the common way of measuring it, and also is the only way to get full areal coverage, or, it can be measured at one site,

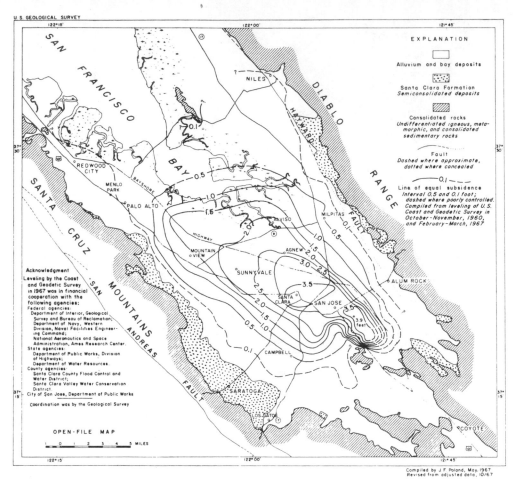

U.S. GEOLOGICAL SURVEY

EXPLANATION

Alluvium and bay deposits

Santa Clara Formation
Semiconsolidated deposits

Consolidated rocks
*Undifferentiated igneous, meta-
morphic, and consolidated
sedimentary rocks*

Fault
*Dashed where approximate,
dotted where concealed*

Line of equal subsidence
*Interval 0.5 and 0.1 foot;
dashed where poorly controlled.
Compiled from leveling of U.S.
Coast and Geodetic Survey in
October–November, 1960,
and February–March, 1967*

Acknowledgment

Leveling by the Coast
and Geodetic Survey
in 1967 was in financial
cooperation with the
following agencies:
Federal agencies:
  Department of Interior, Geological
  Survey and Bureau of Reclamation;
  Department of Navy, Western
  Division, Naval Facilities Engineer-
  ing Command;
  National Aeronautics and Space
  Administration, Ames Research Center.
State agencies:
  Department of Public Works, Division
  of Highways;
  Department of Water Resources.
County agencies:
  Santa Clara County Flood Control and
  Water District;
  Santa Clara Valley Water Conservation
  District.
City of San Jose, Department of Public Works

Coordination was by the Geological Survey

OPEN-FILE MAP

1 0 1 2 3 4 5 MILES

Compiled by J.F Poland, May,1967
Revised from adjusted data, 10/67

FIG. 3. Land subsidence from 1960 to 1967, Santa Clara Valley, California.

by measuring compaction directly. Re-leveling is the basis for knowing how much subsidence has occurred in the San Joaquin Valley. The level net in the subsidence areas plus the ties to bedrock total about 1,500 miles of leveling. Considering that first-order leveling costs about $200 a mile and second-order leveling about $100 a mile, releveling that entire area requires a substantial amount of funds.

Subsidence can be measured at a single point by using what can be ele-gantly called a bore-hole extensometer or can be referred to simply as a compaction recorder. Figure 6 is a simpli-fied diagram of the type of compaction recorder operated in the San Joaquin and Santa Clara Valleys—consisting of an anchor connected to a stainless steel cable that passes over sheaves at the land surface and is kept taut by a counterweight. The cable is connected to a recorder. If there is compaction between the land surface and the an-chor, the cable moves up with respect

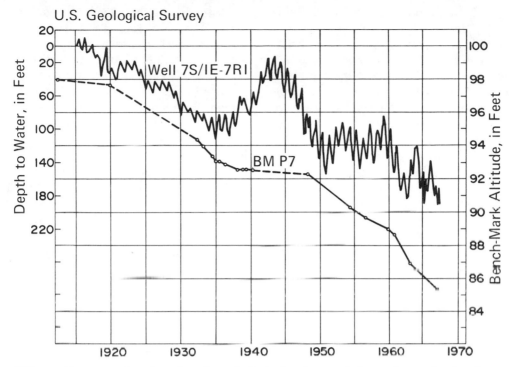

FIG. 4. Change in altitude at bench mark P7 in San Jose and change in artesian head in nearby well.

to the land surface and the magnitude can be recorded. The measured compaction equals land subsidence if the anchor is below the compacting interval.

Figure 7 illustrates a record obtained on the west-central side of Fresno County at Cantua Creek from 1958 to 1966 of compaction in three wells— one about 500 feet deep, another 700, and a third, 2,000 feet deep. At the time the recorders were installed, the 2,000-foot well was almost as deep as any of the water wells nearby. Measured compaction 1958 to 1966 in the 500-foot well was small, in the 700-foot well, about 2 feet, and in the 2,000-foot well, more than 8 feet. The straight line connecting the three dots

shows subsidence of a bench mark on the land surface as determined by leveling from distant stable bench marks and illustrates that the compaction measured in the 2,000-foot well was almost equal to the subsidence of the land surface during this period. This type of multiple-depth installation can be utilized to find the magnitude and rate of compaction between the depth intervals; it can be used also to determine at what depth compaction is occurring.

Problems Caused by Subsidence

If the subsiding area borders the ocean or a bay as in the Santa Clara Valley, levees have to be built and maintained to restrain flooding of lowlands. If yearly high tides happen to coincide with times of excessive stream runoff, levees may be overtopped. The Christmas floods of 1955 caused inundation of the town of Alviso at the south end of San Francisco Bay due to a combination of high tides and heavy stream runoff.

The differential change in elevation of the land surface in subsiding areas creates problems in construction and maintenance of water-transport structures, such as canals, irrigation systems, and drainage systems, and affects stream-channel grade. For example, the California Aqueduct passes through the subsiding areas on the west side of and at the south end of the San Joaquin Valley; also, a peripheral canal, when built, will be about at the east edge of the subsidence in the Delta.

The construction of the San Luis canal section of the aqueduct began in 1963. The map (Fig. 8) illustrates a problem that was faced in planning and construction of the canal in this subsidence area. The map shows subsidence in the 3 years ending in 1963. Obviously, then, planning involves the prediction of future subsidence, but beyond the physical characteristics that have to be considered, the economic and political aspects of the problem are very substantial. For example, how soon will Congress appropriate funds for the construction of distribution systems, and how soon will people who are going to utilize the canal stop pumping ground water and thereby decrease or stop subsidence? These kinds of questions complicate the problem of subsidence prediction.

Another problem that is common to the subsidence areas in the Santa Clara

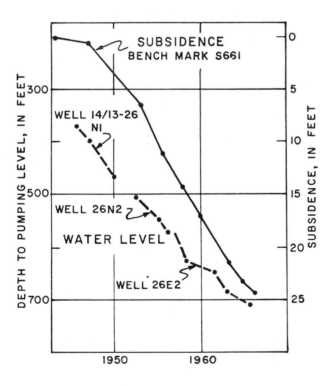

FIG. 5. Subsidence and artesian-head decline 10 miles southwest of Mendota.

and San Joaquin Valleys, and also in south-central Arizona, results from the fact that the compaction of the deposits develops compressive stresses on well casings. Many of the failures have been repaired by swaging out the ruptured casings and inserting liners. The costs of repair or replacement in central California probably have exceeded $10 million.

Subsidence of Oil Fields

Subsidence of a few feet has been noted in many oil fields and probably has occurred unnoticed in many more. The two oil fields in which subsidence has caused or contributed to major problems are the Wilmington and Inglewood oil fields in the Los Angeles coastal plain.

My comments on the Inglewood oil field in the Baldwin Hills area are summarized from a paper by Jansen, Dukleth, Gordon, James, and Shields (1967). These men were all members of the State Engineering Board of Inquiry that investigated the Baldwin Hills Dam failure. In December 1963, the Baldwin Hills Reservoir was destroyed by failure of its foundation. Extensive damage was done to neighboring communities. This reservoir is on the northeast flank of the Inglewood oil field. Subsidence had been observed in the vicinity for many years and was estimated by Jansen and others (1967) to have been 9.7 feet between 1917 and 1963 at a point approximately one-half mile westerly of the reservoir. They concluded that "the earth move-

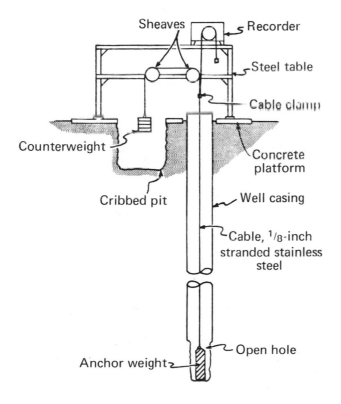

FIG. 6. Compaction-recorder installation.

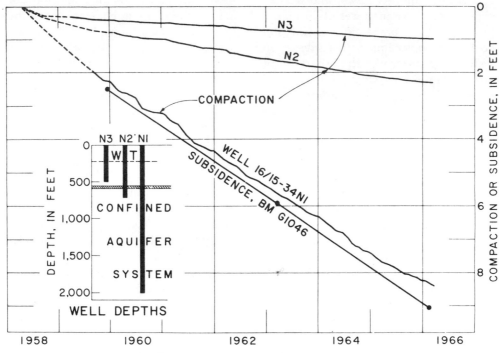

FIG. 7. Compaction and subsidence, Cantua Creek site.

ment which triggered the reservoir failure evidently was caused primarily by
subsidence."

In the Los Angeles–Long Beach
Harbor area, the Wilmington oil field
experienced a costly and spectacular
land subsidence beginning in 1937,
which had reached 29 feet at the
center by 1967. In Fig. 9, the subsidence contours as of 1968 have been
superimposed on an aerial photograph
of the area. The small dimple to the
northeast is the subsidence of the
Long Beach oil field. The main part of
downtown Long Beach, Terminal
Island and Pier A are shown. The area
is intensively industrialized, and this is
one reason why the remedial costs
have been so great. Extensive remedial
measures have been necessary to keep

the sea from invading the subsiding
lands and structures, because much of
the subsiding area initially was only
5 to 10 feet above sea level. The remedial measures for restraining the
sea have been chiefly massive levees,
retaining walls, fill, and raising of
structures. Horizontal as well as vertical movement developed stresses that
ruptured pipelines, oil well casings,
and utility lines, and damaged buildings.

The cost of this remedial work to
maintain structures and equipment in
operating condition had exceeded $100
million by 1962. The Wilmington oil-
field subsidence has been described in
many papers, so I won't discuss it
further except under methods for stopping or reducing subsidence.

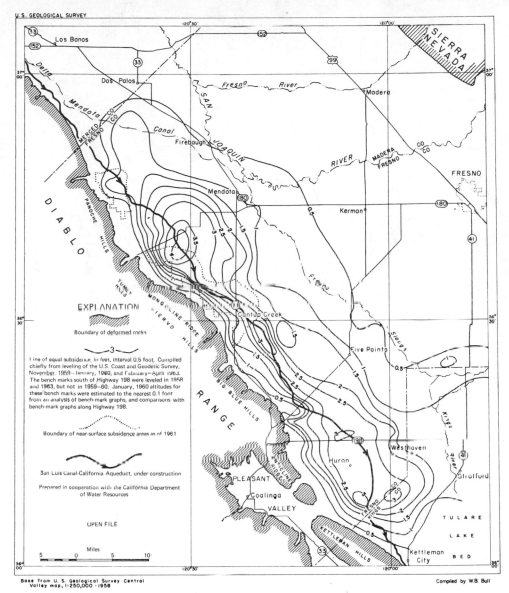

EXPLANATION

Boundary of deformed rocks

Line of equal subsidence, in feet, interval 0.5 foot. Compiled chiefly from leveling of the U.S. Coast and Geodetic Survey, November, 1959–January, 1960, and February–April 1963. The bench marks south of Highway 198 were leveled in 1958 and 1963, but not in 1959–60. January, 1960 altitudes for these bench marks were estimated to the nearest 0.1 foot from an analysis of bench-mark graphs, and comparisons with bench-mark graphs along Highway 198.

Boundary of near-surface subsidence areas as of 1961

San Luis Canal-California Aqueduct, under construction

Prepared in cooperation with the California Department of Water Resources

OPEN FILE

Miles
5   0   5   10

Base from U.S. Geological Survey Central
Valley map, 1:250,000 - 1958

Compiled by W.B. Bull

FIG. 8. Map showing land subsidence in the Los Banos-Kettleman City area, Calif., 1959–63.

Methods for Stopping or Reducing Subsidence

Decreasing fluid pressure in a confined system increases grain-to-grain load and causes compaction; also, increas-ing fluid pressure decreases grain-to-grain load and decreases or stops sub-sidence. In 1958, repressuring of the oil zones at Wilmington began, based on this premise and on the expectancy of increased oil recovery. The bench

FIG. 9. Aerial view of the city of Long Beach, California, showing total subsidence contours (1928–1968). (Photo courtesy of M. N. Mayuga, Dept. Oil Properties, City of Long Beach.)

FIG. 10. Graph of vertical movement of Pier A, Port of Long Beach, 1952–1965.

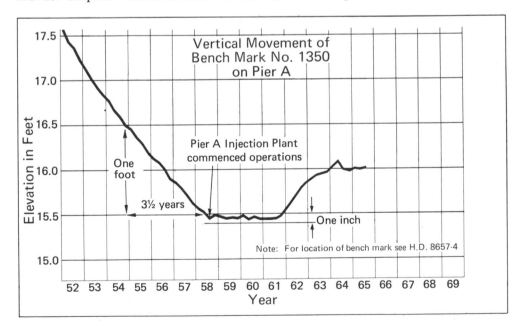

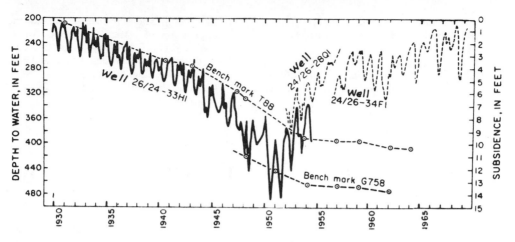

FIG. 11. Correlation of water-level fluctuations and subsidence near center of subsidence south of Tulare.

mark shown in Fig. 10 is on pier A, and you will note that it stopped subsiding in 1958 immediately after injection began nearby. It was essentially stable into 1961 and then rebounded about 0.5 foot by 1964. The maximum rebound of bench marks due to the repressuring as of the present time is on the order of 1.1 foot. Maps prepared by the Department of Oil Properties, City of Long Beach, indicate that by 1968 the subsidence had been stopped in most of the Wilmington oil field by the repressuring operation. I think this is an outstanding demonstration of subsidence control. And I think the people responsible deserve a great deal of credit for overcoming many problems—legal and otherwise—in controlling this subsidence.

Although no subsiding ground-water basins have been extensively repressured through wells, water imported to the Tulare-Wasco area in the southeastern part of the San Joaquin Valley through the Friant-Kern Canal since

1951 has reduced the pumping draft and caused substantial recovery of water level. Figure 11 shows that subsidence of bench marks near Delano, south of Tulare, decreased greatly after 1954, due to recovery of artesian head. Importation of water to the Santa Clara Valley is helping to raise the artesian head and decrease subsidence there, also. As a matter of record, water is or soon will be imported to all the major areas of subsidence due to ground-water withdrawal in California, so that ten years from now subsidence rates in many of these areas probably will be reduced greatly.

References

Bull, W. B., 1964, Alluvial fans and near-surface subsidence in western Fresno County, Calif.: U. S. Geol. Survey Prof. Paper 437-A, p. A1–A71.

Jansen, R. B., Dukleth, G. W., Gordon, B. B., James, L. B., and Shields, C. E., 1967, Earth movement at Baldwin Hills Reservoir: Am. Soc. Civil Engineers Proc., Jour. Soil Mech. Found. Div., SM4, no. 5330, p. 551–575.

Lofgren, B. E., 1960, Near-surface land subsidence in western San Joaquin Valley, Calif.: Jour. Geophys. Research, v. 65, no. 3, p. 1053–1062.

————, 1969, Land subsidence due to the application of water: Geol. Soc. America, Rev. Eng. Geology 2, p. 271–303.

Weir, W. W., 1950, Subsidence of peat lands of the Sacramento–San Joaquin Delta, Calif.: Calif. Univ. Agr. Expt. Sta., Hilgardia, v. 20, no. 3, p. 37–56.

30   Santa Barbara: Oil in the Velvet Playground

Harvey Molotch

Santa Barbara seems worlds apart both from the sprawling Los Angeles metropolis a hundred miles further south on the coast highway and from the avant-garde San Francisco Bay Area to the north. It has always been calm, clean and orderly. Of the city's 70,000 residents, a large number are upper and upper-middle class. They are people who have a wide choice of places in the world to live, but they have chosen Santa Barbara because of its ideal climate, gentle beauty and sophistication. Hard-rock Republicans, they vote for any GOP candidate who comes along, including Ronald Reagan and Max Rafferty, California's right-wing Superintendent of Public Education.

Under normal circumstances, Santa Barbarans are not the sort of people who are accustomed to experiencing stark threats to their survival, or ar-

Molotch, H., 1970, "Santa Barbara: Oil in the Velvet Playground," in *Eco-Catastrophe* by the Editors of *Ramparts*, Harper & Row Publishers, New York, pp. 84–105 (without photographs). Reprinted by permission of the author and the editors of *Ramparts*. Copyright 1970 by the Editors of Ramparts Magazine, Inc.
Professor Molotch is at the State University of New York at Stony Brook and is a specialist in urban ecology.

bitrary, contemptuous handling of their wishes. They are an unlikely group to be forced to confront brutal realities about how the "normal channels" in America can become hopelessly clogged and unresponsive. Yet this is exactly what happened when the Union Oil Company's well erupted in the Santa Barbara Channel, causing an unparalleled ecological disaster, the effects of which are still washing up on the local beaches.

In the ensuing months it became clear that more than petroleum had leaked out from Union Oil's drilling platform. Some basic truths about power in America had spilled out along with it. The oil disaster was more than simply another omen for an increasingly "accident-prone" civilization. Precisely because it was an accident—a sudden intrusion into an extremely orderly social process—it provided Santa Barbarans with sharp insights into the way our society is governed and into the power relationships that dictate its functions.

Across the political spectrum in Santa Barbara, the response has been much the same: fury. Some, including persons who never before had made a political move in their lives, were led from petition campaigns to the picket line and demonstrations, to the sit-down, and even to the sail-in. The position they finally came to occupy shows that radicalism is not, as experts like Bruno Bettelheim have implied, a subtle form of mental imbalance caused by rapid technological change or by the increasing impersonality of the modern world; radicals are not "immature," "undisciplined" or "anti-intellectual." Quite the contrary. They are persons who live in conditions where injustice is apparent, and who have access to more complete information about their plight than the average man, giving them a perspective that allows them to become angry in a socially meaningful way. In short, radicals are persons who make the most rational (and moral) response, given the social and political circumstances. Thus, as recent sociological studies have shown, radical movements like SDS draw their memberships disproportionately from the most intelligent and informed members of their constituent populations.

Optimistic Indignation: Government by the People

For over fifteen years, Santa Barbara's political leaders attempted to prevent the despoilation of their coastline by oil drilling in adjacent federal waters. Although they were unsuccessful in blocking the leasing of *federal* waters beyond the three-mile limit, they were able to establish a sanctuary within *state* waters (thus foregoing the extraordinary revenues which leases in such areas bring to adjacent localities). It was therefore a great irony that the one city which had voluntarily ex-changed revenue for a pure environment should find itself faced, in January of 1969, with a massive eruption which was ultimately to cover the entire city coastline with a thick coat of crude oil. The air was soured for many hundreds of feet inland, and tourism—the traditional economic base of the region—was severely threatened. After ten days, the runaway well was brought under control, only to erupt again in February. This fissure was closed in March, but was followed by a sustained "seepage" of oil—a leakage which continues today to pollute the sea, the air and the famed local beaches. The oil companies had paid a record $603 million for their lease rights, and neither they nor the federal government bore any significant legal responsibility toward the localities which those lease rights might endanger.

The response of Santa Barbarans to this pollution of their near-perfect environment was immediate. A community organization called "GOO" (Get Oil Out!) was established under the leadership of a former state senator and a local corporate executive. GOO took a strong stand against any and all oil activity in the Channel and circulated a petition to that effect which eventually gained 110,000 signatures and was sent to President Nixon. The stodgy Santa Barbara News-Press (oldest daily newspaper in Southern California, its masthead proclaims) inaugurated a series of editorials, unique in their uncompromising stridency and indicative of the angry mood of the community. "The people of the Santa Barbara area can never be repaid for the hurt that has been done to them and their environment," said a front-page editorial. "They are angry—and this is not the time for them to lose their anger. This is the time for them to fight for action that will guarantee absolutely and permanently that there will be no recurrence of the nightmare of the last two weeks. . . ."

The same theme emerged in the hundreds of letters published by the News-Press in the weeks that followed and in the positions taken by virtually every local civic and government body. Rallies were held at the beach, and GOO petitions were circulated at local shopping centers and sent to sympathizers around the country. Local artists, playwrights, advertising men, retired executives and academic specialists from the local campus of the University of California executed special projects appropriate to their areas of expertise.

A GOO strategy emerged for an attack on two fronts. Local indignation, producing the petition to the President and thousands of letters to key members of Congress and the executive, would lead to appropriate legislation. Legal action against the oil companies and the federal government would have the double effect of recouping some of the financial losses certain to be suffered by the local tourist and fishing industries while at the same time serving notice that drilling in the Channel would become a much less profitable operation. Legislation to ban drilling was introduced by Senator Alan Cranston in the U. S. Senate and Representative Charles Teague in the House of Representatives. Joint suits for $1 billion in damages were filed against the oil companies and the federal government by the city and county of

Santa Barbara (later joined by the State of California).

All of these activities—petitions, rallies, court action and legislative lobbying—expressed their proponents' basic faith in "the system." There was a muckraking tone to the Santa Barbara protest: the profit-mad executives of Union Oil were ruining the coastline, but once national and state leaders became aware of what was going on and were provided with the "facts" of the case, justice would be done.

Indeed, there was good reason for hope. The quick and enthusiastic responses of the right-wing Teague and the liberal Cranston represented a consensus of men otherwise polar opposites in their political behavior. But from other important quarters there was silence. Santa Barbara's representatives in the state legislature either said nothing or (in later stages) offered only minimal support. Most disappointing of all to Santa Barbarans, Governor Ronald Reagan withheld support for proposals which would end the drilling.

As subsequent events unfolded, the seemingly inexplicable silence of most of the democratically-elected representatives began to fall into place as part of a more general pattern. Santa Barbarans began to see American democracy as a very complicated affair—not simply a system in which governmental officials carry out the desires of their constituents once those desires become known. Instead, increasing recognition came to be given to the "all-powerful Oil lobby"; to legislators "in the pockets of Oil"; to academicians "bought" by Oil and to regulatory agencies that lobby for those they are supposed to regulate. In other words,

Santa Barbarans became increasingly ideological, increasingly sociological and, in the words of some observers, increasingly "radical." Writing from his lodgings in the Santa Barbara Biltmore, the city's most exclusive residence hotel, an irate citizen penned these words in a letter published in the local paper: "We the People can protest and protest and it means nothing because the industrial and military junta are the country. They tell us, the People, what is good for the oil companies is good for the People. To that I say, Like Hell! . . . Profit is their language and the proof of all this is their history."

Disillusionment: Government by Oil

From the start, Secretary of Interior Walter Hickel was regarded with suspicion, and his publicized associations with Alaskan oil interests did little to improve his image in Santa Barbara. When he called a halt to drilling immediately after the initial eruption, some Santa Barbarans began to believe that he would back them up. But even the most optimistic were quite soon forced to recognize that government policy would indeed confirm their worst fears. For, only one day later, Secretary Hickel ordered a resumption of drilling and production—even as the oil continued to gush into the Channel.

Within 48 hours Hickel reversed his position and ordered another halt to the drilling. But this time his action was seen as a direct response to the massive nationwide media play then being given to the Santa Barbara plight and to the citizens' mass outcry just then beginning to reach Washington. Santa Barbarans were further disenchanted with Hickel and the executive branch both because the Interior Department failed to back any legislation to halt drilling and because it consistently attempted to downplay the entire affair—minimizing the extent of the damages and hinting at possible "compromises" which were seen locally as near-total capitulation to the oil companies.

One question on which government officials systematically erred on the side of Oil was that of the *volume* of oil spilling into the Channel. The U. S. Geological Survey (administered by the Department of the Interior), when queried by reporters, produced estimates which Santa Barbarans could only view as incredible. Located in Santa Barbara is a technological establishment among the most sophisticated in the country—the General Research Corporation, a research and development firm with experience in marine technology. Several officials of the corporation made their own study of the oil outflow and announced findings of pollution volume at a minimum of *tenfold* that of the government's estimate. The methods which General Research used to prepare its estimates were made public. The Geological Survey and the oil interests, however, continued to blithely issue their own lower figures, refusing to provide any substantiating arguments.

Another point of contention was the effect of the oil on the beaches. The oil companies, through various public relations officials, constantly minimized the actual amount of damage and maximized the effect of Union Oil's cleanup activities; and the Department of the Interior seemed determined to support Union Oil's claims. Thus Hickel referred at a press conference to the "recent" oil spill, providing the impression that the oil spill was over at a time when freshly erupting oil was continuing to stain local beaches. When President Nixon appeared locally to "inspect" the damage to beaches, Interior arranged for him to land his helicopter on a city beach which had been thoroughly cleaned in the days just before, thus sparing him a close-up of much of the rest of the county shoreline, which continued to be covered with a thick coat of crude oil. (The beach visited by Nixon has been oil-stained on many occasions subsequent to the President's departure.) Secret servicemen kept the placards and shouts of several hundred demonstrators at a safe distance from the President.

The damage to the "ecological chain," while still of unknown proportions, was treated in a similarly deceptive way. A great many birds died from oil which they had ingested while trying to preen their oil-soaked feathers—a process Santa Barbarans saw in abundant examples. In what local and national authorities called a hopeless task, two bird-cleaning centers were established (with help from oil company money) to cleanse feathers and otherwise minister to injured wildfowl. Spokesmen from both Oil and the federal government then adopted these centers as sources of "data" on the extent of damage to the bird life. Thus, the number of birds killed by oil pollution was computed on the basis of the number of fatalities at the wildfowl centers. It was a preposterous method and was recognized as such. Clearly, the dying birds in the area were provided with inefficient means of pro-

pelling themselves to these designated centers.

At least those birds in the hands of local ornithologists could be confirmed as dead, and this fact could not be disputed by either Oil or Interior. This was not so, however, with species whose corpses are more difficult to produce on command. Several official observers at the Channel Islands, a national wildlife preserve containing one of the country's largest colonies of sea animals, reported sighting unusually large numbers of dead sea lion pups on the oil-stained shores of one of the islands. Statement and counter-statement followed, with Oil's defenders (including the Department of the Navy) arguing that the animals were not dead at all, but only appeared inert because they were sleeping. In a similar case, the dramatic beaching in Northern California of an unusually large number of dead whales—whales which had just completed their migration through the Santa Barbara Channel—was acknowledged, but held not to be caused by oil pollution.

In the end, it was not simply the Interior Department, its U. S. Geological Survey and the President who either supported or tacitly accepted Oil's public relations tactics. The regulatory agencies at both national and state levels, by action, inaction and implication, effectively defended Oil at virtually every turn. In a letter to complaining citizens, for instance, N. B. Livermore Jr. of the Resources Agency of California referred to the continuing oil spill as "minor seepage" with "no major long term effect on the marine ecology." The letter adopted the perspective of Interior and Oil, even though the state was in no way being held culpable for the spill. This tendency was so blatant that it led the State Deputy Attorney General Charles O'Brien, to charge the state conservation boards with "industry domination." Thomas Gaines, a Union Oil executive, actually sits on the state agency board most directly connected with the control of pollution in Channel waters.

Understandably enough, Secretary Hickel's announcement that the Interior Department was generating new "tough" regulations to control offshore drilling was met with considerable skepticism. The Santa Barbara County Board of Supervisors was invited to "review" these new regulations and refused to do so in the belief that such participation would be used to provide a false impression of democratic responsiveness.

In previous years when they were fighting against the leasing of the Channel, the Supervisors had been assured of technological safeguards; now, as the emergency continued, they could witness for themselves the absence of any method for ending the leakage in the Channel. They also had heard the testimony of Donald Solanas, a regional supervisor of Interior's U. S. Geological Survey, who said about the Union platform eruption: "I could have had an engineer on that platform 24 hours a day, seven days a week and he couldn't have prevented the accident." His explanation of the cause of the "accident"? "Mother earth broke down on us." Given these facts, Santa Barbarans saw Interior's proposed regulations— and the invitation to the County to participate in making them—as only a ruse to preface a resumption of drilling.

Their suspicions were confirmed when the Interior Department announced a selective resumption of drilling "to relieve pressures." The new "tough" regulations were themselves seriously flawed by the fact that most of their provisions specified measures (such as buoyant booms around platforms, use of chemical dispersants, etc.) which had proven almost totally useless in the current emergency.

The new regulations did specify that oil companies would henceforth be financially responsible for damages resulting from pollution mishaps. Several of the oil companies have now entered suit (supported by the ACLU) against the federal government, complaining that the arbitrary changing of lease conditions deprives them of rights of due process.

Irritations with Interior were paralleled by frustrations encountered in dealing with the congressional committee which had the responsibility of holding hearings on ameliorative legislation. A delegation of Santa Barbarans was scheduled to testify in Washington on the Cranston bill to ban drilling. From the questions which congressmen asked them, and the manner in which they were "handled," the delegates could only conclude that the committee was "in the pockets of Oil." As one of the returning delegates put it, the presentation bespoke of "total futility."

At this writing, six months after their introduction, both the Cranston and Teague bills, though significantly softened, lie buried in committee with little prospect of surfacing.

Disillusionment: Power Is Knowledge

The American dream is a dream of progress, of the efficacy of know-how and technology; science is seen as both servant and savior. From the start, part of the shock of the oil spill was that such a thing could happen in a country having such a sophisticated technology. The much overworked phrase "If we can send a man to the moon . . ." took on special meaning in Santa Barbara. When, in years previous, Santa Barbara's elected officials had attempted to halt the original sale of leases, "assurances" were given by Interior that such an "accident" could not occur, given the highly developed state of the industry. Not only did it occur, but the original gusher of oil spewed forth completely out of control for ten days, and the continual "seepage" which followed it remains uncontrolled to the present moment—seven months later. That the government would embark upon so massive a drilling program with such unsophisticated technology was shocking indeed.

Further, not only was the technology inadequate and the plans for stopping a leak, should one occur, nonexistent, but the area in which the drilling took place was known from the outset to be extremely hazardous. That is, drilling was occurring on an ocean bottom known for its extraordinary geological circumstances—porous sand lacking a bedrock "ceiling" capable of restraining uncontrollably seeping oil. Thus, the continuing leakage through the sands at various points above the oil reservoir cannot be stopped, and this could have been predicted from the data known to all parties involved.

Another peculiarity of the Channel that had been known to the experts is the fact that it is located in the heart of earthquake activity in a region which is among the most earthquake prone in the country. Santa Barbarans are now asking what might occur during an earthquake; if pipes on the ocean floor and casings through the ocean bottom should be sheared, the damage done by the Channel's thousands of potential producing wells would devastate the entire coast of Southern California. The striking contrast between the sophistication of the means used to locate and extract oil and the primitiveness of the means to control and clean its spillage became extremely clear in Santa Barbara.

Recurrent attempts have been made to ameliorate the continuing seep by placing floating booms around an area of leakage and then sending workboats to skim off the leakage from within the demarcated area. Chemical dispersants of various kinds have also been tried. But the oil bounces over the booms in the choppy waters, the workboats suck up only a drop in the bucket, and the dispersants are effective only when used in quantities which constitute a graver pollution threat than the oil they are designed to eliminate. Cement is poured into suspected fissures in an attempt to seal them up. Oil on the beaches is periodically cleaned by dumping straw over the sands and then raking it up along with the oil which it has absorbed. The common sight of men throwing straw on miles of beaches, within view of complex drilling rigs capable of exploiting resources thousands of feet below the ocean's surface, became a clear symbol to Santa Barbarans. They gradually began to see the oil disaster as the product of a system that promotes research and development in areas which lead to strategic profitability—without regard for social utility.

This kind of subordination of science to profit came out more directly in the workings of the Presidential committee of "distinguished" scientists and engineers (the DuBridge Panel) which was to recommend means of eliminating the seepage under Platform A. When the panel was appointed, hopes were raised that at last the scientific establishment of the nation would come forth with a technologically sophisticated solution to the problem. Instead, the panel—after a two-day session and after hearing no testimony from anyone not connected with either Oil or the Interior Department—recommended the "solution" of drilling an additional 50 wells under Platform A in order to pump the area dry as quickly as possible. One member of the panel estimated that the process would take from 10 to 20 years. Despite an immediate local clamor, Interior refused to make public the data or the reasoning behind the recommendations. The information on Channel geological conditions had been provided by the oil companies (the Geological Survey routinely depends upon the oil industry for the data upon which it makes its "regulatory" decisions). The data, being private property, thus could not be released—or so the government claimed. In this way both parties are neatly protected, while Santa Barbara's local experts remain thwarted by the counter-arguments of Oil/Interior that "if you had the information we have, you would agree with us."

Science played a similarly partisan role in other areas of the fight that Santa Barbarans were waging against the oil companies. The Chief Deputy Attorney General of California, for example, complained that the oil industry "is preventing oil drilling experts from aiding the Attorney General's office in its lawsuits over the Santa Barbara oil spill." Noting that his office had been unable to get assistance from petroleum experts at California universities, The Deputy Attorney General stated: "The university experts all seem to be working on grants from the oil industry. There is an atmosphere of fear. The experts are afraid that if they assist us in our case on behalf of the people of California, they will lose their oil industry grants."

At the Santa Barbara campus of the University, there is little oil money in evidence and few, if any, faculty members have entered into proprietary research arrangements with Oil. Petroleum geology and engineering is simply not a local specialty. Yet it is a fact that oil interests did contact several Santa Barbara faculty members with offers of funds for studies on the ecological effects of the oil spill, with publication rights stipulated by Oil. It is also the case that the Federal Water Pollution Control Administration explicitly requested a U. C. Santa Barbara botanist to withhold the findings of his study, funded by that agency, on the ecological effects of the spill.

Most of these revelations received no publicity outside of Santa Barbara. The Attorney's allegation, however, did become something of a state-wide issue when a professor at the Berkeley campus, in his attempt to refute the charge, actually confirmed it. Wilbur H. Somerton, professor of petroleum engineering, indicated he could not testify against Oil "because my work depends on good relations with the petroleum industry. My interest is serving the petroleum industry. I view my obligation to the community as supplying it with well-trained petroleum engineers. We train the industry's engineers and they help us."

Santa Barbara's leaders were incredulous about the whole affair. The question—one which is asked more often by the down-trodden sectors of the society than by the privileged—was posed: "Whose university is this, anyway?" A local executive and GOO leader asked, "If the truth isn't in the universities, where is it?" A conservative member of the state legislature, in a move reminiscent of SDS demands, went so far as to demand an end to all faculty "moonlighting" for industry. In Santa Barbara, the only place where all of this publicity was appearing, there was thus an opportunity for insight into the linkages between knowledge, the university, government and oil—and into the resultant non-neutrality of science. The backgrounds of many members of the DuBridge Panel were linked publicly to the oil industry. DuBridge himself, as a past president of Cal Tech, served under a board of trustees which included the president of Union Oil and which accepted substantial Union Oil donations.

While "academic truth" was being called into question, some truths not usually dwelt on by Oil's experts were gaining public attention. In another of its front-page editorials, the News-Press set forth a number of revealing facts about the oil industry. The combination of output restrictions, extraordinary tax write-off privileges for drilling expenses, the import quota, and the 27½ per cent depletion allowance creates an artificially high price for U. S. oil—a price almost double the world market price for a comparable product

delivered to comparable U. S. destinations. The combination of available incentives creates a situation where some oil companies pay no taxes whatsoever during extraordinarily profitable years. In the years 1962–1966, Standard Oil of New Jersey paid less than four per cent of its profits in taxes. Standard of California less than three per cent, and 22 of the other largest oil companies paid slightly more than six per cent. It was pointed out again and again to Santa Barbarans that it was this system of subsidy which made the relatively high cost deep-sea exploration and drilling in the Channel profitable in the first place. Thus the citizens of Santa Barbara, as federal taxpayers and fleeced consumers, were subsidizing their own eco-catastrophe.

The Mechanisms of Deception

The way in which federal officials and the oil industry frustrated the democratic process and thwarted popular dissent in Santa Barbara is hardly unfamiliar. But the upper-middle-class nature of the community, and the sharp features of an event which was a sudden disruption of normality, make it an ideal case for illustrating some of the techniques by which the powers that be maintain the status quo.

The first of these has been described by Daniel Boorstin as the technique of the "pseudo-event." A pseudo-event occurs when men arrange conditions to simulate a particular kind of event so that certain prearranged consequences follow as though the actual event had taken place. Several pseudo-events took place in Santa Barbara. From the outset, it was obvious that national actions concerning oil were aimed at freezing out any local participation in decisions affecting the Channel. Thus, when the federal government first called for bids on a Channel lease in 1968, local officials were not even informed. Further, local officials were not notified by any government agency in the case of the original oil spill, nor (except after the spill was already widely known) in the case of any of the previous or subsequent more "minor" spills. The thrust of the federal government's colonialist attitude toward the local community was contained in an Interior Department engineer's memo released by Senator Cranston's office. Written to the Assistant Secretary of the Interior to explain the policy of refusing to hold public hearings prior to drilling, it said: "We preferred not to stir up the natives any more than possible."

The Santa Barbara County Board of Supervisors turned down the call for "participation" in drawing up new "tougher" drilling regulations precisely because they knew the government had no intention of creating "safe" drilling regulations. They refused to utilize "normal channels," refusing thereby to take part in the pseudo-event and thus to let the consequences (in this case the appearance of democratic decision-making and local assent) of a non-event occur.

There were other attempts to stage pseudo-events. Nixon's "inspection" of the Santa Barbara beachfront was an obvious one. Another series of such events were the congressional hearings set up by legislators who were, in the words of a well-to-do lady leader of GOO, "kept men." The locals were allowed to blow off steam at the hearings, but their arguments, however cogent, failed to bring about legislation

appropriate to the pollution crisis. Many Santa Barbarans had a similar impression of the court hearings regarding the various legal maneuvers against oil drilling.

Another technique for diffusing and minimizing popular protest evidenced in the Santa Barbara affair might be called the "creeping event." A creeping event is, in a sense, the opposite of a pseudo-event. It occurs when something *is* actually taking place, but when the manifestations of the event are arranged to occur at an inconspicuously gradual and piecemeal pace, thus avoiding some of the consequences which would follow from the event if it were immediately perceived to be occurring.

The major creeping event in Santa Barbara was the piecemeal resumption of production and drilling after Hickel's second moratorium. Authorization to resume *production* at different specific groups of wells occurred on various dates throughout February and early March. Authorization to resume *drilling* of various groups of new wells was announced by Interior on dates from April 1 through August. Each resumption was announced as a particular safety precaution to relieve pressures, until finally on the most recent resumption date, the word "deplete" was used for the first time in explaining the granting of permission to drill. There is thus no *specific* point in time at which production and drilling were reauthorized for the Channel—and full resumption still has not been officially authorized.

A creeping event has the consequence of diffusing resistance by withholding what journalists call a "time peg" on which to hang the story. By the time it becomes quite clear that "something *is* going on," the sponsors of the creeping event (and the aggrieved themselves) can ask why there should be any protest "now" when there was none before, in the face of the very same kind of provocation. In this way, the aggrieved has resort only to frustration and the gnawing feeling that events are sweeping by him.

A third way of minimizing legitimate protest is by use of the alleged "neutrality" of science and the knowledge producers. I have discussed the "experts" and the University. After learning of the collusion between government and Oil and the use of secret science as a prop to that collusion, Santa Barbarans found themselves in the unenviable position of having to demonstrate that science and knowledge were not, in fact, neutral arbiters. They had to prove, *by themselves*, that continued drilling was not safe; that the "experts" who said it was safe were the hirelings, directly or indirectly, of oil interests; and that the report of the DuBridge Panel recommending massive drilling was a fraudulent document. They had to show that the university petroleum geologists themselves were in league with the oil companies and that information unfavorable to the oil interests was systematically withheld by virtue of the very structure of the knowledge industry. This is no small task. It is a long and complicated story, and one which pits lay persons (and a few academic renegades) against an entire profession and the patrons of that profession. An illustration of the difficulties involved may be drawn from very recent history. Seventeen Santa Barbara plaintiffs, represented by the ACLU, sought a temporary injunction against additional Channel drilling at least until the information utilized by the DuBridge Panel was made public and a hearing could be held. The injunction was not granted, and in the end the presiding federal judge ruled in favor of what he termed the "expert opinions" available to the Secretary of the Interior. Due to limited time for rebuttal, the disorienting confusions of courtroom procedures, and also perhaps the desire not to offend the Court, the ACLU lawyer could not make his subtle, complex and highly controversial case that the "experts" were partisans and that their scientific "findings" followed from that partisanship.

A fourth obstacle was placed in the way of dissenters by the communications media. Just as the courtroom setting was not amenable to a full reproduction of the facts supporting the ACLU case, so the media in general—due to restrictions of time and style—prevented a full airing of the details of the case. A more cynical analysis of the media's inability to make known the Santa Barbara "problem" in its full fidelity might hinge on an allegation that the media were constrained by fear of "pressures" from Oil and its allies. Metromedia, for example, sent to Santa Barbara a team which spent several days documenting, interviewing and filming for an hour-long program—only to suddenly drop the project entirely due to what is reported by locals in touch with the network to have been "pressures" from Oil. Even without such blatant interventions, however, the full reproduction of the Santa Barbara "news" would remain problematic.

News media are notorious for the anecdotal nature of their reporting; even so-called "think pieces" rarely go beyond a stringing together of proximate events. There are no analyses of the "mobilization of bias" or linkages of men's actions with their pecuniary interests. Science and learning are assumed to be neutral; regulatory agencies are assumed to function as "watchdogs" for the public. Information contradicting these assumptions is treated as an exotic exception.

The complexity of the situations to be reported and the wealth of details needed to support such analyses require more time and effort than journalists have at their command. Their recitation would produce long stories not consistent with space limitations and make-up preferences of newspapers, or with analogous requirements within the other media. A full telling of the story would tax the reader/viewer and would risk boring him. The rather extensive media coverage of the oil spill centered on a few dramatic moments in its history (e.g., the initial gusher of oil) and a few simple-to-tell "human interest" stories such as the pathetic deaths of the sea birds struggling along the oil-covered sands. With increasing temporal and geographical distance from the initial spill, national coverage became increasingly rare and sloppy. Interior Department statements on the state of the "crisis" were reported without local rejoinders as the newsmen who might have gathered them began leaving the scene. While the Santa Barbara spill received extraordinarily extensive national coverage relative to other controversial events, this coverage nevertheless failed to adequately inform the American public about a situation which Santa Barbarans knew from first-hand experience.

Finally, perhaps the most pernicious technique of all because of the damage it does to the social conscience, is the routinization of evil. Pollution of the Santa Barbara Channel is now routine; the issue is not whether or not the Channel is polluted, but *how much* it is polluted. A recent oil slick discovered off a Phillips Oil platform in the Channel was dismissed by an oil company official as a "routine" drilling by-product which was not viewed as "obnoxious." That about half of the oil currently seeping into the Channel is allegedly being recovered is taken as an improvement sufficient to preclude the "outrage" that a big national story would require.

Similarly, the pollution of the moral environment becomes routine; it is accepted as natural that politicians are "on the take," "in the pockets of Oil." The depletion allowance remains a question of percentages (20 per cent of 27½ per cent), rather than a focus for questioning the very legitimacy of such special benefits. "Compromises" emerge, such as the 24 per cent depletion allowance and the new "tough" drilling regulations, which are already being hailed as "victories" for the reformers. Like the oil spill itself, the depletion allowance debate becomes buried in its own disorienting detail, in its pseudo-events and in the triviality of the "solutions" which ultimately come to be considered as the "real" options. Evil is both banal and complicated, and each of these attributes contributes to its durability.

The Mechanisms of Change

What the citizens of Santa Barbara learned through their experience was that the parties competing to shape decision-making on oil in Santa Barbara do not have equal access to the means of "mobilizing bias." The Oil/Government combine had, from the start, an extraordinary number of advantages. Lacking ready access to media, the ability to stage events at will, and a well-integrated system of arrangements for achieving their goals (at least in comparison to their adversaries), Santa Barbara's citizens have met with repeated frustrations.

Their response to their relative powerlessness has been analogous to that of other groups and individuals who, from a similar vantage point, come to see the system up close. They become willing to expand their repertoire of means of influence as their cynicism and bitterness increase. Letter writing gives way to demonstrations, demonstrations to civil disobedience. People refuse to participate in "democratic procedures" which are a part of the opposition's event-management strategy. Confrontation politics arises as a means of countering official events with "events" of one's own, thus providing the media with stories which can be simply and energetically told.

Thus, in Santa Barbara, rallies were held at local beaches; congressmen and state and national officials were greeted by demonstrations. (Fred Hartley of Union Oil inadvertently landed his plane in the middle of one such demonstration, causing a rather ugly name-calling scene to ensue.) A "sail-in" was held one Sunday with a flotilla of local pleasure boats forming a circle around Platform A, each craft bearing large anti-Oil banners. City hall meetings were packed with citizens reciting demands for immediate and forceful local action.

A City Council election held during the crisis resulted in a landslide for the Council's bitterest critic and the defeat of a veteran councilman suspected of having "oil interests." In a rare action, the News-Press condemned the local Chamber of Commerce for accepting oil money for a fraudulent tourist advertising campaign which touted Santa Barbara (including its beaches) as completely restored to its former beauty.

One possible grand strategy for Santa Barbara was outlined by a local public relations man and GOO worker, who said, "We've got to run the oil men out. The city owns the wharf and the harbor that the company has to use. The city has got to deny its facilities to oil traffic, service boats, cranes and the like. If the city contravenes some federal navigation laws [which such actions would unquestionably involve], to hell with it. The only hope to save Santa Barbara is to awaken the nation to the ravishment. That will take public officials who are willing to block oil traffic with their bodies and with police hoses, if necessary. Then federal marshals or federal troops would have to come in. This would pull in the national news media."

This scenario has thus far not occurred in Santa Barbara, although the continued use of the wharf by the oil industries has led to certain militant actions. A picket was maintained at the wharf for two weeks to protest the conversion of the pier from a recreation and tourist facility into an industrial plant for the use of the oil companies. A boycott of other wharf businesses (e.g., two restaurants) was urged. The picket line was led by white, middle-class adults—one of whom was a local businessman who, two years earlier, was a close runner-up in the Santa Barbara mayoralty race.

Prior to the picketing, a dramatic Easter Sunday confrontation (involving approximately 500 persons) took place between demonstrators and city police. Just as a wharf rally was breaking up, an oil service truck began driving up the pier to make a delivery of casing supplies for oil drilling. There was a spontaneous sit-down in front of the truck. For the first time since the Ku Klux Klan folded in the '30s, a group of (heavily) middle-class Santa Barbarans was publicly taking the law into its own hands. After much lengthy discussion between police, the truck driver and the demonstrators, the truck was ordered away and the demonstrators remained to rejoice over their victory. The following day's News-Press editorial, while not supportive of such tactics, was quite sympathetic, which was noteworthy given the paper's long-standing bitter opposition to similar tactics when exercised by dissident Northern blacks or student radicals.

A companion demonstration on the water failed to materialize. A group of Santa Barbarans was to sail to the Union platform and "take it," but choppy seas precluded a landing, and the would-be conquerors returned to port in failure.

It would be difficult to predict what forms Santa Barbara's resistance will take in the future. A veteran News-Press reporter who covered the important oil stories has publicly stated that if the government fails to eliminate both the pollution and its causes, "there will, at best, be civil disobedience in Santa Barbara and at worst, violence." In fact, talk of "blowing up" the ugly platforms has been recurrent—and it is heard in all social circles.

But just as this kind of talk is not entirely serious, it is difficult to know the degree to which the other militant statements are meaningful. Despite frequent observations about the "radicalization" of Santa Barbara, it is difficult to determine the extent to which the authentic grievances against Oil have been generalized into a radical analysis of American society. Certainly an SDS membership campaign among Santa Barbara adults would be a dismal failure. But that is too severe a test. People, particularly basically contented people, change their world-view very slowly, if at all. Most Santa Barbarans still go about their comfortable lives in the ways they always have; they may even help Ronald Reagan win another term in the state house. But I do conclude that large numbers of persons have been moved, and that they have been moved in the direction of the radical left. They have gained insights into the structure of power in America not possessed by similarly situated persons in other parts of the country. It can be a revealing shock to experience an event first-hand and then to hear it described, and distorted, by the press and the government. People extrapolate from such experiences to the possibility that official descriptions of other events may be similarly biased and misleading. And when these questions arise, deeper ones follow. As a consequence some Santa Barbarans, especially those with the most interest in and information about the oil spill, while still surrounded by comfort and certainty, have nevertheless come to view power in America more intellectually, more analytically, more sociologically—more radically—than they did before.

31 Environmental Impact Analysis: The Example of the Proposed Trans-Alaska Pipeline

David A. Brew

Introduction

The precedents that have been and will be set by the proposed oil-pipeline system and soon-to-be proposed gas-pipeline system in Alaska will have far-reaching implications for petroleum development in the arctic parts of the Western and possibly the Eastern Hemisphere. Some of the most important precedents will concern the acquisition, analysis, and use of environmental data. The Alaskan example is of interest to all groups involved in arctic resource development because it provides information on predicted environmental impacts and on the methods used in arriving at the predictions.

This paper represents an attempt on the part of the author to summarize pertinent elements of the experience derived from the preparation of a complex environmental analysis for the benefit of others concerned in similar endeavors.

The purposes of this paper are (1) to describe the reasons for analyzing environmental impact and discuss (a) the implications of the National Environmental Policy Act (NEPA) of the United States and of similar laws in

Brew, David A., 1974, "Environmental Impact Analysis: The Example of the Proposed Trans-Alaska Pipeline, *U. S. Geol. Survey Circ.*, *695*, 16 pp.
The author is on the staff of the U. S. Geological Survey.

other countries to governmental and industrial decision-making processes, (b) the economic and public interest factors in the industrial decision-making process, and (c) the basic need to develop ways of minimizing the environmental costs that mankind must pay now and in the future; (2) to describe the general methodology needed to analyze environmental impact rigorously and objectively; (3) to describe in some detail how this methodology was applied to the proposed trans-Alaska pipeline and related systems; (4) to describe the main types of impact predicted from that analysis; (5) to examine the alternatives to the proposed pipeline; and (6) to analyze briefly from the author's viewpoint the approval of the proposed trans-Alaska oil-pipeline system as an example of the degree to which environmental considerations influenced the decision-making process.

It is difficult to discuss these points disinterestedly, without advocating one view or another, because many of the issues and factors are politically sensitive and subject to opposing interpretations when differing value frameworks are used. Nevertheless, because the lessons to be learned from the Alaskan pipeline example are important, the author has attempted to examine the ramifications of the impact analysis and of the decision deliberately and objectively.

This paper is modified from a paper

prepared for presentation to the Fifth International Congress of the Foundation Francaise d'Etudes Nordiques (Brew and Gryc, 1974). The interested reader is referred to that paper for a more complete discussion of the analysis of the government's decision (point 6, above).

Proposed Trans-Alaska Pipeline

The Secretary of the Interior of the United States has granted a permit to the Alyeska Pipeline Service Company for a 48-inch oil-pipeline right-of-way across Federal land in Alaska between a point south of Prudhoe Bay on the North Slope and Port Valdez, an arm of Prince William Sound, on the south coast (Fig. 1). The company will design, construct, operate, and maintain the pipeline system.

The pipeline will be about 789 miles (1,270 km) long, some 641 miles (1,030 km) of which will be across Federal land. The pipeline system will also include pump stations, campsites for use during construction, airfields for use during both construction and operation of the pipeline, a communication system, lateral access roads, and pits or quarries for construction materials. The marine terminal site on Port Valdez will consist of a tank farm, dock, and related facilities. Prior to construction of the pipeline north of the Yukon River, a road will be built for access and the movement of equipment, materials, and personnel during construction. This road, which is proposed to become part of the State of Alaska highway system, will be about 361 miles (580 km) long.

Construction of the proposed pipeline system will result in three additional significant developments not directly included in the pipeline application: (1) an oil field complex at Prudhoe Bay on the North Slope, (2) a probable gas transportation system, and (3) a marine tanker system operating between Port Valdez, Alaska, and various destination ports.

The pipeline and its related developments will constitute a complex engineering system that will result in changes in the existing abiotic, biotic, and social and economic systems of Alaska and adjacent areas. In addition, the pipeline system will affect the economics of energy use and the strategy of energy supply in the United States. The phrase "environmental impact" has gained general use in denoting changes that would occur in existing systems if a proposed course of action were to be adopted.

Reasons for Analyzing Environmental Impact in the Arctic and Other Regions

There are philosophical, economic, social, and legal reasons for attempting to analyze environmental impact in the Arctic and elsewhere. These different reasons are linked together in a complicated way, but the social reasons (those pertaining to the physical well-being of humans and their surroundings) have been dominant and have in some countries led to legal requirements.

People have only recently realized that some of the effects of the industrial revolution are potentially severely detrimental to the life support system that must sustain present and future generations. The natural environment, as contrasted with the social and economic environment that man creates,

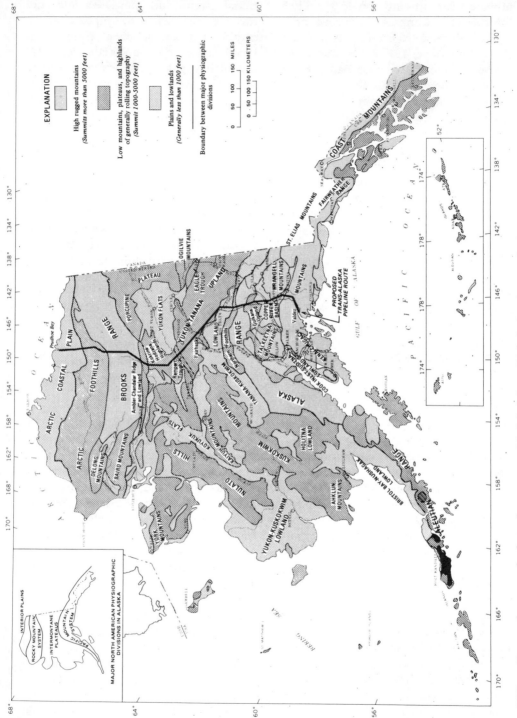

FIG. 1. Route of proposed oil-pipeline system. Modified from Wahrhaftig (1964, pl. 1).

is particularly susceptible to damaging stresses.

Many now believe that the greatest long-term benefits of health and enjoyment are possible only if the natural environment is maintained in a condition as close as possible to that existent before the world population explosion and industrial revolution. If people are to work toward this goal, then it is necessary to strive systematically to repair the damage already done to the natural environment and to avoid or minimize damage from current and future human development.

The Arctic is as yet practically untouched by modern industrial society, and detrimental effects can and should be avoided. If humans are to develop the resources of the Arctic, then they must choose from all the methods of exploration, extraction, and transportation available those that will cause the least environmental damage. The choice must therefore be based on predictions of the consequences to the environment of the various alternative methods. Environmental impact analysis is the process by which these predictions are made.

In addition to these social and philosophical reasons, industry has imposed on itself reasons for predictive analysis relating to the economic advantages of safe operation and of minimization of capital construction and of operating and maintenance costs. These analyses have for many years been an element in decision making by the pipeline and other industries, but it is now becoming clear that there are economic and social advantages in demonstrating that industry has a proper and positive concern for the environment and in particular for the effects that petroleum development, petroleum transportation, and their complex interactions have on the many facets of the environment. As the people of the United States continue to become more environmentally conscious, it will be advantageous for the oil industry to establish and maintain a position of positive environmental consciousness and action.

In the United States the legal requirements for analyzing environmental impact are contained in the National Environmental Policy Act (NEPA) of 1969.[1] The primary purpose of the United States Congress for that enactment was to establish a Federal policy in favor of protecting and restoring the environment. The wording of the act is such that all aspects of man's surroundings are the subject of Federal concern, and the intent is to make environmental considerations a real part of the governmental decision-making process.

The United States' NEPA contains strong directives to Federal agencies to follow this new policy. One section "authorizes and directs that, to the fullest extent possible *** the policies, regulations, and public laws of the United States shall be interpreted and administered in accordance with" the policy of the act. Another section of the act directs agencies to give "appropriate consideration" to environmental values in all decisions. Other sections relate to existing Federal agency policies and other aspects of environmental impact analysis and consideration in Federal authorizations of different types. Yet another section of the act establishes that Federal agencies must predict the environmental effects of proposed actions and of their alternatives and describe them in an "environmental impact statement" at an appropriate time in the decision-making process so that environmental considerations can be an actual part of that decision-making process. The environmental impact statement (U. S. Federal Task Force on Alaskan Oil Development, 1972) on the proposed trans-Alaska pipeline which provides the background for this paper was prepared in compliance with that section of NEPA.

Although Canada does not have an act comparable to the NEPA of the United States, it is clear that the intentions of the Canadian Government are similar to those of the United States Government in requiring that environmental considerations shall be a part of resource development in arctic regions and that legal requirements will be imposed on any applicants who propose pipeline construction and operation in the Canadian Arctic. Those requirements will include specific points considering the preservation and protection of the environment; therefore, the analysis of the environmental impact of any proposed pipeline system in northern Canada will be required.

There are of course both in the United States and in Canada many other laws and regulations which pertain to the construction and operation of pipeline systems. They are only indirectly related to the analysis of environmental impact and are incorporated in all planning and design of pipeline projects for the Arctic.

European countries do not yet have the legal requirements for pipeline systems based on exclusively environmental factors like those just discussed for the United States and Canada.

Nevertheless, there are governmental regulations regarding the design, construction, and operation of pipelines, and those regulations are indirectly related to environmental considerations. The different governmental procedures, regulations, and national codes now existing in Western Europe have been examined in a paper by Watkins (1971). It is impossible from the author's vantage point in the United States to comment on whether environmental impact analysis requirements are likely to become a part of pipeline regulations in Western Europe in the near future. Also, it is not known to the author whether environmental impact analysis of pipeline systems has been practiced or is being practiced in the Soviet Union (Pryde, 1972).

Although increased attention is being given environmental questions in Europe (Verguèse, 1972), the impression is that environmental impact analysis as discussed in this paper has not been practiced in other parts of the world.

A broader and more important reason for analyzing environmental impact transcends specific legal requirements. People appreciate now as never before that they exist on an earth that has finite limits and tolerances. In the present century laymen and scientists alike have recognized many symptoms of environmental perturbation that cause concern. These symptoms, and the technical prediction abilities now available, can be used to demonstrate that people can inadvertently and adversely affect their total environment. If people are to continue to enjoy a healthy existence on earth, those effects must be minimized. The costs of minimizing must themselves also be minimized and must be assigned economically as well as socially.

Environmental impact analysis is a process that uses existing information, existing symptoms, and prediction techniques to forecast what environmental impact effects will be. The control of adverse environmental impact effects must be based on the best information available, and the best information available is obtained through environmental impact analysis.

Environmental Impact Analysis of the Trans-Alaska and Trans-Alaska–Canada Pipeline Systems

The components that are essential in an environmental impact analysis (and the interactions between them) are well illustrated in the example of the proposed trans-Alaska pipeline system and its related developments. Environmental impact analysis requires interrelating several components: analytical method, baseline environmental data, impact linkage data, impacting project data, analysts, and coordination (Fig. 2). To be applicable to geographically large, technologically complex, and environmentally sensitive projects, the analytical method should be formulated for the specific environmental situation and proposed project at hand. The general case methodology requires (1) systematic description of the environment including identification and classification of its sensitive elements, (?) systematic description of the project that would be doing the impacting including identification and classification of the impacting factors inherent

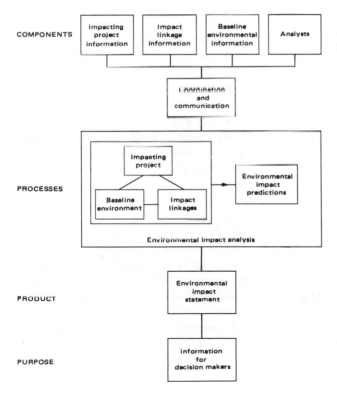

FIG. 2. Components and development of environmental impact analysis.

in it, (3) systematic accumulation of information related to linkages between impacting factors and the environment, (4) analysis of the interrelationships between the sensitive environmental elements and the impacting factors (including indirect and secondary feedback-type relations), (5) prediction of the net effects of those relations, and (6) preparation of an environmental impact report describing the results of the impact analysis. All these components and requirements were successfully included in the analysis of the proposed trans-Alaska pipeline. The actual analysis was made by a task force of resource scientists who were assigned the roles of impact analysts for specific resource topics or disciplines.

The environmental component and the impacting effects information just referred to could be combined to form an information matrix of specific design for the analysis of the impact of the proposed trans-Alaska pipeline and appurtenant systems. Needless to say, the matrix would be complicated and cumbersome, but it would synoptically depict in simplified fashion which impacting effects would impact on which environmental systems or components of those systems. In this regard, it is pertinent to comment on the approach to environmental impact analysis that is contained in U. S. Geological Survey Circular 645 (Leopold and others, 1971). As discussed later under "Guidelines," the methodology used in the trans-Alaska pipeline analysis rigorously excluded value judgments throughout the process with such judgments were unavoidable; then alternative value framework judgments were presented. The approach described in

Circular 645 is quite different in that it presents a nonspecific design approach to impact analysis and in that it admittedly "portrays many value judgments" (p. 1). It was released as a "preliminary effort to fill an interim need" (p. III). The nonspecific design described in that circular may be applicable to many environmental impact situations in which the magnitude and complexity of both the impacting project and of the environmental framework are relatively limited, but it is not well suited to a project with the geographic, ecologic, and engineering complexities of the proposed trans-Alaska pipeline system.

Environment

For the purpose of a comprehensive impact analysis, the environment must be defined and environmental baseline data must be gathered for the total human environment. The total human environment consists of both the biotic and abiotic natural physical systems and the various superimposed socioeconomic systems that are related to people and to their use of the natural physical systems.

Systematic description of the existing environment for impact analysis purposes should accomplish several related purposes: (1) It should inform the reader of the larger environmental framework and ecosystems within which the impact would occur; (2) it should afford the preparer the opportunity to look at a particular topic with the impact potential in mind and to identify sensitive components; (3) it should establish the limitations of the information framework and the degree to which the environmental factors can be quantified; and (4) it should pro-

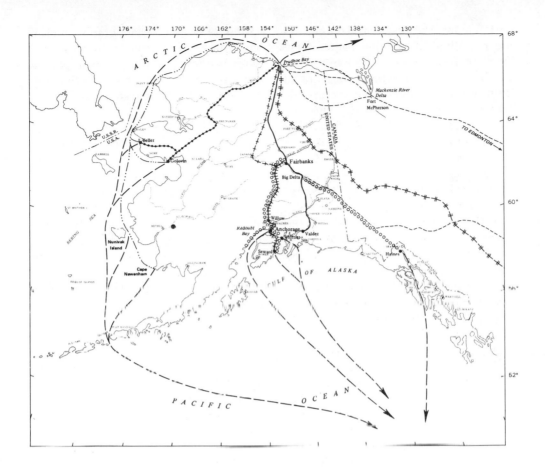

ALTERNATE ROUTES FOR TRANSPORTING
NORTH SLOPE OIL

————————	Proposed trans-Alaska pipeline
+++++++++++++++++	The Alaska Railroad
+ + + + + + +	Alaska Railroad extension
‐‖‐‖‐‖‐‖‐‖‐‖	Trans-Canada resource railroad route
‐‐‐‐‐‐‐‐‐	Trans-Canada corridor
—— — ——	Marine transportation route
ooooooooooooo	Pipeline route to southern Alaska ports
•‐•‐•‐•‐•‐•‐•→	Overland pipeline route to western Alaska ports
——— … ———	Offshore pipeline route to western Alaska ports

FIG. 3. Alaska and northwestern Canada showing alternate routes for transporting North Slope oil.

vide reference to more detailed information if it is available.

In accomplishing these purposes for the analysis of the proposed trans-Alaska pipeline, a task force of experts on different environmental topics developed and compiled descriptive baseline information for the proposed pipeline route from Prudhoe Bay to Port Valdez, the marine tanker route from

385   **Environmental Impact**

Port Valdez to west-coast ports, and the hypothetical pipeline routes from Prudhoe Bay across Alaska into Canada (Fig. 3). These experts were drawn from several Federal agencies including the U. S. Coast Guard, the Environmental Protection Agency, the National Oceanic Survey, the Environmental Data Service, the U. S. Corps of Engineers, the U. S. Geological Survey, the Bureau of Land Management, the Bureau of Out-door Recreation, the Bureau of Indian Affairs, the Bureau of Sport Fisheries and Wildlife, the National Park Service, and the National Marine Fisheries Service. Other baseline data were obtained from the Institute of Social, Economic, and Government Research at the University of Alaska, the Education Systems Resources Corporation of Arlington, Va., and several departments of the State of Alaska government.

Topics considered under natural physical systems for the environment of the proposed pipeline were physiography and geology, climate, air quality, water resources, vegetation, insects, fish and wildlife, and wilderness; topics considered under superposed socioeconomic systems were land use, population and labor force, the Alaskan Native community, composition of income and employment in Alaska, prices and costs, the oil and gas industry in Alaska, mining, fisheries, agriculture, forestry, electrical power systems, and transportation. For the proposed marine tanker transportation route, topics considered under natural physical systems were coastline and marine geology, climate and weather, physical oceanography, chemical oceanography, marine vege-

tation, biological oceanography, marine mammals, terrestrial mammals, and birds; under superposed socioeconomic systems the topics were fisheries, recreation, and marine transportation.

Impacting Project

To evaluate the impact on the environment, the analysts must know what will cause it, how it will occur, and what it will be in both its primary and secondary manifestations. To facilitate analysis the project that will cause the impact should be presented systematically in a project description which has already been reviewed for technical adequacy, agreement with specifications, and conformance with good environmental practice.

For the proposed trans-Alaska pipeline project, the Alyeska Pipeline Service Company prepared two project descriptions, one covering the proposed pipeline system and related structures and one covering the proposed tanker transport system that would connect the terminus of the pipeline with destination ports. The descriptions were reviewed by ad hoc review groups, and the results of those reviews transmitted to the impact analysts and to the company. Following receipt of those reviews, Alyeska provided supplementary project description material which was also used by the impact analysts. The State of Alaska in cooperation with the Alyeska Pipeline Service Company prepared a description of the probable physical developments that would occur in the oil-field area.

Inasmuch as no proposal describing a specific gas transportation system had been received by the Department of the Interior, it was not certain what route or type of system would eventually be proposed. Accordingly, it was necessary to evaluate the impact of four hypothetical gas-pipeline routes: (1) Prudhoe Bay along the Arctic Slope to near the Mackenzie River Delta and on to Fort McPherson and south to Edmonton, (2) Prudhoe Bay across the Brooks Range to Fort McPherson and south to Edmonton, (3) Prudhoe Bay to Port Valdez along the route proposed for the Alyeska oil-pipeline system, and (4) Prudhoe Bay to Big Delta and east to Edmonton.

Identification of Impacting Effects

Just as systematic examination and description of the environment is needed to identify sensitive environmental components, systematic examination of the impacting project is needed to identify, classify, and quantify as much as possible its impacting effects. The review and evaluation of the project description should attempt to classify those effects in terms of their predictability: some effects will be unavoidable and therefore predictable, others will be probabilistic and therefore predictable only statistically, perhaps by comparison with performance records from similar projects. The evaluation should also classify the impacting effects by their time of occurrence, by whether they are direct or indirect, and by whether they are primary, secondary, or tertiary.

The project descriptions of the proposed trans-Alaska pipeline system and associated developments were analyzed to identify and classify the impacting effects that would modify the existing environment. In all cases the unavoidable impact effects were differentiated from the threatened environmental impact effects (defined as effects with a probability of occurrence of less than 1). The effects during the construction, operation, and postoperation phases were differentiated from each other, as were direct and indirect effects. This was done first for primary impacting effects, and a similar process was carried out for secondary impacting effects; where applicable, tertiary impacting effects were also considered.

Within this complicated framework of distribution of effects were considered such primary and secondary effects as those listed subsequently.

Primary and secondary impacting effects associated with proposed trans-Alaska hot-oil pipeline, Arctic gas pipelines, and proposed tanker system

A. Primary effects associated with arctic pipelines:
1. Disturbance of ground
2. Disturbance of water (including treated effluent discharged into water)
3. Disturbance of air (including waste discharged to air and noise)
4. Disturbance of vegetation
5. Solid waste accumulation
6. Commitment of physical space to pipeline system and construction activities
7. Increased employment
8. Increased utilization of invested capital
9. Disturbance of fish and wildlife
10. Barrier effects on fish and wildlife
11. Scenery modification (including erosional effects)
12. Wilderness intrusion

13. Heat transmitted to or from the ground
14. Heat transmitted to or from water
15. Heat transmitted to or from air
16. Heat to or from vegetation
17. Moisture to air
18. Moisture to vegetation
19. Extraction of oil and gas
20. Bypassed sewage to water
21. Man-caused fires
22. Accidents that would amplify unavoidable impact effects
23. Small oil losses to the ground, water, and vegetation
24. Oil spills affecting marine waters
25. Oil spills affecting freshwater lakes and drainages
26. Oil spills affecting ground and vegetation
27. Oil spills affecting any combination of the foregoing

B. Secondary effects associated with arctic pipelines:
1. Thermokarst development
2. Physical habitat loss for wildlife
3. Restriction of wildlife movements
4. Effects on sports, subsistence, and commercial fisheries
5. Effects on recreational resources
6. Changes in population, economy, and demands on public services in various communities, including Native communities, and in Native populations and economies
7. Development of ice fog and its effect on transportation
8. Effects on mineral resource exploration

C. Primary effects associated with tanker system:
1. Treated ballast water into Port Valdez
2. Vessel frequency in Port Valdez, Prince William Sound, open ocean, Puget Sound, San Francisco Bay, southern California waters, and other ports
3. Oil spills in any of those places

D. Secondary effects associated with tanker system:
1. Effects on sports and commercial fisheries
2. Effects on recreational resources
3. Effects on population in Valdez and other communities

Impact Linkage Information

In addition to the baseline environmental and project impact effect data, it is necessary to compile data that pertain to the linkages or paths between and within various kinds of impacting effects and the various environmental topics. The linkages are of many kinds and types. They include all the information needed to actually predict an environmental impact other than the baseline environmental information and project information.

The following example drawn from the Alaska pipeline impact analysis illustrates what is meant by linkage data: Baseline information is available on the distribution of salmon and herring (at various life stages) in time and space in the Port Valdez–Valdez Arm area adjacent to Prince William Sound. Project information provided by Alyeska Pipeline Service Company indicates an estimated 2.4 to 26 barrels of oil per day would be introduced from a ballast-treatment facility into the waters of Port Valdez at a point 100 feet beneath the surface in a concentration intended not to exceed 10 parts per million. The linkage data are those needed to define the spatial and temporal paths that the effluent will take in the dynamic hydroenvironment, the changes it will cause en route in the water's chemical and physical properties, and the effects that the changed water will have on any given salmon or herring resource population at a specific time and place. Linkage data therefore in this case depend on hydrographic information that is properly part of the baseline environment description and also include knowledge of how different concentrations of different hydrocarbons in the water affect the fish population at different life stages.

In the analytical process related to the trans-Alaska pipeline proposal, the compilation of linkage data accompanied compilation of the baseline environmental data and was included both with the baseline data and with the impact analysis results. Where there were conflicting data, the analysts considered all in making the analysis and preparing the results of their analysis.

The limitations on the impact linkage data were the greatest problem encountered in the impact analysis. In many cases the complicated pathways and linkages that would exist between the project and the environment have not yet been studied to the point that predictions can be made with confidence. In such cases the analysts simply stated that rigorous prediction was not possible.

Analysts and the Analysis

Proper execution of an environmental impact analysis depends in a major way on the impartiality of the analysts. Regardless of the actual process used, including the use of predictive mathematical or simulation models, the analytical process is sensitive to the abilities and interests of those responsible for evaluating the interaction of the impacting project and the environment. At the present time the state of the art is such that the actual prediction process is likely to involve subjective steps requiring the judgment of the analyst.

Unfortunately, the educational traditions and occupational roles of scientists and technicians do not prepare them for dispassionate analysis of the type required. Resource scientists typically acquire and maintain strong conservation or development biases that reflect the customary work of their disciplines. Engineers and technicians normally adhere to strong developmental biases. The environmental impact analyst, to arrive at a prediction of impact, must discard prior conviction in favor of careful, thorough, systematic, and objective evaluation.

An example illustrates the problem. A government ornithologist responsible for research on endangered bird species and for enforcement of laws and regulations designed to protect them is given the task of objectively evaluating what will happen to those species if certain endangering transportation developments occur. He immediately faces conflict because the evaluation involves acceptance (for analytical purposes) of events which he has opposed for his entire career. An equally valid hypothetical example can be constructed using a development-oriented mining engineer faced with demonstrating sincere concern for the environment in evaluating the effect of an open-pit mine on the nesting area of an endangered species.

The impact analysis of the proposed trans-Alaska pipeline was made by resource scientists who had been given guidance regarding the analysts' proper function. As they proceeded to determine the type and extent of environmental impact that would occur in their respective fields, they were urged to be as rigorous and objective as possible and to utilize fully all available information. There undoubtedly were minor problems in the impact analysis of the proposed pipeline that arose from conflicts the analysts felt between the bias of traditional roles and the impartiality required in impact analysis.

Coordination and Communication

Coordination and communication compose the last essential component in environmental impact analysis. Coordination is needed to insure that all topics are handled in the same systematic way by all the analysts. Because of the intricate way in which an impacting project can produce reaction chains of impact effects, it is extremely important that preliminary results of analyses be communicated rapidly and fully from one analyst to another. This communication is facilitated by the awareness of all analysts that the results of others may have a direct effect on the analysis that they themselves are making. Careful attention is required to devise a system that provides this communication and that also generates the kind of information needed at the proper time for use of others involved in the analytical process.

Coordination within the impact analysis task force for the proposed trans-Alaska pipeline was accomplished by a core group of five persons including the chairman. Members of the core group worked closely in providing guidance and information to the individual analysts.

A principal effort was to insure that developments from one analysis that might bear on another were communicated rapidly; the draft material was circulated completely, insofar as possible, to all analysts, and all suggestions made by other analysts, the chairman, and the core group were considered before preparing the final draft of the impact statement. This procedure of replicate internal review results in a final report whose parts are the work of individual analysts and not the work or interpretation of the task force chairman or the core group.

Guidelines

Environmental impact analysis requires both philosophical and technical/analytical guidelines. If an analysis and the report of the analysis are to be scientifically, technically, and legally defensible, they must be prepared to the highest standards of objective scientific inquiry. Any attempts to bias the results of an environmental impact analysis cannot escape the notice of careful evaluators of the results.

Inclusion of objective environmental impact analysis information in any complex decision framework adds one more element that possibly conflicts with other elements in the framework. The decision makers of today are (or should be) prepared to evaluate such conflicting elements by applying their values in such a way as to produce a politically, socially, economically, and environmentally just decision. If an impact analysis is to provide this objective information to the decision makers, then the analysts and the analytical process should function in the traditional scientific way.

The technical and analytical guidelines established for any impact analysis should reflect these philosophical points. They should place a high degree of responsibility on the individual analyst for the assembly and compilation of pertinent environmental material and for the understanding of pertinent impacting effects. Similar responsibility exists for preparation of an objective report concerning the results of the impact analysis. Specific guidelines given to the analysts should facilitate preparation of their material in format compatible with that required by any existing laws and suitable for use in communicating with other analysts during the environmental impact analysis process.

A specific guideline worth emphasizing is that, insofar as is possible, value-judgment factors should be omitted from environmental impact analysis; when omission is impossible the specific value framework used should be specified. This is the only way of assuring that the values exercised in the decision are the values of the decision makers rather than the values of those who prepared the environmental impact statement. A related guideline of utmost importance to the impact analysis process is for the analysts to recognize fully and completely that *they* are not to decide the issue.

This discussion of environmental impact analysis would be incomplete without mention of the extremely critical relation between the impact analysis and the "decision point." Stated otherwise, what type and scope of environmental analysis can and should be made at the different "decision points" in the overall decision-making process that accompanies evolution of a project? The information available about a pipeline or any other project varies with time, from a relatively low level in the conceptual stage to a high level in the final construction and operation stages. Depending on the project, its location, the types of impacts possible, and other factors, the pertinent environmental information may or may not follow a similar path. The determination that the available environmental information is adequate in scope and quantity to constitute an element in the decision process depends mainly on the value framework of those responsible for the decision. As environmental awareness and conscience develop, certain critical elements of environmental information should become acknowledged as requirements for just decisions, in the same way that predicted cost and profit data are now universally accepted as critical factors in the analysis of economic feasibility.

In the case of the proposed trans-Alaska pipeline, policymakers in the Department of the Interior decided that the available environmental information was adequate for impact analysis. This was determined before the environmental data had been compiled, and it is therefore questionable to what extent the amount of environmental data actually available influenced the decision to proceed. In retrospect, however, the baseline environmental information available at the start of the impact analysis was approximately comparable in quantity and quality to data available on the proposed pipeline project.

In several ways the completion of the impact analysis of the proposed trans-Alaska pipeline represents a successful endeavor. Because there was no precedent for the analysis, it was necessary to design the procedures to be used, find and assemble the people to work on it, and establish the philosophical and technical guidelines that would result in a scientifically sound product. The methods used in the analysis and in the preparation of the report were rigorous and objective, the analytical group was independent of exterior influence, and the results are a milestone in the developing science of environmental impact analysis.

Main Types of Impact Predicted by The Analysis

The analysis indicated that environmental impact would result from (1) the construction, operation, and maintenance of the proposed oil-pipeline system, including the accompanying highway north of the Yukon River, and of a gas transportation system of some kind, (2) from oil field development, and (3) from the operation of the proposed marine tanker system. Because of the scale and nature of the project, the impact would occur on abiotic, biotic, and socioeconomic components of the human environment far beyond the relatively small area (940 sq. mi. out of 572,000 sq. mi. of land area) of Alaska that would be occupied by the oil-pipeline system and the oil field. The impact paths between the project itself and the affected parts of the environment would be of varying complexity and length and would involve linkage factors that are not all well known.

Of the impact effects that would occur, some, like those associated with wilderness intrusion and public access north of the Yukon River, could be considered either beneficial or adverse depending on the value framework used. Some of the effects on socioeconomic parts of the environment would be classified as beneficial by most persons. Most of the other impact effects would in some way alter the existing environment in a way that was not demonstrably beneficial and would in that sense be adverse. Such effects would occur both on natural physical systems and on the superposed socioeconomic systems.

Some impact effects are unavoidable and can be evaluated with a degree of certainty. Others could result from the occurrence of a threatened event of some kind which would impact the oil or gas transportation systems. These threatened impact effects cannot be evaluated with comparable certainty.

The principal unavoidable effects would be (1) disturbances of terrain, fish and wildlife habitat, and human environs during construction, operation, and maintenance of the oil pipeline, the highway north of the Yukon River, the oil field, and the gas pipeline that would probably follow, (2) the effects of the discharge of effluent from the tanker-ballast-treatment facility into Port Valdez and of some indeterminate amount of oil released into the ocean from tank-cleaning operations at sea, and (3) effects associated with increased human pressures of all kinds on the environment. Other unavoidable effects would be those related to increased State and Native corporation revenues, accelerated cultural change of the Native population, and extraction of the oil and gas resource.

Changes in stable terrain caused by construction and maintenance procedures could produce rapid and unexpected effects, including slope failure, modification of surface drainage, accelerated erosion and deposition, and other disturbances as a result of the permafrost thawing that would follow destruction of the natural insulating properties of the tundra. Placement of gravel pads and berms would especially affect surface drainage. The excavation of borrow materials and placement of the pipeline ditch in and near flood plains and streambeds would also cause changes in stream erosion and deposition. About 83 million cubic yards of construction material, mostly gravel, would be required for the oil pipeline. The general noise, commotion, and destruction of local habitat could cause many species of wildlife to leave an area amounting to about 60 square miles.

Socioeconomic effects during construction would include accelerated inflation, increased pressures on existing communities for accommodations and public services, and job opportunities for perhaps 25,000 persons at peak times (including multiplier effects); unemployment in Alaska, however, would continue to be relatively high.

The main disturbances during operation would be (1) thawing in permafrost leading to possible foundation instability and differential settlement, (2) some barrier effects of aboveground oil-pipeline sections on large mammal (especially caribou) migrations in the Brooks Range, Arctic Coastal Plain, and Copper River Basin areas, and similar effects of any aboveground sections of gas pipeline that would eventually be built, and (3) adverse but unquantifiable effects on the marine ecosystem of Port Valdez and perhaps Valdez Arm and Prince William Sound proper from the discharge of an estimated 2.4 to 26 barrels of oil per day from the ballast-treatment facility and on the marine ecosystem in general from discharge of an indeterminate amount of oil from tank-cleaning operations at sea. These last effects would in turn affect the fishing industry to some unquantifiable extent.

Other main operational effects would include (1) the gradual conversion of about 880 square miles of the North Slope wildlife habitat to an area with widely spaced drilling pads, roads, pipelines, and other structures, with the accompanying adverse effects on the tundra ecosystem, (2) the many diverse effects on wilderness, recreational resources (including hunting and fishing), and general land use patterns that would result from increased public access to the now relatively inaccessible region north of the Yukon River, (3) acceleration of the cultural change process that is already underway among Alaskan Natives and some adverse modification of local Native subsistence-resource base as a result of secondary effects, and (4) additional state revenues of about $300 million per year and subsequent expenditure of those revenues for public works and activities throughout Alaska. Immediately after the end of construction, unemployment would probably increase.

The main threatened environmental effects would all be related to unintentional oil loss from the pipeline, from tankers, or in the oil field. Oil losses from the pipeline could be caused by direct or indirect effects of earthquakes, destructive sea waves, slope failure caused by natural or artificial processes, thaw-plug instability (in permafrost), differential settlement of permafrost terrain, and bed scour and bank erosion at stream crossings. Any of these processes could occur at some place along the route of the proposed pipeline. Oil loss from tankers could be caused by accidents during transfer operations at Valdez and at destination ports like Puget Sound, San Francisco Bay, and Los Angeles, and by tanker or ship casualties resulting from collision, grounding, ramming, or other causes along the tanker routes.

The potential oil loss from pipeline failure cannot be evaluated because of the many variables involved, but perfect no-spill performance would be unlikely during the lifetime of the pipeline. Various models of oil loss from the tanker system indicate that an average of 1.6 to 6.0 barrels per day could be lost from the whole system during transfer operations and an average of 384 barrels per day or about 140,000 barrels per "average" year could be lost from tanker casualties. This modeled loss would occur in incidents of undetermined size at unknown intervals and at unknown locations. This is considered to be a maximum or "worst case" casualty discharge volume.

Oil spilled from the pipeline as a consequence of one of the threats mentioned could, depending on location, volume, time of year, and other factors, result in adverse effects on all the biota involved. Not all the linkages and impact paths are known, but vegetation, waterfowl, and freshwater fisheries could all be affected and then affect Native subsistence use to an unquantifiable extent.

Oil spilled in tanker casualties or transfer operations would affect the marine ecosystem to an extent that would be determined by many variable factors. The salmon and other fishery resources of Prince William Sound would be especially vulnerable to such spills. Over the long term, however, persistent low-level discharge from the ballast-treatment facility and tank-cleaning operations at sea could have a greater adverse effect than short-lived larger spills.

The probable eventual construction and maintenance of a gas pipeline would, if it were not in the oil-pipeline corridor, result in a separate corridor with many of the same effects described for the proposed oil-pipeline corridor. Those effects and those impacts on the environment would be in addition to those predicted for the proposed oil-pipeline system.

Analysis and Comparison of Alternatives

The environmental impact analysis also included consideration of various alternatives to the oil transportation system proposed. The three main types of alternatives examined were those available to the Secretary of the Interior, those concerning alternative routes and transportation systems, and those concerning energy and policy alternatives. The information regarding energy and policy alternatives was compiled and prepared by a special task force made up of representatives of various Federal agencies.

The alternatives considered available to the Secretary of the Interior were granting the permits that had been applied for, denying the permits, or deferring any action. The environmental impact implications of those different actions were examined.

Alternative routes and systems for the transportation of oil included (1) pipelines from Prudhoe Bay to other ice-free ports in southern Alaska such as Redoubt Bay, Whittier, Seward, and Haines, (2) marine transportation systems including ice-breaking and subsurface tankers, (3) both offshore and overland pipelines to terminal ports on the Bering Sea, (4) trans-Alaska–Canada pipelines to Edmonton including coastal offshore and onshore routes to the Mackenzie River Delta, routes inland across the eastern Brooks Range to Fort McPherson, and routes across the central Brooks Range (along the proposed oil-pipeline route) to Fairbanks, Big Delta, and east along Alaska Highway, (5) railroad and highway transportation modes including an Alaska railroad extension from Prudhoe Bay to a southern Alaska port and a new trans-Alaska–Canada railroad route and highway system, and (6) other oil transportation schemes including land, sea, air, and in other energy forms (fig. 3). Some of the alternate oil-pipeline routes that were considered and analyzed are, as noted previously, the same as those routes considered and analyzed for gas pipelines.

The energy and policy alternatives examined were (1) reduction in demand, (2) increased oil imports to the United States, (3) additional production from outer continental shelf and onshore areas, (4) modification of natural gas pricing, (5) nuclear stimulation of natural gas reservoirs, (6) increased use of coal as solid fuel and as source for synthetic fuels, (7) nuclear fuel, (8) synthetic sources, oil shale, tar sands, coal, (9) geothermal power, (10) hydroelectric power, and (11) exotic energy sources and improved efficiency systems.

The analysis of the environmental impact of the alternative trans-Alaska–Canada route and other routes provided information that was used for a comparison between those routes and the proposed trans-Alaska route. This comparison resulted in relative ranking of important impact effects for all the routes. The comparison process included (1) identification of combinations of routes and modes of transportation, (2) identification of specific unavoidable impact effects taking into account the abundance and vulnerability of the resources involved, the length of the route along which they would be affected, and the impact factors that would probably be involved, (3) identification of specific major threatened impact factors, and (4) ranking the different routes against each other on an arbitrary relative-magnitude scale. In the comparison no attempt was made to imply absolute magnitude or to weight any impacts or impact factors in relation to each other.

For the terrestrial environment the unavoidable environmental impacts that were compared included terrain disruption related to oil pipeline, terrain disruption related to terminal, construction material requirements, induced terrain disruption, physical space commitment, surface- and ground-water effects, air-quality effects, vegetation and habitat disruption, and effects on fisheries, on wildlife including birds, on recreation and esthetics, on wilderness, on communities, and on Native culture and subsistence. For the marine environment the unavoidable impacts considered included effects on Alaskan terminal port waters, destination port waters, fisheries, and wildlife including birds. The threatened environmental impact factors that were compared for the terrestrial environment included seismic risk to the pipeline, seismic risk to the terminal, permafrost degradation, slope failure, flooding risk, and, for the marine environment, tanker casualties and oil-transfer operations.

Synthesis of the material included in the comparison of the different routes and transportation modes resulted in several conclusions which were reported in the final environmental impact statement: (1) No single generalized oil-pipeline route appeared to be superior in all respects to any other; (2) in comparing the unavoidable impacts upon the terrestrial abiotic systems, it appeared that all the trans-Alaska routes would have less impact than the trans-Alaska–Canada routes; (3) in comparing the unavoidable impacts upon various terrestrial biotic systems, it appeared that the trans-Alaska route to a Bering Sea port would probably have the least impact and the trans-Alaska–Canada coastal route the next lowest impact; (4) in comparing the unavoidable impacts upon socioeconomic systems, it emerged that the trans-Alaska–Bering Sea port route would probably have the least impact and the trans-Alaska–

Canada coastal route would be next; (5) in comparing unavoidable impacts on the marine environment, all the trans-Alaska–Canada routes would have less impact than the trans-Alaska routes; (6) in comparing the threatened environmental impact factors for the terrestrial environment, the trans-Alaska–Canada coastal and inland routes were found to pose the least threat; and (7) comparing the threatened environmental impact factors for the marine environment, the trans-Alaska–Canada routes would be lowest because no direct marine transportation of oil would be involved.

It should be kept in mind that different levels of information were available for the proposed Alyeska Pipeline Service Company oil-pipeline system, for the alternate oil transportation systems and routes, and for gas transportation systems and routes. The difference affected the analysis and therefore all the comparisons.

The information in the environmental impact statement and in related documents released as a result of legal action after the final statement established that one of the important environmental questions involved comparison of an overland one-corridor oil- plus gas-pipeline transportation system through Alaska and Canada with a two-corridor system involving an oil pipeline through Alaska connecting to a tanker route and a gas pipeline through Alaska and Canada. Although this question was not considered in detail in the final environmental impact statement, the author believes it is important to reiterate here the pertinent facts available during the final decision process and the conclusions he drew from that information. It is emphasized that different conclusions could be (and were) drawn from the same information by other parties and persons.

Any combination of overland pipeline plus tanker systems or of tanker systems alone would impose the threat of oil pollution on the marine environment. The most important causes would be contamination resulting from intentional oil discharge from a ballast-treatment facility and from possible tank-cleaning operations at sea and from unintentional oil loss during transfer operations and from oil-tanker casualties. LNG (Liquefied Natural Gas) tanker systems would impose some threat of unintentional gas loss resulting from ship casualties. If LNG tankers were operating from the same ports as the oil tankers, they would contribute to increased vessel density and thereby indirectly to oil-tanker casualty frequency.

Overland gas- and oil-pipeline systems would impose the threat of environmental impact from rupture and unintentional loss of oil or gas. The most likely cause of rupture would be earthquakes and their attendant ground effects. The most likely impact from gas-pipeline rupture would be fire that could spread into areas adjacent to the pipeline. The most likely effect of oil-pipeline rupture would be oil lost onto the land and into lakes and streams and the various secondary effects that such loss would cause.

Any overland oil- and gas-pipeline systems would intrude the wilderness and would utilize physical space for the pipeline alinement as well as for camps, pump stations, airfields, and so forth; the accompanying roads would provide access along the pipeline corridors. Access would bring with it increased recreational opportunity and increased human pressures on the wilderness resources.

A combination of oil and gas pipelines in one corridor (not necessarily on a single or contiguous rights-of-way) would localize and restrict these effects and thus require less space, cause less wilderness intrusion, provide less access, have less effect on fish and wildlife habitat, and probably have less overall effect on the migration of large animals.

Based on these considerations, and without specifying one or another corridor or transportation mode, it is the author's opinion that one corridor containing both oil and gas pipelines would have less environmental impact and thus incur less environmental cost than would separate corridors.

Considering (1) the threat to the marine environment that any tanker system would impose, (2) the threat that zones of high earthquake frequency and magnitude would impose on pipelines, and (3) the apparent lesser environmental impact of a single corridor as compared with two corridors, it is the author's opinion that environmental impact and cost would be least for a gas- and oil-transportation system that (1) avoided the marine environment, (2) avoided earthquake zones, and (3) placed both oil and gas pipelines in one corridor. The onland trans-Alaska–Canada routes to Fort McPherson and through the Mackenzie Valley to Edmonton would meet these criteria for minimizing environmental impact and would, from that point of view, be preferable. Of the possible onland routes, the inland route across the Brooks Range between Prudhoe Bay and Fort Mc-Pherson appears on some grounds to cause the least overall adverse environmental impact.

These conclusions of the author are subject to one additional qualification. To reach market areas, any solely overland oil and gas transportation system ending near Edmonton would have to be extended beyond the geographic limits that were set for the environmental impact analysis and would thus entail additional environmental impact. The extended construction and operation would, however, be entirely in areas now traversed by oil and gas pipelines and no unusual problems would be encountered nor would any new transportation corridors be created.

As noted earlier, other conclusions are possible, and indeed the official conclusion of the U. S. Department of the Interior and of the U. S. Congress was that the environmental costs of a trans-Alaska–Canada hot-oil pipeline would be approximately the same as those of the proposed trans-Alaska hot-oil pipeline.

Conclusion

To this point this paper has been concerned mainly with the scientific and analytical aspects of environmental impact analysis and with the impact analysis of the proposed trans-Alaska oil pipeline and its alternatives. This final section examines some human and political aspects of this previously discussed material.

The scientist involved in environmental impact analysis should use the same standards and practices that he uses in scientific work. He is not only responsible for using the best avail-able information and using it in the best possible way, but also for making sure that no personal biases enter the analytical procedure. By keeping impact analysis entirely scientific, it is possible to produce information which provides an objective input to the decision process.

Nevertheless, it is likely that almost all environmental impact analysis will be conducted in situations which are influenced by external pressures. These pressures lead to the imposition of time constraints and to requirements that the analysis be made without significant amounts of additional information that would normally be acquired through extensive research. Although the involved scientist will be affected by these pressures, he will not be absolved of the responsibility of conducting the analysis in a rigorous scientific fashion.

The coordination of an environmental impact analysis and the communication of the results to the decision makers will necessarily involve scientists who are in a supervisory role. The external political and economic factors which often are a major part of the decision makers' value framework are likely to be brought to bear directly on those scientists. They therefore have the responsibilities of (1) maintaining the scientific standards of the analytical group against any external pressures and (2) communicating the results of the environmental impact analysis effectively to the decision makers. More and more scientists will have these responsibilities in the future as the world's decision makers require more and better scientific input on questions of critical environmental significance.

The way in which the United States

Government received and used the environmental information of the trans-Alaska pipeline impact analysis is a most important part of this story. The results of the analysis were provided to the decision makers in the written final environmental impact statement and in discussions between the policy makers and the core group of the task force that made the impact analysis. Clear documentation of how the results of the environmental impact analysis and other pertinent information were used in the decision is contained in a document[2] released on May 11, 1972, by the Department of the Interior. This document notes that the major considerations involved in the decision on the proposal were (1) United States energy and crude oil posture, (2) national security aspects, (3) choice of market for North Slope oil, (4) the proposal for the trans-Alaska pipeline, (5) alternative methods of transporting North Slope oil, and (6) further deferral of action. Brew and Gryc (1974) analyzed the document in relation to the information contained in the final environmental impact statement.

The decision document concludes that the environmental consequences of either a trans-Alaska or trans-Alaska–Canada oil-pipeline route are acceptable when weighed against the advantages to be derived from the construction. The Department of the Interior concluded that the Alyeska proposal was acceptable. Similar conclusions are contained in the testimony of Secretary of Interior Morton before the Joint Economic Committee of Congress (U. S. Congress, 1972).

The conflict between environmental values and resource development values that the trans-Alaska pipeline exemplifies demonstrates the continuing need for research on impact analysis and for environmental impact analysis as an essential early component in industrial and governmental decision making and also demonstrates that the scientist can and must interact with the engineer and with those in decision-making roles if the critical human goal of compatibility of environmental and resource-developmental factors is to be achieved.

Notes

[1] 42 United States Code 4332.

[2] "Applications for pipeline right-of-way and ancillary land uses, Prudhoe Bay to Valdez, Alaska," and "Application by State of Alaska for right-of-way for highway—Statement of reasons for approval." U. S. Dept. Interior, Office of Communications, Washington, D.C., May 11, 1972.

References Cited

Brew, D. A., and Gryc, George, 1974, The analysis of impact of oil and gas-pipe-line systems on the Alaskan Arctic environment: Internat. Cong. Foundation Francaise d'Etudes Nordiques "Arctic oil and gas—problems and possibilities," 5th, Le Havre, May 2–5, 1973, Proc. (in press).

Leopold, L. B., Clarke, F. E., Hanshaw, B. B., and Balsley, J. R., 1971, A procedure for evaluating environmental impact: U. S. Geol. Survey Circ. 645, 13 p.

Pryde, P. R., 1972, The quest for environmental quality in the USSR: Am. Scientist, v. 60, p. 739–745.

U. S. Congress, 1972, Natural gas regulation and the trans-Alaska pipeline—Hearings before the Joint Economic Committee, June 7, 8, 9, and 22, 1972: Washington, U. S. Govt. Printing Office.

U. S. Federal Task Force on Alaskan Oil Development, 1972, Final environmental impact statement, proposed trans-Alaska pipeline (6 volumes): U. S. Dept. Interior interagency rept.; available from the Natl. Tech. Inf. Service, U. S. Dept. Commerce, Springfield, Va., 22151, NTIS PB–206921.

Verguèse, Dominique, 1972, Europe and the environment—Cooperation a distant prospect: Science, v. 178, p. 381–383.

Wahrhaftig, Clyde, 1964, Physiographic di-

visions of Alaska: U. S. Geol. Survey Prof. Paper 482, 52 p.

Watkins, R. E., 1971, The influence of governmental regulations on the design, construction, and operation of pipelines in western Europe: Am. Petroleum Inst., 22d Ann. Pipeline Conf., Dallas, Tex., Apr. 26–28, 1971.

Supplementary Readings

(Anonymous), University of California, Santa Barbara, Santa Barbara, California, 1970, *Santa Barbara Oil Pollution, 1969*, Department of Interior, Federal Water Pollution Control Administration.

(Anonymous), *Electric Power and the Environment*—a report sponsored by the Energy Policy Staff, Office of Science and Technology, U. S. Government Printing Office, 1970, 71 pp.

Averitt, P., 1970, Coal Resources of the United States, January 1, 1970, *U. S. Geol. Survey Bull. 1322*, 24 pp.

Barnea, J., 1972, Geothermal Power, *Sci. Amer.* v. 225, n. 1, pp. 70–77.

Barnett, H., 1967, The Myth of Our Vanishing Resources, *Trans-Action*, v. 4, pp. 6–10.

Berryhill, H. L., Jr., 1974, The Worldwide Search for Petroleum Offshore—a status report for the quarter century, 1947–72, *U. S. Geol. Survey Circ. 694*, 27 pp.

Blumer, M., 1971, Scientific Aspects of the Oil Spill Problem, *Environmental Affairs*, v. 1, pp. 54–73.

Brooks, D. B., 1966, Strip Mine Reclamation and Economic Analysis, *Natural Resources Jour.*, v. 6, pp. 13–44.

Brooks, J. W., et al., 1971, Environmental Influences of Oil and Gas Development in the Arctic Slope and Beaufort Sea, *U. S. Dept. Int. Resource Publication 96*, 24 pp.

Brown, T. L., 1971, *Energy and the Environment*, C. E. Merrill, Columbus, Ohio, 141 pp.

Cameron, E. N., ed., 1973, *Mineral Position of the United States—1975–2000*, Univ. Wisconsin Press, Madison, WI., 159 pp.

Cheney, E. S., 1974, U. S. Energy Resources: Limits and Future Outlook, *Amer. Scientist*, v. 62, n. 1, pp. 14–22.

Cloud, P. E., Chr., Committee on Resources and Man, 1969, *Resources and Man: A Study and Recommendations*, W. H. Freeman and Company, San Francisco, Calif., 259 pp.

Davies, W. E., et al., 1972, West Virginia's Buffalo Creek Flood: a study of the hydrology and engineering geology, *U. S. Geol. Survey Circ. 669*, 32 pp.

Dole, H., Chr., 1974, Development of Oil Shale in the Green River Formation, Report of the Committee on Environment and Public Planning, *The Geologist*, supplement to v. 9, n. 4, 8 pp.

Duncan, D. C., and Swanson, V. E., 1965, Organic-Rich Shale of the United States and World Land Areas, *U. S. Geol. Survey Circ. 523*, 30 pp.

Emmett, J. L., et al., 1974, Fusion Power by Laser Implosion, *Sci. Amer.*, v. 230, n. 6, pp. 24–37.

Flawn, P. T., 1966, *Mineral Resources—Geology, Engineering, Economics, Politics, Law*, Rand McNally & Co., New York, N.Y., 406 pp.

Flawn, P. T., 1970, *Environmental Geology: Conservation, Land-Use Planning and Resource Management*, (chap. 4), Harper & Row, New York, 313 pp.

Freeman, S. D., et al., 1974, *A Time to Choose: America's Energy Future*, Ballinger, Cambridge, MA.

Gough, W. C., and Eastland, B. J., 1971, The Prospects of Fusion Power, *Sci. Amer.*, v. 224, n. 2, pp. 56–64.

Gregory, D. P., 1973, The Hydrogen Economy, *Sci. Amer.*, v. 228, n. 1, pp. 13–21.

Hammond, A., et al., 1973, *Energy and the Future*, Amer. Assoc. Advancement Sci., Washington, D. C., 184 pp.

Hill, A., and McCloskey, M., 1971, Mineral King: Wilderness versus Mass Recreation in the Sierra, in *Patient Earth* by J.

Harte and R. H. Socolow, Holt, Rinehart, Winston, pp. 165–80.

Hubbert, M. King, 1971, The Energy Resources of the Earth, *Sci. Amer.*, v. 224, n. 3, pp. 61–70.

Katz, Milton, 1971, Decision-Making in the Production of Power, *Sci. Amer.*, v. 225, n. 3, pp. 191–200.

Legget, R. F., 1968, Consequences of Man's Alteration of Natural Systems, *Texas Quarterly*, v. 11, n. 2, pp. 24–35.

Legget, R. F., 1972, Duisburg Harbour Lowered by Coal Mining, *Canadian Geotechnical Journal*, v. 9, n. 4, pp. 374–83.

Leopold, L. B., Clarke, F. E., Hanshaw, B. B., and Balsley, J. R., 1971, A Procedure for Evaluating Environmental Impact, *U. S. Geol. Survey. Circ. 645*, 13 pp.

Lewis, R. S., and Spinrad, B., eds., 1972, *The Energy Crises*, A Science and Public Affairs Book, Chicago, Educational Foundation for Nuclear Science, 148 pp.

Lovering, T. S., 1968, Non-Fuel Mineral Resources in the Next Century, *Texas Quarterly*, v. 11, n. 2, pp. 127–47.

McDivitt, J. F., and Manners, G., 1974, *Minerals and Men*, Johns Hopkins University Press, Baltimore, Md., 192 pp.

McKelvey, B. E., Tracey, J. I., Jr., Stoertz, G. E., and Vedder, J. G., 1969, Subsea Mineral Resources and Problems Related to Their Development, *U. S. Geol. Survey Circ. 619*, 26 pp.

Meiners, R. G., 1964, Strip Mining Legislation, *Natural Resources Jour.*, v. 3, pp. 442–69.

Murdoch, W. W., ed., 1971, *Environment-Resources, Pollution and Society*, Sinauer Assoc. Inc. Stamford, Conn., 440 pp.

Park, C. F., and Freeman, M. C., 1968, *Affluence in Jeopardy: Minerals & the Political Economy*, Freeman-Cooper, San Francisco, CA., 468 pp.

Park, C. F., and Freeman, M. C., 1975, *Earthbound, Minerals, Energy and Man's Future*, Freeman, Cooper and Co., San Francisco, CA., 279 pp.

Pecora, W. T., 1968, Searching Out Resource Limits, *Texas Quarterly*, v. 11, n. 2, pp. 148–54.

Perry, H., 1974, The Gasification of Coal, *Sci. Amer.*, v. 230, n. 3, pp. 19–25.

Potter, J., 1973, *Disaster by Oil, Oil Spills: Why They Happen, What They Do, How We Can End Them*, MacMillan, 301 pp.

Price, C. A., 1971, The Helium Conservation Program of the Department of the Interior, in *Patient Earth*, J. Harte and R. H. Socolow, pp. 70–83.

Risser, H. E., 1973, Energy Supply Problems for the 1970's and Beyond, *Env. Geol. Notes No. 62*, Ill. State Geol. Survey, Urbana, Ill., 12 pp.

Risser, H. E., 1973, The U. S. Energy Dilemma: the gap between today's requirements and tomorrow's potential, *Env. Geol. Notes No. 64*, Ill. State Geol. Survey, Urbana, Ill. 64 pp.

Risser, H. E., and Major, R. L., 1967, Urban Expansion—an opportunity and a challenge to industrial mineral producers, *Env. Geol. Notes No. 15*, Ill. State Geological Survey, 19 pp.

Rose, D. J., 1974, Energy Policy in the U. S., *Sci. Amer.*, v. 230, n. 1, pp. 20–29.

Ruedisili, L. and Firebaugh, M., 1975, *Perspectives on Energy*, Oxford University Press, N.Y., 475 pp.

Schlee, J., 1968, Sand and Gravel on the Continental Shelf off the Northeastern United States, *U. S. Geol. Survey Circ. 602*, 9 pp.

Starr, Chauncey, 1971, Energy and Power, *Sci. Amer.*, v. 255, n. 3, pp. 36–49.

Steinhart, C. E., and Steinhart, J. S., 1972, *Blowout: a case study of the Santa Barbara oil spill*, Duxbury Press, 138 pp.

Swanson, V. E., Chu, 1974, Environmental Impact of Conversion from Gas or Oil to Coal for Fuel, Report of the Committee on Environment and Public Planning, *The Geologist*, supplement to v. 9, n. 4, 8 pp.

Theobold, P. K., et al., 1972, Energy Resources of the United States, *U. S. Geol. Survey Circ. 650*, 27 pp.

Walsh, J., 1965, Strip Mining: Kentucky Begins to Close the Reclamation Gap, *Science*, v. 150, pp. 36–39.

Warren, K., 1973, *Mineral Resources*, John Wiley and Sons, 272 pp.

Weeden, R. B., and Klein, D. R., 1971, Wildlife and Oil: A Survey of Critical Issues in Alaska, *The Polar Record*, v. 15, n. 97, pp. 479–94.

Weinberg, A. M., 1972, Social Institutions and Nuclear Energy, *Science*, v. 177, pp. 27–34.

Wenk, Edward, Jr., 1969, The Physical Resources of the Ocean, *Sci. Amer.*, v. 221, n. 3, pp. 166–67.

White, Donald, 1965, Geothermal Energy, *U. S. Geol. Survey Circ. 519*, 17 pp.

Yerkes, R. F., Wagner, H. C., and Yenne, K. A., 1969, Petroleum Development in the Region of the Santa Barbara Channel Region, California, *U. S. Geol. Survey Prof. Paper 679-B*, pp. 13–27.

Films

Outlook for the Future

The Atom Underground (U. S. Atomic Energy Commission, 1969: 20 min.)

The Bitter and the Sweet (U. S. Atomic Energy Commission, 1971: 30 min.)

The Bottom of the Oil Barrel (Time-Life Films and BBC-TV, 40 min.)

Energy Crisis (Journal Films, 1972: 13 min.)

Energy for the Future (Encyclopedia Britannica, 17 min.)

The Minerals Challenge (U. S. Bureau of Mines, 1972: 27 min.)

Nuclear Power and the Environment (U. S. Atomic Energy Commission, 1969: 14 min.)

Nuclear Power in the United States (U. S. Atomic Energy Commission, 1971: 28 min.)

Sunbeam Solutions (Time-Life Films and BBC-TV, 38 min.)

Environmental Impact

Alaskan Pipe Dream (Time-Life Films and BBC-TV, 31 min.)

How Safe are America's Atomic Reactors? (Impact Films)

Oil Spill!! Patterns in Pollution (Association-Sterling Films, 17 min.)

The Ravaged Land (John Wiley and Sons, 1971: 15 min.)

Santa Barbara—Everybodys Mistake (National Educational Television, 1971: 30 min.)

Torrey Canyon (Time-Life Films, 1970: 26 min.)

IV. Water Resources

"All the Water in the world is all the water there is."

Water is our most vital resource. Questions concerning its quality, availability, use as a facility for recreation, or diluent for wastes represent critical problems in many areas. A. M. Piper (Reading 32) includes estimates and projections—to the year 2000—of the water supplies and demands of the major drainage basins of the United States. Geographic variations in hydrology are great and frequently match neither present nor prospective patterns of water use. Some basins obviously face a gloomy future, while others have supplies which exceed projected demands. Piper stresses the need for more sophisticated data and prudent and rational management of the nation's water resources if we are to avoid disruptions to the economic and social development of many areas. Time in which to accomplish efficient management is all too short, and no single course of action is seen as a panacea for all water-supply problems.

The outlook for urban water supplies is explored in Reading 33. It appears that, although water resources have been generally sufficient to meet the needs of most cities, shortages result from overtaxed collection, storage, and distribution systems as population growth outstrips development. "Crisis planning," unilateral developments, and apathy have characterized previous approaches to the problem of shortages. Future development of water resources must consider regional demands and resources. Co-ordinated long-range planning among hydrologists, economists, engineers, and local governments is necessary.

C. L. McGuinness explores the advantages and disadvantages of the development of ground water in Reading 34. The ubiquitous occurrence of ground water has enabled Man to occupy large areas that otherwise could not have been settled. But there are many problems associated with the full development of ground water. McGuinness cites the High Plains of Texas as an example of the economic implications of a dramatic contrast between ground water withdrawal and replenishment. The authors of Reading 35 document the response of the hydrologic system on Long Island, New York, to population trends and attendant changes in the use and disposal of water.

Water *quality* is another crucial aspect of the management of water resources. Man has played a well known role in the pollution and purification of ground water and surface water, but bedrock geology also influences water quality. Bedrock geology determines the trace elements which enter the water and are available for plant and animal uptake. The variety of regional diseases which can be related to the

Photo on page 404. Courtesy of John Ward.

geochemistry of trace elements available in local water supplies is explored by Jean Spencer in Reading 36. Spencer also notes that "normal municipal water treatment hardly alters the percentages of the various trace elements in the water distributed to consumers."

On December 17, 1974, President Ford signed into law the Safe Drinking Water Act (Public Law 95523) which is intended to provide for better monitoring, improved treatment, and contamination prevention. The hydrologic implications of waste disposal are presented in Part V.

32 Has the United States Enough Water?

A. M. Piper

Perspective

The destiny of the Nation's water supply is currently a topic of frequent concern in the popular and quasi-technical press. Overly pessimistic writers imply or all but conclude that, within the foreseeable future, much of the United States will have dissipated its available water by consuming it or by grossly polluting it and that consequently industrial expansion must cease at one place or another, irrigated agriculture will wane or even vanish, and social evolution will retrograde. On the other hand, overly optimistic writers foresee no such stringencies within the next several centuries. In considerable part, such implications have come about by treating extreme situations as though they were average or usual, by projecting trends that are not wholly relevant or by assuming that a given volume of water can be "used" only once (the pessimistic view) or can be reused an infinite number of times (the optimistic view).

With an appreciation that he may be oversimplifying, the writer ventures that the United States can be assured of sufficient water of acceptable quality for essential needs within the early foreseeable future, provided that it (1) informs itself, much more searchingly than it has thus far, in preparation for

Piper, A. M., 1965, "Has the United States Enough Water?" U. S. Geol. Survey Water Supply Paper 1797, 27 pp. Figures 1-3 are from River of Life, U. S. Department of the Interior Conservation Yearbook Series, vol. 6. Mr. Piper is on the staff of the United States Geological Survey.

the decisions that can lead to prudent and rational management of all its natural water supplies; (2) is not deluded into expecting a simple panacea for water-supply stringencies that are emerging; (3) finds courage for compromise among potentially competitive uses for water; and (4) accepts and can absorb a considerable cost for new water-management works, of which a substantial part will need be bold in scale and novel in purpose.

Although this general appraisal is derived for the conterminous United States in particular, it is equally valid for Hawaii and Alaska. Components of this generalization now will be examined at some length.

Elements of Water Supply

Nearly all the fresh water naturally available to man is derived from precipitation. Over the United States, excluding Alaska and Hawaii, this ultimate source averages about 1.4 mgd per mi^2 (million gallons per day per square mile), or 30 inches a year. Of this, about 1.0 mgd per mi^2 (21½ inches a year) returns to the atmosphere as water vapor—by evaporation from water surfaces and wetlands and by evapotranspiration of vegetation (native and cultivated). The remainder, about 0.4 mgd per mi^2 (8½ inches a year), sustains the flow of streams and contributes to ground storage (Langbein, 1949). This remainder constitutes the water potentially available for withdrawal to serve man's uses; it is equivalent to constant flow of 1,200,000 mgd (million gallons per day) or 1,900,000 cfs (cubic feet per second).

In this paper, quantities of water are stated usually in millions of gallons per day. Common equivalents of this unit are shown in the following table.

Precipitation

Even in the "normal" year, precipitation on the conterminous United States ranges from more than 4 mgd per mi^2 (85 in. per year) locally in the Pacific Northwest to less than 0.2 mgd per mi^2 (4 in. per year) locally in the Pacific Southwest. (Fig. 1.) Between wet and dry years the range is even greater.

Precipitation is used immediately and directly by man to the extent that it sustains the soil water on which nonirrigated crop plants and native vegetation depend. On the basis of this relation to "use," three precipitation provinces can be discriminated:

1. Over about the eastern half of the United States—that is, over the Atlantic and Gulf Coastal Plains, Appalachian Highlands, Interior Low Plateaus, Interior Highlands, and most of the Central Lowland—average precipitation ranges about from 1 to 3 mgd per mi^2 (20–60 in. per year), changes only gradually from one place to another, and commonly reaches a seasonal maximum at or near the height of the growing season. Ordinarily it is ample for crop plants and for marketable native vegetation. In this province especially, to a certain extent man can manipulate soil-water storage to his advantage by land treatments and by water-retarding structures.

2. Over the western fringe of the Central Lowland and westward across the Great Plains, average precipitation diminishes from about 1 to about 0.5 mgd per mi^2 (20–10 in. per year). The seasonal peak commonly occurs early in the growing season. In most of the province, only water-thrifty crops such as wheat can be grown without irrigation, even in the wetter years.

3. Over the Rocky Mountains, Columbia and Colorado Plateaus, Basin and Range province, Sierra-Cascade Mountains, and most of the Pacific Border, average precipitation ranges

Hydraulic equivalents [Equivalent values are on the same horizontal line]

Million gallons per day (mgd)	Million gallons per year (mgy)	Gallons per minute (gpm)	Cubic feet per second (cfs)	Acre-feet per day (afd)	Acre-feet per year (afy)	Inches on 1 square mile per year (in per mi^2)
1.0	365.0	694.44	1.5472	3.0689	1,120.15	21.002
.0027397	1.0	1.9026	.0042390	.0084079	3.0689	.057541
.0014400	.52560	1.0	.0022280	.0044192	1.6129	.030244
.64632	235.91	448.83	1.0	1.9835	723.97	13.574
.32585	118.96	226.29	.50417	1.0	365.00	6.8433
.00089274	.32585	.61996	.0013813	.0027397	1.0	.018750
.047607	17.377	33.065	.073668	.14612	53.333	1.0

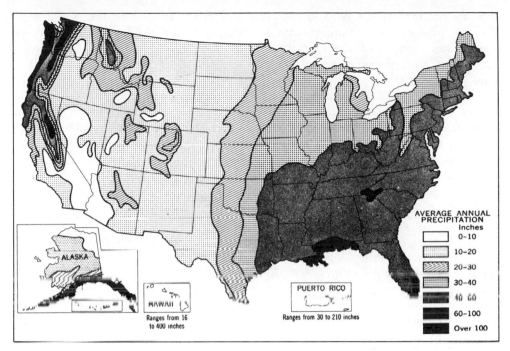

FIG. 1. Average annual precipitation in the U. S.

widely, from about 0.2 to about 4 mgd per mi^2 (4–85 or more in. per year), and the greater amounts fall on the higher parts of the rugged terrain. Seasonal maximum comes in midwinter; summer precipitation is nominal. Variation from month to month and from year to year is extreme. Here, softwood timber thrives on the better watered uplands and affords a profitable crop from lands not suited to most agricultural pursuits. On the lowlands, only the hardiest of forage and grain crops can be grown widely without irrigation. Here the geographic distribution of precipitation and that of arable land are mismatched. In this province, therefore, except in a very local sense, the overriding purpose of management must be so to conserve water that it

can be used at a remote place and a later time, in relation to place and time of precipitation.

It is owing to these and other disparities in precipitation, and in the water supplies which precipitation generates, that the necessities of water-supply management differ so greatly from one region to another.

Evaporation and Transpiration

In the sense that precipitation constitutes gross water supply, evaporation from open-water surfaces—from lakes, reservoirs, streams, ponds, and bogs—and transpiration through vegetation constitute a preemptive, and heavy, tax by Nature. Man can do relatively little to diminish the tax; he gains some advantage from it by substituting marketable vegetation for native species that are not marketable. Man increases the tax whenever he enlarges natural open-water areas or creates such areas artificially and whenever he irrigates land that naturally is "dry." Evapotranspiration that is, the sum of evaporation from wetted surfaces and of transpiration by vegetation—averages about 1.1 mgd per mi^2 (22 in. per year), nearly 75 percent of the precipitation; however, it varies greatly from one place to another.

Potential evaporation from open-water surface ranges about from 1 to nearly 5 mgd per mi^2 (20–90 in. per year). On the Atlantic Slope and Atlantic Coastal Plain, it ranges from 20 inches per year in northern Maine to 54 inches in southern Florida; over the Central Lowland and Great Plains, from 24 to nearly 40 inches per year on the north and 50 to 80 inches across Texas; over the Rocky Mountains, Intermountain Plateaus, and the Pacific Mountains, from 20 inches in northwestern Washington to a maximum of about 90 inches in Death Valley and the lower basin of the Colorado River. Details have been published by the U. S. Weather Bureau (1959).

At such rates, the aggregate loss from open-water surfaces is substantial. Meyers (1962) estimates that it averages 21,100 mgd (23,641,000 acre-feet per year) from the 17 Western States, distributed as follows: From 51 principal reservoirs and regulated lakes, 8,090 mgd or 38 percent of the aggregate; from 600-odd other principal reservoirs and regulated lakes, 2,890 mgd; from other lakes exceeding 500 acres in area, 1,770 mgd; from principal streams and canals, 3,950 mgd; from small ponds and reservoirs, 3,010 mgd;

and from small streams, 1,400 mgd. Per year, this loss from principal reservoirs, regulated lakes, small reservoirs, and ponds amounts to 8.1 percent of the total usable storage capacity.

Potential evapotranspiration—that which would occur under optimum soil-water conditions and optimum vegetal cover—generally is somewhat less than potential evaporation. As estimated by Thornthwaite (1952), potential evapotranspiration ranges about from 18 inches per year in the Rocky Mountain province to 60 inches per year in Death Valley and the lower basin of the Colorado River.

The crucial aspect of evapotranspiration is that it may, and over extensive areas commonly does, exceed precipitation. In oversimplified principle, if potential evapotranspiration exceeds precipitation, the potential moisture requirement of vegetation is not satisfied in full, and water is not available for overland flow to streams. In other words, the climate is arid. Conversely, if evapotranspiration is less than precipitation, runoff is generated perennially. These generalizations are acceptable only as first approximations. Actually, some runoff may occur even though concurrent potential evapotranspiration is not satisfied—perennially or intermittently in the arid regions and intermittently in the humid regions. This situation can occur if: (1) Some runoff is generated by effluent ground-water seepage and (2) if the rate of precipitation exceeds infiltration capacity of the soil so that, however great evapotranspiration may be, part of the precipitation is rejected at the land surface and becomes immediate overland flow.

Figure 2 shows mean potential for perennial yield of withdrawable water —that is, average precipitation minus average potential evapotranspiration. Notable is the relatively large area of water deficiency in the western regions—specifically, the area in which potential evaporation and potential transpiration exceed precipitation and which ordinarily does not contribute perennially to water yield. This area encompasses the westernmost part of the Central Lowland and virtually all the Great Plains; much of the Rocky Mountains, the Columbia and Colorado Plateaus, and the Basin and Range province; and a considerable part of the Pacific Border province in California. Conversely, essentially all the eastern half of the 48 States is an area of potential water surplus which contributes to perennial water yield; there, evaporation and transpiration are exceeded by precipitation.

In the western region of general water deficiency, areas of potential water surplus exist only over the higher and mountainous uplands and over intermountain lowlands northward from San Francisco Bay. These discontinuous and relatively inextensive areas generate nearly all the perennial streamflow in the West.

Being based on average yearly precipitation and evapotranspiration, the areal pattern of Fig. 2 is itself an average. The areas of surplus or deficiency enlarge and diminish reciprocally from one season to another and from a wet year to a dry year. However, the major feature of the pattern persists—a waterplentiful or humid East and a waterdeficient or arid West.

FIG. 2. Water supply and water deficiency in the U. S.

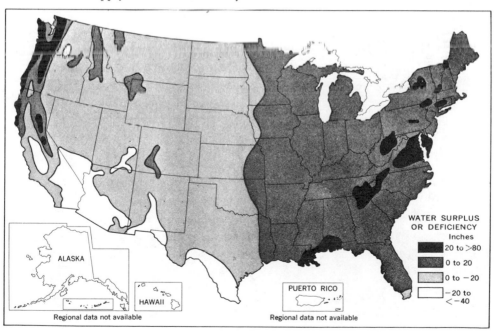

Streamflow

The preemptive tax of evaporation and transpiration having been satisfied, the remainder of the gross water supply (precipitation) sustains the sources from which man can withdraw fresh water for his uses. These sources are the streams, natural lakes, manmade reservoirs, and bodies of ground water. Over any long term of years, neither lakes, reservoirs, nor ground-water bodies increase the fresh-water supply potentially available in the streams, except to the extent that they may be unwatered permanently (a ground-water body thus unwatered is said to be "mined"). Thus, for the purposes of this report, it suffices to measure use and prospective demand of water against streamflow alone.

On the average, aggregate flow of the streams is about 8½ inches a year

or 0.4 mgd per mi^2. This flow is five-fold greater than present withdrawals of water for use and twentyfold greater than consumption in use. However, the comparison is meaningless because both use and supply of water (in this instance, streamflow) are neither uniform from place to place nor constant in time. Indeed, the variability of streamflow is a basic obstacle to full use of all streams; some principal facets of this obstacle are summarized below and are shown by Fig. 3.

Different regions yield greatly different quantities of streamflow: A minimum from the arid Southwest and a maximum from the Pacific Northwest. Among individual stream basins, maximum yield (per unit of area) is roughly 200-fold greater than the minimum. In contrast, in the humid East, maximum yield is less than tenfold greater than

FIG. 3. Average annual run-off in the U. S.

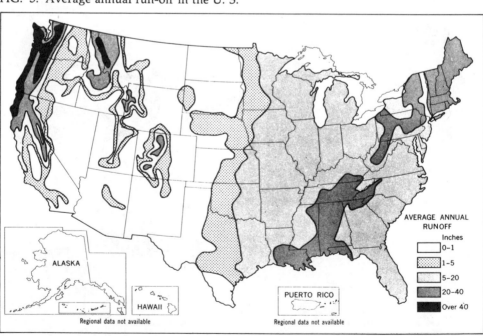

AVERAGE ANNUAL
RUNOFF

Inches

0-1

1-5

5-20

20-40

Over 40

ALASKA

HAWAII

Regional data not available

PUERTO RICO

Regional data not available

the minimum. There are other contrasts of interest: 66 percent of the streamflow occurs east of the Mississippi River (tributaries of the Mississippi from the west excluded); the relatively small Pacific Northwest, which includes the Columbia River and other Pacific slope streams in Washington and Oregon, yields 13 percent of the streamflow from all the 48 conterminous States, and 72 percent of that from all the Pacific slope; this yield of Pacific Northwest streams is 1.1-fold greater than that of all tributaries to the Mississippi from the west and 3.1-fold greater than that of western Gulf streams. These geographic variations in stream yield match neither present nor prospective patterns of water use.

As has been implied, most streamflow in the West is generated on uplands and but little is generated on lowlands. Yet man's occupancy is almost exclusively in the lowlands. Here, then, the water supply must be managed at places remote from points of use.

In virtually all streams, flow varies from one year to another, from one season to another, and even from one hour to another. This variability is of paramount consequence to use of the stream by man because, unless flows are regulated artificially, assured withdrawal can be no more than natural minimum flow and, if the variability is large, a major part of the total flow may pass unused. An example of a river having minimum variability is the St. Lawrence River, whose flow is regulated naturally by the very large storage capacity of the Great Lakes. On this stream, maximum yearly flow is only 1.5-fold greater than the minimum; maximum monthly flow, 2.0-fold greater. In contrast, in numerous principal streams, maximum yearly flow is fivefold or more greater than the minimum, and maximum monthly flow is tenfold or more greater. Flows so variable occur in streams both large and small. They are notably common in streams of the Great Plains province, the western part of the Gulf Coastal Plain, and the southern part of the Basin and Range and Pacific Border provinces.

Variation of flow with the seasons may or may not be a disadvantage—a disadvantage when greatest flow and greatest use occur in different seasons but an advantage when they fall in the same season.

The extreme events of fluctuating streamflow are floods and droughts. Both recur at irregular intervals of time. Floods are of short duration, but commonly their volume is much greater than can be contained practically by reservoirs. In this situation, flood management aims at passing the excess volume downstream with a minimum of damage but, also, with little or no use. The water so passed and unavailable for use may be a considerable part of total streamflow. Floods are especially troublesome in Atlantic slope basins northward from the Chesapeake Bay; in the Ohio River, Missouri River, and lower main-stem segments of the Mississippi River basin; and also in the Columbia River basin and other parts of the Pacific slope.

By definition, drought is an event more prolonged or notably more severe than the ordinary dry season. Thus, even though it may occur infrequently, commonly it induces the greatest withdrawals of water and so limits the assured capability of water-supply systems. Drought has been most notable over parts of the Great Plains, Basin and Range, and southernmost Pacific Border provinces.

To the extent that his requirements exceed natural minimum streamflow, man must suppress these geographic and temporal variations of water yield. The principal and all but exclusive means to this end is detaining streamflow in reservoirs during intervals of surplus flow and releasing the stored water during intervals of deficient natural flow. (See Fig. 4.) Even so, however, all the natural streamflow never can be captured and withdrawn, because reservoirs inevitably increase the open-water area from which evaporation preempts its toll. In other words, the ultimate water-supply capability of a stream basin is something less than its average natural yield. (See also Langbein, 1959.) The difference between supply capability and average natural yield increases as the natural variability in streamflow increases, especially as the range widens between maximum and minimum yearly flows. (Present investigations indicate that, if a fatty-alcohol film can be maintained on the surface of a reservoir, evaporation will diminish moderately but will not be eliminated.)

Reservoirs cost money, and ordinarily the cost per unit volume of water they control increases as successive reservoirs are constructed in a given stream basin. Thus, limits of acceptable cost may also determine the extent to which man will suppress the natural variations of streamflow—that is, will "regulate" the flow—to increase usable water supply. At this economic limit, an appreciable fraction of streamflow ordinarily will remain unused in the wetter years or seasons.

The limit of practicable streamflow regulation to increase dependable yield of water depends upon a complex of conditions unique to each stream basin. For the purposes of this report, it will be assumed that the greatest regulated yield that can be sustained continuously would, under conditions of natural flow, have been exceeded 50 percent of the time—in other words, that the limit of continuous regulated yield is about equal to median natural flow, regionwide. For no major stream of the United States has the water yield yet been so fully regulated; in one basin, that of the Colorado River, works now authorized or under construction will increase aggregate regulating capability almost to the assumed limit.

With water yield at the assumed perennial limit, from one-fourth to three-fourths of natural streamflow may be considered perennially usable; nationwide, somewhat more than half. This degree of perennial yield probably will not be reached on all major streams, but on some it probably can be exceeded feasibly. For clarity, it is emphasized that the preceding discussion of streamflow regulation is wholly about achieving maximum perennial water yield. It should not be overlooked that regulation may be desirable for a purpose other than increased yield or may be justifiable for a purpose that sacrifices potential yield in some measure.

On most major streams, the assumed limit of continuous regulated yield cannot be achieved at a cost that currently is acceptable. However, acceptable cost of managing and regulating water sources will increase, inevitably

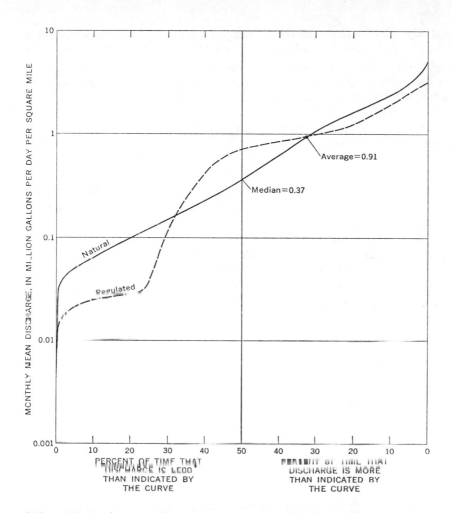

FIG. 4. Natural and regulated streamflow, Merced River at Exchequer, Calif. Usable capacity of the reservoir here is about 29 percent of the average yearly runoff. The streamflow is regulated for generating hydroelectric power in one plant of a wide-flung system; the particular plant operates intermittently to provide "peaking capacity."

Under regulation, both low flows and high flows of the natural regimen are diminished (60 percent of the time), but medium-range flows are increased (40 percent of the time). The regulated flow has been near the natural average 20 percent of the time and greater than the natural median about 60 percent of the time.

If this reservoir were operated to meet a continuous, steady demand (rather than an intermittent, fluctuating demand), the controlled flows would have been substantially less.

and substantially. The writer believes that eventually construction of additional storage for greater regulated yield will be limited principally by major engineering complexities, competition with other potential uses for the land of reservoir sites, or competition with other objectives of stream management.

Water-Supply Elements by Regions

The preceding discussion emphasizes the considerable variation of each water-supply element from one region to another. More meaningful values for the several elements can be derived according to water-resource regions of which each is relatively homogeneous in respect to water yield. Figure 5 shows the water-resource regions that have been adopted for this report; in the main they are coextensive with the

regions adopted by the Select Committee on National Water Resources. Tables 1, 2, and 3 summarize water-supply components by these regions.

Present and Prospective Use of Water

The Overall Situation

As of 1960, the aggregate of all water withdrawals in the 48 conterminous States was about 270,000 mgd, of which about 68,000 mgd was consumed by evaporation in the course of use (MacKichan and Kammerer, 1961). By categories of use, these amounts were distributed as shown in Table 4.

Thus, as of 1960, total consumption of water in the course of use (68,000 mgd) was about 25 percent of the aggregate withdrawn from all water sources (270,000 mgd) but somewhat

FIG. 5. Water-supply and water-use regions of the conterminous United States. Each of the regions outlined either is dominated by a single major source of water or encompasses several sources that are similar in magnitude and variability.

Table 1 Approximate mean water-supply elements, by regions

Region	Area (mi²) (1)	Precipitation (mgd per mi²) (2)	Potential evapotranspiration (mgd per mi²) (3)	Natural depletion (mgd per mi²) (4)	Natural runoff mgd per mi² (5)	Natural runoff mgd (6)	Depleted runoff, as of 1960 Average (mgd) (7)	Median mgd (8)	Per cent (9)
New England	62,500	1.93	1.15	0.84	1.09	67,900	67,200	39,400	59
Delaware-Hudson	36,500	1.97	1.53	1.06	.91	33,300	31,700	18,700	59
Chesapeake	67,600	1.97	1.56	1.20	.77	52,000	51,600	31,700	61
South Atlantic-Eastern Gulf	274,300	2.55	2.07	1.77	.78	214,700	212,000	126,000	59
Eastern Great Lakes	48,300	1.71	1.28	.86	.85	40,900	40,300	19,400	48
Western Great Lakes	89,500	1.37	1.33	.89	.48	43,200	42,500	31,700	75
Ohio	143,400	2.02	1.52	1.24	.78	111,400	110,500	45,900	41
Cumberland-Tennessee	60,300	2.42	1.64	1.42	1.00	60,500	59,800	36,200	60
Upper Mississippi	184,800	1.45	1.55	1.11	.34	63,500	62,400	40,700	65
Lower Mississippi	61,900	2.48	2.13	1.67	.81	50,200	48,800	21,300	44
Upper Missouri-Hudson Bay	509,100	.81	1.86	.75	.058	29,700	18,500	9,050	49
Lower Missouri	54,100	1.67	1.88	1.24	.43	23,100	23,100	5,820	25
Upper Arkansas-Red	171,500	1.07	2.84	.98	.088	15,100	11,000	4,520	41
Lower Arkansas-Red-White	112,600	2.12	2.19	1.42	.70	78,600	76,900	20,000	26
Western Gulf-Rio Grande-Pecos	331,100	1.15	2.93	.98	.17	56,300	46,100	14,200	31
Colorado	255,300	.52	2.67	.48	.044	11,300	3,750	1,680	54
Great Basin	191,800	.48	2.20	.44	.042	8,100	3,750	2,130	57
Pacific Northwest	250,100	1.15	1.39	.54	.61	152,600	143,000	75,600	53
Central and South Pacific	122,000	1.11	2.24	.60	.51	62,500	48,200	15,700	33
Total or mean	3,026,700	1.33	2.05	.94	.39	1,175,600	1,100,500	559,700	51

Column:

1.—After U. S. Dept. of Agriculture (1960) but adjusted to the value given by Douglas (1932, p. 248) for aggregate area of land and water except "that part of the water area of the Great Lakes, the Atlantic Ocean, the Gulf of Mexico, the Pacific Ocean, and the Strait of Juan de Fuca that is under the jurisdiction of the United States."

2 and 3.—After U. S. Weather Bureau (1959, 1960), adjusted to distribute apparent discrepancies among columns 2 to 5.

4.—Column 2 minus column 5.

5 and 6.—Depleted runoff as of 1960 (after Oltman and others, 1960) plus water consumed in use as of 1960 (after MacKichan and Kammerer, 1961) plus depletion by reservoirs (from Table 2). "On-site" consumption of water here is excluded. Such consumption—that is, by land-treatment procedures and structures, by swamps and wetlands, and by fish hatcheries—has been estimated by Eliasberg (1960). As of 1960, however, this consumption is very largely from naturally wet areas and is therefore more a component of Nature's preemptive "take" of water than an effect of activities by man. In other words, current "on-site" use is not chargeable as a depletion or current runoff.

Here and elsewhere in this report, runoff and water yield credited to each of the several regions is that which originates in the particular region. Ten of the regions are parts of two major river basins, those of the St. Lawrence River and the Mississippi River. Thus, runoff credited to the western Great Lakes and eastern Great Lakes cannot be accounted to show main-stem flow, because yield from the part of the basin in Canada is excluded. Main-stem flow of the Mississippi River may be determined by accumulating yields from the eight regions involved, in downstream sequence.

7 and 8.—After Oltman and others (1960).

9.—Per cent of average

Table 2 Reservoirs and regulated lakes, existing and under construction as of 1954

Region	Usable capacity		Surface area (acres)	Effective depth (feet)	Yearly net depletion		
	mg (1)	Days (2)	(3)	(4)	Feet (5)	mg (6)	Per cent (7)
New England	2,898,000	43	840,000	10.6	0.55	149,000	5
Delaware-Hudson	992,400	30	903,000	3.4	.92	270,000	27
Chesapeake	309,100	6	50,500	18.8	.64	10,600	3
South Atlantic-Eastern Gulf	5,334,000	25	1,500,000	10.9	.54	262,000	5
Eastern Great Lakes	543,300	13	261,000	6.4	.71	60,000	11
Western Great Lakes	419,500	10	305,000	4.2	.78	77,400	18
Ohio	1,875,000	17	226,000	25.5	.47	34,900	2
Cumberland-Tennessee	6,957,000	115	895,000	23.9	.42	122,000	2
Upper Mississippi	1,138,000	18	808,000	4.3	.82	216,000	19
Lower Mississippi	1,455,000	29	208,000	21.4	.79	53,800	4
Upper Missouri-Hudson Bay	24,720,000	832	2,140,000	35.4	1.94	1,353,000	5
Lower Missouri	406,000	17	59,700	20.9	1.13	21,900	5
Upper Arkansas-Red	2,472,000	164	317,000	23.9	3.24	335,000	14
Lower Arkansas-Red-White	7,275,000	93	699,000	31.9	1.34	304,000	4
Western Gulf-Rio Grande-Pecos	4,667,000	82	483,000	29.7	3.42	538,000	12
Colorado	11,326,000	1,002	306,000	113.6	3.84	383,000	3
Great Basin	1,659,000	205	398,000	12.8	3.08	400,000	24
Pacific Northwest	9,082,000	60	982,000	28.4	1.50	480,000	5
Central and South Pacific	5,512,000	88	436,000	38.8	2.87	408,000	7
Total or mean	89,040,000	76	11,820,000	23.1	1.42	5,479,000	6

Column:

1.—Summarized from Thomas and Harbeck (1956); includes those reservoirs and regulated lakes whose capacity is 5,000 acre-feet or more, generally without flashboards.

2.—Column 1 divided by column 6 of Table 1. For any single reservoir, this capacity ratio indicates the time required to impound or release a volume of water equal to the usable capacity; it assumes a rate equal to that of mean runoff. Among the 19 regions, only in the upper Missouri-Hudson Bay and Colorado does usable capacity exceed average yearly runoff. In 9 of the 19 regions, usable capacity is less than 10 per cent of average yearly runoff—that is, only a minor part of the water supply is provided by reservoirs. These nine regions span 32 per cent of the Nation's area—all the Atlantic slope and eastern Gulf areas, except New England, and also the Ohio, Upper Mississippi, Lower Mississippi, and Lower Missouri regions.

3.—Summarized from Thomas and Harbeck (1956).

4.—Column 1 divided by column 3, each converted to appropriate units. Other factors being the same, the greater the effective depth, the smaller the proportion of stored water that evaporates.

5.—Potential evaporation minus the depletion that would have occurred naturally had the reservoir not existed. This column is derived from Table 1—specifically, column 3 minus column 4 of that table, or column 3 minus column 2 plus column 5, converted to yearly depth in feet.

less than 6 percent of aggregate stream-flow (1,200,000 mgd). Among the several categories of use, consumption was about 2.3 percent of the withdrawal for self-supplied industry, 17 percent of that for public supplies, 55 percent of that for irrigation, and 78 percent of the small withdrawal for rural uses.

Like streamflow, these uses of water fluctuate. Use from public supplies may increase severalfold during summer, largely for watering grounds and for air conditioning; obviously this seasonal increase is greatest in the warmer and drier regions. As a whole, industrial use is relatively constant throughout the year, although locally and for certain industries—such as food processing—the water requirement is seasonal and fluctuates widely. Use for irrigation is almost wholly within the growing season and is virtually nil in 6 to 9 months of the year.

Seasonal fluctuation in water use is much greater in the West, where most of the irrigation use occurs, and is of small consequence in the industrial East. In both the West and the East, however, a large part of the aggregate water use is focused in relatively small but intensively developed areas—the metropolitan centers, major industrial complexes, and principal irrigated tracts.

Thus, water use varies both in time and in place, and commonly its varia-tions do not match those of the water sources. Water demand commonly is large when yield of the water sources is small, and large demands commonly arise in areas remote from large water sources. This mismatch is an all-pervading problem of water-supply management.

Withdrawal use of water in the United States increases; at the current rate of increase, aggregate use would double in 25 to 30 years. Even greater rates of increase have been projected by Wollman (1960, p. 6, 79–121), who has estimated water withdrawn and water consumed as of 1980 and 2000. Table 5 summarizes his estimates.

The estimates of water withdrawn and water consumed as of 1980 and 2000 are based on medium-level projections of population, economic activity, and water use (Wollman, 1960, p. 5–6). They are accepted by the writer as credible first approximations for comparison with estimates of assured supply. From 1960 to 2000, they embody increases per decade of about 17 percent in population; 19 percent in water withdrawn for public supplies, but 12 percent in water consumed by such use; 47 percent in water withdrawn but 66 percent in water consumed by industry; and 14 percent in water withdrawn but 20 percent in water consumed in irrigation and rural uses.

Certain trends implied by these pro-

6.—Column 3 multiplied by column 5, and the product converted to million gallons a day.
7.—Per cent of usable capacity—that is, column 6 divided by column 1. As has been stated, the greater the effective depth, the less the percentage depletion, other factors being the same. Note in particular that percentage depletion is greatest in the Delaware-Hudson region even though potential evaporation is comparatively small, presumably because effective depth is least. In contrast, percentage depletion is small in the Colorado region even though potential evaporation is large; in this region, effective depth is severalfold greater than in any other of the regions.

Table 3 Reservoirs required to assure flow equal to present median flow

Region	Additional capacity (mg) (1)	Total capacity mg (2)	Total capacity Days (3)	Surface area (acres) (4)	Total yearly net depletion mg (5)	Total yearly net depletion Per cent (6)
New England	8,500,000	11,400,000	170	1,700,000	305,000	3
Delaware-Hudson	3,600,000	4,600,000	140	950,000	285,000	6
Chesapeake	6,500,000	6,800,000	130	1,400,000	292,000	4
South Atlantic-Eastern Gulf	25,400,000	30,700,000	140	3,800,000	669,000	2
Eastern Great Lakes	3,600,000	4,100,000	100	840,000	194,000	5
Western Great Lakes	6,500,000	6,900,000	160	1,400,000	356,000	5
Ohio	9,400,000	11,300,000	100	1,400,000	214,000	2
Cumberland-Tennessee	4,100,000	11,000,000	180	1,400,000	192,000	2
Upper Mississippi	8,500,000	9,600,000	150	2,000,000	534,000	6
Lower Mississippi	4,600,000	6,100,000	120	750,000	193,000	3
Upper Missouri-Hudson Bay	1,900,000	26,600,000	900	2,300,000	1,450,000	5
Lower Missouri	1,700,000	2,100,000	90	320,000	118,000	6
Upper Arkansas-Red	1,100,000	3,600,000	240	440,000	465,000	13
Lower Arkansas-Red-White	7,200,000	14,500,000	180	1,500,000	655,000	5
Western Gulf-Rio Grande-Pecos	3,900,000	8,600,000	150	880,000	981,000	11
Colorado	390,000	11,700,000	1,040	360,000	450,000	4
Great Basin	320,000	2,000,000	250	410,000	411,000	20
Pacific Northwest	15,300,000	24,400,000	160	2,100,000	1,030,000	4
Central and South Pacific	3,600,000	9,100,000	150	700,000	655,000	7
Total or mean	116,000,000	205,000,000	170	24,650,000	9,449,000	5

Column:

1.—After Oltman and others (1960).

2.—Column 1 plus column 1 of Table 2.

3.—To nearest multiple of 10 days. See explanation of Table 2, column 2. Note that, to assure flow equal to present median flow, usable storage capacity must exceed 25 per cent of average natural yearly runoff in all regions, and exceed 50 per cent in 6 of the 19 regions. In two of the latter six—the Upper Missouri-Hudson Bay and Colorado regions—required usable capacity would be 2.5-fold and 2.8-fold greater than average yearly runoff, respectively. Thus, in dry years, most of the streams in most of the regions would need to be regulated continuously to assure flow not less than present median flow. As has been stated elsewhere natural median flow approaches the maximum perennial water supply that can be developed practicably under ordinary environmental and economic circumstances.

4.—Order-of-magnitude estimate only. The estimates take into account the expectation that future reservoirs will have greater effective depth and smaller percentage depletion.

5.—Column 4 multiplied by column 5 of Table 2, and the product converted to million gallons a day.

6.—Column 5 divided by column 2.

Table 4 Water withdrawn and water consumed, 1960 [After MacKichan and Kammerer (1961), modified]

Use	Withdrawn		Consumed	
	mgd	Per cent	mgd	Per cent
Rural	3,600	1.3	2,800	4.1
Public supplies	21,000	7.8	3,500	5.2
Self-supplied industry	140,000	52	3,200	4.7
Irrigation:				
Conveyance losses	23,000	8.5	[1] 7,500	11
Delivered to farms	83,000	31	[2] 51,000	75
Totals (rounded)	[3] 270,000	100	68,000	100

[1] Commonly it is assumed that all the water lost in conveyance by irrigation canals returns ultimately to the streams. However, transpiration by canal-bank vegetation is appreciable in some areas. The writer postulates that, from this cause and others, about one-third of the gross conveyance loss is removed permanently from the stream system.
[2] Water consumed by nonirrigated crops is even greater in amount but is taken from soil water which, in the context of this paper, is not withdrawable.
[3] Includes 32,000 mgd of saline water.

Table 5 Estimated water withdrawn and water consumed, 1980 and 2000 [After Wollman (1960); in millions of gallons per day]

Use	Withdrawn		Consumed	
	1980	2000	1980	2000
Municipal (public supplies)	29,000	42,000	3,500	5,500
Mining, manufacturing, and				
steam-electric (industry)	363,000	662,000	11,000	24,000
Agriculture (rural and irrigation)	167,000	184,000	104,000	126,000
"On site"[1]			71,000	97,000
Totals	559,000	888,000	190,000	253,000

[1] Water consumed by "on-site" uses comprises the effects of land treatment and structures, enlarged swamps and wetlands, and fish hatcheries. In large part, water consumed by such uses is intercepted before it has entered a perennial stream; in other words, streamflow is depleted even though water may not be withdrawn in the usual sense.

Owing to past and present depletion of this kind, accepted values of streamflow as measured and published by the U. S. Geological Survey presumably are smaller than natural flows. Thus, present on-site consumption is not charged as an encumbrance against measured water supply. However, the estimates of on-site consumption as of 1980 and 2000 are for expected increases in such consumption; these must be charged against available supply as now measured.

jections are noteworthy. Per-capita withdrawal for public supplies would increase slightly but per-capita consumption would diminish 15 per cent over the four decades. Such improvement in efficiency of water use is possible and desirable, but it is neither assured nor, in the writer's judgment, easily realized. Per capita withdrawal by industry would increase 2.6-fold,

Table 6 Projected demand and supply of water as of the year 2000, by types of demand and by regions [In millions of gallons per day. After Eliasberg (1960), except as indicated in notes]

Region	Water consumed in off-channel use				Water consumed on site				Dominant in-channel flow		Maximum projected commitment (11)	Potential assured supply (12)	Supply-to-commitment ratio (13)
	Municipalities (1)	Industry (2)	Agriculture (3)	Subtotal (4)	Land treatment (5)	Wetlands (6)	Reservoir depletion (7)	Subtotal (8)	Use (9)	Amount (10)			
New England	200	1,100	300	1,600	500	400	840	1,740	Hp	26,800	30,100	40,000	1.3
Delaware–Hudson	500	1,000	500	2,000	−200	1,300	780	1,880	Fs	23,400	27,300	20,300	.74
Chesapeake	200	600	1,200	2,000	100	900	800	1,800	Fs	33,000	36,800	32,000	.87
South Atlantic-Eastern Gulf	300	3,400	8,100	11,800	900	19,900	1,830	22,630	Hp	67,000	101,400	128,700	1.3
Eastern Great Lakes	400	800	600	1,800	0	1,100	530	1,630	Hp	101,800	105,200	20,000	.19
Western Great Lakes	500	2,500	1,200	4,200	100	3,600	980	4,680	Wd	51,200	60,100	32,400	.54
Ohio	300	2,100	1,800	4,200	500	200	590	1,290	Hp	35,700	41,200	46,800	1.1
Cumberland-Tennessee	(1)	500	400	900	400	100	530	1,030	Hp	47,300	49,200	36,900	.75
Upper Mississippi	300	700	4,600	5,600	600	4,900	1,460	6,960	Nv	48,500	61,100	41,900	.69
Lower Mississippi	100	500	3,100	3,700	300	9,500	530	10,330	Nv	97,100	111,100	22,800	.21
Upper Missouri-Hudson Bay	200	300	20,500	21,000	1,500	17,600	3,970	23,070	Hp	25,000	69,100	20,300	.29
Lower Missouri	(1)	100	1,400	1,500	200	100	320	620	Nv	22,600	24,700	6,100	.25

Region	1	2	3	4	5	6	7	8	9	10	11	12	13
Upper Arkansas-Red	100	900	4,600	5,600	300	1,100	1,270	2,670	Wd	4,600	12,900	8,600	.67
Lower Arkansas-Red-White	(1)	700	3,000	3,700	700	2,000	1,790	4,490	Hp	29,500	37,700	21,700	.58
Western Gulf-Rio Grande-Pecos	500	5,200	14,800	20,500	600	14,300	2,690	17,590	Wd	18,400	56,500	24,900	.44
Colorado	100	1,100	13,200	14,400	100	2,600	1,230	3,930	Fs	15,900	34,200	9,800	.29
Great Basin	100	300	6,100	6,500	( )	5,300	1,130	6,430	Fs	4,000	16,900	6,500	.38
Pacific Northwest	500	900	13,600	15,000	200	1,200	2,820	4,220	Hp	133,900	153,100	85,200	.56
Central and South Pacific	1,200	1,600	27,500	30,300	100	3,800	1,790	5,690	Wd	36,000	72,000	29,800	.41
Total	5,500	24,300	126,500	156,300	6,900	89,900	25,830	122,680	—	821,700	1,100,600	634,700	.58

[1] Less than 50 mgd.

Column:

2.—Manufacturing, 20,900 mgd over all the United States; steam-electric power, 2,800 mgd; mining, 600 mgd.

3.—Chiefly irrigation.

5.—Water that naturally would reach a stream, but that is dissipated by land-treatment practices or structures. Quantities represent increases above those of 1954 and so are chargeable as depletions of runoff. (See note to Table 1, columns 5 and 6.) The negative quantity for the Delaware-Hudson region implies an increase in water yield owing to land-treatment measures.

6.—Water dissipated from manmade wetlands and by fish hatcheries, both constructed after 1954; accordingly, the quantities are chargeable as future depletions of streamflow.

7.—From Table 3, column 5.

9.—Only the largest of potential in-channel water requirements is listed on the assumption that in-channel flow will be sufficient for all if the largest is satisfied. This assumption may or may not be valid. Types of in-channel requirements include: Hp, hydroelectric power; Fs, sport fishing habitat; Wd, waste dilution; Nv, navigation.

11.—Sum of columns 4, 8, and 10. Such summation is valid as a first approximation, provided the column 10 quantity is severalfold greater than the sum of those in columns 4 and 8. If the column 10 component is not severalfold greater, the column 11 summation may be smaller than the flow required to satisfy both off-channel and in-channel uses.

12.—Potential assured supply is assumed equal to median natural flow. As an approximation of this median, the column 12 quantity is equal to column 8 from Table 1, plus water consumed in use as of 1960 (after MacKichan and Kammerer, 1961), plus depletion by reservoirs as of 1954 (Table 2, column 6). The note to Table 1, columns 5 and 6, also applies. In the Mississippi River basin, assured main-stem supply can be approximated by accumulating supplies of the several regions involved, less water consumed off-channel and on-site, in downstream sequence.

13.—Column 12 divided by column 11.

per capita consumption 7.5-fold. These per capita increases seem inordinately large, although industry likely will consume an increasing proportion of its water. Irrigation withdrawals would increase 1.7-fold, and irrigation consumption 2.1-fold. These projections imply that the efficiency of irrigation use will decrease, whereas it should increase under technologic improvements.

According to Wollman's projections, by the year 2000 aggregate withdrawal would be no more than 74 percent of present streamflow; consumption would be 29 percent of withdrawals and 21 percent of streamflow. Of course, these percentages do not indicate that all the projected demands for water can be satisfied without depletion of any stream. Any such inference would be false on several points, including: (1) It would presume that either water or persons and their uses of water can be transported freely and completely in order to balance total water supply against total demand. Transportation so free is not practical. (2) It would presume that all the water yield that is surplus during the wetter seasons and years could be impounded and held for use during the drier seasons and years. As has been shown, the perennially dependable supply is substantially less than the theoretical average supply in all stream basins. (3) It presumes that all water withdrawn but not consumed remains usable for any purpose. Actually, any use of water depreciates the quality of the fraction not consumed; with repeated reuse, progressive depreciation in quality eventually makes some fraction of the supply unusable for many purposes. (4) It does not take into account necessary on-site and in-channel uses—for hydroelectric power, diluting and transporting fluid wastes, navigation, depletion by reservoirs, habitat for fish and waterfowl, and recreation —which, in the aggregate, may be severalfold greater than withdrawal uses.

Demand and Supply by Regions

Tables 6 and 7 present a reasonably realistic comparison of the projected demand and supply of water as of the year 2000, by types of use and by water-resources regions. (See Fig. 5.) Implicit in this comparison are certain generalizations and assumptions, as follows:

1. Assured water supply is equal to median natural streamflow; for all the 48 conterminous States this median would be about 54 percent of total streamflow.

   Wollman (1960) and Eliasberg (1960) derive "maximum low flow(s) that can be sustained" which, for all the 48 conterminous States, aggregate 92 percent of total natural runoff and for certain regions are as much as 98 percent. In the writer's judgment, sustained yields so great would be virtually impossible to achieve regionwide.

2. The potential yield of ground-water bodies can be realized only at the expense of an equal diminution in streamflow, over the long haul. In other words, ground-water sources do not increase the aggregate potential supply of water. This fact would become literally true if total potential yield were being put to use.

3. As derived by Wollman (1960) and Eliasberg (1960) and accepted for this report, projected demands for water are not scaled to supplies.

Rather, each potential use or commitment of water is projected independently, as though it is preemptive; it is also projected according to estimated nationwide or regionwide requirement for the products derivable from the use. This basis leads to certain incongruously large projections, to which further reference will be made.

4. Biological oxygen demand (BOD) of municipal sewage and of industrial waste will be largely removed by treatment, and effluents from treatment plants will be diluted sufficiently to maintain dissolved oxygen at regionwide averages of 4 milligrams per liter (This amount of dissolved oxygen is about the minimum for a satisfactory fish and wildlife habitat.) In the projections by Wollman and Eliasberg, the degree of waste treatment is either that which involves the least cost for treatment plant plus water for dilution or, in certain water-deficient regions, that which requires the least dilution. By these criteria, percentage BOD removal from sewage would range between 80 and 97.5 percent among the several regions; that from industrial wastes, between 50 and 97.5 percent. This degree of BOD removal is far greater than is now achieved regionwide. The greater of these BOD removals may not be achievable at acceptable costs; if not, requirements of water for dilution would be increased commensurately.

5. (a) Water allocated for in-channel uses—for hydroelectric power, waste dilution, navigation, habitat for fish and wildlife, and recreation —also will satisfy all withdrawal uses. (b) The water allocated to the largest in-channel use will suffice for all such uses. (c) In consequence, maximum net commitment against potential supply is the sum of water consumed in off-channel and on-site uses plus that allocated to the largest, or dominant, in-channel use. Strictly, this latter generalization is not valid; as a first approximation, however, it is acceptable.

Table 8 and Fig. 6 summarize the preceding comparison.

Briefly, potential assured supply exceeds projected commitment in three regions: New England, South Atlantic-Eastern Gulf, and Ohio. Only in these three is it expectable that water requirements for the economic and social evolution projected by Wollman and Eliasberg could be realized easily. In the remaining 16 regions, projected commitments exceed assured supply as here defined.

In 7 of the 16 regions of seeming water deficiency, assured supply is greater than projected consumption (off-channel plus on-site) and total streamflow equals or exceeds total commitment. In these seven regions, therefore, most water requirements for the projected economic and social evolution can be realized if virtually complete regulation of streamflow proves feasible. The seven regions are the Delaware-Hudson, Chesapeake, Cumberland-Tennessee, Upper Mississippi, Upper Arkansas-Red, Lower Arkansas-Red-White, and Pacific Northwest.

In the remaining nine regions, total commitment exceeds total streamflow. Projected consumption exceeds assured supply in five of these nine, and exceeds total streamflow in three. Consequently, in these nine regions it is ex-

Table 7 Summary of projected demand and supply of water as of the year 2000, by regions [In million gallons a day per square mile]

Region	Demand						Supply	
	Consumed in use (1)	Consumed on site[1] (2)	Depletion by reservoirs (3)	Subtotal (4)	In-channel commitment (5)	Total (6)	Potentially assured (7)	Total streamflow (8)
New England	0.0256	0.0144	0.0134	0.0534	0.429	0.482	0.640	1.086
Delaware-Hudson	.0548	.0301	.0214	.1063	.641	.748	.556	.912
Chesapeake	.0296	.0148	.0118	.0562	.488	.544	.473	.769
South Atlantic-Eastern Gulf	.0430	.0758	.0067	.1255	.244	.370	.469	.783
Eastern Great Lakes	.0372	.0228	.0110	.0710	2.107	2.178	.414	.847
Western Great Lakes	.0469	.0413	.0109	.0992	.572	.671	.362	.483
Ohio	.0293	.0049	.0041	.0383	.249	.287	.326	.777
Cumberland-Tennessee	.0149	.0083	.0088	.0320	.784	.816	.612	1.003
Upper Mississippi	.0303	.0298	.0079	.0680	.262	.330	.227	.344
Lower Mississippi	.0598	.1584	.0085	.2267	1.569	1.795	.368	.811
Upper Missouri-Hudson Bay	.0412	.0375	.0078	.0865	.0491	.1356	.0399	.0583
Lower Missouri	.0277	.0055	.0059	.0391	.417	.456	.113	.433
Upper Arkansas-Red	.0326	.0082	.0074	.0482	.0268	.0750	.0501	.0880
Lower Arkansas-Red-White	.0328	.0240	.0159	.0727	.262	.335	.193	.698
Western Gulf-Rio Grande-Pecos	.0619	.0450	.0081	.1150	.0556	.1706	.0752	.172
Colorado	.0564	.0106	.0048	.0718	.0623	.1341	.0384	.0443
Great Basin	.0339	.0276	.0059	.0674	.0209	.0883	.0339	.0446
Pacific Northwest	.0600	.0056	.0113	.0768	.535	.612	.341	.610
Central and South Pacific	.2483	.0320	.0147	.2950	.295	.590	.244	.511
Mean	.0516	.0320	.0086	.0922	.271	.363	.210	.388

[1] Land-treatment measures and wetlands only.

Table 8 Projected water demand as of the year 2000 [In percent of potential assured supply]

Region	Consumed off channel	Consumed on site	Dominant in-channel flow	Total
New England	4	4	67	75
Delaware-Hudson	10	9	115	134
Chesapeake	6	6	103	115
South Atlantic-Eastern Gulf	9	18	52	79
Eastern Great Lakes	9	8	509	526
Western Great Lakes	13	14	158	185
Ohio	9	3	76	88
Cumberland-Tennessee	2	3	128	133
Upper Mississippi	13	17	116	146
Lower Mississippi	16	45	426	487
Upper Missouri-Hudson Bay	103	114	123	340
Lower Missouri	25	10	370	405
Upper Arkansas-Red	65	31	53	150
Lower Arkansas-Red-White	17	21	136	174
Western Gulf-Rio Grande-Pecos	82	71	74	227
Colorado	147	40	162	349
Great Basin	100	99	62	260
Pacific Northwest	18	5	157	180
Central and South Pacific	102	19	121	242
Mean	25	19	129	173

pectable that, even with streamflow regulated to the utmost, economic and social evolution will be handicapped moderately to severely. The nine regions in this category are the Eastern Great Lakes, Western Great Lakes, Lower Mississippi, Upper Missouri-Hudson Bay, Lower Missouri, Western Gulf-Rio Grande-Pecos, Colorado, Great Basin, and Central and South Pacific. Together, the nine span 55 percent of the 48 conterminous States.

Courses of Action

Obviously, pure water is becoming a critical commodity whose abundance is about to set an upper limit of economic evolution in a few parts of the Nation and inevitably will do so rather widely within half a century or less. Prudence requires that the Nation learn to manage its water supplies boldly, imaginatively, and with utmost efficiency. Time in which to develop such competence is all too short.

As the basis for water-management decisions that seem imminently necessary, the Nation has only a bare minimum of relevant information. Water facts of all kinds, in ever wider scope and ever greater detail, will be prerequisite to sound decisions. So also will plans for alternative schemes for comprehensive water control and management and for corresponding schedules of cost—in dollars, in economic opportunities created on the one hand and foreclosed on the other, and in "second-generation" problems that can be anticipated. Here the all-embracing plan, immutable for all time, rises as

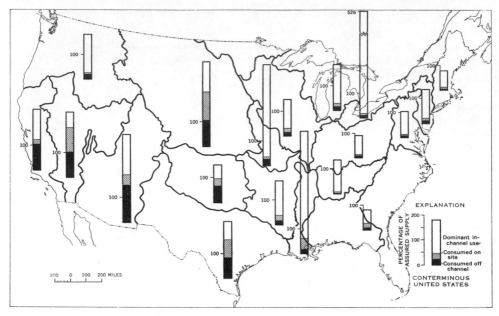

FIG. 6. Projected water demand as of the year 2000. The bar diagrams show, for the water-resources regions, water demand, as projected by Wollman (1960) and Eliasburg (1960), expressed as percentage of assured supply. Thus, in a crude way, the height of bar is proportional to expectable difficulty in satisfying the projected demand.

an enticing will-o'-the-wisp. In actuality, the process of information gathering, decision, and action will never end. Each such cycle inevitably will create the seed of an ensuing cycle, and successive cycles will deal with progressively more complex situations and will be less susceptible to "crash" procedures.

No single course of action can be a panacea for all water-supply ills. Thus, the objectives of water-supply management must be varied from one situation to another.

As one example, consider the case for desalting ocean water or other brines as a "new" source of fresh water, potentially in extremely large volume. Several effective techniques for desalting are established and are being refined. On a pilot-plant scale, the cost approaches but has not yet reached the target of $1 per thousand gallons of fresh-water product. It is reasonable to expect that cost at point of production ultimately can be diminished to and below the target. However, considering the quantity of energy required for separating water from dissolved salts and, further, considering costs at which energy reasonably can be produced and applied to the separation, the writer considers it highly unlikely that the overall cost of desalting ocean water can, in the foreseeable future, be diminished by an order of magnitude below the target—that is, to as little as 10 cents per thousand gallons. Actual use of desalted ocean water will involve an additional increment of cost—

that of pumping from the desalting plant to the place of use against the head necessary for effective distribution.

In contrast, average costs in the United States in 1954 were about 18½ cents per thousand gallons for pure, fresh water from municipal systems, commonly as little as one-tenth that amount for industrial and irrigation water, and about 8 cents for treating sewage. From one place to another, the approximate range in local costs was from 50 to 200 percent of the average. These costs include operation, maintenance, and amortization of capital investment. Those for municipally supplied water and for treating sewage were derived by the writer from data by the U. S. Public Health Service (1960 and 1960a).

Thus, at current and prospective costs as cited above, fresh water obtained by desalting oceanic and other brines seems most unlikely to be universally advantageous. Desalting can, and probably will, compete economically as a source for municipal supply in areas along the immediate coast where water from streams and other conventional sources is unobtainable in adequate volume and where the salts that are removed can be returned to the ocean at little cost. Probably it will compete also in deriving usable supplies from inland brackish waters; at inland sites, however, disposal of the removed salts may be difficult and costly. Elsewhere, "rules of the market place" dictate that the principal course of future action be concerted management of the conventional surface-water and ground-water sources, including those now submarginal in cost.

Much water must be reclaimed from industrial and municipal wastes and reused several times. For such reclaiming, desalting may prove feasible (Oltman and others, 1960). Repeated reuse will become necessary throughout the East if projected consuming uses are to be satisfied from projected in-channel flows. Reuse diminishes withdrawal at the source but does not diminish consumption. Thus, reuse will not modify the demand-supply comparisons of Table 6.

Over most of the West, except only the Pacific Northwest, projected commitment—that is, off-channel and on-site consumption plus dominant in-channel flow—exceeds assured supply. There, the obvious alternatives are either less consumption per unit of product or diminished production. There a considerable part of the commitment, even a major part, is consumption in agriculture, largely in irrigation. There, substantially diminished consumption implies improved efficiency in irrigation. Such improvement must be sought diligently; it will not easily be realized in a large measure.

Of on-site consumption, 68 percent of that projected for improving fish-and-wildlife habitat occurs in four regions—South Atlantic-Eastern Gulf, Lower Mississippi, Upper Missouri-Hudson Bay, and Western Gulf-Rio Grande-Pecos. (See Table 6, column 6.) Only in the first of these regions can this particular projection be realized concurrently with other projected demands, each in full. In the remaining three regions, the respective projections are 42 percent, 87 percent, and 57 percent of potential assured supply (as defined by the writer). In these three, and to a smaller degree in five additional regions—Western Great

Lakes, Upper Mississippi, Lower Arkansas-Red-White, Colorado, and Great Basin—compromise seems ultimately inevitable between an ideal habitat for fish and wildlife on the one hand and the several potentially competing demands for water on the other hand. In this connection, it is emphasized that all the habitat here considered, and covered under Table 6, is that proposed to be created by man.

By the year 2000, estimated reservoir depletion will be only 4 percent of potential assured supply (Table 6, column 7). However, it would exceed 10 percent in five regions—Upper Missouri-Hudson Bay, Upper Arkansas-Red, Western Gulf-Rio Grande-Pecos, Colorado, and Great Basin. Particularly in these five, measures that substantially diminish evaporation would ease prospective deficiencies in water supply. Although results have been disappointing thus far, attempts to discover effective measures and materials should continue as long as there is hope for success.

Depletion by evaporation from water surfaces can, in principle, be diminished also to the extent that streamflow can be regulated in natural underground reservoirs in lieu of man-made reservoirs on the land surface. Capability of underground reservoirs for water-supply management seems potentially large. Field studies to evaluate such capability and to establish procedures are urged.

The potential for salvaging part of the water transpired by noneconomic native vegetation is in a sense analogous to suppression of evaporation from reservoirs, but differs in that a "new" water-supply component would be created. The quantity of this water is large; in the 17 Western States about 20,000 mgd is transpired by phreatophytes, plants withdrawing water that otherwise would reach a stream (Oltman and others, 1960). Methods for eradicating phreatophytes at acceptable cost are under test, principally by the U. S. Army Corps of Engineers and the U. S. Bureau of Reclamation. Field evaluation of the eradication in terms of increased water supply is pending.

A principal concern of the future will be with in-channel flows and, in particular, with flow for diluting wastes. It appears implicit in the projections by Wollman (1960) and by Reid (1960) that nearly all wastes would be commingled with all the available water and that, with certain pretreatment of the wastes, dilution could be sufficient that the mixture would be usable for substantially all purposes. According to the projections in Table 6, however, water for dilution would be insufficient in most regions—definitely in Western Great Lakes, Upper Arkansas-Red, Western Gulf-Rio Grande-Pecos, and Central and South Pacific—and also to a smaller and variable degree in all other regions except the three in which assured supply exceeds projected commitment.

Means must be found to diminish the dilution requirement. Relief will not lie in more inclusive pretreatment of wastes, because the projections already assume a very large percentage removal of BOD. Measures alternative to dilution, that can be considered where and when need arises, include the following:

1. In metropolitan areas, separate distribution of high-purity water for intake by humans and animals, and

of lower purity water for industrial purposes, fire protection, sanitary flushing, and the like. Native stream and ground waters would be conserved for the high-purity system; reclaimed waters could go to the lower purity system. Currently, somewhat less than 10 percent of all water used off-channel is in municipal-supply systems that require high purity.

2. Partial or complete removal of solutes from waste fluids, in effect diluting the waste sufficiently for general reuse. Practical means for so reclaiming waste waters should be sought with some sense of urgency.

3. Waste canals or pipelines, separated from stream channels and leading to off-channel disposal areas where feasible. Part of or all the wastes might be concentrated in some degree prior to disposal or they might even be desiccated.

4. Chemical disintegration or separate disposal, or both, of industrial wastes that do not oxidize under conventional treatment. These would include toxins and "exotic" wastes from the chemical and nuclear-energy industries, wastes that presumably will be produced in ever larger quantities.

Measures such as those just outlined would be simplified if sources of the most troublesome wastes were segregated by area, preferably downbasin. Zoning of this sort has been recommended to delineate and conserve opportunities for outdoor recreation (U. S. Geological Survey, 1962). It might best be realized through the local and State police powers, coupled with conservancy commissions of local, statewide, or even regionwide jurisdiction. Re-

gionwide jurisdictions would preforce rest on interstate negotiations. Whatever its purpose, however, zoning is distasteful; probably, therefore, it will prove to be a last-resort tool in managing water supplies.

Commonly the dominant in-channel projection is for a purpose other than dilution of wastes—for fish and wildfowl habitat, for hydroelectric power, or for navigation. Locally, it might be for recreation. Commonly, also, it exceeds assured supply—for example, the projections for hydroelectric power in the Eastern Great Lakes and Pacific Northwest regions, those for navigation in the Mississippi and Missouri River basins, and that for fish and wildfowl habitat in the Colorado River basin. (See Table 6.) These and other in-channel projections cannot be realized in full. Inevitably, realistic compromises must be reached among off-channel consumption, on-site consumption, and the several in-channel requirements and opportunities.

All these matters concern management of water supply in the engineering sense. Beyond them are related unresolved questions in the field of administrative management. What would be the most appropriate ultimate assignment of responsibility and authority over such unlike matters as inventory of uncommitted water resources, planning and construction for river regulation, allocation of the resource among potentially competitive and mutually exclusive uses, segregation and appropriate treatment or disposal of wastes? Responsibility and authority now rest in many agencies—municipal, State, and Federal, but commonly are either too fragmentary or too specialized to encompass all the necessary courses of action. Is there some reasonable, workable compromise between this presently fractionated concern and overall authority assigned to a single governmental colossus?

Cost of water-supply management as here outlined will be large obviously. How can this large cost be shared equitably among the individual user and taxpayer, the private entrepreneur of commerce or industry, and the many agencies of government?

Current legal rights of the individual to water or to its exclusive use could, if unmodified or unrestrained, greatly complicate water-management procedures of the year 2000. Should these rights, now absolute in most States, be relaxed to the end that a common advantage may be realized from a simpler, more effective procedure? In another context, the writer has concluded that they will be so relaxed, by evolution (Piper, 1959).

The title of this paper is a general question, "Has the United States enough water?" A comprehensive answer, binding as of the year 2000, is not possible from information at hand or in early prospect. However, this paper has served its purpose if it has broken down the general question into correlative aspects and courses of early action. Definitive answers to the numerous residual questions must be found.

References

Douglas, E. M., 1932, Boundaries, areas, geographic centers of the United States and the several States: U. S. Geological Survey Bull. 817, 265 p.

Eliasberg V. F., 1960, Regional water supply and projected uses. In Wollman, 1960 [see below].

Langbein, W. B., 1959, Water yield and reservoir storage in the United States: U. S. Geol. Survey Circ. 409, 5 p.

Langbein, W. B., and others, 1949, Annual runoff in the United States: U. S. Geol. Survey Circ. 52, p. 5.

MacKichan, K. A., and Kammerer, J. C., 1961. Estimated use of water in the United States, 1960: U. S. Geol. Survey Circ. 456, 44 p., 10 fig.

Meyers, J. S., 1962, Evaporation from the 17 Western States: U. S. Geol. Survey Prof. Paper 272-D, p. 93–95.

Oltman, R. E., and others, 1960, National water resources and problems: U. S. Senate, Select Comm. on National Water Resources, 86th Cong., 2d sess., Comm. Print 3, 42 p., 43 fig.

Piper, A. M., 1959, Requirements of a model water law: Am. Water Works Assoc. Jour., v. 51 p. 1211–1216.

Reid, G. W., 1960, Methods of approximating dilution water requirements as a supplemental measure for control of water quality in rivers: U. S. Senate, Select Comm. on National Water Resources, 86th Cong., 2d sess., Comm. Print 29, 28 p.

Thomas, N. O., and Harbeck, G. E., Jr., 1956, Reservoirs in the United States: U. S. Geol. Survey Water-Supply Paper 1360-A, 99 p., 1 pl., 3 fig.

Thornthwaite, C. W., 1952, Evapotranspiration in the hydrologic cycle, in The physical and economic foundation of natural resources: U. S. House of Representatives, Interior and Insular Affairs Comm., v. 2, p. 25–35.

U. S. Dept. Agriculture, 1960, Estimated water requirements for agricultural purposes, and their effects on water supplies: U. S. Senate, Select Comm. on National Water Resources, 86th Cong., 2d sess., Comm. Print 13, 24 p.

U. S. Geological Survey, 1962, Water for recreation—Values and opportunities: Outdoor Recreation Resources Review Comm. Study Rept. 10, 73 p.

U. S. Public Health Service, 1960, Future water requirements for municipal purposes: U. S. Senate, Select Comm. on

National Water Resources, 86th Cong.,
2d sess., Comm. Print 7, 24 p.

———— 1960a, Pollution abatement: U. S.
Senate, Select Comm. on National Water
Resources, 86th Cong., 2d sess., Comm.
Print 9, 38 p.

U. S. Weather Bureau, 1959, Evaporation
maps for the United States: U. S.
Weather Bureau Tech. Paper 37.

———— 1960, in U. S. Dept. Agriculture, 1960
[see above].

Wollman, Nathaniel, 1960, A preliminary report on the supply of and demand for
water in the United States as estimated
for 1980 and 2000: U. S. Senate, Select
Comm. on National Water Resources,
86th Cong., 2d sess., Comm. Print 32,
131 p.

33   Water for the Cities—The Outlook*

William J. Schneider and Andrew M. Spieker

The Problem

If water is used as a criterion of evaluation, we are indeed an affluent
society. All economic levels of our
society use it extravagantly. This is
especially true of the urban dweller
and his suburban neighbor who are
accustomed to an almost unlimited
supply at the turn of a faucet handle.
Our society in 1965 used more than
150 bgd (billion gallons per day) of
water to meet its needs and satiate its
desires, exclusive of rural and agricultural uses. In addition to this direct
use, the social impact of water resources is increasing demands for its
consideration for fish and wildlife conservation, recreation, and aesthetics.
Because water is neither created nor
destroyed in sufficient quantity to alter
significantly its total amount on earth,
our supply is essentially limited. But is

this supply sufficient? Are we running
out of water? To answer this, though,
we must also consider a related question: Why do our cities now face water
problems?

The United States is rapidly becoming an urbanized society. According to
Bureau of Census figures, about 130
million people—two out of every three
persons—lived in metropolitan areas in
1965. Between 1960 and 1965, this urban population increased by more than
11 million people—an increase of over
9 percent. To meet the demands for
this urban population, municipal water
systems are supplying more than 24
billion gallons of water per day.

If population predictions can be relied upon and existing water-use practices are continued, during the next
decade and a half the United States
will be called upon to provide more
than twice this amount of water to
meet the demands of the metropolitan
areas. Population predictions estimate
that by the year 2000, about 280 million people will live in metropolitan
areas—about 85 percent of the population of the United States. Supplying
water for this urban growth will be a

* This paper was presented at a symposium
on "Geology and the urbanization process,"
at a meeting of the Northeastern Section of
the Geological Society of America, Albany,
N. Y., March 14, 1969.

Schneider, W. J. and Spieker, A. M., 1969,
"Water for the Cities—the Outlook," U. S.
Geol. Survey Circ. 601-A, 6 pp.
The authors are affiliated with the United
States Geological Survey.

major challenge to the urban planner, the engineer, and the geologist.

Lewis Mumford (1956, p. 395) sums up the urban water demand as follows:

"Already, New York and Philadelphia . . . find themselves competing for the same water supply, as Los Angeles competes with the whole state of Arizona. Thus, though modern technology has escaped from the limitations of a purely local supply of water, the massing of population makes demands that even apart from excessive costs (which rise steadily as distance increases), put a definite limit to the possibilities of further urbanization. Water shortages may indeed limit the present distribution long before food shortages bring population growth to an end."

Mumford may be overly pessimistic in his outlook, though. Hydrologic data indicate that enough water is generally available for man's needs, but not always where and when he needs it or at a cost he considers reasonable. According to the Water Resources Council's First National Assessment (1968), water demands for all uses totaled 270 bgd in 1965, with a consumptive use of 78 bgd. Projected requirements for the year 2020 show total demands will be at 1,368 bgd and consumptive use, at 157 bgd. This current demand is less than 7 percent of the average of 4,200 bgd precipitation that falls on the conterminous United States, and the projected demand is less than 33 percent of the present average. However, seasonal and spatial variability in precipitation make these figures misleading; the history of water supplies for urban areas has been a constant cycle of shortage and development. A look at the history of municipal supply for two major cities and at the regional effect of the recent Northeast drought will illustrate this point.

Miami, Fla.

Miami, Fla., derives its water supplies from ground water in the Biscayne aquifer—a highly permeable water-bearing limestone that underlies much of southern Florida. The first wells were drilled into the Biscayne aquifer in 1896 to supply water for the newly constructed Royal Palm Hotel and for the Miami Hotel, heralding the start of massive urbanization of the area. In 1900, the local water system served a population of 1,680; by 1925 the population had increased to 30,200. New wells, added in 1907 to the existing location at Spring Garden, supplied municipal water at rates that lowered the water table until salt water encroached on the well field and forced its abandonment in the early 1920's, only 2 years after pumps were added to obtain the necessary flow.

In 1925, the Spring Garden well field was abandoned, and new wells were drilled in the Hialeah-Miami Springs area. However, increased demand for water coupled with the need to lower water levels for flood protection caused salt-water intrusion at this site, and stringent remedial measures have been necessary to insure protection of this source. Only through concerted efforts at preventing overdrainage and controlling water levels through construction of salt-water barriers in drainage canals has further contamination of Miami's water supply been averted.

Despite present conservation measures, increased water use by an expanding population will undoubtedly cause further problems in water availability, in salt-water intrusion, and in pollution. Population estimates by the Dade County Development Department, for example, predict an increase for the Miami area from 1 million people in 1960 to 4 million people in 1995. Daily water use is also expected to rise, from 145 gallons per person in 1960 to 220 gallons per person in 1995. The per capita increase results from a projected expansion in industrial water use. The total increase in water use will require 1.4 bgd as compared with the present use of 230 mgd (million gallons per day).

To supply this 1.4-bgd requirement in the future, Kohout and Hartwell (1967) estimate that the entire amount of rainfall over a 500-square-mile area would need to be collected. They point out, however, that total rainfall is never available for man's use; in the Everglades, almost 80 percent of the rainfall is consumed by evapotranspiration. Therefore, if the remaining 20 percent—10½ inches per year—were diverted to the Miami well fields, it would require an area of 2,800 square miles to supply Dade County alone in 1995. This is an area as large as the entire Everglades from Lake Okeechobee to Cape Sable.

The Miami case is an excellent example of a large metropolitan water system where careful planning has averted shortages and assured an adequate supply to meet future demands. The increased demands will probably be met by water management practices such as reduction of fresh-water discharge to the ocean via canals, by backpumping excess water to inland storage reservoirs, and by reuse of water. Water is a reusable resource, and advanced technology and enlightened water management should insure a continuing supply of fresh water in southern Florida.

New York City

The history of the New York City water-supply system presents a somewhat different situation. Whereas Miami has an abundant supply locally available, New York has had to go to great lengths—literally—to meet its demands.

In its early years, New York's water was supplied by shallow wells and small reservoirs, all privately owned. None of these sources was satisfactory, and epidemics were frequent. By the 1820's it was clear that a public supply was needed, but there were no adequate reservoir sites nearby. New York's population was then approaching 300,000. A proposal to build a 37-mile aqueduct to a reservoir site near Croton was first considered preposterous but gradually became accepted as a necessity. A cholera outbreak in 1832 killed 3,500 people and dramatized the necessity of a new supply, which was authorized in 1834. A disastrous fire in 1835 further demonstrated the desperate need and construction was accelerated. The system was completed in 1842.

At that time the Croton Reservoir was no doubt regarded as the ultimate answer to New York's water needs. Within 20 years, however, it had to be enlarged. Several new reservoirs and a larger aqueduct were needed before the turn of the century. By then, all satisfactory sites in the Croton watershed had been exhausted, and the demand was fast catching up with the available supply. Clearly, new sources of supply would have to be sought.

The Catskill Mountains, about 120

miles from New York, were chosen for the new reservoir sites. Construction began in 1907, and the system was completed in two stages: the Ashokan Reservoir was completed in 1917 and the Schoharie Reservoir, in 1928. Although addition of the Catskill system more than doubled the previous supply, the new supply was barely able to keep up with the rapidly increasing demand. By the late 1920's another water crisis was in sight.

This time alternatives were considered. The Hudson River was ruled out because of its allegedly inferior quality. New Yorkers insist on drinking pure mountain water. The Adirondacks were eliminated because of the excessive distance. In 1928, then, it was decided to expand the Catskill system and to develop new reservoirs in the headwaters of the Delaware River basin. The Delaware River is an interstate stream, so the consent of New Jersey and Pennsylvania was needed to divert water from this basin. The issue was resolved after considerable litigation in 1931 by a decree of the U. S. Supreme Court that allowed New York to divert no more than 440 mgd from the Delaware River basin. First the depression, then World War II delayed construction. The first operational phase of the expansion consisted of an emergency diversion from Rondout Creek to the new Delaware aqueduct from 1944 to 1951.

In the meantime, yet another crisis occurred. The postwar urbanization explosion strained the Croton and Catskill systems almost to their limit. Average pumpage exceeded 1 bgd. Abundant rainfall deferred the day of reckoning until 1949, when reservoir levels dropped to the danger point.

Stringent water conservation measures were enforced, and for the first time the Hudson River was tapped at Chelsea as an emergency source of supply.

Rondout Reservoir, an expansion of the Catskill system, became operational late in 1950 and the diversion from the Hudson was discontinued. Neversink and Pepacton Reservoirs, with their diversion appurtenances, began being used in 1953, but full use of the Delaware system was not achieved until 1955.

History repeats itself. The crisis of 1949 and the forecasts of the even greater population explosion to come made the water planners all too painfully aware that even the Delaware River basin supply system under construction would only temporarily satisfy the city's needs. An additional source would be needed. Thus, planning began for a new reservoir in the Delaware River basin. In 1954 the Supreme Court authorized New York to increase its diversion and in 1955 construction started on the Cannonsville Reservoir. Planners estimated that, with this new addition, the system would have total capacity of 1,800 mgd, sufficient to meet demands through 1980.

The record breaking drought of 1961–66 occurred, however, before the Cannonsville Reservoir was completed. At one time the existing reservoirs were drawn down to 26 percent of capacity (near the minimum safe drawdown for which the system was designed). The most stringent water-use controls in the city's history were put into effect, and the Chelsea pumping station on the Hudson River was rebuilt. By 1967 abundant rainfall eased the crisis, and the situation returned to "normal." But if history can be taken as any guide, it will not be too long before New York is again faced with a water crisis. Indeed, planning has already started on alternative means of meeting expanded needs.

The history of the New York water system has been one of continuing crisis in order to satisfy the demands of the population explosion. Yet part of the water demand might be regarded as unnecessary or artificial. Wasteful and inefficient use of water is encouraged by the absence of metering and unrealistic pricing. While the elaborate network of reservoirs and aqueducts has been built at great cost, the Hudson River, which might supply New York's needs many times over, has, like many other rivers, been allowed to degenerate in quality. The State's Pure Water Program improvements show promise of effecting some regeneration. Planning decisions must be sensitive to economics, politics, and public attitudes. The citizens of New York have become conditioned to drinking "mountain water," and any change in established practices of water supply would require a massive campaign of public information and education.

Northeast Drought of 1961–66

The recent drought in the Northeastern United States points out the regional impact of natural catastrophic events on water for urban areas. In September 1961 precipitation and water levels throughout the northeastern part of the United States fell below normal. Although unheralded at the time, it marked the beginning of a drought— the largest, longest, and most severe in the history of the Northeast United States.

For over 5 years the drought persisted over a 13-state area extending from Maine to North Carolina, an area of more than 400,000 square miles. Each year since 1962 there was a reduction in yields of crops and pasture lands and an increasing threat and occurrences of forest fires. The effects on public water supplies increased with the duration and intensity of the drought. The effect was cumulative from year to year as reserves were depleted and streamflow and groundwater levels dropped to record lows. During the early part of the drought, the effects were largely absorbed by the built in resiliency and planned reserves of the water supply systems. By the summer of 1965, though, about one public water system out of every eight found its reserves at critically low levels.

Drought-related water shortages and problems in 1965 were severe enough to warrant emergency actions by federal, state, and local agencies. In Maine, 21 supply systems restricted water use; more than 50 towns and cities in Massachusetts imposed restrictions; 14 systems in New York faced water shortages; and northern New Jersey, with its interconnected water companies, was also seriously affected. At one time, storage in the New York City reservoir system was reduced to 124 billion gallons, only 26 percent of maximum capacity, and the chloride concentration in the Delaware River at the Philadelphia water intake at Torresdale reached over 50 mg/l (milligrams per liter), with the 250 mg/l isochlor located only 8 miles downstream. At the height of the drought, the water-use habits of more than 20 million people were directly and drastically affected.

Only concerted efforts at all levels

enabled the region to continue to supply the water needs. Stringent conservation measures such as bans on use of water for air conditioning, car washing, and lawn sprinkling were enacted. A "water bank" was established in the New York City reservoir system to retain the 200 mgd which normally would be released for flow augmentation in the Delaware River and permit greater flexibility in management of that system. Emergency actions were taken to rehabilitate the Torresdale water intake for Philadelphia.

Many wells in the region, both individual and public supplies, "went dry" and had to be deepened, redeveloped, or replaced with wells of greater capacity. Here again, these well failures usually did not reflect insufficient sources of supply, but rather inadequately planned or constructed wells.

Despite the critical water shortages, it should be emphasized that never during the drought was there an overall shortage of water in the region. During the entire emergency there was only one outright failure of a city water-supply—that of Lancaster, Pa. The shortage was rather one of facilities for its collection, treatment, storage, and delivery to points of need. The execution of carefully prepared long-range plans can without doubt meet all water requirements of the Northeast for many years.

Outlook

The experiences of Miami, New York, and the Northeast region point out the universal problem of municipal water supply: population growth has tended to outstrip development. In the past, many municipal water systems have operated on marginal conditions. Because of the massive investments involved water utilities seldom manage to keep far enough ahead of our burgeoning population.

These marginal operating conditions suddenly become critical when faced with catastrophic events such as saltwater contamination of a well field or a series of near-dry reservoirs resulting from drought. This situation points more to lack of planning and development rather than to actual water shortages. Water is available for the cities, but the cities must plan effectively and in coordinated fashion if the requirements of all are to be met.

Predicted demands for municipal water are expected to increase from 23.7 bgd in 1965 to 74.3 bgd in 2020, an increase of 213 percent (Water Resources Council, 1968, p. 4–1–4). This demand will strain our ability to meet water requirements for the cities, but the job can and must be done.

Planning will play a major role in insuring adequate water for the cities. Regional planning must supersede local-interest planning as cities are ever increasingly forced to expand their sources of supply. As these sources of supply overlap, jurisdictional disputes will undoubtedly develop. Regional planning must replace uncoordinated unilateral development if chaos is to be avoided.

Moreover, the water-resources planners of the future will have to use considerably more imagination than has been evident in some of the plans of the past and the present if the job is to be done. Management of both the resource and its use may be necessary as the demand approaches the available supply. All alternative sources of supply should be considered in order to arrive at an optimal plan. For example, ground water could be used to supplement a surface reservoir or vice versa. The conjunctive use of surface and ground water should be considered; in many situations this may be the most efficient solution to the water-supply problem. Research is needed in advanced techniques of treatment that could convert marginal or unsatisfactory sources into usable supplies. Desalination, as it becomes economically viable, must be considered as an alternative.

The management of water use could be fully as important as the management of water supplies. It has already been demonstrated that water use can be substantially reduced by judicious management. Industrial water systems can be designed so that most of the water is reused. Saline water could be used in some instances for cooling, which accounts for a large part of industrial water use.

Water-use management need not be confined to industry, however. Municipal supplies can be made more efficient by systematic detection and repair of leaks in water mains. Modern plumbing fixtures generally use less water than outmoded ones. In this regard, building codes can require such fixtures in new construction. Water of less than drinking-water quality could be used for some domestic purposes such as lawn watering and air conditioning.

Realistic pricing would exert a strong influence on water-use habits. Public education and information campaigns might be necessary to gain widespread public acceptance of such changes in traditional water-use practices.

The outlook for water for the cities then, can be regarded as cautiously optimistic. Though the population explosion of the next half century will strain existing systems, the water demands for our cities can be met. To meet these demands, however, coordinated comprehensive planning that gives adequate consideration to all viable alternatives must replace the crisis planning that has characterized much of the water-resources development of the past.

References

Kohout, F. A., and Hartwell, J. H., 1967, Hydrologic effects of Area B Flood Control on urbanization of Dade County, Florida: Florida Geol. Survey Rept. Inv. 47, 61 p.

Martin, R. C., 1960, Water for New York. Syracuse, N. Y., Syracuse University Press, 264 p.

Mumford, Lewis, 1956, The natural history of urbanization, in Thomas, W. L., ed., Man's role in changing the face of the Earth: Chicago, Ill., Univ. of Chicago Press, p. 382–398.

U. S. Water Resources Council, 1968, The nation's water resources—the first national assessment of the Water Resources Council: Washington, D. C., U. S. Govt. Printing Office, 410 p.

34   Ground Water—A Mixed Blessing*

C. L. McGuinness

Introduction

Ground water—the water of wells and springs—is one of the world's most valuable resources. Indeed, in the not distant future it will prove to be not only valuable but vital. Yet, many difficulties will be encountered in the full exploitation of this resource that will be essential in tomorrow's society. It is the purpose of this paper to develop this theme briefly, in terms of conditions in the United States.

First let us define this ground water that is going to occupy a good deal of our attention in the future. Ground water is the water of the zone of saturation as defined by O. E. Meinzer (1923, p. 21); it is the water under hydrostatic pressure in the pores and crevices of the rocks that is free to move under the influence of gravity from places where it enters the zone of saturation to places where it is discharged. It is a phase of the hydrologic cycle, and it is that fact which both makes it a valuable, renewable resource

* Publication authorized by the Director, U. S. Geological Survey.

McGuinness, C. L., 1960, Ground Water—A Mixed Blessing, *Proceedings of Section 20, Twenty-First Session International Geological Congress*, Copenhagen.

Reprinted from *Proceedings of Section 20, Twenty-First Session International Geological Congress*, Copenhagen 1960 by permission of the author and the Danish Geological Survey.

The late Mr. McGuinness was Chief of the Ground Water Branch of the U. S. Geological Survey.

and creates many of the difficulties that attend its full utilization.

Ground water is one of the earth's most ubiquitous resources, and therein lies much of its value. It exists wherever three conditions are met: (1) water from precipitation or streamflow penetrates beneath the surface in quantities sufficient to exceed the field capacity of the soil—that is, moves downward through the zone of aeration under the influence of gravity; (2) the rocks beneath the soil are permeable enough to transmit this water; and (3) the rate of infiltration is sufficient that the zone of saturation formed in the lower part of the permeable rocks will be built up to a perceptible thickness by the time the lateral outflow increases to a rate equal to the rate of infiltration from the land surface. These conditions are met— that is, ground water exists at least intermittently—in a very large part of the world. However, it is only under three further conditions that ground water becomes a usable resource: (1) the rocks in the zone of saturation are permeable enough to yield useful supplies of water to wells, springs, or streams; (2) the zone of saturation is permanent, or at least persists long enough each season to allow practical exploitation; and (3) the mineral substances dissolved by the water as it travels through the ground do not reach such concentrations as to make the water unfit for use at the place where a supply is needed. These further conditions, stringent as they are, are met commonly enough that at least the small quantities of potable water needed for domestic supply are available very widely. Only where impermeable rocks or permanently frozen ground extend to great depths, or where the climate is exceedingly dry, is ground water entirely or practically absent; even in large regions having these characteristics, ground water may be available locally.

It is this near-universality of occurrence that has made ground water so important in the past in enabling human occupation of many large regions that otherwise could not have been settled. As our areal reconnaissances of ground-water geology are extended and as methods of prospecting for and developing ground water are refined, this resource will continue to contribute to the settlement of primitive areas for some time to come. But it is not this aspect of ground-water development that will produce the most headaches; rather, it is in the optimum, or maximum, exploitation of water supplies in areas more abundantly endowed by nature that the principal difficulties have been encountered, and will continue to be.

Full Development of Ground Water— A Future Necessity

The time is coming—coming rapidly—when full exploitation of our water resources will be, not just a desirable objective, but an absolute necessity not only to social progress but even to human survival. Vast water supplies remain nearly or quite untouched, even in some highly developed countries; but, as the world's population continues to increase and the standard of living advances, the margin between supply and demand will become ever narrower. Then, full development will be the order of the day, with all its complexities, its difficulties, and its cost. True, the time may come when advances in nuclear science may provide us an energy source so cheap that sea water can be converted to fresh and piped at reasonable cost anywhere in the world, and when it comes we can forget our water-supply problems. But that happy day is decades off, if not centuries, and our water problems are with us *now*.

Problems and Solutions

It is to be hoped that the reader is now convinced, as is the writer, that the world's supply of usable water will have to be exploited thoroughly and efficiently, and that ground water will have to play its full part. Let us now see what we will have to do to get the ground water we will need.

In many areas, large and small, and for many uses, ground water is by far the most economical source. This situation applies especially where the demand is small or moderate—the few hundred gallons a day needed for a family, or the few tens or hundreds of thousands needed for a town or industry of modest size. Locally, in geologically favorable areas, it applies even to demands of millions or tens of millions of gallons a day. However, surface water commonly is the source of supply for the largest cities and the largest agricultural, industrial, and power-generation projects.

Ground water has many advantages over surface water—it is generally potable and palatable without treatment or can be made so with only simple treatment; its uniform chemical quality and general lack of organic matter simplify any treatment that may be necessary; its uniform temperature makes it attractive as a cooling agent in the summer; it is relatively immune from evaporation and from contamination; and, where the local supply is adequate to meet the demand, the overall cost of obtaining and treating it is generally less than that for surface water.

It is when the demand strains the limits of supply and when surface water is not available at reasonable cost that we begin to realize the mixed nature of the blessing that is ground water. It is then that we become aware that, in comparison to surface water, ground water is more difficult and expensive to locate, to evaluate quantitatively, and to manage. These difficulties are inherent in our lack of detailed knowledge of the places where ground water occurs, of the principles that govern its occurrence and movement in complex geologic situations, of methods for evaluating it quantitatively in these situations which defy practical mathematical analysis, and of methods for exploiting it efficiently under limitations imposed by economics and by law. To obtain the knowledge needed to manage this resource will be much more costly, gallon for gallon, than to learn how to manage surface water—yet, where we must have water and where other sources are not available, we are going to pay the cost or we are going to do without. Our job, then, is to recognize the high cost of optimum ground-water development, and to exert our best efforts to reduce that cost to the minimum.

The Ground-Water Situation in the United States

So far the discussion has been essentially philosophical rather than practical. To get our feet back on the ground, let us describe briefly certain aspects of the ground-water situation in the United States. Then we will have a background for delineating very briefly, and again philosophically, the problems associated with full development of ground water.

Taken as a whole, the United States is abundantly endowed with water. An average of 30 inches of rain and snow falls annually. Of this, about $8\frac{1}{2}$ inches escapes the demands of evapotranspiration and flows back to the sea. This $8\frac{1}{2}$ inches represents our recoverable water supply, except as it might be increased by modifications of vegetal growth to reduce evapotranspiration, by artificially induced increases in total precipitation, or by conversion of saline water.

As measured, the $8\frac{1}{2}$ inches is surface water, but ground water plays no mean part in generating it, for it is the overflow of ground-water reservoirs that maintains most of the fair-weather flow of streams. It has been estimated [W. B. Langbein, U. S. Geol. Survey, oral communication, 1950] that perhaps one-third to two-fifths of the total streamflow in the United States represents ground water whose contribution can be identified in the streamflow graph. A much larger portion of the streamflow—under some conditions virtually all—represents water that has passed beneath the land surface and moved through a shallow, temporary zone of saturation in the soil before entering the streams, but this storm-flow component cannot be distinguished on the hydrograph and, moreover, it hardly constitutes ground water that can be utilized as such.

In the United States the total water supply, as measured by the precipitation, is large in the East and Southeast and decreases generally westward and northward, except in the high mountains of the West and especially of the Pacific Northwest. The geology and the air temperature modify this picture extensively so far as available water supply is concerned, however.

The accompanying map gives a good general idea of the availability of ground water in the United States. It was compiled by Dr. H. E. Thomas of the Geological Survey for his book written for the Conservation Foundation (1951). It is based largely on published reports of the Geological Survey and its cooperating State agencies and on unpublished information in field offices of the Geological Survey. It shows areas where supplies of 50 gallons per minute per well are, or are not, commonly available. It shows also whether the productive aquifers consist of unconsolidated or consolidated rocks, or both.

The map does not show specifically where supplies of hundreds or thousands of gallons per minute are available from single wells. It does so in a general way, however, because in the greatest part of the patterned areas wells may yield several hundred gallons per minute or more. This fact is brought out by a similar map, divided into 10 parts for the principal ground-water regions, prepared by Dr. Thomas for his report to a congressional committee in 1952. This later map shows slightly more detail than the earlier, as

it distinguishes among the principal types of water-bearing rocks—limestone, sandstone, volcanics, and so on. However, the patterned areas, which on the later map show a capability for "moderate to large yields to wells," are very nearly coextensive with those on the accompanying map.

The map shows that almost the entire Atlantic and Gulf Coastal Plain is underlain by productive unconsolidated aquifers—strata of sand and gravel—which are of Mesozoic and Cenozoic age. In Florida and adjacent States large parts of the Coastal Plain are underlain also by consolidated-rock aquifers (largely Tertiary limestone beneath or interbedded with the sand and gravel). The Midwestern States have both unconsolidated (Pleistocene glacial drift) and consolidated (Paleozoic limestone and sandstone) aquifers. The Northeastern States have many small but productive valley deposits of glacial outwash sand and gravel. The entire Mississippi River basin has similar alluvial deposits, shown in solid black. The High Plains have a widespread Tertiary alluvial deposit which yields water to thousands of irrigation wells. The desert valleys of the Basin and Range province of the Southwest and such large valleys as the San Luis Valley of Colorado and the Central Valley of California contain productive alluvial sand and gravel of Tertiary and Quaternary age. The great Tertiary and Quaternary lava plateaus of Idaho and the Pacific Northwest are productive ground-water sources. And, some of the glacial-outwash deposits of the Northwest are among the most permeable aquifers known and are generously recharged.

In most of the areas shown unpat-

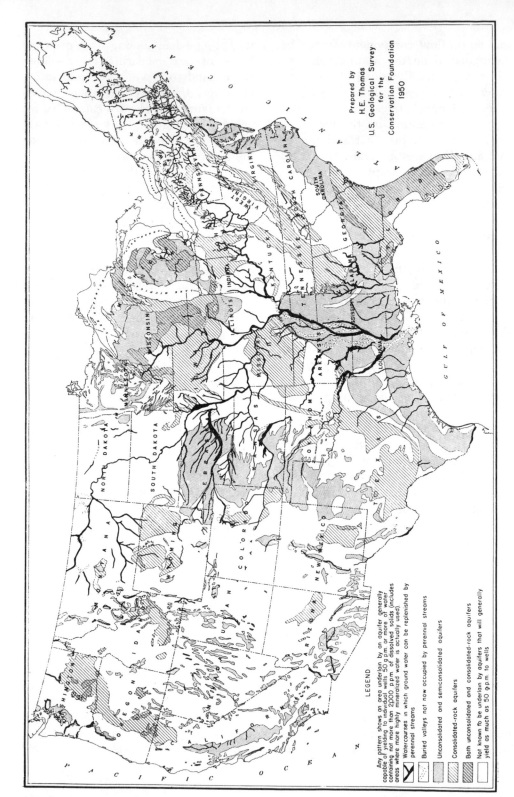

FIG. 1. Ground-Water Areas in the U. S.

Prepared by
H.E. Thomas
U.S. Geological Survey
for the
Conservation Foundation
1950

LEGEND

Any pattern shows an area underlain by an aquifer generally
capable of yielding to individual wells 50 g.p.m. or more of water
containing not more than 2000 p.p.m. dissolved solids (includes
areas where more highly mineralized water is actually used)

Watercourses in which ground water can be replenished by
perennial streams

Buried valleys not now occupied by perennial streams

Unconsolidated and semiconsolidated aquifers

Consolidated-rock aquifers

Both unconsolidated and consolidated-rock aquifers

Not known to be underlain by aquifers that will generally
yield as much as 50 g.p.m. to wells

terned on the map, supplies of ground water adequate for at least domestic use are widely available. One of the most consistently dependable areas for small to moderate supplies is the Piedmont, extending from Alabama to its extension in the New England province, where fractured crystalline bedrocks of Precambrian and Paleozoic age are penetrated by many hundreds of thousands of domestic and small municipal and industrial wells. Locally, supplies of several hundred gallons per minute have been obtained. In the glaciated area which covers New England, New York, and the States to the west as far south as the Ohio and Missouri Rivers, glacial drift and the underlying bedrock yield small to moderate, and locally large, supplies to wells. In the unglaciated Middle West and Midcontinent areas, weathered and fresh sedimentary rocks, largely Paleozoic, generally yield small supplies, but there are some areas where water is difficult to get in more than meager quantities. This difficulty exists also in a considerable part of the glaciated area of western Minnesota and the Dakotas.

In the dry plateau country of the Southwest water is often difficult or expensive to obtain, although the risk of failure can be reduced nearly to zero if the stratigraphy is studied carefully before drilling is attempted. In the mountainous areas, drilled wells are not too successful because the rocks are hard and the fractures tend to be drained, but springs and dug wells supply the relatively sparse rural population, and municipalities use streams, or wells in the larger alluviated valleys, for their supply.

Now we have a general idea where the ground-water resources of the United States are. Where are these resources exploited? Obviously, the large-scale withdrawals are confined to the patterned areas on the map, but where in particular?

In 1955 the total estimated withdrawal of fresh ground water in the continental United States averaged about 45.7 billion U. S. gallons per day [MacKichan, 1957, p. 13]. This was a little more than a fifth of the total of 221 bgd of fresh water withdrawn from all sources for uses other than hydropower generation. We have no more recent figures for the whole country, but this year the 1955 data will be brought up to date, and it will be surprising indeed if they do not show an increase.[1] The 1955 figure for ground water represented better than a 50-percent increase over the comparable figure of 30 bgd for 1950 [MacKichan, 1951, p. 7], and though the increase from 1955 to 1960 may not be as large percentagewise it is virtually certain to be substantial.

The largest single use of ground water is that for irrigation 30 bgd in 1955. A third of the total was pumped in California; Texas was next with 6.5 bgd, and Arizona third with 4.7 bgd. Thus more than two-thirds of the total for irrigation was pumped in 3 of the 48 States.

Industrial use of fresh ground water, including fuel-electric power generation, averaged 9.2 bgd in 1955. The use was greater in the East than in the West but was still substantial in two of our previously named Western States—about half a billion gallons per day each in Texas and California. Industrial use is growing all over the country, but perhaps especially in the South and West.

Public-supply use of ground water was 4.7 bgd in 1955. It of course accorded with population distribution and was greatest in the Northeast and Middle West. Here again, however, Texas and California were leading States—first and second, respectively.

Rural use of ground water, the smallest of the four major categories, was 1.8 bgd in 1955. It was rather evenly distributed, being larger than average in the populous Middle Western and Northeastern States and— again—in Texas and California, and smallest in the small New England States and thinly populated Western States.

Thus, in 1955 we had 10 States each pumping more than a billion gallons per day, and 3 more very close to that total and no doubt over it by now. Of the 13 only 3—California, Texas, and Arizona—exceeded 1.5 bgd, but these did it handsomely, with totals of 11.1, 7.2, and 5.0 bgd.

Of our 13 leading States 8, including the top 6, are among the 17 Western States—the States where the precipitation is prevailingly less than the national average. This fact is a tribute to the productive aquifers that nature has placed in the West, in spite of the reduced precipitation, but it has a sinister meaning also. It means that a large part of the Nation's serious water problems are to be found in these water-rich yet water-poor States. Just a quick look at one of these problems will show how important and how serious they are.

An Example of a Water-Supply Problem

About as spectacular a case as any is that of the southern High Plains of Texas—the so-called "South Plains."

The aquifer of the South Plains and the adjacent area in New Mexico is a remnant of a formerly continuous alluvial apron which in Pliocene time extended for hundreds of miles east of the Rocky Mountains but which since has been cut off from the Rockies by erosion and has itself been cut into segments. The aquifer in the South Plains of Texas contains an enormous amount of ground water in storage— about 200 million acre-feet, or about 65 million million U. S. gallons, as of 1957–58 [J. E. Cronin, U. S. Geol. Survey, written communication, 1959]. But this aquifer, in common with its related parts in much of the rest of the High Plains, has one distinguishing feature—an extremely low rate of replenishment. This rate is estimated to be something like 50,000 acre-feet per year in the Texas portion of the southern High Plains. Both storage and recharge in the New Mexico portion are perhaps a third as great as in the Texas counterpart. Thus we have an aquifer which contained 250 to 275 million acre-feet of water in storage as of 1957–58, and from which something like 40 million acre-feet of water had already been pumped, but the replenishment of which currently is at a rate equivalent to less than 1 percent of the withdrawal. Furthermore, because of the vastness of the aquifer the current pumping, heavy as it is, has not yet reduced the natural discharge at the edges of the Plains; thus the withdrawal to date has come wholly from storage.

The economy of the South Plains is based largely on irrigation with ground water, which in recent years has grown at a rate unparalleled elsewhere in the country. But the ground water is being "mined." Surface water is not the answer—there is very little of it in the region, and under present economic conditions the amount that could be developed would meet only a very small fraction of the total water demand. Artificial recharge through wells of a part of the rainwater that gathers in many ponds or "sinks" in wet weather is being investigated actively and will be helpful locally, but it is no more an answer to the total problem than is water from streams. In the same class so far as a permanent solution is concerned are conservation measures to reduce waste of the pumped water: these will help to prolong the life of the ground-water supply, but no measures that are practical under present conditions can prolong it indefinitely at the current rate of withdrawal. On the other hand, to leave the water in the ground means losing the wealth which it, like any other minable resource, is capable of creating. How the South Plains will adjust economically to the depletion of the ground-water resource has yet to be determined, but that a problem of the first magnitude is involved is obvious.[2]

The case of the South Plains is exceptional in the rate of increase in withdrawal and in the dramatic contrast between withdrawal and replenishment, but as a problem of shortage of water to meet future demands it is anything but unique. Many ground-water basins in the arid Southwest are currently being overdrawn, even though they may be replenished at rates that are equivalent to a very substantial part of the withdrawal. Similar problems of at least local shortage exist in many of the heavily pumped urban areas of the East. In both East and West, many problems of shortage in quantity are created or

complicated by the threat of encroachment of saline water due to pumping— and this in such inland areas as the Tularosa Basin—Hueco Bolson area of New Mexico and Texas just as truly as in the heavily pumped coastal areas of California, Texas, Florida, and Long Island, New York. [See Reading 35.]

The Basic Problem of the Future

Perhaps we have made our point that many serious problems of ground-water availability and quality exist in the United States. There are even more important problems, however— those involved in finding ways to make ground water meet its full share of the responsibility for satisfying our water demands of the future. These latter problems can be characterized briefly as follows:

1. Evaluating aquifer systems.
2. Devising methods of water management that are compatible with both hydrologic and social realities, or can be made so by means that can reasonably be achieved.

The first task is that of the geohydrologist—that geologic and hydrologic expert who represents a synthesis of the ground-water geologist, the chemist, the physicist, the mathematician, the meteorologist, and the engineering scientist. The task, in a word, is to describe specific aquifer systems in terms of their geologic and hydrologic boundaries and of their response to external forces, as a basis for predicting reliably their hydrologic behavior under any condition that may be assumed to be likely in the future.

Quantitative ground-water hydrology has come a long way in recent decades in Europe, in America, and elsewhere. Aquifer-test methods for non-steady-state conditions became a reality in the United States with the work of C. V. Theis (1935). His basic equation for an infinite and isotropic aquifer and a steady pumping rate has been modified by many later workers to provide useful means for handling aquifers, and problems, whose departures from the stringent assumptions of the original Theis equation can be assigned specific values.

But all this is not enough. As every geologist knows, variations in the lithology and dimensions of permeable rocks, as of other rocks, are infinitely complex. It is easy to show that problems can be set up in which difficulties introduced by even modest variations in permeability and storage coefficient, in dimensions, and in boundary conditions of an aquifer are beyond the ability of even the most refined mathematics to solve in a reasonable time. The answer to this seemingly unscalable obstacle is the analog model, of which the electrical model appears to be more promising than the hydraulic or heat-flow model. Set up on the basis of geologic and hydraulic information obtained by conventional means, the model will show the response of complex aquifer systems with a reliability that depends solely on the amount and accuracy of data fed into it. And herein is our problem as ground-water geologists and hydrologists. The more complex problems need a lot of data, and data cost money. Yet, decisions are going to have to be made, and they will be made either on the basis of scientific data or on the basis of social or political judgment which may or may not prove to be sound.

The problem of getting enough data

for aquifer-system description is one that ground-water geologists and other water-oriented scientists can get their teeth into, but they will not find it easy to solve. That geologic complexities will make aquifer-system analysis difficult and costly is the most important of what might be called the natural reasons why ground water is a mixed blessing. Other problems are man-caused, or at least strongly man-influenced. These are economic, legal, psychological—what might be called social problems. Let us mention the most important ones briefly.

Perhaps one of the most urgent problems is the need for wide public recognition of the extent to which ground water and surface water are interconnected and interdependent, and the extent to which it will be necessary to develop them on a coordinated, integrated basis to meet the maximum water demands of the future. In such developments ground water will have a most vital part to play, because ground-water reservoirs comprise by far the greatest part of the total storage facilities available for evening out the effects of fluctuations in replenishment and in demand. Evaluating their storage capacity and devising means for getting water into and out of them at the proper times are a part of the task of the geohydrologist and the water-management engineer.

This enormous storage capacity of the ground-water reservoirs, which is potentially so important to the water management of the future, is responsible for some of today's problems, however. Where unplanned, unrestricted development has taken place, it has tended to encourage withdrawal at a rate that cannot be sustained indefinitely except by means, such as artificial recharge, which cost money that the initial developers never contemplated spending. Still, this can be considered only one phase of the difficulties involved in achieving public understanding of the procedures necessary for optimum water management.

The physical problems of water management, even when all the necessary data are at hand, are staggering. In effect, they will require setting up a second analog model, into which can be fed the data on ground water and on the streams, which, so far as the aquifers are concerned, are a part of the boundary conditions determining aquifer system response. To these geohydrologic data must be added information on expected places and amounts of water withdrawal and disposal. This information, like all the rest, obviously is only as dependable as the means by which it is generated, but nevertheless it must be given numbers.

But suppose we have all the hydrologic data we need, including reliable predictions of future needs, and the master model or computer by means of which the procedures necessary for efficient water management can be indicated readily and clearly. Let us make another very optimistic assumption and say that we have found economical means of performing each of the operational steps of management. Have we won the battle? Not yet. We still have the social problems resulting from the facts that aquifers and streams cross jurisdictional lines, and that water laws in adjacent jurisdictions may be based on conflicting legal principles and may incorporate incorrect hydrologic concepts. We might point out that aquifers and river basins often do not coincide, but this is a physical rather than a social problem and can be handled scientifically if enough data can be obtained.

So here is the crux of our problem: It is the need for vastly accelerated scientific studies of the geology of water, and for extensive interpenetration of the knowledge and the thinking of all concerned with water—geologists and other scientists, water-management authorities, lawyers and legislators, and the general public. The problems of ground water in particular and of water in general are many and serious and will grow more numerous and more serious before we begin to get them under control. But the very fact that we can recognize and analyze them signifies that we have the intellectual means for solving them, and we will have only ourselves to blame if we fail to do so.

Notes

1 In 1970 the total estimated withdrawal of fresh ground water in the continental United States averaged about 67.8 billion U. S. gallons per day (C. R. Murray and F. B. Reeves, 1972, Estimated Use of Ground Water in the United States, 1970: *U. S. Geol. Survey Circ. 676*). This was a little more than a fifth of the total of 320 bgd of fresh water withdrawn from all sources for uses other than hydropower generation. The 1970 figure for ground water represented better than a 67 per cent increase over the comparable figure of 45.7 bgd for 1955. The largest single use of ground water continued to be for irrigation—45 bgd in 1970. Industrial use of fresh ground water, including fuel-electric power generation averaged 9.4 bgd in 1970. Public-supply use of ground water was 9.4 bgd in 1970 while rural use of ground water was 3.6 bgd in 1970. These two uses record a doubling of the 1955 figures. [Ed.]

2 Pumping, from 1953–1961, averaged 5 mil-

lion acre-feet per year. Pumping in 1973 was 4.1 million acre-feet, and the estimated supply at that time was 176 million acre-feet. By the year 2015, pumping is predicted to decrease to 95,000 acre-feet per year, and less than 2½ per cent of the supply of 1973 will exist. Precipitous declines in agricultural production are forecast by 1990 and it is predicted that irrigated acreage will decline from 4 million acres at present to 125,000 acres by 2015. (*Water Policies for the Future*, Final Report to the President and to the Congress of the U. S. by the Nat'l Water Comm., U. S. Govt. Printing Office, Wash., D. C. June, 1973, 239 pp.) [Ed.]

References

MacKichan, K. A. (1951): Estimated use of water in the United States, 1950: *U. S. Geol. Survey Circ. 115*, 13 p.

MacKichan, K. A. (1957): Estimated use of water in the United States, 1955: *U. S. Geol. Survey Circ. 398*, 18 p.

Meinzer, O. E. (1923): Outline of ground-water hydrology, with definitions: *U. S. Geol. Survey Water-Supply Paper 494*, 71 p.

Theis, C. V. (1935): The relation between the lowering of the piezometric surface and the rate and duration of discharge of a well using ground-water storage: *Am. Geophys. Union Trans.*, p. 519–524.

Thomas, H. E. (1951): The conservation of ground water: New York, McGraw-Hill, 327 p.

Thomas, H. E. (1952): Ground water regions of the United States—their storage facilities; The Physical and Economic Foundation of Natural Resources, v. 3: *U. S. Cong., Interior and Insular Affairs Comm.*, Washington, U. S. Govt. Printing Office, 78 p.

35 The Changing Pattern of Ground-Water Development on Long Island, New York

R. C. Heath, B. L. Foxworthy, and Philip Cohen

Introduction

Even before the severe drought that is now (1965) affecting the Northeastern United States, Long Island was well known among water specialists for its underground-water resource, mainly as a result of both the magnitude of the ground-water resource and the unique aspects of man's utilization of that resource. The current drought has focused increased attention upon the vast amount of ground water in storage on

Heath, R. C., Foxworthy, B. L., and Cohen, Philip, 1966, "The Changing Pattern of Ground-Water Development on Long Island, New York," *U. S. Geol. Survey Circ. 524*, 10 pp.
The authors are on the staff of the United States Geological Survey.

Long Island and upon the large quantity of water being pumped from the system. In 1963, for example, an average of about 380 mgd (million gallons per day) was pumped from Long Island wells; these wells tap a fresh ground-water reservoir that has an estimated storage capacity of 10 to 20 trillion gallons. Nearly all the water pumped was for domestic and industrial use, and this pumpage probably represents one of the largest such uses of a single well-defined ground-water reservoir anywhere in the world.

The history of ground-water development on Long Island has been thoroughly documented, largely as a result of studies made by the U. S. Geological Survey in cooperation with the New York State Water Resources Commission and Nassau and Suffolk Counties. The water development has followed a general pattern which, although somewhat related to population density and local waste-disposal practices, has been controlled largely by the response of the hydrologic system to stresses that man has imposed upon the system. The purpose of this report is to summarize the highlights of the historical pattern of ground-water development on Long Island and to consider briefly the insight that the history of development affords regarding the future development and conservation of Long Island's most valuable natural resource.

Geologic Environment

Long Island (Fig. 1) has a land area of about 1,400 square miles and is geographically a large detached segment of the Atlantic Coastal Plain. The island is underlain by crystalline bedrock, the uppermost surface of which ranges in altitude from about sea level at the northwest corner of the island to about 2,000 feet below sea level in the southeastern part of Suffolk County (Fig. 2).

The bedrock is overlain by a wedge-shaped mass of unconsolidated sedimentary deposits that attain a maximum thickness of about 2,000 feet. These deposits constitute the ground-water reservoir of Long Island and can be divided into six major stratigraphic units, which differ in their geologic ages, mineral composition, and hydraulic properties. These units are, from oldest to youngest, (1) Lloyd Sand Member of the Raritan Formation, (2) clay member of the Raritan Formation, (3) Magothy Formation, (4) Jameco Gravel, (5) Gardiners Clay, and (6) glacial deposits. (Suter and others, 1949). The first three units listed are of Cretaceous age, and the last three are of Pleistocene age.

The Lloyd Sand Member of the Raritan Formation has a maximum thickness of about 300 feet and consists mainly of fine to coarse sand and some gravel and interbedded clay. It forms

FIG. 1. Long Island and vicinity.

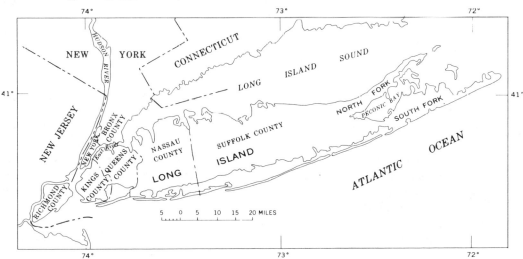

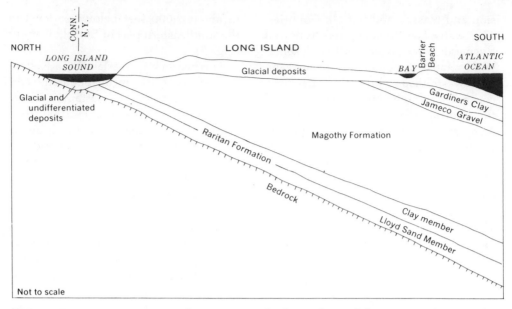

FIG. 2. Diagrammatic section showing general relationships of the major rock units of the ground-water reservoir in Nassau County.

the basal water-bearing unit of the ground-water reservoir. The clay member of the Raritan Formation is composed mainly of clay but locally contains considerable sand; it also has a maximum thickness of about 300 feet. Hydraulically, the clay member is a leaky confining layer for the Lloyd Sand Member—retarding, but not preventing, vertical leakage of water to and from the Lloyd.

The Magothy Formation on Long Island is partly correlative with the Magothy formation in New Jersey. It consists of complexly interbedded layers of sand, silt, and clay and some gravel in the lower part. The complexity of the interbedding and the character of fossils it contains suggest that the formation was mainly laid down under continental (flood-plain) conditions. The Magothy Formation is the thickest unit of the ground-water res-

ervoir on Long Island, attaining a maximum thickness of about 1,000 feet. Its horizontal permeability differs widely from place to place and is considerably higher than its vertical permeability. It commonly yields more than 1,000 gpm (gallons per minute) per well. Water in the formation is largely under artesian conditions.

Near the north and south shores of the island, the Magothy Formation locally is overlain by the Jameco Gravel. The maximum thickness of the Jameco is about 200 feet. It consists mainly of medium to coarse sand, but locally contains abundant gravel and some silt and clay. The Jameco Gravel is moderately to highly permeable and yields as much as 1,500 gpm per well. Water in the formation occurs under artesian conditions.

The Gardiners Clay is mainly restricted in extent to two moderately narrow bands that parallel the north and south shores, and it is commonly underlain by either the Jameco Gravel or the Magothy Formation.

The surface of Long Island is composed mostly of material deposited either directly by Pleistocene continental ice sheets or by melt water derived from the ice sheets. These glacial deposits consist mainly of sand and gravel outwash in the central and southern parts of the island, and mixed till and outwash atop and between the hills in the northern part of the island. The glacial outwash deposits are highly permeable and therefore permit moderately rapid infiltration of precipitation.

Hydrologic System

The four major water-bearing units of the ground-water reservoir of Long Island are the glacial deposits, Jameco Gravel, Magothy Formation, and Lloyd Sand Member of the Raritan Formation (Fig. 2). These four units contain mostly fresh ground water; however, locally they contain salty ground water or they are hydraulically connected with salty water of the ocean, sound, or bays. Under natural conditions recharge to the ground-water reservoir resulted entirely from the infiltration of precipitaton, which is estimated to have averaged roughly 1 mgd per square mile (Swarzenski, 1963, p. 35). Most of the ground water moved laterally through the glacial deposits and discharged into streams or into bodies of salt water bordering the island without first reaching deeper water-bearing zones. Most of the remainder of the ground water moved downward through the glacial deposits into the Jameco Gravel or Magothy Formation, and from there part flowed laterally to the ocean and the remainder flowed downward through the clay member of the Raritan Formation into the Lloyd Sand Member. (See Fig. 4.)

Estimates of ground-water discharge under natural conditions can be developed by extrapolation of data listed by

FIG. 3. Generalized contours on the water table (the upper surface of the ground-water reservoir) in 1961.

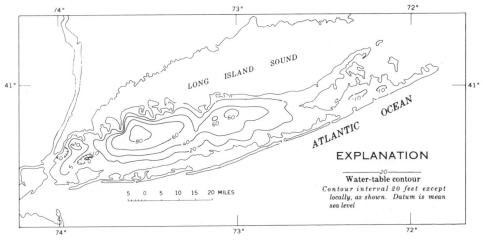

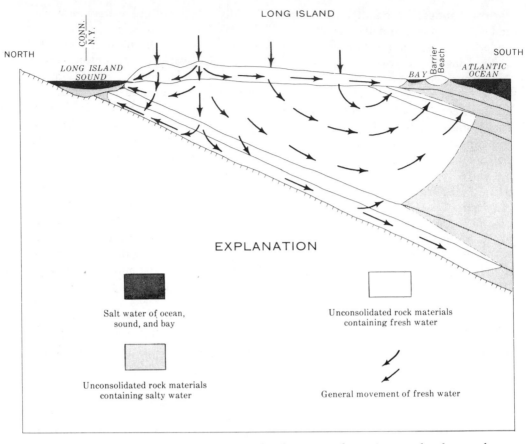

EXPLANATION

Salt water of ocean, sound, and bay

Unconsolidated rock materials containing fresh water

Unconsolidated rock materials containing salty water

General movement of fresh water

FIG. 4. Diagrammatic section showing predevelopment (phase 1) generalized ground-water conditions. Contacts between rock units are as shown in Fig. 2.

Pluhowski and Kantrowitz (1964, p. 38–55) for the Babylon-Islip area, a large and reasonably representative part of Long Island. Those data suggest that about 90 percent of the total recharge ultimately discharged from the glacial deposits (mainly by seepage to streams), and about 10 percent discharged by subsurface outflow from the Magothy Formation, the Jameco Gravel, and the Lloyd Sand.

The water table on Long Island (Fig. 3) and also the piezometric (pressure) surfaces of the underlying artesian aquifers (which have about the same general shape as the water table) form elongate mounds following roughly the configuration of the land surface. Two prominent highs characterize the water table—one centered in Nassau County and one centered in Suffolk County. Northwestern Queens County also has a small high in the water table. Other notable features are the cones of depression that extend below sea level in Kings and Queens Counties; these cones are in areas of past or current local overdevelopment of ground water.

Changes in Ground-Water Development with Time

Phase 1—Predevelopment Conditions

Ground-water development on Long Island has progressed and is progressing through several distinct phases. Under natural or predevelopment conditions (Fig. 4), the hydrologic system was in overall equilibrium and long-term average ground-water recharge and discharge were equal. The general positions of the subsurface interfaces between fresh and salty water in each of the previously described geologic units were stable, reflecting the over-all hydrologic balance. The interfaces were virtually at the coasts in the glacial deposits and were off-shore in the underlying units.

Phase 2

In the initial stage of development (Fig. 5), which began with the arrival of the first European settlers, virtually every house had a shallow well draw-

FIG. 5. Diagrammatic section showing generalized ground-water conditions during phase 2 of ground-water development (shallow supply wells and waste disposal through cesspools). Contacts between rock units are shown in Fig. 2.

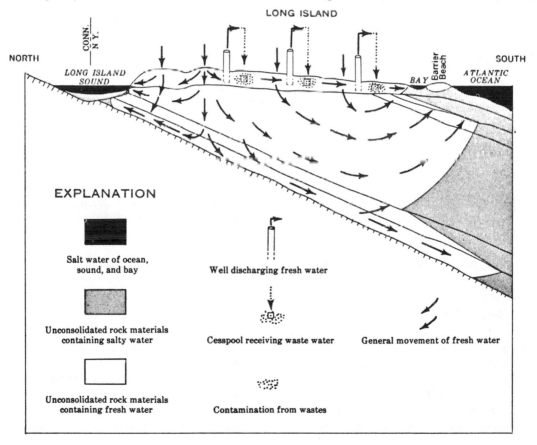

LONG ISLAND

NORTH   SOUTH

LONG ISLAND SOUND   ATLANTIC OCEAN   BAY   Barrier Beach

CONN. N.Y.

EXPLANATION

Salt water of ocean, sound, and bay

Unconsolidated rock materials containing salty water

Unconsolidated rock materials containing fresh water

Well discharging fresh water

Cesspool receiving waste water

Contamination from wastes

General movement of fresh water

ing water from the glacial deposits and a cesspool returning waste water to the same deposits. As the population increased, individual wells were abandoned and public-supply wells were installed in the glacial deposits. The individual cesspools, however, were retained and little water was lost from the system during use. Although a considerable amount of ground water was being withdrawn, practically all of it was returned to the same aquifer from which it was removed. In general, therefore, the system remained in balance, and the positions of the interfaces between fresh and salt water remained practically unchanged. However, this cycle of ground-water development and waste-water disposal resulted in the pollution of the shallow ground water in the vicinity of the cesspools.

Phase 3

In time, as the cesspool pollution spread, some shallow public-supply wells had to be abandoned and these were replaced with deeper public-supply wells, most of which tapped the Jameco Gravel and the Magothy Formation. Supply wells were also constructed in the deeper units at places where the glacial deposits contained water with objectionable amounts of dissolved iron or other troublesome natural constituents. Most of the water withdrawn from the deeper units was returned to the shallower glacial deposits by means of cesspools, and subsequently discharged to the sea by subsurface outflow or by seepage to streams (Fig. 6).

As a result of the withdrawal of water from the Magothy Formation and the Jameco Gravel, and the concurrent decrease in hydraulic heads in these units, the downward movement of ground water from the overlying glacial deposits locally was increased. However, the increased downward movement only partially compensated for the withdrawals of water from the Magothy and Jameco deposits. Locally, a hydraulic imbalance developed in the Magothy and Jameco deposits and caused a decrease in the amount of fresh ground water in storage and a landward movement of salty water.

Phase 4

The next major phase in the development of ground water on Long Island (Fig. 7) was the introduction of large-scale sewer systems—notably in that portion of Long Island that is part of New York City (Kings and Queens Counties). Most of the pumped ground water that previously had been returned to the ground-water reservoir by means of cesspools was thereafter discharged to the sea through the sewers. Whereas the net draft on the ground-water system during the preceding phases of development was negligible, virtually all the ground water diverted to sewers during phase 4 represented a permanent loss from the system. The newly imposed stress on the ground-water system locally resulted in a rapid landward encroachment of salty water into the previously fresh ground-water reservoir. The most dramatic example occurred during the 1930's in Kings County (the Borough of Brooklyn), which by that time had been completely sewered for many years. In 1936, decreased natural recharge owing to urbanization and increased ground-water withdrawals, which during the previous few years

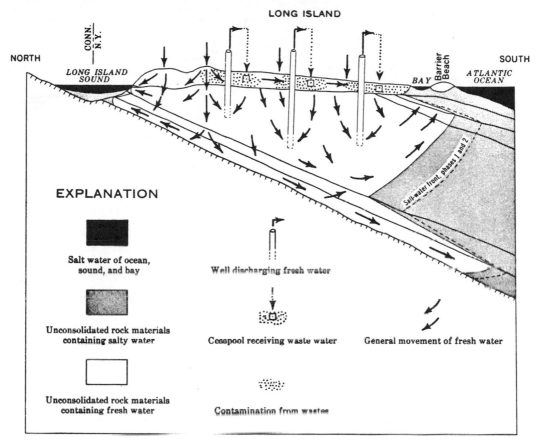

FIG. 6 Diagrammatic section showing generalized ground-water conditions during phase 3 of ground-water development (deep supply wells and waste disposal through cesspools). Contacts between rock units are as shown in Fig. 2.

averaged more than 75 mgd, caused ground-water levels in Brooklyn locally to decline to as much as 35 feet below sea level (Lusczynski, 1952, pls. 1 and 2). This local overdevelopment caused contamination of large parts of the ground-water reservoir in that area from sea-water encroachment.

In 1947 virtually all pumping for public supply in Kings County was discontinued and the Borough was thereafter supplied with water from the New York City municipal-supply system, which utilizes surface-water reservoirs in upstate New York. A notable exception was ground-water withdrawal for air-conditioning use. Such usage was permitted, however, only under the condition that the water was returned to the ground-water reservoir by means of injection wells (locally referred to as "diffusion' wells).

Present Areal Differences in Ground-Water Development

The present pattern of ground-water development on Long Island affords an

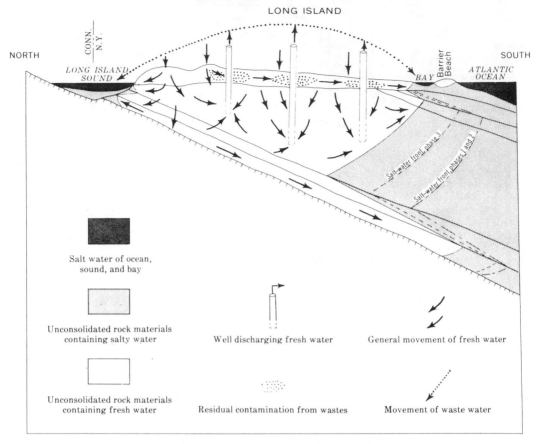

FIG. 7. Diagrammatic section showing generalized ground-water conditions during phase 4 of ground-water development (deep supply wells and waste disposal through sewers to adjacent salt-water bodies). Contacts between rock units are as shown in Fig. 2.

excellent opportunity to observe and evaluate the historic trend of that development, because all the major phases of development described herein, except the predevelopment phase, can be observed now in different subareas of the island (Fig. 8). Moreover, once the transitory status of present development in each subarea is recognized in relation to the pattern of historical trends, it becomes possible to predict and perhaps forestall some of the undesirable aspects of those trends.

Subarea A (Fig. 8) includes roughly

the eastern two-thirds of Suffolk County. Except for several small communities, the subarea is largely rural and has the lowest population density on Long Island. On the whole, the subarea can be characterized as being in phase 2 of ground-water development (Fig. 5)—that is, most of the wells in the subarea tap the shallow glacial deposits and supply water to single-family dwellings. The bulk of this water is returned to the glacial deposits through individually owned cesspools, and in overall aspect the ground-water system is still in hydraulic balance.

Subarea B, in central Suffolk County, is experiencing the impact of the suburban expansion associated with the entire New York City metropolitan area. Farms and woodlands are giving way to housing developments, and

FIG. 8. Water-development subareas in 1965.

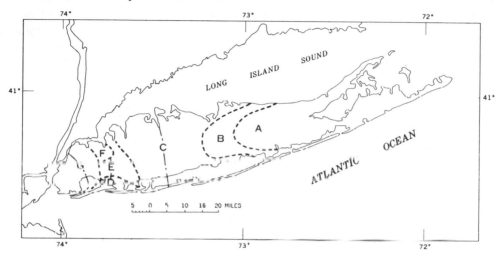

EXPLANATION

Subarea   Characteristics

A   Phase 2 of development. Pumpage mainly from shallow privately owned wells. Waste water returned to shallow glacial deposits through cesspools; local contamination of glacial deposits by cesspool effluent. System virtually in balance; positions of salt-water fronts unchanged.

B   Transition between phase 2 and 3. Pumpage from privately owned and public-supply wells. Waste water returned to shallow glacial deposits by way of cesspools; areas of cesspool-effluent contamination spreading. System virtually in balance.

C   Phase 3 of development. Pumpage mainly from deep public-supply wells; waste water returned to shallow glacial deposits by way of cesspools. System locally out of balance, causing local salt-water intrusion.

D   Phase 4 of development. Pumpage almost entirely from deep public-supply wells; waste water discharged to the sea by way of sewers. System out of balance; salty water actively moving landward.

E   Phase 4 of development. Pumpage almost entirely from deep public-supply wells; waste water discharged to the sea by way of sewers. System out of balance; may be subject to salt-water intrusion in the future.

F   Very little ground-water development. Water supply derived from New York City municipal-supply system; waste water discharged to the sea by way of sewers. System in balance.

G   Very little ground-water development. Water supply derived from New York City municipal-supply system; waste water discharged to the sea by way of sewers. Large areas contain salty ground water owing to former intensive ground-water development and related salt-water intrusion.

most of the pumpage in the subarea is now from large-capacity public-supply wells that tap the glacial deposits. However, most of the sewage disposal is still through individually owned cesspools. Thus, the area is in a transition between phase 2 and phase 3 of development. Cesspool pollution still is not widespread, but is substantial enough to be of concern to local government agencies. Accordingly, plans are currently (1965) being made to construct sewers in the area and to gradually replace the wells that tap the glacial deposits with wells that will tap the Magothy Formation.

Subarea C includes the westernmost part of Suffolk County and the eastern two-thirds of Nassau County. Mainly because it is closer to New York City, this subarea was subjected to intensive suburban development earlier than was subarea B. Therefore, the population density and, accordingly, the water requirements in subarea C are substantially greater than in subarea B. Virtually the entire water supply for subarea C is obtained from large-capacity public-supply wells. The part of the subarea that is in western Suffolk County obtains most of its water supply from public-supply wells, of which about half tap the glacial deposits and most of the remainder tap the Magothy Formation. In the part of the subarea that is in Nassau County, most of the public-supply wells tap the Magothy Formation.

Except for a few communities along the coast, most of subarea C is not sewered; practically all the domestic sewage is disposed of through individually owned cesspools. Thus, on the whole the subarea is in phase 3 of development (Fig. 6). The system locally

is out of balance owing to this development; however, substantial widespread salt-water encroachment has not yet occurred. Plans are being made to install sewers throughout the subarea.

Subareas D and E, which include parts of western Nassau and southeastern Queens Counties, are moderately to highly urbanized and are almost completely sewered. Practically the entire water supply for these subareas is derived from wells tapping the Magothy Formation, Jameco Gravel, and the Lloyd Sand Member of the Raritan Formation. Thus, these subareas are mainly in phase 4 of development and are characterized by a hydrologic imbalance (Fig. 7). The imbalance, which is accentuated because more than 70 mgd of water derived from the ground-water reservoir of these subareas currently is being discharged to the sea by way of sewage-treatment plants, is most clearly manifested in subarea D, where salty water is moving landward (Lusczynski and Swarzenski, 1960; Perlmutter and Geraghty, 1963). If the present trend continues, subarea D (the area of active salt-water encroachment) probably will expand at the expense of subarea E.

Subarea F, in northeastern Queens County, receives nearly its entire water supply from the New York City municipal-supply system. The subarea is sewered; however, because ground-water pumpage is negligible, the ground-water system is largely in balance.

Subarea G is the most highly urbanized and receives virtually all its water from the New York City municipal system. The entire subarea is sewered. As previously noted, large areas in

Kings County were invaded by salty water because of substantial overdevelopment and the resulting decline in ground-water levels. Similarly, salty water had invaded the ground-water reservoir in parts of western Queens County. Water levels in Kings County have recovered appreciably since the mid 1940's, when the consumptive ground-water uses were drastically reduced. Presumably, the salty water is retreating seaward and is being diluted by recharge derived from precipitation, but precise data regarding these changes are lacking.

Conclusion

Ground water probably will continue to be the major source of water for most of Long Island (except for Kings and Queens Counties) for at least the next several decades. Moreover, if the present trends continue, the ground-water resources of the island probably will continue to be depleted perhaps at an accelerated rate. The historic trends of ground water development and the present status of development strongly suggest that such depletion will in time cause salt-water contamination of larger and larger parts of the ground-water reservoir. Moreover, the areas in which such contamination occurs, in addition to extending inward from the coasts, probably will also extend farther and farther eastward as the population continues to expand in that direction.

Several alternative methods of conserving and augmenting the ground-water resources of Long Island are currently being considered. These include, among others, desalting of sea water with the use of atomic energy, artificial recharge, and the reclamation of water from sewage. The consequences of such possible meaures are highly significant inasmuch as the future well-being of several million people is at stake. However, even with the most promising of conservation methods, wise management will be required to gain the fullest use from the available fresh-water supply while also preventing undue hardships resulting from local over-development of the ground-water reservoir. Fully effective management requires:

1. Recognition of the unity of the hydrologic system of Long Island.

2. The best obtainable scientific information about the system and how it functions.

3. Sound evaluation of the various alternative methods of water development and conservation, guided by available scientific information— including the hydrologic consequences of the historic and present-day changing pattern of ground-water development on Long Island.

References

Lusczynski, N. J., 1952. The recovery of ground-water levels in Brooklyn, New York from 1947 to 1950: U. S. Geol. Survey Circ. 167, 29 p.

Lusczynski, N. J, and Swarzenski, W. V., 1960, Position of the salt-water body in the Magothy(?) Formation in the Cedarhurst-Woodmere area of southwestern Nassau County: N. Y. Econ. Geology, v. 55, no. 8, p. 1739–1750.

Perlmutter, N. M., and Geraghty, J. J., 1963, Geology and ground-water conditions in southern Nassau and southeastern Queens Counties, Long Island, New York: U. S. Geol. Survey Water-Supply Paper 1613-A, 205 p.

Pluhowski, E. J., and Kantrowitz, I. H., 1964, Hydrology of the Babylon-Islip area, Suffolk County, Long Island, New York: U. S. Geol. Survey Water-Supply Paper 1768, 119 p.

Suter, Russell, de Laguna, Wallace, and Perlmutter, N. M., 1949, Mapping of geologic formations and aquifers on Long Island, New York: New York State Power and Control Comm. Bull. GW-18, 212 p.

Swarzenski, W. V., 1963, Hydrology of northwestern Nassau and northeastern Queens Counties, Long Island, New York: U. S. Geol. Survey Water-Supply Paper 1657, 90 p.

36   Geological Influence on Regional Health Problems

Jean M. Spencer

Introduction

Medical geology, regional pathology, and geographical disease all describe the relationship between health and geology. In the past, certain localities were regarded with suspicion as areas with high percentages of particular types of disease. Current investigation into many of these suspicions demonstrates a decided link between various chronic diseases and particular geological environments.

Iodine Deficiency

Perhaps the best known relationship between a disease and geology is that of thyroid disease caused by an environmental iodine deficiency. Iodine is essential to normal function of the thyroid gland which is located at the base of the neck. Iodine is also present in tissue and blood. Its deficiency causes goiter or enlargement of the thyroid in many persons living in iodine-deficient areas. The term "Derbyshire neck" reflects the frequency of goiter cases in Derbyshire, England.

If a pregnant woman has a severe iodine deficiency, her child may be born a cretin, as were common at one time in high goiter-rate areas of Switzerland and Mexico. A cretin is an idiotic dwarf, small in stature, who rarely reaches or exceeds a mental age of 10.

Much of the northern United States, especially the Great Lakes region and the northwestern states, has iodine-deficient soils and water, reflected in the high goiter rate before the use of iodized salt. Similar relationships exist throughout the world as in Central Mexico, Great Britain, Nepal, and Switzerland.

The National Nutrition Survey found goiter incidence increasing in the United States because iodized salt is not used as widely as before World War II. In some areas of the United States goiter is still endemic, particularly among the poor (Schaefer and Johnson, 1969).

Reprinted from *The Texas Journal of Science,* v. 21, p. 459–469 (1970) with permission of the author and the Texas Academy of Science.

Ms. Spencer is on the faculty at Baylor University.

Iodine also appears to play an important role in the incidence of female breast cancer. In the United States breast cancer is the leading cause of death for women between 40 and 44, and the leading cause of death for women dying from all types of cancer between the ages of 35 and 55. The death rate from female breast cancer is higher in iodine-deficient areas than in other areas (Fig. 1). This relationship is observed in other countries as well as in the United States. Countries with high incidences of goiter and breast cancer include Thailand, Mexico, England, Wales, the Netherlands, and Switzerland. Countries with low incidences of goiter and breast cancer include Japan, Chile, and Iceland (Bogardus and Finley, 1961).

Fluorine Deficiency

Fluorine, another environmental halogen, is the object of much investigation. This element is known to produce strong teeth mottled with brown in children raised where the natural fluorine concentration in the water supply is well above that recommended by the U. S. Public Health Service. This condition is common to some areas of west Texas. Where fluorine is deficient in the water supply (considerably below one part per million) children develop soft teeth that decay easily.

Not so well known perhaps, is the fact that the elderly also need fluorine to maintain good bone density. Bone is composed of the protein collagen,

FIG. 1. Distribution of death rate in the United States for female breast cancer. *After* Bogardus and Finley, 1961 —Breast cancer and thyroid disease. *Surgery,* 49 (4): 464.

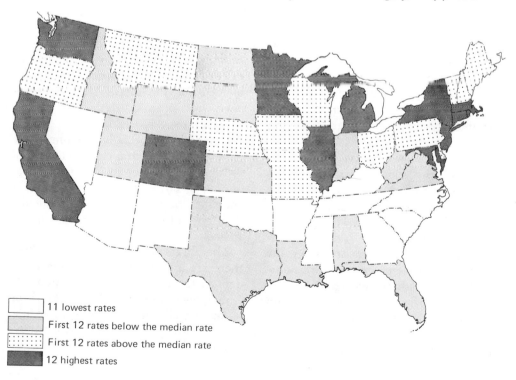

☐ 11 lowest rates
▨ First 12 rates below the median rate
⣿ First 12 rates above the median rate
■ 12 highest rates

which acts as reinforcing material, and the mineral apatite, which gives strength to the bone. Calcium found in bone is present in apatite crystals.

Apatite, with a composition of $Ca_5(OH, F, Cl)(PO_4)_3$, accepts either fluorine or the hydroxyl radical into its crystal lattice in bone. When fluorine is present, apatite crystals are larger, more perfect, and the bone is more resistant to degeneration. More calcium remains in the bone, and density is maintained. When the hydroxyl radical substitutes for the fluoride ion, degeneration occurs more readily, and various types of bone fractures become more common.

Gradual loss of bone density in men and women over 40 can result in loss of as much as half the total skeletal mass by age 70. This loss of bone density leads to the condition known as osteoporosis. The bent-over little old ladies of the 6th decade and beyond, many with what is called a "dowager's hump," are suffering from collapse of the spinal vertebrae due to osteoporosis and subsequent breaking. The incidence of collapse and fracture doubles during each 5-year period after age 40 among women and after 50 among men.

Two regional studies comparing high and low fluoride areas show osteoporosis higher in the low fluoride areas and rare in high fluoride areas (Bernstein, *et al.*, 1966). However, the amount of fluoride in drinking water needed to avoid osteoporosis in the elderly is high enough to cause some mottling of teeth in children.

While osteoporosis is more common among elderly women, the calcium released by loss of bone density frequently deposits in and lines the aortas of men, producing aortic calcification and subsequent narrowing of the aorta, the major artery leading from the heart. Adult men, in every age group, living in low fluoride areas have 2 to 3 times more aortic calcification than those living in high fluoride areas (Anon., 1967). Aortic calcification in turn, often produces aneurysms or dilation of the calcified blood vessels causing other cardiovascular problems.

Calcium Deficiency

A disease produced by an environmental calcium deficiency is the Urov disease of the Eastern Transbaikal of the Soviet Union and northern China (Fig. 2). In these areas people and domestic animals gradually develop enlarged and stiffened joints early in life. Bone growth is arrested. In one village in the Amur province 44% of the population was afflicted. Most of these were children 11 to 15 years of age (Khobot'ev, 1960).

While various other elements (lead, cadmium, gold, iron, radium), organic matter, and iodine deficiency have been blamed for the disease, these causes have not been proved. The "sick" water, however, "is deficient in dissolved solids, especially calcium, while 'healthy' water contains more dissolved solids and is richer in calcium" (Khobot'ev, 1960). Where the disease is endemic, waters are not only calcium deficient but strontium and barium enriched.

The disease does not occur where there are limestone outcrops but is endemic to marine Jurassic deposits (sandstones and shales) and zones of igneous rocks including a granite unusually low in calcium (Khobot'ev, 1960).

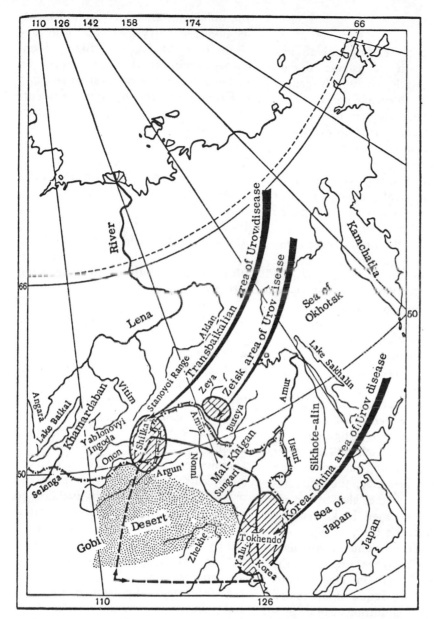

FIG. 2. Distribution of Urov endemic areas in the Far East. *From* Khobot'ev, 1960—Bio-geochemical provinces with calcium deficiency. *Geochemistry*, 8: 831.

Other Factors

In west Devonshire, England an uneven distribution of cancer deaths prompted a study in which cancer deaths for a 20-year period were plotted on a geologic map of the area. This study demonstrated an extraordinary distribution of cancer deaths for those persons living on certain geologic formations (notably Devonian sandstones). These death rates were not matched for persons living on adjacent areas (Allen-Price, 1960).

Many soils in the high cancer areas proved to have high concentrations of lead—100 ppm, with some samples containing more than 1000 ppm lead. Vegetables grown on these soils have high lead contents, none less than 10 ppm in the ash (Warren, 1963).

The development of highly sophisticated analytical techniques, such as the atomic absorption spectrophotometer, permits rapid microchemical studies of cells, soil, and water. This analytical progress facilitates investigation into the sources of trace elements and their actual role in physiological function.

To function properly, the body requires a number of trace elements in addition to the so-called bulk elements (those found in the body in high concentrations). Trace elements are usually, though not always, present in the body in parts per million. The amounts of trace elements required are small and pathological conditions can be produced either by a slight deficiency or a slight excess of a particular element, as in the case of selenium and fluorine.

Of the trace elements, manganese, iron, cobalt, copper, zinc, and molybdenum are most commonly associated with enzyme activity. Enzymes act as catalysts in biochemical reactions, and the poisoning effects of such elements as silver, mercury (+2), and lead may stem from the fact that they are enzyme-inhibitors when present in an enzyme in place of the desired element.

Diseases caused by trace elements were first known among miners. Symptoms were caused by constant contact with large amounts of a particular element over a long period of time. Pitchblende miners in Austria acquired a condition called "Bergkrankheit"— mountain disease—from inhalation of the radio-active gas radon, which emits alpha particles. Mortality rate from lung cancer among these miners was 50 times that of the rest of the population (Alexander, 1959).

Elements can be inhaled, as in the case of the miners suffering from "Bergkrankheit," but normally they are ingested with food and water. The geology of an area, in the form of its rocks and sediments, is the source of the elements that enter soil and water and are made available to man and the plants and animals of his food supply.

However, the fact that an element is present in soil or rocks does not mean that it is necessarily available to plants or that it will dissolve in water. Its physical state and whether it is tightly bound in a mineral lattice or held to clay particles will determine its availability.

Deficiencies and poisonings in plants and domestic animals have been known and treated for many years. Many areas of the world with excesses or deficiencies of various trace elements are known. Figure 3 shows areas of animal diseases due to mineral deficiencies and poisonings in the United States.

Because in the United States our

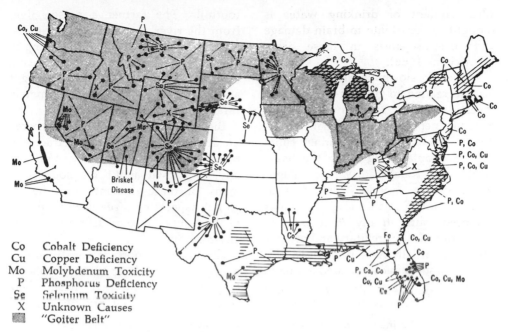

Co	Cobalt Deficiency
Cu	Copper Deficiency
Mo	Molybdenum Toxicity
P	Phosphorus Deficiency
Se	Selenium Toxicity
X	Unknown Causes
▓	"Goiter Belt"

I. Known areas in the United States where mineral-nutritional diseases of animals occur. The dots indicate approximate locations where troubles occur. The lines not terminating in dots indicate a generalized area or areas where specific locations have not been reported.

FIG. 3. Mineral nutritional diseases in animals. *From* Beeson, 1957—Soil management and crop quality, in *Soil, The 1957 Yearbook of Agriculture.* U. S. Dept. of Agriculture, 259.

food supplies come from many sources rather than local kitchen gardens, water is probably the major source of inorganic ions that reaches almost 100% of a resident population. It is therefore important to know what elements are present or lacking in a given water supply, the source of these elements, and their geochemistry and biochemistry. Normal municipal water treatment hardly alters the percentages of the various trace elements in the water distributed to consumers.

Studies into the physiological effects of hard and soft municipal water demonstrate a relationship between soft water and high cardiovascular death rate for those of middle and old age. None of the water supplies studied contained any elements considered toxic or in dangerous concentrations, and no element was found to be particularly significant as the cause of cardiovascular disease (Crawford, 1968). Crawford, working in England and Wales, found concentrations of manganese and aluminum higher in soft water-high cardiovascular areas and concentrations of boron, iodine, fluorine, and silica higher in hard water-low cardiovascular areas. In the United States similar studies also demonstrate that the softer the water the higher the death rate from cardiovascular disease (Schroeder, 1966).

In certain areas of Japan the high

silica content of drinking water is thought to contribute to brain damage and arteriosclerosis in these areas (Henschen, 1966).

A chronic, slowly progressive kidney disease related to river areas is under investigation in Yugoslavia. Chronic endemic nephropathy, or Balkan nephritis, gradually reduces kidney function of people living along the Sava, Drina, and Kalabara rivers of Yugoslavia and in very localized areas of Bulgaria and Romania (Fig. 4). It has not been found in any other areas of these countries. Hereditary and organic causes essentially have been ruled out. The disease is most common among those who live in the river valleys but not among those who live in nearby foothills. The farther a person lives from the river, the less severe the disease. Medical studies are attempting to implicate lead, uranium, cadmium, and nickel, but with no success (Griggs and Hall). The cause of this ultimately fatal disease is still unknown.

Biological data are being gathered on the effects of many other trace elements in the human body. Little, if any, is known about the sources of many of these elements and the regional aspects of disease with respect to their abundance or deficiency in the environment.

Zinc is an important constituent of many enzymes. It appears to concentrate in parts of the body where there is an increase in cell growth, such as

FIG. 4. Outline map of Yugoslavia and surrounding countries. Dotted lines indicate areas of chronic endemic nephropathy. *From* Griggs and Hall— Investigation of chronic endemic nephropathy in Yugoslavia, in *15th Annual Conference on the Kidney Proc.* National Kidney Foundation, 313.

in healing wounds and burns. Given in large amounts, it speeds wound healing (Pories, 1967).

Zinc-deficient diets in pregnant rats produce such birth defects as cleft lip, missing digits, and clubbed feet. These congenital malformations are also found in human infants, although no relationship to zinc has been established (Hurley, 1968).

Zinc-deprived humans have retarded longitudinal growth and physical maturing. In a group of zinc-deprived Egyptian boys who were also heavily infected with parasites and suffered from general malnutrition, only the institution of zinc therapy produced growth and physical maturing (Sandstead, et al. 1968).

The presence of zinc in thermal springs in Germany has been implicated as an important factor in the sexual rejuvenation properties attributed to many of these springs.

Cadmium is apparently an antimetabolite for zinc. An elevated renal cadmium-to-zinc ratio often appears in persons dying of hypertensive disease. Cadmium is not present in the body at birth but increases in concentration with age. An increase in cadmium parallels an increase in hypertension (Schroeder, 1965). Coffee and tea are sources of cadmium, but what about its natural sources in soil and water?

These are only a few of the relationships, understood and unclear, between geology and health. Medical personnel are aware of many deviations from "normal" metabolism by excesses or deficiencies of trace elements. They are not, however, trained to recognize sources and geologic relationships of these elements. It is, therefore, the responsibility of those who are trained in the study of the earth to contribute their knowledge to this field that is important to all of us—health.

Literature Cited

Alexander, P., 1959—*Atomic Radiation and Life.* Penguin Books, Harmondsworth, Middlesex, England.

Allen-Price, E. D., 1960—Uneven distribution of cancer in west Devon. *Lancet,* June 1960: 1235–1238.

Anonymous, 1967—Fluoride: Deficiency held a factor in osteoporosis. *Medical Tribune,* 8 (57): 12.

Beeson, K. C., 1957—Soil management and crop quality, in *Soil, The 1957 Yearbook of Agriculture.* U. S. Dept. of Agriculture, 258–267.

Bernstein, D. S., N. Sadowsky, D. M. Hegsted, C. D. Guri, and F. J. Stare, 1966—Prevalence of osteoporosis in high- and low-fluoride areas in North Dakota. *Jour. Amer. Med. Assoc.,* 198 (5): 499–504.

Bogardus, G. M., and J. W. Finley, 1961—Breast cancer and thyroid disease. *Surgery,* 49 (4): 461–468.

Crawford, M. D., M. J. Gardner, and J. N. Morris, 1968—Mortality and hardness of local water-supplies. *Lancet,* April 1968: 827–831.

Griggs, R. C., and P. W. Hall, Investigation of chronic endemic nephropathy in Yugoslavia, in *15th Annual Conference on the Kidney Proc.* National Kidney Foundation: 312–328.

Henschen, F., 1966—*The History and Geography of Disease.* Delacorte Press, New York.

Hurley, L. S., 1968—The consequences of fetal impoverishment. *Nutrition Today,* 3 (4): 2–10.

Hurley, L. S., and H. Swenerton, 1966—Congenital malformations resulting from zinc deficiency in rats. *Soc. for Experimental Biology and Medicine Proc.,* 123: 692–696.

Khobot'ev, V. G., 1960—Biogeochemical provinces with calcium deficiency. *Geochemistry*, 8: 830–840.

Pories, W. J., 1967—Acceleration of healing with zinc sulfate. *Ann. Surg.*, 165: 432–436.

Sandstead, H. H., A. S. Prasad, A. R. Schulert, Z. Farid, A. Miale, Jr., S. Bassilly, and W. J. Darby, 1967—Human zinc deficiency, endrocrine manifestations and response to treatment. *Amer. Jour. Clinical Nutrition*, 20 (5): 422–442.

Schaefer, A. E., and O. C. Johnson, 1969— Are we well fed? The search for the answer. *Nutrition Today*, 4 (1): 2–11.

Schroeder, H. A., 1965—Cadmium as a factor in hypertension. *Jour. Chronic Dis.*, 18: 647–656.

———, 1966—Municipal drinking water and cardiovascular death rates. *Jour. Amer. Med. Assoc.*, 195 (2): 81–85.

Warren, H. V., 1963—Trace elements and epidemiology. *Jour. Coll. Gen. Practit.*, 6: 517–531.

Supplementary Readings*

Ackermann, W. C., 1971, The Oakley Project—a Controversy in Land Use, in *Env. Geol. Notes No. 46*, (R. E. Bergstrom ed.), pp. 33–39, Ill. State Geol. Survey.

Davis, G. H., and Wood, L. A., 1974, Water Demands for Expanding Energy Development, *U. S. Geol. Survey Circ. 703*, 14 pp.

Deming, H. G., Gilliam, W. S., and McCoy, W. H., 1975, *Water*, Oxford Univ. Press, N.Y., 350 pp.

Durfor, C. N., and Becker, E., 1964, Public Water Supplies of the 100 Largest Cities in the United States, 1962, *U. S. Geol. Survey Water-Supply Paper 1812*, 364 pp.

Goldman, C. R., et al., eds., 1973, *Environmental Quality and Water Development*, W. H. Freeman and Co., San Francisco, Calif., 510 pp.

Hackett, O. M., 1966, Ground-Water Research in the United States, *U. S. Geol. Survey Circ. 527*, 8 pp.

Harte, J., and Socolow, R. H., 1971, The Everglades: Wilderness versus Rampant Land Development in South Florida, in *Patient Earth* by J. Harte and R. H. Socolow, Holt, Rinehart, Winston, pp. 181–202.

Hasler, A. D., 1947, Eutrophication of Lakes by Domestic Drainage, *Ecology*, v. 28, n. 4, pp. 383–95.

Jenkins, D. S., 1957, Fresh Water from Salt, *Scientific American*, v. 196, n. 3, pp. 37–45.

Jones, D. E., 1967, Urban Hydrology—a redirection, *Civil Engineering*, v. 37, n. 8, pp. 58–67.

Leopold, L. B., 1968, Hydrology for Urban Land Planning—A Guidebook on the Hydrologic Effects of Urban Land Use, *U. S. Geol. Survey Circ. 554*, 18 pp.

Leopold, L., 1974, *Water—a primer*, W. H. Freeman and Co., San Francisco, Calif., 172 pp.

Lohman, S. W., et al., 1972, Definitions of Selected Ground-Water Terms—revisions and conceptual refinements, *U. S. Geol. Survey Water-Supply Paper 1988*, 21 pp.

Maxwell, J. C., 1965, Will There Be Enough Water?, *Amer. Scientist*, v. 53, pp. 97–103.

McGuinness, C. L., 1969, Scientific or Rule-of-Thumb Techniques of Ground-Water Management—Which Will Prevail? *U. S. Geol. Survey Circ. 608*, 8 pp.

Nace, R. L., 1967, Are We Running Out of Water? *U. S. Geol. Survey Circ. 536*, 7 pp.

Peixoto, J. P., and Kettani, M. A., 1973, The Control of the Water Cycle, *Sci. Amer.* v. 228, n. 4, pp. 46–61.

Pluhowski, E. J., 1970 Urbanization and Its Effect on the Temperature of the Streams on Long Island, New York, *U. S. Geol. Survey Prof. Paper 627-D*, 110 pp.

Rickert, D. A., and Spieker, A. M., 1971,

* References to the hydrologic implications of waste disposal are included in the supplementary readings in Part V.

Real-Estate Lakes, *U. S. Geol. Survey Circ. 601-G*, 19 pp.

Sayre, A. N., 1950, Ground Water, *Sci. Amer.*, v. 183, n. 5, p. 14–19.

Schneider, W. J., Rickert, D. A., and Spieker, A. M., 1973, Role of Water in Urban Planning and Management, *U. S. Geol. Survey Circ. 601-H*, 10 pp.

Seaburn, G. E., 1969, Effects of Urban Development on Direct Runoff to East Meadow Brook, Nassau County, Long Island, New York, *U. S. Geol. Survey Prof. Paper 627-B*, 14 pp.

Seaburn, G. E., 1970, Preliminary Results of Hydrologic Studies at Two Recharge Basins on Long Island, New York, *U. S. Geol. Survey Prof. Paper 627-C*, 17 pp.

Smith, W. C., 1966, Geologic Factors in Dam and Reservoir Planning, *Ill. Geol. Survey, Env. Geol. Note 13*, 10 pp.

Spencer, J. M., 1974, Geology, Health, and Phosphorus, *Jour. Geol. Education*, v. 22, n. 3, pp. 93–96.

Spieker, A. M., 1970, Water in Urban Planning, Salt Creek Basin, Illinois, *U. S. Geol. Survey Water-Supply Paper 2002*, 147 pp.

Thomas, H. E., and Leopold, L. B., 1964, Ground Water in North America, *Science*, v. 143, n. 3610, pp. 1001–1006.

Thomas, H. E., and Schneider, W. J., 1970, Water as an Urban Resource and Nuisance, *U. S. Geol. Survey Circ. 601-D*, 9 pp.

Walker, W., 1969, Illinois Ground Water Pollution, *Jour. Amer. Water Works Assoc.*, v. 61, pp. 31–40.

Weinberger, L. W., Stephan D. G., and Middleton, F. M., 1966, Solving Our Water Problems—Water Renovation and Reuse, *Annal N.Y. Acad. Sciences*, v. 136, art. 5, pp. 131–54.

Films

The First Pollution (Stuart Finley, Inc., 26 min.)

Ground Water—The Hidden Reservoir (John Wiley and Sons, 1971, 19 min.)

Photo by Ted Jones courtesy of Stuart Finley, Incorporated.

V. Waste Disposal

"We might someday be known as the generation that stood knee deep in garbage while firing rockets at the moon."

For many people, today's world is an urban world. Approximately 70 per cent of the United States population lives in urban areas. Furthermore, it is anticipated that most of our future population increase will be absorbed by cities. The implications of population growth and settlement patterns in terms of demands on the physical environment are overwhelming. It has, therefore, become necessary to anticipate and recognize the resultant problems and to plan intelligently to cope with them. Urban geology—a field of applied geology—can contribute significantly to the solution of many problems associated with urbanization.

Some of the urban land-use problems are related to natural geologic hazards inherent in the environment. Volcanism is a potential threat to Seattle (Reading 4). Earthquake activity presents problems for San Francisco and Los Angeles (Reading 6). Venice is plagued by subsidence and sea level changes (Reading 41) and Anchorage by quick clay deposits (Reading 2). Floods are a hazard in the Chicago metropolitan area (Reading 21). The poorly planned exploitation of natural resources has had a negative impact on such urban areas as Long Beach (Reading 29) and Long Island (Reading 35). These aspects of urban geology are dealt with in other sections of this anthology. This section deals with another product of urbanization—the generation of waste.

Solid wastes are accumulating at the rate of more than 1400 million pounds per day in the United States and the rate of production is increasing at 4 per cent per annum. The per capita production of waste is highest in urbanized areas where diverse industrial wastes are added to the garbage and rubbish generated by individuals. The disposal of this material is one of the most serious problems confronting many municipalities. The current annual cost of waste collection and disposal is over three billion dollars. Among public services this amount is exceeded only by expenditures for schools and roads. Safe disposal sites are at a premium in many areas, and indiscriminate disposal can lead to serious health and environmental problems. What are the principal methods of solid-waste disposal? What are the critical elements of the geologic environment which govern the suitability of a disposal site? What are the hydrologic implications of solid-waste disposal? These questions and others are considered by William Schneider in Reading 37.

Most communities continue to employ disposal methods that waste vast quantities of energy and resources that could—and should—be recovered and reused. The technology for the recovery of ferrous metals, aluminum, glass, and paper is now available and in some cases the high BTU value of shredded garbage is being used as a supplementary source of energy. Self-contained recovery—recycling—marketing systems are available and could relieve municipalities of burdensome disposal problems and alleviate the demand on virgin resources. The Resource Recovery Act of 1970 encourages recycling of wastes. Financial support for the employment of innovative recovery systems may be available from the Environmental Protection Agency.

In addition to solid wastes, urbanized areas generate large volumes of exotic liquid wastes. These wastes may be disposed of by underground injection, surface irrigation, or septic tanks. Each of these methods has inherent advantages and dangers. The subsurface disposal of liquid waste at the Rocky Mountain Arsenal well near Denver, for example, led to the development of earthquake swarms (Reading 8) and revealed our limited understanding of safe injection pressures. In other cases subsurface disposal has interfered with natural zones of ground water circulation and has proven to be a health hazard.

The advantages and disadvantages of irrigation are reviewed in Reading 38. Although this method has the potential for disposing of large volumes of both municipal and industrial wastes while at the same time recharging the ground water system, the danger of contaminating ground water cannot be overemphasized.

In areas where the rate of urban development has outpaced the installation of city sewer lines, septic tank systems have been installed to handle liquid wastes. In some areas local soils cannot properly absorb the septic tank effluent, and disposal becomes unsafe or the system fails to operate efficiently. The relationship among soil conditions, septic tank design, and the disposal of septic tank effluent is outlined in Reading 39.

Industry generates a variety of toxic wastes that are better handled through carefully designed "management programs" rather than through attempts at "safe," permanent disposal. Much concern has been expressed about radioactive wastes. Radioactive wastes are an essential part of nuclear power development, and methods for handling this product have been the subject of much debate and major research efforts. In Reading 40 Chauncy Starr and R. Philip Hammond argue for "perpetual, flexible management" and present an interesting perspective on the problem of nuclear waste.

37 Hydrologic Implications of Solid-Waste Disposal

William J. Schneider

Introduction

The disposal of solid-waste material—principally garbage and rubbish—is primarily an urban problem. However, unlike liquid waste disposal of sewage and industrial effluents, the problem has received only limited recognition. It is common practice in many metropolitan areas to overlook or ignore the consequences of waste-disposal programs. The full scope of the problem, though, cannot be ignored.

The urban population of the United States is now producing an estimated 1,400 million pounds of solid wastes each day. Disposal of these wastes is a major problem of all cities. In many instances, seemingly endless streams of trucks and railroad cars haul these wastes long distances—as much as hundreds of miles—to disposal sites. Based on a volume estimate of 5.7 cubic yards per ton of waste, this refuse is sufficient to cover more than 400 acres of land per day to a depth of 10 feet. Local governments spend an estimated $3 billion each year on collection and disposal, a sum exceeded in local budgets only by expenditures for schools and roads.

The disposal of these solid wastes poses many problems to local government agencies. Unfortunately, the prob-

Schneider, W. J., 1970, "Hydrologic Implications of Solid-Waste Disposal," *U. S. Geol. Survey Circ. 601-F*, 10 pp. Reprinted by permission of the author.
Mr. Schneider is on the staff of the United States Geological Survey.

lem is handled by many governments on the basis of expediency without due regard to environmental considerations. Garbage and rubbish are collected, hauled minimum distances commensurate with public acceptance, and dumped. Occasionally, the waste is either burned or mixed with soil to provide landfill. As long as the procedure removes the refuse and as long as the disposal site is not a health hazard and does not offend esthetic values too greatly, the operation is considered successful. Overlooked or even ignored is the effect of the disposal on the total environment, including the water resources of the area. Although the disposal of solid wastes can create many serious health, esthetic, and environmental problems, only the hydrologic implications—the effect upon water resources—are considered in this report.

Types of Solid Wastes

Our urban society generates many types of solid wastes. Each may exert a different influence on the water resources of an area. In order to understand the effect of each type, it is necessary to identify the various types as to the principal constituents. Table 1 lists the various categories and sources of refuse material primarily generated by urban activities. Not included are wastes from industries and processing plants; hazardous, pathological, or radioactive wastes from institutions and industries; solids and sludge from sewage-treatment plants; and other special types of solid wastes. These

Table 1 Classification of refuse materials [Adapted from American Public Works Association (1966)]

Kind of refuse	Composition	Source
Garbage	Wastes from preparation, cooking, and serving of food; market wastes; wastes from handling, storage, and sale of produce.	Households, restaurants, institutions, stores, and markets.
Rubbish	Combustible: paper, cartons, boxes, barrels, wood, excelsior, tree branches, yard trimmings, wood furniture, bedding, and dunnage. Noncombustible: metals, tin cans, metal furniture, dirt, glass, crockery, and minerals.	Do.
Ashes	Residue from fires used for cooking and heating and from onsite incineration.	Do.
Trash from streets	Sweepings, dirt, leaves, catch-basin dirt, and contents of litter receptacles.	Streets, sidewalks, alleys, vacant lots.
Dead animals	Cats, dogs, horses, and cows	Do.
Abandoned vehicles	Unwanted cars and trucks left on public property	Do.
Demolition wastes	Lumber, pipes, brick, masonry, and other construction materials from razed buildings and other structures.	Demolition sites to be used for new buildings, renewal projects, and expressways.
Construction wastes	Scrap lumber, pipe, and other construction materials	New construction and remodeling.

items usually pose special handling problems and are usually not a part of normal municipal solid-waste-disposal programs. The following descriptions of the categories of solid wastes are abbreviated from descriptions by the American Public Works Association (1966).

Waste refers to useless, unused, unwanted, or discarded materials including solids, liquids, and gases.

Refuse refers to solid wastes which can be classified in several different ways. One of the most useful classifications is based on the kinds of material: garbage, rubbish, ashes, street refuse, dead animals, abandoned automobiles, industrial wastes, demolition wastes, construction wastes, sewage solids, and hazardous and special wastes.

Garbage is the animal and vegetable waste resulting from the handling, preparation, and cooking of foods. It is composed largely of putrescible organic matter and its natural moisture. It originates primarily in home kitchens, stores, markets, restaurants, and other places where food is stored, prepared, or served.

Rubbish consists of both combustible and noncombustible solid wastes from homes, stores, and institutions. Combustible rubbish is the organic component of refuse and consists of a wide variety of matter that includes paper, rags, cartons, boxes, wood, furniture, bedding, rubber, plastics, leather, tree branches, and lawn trimmings. Noncombustible rubbish is the inorganic component of refuse and consists of tin cans, heavy metal, mineral matter, glass, crockery, metal furniture, and similar materials.

Ashes are the residue from wood, coke, coal, and other combustible materials burned in homes, stores, institutions, and other establishments for heating, cooking, and disposing of other combustible materials.

Street refuse is material picked up by manual and mechanical sweeping of streets and sidewalks and is the debris from the public litter receptacles. It includes paper, dirt, leaves, and other similar materials.

Dead animals are those that die naturally or from disease or are accidentally killed. Not included in this category are condemned animals or parts of animals from slaughterhouses which are normally considered as industrial waste matter.

Abandoned vehicles include passenger automobiles, trucks, and trailers that are no longer useful and have been left on city streets and in other public places.

Methods of Solid-Waste Disposal

The disposal of these solid wastes generated by our urban environment is generally accomplished by one or more of six methods. All are currently in use to one degree or another in various parts of the United States. To a large extent, the method of waste disposal in any particular area depends upon local conditions and, to some extent, upon public attitude. In many areas several methods are employed. Each has its unique relation to the water resources of the area. The six general methods of solid waste disposal are:

1. Open dumps.
2. Sanitary landfill.
3. Incineration.
4. Onsite disposal.
5. Feeding of garbage to swine.
6. Composting.

Open Dumps

Open dumps are by far the oldest and most prevalent method of disposing of solid wastes. In a recent survey, 371 cities out of 1,118 surveyed stated that this method was emphasized within their jurisdictions. In many cases, the dump sites are located indiscriminately wherever land can be obtained for this purpose. Practices at open dumps differ. In some dumps, the refuse is periodically leveled and compacted; in other dumps the refuse is piled as high as equipment will permit. At some sites, the solid wastes are ignited and allowed to burn to reduce volume. In general, though, little effort is expended to prevent the nuisance and health hazards that frequently accompany open dumps.

Sanitary Landfill

As early as 1904, garbage was buried to provide landfill. Although in subsequent years, the practice was used by many cities, the technique of sanitary landfill as we know it today did not emerge until the late 1930's. By 1945, almost 100 cities were using the practice, and by 1960 more than 1,400 cities were disposing of their solid wastes by this method.

Sanitary landfill consists of alternate layers of compacted refuse and soil. Each day the refuse is deposited, compacted, and covered with a layer of soil. Two types of sanitary landfill are common: area landfill on essentially flat land sites, and depression landfill in natural or manmade ravines, gulleys, or pits. Depth of the landfill depends largely on local conditions, types of equipment, availability of land, and other such factors, but it commonly ranges from about 7 feet to as much as 40 feet as practiced by New York City.

In normal operation, the refuse is deposited and compacted and covered with a minimum of 6 inches of compacted soil at the end of each working period or more frequently, depending upon the depth of refuse compacted. Normally about a 1:4 cover ratio is satisfactory; that is, 1 foot of soil cover for each 4-foot layer of compacted refuse. Ratios as high as 1:8, however, have been used. The final cover is at least 2 feet of compacted soil to prevent the problems associated with open dumps.

Incineration

Incineration is the process of reducing combustible wastes to inert residue by burning at high temperatures of about 1,700° to 1,800°F. At these temperatures all combustible materials are consumed, leaving a residue of ash and noncombustibles having a volume of 5 to 25 percent of the original volume.

Although incineration greatly reduces the volume and changes the material to inorganic matter, the problem of disposal is still present. Much of the residue is hauled to disposal sites or is used for landfill, although the land required for disposal of the residue is about one-third to one-half of that required for sanitary landfill. Some cities require that combustible materials be separated from noncombustibles prior to collection, while others use magnetic devices to extract ferrous metal for salvage.

The combination of urban growth, increasing per-capita output of refuse, and the rising costs of land for sanitary landfills has stimulated the use of incineration for solid-waste disposal. Today, there are an estimated 600 central-incinerator plants in the United States with a total capacity of about 150,000 tons per day.

Onsite Disposal

With the increasing rate of production of solid wastes in the urban environment, there is a growing trend toward handling this waste in the home, apartment, and institution. Onsite disposal has become increasingly popular during the past decade as a way of minimizing the waste problem at its source. Most widely used devices for onsite disposal are incinerators and garbage grinders.

Onsite incineration is used widely in apartment houses and institutions. The incinerators do, however, require constant attention to insure proper operation and complete combustion. Domestic incinerators for use in individual homes are not a major factor in solid-waste disposal, nor are they likely to be a major factor in the near future. Maintenance and operating problems are usually considerable.

Garbage grinders, on the other hand, are becoming increasingly prevalent in homes for disposal of kitchen food wastes. It is estimated that more than a million grinders are now in home use. The grinders are installed in the waste pipe from the kitchen sink; food wastes are simply scraped into the grinder, the grinder is started, and the water turned on. The garbage is ground and flushed into the sanitary-sewer system. In some local communities, garbage grinders have been installed in every residence as required by local ordinance.

Swine Feed

The feeding of garbage to swine has been an accepted way of disposing of the garbage part of solid wastes from urban areas for quite some time. Even as late as 1960, this method was employed in 110 American cities out of 1,118 cities surveyed on their solid-waste-disposal practices. In addition to the municipal practices of using garbage for swine feed, many cities and municipalities permit private haulers to service restaurants and institutions to collect garbage for swine feed. The feeding of raw garbage led to a widespread virus disease in the middle 1950's, which affected more than 400,000 swine. As a result, all States now require that garbage be cooked before feeding to destroy contaminating bacteria and viruses. However, according to the American Public Works Association (1966), more than 10,000 tons of food wastes—about 25 percent of the total quantity of garbage produced—is still used daily in the United States as swine feed.

Composting

Composting is the biochemical decomposition of organic materials to a humuslike material. As practiced for solid-waste disposal, it is the rapid but partial decomposition of the moist, solid-organic matter by aerobic organisms under controlled conditions. The end product is useful as a soil conditioner and fertilizer. The process is normally carried out in mechanical digesters.

Although popular in Europe and Asia where intensive farming creates a demand for the compost, the method is not used widely in the United States at this time. Composting of solid-organic wastes is not practiced on a full-scale basis in any large city today. Although there are several pilot plants in operation, it does not seem likely that com-

posting will be a major method of solid-waste disposal.

The selection of one or more of these methods of solid-waste disposal by a municipality depends largely on the character of the municipality. Geographic location, climate, standard of living, population distribution, and public attitudes play important roles in the selection. In general, the natural resources and environmental factors have been given only small recognition in this selection. Only recently has there been a considerable upsurge of scientific interest in the effects of solid-waste disposal on our water resources.

Hydrologic Implications

Types of Pollution

The disposition of solid wastes in open areas carries with it an inherent potential for pollution of water resources, regardless of the manner of disposal or the composition of the waste material. Of the six principal methods of solid-waste disposal, only swine feeding and composting offer no direct possibility of pollution of water resources from the waste material itself. Quite the contrary: properly composted garbage is a soil conditioner that improves the permeability of the soil and may actually assist in improving the quality of water that percolates through it. Although the cooked garbage that is fed to swine does not directly contribute to pollution of water resources, the manure from the feedlots may cause serious problems if not managed properly.

The type of pollution that may arise is directly related to the type of refuse and the manner of disposal. Leachates from open dumps and sanitary landfill usually contain both biological and chemical constituents. Organic matter, decomposing under aerobic conditions, produces carbon dioxide which combines with the leaching water to form carbonic acid. This, in turn, acts upon metals in the refuse and upon calcareous materials in the soil and rocks, resulting in increasing hardness of the water. Under aerobic conditions, bacterial action decomposes organic refuse, releasing ammonia, which is ultimately oxidized to form nitrate. In both landfills and open dumps, where decomposition is accomplished by bacterial action, the leachate has a high biochemical oxygen demand (BOD).

Table 2 indicates the magnitude of the constituents leached from solid wastes under various conditions. These data were compiled by Hughes (1967) from various sources.

Relation to Hydrologic Regimen

That part of the hydrologic regimen associated with pollution from solid-waste disposal begins with precipitation reaching the land surface and ends with the water reaching streams from either overland or subsurface flow. The manner in which this precipitation moves through this part of the cycle determines whether or not the water resource will become polluted.

Table 2 Percentages of materials leached from refuse and ash, based on weight of refuse as received [Adapted from Hughes (1967)]

Material leached	Percentage leached under given conditions*					
	1	2	3	4	5	6
Permanganate value 30 min	0.039					
Do 4 hr	.060	0.037				
Chloride	.105	.127		0.11	0.087	
Ammonia nitrogen	.055	.037		.036		
Biochemical oxygen demand	.515	.249		1.27		
Organic carbon	.285	.163				
Sulfate	.130	.084		.011	.22	0.30
Sulfide	.011					
Albumin nitrogen	.005					
Alkalinity (as $CaCO_3$)				0.39	0.042	
Calcium				.08	.021	2.57
Magnesium				.015	.014	.24
Sodium			0.260	.075	.078	.29
Potassium			.135	.09	.049	.38
Total iron				.01		
Inorganic phosphate				.0007		
Nitrate					.0025	
Organic nitrogen	.0075	.0072		.016		

* Conditions of leaching:
1. Analyses of leachate from domestic refuse deposited in standing water.
2. Analyses of leachate from domestic refuse deposited in unsaturated environment and leached only by natural precipitation.
3. Material leached in laboratory before and after ignition.
4. Domestic refuse leached by water in a test bin.
5. Leaching of incinerator ash in a test bin by water.
6. Leaching of incinerator ash in a test bin by acid.

Precipitation on the refuse-disposal site will either infiltrate the refuse or run off as overland flow. In open dumps, there is little likelihood of direct runoff unless the refuse is highly compacted. In sanitary landfills, the rate of infiltration is governed by the permeability and infiltration capacity of the soil used as cover for the refuse. A part of the water entering the refuse percolates downward to the soil zone and eventually to the water table. If the water table is above the bottom of the refuse deposit, the percolating water travels only vertically through the refuse to the water table. During the vertical-percolation process the water leaches both organic and inorganic constituents from the refuse.

Upon reaching the water table, the leachate becomes part of and moves with the ground-water flow system. As part of this flow system, the leachate may move laterally in the direction of the water-table slope to a point of discharge at the land surface. In general, the slope of the water table is in the same direction as the slope of the land. The generalized movement of leachate in this part of the hydrologic cycle is shown in Fig. 1.

There are several well-documented cases of pollution caused by leachates from solid-waste-disposal sites, especially those compiled by the California Water Pollution Control Board (1961). Most of these studies, however, were able to determine only that the pollution originated from solid-waste-disposal sites; few, if any, data on the gross magnitude of the pollution and its fate in the hydrologic cycle are available.

One well-documented case is that of pollution from about 650,000 cubic yards of refuse deposited in a garbage dump near Krefield, Germany, over a 15-year period in the early 1900's. High salt concentrations and hardness were detected in ground water about a mile downgradient from the site within 10 years of operation. Concentrations

FIG. 1. Generalized movement of leachate through the land phase of the hydrologic cycle.

up to 260 mg/l (milligrams per liter) of chloride and a hardness of 900 mg/l were measured—an increase of more than sixfold in chloride concentration and fourfold in hardness. The pattern of pumping of wells in the area precludes detailed understanding of the course of the pollution in the ground water, but wells near the dumping site were still contaminated 18 years later.

In Schirrhof, Germany, ashes and refuse dumped into an empty pit extending below the water table resulted in contamination of wells about 2,000 feet downstream. The contamination occurred 15 years after the dump was covered; measures of hardness up to 1,150 mg/l were recorded as compared with 200 mg/l prior to the contamination.

In Surrey County, England, household refuse dumped into gravel pits polluted the ground water in the vicinity. Refuse was dumped directly into the 20-foot-deep pits where water depth averaged about 12 feet. Maximum rate of dumping was about 100,000 tons per year over a 6-year period, and this occurred during the latter part of the period of use (1954–60). Limited observations on water quality extending less than a year after the closing of the pits showed chloride concentrations ranging from 800 mg/l at the dump site, through 290 mg/l in downgradient adjacent gravel pits, to 70 mg/l in pits 3,500 feet away. Organic and bacterial pollution were detected within half a mile of the dumping sites, but not beyond. Because of the limited study period and the slow travel of the pollutants, the maximum extent of pollution was not determined.

More recently, a study was made of the ground-water quality associated with four sanitary landfill sites in northeastern Illinois (Hughes and others, 1969). At the DuPage County site, total solids of more than 12,500 mg/l and chloride contents of more than 2,250 mg/l were measured in samples collected about 20 feet below land surface under the fill. These were by far the highest concentrations measured at any of the four sites. In general, total solids ranged from 2,000–3,000 mg/l under the fill to as low as 223 mg/l adjacent to the fill.

Hydrologic Controls

The movement of leachate from a waste-disposal site is governed by the physical environment. Where the wastes are above the water table, both chemical and biological contaminants in the leachate move vertically through the zone of aeration at a rate dependent in part upon the properties of the soils. The chemical contaminants, being in solution, generally tend to travel faster than biological contaminants. Sandy or silty soils especially retard particulate biological contaminants and often filter them from the percolating leachate. The chemical contaminants, however, may be carried by the leachate water to the water table where they enter the ground-water flow system and move according to the hydraulics of that system. Thus, the potential for pollution in the hydrologic system depends upon the mobility of the contaminant, its accessibility to the ground-water reservoir, and the hydraulic characteristics of that reservoir.

The character and strength of the leachate are dependent in part upon the length of time that infiltrated water is in contact with the refuse and the amount of infiltrated water. Thus, in areas of high rainfall the pollution potential is greater than in less humid areas. In semiarid areas there may be little or no pollution potential because all infiltrated water is either absorbed by the refuse or is held as soil moisture and is ultimately evaporated. In areas of shallow water table, where refuse is in constant contact with the ground water, leaching is a continual process producing maximum potential for ground-water pollution.

The ability of the leachate to seep from the refuse to the ground-water reservoir is another factor in the degree of pollution of an aquifer. Permeable soils permit rapid movement; although some filtering of biological contamination may take place, the chemical contamination is generally free to move rapidly under the influence of gravity to the water table. Less permeable soils, such as clays, retard the movement of the leachate, and often restrict the leachate to the local vicinity of the refuse. Under such conditions, pollution is frequently limited to the local shallow ground-water reservoir and contamination of deeper lying aquifers is negligible.

Leachate that does reach the water table and enters an aquifer is then subject to the hydraulic characteristics of the aquifer. Because the configuration of the water table generally reflects the configuration of the land surface, the leachate flows downgradient under the influence of gravity from upland areas to stream valleys, where it discharges as base flow to the stream systems. The rate of flow is dependent upon the permeability of the rock material of the aquifer and on the slope of the water table. In flat areas or areas of gentle relief, minor local topographic variations may have no effect on the configuration of the water table, and

movement of ground water may be uniform over large areas.

In some places dipping confined aquifers crop out in upland areas and thus are exposed to recharge. Contaminants entering the aquifer in these areas move downgradient into the confined parts of the aquifer. Although there is usually some minor leakage to confining beds above and below the aquifer, the contaminants in general will be confined to the particular aquifer, and water-supply wells tapping that aquifer will thus be subject to contamination to the extent that the contaminants are able to move from the outcrop to the wells.

Optimum conditions for pollution of the ground-water reservoir exist where the water table is at or near land surface, subjecting the solid waste to continual direct contact with the water. Such conditions commonly exist where abandoned quarries that penetrate the ground-water reservoir are used as refuse-disposal sites. The continual contact of the water with the refuse produces a strong leachate highly contaminated both biologically and chemically. Under hydrogeologic conditions of permeable materials and steep hydraulic gradients, the leachate may move rapidly through the ground-water system and pollute extensive areas. The hydrologic effects of solid-waste disposal in four geologic environments are shown in Fig. 2.

Figure 2A illustrates a waste-disposal site in a permeable environment. The waste is shown in contact with the ground water in a permeable sand-and-gravel aquifer underlain by confining beds of relatively impermeable shale. In this case, the potential for pollution is high because conditions of both high

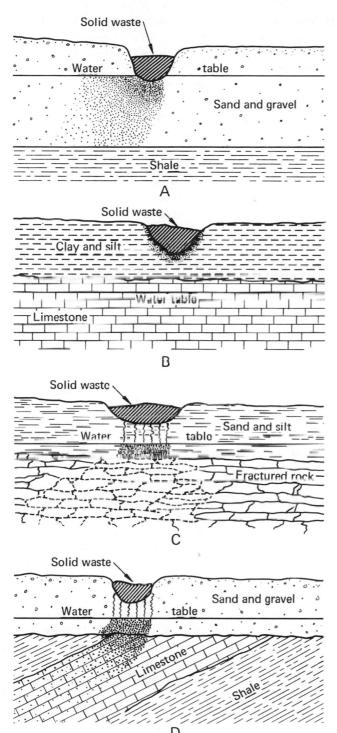

FIG. 2. Effects on ground-water resources of solid-waste disposal at a site (A) in a permeable environment, (B) in a relatively impermeable environment, (C) underlain by a fractured-rock aquifer, and (D) underlain by a dipping-rock aquifer. Leachate shown by dots.

infiltration and direct contact between wastes and ground water exist. Because of the permeability of the aquifer, the contaminants move downgradient with the water in the aquifer and are diffused and diluted during this movement. In areas where the water table is below the bottom of the waste material, the degree of contamination is lessened because the wastes are no longer in direct contact with the ground water. In this case, leachate from the wastes moves vertically through the zone of aeration to the water table. It then enters the ground water and moves downgradient as in the case of a shallow water table.

Figure 2B illustrates a waste-disposal site in a relatively impermeable environment. In humid areas, the water table may be near land surface, and the disposed waste may or may not be in direct contact with the ground water. In the illustration, ground water is shown confined to the underlying limestone aquifer. The relative impermeability of the overburden prevents significant infiltration of the rainfall; consequently there is only minor leaching of contaminants from the wastes. Pollution is confined locally to the vicinity of the waste-disposal site; movement in all directions is inhibited by the inability of the water to move through the tight soils. If significant amounts of rainfall penetrate the wastes, a local perched water table may develop in the vicinity of the fill, and that water will likely be highly contaminated, both chemically and bacteriologically.

Figure 2C illustrates a waste-disposal site above a fractured-rock aquifer. The position of the water table in the overburden relative to the waste-disposal site is dependent upon the amount of infiltration and the geometry of the ground-water flow system. The water table shown here is below the body of waste. In this case, the potential for pollution is not high because of limited vertical movement of the leachate to the water table. However, the contaminants that reach the fractured-rock zone may move more readily in the general direction of the ground-water flow. Dispersion of the contaminants is limited because the flow is confined to the fracture zones. A thin, highly permeable overburden with a shallow water table (similar to that shown in Fig. 2A) overlying the fractured rock would provide an ideal condition for widespread ground-water pollution.

Figure 2D illustrates a waste-disposal site in a geologic setting in which dipping aquifers are overlain by permeable sands and gravels. In this illustration, the waste-disposal site is shown directly above a permeable limestone aquifer. Here leachate from the landfill travels through the sand and enters the limestone aquifer as recharge. Again, the strength of the leachate depends in part upon whether the water table is in direct contact with the waste. Leachate will move downgradient with the ground-water flow in both the sands and gravels and the limestone, as shown in the illustration. If the waste-disposal site were located above the less permeable shale, most of the leachate would move downgradient through the sand and gravel, with very little penetrating the relatively impermeable shale as recharge. However, in its downgradient movement, it would enter any other permeable formations as recharge.

A high pollution potential exists also where waste-disposal sites are located on flood plains adjacent to streams.

Water-table levels generally are near land surface in flood-plain areas, especially during the usual period of high water in winter and spring throughout much of the humid areas of the United States. In such environments the water may have contact with the refuse for extended periods, giving rise to concentrated leachate. The contaminated water moves through the flood-plain deposits and discharges into the stream during low-flow periods when the bulk of the streamflow is from ground-water discharge. The degree of pollution of the stream depends upon the concentration of the leachate, the amount of leachate entering the stream, and the available streamflow for dilution.

Hydrologic Considerations in Site Selection

It is obvious that our current national policy of pollution abatement and protection of our natural environment requires full consideration of the water resources in selection of sites for solid-waste disposal. To date, with few exceptions, these considerations have been on a local scale, dealing primarily with the hydrological characteristics of the immediate site.

The American Society of Civil Engineers in a manual on sanitary landfill (American Society of Civil Engineers, 1959) discussed site selection from a hydrologic standpoint as follows:

In choosing a site for the location of a sanitary landfill, consideration must be given to underground and surface water supplies. The danger of polluting water supplies should not be overlooked.

The report states further that:

Sufficient surface drainage should be provided to assure minimum runoff to and into the fill. Also, surface drainage should prevent quantities of water from causing erosion or washing of the fill . . . Although some apprehension has been expressed about the underground water supply pollution of sanitary landfills, there has been little, if any, experience to indicate that a properly located sanitary landfill will give rise to underground pollution problems. It is axiomatic, of course, that when a waste material is disposed of on land, the proximity of water supplies, both underground and surface, should be considered . . . Also, special attention should be given areas having rock strata near the surface of the ground. For example, limestone strata may have solution channels or crevices through which pollution contamination may travel. Sanitary landfills should not be located on rock strata without studying the hazards involved. In any case, refuse must not be placed in mines or similar places where resulting seepage or leachate may be carried to water-bearing strata or wells . . . In summary, under certain geological conditions, there is a real potential danger of chemical and bacteriological pollution of ground water by sanitary landfills. Therefore, it is necessary that competent engineering advice be sought in determining the location of a sanitary landfill.

Consideration of hydrology in site selection is required by law in several States. Section 19–13–B24a of the Connecticut Public Health Code requires that:

No refuse shall be deposited in such manner that refuse or leaching from it shall cause or contribute to pollution or contamination of any ground or surface water on neighboring properties. No refuse shall be deposited within 50 feet of the high water mark of a watercourse or on land where it may be carried into an adjacent watercourse by surface or storm water except in accordance with Section 25–24 of the General Statutes which require approval of the Water Resources Commission.

The rules and regulations of the Illinois Department of Public Health require that:

The surface contour of the area shall be such that surface runoff will not flow into or through the operational or completed fill area. Grading, diking, terracing, diversion ditches, or tilling may be approved when practical. Areas having high ground water tables may be restricted to landfill operations which will maintain a safe vertical distance between deposited refuse and the maximum water table elevation. Any operation which proposes to deposit refuse within or near the maximum water table elevation shall include corrective or preventive measures which will prevent contamination of the ground-water stratum. Monitoring facilities may be required.

Other States have similar regulations.

A common denominator in these sets of recommendations is the general concern for the onsite pollutional aspect. This is characteristic of most current approaches, especially from the engineering and legislative viewpoints. Another characteristic is the restrictive approach to the problem. Hydrologic conditions are documented under which disposal of solid wastes is either discouraged or prohibited. In general, the pollutional problem is treated more in local than in regional context. These are, of course, important considerations and should be followed in any site selection. In fact, even stronger guidelines are desirable, to the extent of requiring detailed knowledge of the extent and movement of potential pollution at any site before the site is activated.

The water resource, however, must be considered also as a regional resource, not just a localized factor. As such, it should be considered in a regional concept in its relation to solid-waste disposal. This, of course, requires that adequate regional information on the water resource is available. Given such information, the planner can weigh all available alternatives and insure that the final site selection is compatible with comprehensive regional planning goals and environmental protection. The Northwestern Illinois Planning Commission followed this comprehensive approach in developing its recommendations on refuse-disposal needs and practices in northeastern Illinois (Sheaffer and others, 1963).

It is, of course, quite possible that, in the comprehensive approach, some otherwise optimum sites for solid-waste disposal may be only marginally acceptable from a hydrologic viewpoint. Under such conditions detailed information on the hydrology should be obtained and detailed evaluations made of the impact of the potential waste disposal before the site is put into use; the actual impact should then be monitored during and after use. In general, although such studies are desirable for all solid-waste-disposal sites, they are essential where geologic, hydrologic, or other data indicate a possibility of undesirable pollutional effects.

The problem of solid-waste disposal is one of the most serious problems of urban areas. The ever-increasing emphasis on protection and preservation of natural resources through regional planning is evident today. The implementation of these commitments and goals can insure adequate protection of vital water resources from pollution by disposal of solid wastes.

References

American Public Works Association, 1966, Municipal refuse disposal: Chicago, Ill., Public Adm. Service, 528 p.

American Society of Civil Engineers, Committee on Sanitary Landfill Practices, 1959, Sanitary landfill: Am. Soc. Civil Engineers Eng. Practices Manual 39, 61 p.

Anderson, J. R., and Dornbush, J. N., 1967, Influence of sanitary landfill on ground water quality: Am. Water Works Assoc. Jour., April 1967, p. 457–470.

California Water Pollution Control Board, 1961, Effects of refuse dumps on ground water quality: California Water Pollution Control Board Pub. 24, 107 p.

Hughes, G. M., 1967, Selection of refuse disposal sites in northeastern Illinois: Illinois Geol. Sur. Environmental Geology Note 17, 18 p.

Hughes, G. M., Landon, R. A., and Farvolden, R. N., 1969, Hydrogeology of solid waste disposal sites in northeastern Illinois: Washington, D. C., U. S. Public Health Service, 137 p.

Sheaffer, J. R., von Boehm, B., and Hackett, J. E., 1963, Refuse disposal needs and practices in northeastern Illinois: Chicago, Ill., Northeastern Illinois Metropolitan Area Planning Comm. Tech. Rept. 3, 72 p.

38 Hydrogeologic Considerations in Liquid Waste Disposal

S. M. Born and D. A. Stephenson

Municipal wastes have been disposed of by irrigation on sewage farms for almost a century, but the idea of disposing of industrial wastes by irrigation has evolved primarily since World War II.

The earliest irrigation disposal method was ridge-and-furrow irrigation, a process by which wastes are transported to furrowed plots of land and allowed to infiltrate the soil. But

Born, S. M. and Stephenson, D., 1969, "Hydrogeologic Considerations in Liquid Waste Disposal," *Jour. Soil and Water Conservation*, vol. 24, no. 2. Reprinted by permission of the authors and the Soil Conservation Society of America. Copyright 1969 by S. C. S. A.
Dr. Born is Director, State Planning Office, Madison, Wisconsin. Dr. Stephenson is Chairman of the Environmental Resources Unit, University of Wisconsin—Extension.

ridge-and-furrow irrigation has several serious shortcomings. A comparatively large amount of reasonably level land is required for the disposal site, and the site requires clearing and preparation prior to the application of waste water. The ridge-and-furrow method is also prone to flooding, which creates odors and may damage crops. In recent years, pressing demands for more intensive use of land have further diminished the popularity of the system for disposal of industrial wastes. It is still used locally, however, for disposal of stabilized municipal wastes.

An improved technique for waste-water irrigation was developed in 1947 and was first used by a canning company in Hanover, Pennsylvania.[3] Effluent water was applied to the land by sprinklers, giving rise to the name "spray irrigation." Waste water is thus disposed of by infiltration and evaporation.

Spray-irrigation disposal systems have numerous advantages: (1) The possibility of creating odor nuisances is minimized since the waste water is aerated during the application process, and oxygen-deficient conditions resulting from ponding and surface flooding at the irrigation site can be avoided due to the mobility of the sprinkler system. (2) No special land preparation may be necessary, and sloping areas and woodlands can be irrigated. (3) Spray-irrigated land can be farmed. (4) The spray system is readily expanded to accommodate increased volumes of effluent, and the distribution system can be salvaged.

The method is not without its disadvantages. Unfavorable sites or poor management practices can lead to surface runoff from spray-irrigation areas. This runoff may be of sufficient magnitude to condemn the method. Wind can transport both sprayed effluent and odor to unwanted places. Some waste water cannot be sprayed without extensive pre-treatment, such as sedimentation with or without flocculants, cooling, and screening. Clogging of sprinkler nozzles by solids in the effluent or by precipitated chemicals can decrease disposal efficiency. Where practicable, however, spray irrigation is a satisfactory means of disposing of liquid wastes on land.

Spray-irrigation disposal systems vary widely in design, cost, and capacity. Choice of a system is largely controlled by the physical characteristics of the site. One efficient system, located at Seabrook Farms in New Jersey, disposes of 5 to 10 million gallons of process water daily on 84 wooded acres of loamy sand.[3] Total cost of the Seabrook installation was about $150,000.

Waste disposal by irrigation has benefits other than the immediate one of protecting surface-water quality. In some cases, nutrient-charged waste water can be used to fertilize cultivated lands. A team of scientists and engineers at Pennsylvania State University recently demonstrated that the application of treated sewage effluent to croplands increased hay yields 300 percent, corn yields 50 percent, corn silage yields 36 to 103 percent, and oat yields 17 to 51 percent.[4] Concentrations of various nutrients originally in the effluent were essentially removed from the plot. The crop functioned as a "living filter."

Augmentation of groundwater recharge by treated effluent water is another important potential benefit of irrigation with waste water. Regions long dependent on groundwater supplies are experiencing an overdraft on these reserves. The overdraft is expressed in terms of a declining water table, increased water cost, local water quality deterioration, and even a water shortage. Recharge by irrigation with waste water can provide a partial answer to this problem of depleted groundwater supplies. In the Pennsylvania State University experiment, 60 to 80 percent of the applied effluent entered the groundwater reservoir relatively free of nutrients. However, the potential danger of contaminating groundwater cannot be overemphasized.

The ideal approach to irrigation disposal of liquid wastes is to derive secondary benefits from the operation and simultaneously guard against endangering the quality of groundwater supplies. Careful selection of the disposal site and wise management of the irrigation installation maximizes the chance of achieving both of these goals. Fortunately, nature has provided a remarkable purification system of its own. Removal of solids and nutrients from effluent water is accomplished by the microbial population in the soil and by the soil and rock medium itself through adsorption by clays, ion exchange, precipitation, and filtration. Man can supplement the natural purification of irrigated waste water by renovation techniques such as the cropping practice mentioned previously.

Pollution from irrigated areas can be controlled by adequate preliminary evaluation of the proposed site with due consideration given to the geologic and hydrogeologic environments. These physical environments should be influential factors in the design of a waste-disposal system.

Determining Flow Systems

Definition of a groundwater flow system allows an operator of a plant producing liquid wastes to select the optimum disposal site available on his land and further permits him to know in which direction effluent waters will travel in the ground, at what rate they travel, and where they will surface. In general, the flow system of interest for irrigation purposes is a local (shallow) system; however, in some geologic environments, the local system is only a small element of a larger regional system where the flow path of the effluent is governed by a deeper flow pattern.

Until recently, surface-water bodies have been studied as entities separate from groundwater; now these systems are recognized as being interconnected and are studied as such. Groundwater is derived from surface water by infiltration through the soil and includes all water within the saturated zone below a water table. Thus, the upper limit of this zone of saturation defines the water table, which is a subdued replica of surface topography. A water table is high under uplands, and slopes toward lowlands. Where the land surface intersects the water table, a surface body of water is present.

Water in the ground ultimately returns to the surface and becomes runoff in the lowlands. Movement in a groundwater flow system is along flow paths from areas of high potential (upland or recharge zone) to areas of lower potential (lowland or discharge zone). Potential is water elevation expressed as feet above sea level. Lines connecting points of equal potential are called equipotential lines.

In a recharge zone, the groundwater gradient is downward from the water table; in a discharge zone, it is up toward the water table (Fig. 1). Evidence of a groundwater discharge zone is commonly a wetland area or marsh in humid regions and a playa or "alkali flat" in arid zones. Water may be present perennially in a discharge area because of the upward movement of groundwater. Irrigation, therefore, must be undertaken with caution in a discharge area because infiltration is at a minimum and the effluents remain on or near the surface.

The pattern of groundwater flow from a recharge to a discharge area constitutes a dynamic flow system.[5] A flow system is controlled by topog-

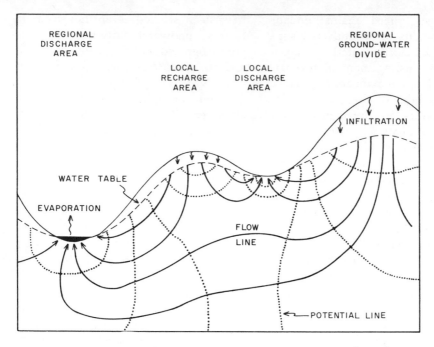

FIG. 1. Idealized groundwater flow system, homogenous soil conditions.

raphy but modified in flow direction and flow rate by the soil-rock conditions prevailing along individual flow paths. Groundwater flow systems can be defined in the field with empirical geologic and hydrogeologic techniques.

Each geographic area has unique rock-soil-water relationships since geology, topography, and climate vary regionally. On a gross pattern, however, it is likely that conclusions regarding flow systems for one area can be extrapolated to areas of similar or like environments. A mapped system has numerous applications with respect to water quality and quantity problems, including more efficient use of land for developmental, waste-disposal, and water supply purposes.

Effluent Infiltration and Movement

The ability of water to permeate the surface (infiltration capacity) is the critical element in efficient irrigation disposal operations. Successful disposal of waste water, especially by spray or ridge-and-furrow irrigation, allows the effluent to infiltrate the ground and undergo natural purification (particularly clarification) while percolating through the geologic medium prior to being discharged from the area. This minimizes malodorous effects and the possibility of surface water contamination at the discharge point.

Infiltration capacity is controlled by a number of variables.[7] Topographic relief controls the disposition of surface runoff and, therefore, to a large degree, the amount of water available for infiltration at a given location. As noted previously, topography further controls groundwater gradients and, hence, how the flow system operates at any specified point. Infiltration in discharge areas of humid and subhumid regions is sometimes limited by a prevailing upward gradient and saturation of the soil due to a frequent vertical proximity of the water table and ground surface. In recharge portions of the flow system, the limiting factor controlling water intake is geological, that is, the nature of the surface material (Fig. 2).

Infiltration is also influenced by rock type and the rock's weathering history which determine the nature and extent of pore space, the depth to impermeable zones, and the texture of the ground surface. Rates of infiltration are further reduced by mechanical compaction (by livestock, man, machines, and rain) and by pore clogging resulting from the erosion of natural materials and the in-wash of organic materials and solids in many industrial effluents. Surface runoff, which increases the chance of direct surface-water pollution, is one by-product of reduced infiltration.

Another influence on infiltration is the soil's state of saturation. Water is removed naturally from the soil profile by evaporation through the air-soil interface and by transpiration through vegetation. This removal produces a soil moisture deficiency which benefits the infiltration of effluent disposed of by irrigation. A dry soil will generally absorb at least twice as much water as a wet one. This fact explains the sometimes rapid decline in infiltration capacity that occurs under continued irrigation.

Having long-term records of rainfall and climate available is desirable so that pre-irrigation soil moisture conditions can be anticipated; such records

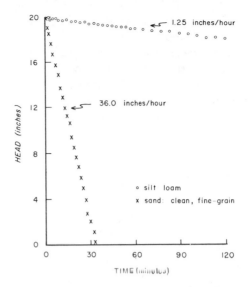

FIG. 2. Infiltration rate curves for two markedly different geologic materials (data from infiltration ring studies in northern Wisconsin by the authors).

are maintained by the U. S. Weather Bureau. A disposal site must be able to accommodate a volume of waste water over and above the natural "background" of precipitation. This consideration is especially important in designing a spray-irrigation system for a humid region.

In many operations, generation of waste water is almost continuous. Variations in precipitation and soil moisture—and, therefore, infiltration capacity—must be provided for in the system, either by creating temporary holding capacity and thereby reducing discharge during periods of rainfall, or by utilizing sufficient acreage to cope with precipitation and liquid-waste disposal simultaneously.

Once effluent infiltrates the ground, it eventually enters a groundwater flow system. Velocity of water within the saturated zone is controlled by permeability and gradient (Darcy's Law). The permeability of a material is defined as "the ability of a soil or rock to transmit fluids." Permeability in rocks and soils is controlled by the nature of the interconnected open space, either as pores between the grains, or fractures, or solution cavities.

Permeability of soil or rock samples collected in the field can be routinely measured in a laboratory with an instrument known as a permeameter. However, laboratory testing may not be accurate because the natural packing of the sample material is difficult to duplicate in the testing apparatus, and a small sample may not be representative of field conditions where discontinuities in the soil or rock medium frequently occur. Where accurate data are mandatory, pumping tests of wells must be conducted. The groundwater gradient can be determined in the field by monitoring groundwater levels in a group of sand-point observation wells.

Calculating the velocity of effluent movement in the ground permits disposal-site operators to predict the length of time required for decay of groundwater mounds built up during irrigation. In a sprinkler rotation system, such predictions enable scheduling of "rest periods" for different parts of the site. Knowing the velocity and direction of groundwater flow also enables the operator to predict where and when effluent which has entered the ground will discharge. By monitoring groundwater quality along its flow path, the operator can ensure that waste water is renovated and that contaminated water is not entering surface water at the point of discharge. In view of the present outcry over polluted water and the

strong legislative response by state and federal governments, such information may prove valuable should the concerned industry become involved in pollution litigation.

Evaluating a Disposal Site

A thorough knowledge of geologic conditions is necessary where waste water is to be disposed of by irrigation. Of particular importance is the geology of unconsolidated, surficial deposits. The thickness, nature and distribution of these deposits define the effectiveness of filtration of effluent water, the adsorptive capacity of soil types present for the removal of specific constituents in the effluent, and the location of impermeable horizons which impede downward movement of the waste water. The amount of pore space in the geologic medium above the water table permits the geologist to calculate the storage capacity of the unsaturated portion of the soil profile. This potential storage volume, together with the rates of infiltration and ground-water movement, limits the application of effluent on the disposal site.

Infiltration rates can be determined in situ with an infiltrometer.[2] Reasonable estimates of infiltration and permeability can also be determined by comparing textural properties of sediments at the site (grain size, shape, amount of clay and silt) with known hydraulic characteristics for given sediment types. Where relatively crude data are acceptable, such information can be derived by microscopic inspection of samples, thereby saving the cost of laboratory permeameter tests or expensive well pumping tests.

Occurrence of bedrock valleys of

glacial or alluvial origin may permit the location of a satisfactory disposal site in otherwise unacceptable terrain. The existence of such valleys has been documented in geological studies of many areas. Relatively simple geophysical surveys can be used to define them where they are likely to be present.[1]

Zones of increased weathering, solution, and high permeability commonly are localized along fractures in geologic materials. Permeability along bedrock fractures is often many times greater than in adjacent, unfractured bedrock; velocity of groundwater movement is fast; and very little filtration may occur. Therefore, fractured bedrock, particularly limestone and dolomite, near the surface of a disposal site may provide "avenues of pollution" for downward-moving waste water. Fracture patterns oftentimes can be identified by field investigations and mapped on aerial photographs. The disposal site can then be positioned to minimize the danger of largely unfiltered, contaminated water being discharged from the area by these routes.

It was noted earlier that flow systems exist that are larger than local systems, in which case the discharge area is not necessarily the lowland adjacent to an upland recharge area. Instead, downward-moving water may follow a deeper flow system along fractures or solution channels and travel many miles along an unfiltered path to a regional discharge area[6] (Fig. 1). The source of pollutants at such a discharge point may be more difficult to locate, but the resulting pollution is of no less concern. Carbonate and volcanic terrains are especially susceptible to rapid travel of effluents. Regional geologic studies can be used to define

such areas and prevent their use for disposal sites.

Preliminary Studies Imperative

National concern over the deteriorating quality of our surface water resources has resulted in federal and state laws for regulating the disposal of polluting effluents. Many small industries have been affected and, of necessity, have considered land disposal of process waters. A common method adopted by these industries has been disposal of effluent onto an irrigation plot. This practice can and does degrade both surface water and groundwater at irrigation sites where inadequate technical consideration has been given to location and maintenance.

Giving adequate consideration to geologic and hydrogeologic factors in selecting and operating disposal sites for liquid wastes minimizes the pollution potential. Costs associated with preliminary investigations can be high; but weighed against the consequence of inadequate planning, these costs may never be cheaper and should be an inherent part of any budget for an irrigation disposal facility.

Notes

[1] Drescher, William J. 1956. *Ground water in Wisconsin.* Inf. Circ. No. 3. Wisc. Geol. Surv., Madison, Wisc. 37 pp.

[2] Johnson, A. I. 1963. A *field method for measurement of infiltration.* Water-Supply Paper 1544-F. U. S. Geol. Surv., Washington, D. C. 27 pp.

[3] Lawton, G. W., L. E. Engelbart, G. A. Rohlich, and N. Porges. 1960. *Effectiveness of spray irrigation as a method for the disposal of dairy plant waste.* Res. Rept. No. 6. Wisc. Agr. Exp. Sta., Madison, Wisc. 59 pp.

[4] Parizek, R. R., L. T. Kardos, W. E. Sopper, E. A. Myers, D. E. Davis, M. A. Farrell,

and J. B. Nesbitt. 1967. *Waste water renovation and conservation*. Study No. 23. Penn. State Univ., University Park, Penn. 71 pp.

[5] Toth, J. 1962. *A theory of ground water motion in small drainage basins in Central Alberta, Canada*. J. Geophys. Res. 67(11): 4375–4387.

[6] Winograd, I. J. 1962. *Interbasin movement of ground water at the Nevada Test Site*. Prof. Paper 450-C. U. S. Geol. Surv., Washington, D. C. pp. C108-C111.

[7] Wisler, C. O., and E. F. Brater. 1959. *Hydrology*. John Wiley and Sons, New York, N. Y.

39 Disposal of Septic Tank Effluent in Soils

John M. Cain and M. T. Beatty

Before World War II, septic tank systems were used mainly on farms and for widely separated residences in largely rural areas. During the postwar building boom, septic tanks were employed in many subdivisions as areas beyond city sewage disposal facilities were rapidly developed. At present, it is estimated by Bendixen[3] that 25 percent of the nation's population depends on waste disposal through soil absorption.

The septic tank used today for individual homes is essentially the same in form as that used in the early 1920's.[10] Now, as then, all private liquid waste disposal systems do not operate perfectly. McGauhey and Winneberger[11] found that as many as one-third of the septic tank systems in a single subdivision failed during the first 3 or 4 years

Cain, J. M. and Beatty, M. T., 1965, "Disposal of Septic Tank Effluent in Soils," *Jour. Soil and Water Conservation*, vol. 20, no. 3, pp. 101–5. Reprinted by permission of the authors and the Soil Conservation Society of America. Copyright 1965 by S. C. S. A.
John Cain is on the staff of the Wisconsin Department of Natural Resources, Madison, Wisconsin. Dr. Beatty is Professor of Soil Science at the University of Wisconsin and Chairman, Environmental Resources Unit, University Wisconsin-Extension, Madison, Wisconsin.

of use. In one case, wholesale failure of septic tank systems in an entire subdivision meant that all of the more than 1,000 homes in the subdivision had to be repossessed, then refinanced and resold after the septic tank systems had been rebuilt.

Functions of a Septic Tank

In its simplest form, a septic tank is a water-tight container with an inlet and an outlet. The function of the septic tank[20] is to condition the sewage so that it may be more readily percolated into the subsoil. Biological decomposition of solids by anerobic bacteria takes place in the septic tank; part of the solids are retained in the tank. Contrary to popular belief, the septic tank does not remove a large proportion of harmful microorganisms from the waste.

Effluent from the septic tank is discharged into the soil by means of a seepage pit, seepage bed, or seepage trench. The rate at which the soil absorbs the effluent is critical to the operation of the sewage disposal system. If the effluent is not absorbed rapidly enough, it may back up into the drains in the home and eventually it may rise to the surface of the ground over the seepage area. If the effluent drains through the soil too rapidly, it may travel unfiltered into wells or surface-water supplies and contaminate them with various types of disease-bearing organisms.

Soil Permeability

The approach to design of sewage effluent absorption systems has been based on an estimate of soil permeability. The first attempt at quantitative evaluation of soil permeability in relation to septic tank effluent was made by Ryon[18] in 1928. From 50 septic tank systems that were operating at full capacity or had overflowed, he collected information on the amount of effluent applied per square foot of bottom area of the seepage system. He also conducted percolation tests at each sewage disposal system site. First, he saturated the soil around a 1-foot square hole about 18 inches deep with water. Then, after placing 6 inches of water in the hole, he recorded the time required for the water level to drop 1 inch. On the basis of information obtained in this study, he developed a relationship among percolation rate, water use, and bottom area of the seepage system. Thereafter, this relationship was used for septic tank system design purposes.

Ryon's work was widely accepted and served as the standard for evaluation by most agencies responsible for control of sewage disposal practices. The same type of percolation test, with some modifications, is given as the standard in the *Manual of Septic Tank Practice*.[20] The results of this test are reported in terms of the number of minutes it takes the water level to drop 1 inch in the hole. The lower the value

in minutes per inch, the greater the permeability of the soil.

Another method of measuring soil permeability involves taking an undisturbed soil core and in the laboratory determining the rate of water movement through it under a one-half inch head of water. The rates measured by this method are called the hydraulic conductivity of the soil and are expressed in terms of the number of inches of water that move through the soil core per hour. The higher the value in inches per hour, the greater the permeability of the soil.

A third method of estimating soil permeability is outlined by O'Neal.[14] With this method an attempt is made to relate soil characteristics observable in the field to measured hydraulic conductivity. O'Neal found that though permeability could not be estimated on the basis of any one characteristic, soil structure is the most important single characteristic influencing it. Other observable soil characteristics that affect permeability are soil texture, the relation between horizontal and vertical axes of aggregates, the amount of overlap of aggregates, mottling, size and number of visible pores, and direction of easiest natural fracture.

Devereux, Steele, and Turner[8] reported on the use of O'Neal's system on the soils of Virginia. In most cases, predictions of permeability based on carefully written field descriptions correlated closely with the results of laboratory tests. Devereux and his coworkers conclude, "It is believed that this technique can be developed sufficiently for all interested technicians to make reasonably accurate field estimates." At least, the technician can arrive at an estimate that is as useful and as meaningful as the results of a percolation test.

One reason that it is difficult to measure soil permeability accurately is that the percolation rate changes with time. Christiansen,[6] Allison,[1] Sillanpaa,[19] and Muckel,[12] working with various kinds of soil under both field and laboratory conditions, found that during a prolonged testing period the permeability varies in three distinct phases. Phase one is a period of initial decrease in percolation rate, phase two a period of increase in rate, and phase three a period of gradual but steady decrease in rate (Fig. 1).

The initial decrease in percolation rate probably is due to swelling of soil particles and dispersion of soil aggregates. The increase in rate during phase two is attributed to an increase in the amount of pore space available for water movement, which occurs as a result of the dissolving of entrapped air. The gradual reduction in permeability during phase three, which is the aspect of this soil property important insofar as septic tank operation is concerned, is due to (a) mechanical disintegration of soil aggregates, (b) clogging of soil pores by biological material, and (c) dispersion of soil aggregates by microorganisms.

Allison[1] demonstrated that the reduction in percolation rate did not take place in a sterile system during a 70-day test. He concluded that the rate reduction that normally occurs is due to microbial action and that the clogging material probably consists of microbial cells, slimes, and polysaccharides.

The changes of permeability with time suggest a number of limitations to the usefulness of the percolation test. Among them are the following:

1. Data from the tests are not applicable if there is a fluctuating water table near the soil surface or if there are abnormal situations such as root channels, large soil cracks, or small animal burrows in the test area.

2. The test cannot be performed on frozen ground and is not reliable when run on dry soil.

3. There is considerable variation in the techniques used in performing the test; often, it may be run improperly.

4. There is no valid reason for assuming that the percolation rate from a carefully prepared test hole will be

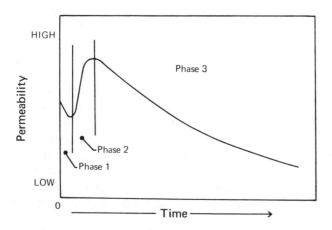

FIG. 1. The effect of prolonged submergence on permeability of soil.

the same as that from an absorption area constructed on the same soil with heavy machinery.

5. It is quite likely that there may be no relationship between the ability of the soil to accept water for a short period of time and its ability to accept sewage effluent for a long period. The research on soil clogging shows that a number of factors other than initial soil permeability affect clogging and the ultimate percolation rate.

Soil Clogging

Since soil permeability gradually decreases with time, even when distilled water is used, it appears logical that this decrease would proceed at an increasingly rapid rate when the soil receives septic tank effluent, which contains suspended solids, a variety of chemicals, and a large and varied microbial population. The possibility that soil pores may be clogged by septic tank effluent has been mentioned by several workers, but very little quantitative research has been done in this area until recently.

For discussion purposes, soil clogging can be divided into three types—physical, chemical, and biological—although they actually are interrelated. Physical clogging occurs when solid material carried in the effluent is deposited in the pores of the soil. As the pores are filled, the percolation rate is lowered until the absorptive surface becomes sealed. Orlob and Butler[15] and Orlob and Krone[16] found that organic matter generally is deposited near the absorbing surface of the soil; for example, on the wall of a seepage trench. The coarser the soil, the deeper the organic matter will penetrate. In fine-textured soil, most of the organic matter is deposited within one-half inch of the absorbing surface. Bendixen and his co-workers[4] report that the rate of clogging is proportional to the amount of suspended solids in the effluent.

Since soil clogging is due in part to suspended solids in the effluent, it seems that serious consideration should be given to septic tank design that will reduce the solids content. Baumann and Babbitt[2] studied the operation of six different septic tanks; they found considerable variation in the quality of effluent, both from day to day for any one septic tank and in the average between septic tanks. During an 8-month test period, 85 percent of the suspended solids were removed by the best tank and only 68.2 percent were removed by the poorest tank.

Baumann and Babbitt point out that at certain times gas bubbles cause turbulence in the septic tank and this results in abnormally large amounts of solids being carried out in the effluent. Effluent collected during these periods of "sludge unloading" showed a greater clogging tendency than normal effluent in sand filter tests. Certain of the septic tanks were equipped with a gas baffle, which is a slanted plate mounted below the outlet to divert the gas bubbles and solids away from the outlet. The three septic tanks with gas baffles did not exhibit sludge unloading.

This type of evidence accentuates the importance of sound sanitation ordinances, strictly enforced to insure that properly designed septic tank systems are installed.

Soil clogging also may be caused by chemicals that are able to alter the composition of the soil and break down the natural soil structure. Sodium is one ion that can cause soil structure to break down, but not enough presently is known about its effects in septic tank absorption fields to permit soil scientists to make a definitive assessment.

Biological materials seem to be the most important cause of soil clogging. The exact nature of the clogging material is not known, but McGauhey and Winneberger[11] have found deposits of ferrous sulfide where effluent is absorbed into the soil and they believe this is an important clogging material. The insoluble ferrous sulfide precipitate is probably a result of anaerobic bacteria acting on organically bound iron and sulfur. Under aerobic conditions, the ferrous sulfide is oxidized to the soluble sulfate form. Allison[1] indicates that clogging is probably due to products of microbial growth. Although it is desirable to know more about the exact nature of the clogging material, the important fact is that clogging takes place mainly under anaerobic conditions.

Research by a number of workers indicates that when clogged soil is allowed to dry, permeability is partially restored. During this resting period under aerobic conditions, the clogging material is oxidized and in some cases the microbial activity may result in better soil aggregation and increased permeability.

One of the most promising areas for research in improved septic tank system design appears to be that of devising some type of field rotation in the absorptive phase. In 1924, Hardenbergh[10] prepared a diagram for a distribution box with stop blocks so effluent could be directed into or away from three separate sections of a tile drain field. The dosing chamber and automatic dosing siphon, which have been given consideration in the past, apparently are being overlooked at present. Use of paired tile lines, seepage beds, or pits seems to be worth further study and may provide a method for making marginal soils safer for septic tank systems and for prolonging the useful life of systems on suitable soils.

The necessity for aerobic conditions to minimize soil clogging makes it imperative that the depth to water table in the soil be evaluated. Below the water table, anaerobic conditions exist. Above the water table is a capillary fringe where the soil is nearly saturated. In most soils, the depth to water table fluctuates during the year. If the water table is at or near the level of the absorption system for even part of the year it can cause soil clogging to start. Once started, soil clogging can be self perpetuating, since the effluent will pond in the trench, bed, or pit and maintain anaerobic conditions even after the water table drops.

Defects in Septic Tank Systems

Not all failures of septic tank systems are due to soil factors; many can be traced to faulty design and improper construction practices. Numerous faulty septic tank systems are installed because builders are unaware of the importance of certain construction features, enforcement of local health and building codes is difficult, and prospective buyers do not recognize the importance and the value of a well-designed and correctly installed system.

McGauhey and Winneberger[11] cite examples of septic tank failure caused by the practice of laying tile directly on the soil and then covering it with only a thin layer of gravel. Coulter, Bendixen, and Edwards[7] were able to relate septic tank system failure to amount of water used. In a survey of seepage beds in Knox County, Tennessee, they found that as water use increased the percentage of systems failing increased. Bendixen and his co-workers[4] found that homes with food waste grinders should have increased septic tank capacity and increased absorption areas to take care of the additional load.

If a septic tank is not cleaned out when it should be, sludge and scum may flow into the absorption area and cause clogging of the soil.

One factor that has not been evaluated quantitatively is the damage done to soil structure by construction machinery. Heavy machinery may smear the sidewalls and compact the bottom of trenches if the soil is wet during construction. If this happens, a seepage system may never attain its full absorptive capacity.

Ground Water Contamination

Fear that effluent from septic tanks may contaminate ground water has been expressed frequently. However, very little information on this subject has been available until recently. When septic tanks were widely scattered, distance and the opportunity for effluent dilution prevented contamination of water supplies from becoming a widespread or serious problem. But awareness of the potential pollution problem has increased with the use of septic tanks in crowded subdivisions and the widespread use of household detergents not easily decomposed by microorganisms.

Woodward, Kilpatrick, and Johnson[22] surveyed 63,000 wells in 39 communities in Minnesota; they found that 13,800, or 21.8 percent, of them contained measurable quantities of synthetic detergents. Campenni[5] tested half of the wells in a 50 home subdivision in Rhode Island; he found that all but one contained synthetic detergents.

Nichols and Koepp[13] tested 2,167 samples from privately owned wells in Wisconsin. They reported that 32.1 percent of the samples contained measurable amounts of detergents. Even more important, 20.3 percent of the samples that contained synthetic detergent were unsafe for human use from a bacteriological standpoint; only 9.2 percent of the samples without synthetic detergent were unsafe. This study indicates that there may be some relation between the presence of synthetic detergents in wells and bacteriological contamination of them.

Not a great deal of precise information is available on the ability of different kinds of soils to filter septic tank effluent or on the exact processes that take place during filtration. Robeck and his co-workers[17] found that synthetic detergents and other organic compounds are adsorbed by the soil particles and are decomposed by microorganisms. They indicate that the greatest degree of purification occurs near the point where the effluent is absorbed and that it is important to maintain an aerobic environment for proper microbial decomposition. They conclude that the best soil for filtering is one that will accept effluent at a reasonably rapid rate, has an ample adsorption surface, and has permeability characteristics that allow adequate time for microbial decomposition.

The main attempts to prevent well water contamination by septic tank effluent have been directed toward establishment of minimum lot size requirements and minimum spacings between septic tanks, wells, and lot boundaries. The studies by Flynn, Andreoli, and Guerrara,[9] Vogt,[21] and Campenni,[5] seem to indicate that this alone is not the answer. Although adequate spacing is desirable and in many cases may help prevent contamination, spacing regulations by themselves will not prevent ground water contamination; consideration must also be given to soil, ground water, and geologic conditions.

General Summary of Problems

Most of the problems associated with septic tank use can be grouped into three general categories. The first category involves problems related to the use of septic tanks on small lots in crowded subdivisions. Under such conditions, there often is either an inadequate area for disposal of effluent or contamination of ground water supplies. Not infrequently, the houses in attractive subdivisions with private wells and septic tanks must be connected to public sewer and water facilities soon after the subdivision is completed. This means that roads must be torn up, lawns disturbed, and additional expense incurred by all the homeowners. Problems of this type can be avoided by good community planning.

Many areas have restricted use of septic tanks to homes on lots that are considerably larger than conventional city lots. The objective of this restriction is to provide space for a new seepage system if the original one fails and to assure that distances between sewage disposal systems and wells are great enough to prevent ground water

contamination. However, these large lots also introduce many new problems, for they result in such a low population density that it may never be economical to connect the homes on them to the municipal sewer and water facilities. Also, other community facilities, such as utilities, police and fire protection, roads and transportation, and other services, will be unduly expensive throughout the life of the community. All communities should consider carefully how much of this type of urban sprawl they can afford, both in terms of the best use of available land resources and the continuing cost of community services.

The second category involves problems resulting from failure of septic tank systems due to faulty design and construction. Such problems can be caused by septic tanks or absorptive areas of inadequate size or by other defects in design and construction. Problems of this type can be controlled by the strict enforcement of good sanitation ordinances.

The third type of problem has to do with the installation of septic tank systems in soils not suited to use for waste disposal. This can result in the development of an ill smelling, unhealthful bog if the soil is so impermeable that the effluent rises to the surface of the lawn. Conversely, the soil may be so permeable that it accepts effluent too rapidly to provide sufficient filtration; this results in the contamination of ground water.

All of the aforementioned problems stem from lack of adequate control over the installation of septic tank systems. To be adequate, control must involve both the mechanical aspects of a system—size, shape, and type of construction—and the conditions under which septic tank systems are permitted. Control in the first instance is accomplished by sanitation ordinances and in the second by both sanitation ordinances and sound land use planning and zoning.

An especially useful tool to assist community leaders, planners, and sanitarians in better planning and control is the soil survey report, including maps, prepared by soil scientists.

Using Soil Survey Information

With a soil map and the related interpretive information on the soils, it is possible to delineate areas where septic tank systems cannot be used successfully. These areas include poorly drained soils, very fine textured soils, rock outcrops, very steep slopes, and flood plains. Also easily outlined on soils maps are areas where the use of a septic tank system is limited; such areas include somewhat poorly drained soils, slowly permeable soils, and highly variable soils. If a community decides that it is necessary to allow some areas to develop with septic tanks, the areas with soils suited for such development can be selected readily with the help of a soil map. These areas include soils that are permeable, have a deep water table, and have demonstrated an ability to function well for effluent disposal purposes.

The soil map is useful for describing soil conditions over large areas, but small inclusions of different soils may not be shown on the map. Where a large investment is planned, such as a septic tank seepage field, it is advisable to make an on-site evaluation. Such an on-site investigation can be performed by someone trained in the techniques used by soil scientists. This approach is unique, for it makes possible interpretations based on observable morphological characteristics of the soil at the site and also on the relationship of this soil to others with similar morphology that have been studied elsewhere. The findings from field and laboratory studies that have been performed on similar soils can then be related to the soil at the site. The use of soil survey information can contribute much to sound community planning, land use control, and development of regulations for land use applicable to each local situation.

Notes

[1] Allison, L. E. 1947. *Effect of microorganisms on permeability of soil under prolonged submergence*. Soil Sci. 63: 439–450.
[2] Baumann, E. R., and H. E. Babbitt. 1953. *An investigation of the performance of six small septic tanks*. Bul. No. 409. Engineering Experiment Station, University of Illinois, Urbana. 75 pp.
[3] Bendixen, T. W. 1962. *Field percolation tests for sanitary engineering application*. Special Tech. Publ. No. 322. American Society for Testing and Materials, Philadelphia, Pa. pp. 3–6.
[4] Bendixen, T. W., M. Berk, J. P. Sheehy, and S. R. Weibel. 1952. *Studies on household sewage disposal systems, part II*. U. S. Govt. Printing Office, Washington, D. C. 94 pp.
[5] Campenni, L. G. 1961. *Synthetic detergents in ground waters, part 2*. Water and Sewage Works 108: 210–213.
[6] Christiansen, J. E. 1944. *Effect of entrapped air upon the permeability of soils*. Soil Sci. 58: 355–365.
[7] Coulter, J. B., T. W. Bendixen, and A. B. Edwards. 1960. *Study of seepage beds*. Robert A. Taft Sanitary Engineering Center, U. S. Public Health Service, Columbus, Ohio. 62 pp.
[8] Devereux, R. E., F. Steele, and W. L. Tur-

ner. 1950. *Permeability and land classification for soil and water conservation.* Soil Sci. Soc. Am. Proc. 15: 420–423.

[9] Flynn, J. M., A. Andreoli, and A. A. Guerrara. 1958. *Study of synthetic detergents in ground water.* J. Am. Water Works Assoc. 50: 1551–1562.

[10] Hardenbergh, W. A. 1924. *Home sewage disposal.* J. B. Lippincott Co., Philadelphia, Pa. 66 pp.

[11] McGauhey, P. H., and J. H. Winneberger. 1963. *Summary report on causes and prevention of failure of septic tank percolation systems.* Report No. 63-5. Sanitary Engineering Research Laboratory, University of California, Berkeley. 66 pp.

[12] Muckel, D. C. 1953. *Research in water spreading.* Trans. Am. Soc. Civil Eng. 118: 209–219.

[13] Nichols, M. S., and E. Koepp. 1961. *Synthetic detergents as a criterion of Wisconsin ground water pollution.* J. Am. Water Works Assoc. 53: 303–306.

[14] O'Neal, A. M. 1949. *Some characteristics significant in evaluating permeability.* Soil Sci. 67: 403–409.

[15] Orlob, G. T., and R. G. Butler. 1955. *An investigation of sewage spreading on five California soils.* Sanitary Engineering Research Laboratory, University of California, Berkeley. 53 pp.

[16] Orlob, G. T., and R. B. Krone. 1956. *Movement of coliform bacteria through porous media: final report.* Sanitary Engineering Research Laboratory, University of California, Berkeley. 42 pp.

[17] Robeck, G. G., J. M. Cohen, W. T. Sayers, and H. L. Woodward. 1963. *Degradation of ABS and other organics in unsaturated soils.* Water Pollution Control Federation J. 35: 1225–1236.

[18] Ryon, H. 1928. *Notes on the design of sewage disposal works, with special reference to small installations.* Published by the author, Albany, N. Y.

[19] Sillanpaa, M. 1956. *Studies on the hydraulic conductivity of soils and its measurement.* Published by the author, Helsinki, Finland. 109 pp.

[20] United States Department of Health, Education and Welfare. 1960. *Manual of septic tank practice.* Public Health Service Publ. No. 526. U. S. Govt. Printing Office, Washington, D. C. 93 pp.

[21] Vogt, J. E. 1961. *Infectious hepatitis epidemic at Posen, Michigan.* J. Am. Water Works Assoc. 53: 1238–1242.

[22] Woodward, F. L., F. J. Kilpatrick, and P. B. Johnson. 1961. *Experiences with ground water contamination in unsewered areas in Minnesota.* Am. J. Public Health 51: 1130–1136.

40 The Nuclear Waste Problem In Perspective

Chauncey Starr and R. Philip Hammond

Reprinted from *Science*, v. 177, no. 4051, p. 744–45 by permission of the senior author and the American Association for the Advancement of Science. Copyright 1972 by AAAS.
Dr. Starr was at the School of Engineering and Applied Science, University of California, Los Angeles and R. Philip Hammond was at Oak Ridge National Laboratory, Oak Ridge, Tennessee when this article was written.

In public discussion of nuclear power and public safety, much concern is expressed about the need for storing the radioactive waste for centuries. While such long-term storage is an essential part of nuclear power development, the projected public safety involved is minimal, compared with other environmental problems.

The fact is that a completely adequate waste storage system is trivial in scope and cost, although not in importance. As with the oil filter in an automobile engine, we depend upon its being there and functioning properly, and would suffer hazard and expense if it were not; but it is not a significant item in cost or difficulty. Because of the very long radioactive lifetime of nuclear waste, we are of necessity handing onto future generations a problem which we have "wrapped up" in one form or another.

There is some ambiguity and confusion at present as to what this form should be, deriving mainly from a lack of clear distinction between the concepts of "waste disposal," and "waste management." We believe that perpetual, flexible, management is essential, so that future generations can have the option of choosing new solutions as new conditions and new technologies appear. Such perpetual care is not difficult nor costly, chiefly because the inherent volume of nuclear waste is so very small.

Each citizen of the United States consumes about 7,000 kilowatt hours of electricity per year, on the average, and it so happens that this amount of power is obtained from the fissioning of about one gram of nuclear fuel, equal to the weight of three aspirin tablets, but with a volume less than one aspirin. Thus if the electric source is nuclear, there is created about a gram of fission products to be stored per year per person.

The waste concentration process is carefully arranged to remove the valuable plutonium for fuel purposes, but there is a certain amount of other inert material which is too much trouble to remove. The safest way to handle the final mixture is to drip it in liquid form into a small pot, heated by electric coils, where it boils dry and then melts to form a glass-like ceramic clinker which is insoluble in water. This operation is done in a sealed chamber behind heavy walls, and watched and controlled with telescopes.

After firing and cooling is completed, the clinker, pot and all, is sealed up inside a tight can, and then into another. It then can be safely moved in a thick-walled shipping cask to a final storage place. (The casks are designed to survive all expected shipping accidents.)

In clinker form, the one gram of fission products and its accompanying inert material (representing about one man-year of electricity use) will occupy about 1/10 of an ounce, volume measure, and the total cost of processing, transport, and permanent storage will amount to about 14 cents.[1] The heat emitted is 1/40 of a watt, or about 1/10 the energy of a penlight flashlight.

For a city like New York the perspective is also interesting, although the numbers are larger. If entirely nuclear powered, New York City would have fission wastes, including inert materials, of about the volume of the mayor's limousine each year (800 cu. ft.).[2] They would give off enough heat to warm a small building (250 kw.). The vaults of the Chase Manhattan Bank would have the capacity to store the city's nuclear wastes for about a thousand years, although they are much more useful for storing gold, which we also wish to keep in perpetuity.

The volume to be stored is trivial, and the cost of storage is a fraction of a percent of the value of the power, but the wastes last a long time, must be kept behind thick walls, and must get rid of a certain amount of heat. Nuclear wastes accumulated for one year emit 10 watts of heat for each megawatt (1,000 kw.) of heat emitted while in the reactor. If wastes from the same power source continuously are added to the storage vault, a steady state heat output is reached of 550 watts per megawatt, since the older residues are decaying.[3]

Where would we store such wastes? How can we contemplate a continuity of protection and integrity of containment which will extend over hundreds of generations? Has anyone ever made such commitments before? The answer is yes—in Egypt and with rather remarkable success. Wooden chests and sarcophagi removed from the Egyptian pyramids are perfectly preserved, and look like new wood after 5,000 years in the desert. Metal, ceramic, and glass objects are, of course, unchanged also. Can we not do as well?

Thus in a lifetime of 70 years, each person (if fully nuclear powered) would account for a nuclear waste accumulation of less than half a pint in volume. The value of the electric power consumed in his life would be $10,000 at 2¢ per kilowatt hour, and the cost of the nuclear waste storage would be $10 of this. But it would not be of great economic moment if it were $20, or $30, as long as it is done well.

The stone of the great pyramid of Cheops, which is about 750 feet square at the base, could be arranged to form a series of smaller vaults which would house the wastes of the present United States generating capacity, if entirely nuclear powered, for over 5,000 years. (Volume 8×10^7 cubic feet, heat dissipation 275 megawatts, which is a small load for 750 feet square "dry cooling tower.") By then some spent waste could be removed for simple burial to make room for new, so that in fact a perpetual capacity would exist for our present rate of electricity use.

New pyramids would be needed as loads increased, perhaps one every decade or so. To compare with such a 750 foot square pyramid, consider the equivalent energy in strip-mined coal, which would mean handling a volume of fuel and overburden 750 feet in width, 300 feet deep and 200,000 miles long!

We recognize that an engineered storage facility with appropriate handling and cooling facilities would require additional volume and might look more like the Pentagon Building than a pyramid. The point of these examples is to give perspective to the quantities of waste to be managed, which are indeed tractable and feasible. We are not seriously suggesting that pyramids in the desert are the best way to store nuclear wastes. Other places, such as salt mines, are perhaps better. But if all else fails, they would work, they could be safe and attractive, and they would not be forgotten.[4]

What about the cans? Will they last 5,000 years? It is not really very important whether they do or not, although those of the Pharaohs did. The main thing we must do is give our successors the freedom to change the plan if they find a better one, or if conditions change. The containers are large enough so the number of items to be accounted for is reasonable, just as we account for gold bricks. Unlike gold, however, the waste provides no incentive for theft, and is inventoried only for safety reasons. Inside the vaults, the containers can be arranged so that we can monitor for leaks or deterioration, and remove and renew the cans if necessary, or change to a different storage site if we wish. If this is done, nuclear waste storage will remain a trivial, though still important problem.

Notes

[1] Belter, W. G., "Report on the 1968 Symposium on Solidification and Long-Term Storage of Highly Radioactive Wastes," Nuclear Safety, Vol. 8, No. 2, p. 174 (1966).

[2] McClain, W. C., and Bradshaw, R. L., "Status of Investigations of Salt Formations for Disposal of Highly Radioactive Power-Reactor Wastes," Nuclear Safety, Vol. 11, No. 2, p. 131 (1970).

[3] Weinberg, A. M., and Hammond, R. P., "Global Effects of Increased Use of Energy," Fourth International Conference on Peaceful Use of Atomic Energy, Geneva, Sept. 5, (1971).

[4] Since the above was written, we note that the AEC has announced plans for vault storage, while continuing research on other modes: Chauncey Starr and R. Philip Hammond.

Supplementary Readings

Andersen, J., and Dornbush, J., 1967, Influence of Sanitary Landfill on Ground Water Quality, Amer. Water Works Assoc. Jour., v. 59, n. 4, pp. 457–70.

Bascom, W., 1974, The Disposal of Waste in the Ocean, Sci. Amer., v. 231, n. 2, pp. 16–25.

Bergstrom, R. E., 1968, Disposal of Waste: Scientific and Administrative Considerations, Environ. Geol. Notes No. 20, Ill. State Geol. Survey, 12 pp.

Cartwright, K., and Sherman, F. B., 1969, Evaluating Sanitary Landfill Sites in Illinois, Env. Geol. Notes No. 27, 15 pp.

Council on Environmental Quality, 1970, Ocean Dumping—A National Policy, U. S. Gov. Printing Office, Wash. D. C.

Fox, C. H., 1969, Radioactive Wastes, U. S. Atomic Energy Comm., Wash. D. C.

Franks, A. L., 1972, Geology for Individual Sewage Disposal Systems, California Geology, v. 25, n. 9, pp. 195–203.

Galley, J. E., ed, 1968, Subsurface Disposal in Geologic Basins—A Study of Reservoir Strata, Amer. Assoc. Petroleum Geol. Memoir 10, 253 pp.

Gross, M. G., 1970, New York Metropolitan Region—a major sediment source, Water Resources Research, v. 6, pp. 927–31.

Hopkins, G., and Popalisky, J., 1970, Influence of an Industrial Waste Landfill Operation on a Public Water Supply, Water Pollution Control Fed. Jour., v. 42, n. 3, pp. 431–36.

Landon, R. A., 1969, Application of Hydrology to the Selection of Refuse Disposal Sites, Ground Water, v. 7, n. 6, pp. 9–13.

McGauhey, P. H., 1968, Earth's Tolerance for Waste, Texas Quarterly, v. 11, n. 2, pp. 36–42.

National Academy of Sciences—National Research Council, 1972, An Evaluation of the Concept of Storing Radioactive Wastes in Bedrock Below the Savannah River Plant Site, Wash., D. C.

Pierce, W. G., and Rich, E. I., 1962, Summary of Rock Salt Deposits in the United States as Possible Storage Sites for Radioactive Waste Materials, U. S. Geol. Survey Bull., 1148.

Piper, A. M., 1969, Disposal of Liquid Wastes by Injection Underground—Neither Myth nor Millennium, U. S. Geol. Survey Circ. 631, 15 pp.

Summers, C. M., 1971, The Conversion of Energy, Sci. Amer., v. 224, n. 3, pp. 149–60.

Films

Clean Town, U. S. A. (Atlantic-Richfield Co., 16 min.)

Cloud Over the Coral Reef (Moonlight Productions, 1972: 27 min.)

Cycles (Association-Sterling Films, 14 min.)

A Day at the Dump (Stuart Finley, Inc., 15 min.)

Safety in Salt: the transportation, handling and disposal of radioactive waste (U. S. Atomic Energy Commission, 1971: 29 min.)

Sanitary Landfill—one part earth to four parts refuse (Bureau of Solid Waste Management, 1969: 24 min.)

Wealth Out of Waste (U. S. Bureau of Mines 1974: 27 min.)

The 3rd Pollution (Stuart Finley, Inc., 23 min.)

Epilogue

"If Man is to survive as a species, we must quite soon accept the idea that every nation holds its realm in trust for all mankind, and for all future generations."

Donald Gould

Aerial view of St. Mark's Square, Venice. Photo courtesy of Italian Government
Travel Office.

It seemed appropriate to organize this collection of readings in sections dealing with the role of geology in four major problem areas: (1) the recognition of geologic hazards (Part II), (2) assessment of the magnitude of mineral resources and analysis of the environmental impact of exploiting these resources (Part III), (3) management of water resources (Part IV), and (4) evaluation of the limitations of the earth to absorb waste products (Part V). These problem areas, however, frequently overlap one another and thereby pose special challenges to Man's technological ingenuity. Waste disposal practices can influence the quality of our water resources, cause earthquakes, or augment our mineral base through recycling. Volcanism can produce earth tremors, landslides, or even catastrophic flooding. The impact of mining goes well beyond the mine site and influences the hydrosphere, atmosphere, and biosphere.

The interaction of Man and a variety of natural processes not only challenges our technological ingenuity, but may also pose special questions involving critical value judgments. Venice was founded 1400 years ago on low land in the middle of a shallow lagoon. Throughout its history it has been particularly vulnerable to the destructive forces of erosion, flooding by storm waves, and the long-term effects of a eustatic rise in sea level. At the same time, the island setting afforded a measure of security against hostile neighbors and the city's artesian aquifers furnished abundant and high quality water. Venetians could also rely on the waters of the lagoon and the tides to dilute and flush their wastes. But during the twentieth century, nearby industrial construction and intensive pumping of water, oil, and gas combined to cause subsidence and increase the city's vulnerability to flooding. Industrial wastes have defiled the lagoon, and acid vapors foul the atmosphere. The unique landscape and artistic treasures of Venice are clearly threatened. There are those who argue for immediate action and preservation at all cost. On the other side, however, are those who argue that Venice cannot survive as a viable city without continued industrial development of the port and the nearby mainland. Even interim measures, as well as possible long-term solutions, appear to be incompatible with both the preservation of Venice and the continued development of the port and mainland. In this respect the controversy is similar to many involving preservationists and developers. But this is more than a local dispute over the solution to a complex environmental problem. ". . . Venice is not only an Italian but a world-wide patrimony. . ." Carlo Berghinz explores the physical problems facing Venice and the controversy over the proposed solutions in the closing reading in this anthology.

41   Venice Is Sinking into the Sea

Carlo Berghinz

The flood caused by a storm surge of extraordinary height early in November 1966, during which more than eighty percent of Venice was submerged, suddenly called the world's attention to the city. The problem of Venice's survival appeared dramatically urgent. The inventory of the damages to the town and to its artistic patrimony, evaluated at more than $70 million, and the increasing frequency of such catastrophes, were too serious to allow further delays.

What is the real danger menacing Venice, and why is it becoming more and more serious?

Venice and its Lagoon

Venice was founded in the seventh century A.D. by the mainland population in the middle of a large lagoon in order to ensure safety.

The Venetian people prevented siltation by diverting the three rivers (Brenta, Sile and Piave) that flow in the lagoon, and built wall protections (the "murazzi") along the seaward side of the lagoon. Venice has always been "wed to the sea" and only in the past century has it been connected with the mainland (Poro Marghera and Mestre) with a 3-mile railroad bridge. In 1935 a highway bridge was built.

The lagoon extends along the Adri-

Reprinted from *Civil Engineering*, v. 41, pp. 67–71, 1971, by permission of the author and the American Society of Civil Engineers. Copyright 1971 by A.S.C.E.
Mr. Berghinz is Director, Electroconsult, Milan, Italy.

atic sea for 35 miles and is some 6 miles wide (see Fig. 1). Total area is about 210 square miles. Tidal surges flow in the lagoon through three inlets: Lido, Malamocco and Chioggia. The tide entering from each inlet commands a defined part of lagoon, which is therefore considered as divided in three basins.

One-third of the lagoon is occupied by large shallow permanent pools and by a system of canals, partly natural and partly artificial, ranging from 3 ft to more than 50 ft of depth. Some 20 percent of the area, located mainly north and southwest, has been gradually enclosed by dikes and transformed into fishery ponds. Toward the mainland the lagoon bottom rises and lies within the range of normal tide fluctuations, giving birth to mud and sand flats, called "barene." The wet barene are submerged by each tide, the dry barene only during spring tides. The barene cover more than 40 percent of the lagoon; a part of them has been reclaimed to expand the Marghera's industrial zone. Some 5 percent of the lagoon is covered by a number of small flat islets. Venice is built on pileworks driven in some of these islets as well as in the surrounding lagoon.

The "Acqua Alta"

Storm surges, locally called "acqua alta" (high water) are a centuries-old phenomenon in Venice. But never has their intensity and frequency reached the level of the last few years.

An acqua alta depends on the simul-

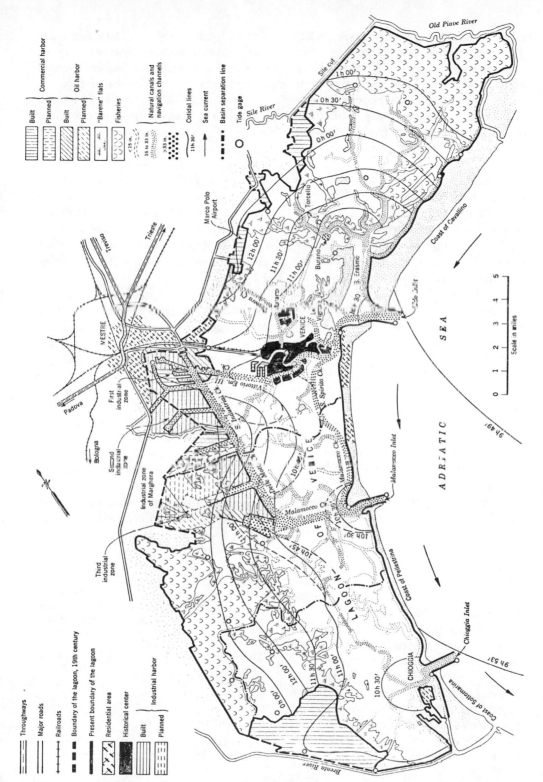

FIG. 1. The Venice lagoon—main hydraulic features and manmade changes.

taneous action of several causes, in addition to normal tide fluctuation, that raise the sea water to an abnormally high level, thus flooding the city of Venice. Among them, atmospheric pressure, rain, wind and mass oscillations of the Adriatic sea are most important.

Tides flow in and out from the lagoon through the three inlets. The maximum tidal prism has been estimated at 260,000 acre-ft, out of which 115,000 is in the Lido basin. The corresponding water level rise averages 2 ft. At the end of the channel, especially where the "barene" have been reclaimed and substituted with embankments that suddenly stop tide flow, additional rises of two to six in. over normal tide level, basically due to kinetic energy mobilization, have been recorded. In the meandering network of narrow and shallow canals of the city, the tidal rise speed lowers to less than 20 in. per second: a minimum tide speed (although always detrimental to building foundations), is indispensable because it ensures canal cleaning and permits the town to exist without sanitary sewers.

Abnormal drops of atmospheric pressure (in Venice a minimum of less than 29 in. of mercury have been registered) can raise the sea level four to eight in. and, exceptionally, more than 12 in.

The winter concentration of precipitation on the Northern Adriatic sea and on the basins of the inflowing rivers causes seasonal rises of the sea level of about four to eight in.

The south-east wind ("scirocco"), blowing the sea waters towards the lagoon, is among the main causes of the "acqua alta." A 6 mph wind raises the water four in. and 35 mph wind, more than three ft.

And finally, in the Adriatic sea, mass oscillations—seiches—are very important and can raise the water level up to 15 to 25 in. with peaks of three ft.

The "acqua alta", as a compound effect of the above causes, reaches high levels in the measure in which the different components attain simultaneously the highest values. An estimate allows comparison of the 1966 flood with the flood that could occur in the case that the different components attain simultaneously the highest values recorded (water elevation in inches above the mean sea level). (See Table 1.)

If for each component the theoretical peak value is assumed, the "acqua alta" would reach an even higher level, 120 in.; the probability of such a disaster is every 10,000 years, but the 1966 flood probable frequency is less than 250 years, and "acque alte" of less than 60 in. are common. Since nearly 70 percent of Venice lies less than 50 in. above mean sea level, the danger is easily appreciated.

However, the greatest worry is not the "acqua alta" itself, but its greatly increasing frequency. Out of 58 "acque alte" recorded in the past hundred years, 48 occurred in the last 35 years,

Table 1

	Nov. 1966	Highest "Acqua Alta" recorded
Tides	10	24
Atmospheric pressure	6	8
Rainfall	8	8
Winds	33	35
Mass oscillations	20	25
	77	100

and 30 in the last 10 years. In other words, in the first 65 years one "acqua alta" every 5 years, in the following 25 years almost one "acqua alta" per year, and in the last 10 years three "acque alte" per year have been suffered by Venice.

Sinking of the Town

Land level is dropping relative to sea level. In reality two distinct movements, with additive effects, have been recognized: the gradual rising of sea level (eustatism), and the progressive sinking of the lagoon bottom (subsidence).

Eustatism happens all over the world as a consequence of the polar caps and glaciers melting, due to the increasing of earth temperature (0.1 deg C each century). An eustatism of nearly 0.06 in. per year, i.e. about 6 in. per century, has been observed at Venice.

Subsidence (absolute, not compared with the mean sea level) is nothing new in the history of Venice lagoon. Subsidence of 140 to 240 in. has been observed, through archeological findings, from prehistoric time, and of 70 to 120 in. from Roman time. Average subsidence value for earlier centuries is estimated at 4 in. per century with a practically constant trend. In recent years, however, subsidence has acquired a progressive and definitely worrying trend. The few available data are sufficient to focus the problem; for instance, measurements conducted systematically at Palazzo Loredan (Venice Townhall) show the following subsidence values (see Table 2).

While the slow subsidence of earlier centuries has been always interpreted as the natural settlement of the loose material layers forming the lagoon's

Table 2

Period	Total subsidence in.	Mean annual subsidence in.
1908–1925	0.7	0.04
1926–1942	1.5	0.09
1943–1952	1.4	0.14
1953–1961	1.8	0.20

bottom for a depth of several hundred yards, no agreement has been reached on the reasons of the rapid increase of the subsidence rate observed during the last decades, and a passionate debate is still going on. Several explanations have been imagined, including movements of the deep rock formations supporting the above mentioned loose materials, natural gas exploitation in the Po river delta (carried out mainly between 1935 and 1955 and later forbidden), and man-made alterations to the lagoon's natural behavior. From a comparative analysis of the different theories, the most important cause of subsidence is likely the increased aquifer exploitation from wells located around and inside the lagoon, and in the additional load of extensive recent building, both connected with the Porto Marghera and Mestre industrial and urban development.

In effect, while detailed leveling surveys have shown that the direct influence of the gas exploitation in the Po delta stops before reaching the southern borders of the lagoon many miles from Venice, which therefore is not affected, on the contrary several observations, even if not exhaustive, show that a direct correlation exists between subsidence and aquifer exploitation (more than 200 cfs from 7,000 wells).

As a result, the aggregate of eustatism and subsidence leads to a progressive sinking of Venice, of more than 0.25 in. per year and, what is worse, this rate is steadily increasing. Seventy percent of Venice lies between 3.5 and 4.5 ft above mean sea level. Because of the town's sinking, these elevations are reached by the "acqua alta" with increasing frequency. As a consequence the surface of the flooded area goes on extending at a much higher rate than in the past, and damages become more and more heavy.

Porto Marghera Industrial Development

Marghera's port was built in the first half of this century with the distinguishing target, in comparison with other Italian ports, to allow the industrial transformation of raw materials locally. It became a clearly defined industrial port. A navigation channel between Marghera and Venice made Marghera accessible from the Lido inlet, and a first industrial zone of some 1,300 acres was built between 1919 and 1932, partly on mainland and partly on land taken from the "barene". A second industrial zone of 2,700 acres was built between 1959 and 1961.

Recently the works for a new industrial zone of 10,000 acres have begun. With the third zone the Marghera port (whose present yearly movement is more than 20 million tons) would become one of the major commercial, industrial and oil centers of South Europe; a new waterway should in fact link Venice to Milan and a motorway from Venice to Munich has been planned. The major installations of the third zone should be a new 2,000 mw thermal power plant,

a 2 million ton per year steel mill, the extension of existing aluminum and chemical industries, and an oil terminal with 16 berths and a new oil refinery. In addition to the third zone a new navigation channel is under excavation and nearly finished. This channel, 11 miles long, 600 ft wide and 50 ft deep, will link directly the industrial zones with the Malamocco inlet and so, avoiding Venice, will allow the passage of ships up to 60,000 tons.

The third industrial zone and the Malamocco channel are the object of passionate controversies. While from one side their clear economic importance is pointed out, from the other side questions are raised upon the effects that such works might have on the lagoon's internal balance. The third zone, in particular, is under discussion: the earthfilling will involve nearly 10 percent of the lagoon's surface, and almost 20 percent of the "barene" zone. There is concern about the detrimental effect the earthfilling might have on the "acqua alta"; there is fear also that new heavy installations might increase subsidence.

The Malamocco channel itself has been at first discussed, because it was said that, by increasing tide flow in the Malamocco basin, the channel would cause a shifting towards Venice of the Lido and Malamocco basins' separation line. As a consequence a possible increased tide rise in Venice together with a fall of tide speed and with pollution danger were feared. But, on the other hand, the channel has the clear advantage of detouring from Venice today's very dangerous tanker traffic passing from the Lido inlet, and this consideration has prevailed.

Perspectives and Actions

The rescue of Venice from its present progressive decay, and the contemporary development of the Porto Marghera industrial area are the factors in the complex problem of the lagoon. Everybody, and first of all the Venetians, agree on the necessity of rescuing Venice, but opinions differ on the way to do it.

On one side a numerous group of persons joined up in the "Italia Nostra" Association, are fighting a strenuous struggle, whose main objective is the preservation of the artistic patrimony of Venice, including its unique landscape. They therefore insist on the immediate cessation of the indiscriminate development of the industrial port, to avoid possible harmful impacts on the lagoon's internal equilibrium and to prevent the further spoiling of the town and its surroundings.

On the other side, the Port Authority and the Industrialists' Association of Marghera are convinced that the survival of Venice as a town without further industrial development cannot be conceived and therefore, in their opinion, the construction of the third industrial area and of the Malamocco channel should no more be delayed.

These two tendencies will have to meet to allow Venice to be saved.

Many individual initiatives have been started in the last few years for the rescue of Venice. Defenses from the sea have been studied as, for example, a system of forecast and alarm for the "acqua alta". Proposals have been made for different types of barriers such as a circular barrier inside the lagoon around Venice, translagunar barriers aiming at separating the Lido basin from that of Malamocco, belt-barriers for the defense of the entire lagoon. The possible closure of the lagoon outlets by stormgates in case of exceptional events has also been considered. Since all these works would limit the regular tide flow, the necessity would arise of providing Venice with an adequate sewerage system.

Communication between Venice and the mainland has also been the object of studies and proposals; the construction of translagunar highways has been examined but it is not likely to take place for the disfigurement which would be caused to the town. Preference is given to underground transportation and various projects provided for the construction of sublagunar highways and railways. The improvement of existing translagunar transportation as well as the linkage of the lagoon with a system of waterways on the mainland has been planned.

Various projects for the construction of new aqueducts from the mainland have been proposed with a view of substituting pumping from wells situated in the lagoon area.

The transformation of ancient Venetian palaces into office buildings without spoiling their character is also under consideration.

Unfortunately, few initiatives have so far materialized due to inadequate coordination of the different actions, and to the insufficient knowledge of the lagoon problems.

Recently, an Interministerial Study Committee for the Defense of Venice has been constituted and is already carrying out investigations in the fields of town planning and construction, sanitation and biology, sub-soil geology, geophysics and geotechnics, hydraulics (including models of the lagoon and studies on possible water table recharge), oceanography and meteorology, and administrative and legislative aspects. The studies are carried out in collaboration with various international and national bodies such as UNESCO, CNR (National Research Council), universities and private companies.

Progressive closure of existing artesian wells, prohibition of natural gas or oil drilling in proximity of Venice and, recently, submittal of any initiative in the Venice Lagoon to an appropriate Committee for control and approval are the provisional emergency measures being taken pending the findings of these investigations.

All these efforts are expected to give rise to the appropriate solutions of the various problems for Venice revival. The work is hard, and, as Venice is not only an Italian, but a worldwide patrimony, the many proposals of international scientific collaboration have been and are gratefully accepted.

Editor's note: In April 1973 the Italian government passed a long-delayed 510 million dollar law to safeguard Venice. The Bill provides funds for the restoration of paintings, frescoes, sculptures, Renaissance palaces, and unpalatial homes. There are also provisions for a sewerage system and laws against dumping noxious wastes into the surrounding water. Domestic heating units would be converted from sulphurous fuels to methane, and a 10 million dollar aqueduct from the Sile River would replace artesian wells. An 80 million dollar set of moveable dikes would be installed to hold back flood waters. Further filling of the Venetian Lagoon would be prohibited.

Appendix A: Geologic Time Scale

RELATIVE GEOLOGIC TIME			*ATOMIC TIME
ERA	**PERIOD**	**EPOCH**	
Cenozoic	Quaternary	Holocene	
	Quaternary	Pleistocene	
			2-3
	Neogene	Pliocene	
			12
		Miocene	
			26
	Tertiary	Oligocene	
			37-38
	Paleogene	Eocene	
			53-54
		Paleocene	
			65
Mesozoic	Cretaceous	Late / Early	
			136
	Jurassic	Late / Middle / Early	
			190-195
	Triassic	Late / Middle / Early	
			225
Paleozoic	Permian	Late / Early	
			280
	Carboniferous / Pennsylvanian	Late / Middle / Early	
	Carboniferous / Mississippian	Late / Early	
			345
	Devonian	Late / Middle / Early	
			395
	Silurian	Late / Middle / Early	
			430-440
	Ordovician	Late / Middle / Early	
			500
	Cambrian	Late / Middle / Early	
			570
Precambrian			3,600 +

* Estimated ages of time boundaries (millions of years)
From *Geology* by W. C. Putnam, 2nd ed., revised by A. Bassett, Oxford University Press, 1971.

Appendix B: Metric Conversions

Linear Measure

1 millimeter (mm)	= 0.039 inch
1 centimeter (cm)	= 0.39 inch
1 meter (m)	= 39.4 inches = 3.28 feet = 1.09 yards

1 inch	= 2.54 centimeters
1 foot (ft.)	= 30.5 centimeters
1 yard (yd.)	= 0.91 meter
1 mile (mi.)	= 5,280 feet = 1.61 kilometer
1 kilometer (km)	= 1,000 meters = 0.62 mile

Area Measure

1 square yard	= 0.836 square meters
1 square mile	= 640 acres = 2.6 square kilometers
1 acre	= 43,560 square feet = 0.4 hectare
1 hectare (ha)	= 2.5 acres
1 square kilometer	= 0.4 square mile = 100 hectares

Volume

1 quart (qt.)	= 2 pints = 0.95 liters
1 liter (l)	= 1.06 quarts = 0.26 gallons
1 gallon (U. S.)	= 4 quarts = 3.8 liters
1 barrel (oil)	= 42 gallons = 159.6 liters
1 cubic yard	= 27 cubic feet = 0.76 cubic meters
1 cubic meter	= 35.3 cubic feet = 1.31 cubic yards

Weights and Masses

1 gram	= 15.43 grains = 0.035 ounce (avoirdupois)
1 kilogram (kg)	= 2.20 pounds
1 pound (lb.)	= 453.59 grams = 0.45 kilograms
1 short ton	= 2,000 pounds = 907.2 kilograms
1 long ton	= 2,240 pounds = 1,016.1 kilograms
1 metric ton	= 2,205 pounds = 1,000 kilograms

Temperature

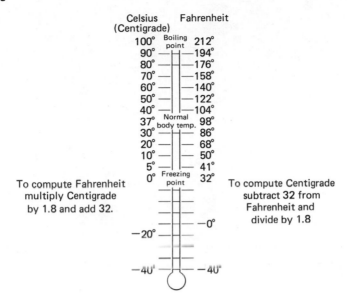

Celsius (Centigrade) / Fahrenheit

Celsius		Fahrenheit
100°	Boiling point	212°
90°		194°
80°		176°
70°		158°
60°		140°
50°		122°
40°		104°
37°	Normal body temp.	98°
30°		86°
20°		68°
10°		50°
5°		41°
0°	Freezing point	32°
		—0°
—20°		
—40°		—40°

To compute Fahrenheit multiply Centigrade by 1.8 and add 32.

To compute Centigrade subtract 32 from Fahrenheit and divide by 1.8

Other Measures

1 kilowatt-hour	= 3,413 BTU = 3.6×10^{13} ergs = 860,421 calories
1 BTU	= 2.93×10^{-4} kilowatt-hours = $1,0548 \times 10^{10}$ ergs = 252 calories
1 watt	= 3,413 BTU/hour
1 horsepower	= 0.746 kilowatt
1 gallon/minute	= 8.0208 cu. ft./min.
1 acre foot	= 1,233.46 cubic meters

Appendix C: Glossary

A A LAVA A lava flow characterized by a rough clinkery surface.

ACCELOGRAPH An instrument for recording the acceleration in velocity of earthquake vibrations.

ADIT A tunnel or passage way by which a mine is entered.

AEROBIC CONDITION Characterized by presence of free oxygen.

AGGRADATION The general building up of the land by depositional processes.

ALLUVIAL (ALLUVIUM) Pertains to material deposited by moving water. The deposits may assume a fan shape where a mountain stream enters a flat plain (alluvial fan).

ANAEROBIC CONDITION Characterized by absence of air or free oxygen.

ANASTOMOSING Branching or interlacing with a braided appearance.

ANDESITIC BASALT A fine-grained extrusive igneous rock composed of plagioclase feldspars and ferromagnesian silicates.

ANTHRACITE COAL = "hard coal" A hard, black, lustrous coal containing a high percentage of fixed carbon and a low percentage of volatile matter.

ANTICLINE A fold in which the rocks are bent convex upward.

AQUIFER A water bearing rock formation.

AQUITARD A rock formation which retards the flow of water. A body of impermeable material stratigraphically adjacent to an aquifer. A confining bed.

ARTESIAN HEAD The level to which water from a well will rise when confined in a standing pipe.

ARTESIAN WELL A well in which water rises above the top of the aquifer. In some cases the well may flow without the aid of pumping. The water is being derived from a confined water body.

AUGER MINING A method of extracting ore by boring horizontally into a seam much like a carpenter bores a hole in wood.

BASALT A fine-grained, extrusive, basic igneous rock.

BENCH MARK A mark on a fixed object indicating a particular elevation.

BIOSPHERE Zone at and adjacent to the earth's surface including all living organisms.

BITUMINOUS COAL = "soft coal" A coal which is high in carbonaceous matter and having between 15 per cent and 50 per cent volatile matter.

BOD (biochemical oxygen demand) The oxygen used in meeting the metabolic needs of aquatic aerobic microorganisms. A high BOD correlates with accelerated eutrophication.

BOMB, VOLCANIC Detached mass of lava or solid fragment ejected from a volcano. They range from 32 mm to several meters in length.

BOUGUER GRAVITY ANOMALY The gravity value after a correction has been made for the altitude of the station and the rock between the station and sea level.

BRACKISH WATER Water with a salinity intermediate between that of fresh water and sea water.

BREAKWATER A structure protecting a harbor, shore area, inlet or basin from waves.

BRECCIA A rock made up of angular fragments. It may be produced by sedimentary, volcanic, or tectonic processes.

BREEDER REACTOR A nuclear reactor capable of producing fissionable fuel as well as consuming it, especially one that creates more than it consumes.

BTU (British thermal unit) The quantity of heat needed to raise the temperature of one pound of water one degree Fahrenheit.

BURNER REACTOR See converter reactor.

CALDERA A large semicircular volcanic depression commonly found at the summit of a volcano.

CARBONACEOUS SHALE An organic-rich shale containing coaly material, graphitic material, or other carbonaceous matter that is presumed to be predominantly nonvolatile.

CARCINOGEN Any substance which tends to produce a cancer in a body.

CESSPOOL A pit for retaining the liquid waste from household sewage.

CINDER CONE A conical structure composed of volcanic ash and cinders.

CIRCUM-PACIFIC BELT A belt of modern earthquake and volcanic activity which includes the margins of the Pacific Ocean basin.

COLLUVIAL Loose, heterogeneous material deposited at the base of a steep slope by agents of mass-wasting.

CONE OF DEPRESSION The roughly conical depression produced in the water table by pumping.

CONTINENTAL SHELF The gently sloping zone bordering a continent and extending from low tide to the depth where there is a marked increase in the slope of the ocean bottom. The greatest average depth is 600′ (100 fathoms).

CONVERTER REACTOR (1) A nuclear reactor that produces some fissionable material, but less than it consumes. (2) A reactor that produces a fissionable material different from the fuel burned, regardless of the ratio.

CREEP (1) Gravitational creep is the slow downslope movement of soil or other surficial material. (2) Tectonic creep is slight, apparently continuous movement along a fault.

CREST-STAGE Refers to the highest point of a flood.

CULM BANK Refuse coal screenings often piled in heaps or banks.

CURIE POINT That temperature below which a substance ceases to be paramagnetic.

DARCY'S LAW A derived formula applied to the flow of fluids.

DDT (dichloro diphenyl trichloroethane) An insecticide. One of several chlorinated hydrocarbons.

DEGRADATION The general lowering of the land by erosional processes.

DEPLETION ALLOWANCE A proportion of income derived from mineral production that is not subject to income tax.

DESALINATION Any process capable of converting saline water to potable water.

DETRITAL Relates to deposits formed of minerals and rock fragments transported to the place of deposition.

DIASTROPHISM The process by which the earth's crust is deformed. Includes folding, faulting, warping, and mountain building

DILATANCY Refers to the increase in bulk volume which occurs during deformation.

DIP The angle at which a rock surface departs from a horizontal plane.

DUNITE An ultrabasic igneous rock composed almost entirely of olivine.

EARTHQUAKE Natural vibrations or tremors which are generated by the rupturing of rocks.

EFFLUENT Anything that flows forth; a stream flowing out of another, a lava flow discharged from a volcanic fissure, discharge from sewage treatment facilities, and so on.

EJECTA Solid material thrown out of a volcano. It includes volcanic ash, lapilli, and bombs.

ELASTIC DEFORMATION A non-permanent deformation which returns to its original shape after the load is released. Elastic energy is released during return to original shape and this may produce tremors.

ELECTROLYTE A conducting medium involving the flow of current and movement of matter.

ELECTROLYTIC HYDROGEN Hydrogen derived from water through the application of high current electrodes.

ENDEMIC Refers to organisms that are restricted to a particular region or environment.

EN ECHELON Offset but parallel structural features.

EPHEMERAL May refer to a temporary or intermittent lake or stream.

EPICENTER The point on the earth's surface directly above the point of origin of an earthquake.

ESCARPMENT The steep face of a ridge.

EUGEOSYNCLINE An elongate downwarping of the crust in which volcanism is associated with clastic sedimentation.

EUSTATIC Refers to worldwide and simultaneous changes in sea level.

EUTROPHICATION A process whereby natural bodies of water rich in plant nutrients and organisms become deficient in oxygen.

EVAPOTRANSPIRATION The sum of evaporation from wetted surfaces and of transpiration by vegetation.

FANGLOMERATE Alluvial fan deposits which have been cemented into solid rock.

FAULT SCARP A cliff formed by a fault. It is the topographic expression of vertical displacement within the crust of the earth.

FIRN LINE The edge of the snow cover at the end of summer season.

FISSION The splitting of heavy nuclei and accompanying release of energy.

FLOOD-PLAIN The area bordering a stream which becomes flooded when the stream overflows its channel.

FOCUS The point of origin of an earthquake.

FUMAROLE A hot spring or geyser which emits gaseous vapor.

FUSION The combination of two light nuclei to form a heavier nucleus.

GABBRO A coarse-grained, basic, intrusive igneous rock.

GEODETIC STATION A station which is used to record changes in the shape and dimensions of the earth.

GEODIMETER An electronic-optical instrument that measures distance on the basis of the velocity of light.

GEOTHERMAL Refers to heat in the earth's interior.

GLACIAL DRIFT A general term applied to sedimentary material transported and deposited by glacial ice.

GNEISS A textural term which refers to coarse-grained, banded metamorphic rocks.

GNP (Gross National Product) The total market value of all the goods and services produced by a nation during a specified period of time.

GOUGE A layer of soft material occurring along the wall of a fault.

GRABEN A down faulted block. May be bounded by upthrown blocks (horsts).

GROIN A shore-protection structure built to trap littoral drift. It extends perpendicular from the shoreline out into the water. Some groins are permeable and permit the circulation of water through them.

GROUND WATER Water located beneath the surface and within the zone of saturation.

GROUT A fine mortar for finishing surfaces.

HORST An up faulted block. May be bounded by downthrown blocks (grabens).

HUMMOCKY Refers to uneven topography dominated by knolls and mounds.

HYDROCARBON Organic compounds containing only carbon and hydrogen. Commonly found in petroleum, natural gas, and coal.

HYDROGRAPH A chart which records the changing level of water in a stream, reservoir, or well.

HYDROLOGIC Relates to the properties, occurrence, and movement of water.

HYDROLOGIC CYCLE The complete cycle of phenomena through which water passes from the atmosphere to the earth and back to the atmosphere.

HYDROSPHERE The aqueous portion of the earth. Includes the waters of the oceans, lakes, streams, ground water, and atmospheric water.

HYDROSTATIC PRESSURE Relates to pressures exerted by liquids.

HYPOCENTER (1) The region where an earthquake is initiated. (2) The point on the earth's surface directly below the center of a nuclear bomb explosion.

ILLITE A general name for a group of mica-like clay minerals.

IMPERMEABLE Impervious to the natural movement of fluids.

INFRARED SENSING Detection of invisible radiation of greater wavelength than that of red light.

Infrared rays can be detected by use of special film.

IONOSPHERE The uppermost ionized layer of the earth's atmosphere.

ISOSTACY A condition of balance or equilibrium in large areas of the earth's crust.

JETTY A structure extending into a body of water to direct and confine the stream or tidal flow to a selected channel. They are built at the mouth of a river or entrance to a bay to help deepen or stabilize a channel.

KARST A type of topography characterized by closed depressions (sinkholes), caves, and subsurface streams.

KINEMATIC PROCESSES Includes processes dealing with aspects of motion apart from considerations of mass and force.

LAPILLI Pea-sized volcanic ejecta. Accretionary lapilli experience a natural increase in size through the addition of extraneous material.

LAVA Molten material derived from a volcanic eruption or a rock which solidifies from such molten material.

LEACHATE The liquid material which has filtered through deposits of solid waste.

LEVEE An embankment confining a stream channel and limiting flooding.

LEVELING The process of establishing the elevations of different points on the surface of the earth by use of the surveyor's level.

LITHOLOGY Refers to a description of the physical characteristics of a rock.

LITHOSPHERE The solid or rocky portion of the earth.

LITHOSTATIC PRESSURE Pressure related to the weight of overlying rocks.

LITTORAL The bottom environment between the limits of high tide and low tide.

LNG (liquefied natural gas) Natural gas which is liquefied by lowering its temperature to $-259°$ Fahrenheit. The liquid occupies $\frac{1}{632}$ the volume of the equivalent vapor.

LOESS Refers to homogeneous deposits of silt deposited primarily by wind.

MAGMA A naturally occurring silicate melt.

MALTHUSIAN Refers to the doctrine of Malthus which states that population tends to increase at a faster rate than its means of subsistence.

MANTLE (1) The layer of the earth between the crust and the core. (2) Loose, unconsolidated surficial deposits overlying bedrock (=Regolith).

MARL A calcareous clay, silt, or fine-grained sand.

MASS MOVEMENT Movement of earth materials as a unit or *en masse*.

MEDIAL MORAINE An elongate glacial deposit formed below the junction of two coalescing valley glaciers.

MERCALLI SCALE A scale of earthquake intensity ranging from I to XII. Based on observable effects at a given place (compare with Richter scale).

MONTMORILLONITE A group of clay minerals with an expanding lattice which leads to swelling on wetting.

MUDFLOW A flowage of a mixture of rock, soil, and water.

NUCLEAR REACTOR A device in which a fission chain reaction can be initiated, maintained, and controlled.

OIL-SHALE Any part of an organic-rich shale deposit that yields at least 10 gallons (3.8 per cent) of oil per short ton of shale by conventional methods of destructive distillation is considered to be an oil-shale.

OLIVENE A green, silicate mineral commonly found in basic or ultrabasic igneous rocks.

OPEC (Organization of Petroleum Exporting Countries) The members of OPEC are: Saudi Arabia, Iran, Venezuela, Nigeria, Libya, Kuwait, Iraq, United Arab Emirates, Algeria, Indonesia, Qatar, Ecuador, and Gabon, which is an associate member. The United Arab Emirates is a federation of Abu Dhabai, Dubai, Sharjah, Ajman, Umm al Quwain, Ras al Khaimah, and Fujairah. Trinidad-Tobago is an observer. The organization was founded in 1960 and accounts for about 90 per cent of the oil moving in world trade.

ORE A "mineral" deposit which can be mined at a profit. Includes metals, fossil fuels, and non-metalliferous deposits.

OVERBURDEN (1) Material over-lying an ore deposit (=spoil). (2) Unconsolidated materials overlying bedrock.

PAHOEHOE Lava flow characterized by a smooth, ropy surface.

PEAT Partly decayed plant matter found in bogs or swamps. May be used as a fuel or soil conditioner.

PEGMATITE Very coarse-grained igneous rocks usually found as dikes associated with a large mass of intrusive igneous rock. Some pegmatites may contain a variety of rare minerals.

PERCOLATION TEST A test used to determine the rate at which water percolates through the soil.

PERMAFROST Permanently frozen ground.

PERMEABILITY A measure of the ability of a rock to transmit fluids. Effective porosity.

PESTICIDE Any chemical used for killing noxious organisms.

PETROGRAPHY The branch of geology dealing with the description and classification of rocks.

PHENOCRYST A large crystal set in a fine-grained matrix.

PHYSIOGRAPHIC PROVINCE A region characterized by its geologic structure, climate, landforms, and geomorphic history.

PHYSIOGRAPHY Refers to the descriptive study of landforms.

PIEZOMAGNETIC Refers to stress dependence of magnetic properties.

PIEZOMETRIC SURFACE The surface to which water from a given aquifer will rise under its full head. Also referred to as the potentiometric surface.

PILLOW LAVA Refers to those

lavas having a pillow-like structure which probably formed in a subaqueous environment.

PLANIMETRIC MAP A map presenting the relative horizontal positions of natural and cultural features.

PLAYA Desert lake basin.

POROSITY The percentage of void space in a rock.

PORPHYRITIC A textural term for igneous rocks which contain larger crystals (phenocrysts) set in a finer matrix. A copper porphyry would contain disseminated copper minerals in a large body of porphyritic rock.

PRORATION A legal restriction of oil production to some specified fraction of potential production.

PROTORE Low-grade mineral deposits which can be concentrated by natural surface processes to become ore.

PUMICE A light-colored volcanic froth which is cellular in texture.

QUICK CLAY Deposits of clay or soil which quickly change from a solid to a liquid state when suddenly jarred.

RESISTIVITY Refers to the resistance of material to electrical current. The reciprocal of conductivity.

RESONANCE Amplification by reinforcing vibrations.

REVETMENT A facing of stone or other resistant material built to protect an embankment from wave erosion.

RICHTER SCALE A scale of earthquake magnitude based on the logarithm (base 10) of the ampli-

tudes of the deflections created by earthquake waves and recorded by a seismograph. (See Mercalli scale.)

RIFT-VALLEY A graben or elongated valley formed by down faulting.

RIGHT-LATERAL MOVEMENT A fault with movement parallel to strike and right-handed separation. A reference point on the side opposite the observer appears to have moved toward the right of the observer.

RIPARIAN LAND Land situated along the bank of a body of water.

RIPRAP A layer, facing, or protective mound of stones randomly placed to prevent erosion or scour of an embankment.

RIVERINE Located along the banks of a river or a feature formed by a river.

ROCK FLOUR Finely ground rock fragments produced by glacial abrasion.

RUBBLE Loose, angular, and water-worn stones along a beach.

SAG POND Ponds formed by the uneven settling of the ground.

SANITARY LANDFILL A disposal area for solid wastes consisting of alternate layers of compacted refuse and soil.

SCARP A cliff or steep slope which may be produced by a fault in the earth's crust.

SCHIST A textural term referring to coarse-grained metamorphic rocks displaying a foliated structure.

SCORIA A vesicular, cindery crust on the surface of a lava flow.

SEAWALL A structure built along a portion of a coast primarily to prevent erosion and other damage by wave action. It retains earth against its shoreward face.

SEICHE A periodic oscillation of a body of water.

SEISMIC ACTIVITY Pertains to earth vibrations or disturbances produced by earthquakes.

SEISMIC SEA WAVES See tsunami.

SEISMIC TREMORS Earth vibrations.

SEISMOGRAPH An instrument for recording earth vibrations (syn. seismometer).

SEPTIC TANK A tank receiving solid and liquid wastes. The wastes are temporarily retained and decomposed by anaerobic bacteria.

SERPENTINE A silicate mineral associated with metamorphic rocks.

SHEARING STRENGTH The internal resistance offered to tangential stress.

SHUTTERRIDGE A ridge formed by displacement on a fault which cuts across ridge-and-valley topography.

SINKHOLE A topographic depression developed by the solution of limestone, rock salt, or gypsum bedrock.

SOLIFLUCTION The slow, viscous downslope flow of saturated surficial material.

SORB To take up and hold either by adsorption or absorption.

SPOIL See overburden.

STRAIN Changes in the geometry of a body which result from applied forces.

STRATIFICATION The structure produced by a series of sedimentary layers or beds (strata).

STRESS Forces that act to change the geometry of a body. Forces may be compressional, tensional, or tortional.

STRIKE The bearing or direction of the line of intersection of an inclined stratum and a horizontal plane.

STRIKE-SLIP FAULT A fault in which movement or slip is parallel to the strike of the fault.

SUBSIDENCE A sinking or settling of a large part of the earth's crust.

SURFICIAL Pertains to the surface of the earth.

TAILINGS (1) Those portions of washed ore that are regarded as too poor to be treated further. (2) The sand, gravel, and cobbles which pass through the sluices in hydraulic mining.

TALUS DEBRIS Unconsolidated rock fragments which form a slope at the base of a steep surface.

TECTONIC Refers to deformation of the earth's crust through warping, folding, or faulting.

TECTONIC CREEP Slight, apparently continuous movement along a fault.

TELEMETRY The automatic transmittal of data to a point remote from the sensing instrument.

TENSILE STRENGTH A measure of the ability of materials to resist forces tending to pull them apart.

TEPHRA A general term referring to the pyroclastic material of a volcano. It includes volcanic dust, ash, lapilli, and larger particles.

TERRACE Relatively flat, horizontal, or gently inclined surfaces which are bounded by steeper slopes. May be produced by stream or wave activity.

THERMOCOUPLE A device consisting of two dissimilar metallic conductors which produces a thermoelectric current when there is a difference in temperature between the ends of the conductors.

THERMOGRAPH A self-registering thermometer.

THERMOKARST Karst-like topographic features produced by local melting of ground ice in a permafrost region.

TILL Unstratified and unsorted sediments deposited by glacial ice.

TILTMETER An instrument used to detect changes in the slope of the ground surface. Measures horizontal displacement and can be used to indicate impending volcanic or earthquake activity.

TOMBOLO A sand bar connecting the island with the mainland.

TRANSFORM FAULT A fault displaying a change in structural style, for example, strike-slip to ridge-like structures.

TSUNAMI A large ocean wave produced by earthquake activity. Also referred to as a tidal wave or seismic seawave.

VESICULAR A textural term indicating the presence of many small cavities in a rock.

VISCO-ELASTIC Materials exhibiting viscous and elastic properties.

WATER TABLE The surface marking the boundary between the zone of saturation and the zone of aeration. It approximates the surface topography.

ZONE OF AERATION The zone in which the pore spaces in permeable materials are not filled (except temporarily) with water. Also referred to as unsaturated zone or vadose zone.

ZONE OF SATURATION The zone in which pore spaces are filled with water. Also referred to as phreatic zone.

Appendix D: Review Questions

1. What geologic data are necessary for comprehensive land-use planning? How can this data be presented for effective use by groups not trained in the earth sciences? What other types of data are necessary for effective land-use planning? Describe the status of land-use planning in your community. What role has geology played in guiding this planning?

2. What specific geologic evidence do D. Crandell and H. Waldron cite in Reading 4 to support their contention that there are hazards in the Cascade Range? What has Man done to compound the natural hazards of the Cascades area? In addition to issuing a general warning, what might be done to minimize the impact of the hazards?

3. Recent advances in seismology have enabled seismologists to predict earthquakes in Russia, New York, and California. Experience with fluid injection in Denver and Rangely, Colorado, has suggested a method of releasing strain in a fault system and thereby controlling earthquake activity. Suppose that within a decade both our ability to predict and control earthquakes improves and that there are predictions of a large earthquake in the Los Angeles area. How much publicity should be given to the prediction? What are some of the scientific, sociological, and economic considerations involved in deciding on the feasibility of initiating a strain-release program in this situation?

4. What are some of the factors which may lead to mass movement of material? Which of these factors were responsible for mass movement at Vaiont? (Reading 13) Vaiont is located in one of the world's major earthquake belts. What evidence can you cite to prove that an earthquake was not responsible for the final failure of rocks at Vaiont?

   The engineers at Vaiont were well aware of the historical record of landslides in this area and even documented creep activity prior to final failure. What reason(s) can you give for their failure to alert the citizens in ample time to evacuate the area and minimize the loss of lives?

5. Given the fact that floodplain occupancy is a characteristic of all major industrialized and preindustrialized societies: Who should bear the major cost of systems for forecasting and warning of floods? for modifications of stream channels? for watershed treatment? for floodproofing buildings? for flood insurance? for emergency assistance to flood victims? What are the implications

of your answer for further development of the assets of the floodplain? for reduction of losses when floods do occur?

6. Rigorous zoning laws have been proposed by those involved in land-use planning for flood plains. Do you think that this approach should be expanded to include other geologic hazards such as volcanism, earthquakes, tectonic movements and landslides? Are any aspects of these hazards unique so as to call for radically different approaches? Should the application of zoning restrictions be retroactive? Should resettlement be allowed after a disaster? What factors must be considered in deciding whether resettlement should be permitted?

7. The policy of some land management agencies is to control those natural processes which have proven to be destructive. Cite some examples of the techniques which have been employed to control natural hazards in the coastal setting.

 Others involved in land management argue that natural change, even when destructive, is essential to the maintenance of ecologic systems; that attempts to interfere with the natural processes can lead to the loss of these systems and to responses which are undesirable to Man. Cite some examples which support this point of view.

 Give examples to demonstrate that these two points of view can be reconciled.

8. What developments could lead to a reclassification of a "submarginal proven resource" to a "recoverable proven resource"?

9. What problems may accompany the development of new energy resources?

10. What role would zero population growth play in alleviating the energy crisis?

11. What geological considerations appear to argue against the premise that technology will significantly expand our resource base?

12. What are some of the environmental costs of consuming more energy? In your opinion, are current environmental standards which inhibit coal-burning, construction of new power plants, strip-mining, offshore oil drilling, and so on, justified while fuel is in short supply?

13. What are some of the economic and trade problems that could arise if U. S. industry passes along the necessary costs involved in

protecting the environment? Do these costs always result in a net loss or do some safeguards or rehabilitation practices lead to marketable assets or other gains to industry?

14. In the concluding section of Reading 31 David Brew lists six major considerations involved in the decision on the proposed Trans-Alaska pipeline. List these according to your priorities and defend your decisions.

15. Do you think that we should continue to expand our nuclear power facilities while we cannot agree on a method for handling nuclear waste materials?

16. What are some of the different uses of water in a single river? What are the implications of this in terms of predicting supply and in terms of water management?

17. What are the advantages of ground water over surface water? What problems are associated with the development of ground water reservoirs? How can these problems be solved? To what extent are these problems multidisciplinary?

18. What methods does your local community employ for disposing of its waste? What are the hydrologic implications of these methods? How safe are they? How much do they cost in comparison to other municipal services? What materials are recycled?

19. In Reading 41 Carlo Berghinz argues that, "Venice is not only an Italian but a world wide patrimony. . ." Do you think that this argument can be applied equally to wilderness areas? Why or why not? Would you argue for preservation of vast wilderness areas as a trust for all mankind? Cite examples of serious conflict between the needs of the present generation and its responsibility to future generations.